RORSCHACH HANDBOOK OF CLINICAL AND RESEARCH APPLICATIONS

RORSCHACH HANDBOOK

MARVIN R. GOLDFRIED
State University of New York at Stony Brook

GEORGE STRICKER
Adelphi University

IRVING B. WEINER
University of Rochester School of Medicine and Dentistry

OF CLINICAL
AND
RESEARCH
APPLICATIONS

Prentice-Hall, Inc., Englewood Cliffs, New Jersey

RORSCHACH HANDBOOK OF CLINICAL AND RESEARCH APPLICATIONS

Marvin R. Goldfried
George Stricker
Irving B. Weiner

Prentice-Hall Series in Personality, Clinical and Social Psychology
Richard S. Lazarus, Series Editor

ISBN: 0-13-783225-7

Library of Congress Catalog Card Number: 79-146644

Printed in the United States of America

10 9 8 7 6 5 4 3 2

PRENTICE-HALL INTERNATIONAL, INC., *London*
PRENTICE-HALL OF AUSTRALIA, PTY. LTD., *Sydney*
PRENTICE-HALL OF CANADA, LTD., *Toronto*
PRENTICE-HALL OF INDIA PRIVATE LIMITED, *New Delhi*
PRENTICE-HALL OF JAPAN, INC., *Tokyo*

CONTENTS

PREFACE

During the years in which the Rorschach has been used, it has been employed to predict success in therapy, to detect organic brain damage, to assess the level of anxiety and hostility, to determine developmental level of functioning, and to measure a variety of other characteristics. The purpose of this handbook is to present and evaluate several of these clinical and research applications of the Rorschach.

The applications of the Rorschach to be discussed in this book have appeared in a variety of scattered sources, and a fair amount of research has been carried out on most of these approaches. Some of the research was designated specifically to test the validity of the approach. Other studies have used a particular approach to the Rorschach as a measure, the purpose of the studies being an investigation of how the variable related to some other problem area. Although it may not have been the original intent of these latter studies, they nevertheless may be considered indirect or construct validations of this particular use of the Rorschach.

All of those applications of the Rorschach which will be described and evaluated in this book share a common characteristic in that they make use of the test to measure some specific potential or variable. Further, they are alike in that the assessment of this variable is reflected in the scoring itself, so that relatively little is required in the *interpretation* of the final score or pattern of scores. For example, in using the Rorschach for measuring hostility, statements regarding the level of hostility are directly reflected in the frequency of relevant indicators present in the protocol. Interpretations may be involved in deciding whether or not a given response should be scored in a certain way, but once the responses have been scored, the protocol is used in a more or less straightforward psychometric fashion.

There are a small number of Rorschach scoring systems which have been omitted from our discussion. Most notably these include the Holt Primary Process Scoring System, Witkin's approach to scoring the Rorschach for Field dependence-independence, and Levine and Spivack's Rorschach Index of Repressive Style. While these systems, and other less prominent ones, are descriptively similar to those which have been included, they tend to be parochial, having been developed and applied largely within a single setting. Each of the authors has summarized most of the available information in their presentation of the system, and much of that information is from their own work and the work of their students. We were more interested in evaluating systems of more widespread use, where existing summaries are not adequate for presentation of the system to the uninitiated reader. However, the interested reader can be referred to Holt and Havel (1960), Holt (1966), Witkin, Lewis, Hertzman, Machover, Meissner and Wapner (1954), Witkin, Dyk, Faterson, Goodenough and Karp (1962) and Levine and Spivack (1964).

The need for a handbook of this type is threefold. First, it provides the student and practicing clinician with a set of manuals for the various applications of the Rorschach. Second, the researcher may find this book useful in selecting some of the measures needed for carrying out research in a variety of problem areas. Finally, this book would be of interest to those involved with the question of test evaluation.

In many respects, the handbook may be seen as a much-needed step in the direction of unraveling the complex question: "Is the Rorschach valid?" Much confusion in the attempt to determine the validity of the Rorschach has stemmed from the way in which this question has been put. Thus, instead of asking if the Rorschach is valid, we are posing a series of more specific questions, such as: "Is the Rorschach valid for measuring developmental level?" "Can it detect organic brain damage?" "Is it a good measure of homosexual tendencies?" "Is the Rorschach useful for predicting suicide?" What we have attempted to do, therefore, is present a step-by-step approach to determining some of the limits of validity and usefulness of the Rorschach as a clinical and research instrument.

ACKNOWLEDGEMENTS

The financial and moral support for the completion of this handbook has come from a variety of different sources. We would like to acknowledge the grant support received from the National Institute of Mental Health (Grant MH11654 and MH12000) and the Research Foundation of the State University of New York. We are particularly grateful to Philip A. Goldberg and Stanley Kissel for their contribution to the original conception of this approach to the evaluation of the Rorschach. We would also like to extend our thanks to Howard Friedman, Leslie Phillips and Seymour Fisher who read and commented on earlier versions of those chapters dealing with their scoring systems, and to Richard S. Lazarus for his careful and critical evaluation of the entire manuscript. Acknowledgement is also due to several of the graduate students who assisted us in the very arduous task of conducting the literature search.

For the typing and editorial work on the manuscript, we are deeply indebted to the very competent, patient, and persevering efforts of Rosemary Cascardi, Jacqueline Russom, Audrey Cunningham, Margaret McNeill, Joan Reynolds, and Chris McClelland. Above all, we would like to acknowledge the role played by our wives, Anita, Joan, and Fran, whose understanding and encouragement carried us through to the final completion of the book.

The authors are finally pleased to acknowledge permission to quote or reproduce various copyrighted materials. The following Rorschach scoring systems are presented in detail in the text:

Friedman's Developmental Level Scoring. From Howard Friedman, "Perceptual Regression in Schizophrenia: An Hypothesis Suggested by the Use of the Rorschach Test." *Journal of Projective Techniques,* 1953, **17**, 171-85.

Phillips' Developmental Level Scoring. From Leslie Phillips, Stanley E. Kaden, and Marvin Waldman, "Rorschach Indices of Developmental Level." *Journal of Genetic Psychology,* 1959, **94**, 267-85.

Elizur's Hostility and Anxiety Scoring. From Abraham Elizur, "Content Analysis of the Rorschach with Regard to Anxiety and Hostility." *Rorschach Research Exchange and the Journal of Projective Techniques,* 1949, **13**, 247-84.

Fisher and Cleveland's Body-Image Boundary Scoring. From *Body Image and Personality* by Seymour Fisher and Sidney E. Cleveland, Copyright © 1958, by Litton Educational Publishing, Inc., by permission of Van Nostrand Reinhold Company.

Wheeler's Scoring for Homosexuality. From William M. Wheeler, "An Analysis of Rorschach Indices of Male Homosexuality." *Rorschach Research Exchange and the Journal of Projective Techniques,* 1949, **13**, 97-126.

Klopfer's Prognostic Rating Scale. From Bruno Klopfer, Frank J. Kirkner, Wayne Wisham, and Gertrude Baker, "Rorschach Prognostic Rating Scale." *Journal of Projective Techniques,* 1951, **15**, 425-28.

The following three chapters of the text are extended versions of previously published articles:

Chapter 1 is an extended version of "A Suggested Approach to the Evaluation of Projective Techniques," by Marvin R. Goldfried, published in *Psychological Reports,* 1966, **18**, 111-14, and reprinted with permission of the author and publisher.

Chapter 5 is an extended version of "The Assessment of Anxiety by Means of the Rorschach," by Marvin R. Goldfried, published in the *Journal of Projective Techniques and Personality Assessment,* 1966, **30**, 364-80, and reprinted with permission of the author and publisher.

Chapter 7 is an extended version of "On the Diagnosis of Homosexuality from the Rorschach," by Marvin R. Goldfried, published in the *Journal of Consulting Psychology,* 1966, **30**, 338-49, Copyright © 1966 by the American Psychological Association and reproduced by permission.

Chapter 1

THE PROBLEM OF EVALUATING THE RORSCHACH

Since Hermann Rorschach first published his monograph, "The Form Interpretation Test," in 1921, the Rorschach has become one of the most heavily researched and most widely disagreed-upon instruments to appear on the psychological scene. Despite accusations that it has done little else during the past half decade, the Rorschach has unquestionably generated research. At the time of this writing the number of publications on the Rorschach had gone beyond the 3000 mark.

Despite all this research, or perhaps because of it, most psychologists seem to remain in one of two camps: *believers* or *nonbelievers.* We purposely use the terms "believers" and "nonbelievers" because they connote strong personal convictions rather than logical evaluations in the light of research data. These convictions may have evolved either through the success or failure of personal experiences with the Rorschach, or through the simple acceptance of attitudes communicated by role models in graduate school.

Extrapolating from the way things have been going for the past 3000 studies or so, it seems highly unlikely that these two divergent views of the Rorschach will converge in the future. The usual recommendation that "more research is needed in this area" would be what Goldberg (1959) has termed the "Newcastle approach" to Rorschach evaluation. Some may argue that all the research data needed to validate the Rorschach are in and that the reason many still use the Rorschach is that they simply do not read the literature. Those who use the Rorschach counter this argument by pointing out that the so-called validation research does not accurately test the Rorschach in the way in which it is used clinically.

Chapter 1 is reprinted in part, with permission of author and publisher, from Goldfried, M. R. A suggested approach to the evaluation of projective techniques. *Psychological Reports,* 1966, 18, 111–114.

CHARACTERISTICS OF RORSCHACH VALIDITY RESEARCH AND RESEARCHERS

This description of the controversy over acceptance of the Rorschach as a valid and useful instrument is actually somewhat oversimplified. In addition to considering one's *acceptance* of the Rorschach, one might more accurately understand the present state of affairs by looking at the partially overlapping dimension of one's *orientation* to the Rorschach as well. By orientation we mean the general use to which the Rorschach is seen as being most appropriate. For example, practicing clinicians tend to view the Rorschach as a useful instrument for diagnosis and prediction. Academicians, on the other hand, if they accept the Rorschach at all, are more likely to view it as one of the measures available for pursuing problems of "basic" research.

The very interesting interaction which occurs between the acceptance and orientation variables is reflected in a study by Levy and Orr (1959). Following their interest in what they call "the social psychology of Rorschach validity research," Levy and Orr searched the literature on Rorschach validity to determine the relationship among three variables: (1) the type of *institutional setting* in which the study was conducted (academic vs. nonacademic), (2) the *type of validity study* ("theoretical," i.e., construct validity, vs. "criterion," i.e., predictive and concurrent validity), and (3) the *outcome* of study ("for" or "against" the validity of the Rorschach). Levy and Orr searched each issue of the *Journal of Abnormal and Social Psychology, Journal of Clinical Psychology, Journal of Consulting Psychology,* and *Journal of Projective Techniques* for the years 1951–1955, and came up with a total of 168 validity studies.

The findings of their study are summarized in Table 1.1. Their results, which were tested for statistical significance by chi square analyses, indicate that studies conducted in academic settings are more frequently of the construct- than of the criterion-validity type. The converse was true for studies done in nonacademic settings. These findings not only confirm the expected difference between academicians and nonacademicians in their orientations to the Rorschach, but also reflect a very practical difference, namely, that criterion groups are more accessible in nonacademic than in academic settings.

TABLE 1.1
Distribution of Studies Among Variables of Setting, Type of Study, and Outcome[a]

	Academic		Nonacademic	
	Construct	*Criterion*	*Construct*	*Criterion*
Favorable	51	12	14	19
Unfavorable	22	23	14	13

[a] From Levy and Orr, 1959, p. 82.

A second very interesting finding of Levy and Orr seems to reflect the interaction between what we have described as orientation to, and acceptance of, the Rorschach. Their results indicate that research done in academic settings was more than twice as likely to yield *positive* results when the study was of the *construct type,* and almost twice as likely to yield results *unfavorable* to the validity of the Rorschach when the study was of the *criterion type.*

Thus, Levy and Orr found that the likelihood of obtaining positive or negative results for the validity of the Rorschach depended upon *both* the type of study and the institutional affiliation of the researcher. In interpreting these results, it is important to make a distinction not made by Levy and Orr. When the authors talk about the "outcome" of a validity study, they are referring to the researcher's interpretation of his results. Although most researchers show a relatively high degree of agreement in reporting *results,* concurrence starts to break down when it comes to *interpreting* what these results mean. In studies where the results are ambiguous (as they often are with the Rorschach), the way a researcher interprets his findings will probably be colored by his own prior orientation to and acceptance of the Rorschach. Thus, the results of Levy and Orr's study might in part reflect the biases of each researcher in the *interpretation* of his data—that is, whether the findings should be entered on the asset or liability side of the validity ledger.[1]

Let us carry this point about variable interpretation a bit further. Piaget, in conceptualizing an individual's cognitive activity and its relationship to the external environment, has distinguished between what he calls "accommodation" and "assimilation" (Flavell, 1963). A person is said to accommodate to his environment when he changes his own internal schema or set in light of changes in his environment. Assimilation, on the other hand, occurs when the person cognitively modifies the external environment so that *it* becomes consistent with his own internal schema. Applying these concepts to the social psychology of Rorschach validation, one may hypothesize that few psychologists have accommodated to the some 3000 studies on the Rorschach. Those who "believe" the Rorschach is useful for certain purposes recognize confirming studies and "assimilate" those studies with unfavorable results, indicating that this research is naive and irrelevant. On the other hand, "nonbelievers" retain their view that the Rorschach is of little value, and point out that the research evidence confirms their conclusions. Consequently, since few psychologists shift their view of the Rorschach, the validity research seems to continue largely on a functionally autonomous basis.

A good deal of this confusion seems to be perpetuated by the unsystematic approach which has been taken in the attempt to "validate" the Rorschach. This lack of direction in research, as well as in the periodic reviews of the literature, may be attributed to the very elusive nature of the question that has been asked about the Rorschach: "Is the Rorschach

1 For a comprehensive and scholarly coverage of experimenter bias in behavioral research the reader is referred to Rosenthal (1966).

valid?" Approaches to the evaluation of the Rorschach have been guided—at least *implicitly*—by this vague and global question, and too much room has consequently been left for variability as to what is actually being asked.

The Validity of the Rorschach for What?

In pausing for a moment to try to gain a little more perspective on this issue of the Rorschach's validity, one is confronted with an obvious, although embarrassingly relevant fact, namely, the Rorschach consists of only 10 inkblots. Looking at things from a very simplistic point of view, it seems that there must be *limits* as to what can be determined about a person from this very brief and unique sample of his behavior.

In the past, the classic analogy about projective tests in general, and the Rorschach in particular, was that they were like psychological X rays. Projective tests were seen as being the ideal method for bypassing a person's defenses and inhibitions and getting information as to what he was "really" like. Few psychologists today would accept this rather unsophisticated analogy, but allow us to retain this simple comparison for a moment to make our point. If one had occasion to question the validity of the X ray itself, any technician would admit readily that his device is useful only for certain purposes; clearly X rays are not able to measure everything under the skin. The implication for the Rorschach seems obvious. And yet, when it comes down to the task of evaluating the Rorschach, the *tacit* assumption seems to be that if it is to be valid, it must measure practically everything about a person psychologically. If this is the job the Rorschach is supposed to do chances are that it will never be shown to be "valid." The job of measuring this vague and global construct "personality" may simply be too large for any test, let alone a mere handful of inkblots.

The question "Is the Rorschach valid?" actually implies many subquestions. One approach in trying to cut down this larger question into more manageable portions has been the attempt to validate specific hypotheses about the Rorschach, such as the hypothesis that a high F% indicates constriction. Validity research of this fragmented type has been criticized severely on the grounds that this does not represent the way the Rorschach is used; single scores in themselves are used only in the context of the total protocol.

Rather than focusing on the interpretive significance of isolated aspects of a protocol, a more meaningful and yet manageable way to approach the validity question is to use the personality characteristic, and not the test, as the point of departure. In other words, the relevant validity question which should be asked is: "*What* is the Rorschach valid *for*?" Harris (1960), in a very stimulating paper on the problem of Rorschach validity, has come close to adopting this orientation.

> The search for validity of personality description from Rorschach data seems, then, to require not so much the splitting apart of primary traits or tendencies into infinitesimal units, as a conservative retention of larger traits

> (which may change with the development of theory) and an empirical specification of the major environmental situations in which these traits usually express themselves (p. 414).

In asking *what* the Rorschach is valid for, the kinds of questions which need to be asked are as follows: "Is the Rorschach a valid indicator of homosexuality?" "Can the Rorschach be useful in predicting success in psychotherapy?" "Is the Rorschach a good measure of a person's defensive style?" "Is the Rorschach a valid measure of degree of hostility?" "Can it detect organic brain damage?" One can continue to pose as many questions as there are uses for the Rorschach. The list of questions will undoubtedly grow as more and more varied uses are made of the Rorschach. And yet it is only by asking these specific questions that we shall determine those areas in which the Rorschach may and may not be validly applied. This book will raise and, hopefully, answer some of these questions.

In reducing the larger question of Rorschach validity to questions of validity in specific areas, the vagueness of *what* is being measured is reduced, but by no means eliminated. The theoretical or even behavioral nature of many of the constructs which the Rorschach is purported to measure is often loosely defined. For example, in using Elizur's (1949) approach in scoring for "anxiety," one may question: Is it the subject's transitory anxiety state which is reflected in the final score, or is it the more long-term, chronic level of anxiety which is being measured? Further, does the "anxiety" being measured by this scoring refer to the individual's conscious, experiential state, or does it refer to the pervasiveness of signal anxiety, which is never experienced but which serves to evoke defenses?

Not all areas of Rorschach applicability involve this problem of definition. In some approaches, the definition of the construct being measured is delineated better by theory. An example of this approach would be Friedman's (1953) scoring for developmental level, in which the definition of the construct comes directly from Werner's (1948) theory of development. In still other Rorschach approaches, that which is being measured is defined behaviorally. Thus, if one scores the Rorschach for suicide indicators, the question of what is being measured is less likely to involve problems of definition. The general issue of delineating the construct which is being measured, or the criterion against which a test should be validated, is a problem encountered in trying to establish the validity of most tests, and will be discussed in greater detail later in the chapter.

Some Considerations in Using the Rorschach

In deciding whether to use the Rorschach to assess a given characteristic for which it has been shown to be a valid measure, it is important to recognize certain practical considerations. One obvious consideration is that there may be other instruments available which can do a better job than the Rorschach. Or perhaps there are other measures which are as good as the Rorschach for a given purpose, but which require less time and skill.

Considering the usual 1½–2 hours taken for administration and scoring, it seems only reasonable to admit that the Rorschach may not always be the most practical measure.

Although there are some practical limitations which can make the Rorschach a less attractive instrument, it unquestionably possesses assets which few other measures share. Whereas other measuring instruments tend to be limited in their range of applicability, the Rorschach's scope is indeed wide. Given the same set of responses to the same 10 cards, there are innumerable ways in which to evaluate any given protocol. This multidimensional characteristic is shared by the MMPI, which undoubtedly accounts for its popularity.[2] Thus, what seems at first to be a very cumbersome, painstaking task of asking several "validity for what?" questions about the Rorschach actually turns out to be a manifestation of its varied usage and potential.

A prime illustration of the potential of a given Rorschach protocol is seen in the work of Fisher and Cleveland (1958). In their book on body image, they report results of several studies done by other authors for other purposes. As these studies were relevant to their concept of body image, Fisher and Cleveland obtained these Rorschach records and rescored them according to the body-image scoring system. In comparison with those other body-image measures, which would have necessitated the actual replicating of these studies, the minimal amount of time taken to rescore the available Rorschachs clearly makes this the most efficient instrument to use.

The practice of rescoring Rorschach protocols obtained for other purposes is certainly legitimate, but for some reason has not been employed nearly as much as it might be. It is also likely that much profitable data would emerge if all those Rorschach protocols in clinic and hospital files were rescored for various specific personality characteristics, and if these were then related to other variables. Needless to say, the usual caution concerning the selectivity of patients who tend to be referred for testing should be kept in mind in this type of "file research."

For any particular problem area, the Rorschach may have a clinical and/or a research application. In a way, this extends the question of Rorschach validity to "validity for what *and when*?" More is required of the Rorschach if it is to be applied clinically than if it is to be used only for research. In addition to the requirements of prediction to a criterion involved in clinical validation, there is the very knotty problem of overlap between groups. The Rorschach may be an excellent measure of certain characteristics when used for research purposes, where differences between groups may be found to be statistically significant. But in the clinical setting the use of the Rorschach as a measure of these same characteristics may prove of little idiographic value.

Even when the amount of overlap among groups is minimal, the clinical application of the Rorschach additionally requires the existence of normative

2 There have been over 200 scales devised from the basic 550 MMPI items (Dahlstrom and Welsh, 1960).

data. The need for objective Rorschach norms has always been great, but has never been really adequately met. In the context of our orientation toward Rorschach validity, what is needed are individual sets of norms for each special application of the Rorschach. More will be said concerning norms later.

FRAMEWORK FOR EVALUATING THE RORSCHACH

The overall framework within which we shall present and evaluate the several applications of the Rorschach is based on the basic guidelines originally set by the American Psychological Association (1954) in the *Technical Recommendations for Psychological Tests and Diagnostic Techniques,* and later revised in the *Standards for Educational and Psychological Tests and Manuals* (American Psychological Association, 1966). The basic thesis of the *Standards* is that "a test manual should carry information sufficient to enable any qualified user to make sound judgments regarding the usefulness and interpretation of the test" (p. 2). The term "test" is used here in the broadest sense of the word, and refers to most types of diagnostic and evaluative tests and techniques. Despite many of the difficulties inherent in the evaluation of a projective technique such as the Rorschach, there are, nevertheless, many aspects of the Rorschach which are amenable to a quantitative evaluation. The authors of the *Standards* were quick to recognize this issue. They note:

> Many users of projective devices aim at idiographic analysis of an individual. Since this kind of analytical thinking places heavy reliance on the creative, artistic activity of the clinician, not all of this process can be covered in test standards. That is, the recommendations herein presented are necessarily of a psychometric nature and should not be interpreted as necessarily applying to all users of projective techniques. Nevertheless, proposals for arriving at such unique idiographic interpretations are almost always partially based upon some nomothetic premises, for example, that a Rorschach determinant tends to correlate with a specified internal factor. There is no justification for failure to apply the usual standards in connection with premises of this kind. Therefore, although these devices present unusual problems, the user of projective techniques requires much of the same information that is needed by users of other tests (p. 4).

Although some of the suggestions offered in the *Standards* do not apply to the Rorschach, the large majority of them do.

The recommendations outlined in the *Standards* vary as to their level of importance. The *essential* recommendations are those which reflect "...the consensus of present-day thinking concerning what is normally required for operational use of a test" (p. 5). The second level of recommendation includes those suggestions which are *very desirable.* A guideline was placed at this level, either because it was not unanimously agreed that the information was essential, or because the information was seen as being very difficult to obtain practically. The third and lowest level recommendations are those considered *desirable.* This includes information that is helpful in the use of the test although neither *very desirable* nor *essential.*

The specific basis for the evaluation of each of the Rorschach approaches will involve the criteria of *validity, reliability, scoring,* and *normative data.* Each of these criteria is described in detail below.

Validity

The most basic and important question that must be considered in the evaluation of any instrument is the test's validity. The *Standards* have gone beyond the simple definition of validity as being whether or not a test measures what it purports to measure. The definition of validity has not actually *changed,* but rather has been elaborated upon so as to include three different types of validity: *content validity, criterion-related validity,* and *construct validity.* Each type of validity and its relevance to Rorschach evaluation is discussed below.

Content Validity

This approach to validity refers to the adequacy with which the test has sampled the situation or characteristics which it purports to measure. In deciding whether or not content validity applies to the evaluation of the Rorschach, it might be helpful to note the distinction made by Goodenough (1949) between the "sample" and "sign" approach in the interpretation of a test.

Goodenough's definition of the sample approach is much the same as that given for "content validity"—the test consists of a sampling of behaviors, interests, beliefs, or any other characteristic selected from a larger population of similar characteristics. A test sign, on the other hand, does not necessarily resemble the characteristic it purports to measure. In her discussion of the Rorschach, Goodenough classifies it as being a sign approach, and stresses that the universe of characteristics reflected by these signs must be determined empirically. Although we would not disagree with her last point, Goodenough's description of the Rorschach as being solely a sign approach is not entirely accurate.

Rorschach "signs" typically have referred to the nontheoretical, empirically derived scoring categories which have been found to be related to certain overt behavior or personality characteristics. In contrast to these *empirical* Rorschach signs are those Rorschach systems which have been derived on a *theoretical* basis. The developmental scoring system (Friedman, 1953) is one example of this approach. Based on Werner's (1948) theory of cognitive development, Friedman interprets responses to the Rorschach blots as being a *sample* of the subject's level of perceptual and cognitive functioning. Another instance of the use of the Rorschach as a sample is in Holt's primary process scoring (Holt and Havel, 1960). According to Holt, the very unstructured and ambiguous nature of the Rorschach blots is such that they elicit a sample of the adequacy with which an individual functions at a primary process level. Thus, the Rorschach may be more accurately viewed as *both* a sign and a sample approach, depending upon how the responses are evaluated.

Despite the fact that certain applications of the Rorschach may be interpreted as sample approaches, content validation would not be a particularly meaningful way in which to evaluate these approaches. The blots comprising the Rorschach were selected long before these various sample approaches were formulated, and while the Rorschach stimuli may actually sample certain areas, it would be very difficult to determine their representativeness. What appears to be more amenable to the criterion of representativeness is the sampling of the scoring categories used in each of these systems, but this would not refer to the Rorschach's content validity. Consequently, the category of content validity may be considered as being of little value in the evaluation of the Rorschach.

Criterion-Related Validity

Criterion-related validity refers to the demonstration that the test in question is related to some external criterion data, which are believed to reflect directly the behavior or characteristic the test purports to measure. When one's interest is in the evaluation of a measure for the assessment of current status, the test scores and the external criteria are obtained at approximately the same time, providing information about the test's *concurrent* validity. If the question of the test's *predictive* validity is relevant, the criterion measure is obtained at some subsequent time. Except for the time at which the criterion measure is obtained, the operations for establishing the current or predictive validity of a test are the same.

In attempting to establish the concurrent and predictive validity of the Rorschach, several problems present themselves. Some of these difficulties are specific to the Rorschach, but the majority are inherent in determining the criterion-related validity of most measures. Among the difficulties which must be recognized and dealt with are the problems associated with (1) the criterion measure, (2) base rates, (3) the overlap between groups, and (4) the presence of unmeasured variables.

1. The Criterion Measure. The specification of an acceptable criterion measure can at times be most difficult. What can we use as a criterion measure for the primary process scoring? What constitutes "success" in psychotherapy? Even criteria which at first might seem relatively simple to determine can involve problems of definition. For example, Hooker (1959) has raised the question, "What is a homosexual?"

The *Standards* note the difficulties in defining the criterion, agreeing that "no one criterion is uniquely appropriate" in the validation of any test. At our present level of knowledge, the theoretical and behavioral specifications of many of the characteristics we attempt to measure are limited. At the very best, we are forced to use whatever criterion measures we have at present, with full realization that we are not likely to find a single criterion that suits our needs. Consequently, the definition of the criterion measure, or the composition of the criterion group, needs to be spelled out as much as possible, so that the results may be differently interpreted with our changing conceptions of the particular criterion.

2. THE PROBLEM OF BASE RATES. The necessity of paying attention to base rates has been emphasized in the classic article by Meehl and Rosen (1955). By base rates, Meehl and Rosen mean simply the probability of a statement or prediction about something being correct, based purely on the empirical occurrence of this particular characteristic or outcome in the population. For example, if approximately 85% of all patients in a given hospital tended to be schizophrenic, one could be a very accurate diagnostician by calling every incoming patient schizophrenic; one would be wrong only 15% of the time. Further, depending upon the base rates, the use of the Rorschach may improve or impair diagnostic efficiency. Suppose the Rorschach's ability to diagnose schizophrenia proved to be accurate in 75 out of every 100 cases. Although the figure of 75% accuracy seems impressive, a secretary instructed to label all new admissions "schizophrenic" would still prove to be more accurate and efficient in our hypothetical hospital. On the other hand, if the patient population of this hospital was made up of only 40% schizophrenics, then the Rorschach would prove to be more accurate than our secretary with her rubber stamp.

In general, a clinician's or researcher's success or failure in making an accurate statement on the basis of the Rorschach either may be demonstrating the sensitivity or insensitivity of the Rorschach, or may be simply reflecting whether the Rorschach is moving with or against the base rates.

In clinical practice, as in research, it is important to specify the population in which the Rorschach is being used, as base rates will vary from one population to another. This variation may even involve as fine a distinction as that between the base rates for the psychiatric population within a given hospital, and the base rates of those patients in the same hospital who typically are *referred for testing.*

An implication of Meehl and Rosen's discussion of base rates is that one cannot set hard and fast cutoff scores when using the Rorschach for diagnostic and predictive purposes. Rather, the particular cutoff score selected must be determined in light of the base rates for the specific population in question.

3. THE PROBLEM OF OVERLAP. In trying to determine from the Rorschach whether there are differences among groups or whether certain events will or will not occur, the problem of overlap must be recognized as a potential limitation. Statistical significance by no means implies concurrent or predictive validity.

Meehl and Rosen (1955) have pointed out that one way of trying to contend with this problem of overlap, and with the relative frequency of *false positives* and *false negatives,* is by either raising or lowering one's cutoff scores. Whether one type of "error" is more tolerable than the other depends on the particular situation. For some purposes, the primary emphasis will be on the reduction of the number of false positives—that is, eliminating as much as possible those individuals who are predicted on the basis of the Rorschach as reacting in a certain way, but who fail to show this response. Thus, in trying to predict prognosis for therapy in a clinical situation where the number of therapeutic hours is at a premium, one would want to set the cutoff score high, so as to eliminate as many false positives as possible. The resulting number of false negatives would be less important in this situation. In other situations, emphasis will be on the elimination of false negatives—those who show a given reaction even though the Rorschach has failed to predict it. For example, in looking for suicide indicators on the Rorschach, one might be more willing to lower the cutoff score and decrease the number of false negatives, even though it would be at the cost of being unduly cautious in watching the false positives who never actually attempt suicide.

4. The Problem of Unmeasured Variables. The predictive validity of the Rorschach, or of any test for that matter, is limited by the extent to which the test fails to measure all the relevant variables. In many instances, however, the number and type of variables needed for an accurate prediction are just not known. An otherwise accurate prediction on the basis of the Rorschach can turn out to be wrong because of some "divergent" and unexpected event in the environment which happens to affect relevant variables (cf. London, 1946).

Aside from the interference of extratest variables, a prediction can fail because all the variables related to the criterion itself were not sampled. For example, Purcell (1958) has offered an interpretation of why some projective instruments may fail in their predictions to a criterion. Based on Dollard and Miller's (1950) approach-avoidance theory of conflict, Purcell reasons that in using a projective test to measure some personality characteristic, one is apt to assess the individual's approach tendencies (e.g., aggressiveness), but to miss the presence of the avoidance tendencies (e.g., anxiety over aggression). This reduction of the avoidance tendency stems presumably from the disguised nature of the tests. Thus, in using the test performance to predict how an individual will act in a real-life situation, one has information on only half the story—the approach tendency. To make a more accurate prediction, it is necessary to take into account the avoidance tendencies as well. Purcell suggests ways of attempting to determine the net strength of an individual's approach reaction. For example, one may attempt to estimate the probability of response evocation by such variables as the *frequency* with which a sign occurs and the *latency* of its occurrence (i.e., how soon in the protocol it appears).

Although Purcell has raised an interesting problem, his suggestions for achieving greater precision in prediction are not very satisfying insofar as the Rorschach is concerned. The frequency variable is already used in practically all the various applications of the Rorschach. The more indicators present in a protocol, the greater the likelihood that the individual will manifest a given characteristic. The use of Purcell's latency criterion might be worthwhile, although latency of response would probably be determined in part by card pull.

In a most provocative paper, Wallace (1966) has argued that a highly relevant but conspicuously absent component in most projective tests is *situational variables.* To predict how an individual might behave in a given situation, it would seem to make sense that the measuring instrument should include stimuli which represent samples of the situation. In this respect, the Rorschach is severely limited. It clearly consists of ambiguous stimuli, and the speculations of some clinicians regarding specific card pull notwithstanding, the blots themselves cannot be construed as representing specific situations.

In the absence of any method of refining the Rorschach scoring to take into consideration the strength of avoidance tendencies or the modification of the blots themselves so that they more adequately approximate real-life situations, the evaluation of the Rorschach's value for making certain types of predictions must, in the final analysis, be purely *empirical*—even if we think we know why it might not work.

Construct Validity

The formalization of construct validity as a legitimate approach to test validation occurred with the publication of the *Technical Recommendations* (American Psychological Association, 1954). Impetus for this approach to validation arose from the frustration occurring in those situations where it was not very clear what the criterion measure might be. An example of this might be in a test of "ego strength." Rather than attempt to dream up some criterion measure, the construct-validity approach would operate as follows: First, an hypothesis derived from theory would be stated; for example, "People with good 'ego strength' tend to function better under stress than people with poor 'ego strength.'" Then, by using the test to preassess "ego strength," this hypothesis would be tested in an actual experiment.

In trying to determine the construct validity of a test, if a prediction from theory is confirmed in a study using a particular measuring instrument, then there is evidence not only for the validity of the *test* but for the *theory* as well. The situation is not as clear cut if the study reveals negative results. Assuming the study were otherwise methodologically sound, negative results might lead one to question and possibly modify the theory, the measuring instrument, or both. The decision as to what should be done is not an easy one to make, and much will depend on the relative amount of previous confirming evidence for both theory and test.

Constructs, which have been defined by Cronbach and Meehl (1955) as "postulated attribute[s] of people, assumed to be reflected in test performance" (p. 283), can vary as to their ambiguity as well as the extent and systematization of their theoretical underpinnings. Shneidman (1959) has described the task of trying to validate a test which measures some loose and changing theoretical construct as being "in some way similar to measuring a floating cloud with a rubber band—in a shifting wind" (p. 261). The *Standards* recognize this difficulty and consequently state that it is "essential" that the theoretical structure to which the particular construct is related be presented so as to make relatively clear the way in which the construct may be used.

In their elaboration of the theoretical reasoning behind the construct-validity approach, Cronbach and Meehl (1955) discuss the relationship between a construct and its *nomological network*. This concept refers to "the interlocking system of laws which constitute a theory" (Cronbach and Meehl, 1955, p. 290). These particular "laws" refer to (a) the relationship among theoretical constructs, (b) the relationship between theoretical constructs and observables, and (c) the relationship among observables themselves. So that the construct does not remain floating around in theoretical space, it is important that some of the laws in the nomological network involve observables. The more the network is filled out both empirically and theoretically, the easier it is to determine whether or not a test measures a particular construct.

Bechtoldt (1959) has argued that the very basic assumption underlying construct validity is illogical, in that one is said to have confirmed the validity of both theory and test by the successful prediction of a hypothesized outcome. To demonstrate his point, Bechtoldt cites the following syllogism of Johnson (1954):

> If "Old Dog Tray" was run through a large and powerful sausage-grinder, he is dead; he is dead, therefore he was sausaged (p. 723).

As Campbell (1960) has quite correctly pointed out, however, this break in the reasoning process is not specific to construct validity, but is basic to our very thinking about theory testing. And just as we would not be likely to "validate" a theory if it has generated one empirically confirmed hypothesis, so would it be naive if we expected that a single successful construct-validity study would give a test construct validity. Instead, one must look toward the "batting average" to note the degree to which confirmation has occurred, not just the simple average of "hits" and "misses," as some hypotheses can be more crucial than others. Thus, if we find that our "Old Dog Tray," although he has passed on, is not in little bits and pieces, we are not very likely to retain our original hypothesis.

METHODS OF ESTABLISHING CONSTRUCT VALIDITY. The method by which the construct validity of a test may be established can vary. Cronbach and Meehl (1955) have indicated that construct validity can be determined by any of five ways: (1) the prediction of behavioral or attitudinal differences between groups at different test-score levels, or an investigation of the hypothesis that certain groups of individuals should differ in the scores they obtain; (2) the correlation of the test with a second test purporting to measure the same construct; (3) factor analysis, which is actually an extension of the above method to determine the hypothesized relationship among a number of tests; (4) determining the internal structure of the test to see if it is consistent with the hypothesized heterogeneity or homogeneity of the construct; (5) noting predicted changes in the test score either as a function of some experimental manipulation or, for some constructs, simply of the time elapsed.

As in the case of criterion-related validity, it is desirable to represent construct validity numerically. A numerical estimate of a test's construct validity would refer to "the proportion of the test-score variance that is attributable to the construct variable" (Cronbach and Meehl, 1955, p. 289). Cronbach and Meehl recognize that the construct "loading" cannot be represented very easily in a single score. However, the *upper* and *lower* limits of the loading can be estimated by means of the correlation with other tests, which theoretically *do* and *do not* purport to measure the construct in question.

Two Types of Construct Validity. In addition to the specific operations involved in conducting the validity research, construct-validity studies vary in the extent to which theory is involved. Along these lines, Campbell (1960) has distinguished between two types of construct validity—*nomological validity* and *trait validity.*

By nomological validity, Campbell is referring to what most people think of when they speak of construct validity—namely, the use of the measuring instrument to test the accuracy of a theoretical prediction. Trait validity, on the other hand, typically involves the correlation of the test purporting to measure a particular trait with other measures of this same or theoretically related trait. Possibly, although not necessarily, because of an undeveloped theoretical system underlying the construct, the amount of inference from theory in the trait-validity approach is minimal.

In his discussion of trait validity, Campbell suggests several requirements which he believes to be important for test validation. His suggestions are based mainly on the general concept of discriminant validity (Campbell and Fiske, 1959), which requires that several measures of the same trait correlate higher with each other than they do with measures of different traits.[3] In order to approach an acceptable level of discriminant validity, Campbell offers a number of recommendations; only those that are relevant to Rorschach validation will be mentioned here.

1. *Correlations with tests of intelligence should be noted.* This recommendation is relevant particularly to those Rorschach approaches which attempt to measure level of cognitive functioning (e.g., developmental level or primary process level), prognosis for therapy, and similar characteristics. The degree to which a measure of a given construct is expected to relate to measures of intelligence depends on the theoretical conceptualization of the construct.
2. *Correlations with measures of social desirability should be noted.* The relevance of this suggestion to Rorschach validation may not seem as clear cut. Nevertheless, research along these lines might prove fruitful. For example, this recommendation might apply to certain scoring systems which rely on content (e.g., hostility indices), where there exists the possibility of the subject "faking good."
3. *Validity coefficients should be higher than those obtained by self-ratings.* The implication here is obvious. If a particular approach to the Rorschach fares no better than simple self-ratings of behavior

[3] Discriminant validity is very similar to Cronbach and Meehl's (1955) suggestion that one attempt to establish the upper and lower limit of a test's construct "loading."

relevant to the trait, then this particular Rorschach score is of minimal value. Admittedly, the enjoyment of measurement would be less in the use of self-ratings—but so would the time involved. In reviewing a variety of assessment techniques, Kelly has suggested something similar: "If you don't know what is going on in a person's mind, ask him; he may tell you" (1958, p. 330).

4. *Multitrait-multimethod matrix designs should be used.* The description of this approach has been presented in detail by Campbell and Fiske (1959). A multitrait-multimethod matrix design in validity research requires that *more than one method* be used in measuring a given trait, and also that an attempt be made to measure *more than one trait* by these various methods. According to Campbell and Fiske, this is the experimental design *par excellence* for determining the discriminant validity of a measuring instrument.

The Role of Theory in Test Construction. In most discussions of construct validity (American Psychological Association, 1954, 1966; Bechtoldt, 1959; Campbell, 1960; Cronbach and Meehl, 1955), the role of theory typically has been viewed as the means by which testable hypotheses are generated. Jessor and Hammond (1957), however, in their critique of the Taylor anxiety scale, extend the function of theory in construct validity. They maintain that construct validity should require that theory be involved in the actual *construction* of the test. Loevinger (1957) and Liverant (1958) similarly have presented strong arguments in favor of using theory in the construction of tests.

With respect to the Rorschach, it is obvious that the suggestions of Jessor and Hammond, Loevinger, and Liverant cannot be applied very easily to the construction of the blots themselves. On the other hand, the various approaches to the Rorschach *can* be evaluated as to the extent to which theory was utilized in the construction of each of the *scoring systems.* In the final analysis, however, the validity of the various Rorschach approaches should be determined by the results of validation studies—regardless of how the particular approach originated.

Reliability

The concept of reliability can be more varied in meaning than that of validity. Although reliability refers to the amount of error variance associated with the test score, the *Standards* discuss three approaches to reliability, each of which differs as to its method and purpose. The three ways of studying test reliability—*comparability of forms, internal consistency,* and *comparisons over time*—are described below, together with the relevancy of each to the Rorschach.

Approaches to Reliability

Comparability of Forms. This approach to reliability refers to the extent to which alternate forms of the same test correlate. Because of the variable card pull in the Rorschach blots, it would be extremely difficult to construct a set of blots that are equivalent in all those aspects to which the subject might respond. Consequently, this approach to reliability does not seem to be useful in Rorschach evaluation.

Internal Consistency. On the assumption that the test measures some homogeneous trait, this method of investigating reliability utilizes the split-half or odd-even method in correlating the two halves of the test. With respect to the Rorschach, however, this approach also seems of little use. The lack of applicability is based not only on the fact that many of the Rorschach approaches measure heterogeneous traits, but also on the very practical limitations imposed by differential card pull (cf. Goldfried, 1962b) and minimal size of the card sample.

Comparisons over Time. This approach to reliability, which involves the instrument's test-retest correlation, also presents problems in the case of the Rorschach. If a subject's performance on the Rorschach shows changes in the second administration, the question of whether this change reflects the instability of the Rorschach or a change in personality characteristics is not an easy one to unravel. In trying to minimize the likelihood of personality change by means of shorter time intervals between the two administrations, one encounters the problem of memory factors influencing the second protocol.

Whether or not a comparison over time applies to Rorschach evaluation depends upon the constancy of the characteristic which the particular Rorschach approach purports to measure. For example in the use of the Rorschach to measure transitory anxiety, or to determine suicide indicators, test-retest correlations would be of little value. For the use of the Rorschach in the measurement of other characteristics, such as general personality orientation (e.g., defensive style), the assessment of stability would indeed be appropriate. For still other approaches to the Rorschach in which changes are *expected* to occur over time (e.g., developmental scoring), test-retest correlations would not be appropriate as a measure of reliability. Rather, if one predicts a change in a particular characteristic, then the test-retest procedure would more accurately be used for construct validation (Cronbach and Meehl, 1955).

In those approaches to the Rorschach where the estimate of stability over time *is* applicable, an important factor to be considered is the composition of the sample upon which the reliability estimate is based. A sample which is homogeneous with respect to the particular characteristic is apt to yield a spuriously low correlation, whereas too heterogeneous a sample will tend to inflate the reliability coefficient. In addition, in evaluating the stability of a test, the *Standards* have pointed out the necessity of obtaining data on any changes in the means or standard deviations, as well as the usual information on the correlation between the two administrators.

On the Importance of Rorschach Reliability

But how may an estimate of reliability be obtained for Rorschach approaches in which a comparison over time is *not* applicable? The comparability of forms or the internal consistency methods do not present themselves as satisfactory alternatives.

Holzberg (1960) has suggested a different approach for determining the reliability of the Rorschach. He proposes that the consistency of perceptual and conceptual functioning on the Rorschach be related to performance on a variety of other similar tasks. Although this suggestion is a valuable one, it is doubtful that this would provide a measure of reliability in any of the ways in which reliability typically has been conceptualized. In fact, Holzberg's suggestion would be more appropriate as a method of determining construct validity (American Psychological Association, 1966; Campbell, 1960; Cronbach and Meehl, 1955).

The problem of determining the reliability of projective techniques in general has been discussed at length by MacFarlane and Tuddenham (1951). They acknowledge the many difficulties involved in determining the reliability of such instruments as the Rorschach. Although these difficulties cannot easily be overcome directly, we would agree with MacFarlane and Tuddenham, who maintain that the problem of Rorschach reliability can be handled indirectly. Consequently, for those Rorschach approaches where reliability coefficients cannot meaningfully be obtained, reliability can be *assumed* to exist if validity can be established. The limitation of this approach, of course, is that if the validity studies on a particular Rorschach approach fail to yield positive results, one is then hard put to explain just why this has occurred.

Scoring

The *Standards* have made some very simple and straightforward suggestions regarding the presentation of a test's system of scoring. In the case of the various Rorschach approaches, where scoring involves subjective judgments, the scoring criteria should be presented in sufficient detail so as to allow other individuals to learn the system.

The various scoring systems to be presented in this book vary as to their length, complexity, and ease in learning and application. In all instances, the entire scoring system, as well as sample responses will be presented. For all of the Rorschach systems evaluated in this book, the interscorer reliability, as well as a more general evaluation of the scoring procedures, will be presented.

Normative Data

Normative data or, more accurately, the lack of these data, have been a perennial problem in the use of the Rorschach. And yet without these data, the clinical use of the Rorschach must depend on the subjective, biased, and variable "internal norms" of each individual clinician.

In establishing normative data for a measuring instrument, there exists the problem of the representativeness of the sample upon which they are based. The sampling of the population to which each Rorschach approach is likely to be applied should, at the very least, include such variables as age, sex, I.Q., and educational level. Other variables may be relevant as well, depending upon the particular approach in question.

Rorschach norms gathered from patient populations present an additional problem. If the data were obtained from those Rorschach protocols available in the files, then these norms can be applied at best to those patients who are likely to be referred for testing. For most clinical purposes, however, this is the population for which norms are needed.

It would be a very nice state of affairs if, for each Rorschach approach, there were different sets of norms available for different levels of total response, as scores often vary as a function of length of protocol. Unfortunately, it is the rare study that presents sufficient data relevant to the relationship between the Rorschach scoring category and total R to allow us to obtain such information.

THE AIM OF THE BOOK RESTATED

For the past 40 years or so, the Rorschach has been employed for a number of special purposes, although the validity of these various applications has not always been clear. This book will present and evaluate some of these clinical and research applications of the Rorschach within the framework established by the APA *Standards*. And, from a broader perspective, the aim of this book may be viewed as a presentation of a step-by-step approach to determine some of the limits of the Rorschach's validity.

Chapter 2

FRIEDMAN'S DEVELOPMENTAL LEVEL SCORING

The use of the Rorschach as a measure of developmental level probably represents both the most original and useful application to which the test has been put. The term "developmental level" is misleading, in that it implies a concept to be used primarily with children. As will become increasingly evident in this chapter, this is far from being the case. More often than not, the concept of developmental level is used as a means of evaluating the adequacy of an individual's cognitive functioning. Hence, it has relevancy to such areas as schizophrenia, brain damage, mental deficiency, and other problems in which cognitive functioning might be impaired. Despite these diverse uses to which the developmental scoring of the Rorschach may be put, it nonetheless refers to a relatively clear-cut and theoretically consistent construct.

This chapter begins with a description of the theoretical basis for Friedman's scoring system. Following this, the actual scoring criteria are outlined. The available normative data are presented next, together with a description of the samples on which they were based. Research relevant to the reliability and validity of the developmental scoring is reviewed, and the chapter concludes with an overall evaluation of the strengths and weaknesses of this approach to the Rorschach.

THEORETICAL BACKGROUND

The concept of developmental levels as employed by Friedman (1952, 1953) is based on Werner's (1948, 1957) theory of cognitive development. According to Werner, development from children to maturity follows an *orthogenetic principle.* That is, development "precedes from a state of relative globality and lack of differentiation to a state of increasing differentiation, articulation, and hierarchic integration" (Werner, 1957, p. 126). In particular, the developmental sequence progresses along several bipolar continua: syncretic-discrete, diffuse-articulated, labile-stable, and rigid-flexible.

The developmentally early *syncretic* mode of functioning refers to the fused nature of the content of cognitions. An example of this would be synaesthesia, in which the sensory modalities are fused. Syncreticism is also seen in primitive emotions, where at early stages of development the distinction in feeling states goes no further than positive and negative excitation. The *diffuseness* characteristic of early development refers more to the structure or organization of cognitive functioning. That is, it points to the fact that the formal aspects of thought and cognition are as yet undifferentiated. Werner used the term *lability* to describe the unstable and highly changeable characteristic of primitive functioning; the *rigidity* seen at early stages, on the other hand, refers to the difficulty in adapting to changes in the surrounding environment. According to Werner, development progresses along these several bipolar continua toward a more differentiated and integrated mode of functioning, which is discrete, articulate, stable, and flexible.

By the term "hierarchic integration" Werner meant that through the process of development, certain functions become subordinated by more highly developed abilities, and that the individual becomes more conceptual and less stimulus-bound. As Werner himself has stated: "Thus, emotions become intellectually controlled, abstract conceptualization of the environment replaces concrete perceptual organization, and so on" (Werner, 1948, p. 56b).

Werner has indicated that an important determinant of the child's initial globality in cognition is the absence of any clear-cut distinction between self and environment. In general, "the younger the child the 'nearer' it is [to its world], and the distance separating subject and object increases with age" (Werner, 1948, p. 383). Werner has used the concept "ego-halo" to refer to the indefinite boundary between self and external world, adding that this ego-halo is more extended for the child than it is for the adult.

Some of Werner's theoretical concepts are admittdly somewhat abstract and elusive. As we describe the interpretative significance of each of Friedman's developmental scoring categories, however, they should become more clear.

As we have noted, Werner's theory should be viewed not only as an explanation of the sequence of development in children, but also as an *approach* to the understanding of the adequacy of cognitive functioning in normal and pathological adults. From a developmental point of view, schizophrenics are seen being in a state of regression, and consequently are functioning at developmentally lower levels. However, just as later stages of development can be found to show some remnants of earlier levels of development, the regressed individual may be expected to possess residuals of more mature levels of functioning. Consequently, although schizophrenics are believed to be functioning at developmentally lower levels, their functioning should be similar, but not identical, to that of children.

It should be noted that Werner did not conceive of an individual's developmental level of functioning as being represented by a single point on a continuum. Rather, people may be characterized more appropriately as having a *range* of developmentally different operations at their disposal. In fact, Werner has maintained that the wider the range of developmental operations, the more mature the person. For example, creative activities often reflect a syncretic approach to functioning, such as those physiognomic observations in which emotional qualities are attributed to inanimate objects (e.g., a "sad" sunset). In this respect, there are some bases for comparison between Werner's developmental theory and the "primary process" construct used by Holt in his scoring system (Holt and Havel, 1960).

From a general point of view, Werner's approach to development may be characterized as being somewhat nativistic. Because of his sympathy to Gestaltist orientation, the possible role of learning and experience in the development of cognitive functioning was deemphasized. The maturation vs. learning controversy is of less concern if we view the concept of developmental level in a descriptive sense—namely, as the demarcation of the various stages in which the developmental sequence progresses.

This, in brief, is the theoretical structure underlying Friedman's developmental scoring system. There are several implications of the theory which we have not yet mentioned. These additional aspects, however, are best presented later in this chapter in connection with the interpretive significance of the developmental scoring categories, together with the assumptions underlying some of the validity studies.

FRIEDMAN'S DEVELOPMENTAL SCORING SYSTEM

Friedman has used Werner's theory to define not only the construct "developmental level," but also to develop the scoring system itself. Drawing on the work of Beck, Dworetski, and Rapaport, Friedman 1952, 1953) has developed a simple scoring of the Rorschach which takes into account only the structural and organizational aspects of the percept. In a sense, a subject's protocol is viewed as being comprised of perceptual-cognitive responses. Only location scores are used (as defined by Beck, 1949, 1961), which are then further classified according to the percept's level of diffuseness, articulation, integration, and so on. Where form-level judgments are required, Friedman suggests the use of Beck's (1949, 1961) or Hertz' (1951) tables. All the scores in Friedman's approach fall into either the *developmentally high* (*or mature*) or *developmentally low* (*or immature*) classification.

The following is a description of the *scoring criteria* for each of the scoring categories within the developmentally (or genetically) high and low classifications, together with sample responses for each scoring category.[1] Following this is a discussion of the theoretical and empirical *interpretive significance* of these scores, the possible ways of arriving at *summary scores* for a protocol, and the *interscorer reliability*.

Scoring Criteria for Developmentally High Scores

1. W++

"A response in which a unitary blot is perceptually articulated and then reintegrated into a well-differentiated unifying whole, the specific form of which matches the blot" (Friedman, 1953, p. 173). A W + +, since it involves the breaking down of a uniform total blot area, can occur only on "unbroken blots" (Cards I, IV, V, VI, and IX). Friedman defines an unbroken blot as one in which there is a minimum of white space separating the Usual Detail (D) areas. "Broken blots," on the other hand, are those blots where all or most of a D area is separated from the rest of the blot by white space, or where the two lateral halves of the blot are separated by a large amount of white background (Cards II, III, VII, and X).

Sample W + + responses are as follows:

Card I: "Two figures holding onto a woman."
Card IV: "A man sitting on a stool."
Card V: "Two people sleeping back to back."
Card VI: "A lighthouse on a rock."
Card IX: "Witches brewing a potion."

2. D++

A response to a D location where there is both the articulation and reintegration into a percept of good form level.

Sample D + + responses are as follows:

Card I, D4: "Two women with their arms around each other."
Card III, D2: "A parrot on a swing."
Card VII, D2: "A clown about to throw a stick."
Card IX, D3: "A man blowing a bugle."
Card X, D9: "A puppet sticking out of a stocking."

3. W+

"A response in which all the discrete portions of a broken blot are combined into a unifying whole, and in which the specific form implied in the content matches the blot" (Friedman, 1953, p. 173). Since a W + response involves the integration of blot areas already broken down, this score can be obtained only on broken blots.

[1] In the case of responses presenting particular scoring problems, see the more elaborate criteria presented by Phillips' system in Chapter 3.

Sample W + responses are as follows:

Card II: "Two clowns dancing together."
Card III: "Two people decorating a room for a party."
Card VII: "Two women talking."
Card VIII: "Sailboat"; "lions climbing a hill."
Card X: "An aquarium."

4. D+

"A response in which two or more discrete blot areas (two or more D) are combined into one percept, the specific form of which matches the blot" (Friedman, 1953, p. 174). It is essential that the areas be *integrated meaningfully.* Thus, "two bears" to Card VII, DI, should be scored Dm (see below), as integration is not indicated.

Sample D + responses are as follows:

Card II, D6: "Two bears rubbing noses."
Card III, D1: "Cannibals standing over a pot."
Card VII, D2: "Indians arguing."
Card VIII, D1 and D8: "Two animals climbing a tree."
Card X, D1 and D12: "A crab who just caught a fish."

5. Wm

"A mediocre response in which the gross outline and articulation of an unbroken blot are taken into account so that the specific form implied in the content matches the blot" (Friedman, 1953, p. 173). The Wm response is the "cheap" or lazy" W response which has certain fairly definite form demands on the content. While a Wm response is usually obtained on unbroken blots, there is one exception: responses to Card VII which imply a definite "U" shape. Examples of this are cited below.

Sample Wm responses are as follows:

Card I: "Bat"; "cat's face"; "airplane."
Card IV: "Butterfly"; "bear."
Card V: "Bat"; "butterfly."
Card VI: "Animal hide"; "large violin."
Card VII: "Bowl"; "harbor."
Card IX: "Water fountain."

6. Dm

An F + response to a single D area, where the content has definite form requirements, but where the blot is not broken down and reintegrated.

Sample Dm responses are as follows:

Card I, D4: "Woman with her hand raised."
Card III, D3: "Bow tie."

Card IV, D1: "Cow's head."
Card VI, D3: "Butterfly."
Card X, D9: "Sea horse."

Scoring Criteria for Developmentally Low Scores

1. Wv

"A vague response in which there is a diffuse general impression of the blot. Although some form element is present, it is of such an unspecific nature that almost any perceptual form is adequate to encompass the content" (Friedman, 1953, p. 173). It should be noted that despite the fact that vague responses typically (although not always) receive plus scorings on a normative basis, this type of response is considered to be developmentally low. The essence of the vague response is that it can conceivably be attributed to any of the 10 blots.

Sample Wv responses are as follows:

Card I: "A map."
Card II: "A rock formation."
Card IV: "An island"; "emblem."
Card VII: "Clouds"; "torn paper."
Card IX: "Insides of a body."

2. Dv

A vague response to a D area, the content of which involves unspecific form demands. Analogous to the Wv response, the Dv response may be attributed to practically any D area.

Sample Dv responses are as follows:

Card II, D3: "Explosion."
Card III, D2: "Splotches of blood."
Card VI, D1: "A piece of land."
Card VIII, D2: 'Ice cream."
Card IX, D1: "Clouds."

3. Wa

"An amorphous response in which the shape of the blot plays no determinable role. Such responses are based solely on chromatic or achromatic aspects of the blot, and in customary scoring procedure no form element would be included in the score" (Friedman, 1953, p. 173).

Sample Wa responses are as follows:

Card I: "Black paint."
Card II: "Ink mixed with blood."
Card IV: "Night."

Card VIII: "Colors of the rainbow."
Card X: "Colors on an artist's palette."

4. Da

An amorphous response given to a D location.
Sample Da responses are as follows:

Card II, D2: "Blood."
Card III, D2: "Fire."
Card VII, D5: "Smoke."
Card VIII, D5: "Grass."
Card IX, D1: "Green water."

5. W−

"A response in which the content produced requires a definite specific form, which, however, is not provided by the blot" (Friedman, 1953, p. 173). The normative tables for plus and minus scoring are used to determine whether or not the content matches the blot.

Sample W − responses are as follows:

Card I: "A man riding a bike."
Card III: "A spider."
Card V: "A map of the United States."
Card VIII: "Statue."
Card IX: "Butterfly."

6. D−

A response to a D location which, according to normative tables, is classified as being minus.

Sample D − responses are as follows:

Card I, D4: "A cat."
Card II, D3: "Crab."
Card IV, D1: "A snail."
Card VII, D1: "A duck."
Card X, D2: "Chicken."

7. DW

A confabulatory response, where the content is generalized to the whole blot on the basis of what is seen in a D area. To score DW, it is essential to determine, from either the free association or the inquiry, that the entire percept was indeed based on the subject's response to the D area.

Sample DW responses are as follows:

Card I: "A bird, because of the wings (D8)."
Card III: "A cat's face, because of the nose (D3)."

Card IV: "A dog, because here are the ears (D4)."
Card V: "A rabbit, because this is his head (D6)."
Card VI: "A cat, because of his whiskers (D6)."

8. DdD

A confabulatory response, where the response to a D area is generalized from what is seen in a Dd area. As is the case with the DW score, it is important to determine that the Dd percept was in fact responsible for the response to the D area.

Sample DdD responses are as follows:

Card I, D4: "A cat, because of its tail (Dd31)."
Card II, D1: "A monkey, because of his ear (Dd31)."
Card VI, D4: "A boat, because of this gun (Dd25)."
Card IX, D6: "A bird, and here are his feet (Dd21)."
Card X, D9: "A bear, because of its face (Dd25)."

9. FabC

A fabulized combination response, in which two or more separately interpreted areas are combined on the basis of their spatial relationship; the resulting response is a percept which does not usually occur in nature.

Sample FabC responses are as follows:

Card II: "A leg (D2) on the head of a bear (D1)."
Card V, W: "A rabbit (D7) with wings (D4)."
Card VII, W: "Two rabbits (D1), sitting on two masks (D3), sitting on two rocks (D10)."
Card VIII: "Two bears (D1) waving blankets (D5)."
Card X: "Puppets (D9) blowing glass (D6), with bugs controlling the strings (D11)."

10. ConR

A contaminated response, in which two separate responses are fused, and attributed to the *same* blot area.

Sample ConR responses are as follows:

Card IV, W: "Front of a bug-ox" (W both front of a bug and front of an ox).
Card V, D4: "Two figures lying in a forest" (D4 both figures and forest).
Card VIII, D5: "Flags flying in the sky" (D5 both flags and sky).
Card IX, D1: "Two gnomes sitting on the grass" (D1 both gnomes and grass).
Card X, D1: "A spidery elf" (D1 both spider and elf).

Once a protocol is scored according to the criteria presented above, the task of summarizing the scores is relatively straightforward. Actually, one has a choice of two general approaches in summarizing a record. Before describing these methods, however, we shall outline the interpretive significance—based upon the theoretical underpinnings of the system as well as actual research findings—for each of the developmentally high and low scores.

Interpretive Significance of Developmentally High Scores

1. W++

A response of this type reflects both a differentiation as well as a reintegration of parts. Normal adults obtain significantly more W + + scores than children and, at a lower significance level (p between .05 and .10), than hebephrenic and catatonic schizophrenics. Children and schizophrenics do not differ as to the frequency of this response (Friedman, 1952).

2. D++

This type of response occurs infrequently, as does the W + + response. Friedman (1952) implies that because of the fine degree of articulation and integration required to produce a D + + response, one would expect to find it only in the records of individuals with a very high developmental level of functioning.

3. W+

The primary significance of this type of response is the integration it requires. Friedman (1952) found that although regressed schizophrenics and children did not differ in the frequency of this response, normal adults produced significantly more than children. The greater frequency of this response in normals as opposed to regressed schizophrenics "approached" significance (p between .05 and .10). W + responses were also found to occur significantly more often for normals than for neurotics (Frank, 1952).

4. D+

The D + response reflects an integrative capacity, but one of a lesser degree than the W + response. Friedman (1952) found that normals produced the D + response significantly more often than regressed schizophrenics. The schizophrenics obtained this score more often than children, which Friedman interprets as being consistent with Werner's contention that regressed individuals retain some remnants of their higher levels of development. The D + response was also found to occur less frequently in neurotics than in normals (Frank, 1952).

5. Wm

Although classified as a developmentally high response, the Wm score reflects little organization. Rosenblatt and Solomon (1954) found no difference in the frequency of this type of response betwen normals and mental defectives. Nevertheless, Friedman (1952) reports that this was the only W score which differentiated among normals, schizophrenics, and children; normals produced more Wm responses than schizophrenics, and schizophrenics more than children. In trying to explain why normals and schizophrenics differ on this developmentally high W score, but only *approach* a significant difference on the W + + and W + scores, Friedman (1952) hypothesizes that Wm responses occur less frequently in schizophrenics because "the relatively frequent Wv in the schizophrenics is the result of regressive diffuseness and vagueness interfering with percepts which, in the absence of such a process, might have been Wm responses" (p. 90). For a more complete discussion of the relationship between mediocre and vague responses, see the description below of the interpretive significance of the Dv response.

6. Dm

As was the case with the Wm score, Dm was found by Friedman (1952) to occur most often in normals, less often in schizophrenics, and least often in children. The relationship between Dm and Dv is discussed below under the interpretive description of the Dv score.

Interpretive Significance of Developmentally Low Scores

1. Wv

This developmentally low response differs from Wa responses in that the Wv score reflects some minimal form requirements for the percept. Friedman (1952) interprets Wv responses as indicating a "less specifically structured" view of the world, which reflects the *regressive* nature of the individual's level of functioning. Accordingly, studies have found that Wv responses are relatively rare in normal adults, neurotics, children, and mental defectives (Frank, 1952; Friedman, 1952; Rosenblatt and Solomon, 1954). Wv responses *do occur,* however, among individuals who are believed to have regressed in their functioning—paranoid schizophrenics, hebephrenic and catatonic schizophrenics, and brain damaged (Friedman, 1952; Peña, 1953; Siegel, 1953). Although Wv responses presumably reflect the regressive characteristics of the subject, the regression is not as severe as that reflected in such primitive scores as Wa, W −, DW, ConR, and so on. The Wv presumably reflects the individual's attempts to use whatever remaining cognitive processes he has in order to cope with the regression.

2. Dv

Although normals, schizophrenics, and children were not significantly different in the frequency of Dv responses, the relative distribution among the three groups was similar to the distribution for Wv (Friedman, 1952). No difference was found between normals and neurotics in this scoring category (Frank, 1952). Peña (1953), however, found that hebephrenic and catatonic schizophrenics produced more Dv responses than brain-damaged subjects.

Friedman[2] has suggested an interesting hypothesis for interpreting the relationship between mediocre and vague responses in each of the W and D location areas. Although both Wm and Dm responses are believed to be replaced by Wv and Dv, respectively, during regression to earlier levels of functioning, the sequence of change may be expected to differ for the two location scores. According to Werner's (1948, 1957) theory, the sequence of cognitive development progresses from an undifferentiated, global condition (i.e., developmentally low W response), to an articulation of parts (i.e., developmentally high D responses), and finally to an integration of parts into a larger whole (i.e., developmentally high W responses); this developmental sequence has been confirmed empirically (Hemmendinger, 1953). Based on both theory and empirical evidence that developmentally high D scores (in this instance Dm) occur earlier than high W scores in the developmental sequence (see Figures 2.1 and 2.2, pp. 41–42), Friedman hypothesizes that mature D scores are most resistant to change. Developmentally high W scores (in this instance Wm), because of their relatively later development, represent less firmly established cognitive processes than the mature D scores. Consequently, one might expect that under conditions of regression, Wv responses would replace Wm responses sooner than Dv would replace Dm responses. Conversely, under conditions of remission Wv would be expected to disappear before Dv. Thus, because of their more recent developmental acquisition relative to Dm responses, Wm responses are the *first to go during regression,* but also the *first to return during remission.*

In comparing the relative frequency of Wv and Dv scores in a given protocol, Friedman suggests the following interpretations:

1. *Low Wv%* and *low* Dv% [i.e., (Wv) (Dv)] indicates the *absence* of regression.
2. *High* Wv% and *low* Dv% [i.e., (Wv) (Dv)] reflects the *beginnings* of regression.
3. *High Wv%* and *high* Dv% [*i.e.,* (Wv!) (Dv!)] indicates that the person is in a more *severe* state of regression, or has only partially recovered from a regressed condition (Dv still present) and is now again *moving into* (Wv reappearing) a regressed state.
4. *Low* Wv% and *high* Dv% [i.e., (Wv) (Dv!)] reflects the process of *remission* from a regressed condition.

By "high" and "low" is meant the higher or lower Wv% or Dv% obtained relative to the percentage scores for normal subjects. For normative data on each of the developmental scoring categories, see Table 2.4.

Although no direct empirical test of these hypothesized relationships has been carried out, there are some indirect data which partially confirm some of the interpretations. For example, Peña (1953) found that hebephrenic and catatonic schizophrenics, who presumably are more severely

[2] Personal communication, May 10, 1963.

regressed than organics, did not give more Wv responses but *did* obtain more Dv responses. Even more indirect evidence was obtained by Rochwarg (1954), who found that integrated W responses (i.e., W + + and W +) disappeared completely during old age, while integrated D responses (i.e., D + + and D +) only declined to the 8- to 9-year-old levels.

Findings relevant to these hypothesized relationships have also been reported by Siegel (1953), who compared three groups which presumably represent three levels of regression—normals, paranoid schizophrenics, and catatonic and hebephrenic schizophrenics. The data on the median Wv% are as follows: 0% for normals, 26.5% for paranoid schizophrenics, and 17.0% for hebephrenics and catatonics. The difference between normals and paranoids is statistically significant (p between .02 and .05), while the difference between normals and hebephrenics and catatonics only approaches significance (p between .05 and .10). Although the Wv% is lower for hebephrenics and catatonics than for paranoids, the difference between the two groups was not significant. It should be noted that for genetically lower W scores (W − and DW), hebephrenic and catatonic schizophrenics were found to be more regressed. The data for Dv% reported by Siegel are as follows: 5.0% for normals, 5.5% for paranoid schizophrenics, and 11.5% for hebephrenic and catatonic schizophrenics. The only difference that even approached significance (p between .05 and .10) was between the normals and hebephrenics and catatonic schizophrenics, which partially confirms the hypothesis that Dv scores appear only when regression is more severe.

The support for Friedman's hypotheses is indirect and only minimal. A more direct test, preferably a longitudinal study which would follow pathological groups through regression and remission, is needed to help clarify the relationship between vague and mediocre responses in W and D locations.

3. Wa

The Wa score reflects the most diffuse, global level of perception. Friedman (1952) found that although children and regressed schizophrenics could not be distinguished on the basis of this score, both groups obtained significantly more Wa responses than normals.

4. Da

The developmental progression of this type of response is not clear cut, and Friedman (1952) reasons that once perception has reached the stage where discreteness occurs, the amorphous quality of perception apparently begins to disappear.

5. W−

Friedman (1952) interprets this score as reflecting what Werner (1948) has called the "syncretic" mode of cognitive functioning. That is, it depicts the blending of several modes of functioning (e.g., affective, sensory, motor) in such a manner that one's inner condition strongly determines the way in which an individual reacts to the world. Consequently, the Rorschach percept is less likely to conform to the demands made by the blot structure. Friedman (1952) found that while children and regressed schzophrenics do not differ in their W −%, both groups obtain significantly higher scores than normals.

6. D−

The D − score, like the W −, reflects the syncretic mode of functioning. Normals give fewer D − scores than children, schizophrenics, or brain damaged (Friedman, 1952; Peña, 1953). The finding that schizophrenics do not obtain this type of response as often as children also serves to confirm Werner's (1948) hypothesis that regressed individuals possess residuals of higher levels of functions (cf. interpretive significance of D + responses).

7. DW

This confabulatory response for the W location is interpreted in light of Werner's (1948) concept of *pars pro toto*—any given part implies the quality of the whole. Although children and schizophrenics do not differ as to the frequency of this response, both groups obtain significantly more DW responses than normals (Friedman, 1953).

8. DdD

The confabulatory response for the D location occurs infrequently in children, normals, and schizophrenics (Friedman, 1953), which is what accounts for the failure of this response to differentiate among these three groups.

9 and 10. FabC and ConR

Both the fabulized combination (two percepts combined into one on the basis of contiguity) and the contaminated response (two percepts fused into the same area) are interpreted by Friedman as reflecting Werner's (1948) description of the "magic of contiguity." These primitive responses may also be seen as an indication of the parataxic mode (Sullivan, 1953). Because of the relative infrequence of the FabC and ConR, Friedman (1952) combined the two scores in comparing normals, children, and schizophrenics. In accordance with theoretical expectation, both children and schizophrenics failed to differ in the production of these scores, but each produced more than normals.

Summary Scores

There are two general approaches in summarizing a record; one involves the use of percentage scores, and the other the differential weighting of the several scoring categories.

Percentage Scores

A convenient way to summarize most of the developmentally high and low scores for clinical usage is to compute the per cent of each W and D

TABLE 2.1
Sample Table for Summarizing Per Cent of Developmentally Mature and Immature Whole (W) and Usual Detail (D) Location Scores[a]

	Mature				Immature				
	++	+	*m*	*Total % Mature*	–	*v*	*a*	*DW* or *DdD*	*Total % Immature*
W	6.1	16.5	42.4	65.0	13.5	18.2	2.2	1.1	35.0
D	1.0	17.1	56.6	74.7	16.1	7.7	0.9	0.6	25.3

[a] The percentages are based on the proportion of each scoring category to the relevant location score in general (e.g., W ++/total W, D ++/total D, etc.).

scoring category to all W and D scores, respectively. Thus, W + +% = W + +/total W, D + +/total D, and so forth. The final summary of all the resulting scores can be included in a table such as that presented in Table 2.1. The data in Table 2.1 are fictitious, and are presented for illustrative purposes only. The summary table includes information as to the per cent of each of the location scores in the protocol, as well as the per cent of developmentally high and low W and developmentally high and low D. Normative data for the type of scores summarized in Table 2.1 are presented in Tables 2.4 and 2.5.

INDEX OF INTEGRATION. Because of the somewhat intermediate developmental level of functioning represented by the Wm and Dm scores, several workers have eliminated these two scores in order to compute a more refined index of the subject's capacity for developmentally high function. This final score, referred to as the *index of integration,* is computed by the following formula:

$$\text{Index of Integration} = \frac{(\text{W}{+}{+}) + (\text{W}{+}) + (\text{D}{+}{+}) + (\text{D}{+})}{\text{all } (\text{W} + \text{D})} \times 100$$

INDEX OF PRIMITIVE THOUGHT (IPT). The index of primitive thought reflects what is believed to be the developmentally lowest level of functioning. The following formula is used to compute this index:

$$\text{IPT} = \frac{\text{FabC} + \text{ConR} = \text{DW} + \text{DdD}}{\text{total R}} \times 100$$

Weighting of Scores

On the basis of developmental theory as well as previous research findings, Becker (1956) has devised a system of weighting the developmental scoring categories. By means of Becker's approach, a single developmental level (*DL*) score may be obtained to summarize the entire protocol. Each of the scores in a protocol is assigned a weight from 1 to 6 (see Table 2.2) and all weights are summed and then divided by the number of weights totaled. In other words, the final *DL* score represents the *average weighting* for the entire protocol.

TABLE 2.2
Becker's Weightings of Friedman's Developmental Scoring Categories

Scoring Categories	*Weight Assigned*
Wa, W −, DW, ConR, FabC, Rejection[a]	1
Da, DdD, D −, Dv, Dd −[b]	2
Wv, Dd +[b]	3
Dm, Wm	4
D +, W +	5
D ++, W ++	6

[a] Wilensky (1959b) has suggested that card rejections be given a weight of 1.
[b] Not part of Friedman's original scoring system, but a score suggested by Becker (1956).

Wilensky (1959a) has suggested that the final *DL* as computed by Becker's approach may be affected by the number of responses. Specifically, Wilensky maintains that as productivity increases, more mediocre responses, which are assigned a weight of 4, are given. This results in a ceiling effect, which in turn makes for a less variable distribution of *DL* scores for a group of subjects. Wilensky offers an alternative method of computing the final *DL* score, which minimizes the ceiling effect produced by the increase in number of responses—particularly the large number of mediocre responses to Card X. The Wilensky method of computing the *DL* score, while it uses the weights suggested by Becker, requires that an average developmental score be first obtained for *each card*. The 10 scores are then totaled and an average score is arrived at for the entire protocol.

As might be expected, the Becker and Wilensky approaches to computing the *DL* score are highly correlated. Wilensky (1959a), using protocols from a schizophrenic sample, obtained a .95 correlation between the two methods. Goldfried (1962b) similarly found the two approaches to be correlated significantly ($r = .89$) within a psychiatric population. Using this same sample of patients, Goldfried (1962b) confirmed that the Wilensky method produced a more variable distribution of DL scores ($p < .05$) than the Becker approach.

The method of summarizing a protocol by means of a single score, although extremely convenient for research purposes, nevertheless has both theoretical and empirical drawbacks. From the theoretical viewpoint underlying the concept of developmental level (Werner, 1948, 1957), one may argue that this single summary score obscures the hierarchic integration of developmentally high and low modes of functioning which characterize the individual. Further, from an empirical standpoint, results have indicated that some groups differ not so much in their overall developmental level, but in their differential *patterning* of developmentally high and low W and D scores.

Which Type of Summary Score to Use

The problem of whether or not a developmentally scored Rorschach protocol is best represented by an overall summary or by summaries of the constituent scoring categories is much like the question that has been raised with regard to the results of an I.Q. test. Just as two individuals with the same I.Q. score can differ in their patterning of intellectual strengths and weaknesses, so can two people with a similar overall developmental level of functioning differ in the patterning of functioning that the final score summarizes.

The decision as to which type of summary score to use depends in part upon whether the developmental scoring is to be used for clinical or research purposes. For the *clinical* use of the developmental scoring system, the percentage-score approach as illustrated in Table 2.1 is probably the most useful. This approach gives not only the patterning of individual scores in the protocol, but summaries of the entire record as well. Actually the final summary can be represented by two scores: *per cent mature W* and *per cent mature D*. The additional use of per cent of immature W and immature D would be superfluous, as these scores are always equal to total W minus mature W/total W, and total D minus mature D/total D, respectively.

For *research* purposes, it is also convenient to summarize the protocol with the mature W per cent and mature D per cent scores. Similarly, one can conduct studies in which groups are compared on the percentage scores of the specific scoring categories (e. g., W +, Wm, etc.). Perhaps the most convenient of all approaches, however, would be to use the weighting method, as this yields a single *DL* score. Because of the theoretical and empirical limitations to this method discussed above, the use of this summary score would probably depend on the particular research problem. Obviously, if the study involved the comparison of two groups as to their range or patterning of functioning on cognitive tasks, the single summary score would tend to mask differences. If, on the other hand, the study was designed to assess differences in some overall level of cognitive development, the total *DL* score would be more appropriate (cf. Kissel, 1965).

Interscorer Reliability

Friedman's scoring system is a relatively simple one to learn, and the time required for scoring an actual record is minimal. As to the interscorer reliability of the system, results of studies have shown it to be quite favorable. With two judges independently scoring the same protocols, the mean per cent of agreement is 93.5, with a range of 89.7–96.0 (Friedman, 1953; Goldfried, 1961; Hurwitz, 1954; Lofchie, 1955; Misch, 1954; Zimet and Fine, 1959). For three independent judges, the mean per cent of agreement is 93.6, with a range of 91.3–95.6 (Frank, 1952; Siegel, 1953). Thus, all these studies have typically found interscorer reliability to be quite high—in most instances, beyond 90% agreement.

One exception to this high degree of agreement, however, is reported in a study by Margolis, Engelhardt, Freedman, Hankoff, and Mann (1960) in which only 70% agreement is reported. Although it is not stated explicitly, this figure presumably was based on agreement among five judges. In light of the high reliability scores found in other studies, it seems unlikely that the lower agreement found by Margolis et al. was due entirely to the greater number of judges involved. One might speculate that the lower reliability could also have been a function of the relative lack of experience that these judges had with the Rorschach—only two of the five judges had a Ph.D., one had a B.A., and the other two had M.D.s.

Apart from the 70% agreement reported by Margolis et al. (1960), the large majority of results clearly indicate that the interscorer reliability for Friedman's scoring system is quite good.

NORMATIVE DATA

The normative data in this section were culled from those validation studies reporting group data for each of the developmental scores. Before presenting the actual data, the nature of the sample is described in enough detail to make the range of applicability reasonably clear.

Nature of the Sample

The data were obtained for children between the ages of 3 and 10 (Hemmendinger, 1953), adult mental defectives at several mental age levels (Rosenblatt and Solomon, 1954), normal adults (Friedman, 1952), neurotics (Frank, 1952), schizophrenics (Siegel, 1953), and brain damaged (Peña, 1953). A description of the characteristics of each of these samples is presented in Table 2.3

One of the most obvious restrictions of the sample is that, except for the mental defectives, the group consists of white males. Most of the studies indicate additionally that their subjects were American born. The question as to whether or not the normative data in this section can be appropriately used to interpret the protocols of female subjects cannot be answered unequivocally. Only one study (Wilson, 1954) has been done to compare males and females as to their developmental levels of functioning. In this study, Wilson found that boys and girls between the ages of 6 and 17 did *not* differ on overall developmental level of functioning. No comparisons were made between the sexes for each of the separate scoring categories.

Other limitations in the sample include the size of each group. Thirty and even fewer subjects is somewhat of a small *N* to allow for a confident generalization to each of the separate populations. A less serious restriction is in the I.Q. scores reported; these values were based on a variety of measures, such as the Wechsler–Bellevue (Forms I and II), Stanford–Binet, the vocabulary subtests of these tests, the Otis, and so on. However, the general I.Q. range of the subjects in each group probably would have differed only minimally had a single uniform measure of I.Q. been used throughout.

For most of the groups, the inquiry was conducted after all 10 cards. This procedure was modified in the case of the children, where the inquiry was conducted after each card, and in the case of some of the less intelligent mental defectives, where the inquiry was conducted after each response. Most of the studies included only those subjects who obtained at least a minimal number of responses (usually 8 or 10) for the entire record.

TABLE 2.3
Characteristics of the Normative Data Sample

	Sex			Age			I.Q.			Mean M.A.	Years of Education	
Group	*N*	*Male*	*Female*	*Mean*	*Median*	*Range*	*Mean*	*Median*	*Range*	*in Months*	*Median*	*Range*
Normal Children (Hemmendinger, 1953)												
3-Year-Olds	20	20	0	3:5.9	—[a]	3:0–3:11	107.5	—	93–120	—	—	—
4-Year-Olds	20	20	0	4:5.9	—	4:0–4:11	112.3	—	87–120	—	—	—
5-Year-Olds	20	20	0	5:5.5	—	5:0–5:11	103.0	—	89–120	—	—	—
6-Year-Olds	20	20	0	6:5.6	—	6:0–6:11	109.9	—	88–120	—	—	—
7-Year-Olds	20	20	0	7:6.8	—	7:0–7:11	106.1	—	92–120	—	—	—
8-Year-Olds	20	20	0	8:5.1	—	8:0–8:11	108.8	—	96–120	—	—	—
9-Year-Olds	20	20	0	9:4.1	—	9:0–9:11	103.1	—	85–120	—	—	—
10-Year-Olds	20	20	0	10: 4.3	—	10:0–10:11	103.8	—	91–116	—	—	—
Adult Mental Defectives (Rosenblatt and Solomon, 1954)												
Average M.A. of 5:1	16	8	8	30.8	—	22–53	—	—	28–35	61	—	—
Average M.A. of 6:11	16	8	8	29.3	—	19–50	—	—	40–45	81	—	—
Average M.A. of 8:5	16	8	8	28.9	—	19–40	—	—	50–55	101	—	—
Average M.A. of 9:11	16	8	8	29.0	—	19–55	—	—	60–65	119	—	—
Average M.A. of 11:11	16	4	12	27.3	—	20–45	—	—	70–81	143	—	—
All five M.A. Levels Combined	80	36	44	29.0	—	19–55	—	—	28–81	101	—	—
Normal Adults (Friedman, 1953)	30	30	0	29.4	29	22–40	104.9	106.0	88–120	—	12.0	10–16
Neurotics (Frank, 1952)	30	30	0	29.6	31	20–40	107.0	105.5	91–120	—	11.5	6–16
Paranoid Schizophrenics (Siegel, 1953)	30	30	0	27.7	26	21–36	104.0	105.0	87–120	—	12.0	6–16
Hebephrenic and Catatonic Schizophrenics (Siegal, 1953)	30	30	0	27.4	26	20–39	99.9	101.0	85–118	—	10.0	7–16
Brain Damaged (Peña, 1953)	30	30	0	29.8	30	20–40	104.6	106.5	86–120	—	10.5	8–16

[a] A dash (—) indicates that these data were not available.

However, no information is reported as to the number of cases that had to be eliminated because of this criterion.

Additional information on the composition of some of the subsamples described in Table 2.3 should be mentioned. The 80 adult defectives represent a fairly homogeneous grouping of the "familial" type of mental deficiency; that is, there was no discernible evidence of any organic impairment (Rosenblatt and Solomon, 1954). The group of neurotics consisted of 20 anxiety neurotics, six conversion reactions, three phobic reactions, and one dissociative reaction. These patients had been hospitalized, and their diagnoses were based on the final discharge summaries (Frank, 1952). The groups of paranoid schizophrenics and of hebephrenic and catatonic schizophrenics were composed of patients who had been diagnosed at staff conferences (Siegel, 1953). The brain-damaged group consisted of individuals with extensive and irreversible damage, as judged by both a neurologist and neurosurgeon; patients who manifested neurotic or psychotic characteristics were excluded from this sample (Peña, 1953).

Data on Developmental Scores

The per cents for each of the developmental indices on each of the subsamples are presented in Table 2.4. Each score in this table represents the median value within each of the subsamples. For those scores in which less than 50% of the subsample failed to obtain a given score, the median score entered in the table consequently is zero. Whenever the information was available, the *per cent of subjects* obtaining a score which has a median value of zero is indicated in parentheses. For example, as Table 2.4 indicates that the median Wa% for 3-year-old children is zero, the information in parentheses shows that 20% of the subjects (i.e., four of the sample of 20) gave at least one Wa response.

In Table 2.5, data are presented on the per cent of developmentally high W and high D, as well as developmentally low W and low D for each of the subsamples. In computing the high and low scores for a given protocol, high and low W should total 100%, as should high and low D. This should be fairly evident, inasmuch as the total of all the developmentally high and low W (or D) scores are equivalent to total number of W (or D) obtained. It should be noted, however, that the norms in Table 2.5 for the high and low location scores within each subsample do *not* always add up to 100%. While the values for a *given subject* should always total 100, the *median* per cent scores for a *group* need not. One would expect that as the number of subjects within each group increased, the total of the high and low location scores should approach 100%.

The median per cent developmentally high W and D scores for each of the subsamples are presented graphically in Figs 2.1 and 2.2 The groups are arranged according to *increasing* level of development for the normal samples (children and normal adults), and then decreasing level of development for the pathological groups (neurotics, paranoid schizophrenics, brain damaged, mental defectives, and hebephrenic and catatonic schizophrenics). In comparing the sequence of development and regression for

TABLE 2.4
Median Per Cent of Each of the Developmental Scoring Categories and R for Several Samples[a]

	Developmentally High Scores					
Group	*W++%*	*D++%*	*W+%*	*D+%*[b]	*Wm%*	*Dm%*[b]
Normal Children (Hemmendinger, 1953)						
3-Year-Olds	0(0.)[c]	0(0.)	5.0	0(—)	13.4	18.0
4-Year-Olds	0(0.)	0(0.)	0(—[d])	0(—)	10.3	20.0
5-Year-Olds	0(10.)	0(0.)	8.5(—)	9.5	21.0	33.3
6-Year-Olds	0(5.)	0(5.)	0(—)	3.0	28.0	46.5
7-Year-Olds	0(10.)	0(5.)	0(—)	4.5	34.5	52.5
8-Year-Olds	0(10.)	0(15.)	0(—)	7.0	46.5	48.0
9-Year-Olds	0(35.)	0(30.)	0(—)	8.5	41.5	51.5
10-Year-Olds	0(25.)	0(25.)	4.0	11.5	33.0	51.0
Adult Mental Defectives (Rosenblatt and Solomon, 1954)						
Average M.A. of 5:1	0(0.)	0(0.)	0(6.)	0(0.)	21.0	52.0
Average M.A. of 6:11	0(6.)	0(0.)	0(0.)	0(0.)	38.0	67.0
Average M.A. of 8:5	0(0.)	0(0.)	0(6.)	0(12.)	53.0	71.0
Average M.A. of 9:11	0(6.)	0(0.)	0(18.)	0(36.)	53.0	67.0
Average M.A. of 11:11	0(6.)	0(0.)	0(12.)	0(12.)	53.0	74.0
All five M.A. levels combined	0(4.)	0(0.)	0(9.)	0(13.)	50.0	67.0
Normal Adults (Friedman, 1953)	0(27.)	0(13.)	13.0	18.0	50.0	60.0
Neurotics (Frank, 1952)	0(17.)	0(13.)	0(0.20)	9.5	50.0	59.5
Paranoid Schizophrenics (Siegal, 1953)	0(17.)	0(10.)	0(—)	13.0	41.5	50.0
Hebephrenic and Catatonic Schizophrenics (Siegel, 1953)	0(10.)	0(0.)	0(43.)	10.5	31.5	45.0
Brain Damaged (Peña, 1953)	0(7.)	0(7.)	0(43.)	15.5	46.4	47.8

[a] The per cent scores are based on the proportion of scoring category to location score in general (e.g., W ++% = W ++/total W, D ++% = D ++/total D, etc.). The one exception to this is FabC and/or ConR% = FabC + ConR/R.

[b] The scoring criteria for D + and Dm in the mental-defective sample (Rosenblatt and Solomon, 1954) differed somewhat from those outlined in this chapter. Rosenblatt and Solomon scored responses to Card VIII that involved

TABLE 2.4 (*cont.*)

				Developmentally Low Scores					
Wv%	*Dv%*	*Wa%*	*Da%*	*W−%*	*D−%*	*DW%*	*DdD%*	*FabC and/or ConR%*[a]	*Median Number of Responses*
0(—)	0(—)	0(20.)	0(20.)	57.8	53.5	11.1(65.)	0(5.)	0(10.)	13.0
11.8	0(—)	0(40.)	0(35.)	34.0	54.0	9.0(55.)	0(25.)	0(45.)	15.0
0(—)	10.0	0(30.)	0(15.)	31.0	33.8	6.0(50.)	0(25.)	0(35.)	17.0
11.0	5.5	0(40.)	0(30.)	19.0	31.0	0(15.)	0(35.)	0(20.)	17.0
4.5	11.0	0(10.)	3.0(60.)	8.5	22.0	0(0)	0(30.)	0(35.)	35.5
0(—)	10.5	0(0)	0(20.)	5.5	25.0	0(5.)	0(25.)	0(30.)	34.5
0(—)	8.0	0(5.)	0(10.)	6.5	23.5	0(5.)	0(15.)	0(20.)	27.5
0(—)	8.0	0(5.)	0(40.)	20.0	23.5	0(5.)	0(10.)	0(10.)	27.5
0(18.)	0(6.)	0(6.)	0(37.)	50.0	37.0	0(42.)	0(18.)	—[d]	13.0
0(24.)	0(6.)	0(18.)	0(12.)	28.0	33.0	10.0	0(12.)	—	11.5
0(18.)	0(12.)	0(6.)	0(6.)	25.0	22.0	0(36.)	0(24.)	—	11.0
0(24.)	0(36.)	0(0)	0(6.)	18.0	21.0	0(24.)	0(12.)	—	15.0
0(24.)	0(6.)	0(6.)	0(18.)	0(42.)	23.0	0(18.)	0(12.)	—	13.5
0(22.)	0(14.)	0(6.)	0(15.)	25.0	25.0	0(36.)	0(16.)	—	12.8
0(43.)	5.0	0(0)	0(7.)	0(0)	16.0	0(0)	0(7.)	0(3.)	19.0
0(46.)	7.0	0(3.)	0(20.)	0(17.)	19.0	0(0)	0(0)	0(3.)	25.0
26.5	5.5	0(17.)	0(37.)	0(—)	19.0	0(0)	0(3.)	0(23.)	26.5
17.0	11.5	0(37.)	0(17.)	22.0	20.0	4.0(50.)	0(13.)	0(30.)	20.0
22.2	0(—)	0(20.)	0(10.)	4.6	25.0	0(17.)	0(10.)	0(13.)	14.5

two animals climbing something as Dm rather than D +. Their reasoning was that such a response occurred too often in the mental-defective sample (given by 28% of the group) to reflect as high a score as D +.

[c] Those instances in which the median per cent is zero indicate that less than 50% of the cases obtained this score, and *not* that the score failed to occur in the sample. Wherever possible, the *per cent of subjects* obtaining at least one such score is indicated in parentheses.

[d] A dash (—) indicates that these data were not available.

TABLE 2.5
Median Per Cent of Developmentally High and Low W and D Scores for Several Samples[a]

Group	*% Genetically High W*	*% Genetically Low W*	*% Genetically High D*	*% Genetically Low D*
Normal Children (Hemmendinger, 1953)				
3-Year-Olds	22.2	75.0	25.0	64.8
4-Year-Olds	17.2	64.8	25.0	62.5
5-Year-Olds	35.4	46.5	37.5	43.8
6-Year-Olds	38.9	33.0	50.0	36.0
7-Year-Olds	50.0	8.5	60.0	30.5
8-Year-Olds	66.7	5.5	58.0	25.0
9-Year-Olds	61.7	6.3	64.0	27.5
10-Year-Olds	63.4	20.0	61.5	30.0
Adult Mental Defectives (Rosenblatt and Solomon, 1954)				
Average M.A. of 5:1	52.0	—[b]	25.0	—
Average M.A. of 6:11	40.0	—	67.0	—
Average M.A. of 8:5	61.0	—	71.0	—
Average M.A. of 9:11	71.0	—	75.0	—
Average M.A. of 11:11	69.0	—	67.0	—
All five M.A. levels combined	47.0	—	67.0	—
Normal Adults (Friedman, 1953)	83.0	12.0	76.0	24.0
Neurotics (Frank, 1952)	67.0	26.5	75.0	27.0
Paranoid Schizophrenics (Siegel, 1953)	60.0	40.0	67.0	33.0
Hebephrenic and Catatonic Schizophrenics (Siegel, 1953)	38.0	62.0	57.5	41.0
Brain Damaged (Peña, 1953)	58.6	41.4	66.3	33.7

[a] The four summary scores are computed as follows: % high W = (W ++, W +, and Wm/all W) × 100; % high D = (D ++, D +, and Dm/all D) × 100; % low W = (Wv, Wa, W −, and DW/all W) × 100; % low D = (Dv, Da, D −, and DdD/all D) × 100.
[b] A dash (—) indicates that these data were not available.

the high W and D responses, it should be noted that relative to mature D responses, developmentally high W responses develop later in the sequence, and are more readily impaired under conditions of disturbance.

The Problem of Overlap. The data in Tables 2.4 and 2.5 do not include any information on the amount of overlap for each score across the several subsamples. Although the clinical use of the scoring system can be facilitated by these tables of norms, the decision as to what constitutes a meaningfully "high" or "low" score must be based on the clinician's "internal" norms for the scoring system. Clearly, any additional normative data collected on the developmental scoring should include information about the *distribution* of each score within each subsample as well.

Norms for Different Levels of R. Whether or not separate sets of norms are required for different levels of the total number of responses depends upon the nature of the relationship between *R* and each scoring

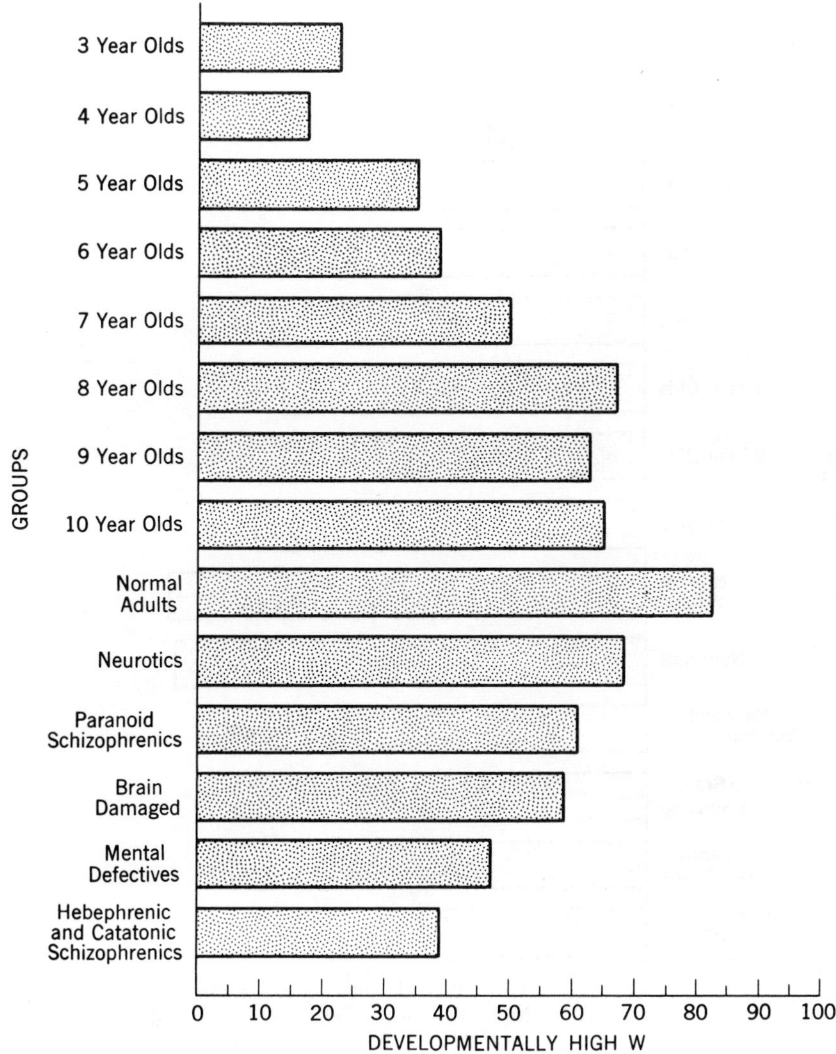

FIGURE 2.1
Median Per Cent Developmentally High W Response for Each Group

category. Summarizing the scoring categories by comparing them to the total number of relevant location scores in the record (e.g., D+% = D+/total D), or even the use of the average weighting method of computing *DL* would seem to provide adequate control for protocol length. Little has been done empirically, however, to determine whether or not this is indeed the case. Wilensky (1959a) did fail to obtain any significant relationship between *DL* and total R among three separate groups of schizophrenics, but the number of subjects used in his study was small. No

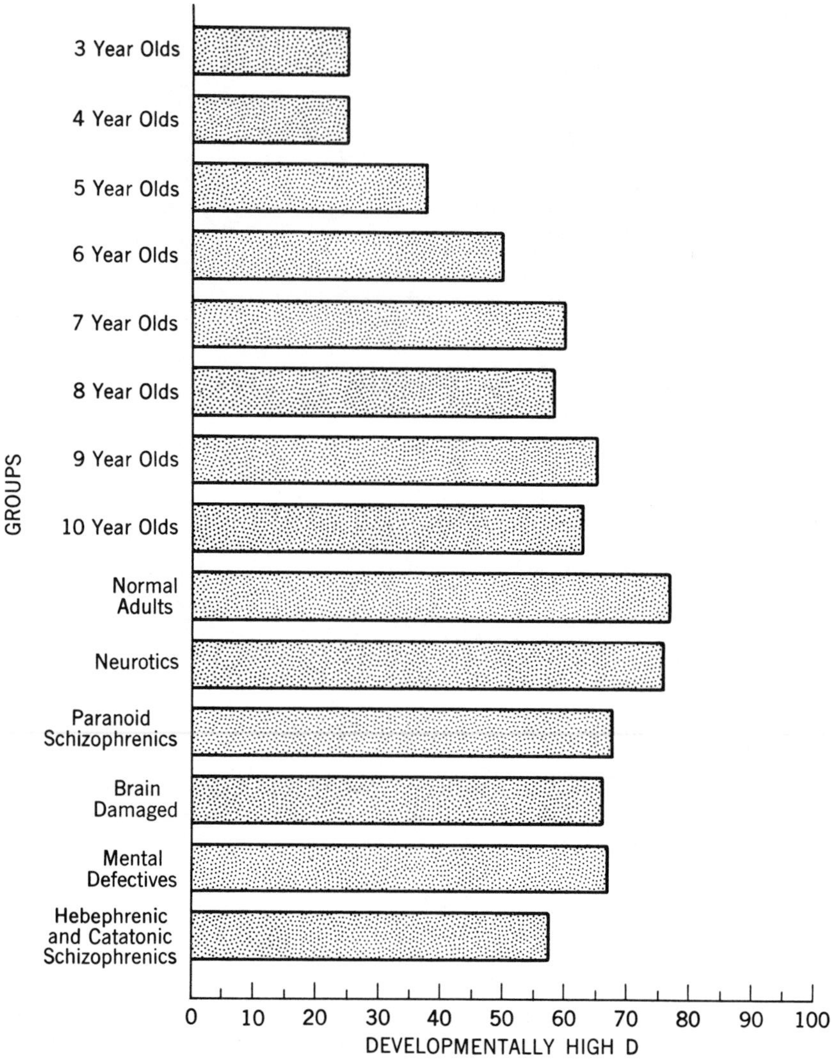

FIGURE 2.2
Median Per Cent Developmentally High D Response for Each Group

data at all are available on the correlation between length of protocol and the various percentage scores.

RELIABILITY

Very little research has been done to study the stability of developmental scores over time (Wilensky, 1959b). Although Werner (1948, 1957) might argue that an individual's developmental level of functioning changes to meet the demands of a changing environment, the study of the test-retest reliability of the *overall* level of functioning seems appropriate.

Wilensky (1959b) reports some findings on the stability of the overall *DL* scores (as computed by his method, described on p. 32) for two groups of chronic schizophrenic patients. The patients used for this study were selected from a larger group of chronic schizophrenics; the time since their first hospitalization ranged from 5 to 10 years. Approximately one-third of the original group were eliminated because they were either untestable or obtained too few (less than eight) responses on the Rorschach. With a one-month interval between testings, the test-retest correlation obtained for a group of 41 patients was .75. For a smaller group (17 patients), the correlation with a 12–18 month interval was .68. No information is reported as to whether or not there were changes in the mean *DL* for the groups from one testing to the other.

Considering that the samples used in Wilensky's study were relatively homogeneous with respect to developmental level of functioning, these correlations seem impressively high. However, homogeneity of distribution per se need not always imply that a low correlation may be expected. This is particularly true in the case of Wilensky's groups, where the chronicity of their disturbance has probably resulted in a developmentally low, but *consistent* level of functioning. This interpretation of the obtained correlations, of course, assumes that the *DL* score *is, in fact,* a valid measure of developmental level. Carrying this explanation one step further, one might expect to find lower test-retest correlations on a similarly homogeneous, but developmentally higher group of subjects. Such a finding would add to the construct validity of the scoring system.

VALIDITY

Validity research on Friedman's developmental scoring system has been extensive. This seems to be due to the fact that Werner's developmental theory has been used not only as an approach to development, but also as a point of view in characterizing the adequacy of cognitive functioning. Thus, the developmental scoring of the Rorschach, in addition to being used to study the process of development in children, has also been used in the study of such problem areas as psychopathology, organicity, mental deficiency, old age, social adequacy, hospital ward adjustment, and creativity.

The validation studies discussed in this section are arranged according to the criterion-related (concurrent and predictive) and construct-validity classifications. Strictly speaking, the most appropriate type of validity study for the developmental scoring system is construct validation. As *developmental level* refers more to an unobservable construct than to any specific criterion groups, concurrent or predictive validity studies do not seem very appropriate. Nevertheless, a few studies done with the developmental scoring system may be considered relevant to concurrent or predicitive validation. Specifically, a study may be said to represent the concurrent-validity type if, with little knowledge of the theoretical construct, one would expect certain groups to represent different levels of development. Thus, the comparison of children at different age levels may be considered to represent a concurrent validation of the scoring system. Studies may be judged to represent predictive validation if the developmental scoring is clearly used as a prognostic indicator, even if the criterion measure does not directly reflect level of development (e.g., length of hospitalization).

Criterion-Related Validity

Concurrent Validity

Hemmendinger (1953) used the scoring system to study the developmental levels of functioning for 160 boys between the ages of 3 and 10. He found that developmentally high W and D scores increased and developmentally low W and D scores decreased with age. The developmental sequence was not gradual and regular, as may be seen in Figures 2.1 and 2.2, where Hemmendinger's data are presented graphically. These figures also illustrate how the developmentally high D scores develop at a faster rate than the high W scores.

The developmental levels of mental defectives of different mental ages were studied by Rosenblatt and Solomon (1954). Rosenblatt and Solomon used a sample of 80 adult male and female mental defectives of the "familial" type (i.e., no discernible evidence of the presence of organic impairment), and divided them into five groups of increasing mental age (5:1, 6:11, 8:5, 9:11, and 11:11). The results indicated that defectives of lower mental ages functioned at significantly lower developmental levels on the Rorschach.

The two studies cited above, then, offer confirming evidence that Friedman's developmental scoring system is a valid indicator of different levels of development.

Predictive Validity

The developmental scoring system has been used to predict length of hospitalization, the social participation of chronic schizophrenics, and success in the placement of mental defectives.

Levine (1959) compared two groups of male psychiatric patients as to their Rorschach developmental level: one group consisted of 24 patients who had been discharged within one year after admission, and the other group was composed of 24 patients who had been hospitalized continuously for one year. Although the patients were not necessarily first admissions, none of them had been hospitalized for a period of more than 90 days within six months prior to the admission date used in the study. Both groups were comparable as to age, diagnosis, education, and marital status. Levine found that the overall developmental level upon admission was significantly higher for those patients who were discharged at the end of one year. Levine concludes that whereas the prognostic use of the Rorschach with traditional approaches to scoring has failed, the developmental approach has succeeded. While the developmental scores of the two groups differed significantly, the *overlap* between groups was great. Using Becker's (1956) system of weighting, Levine found that the mean and standard deviation, respectively, were 3.41 and 0.391 for the discharged group, and 3.04 and 0.480 for the continuously hospitalized group. In order to make successful predictions (e.g., being in error only once in 100) for populations having similar base rates (whatever they might have been in Levine's study), one would have to use a cutoff score of approximately 4.48. However, as a score at this level or higher can be expected to occur for less than 5% of those discharged at the end of the year, the clinical application of the scoring system for this purpose is limited.

Although not designed specifically as a predictive study, some findings by Wilensky (1959a) have clear implications for the predictive validity of the scoring system. Wilensky was interested in studying the relationship between developmental level and the social participation of chronic schizophrenics in a small-group, problem-solving situation. Wilensky found that inasmuch as most of the subjects were initially unresponsive, ratings of their social participation were not related to developmental level. However, approximately four weeks later, after the subjects had had a chance to become familiar with the task, developmental level showed a significant positive relationship to the observed social participation ($r = .86$ and .58 for participation with acquaintances and strangers, respectively). The interesting thing to note is that despite the same initial reaction of all patients, the developmental score was able to distinguish between those who would and those who would not be able to adjust to the social situation.

Solomon (1955) used the scoring system to try to predict the success of community placement for a group of male and female mental defectives. "Successful" and "unsuccessful" subjects were classified on the basis of whether or not they had remained in the same placement situation after eight months. The two groups did not differ as to age, sex, or I.Q. Unfortunately, they failed to differ in level of development as well. The results were in the expected direction, but the p levels were only around the .20 level. One may question the adequacy of the "success" criterion, as it is not clear just why a subject might have left the original placement. Relating developmental level to some independent rating of adjustment in the placement situation might have yielded more favorable results.

In general, the developmental scoring system seems to have some use as a predictive measure for the estimation of length of hospitalization and social participation in chronic schizophrenics, but not to predict the successful community placement of mental defectives. Because of the overlap between groups, however, the clinical use of the system should be carried out only in conjunction with other relevant prognostic indicators.

Construct Validity

The construct validity studies of the nomological type (i.e., involving theoretically predicted differences among groups or conditions) are discussed separately from those of the trait validity type (i.e., the relationship to other measures).

Nomological Validity

The section which follows includes studies in which the developmental scoring of the Rorschach was used to test (1) hypothesized developmental differences among various pathological groups, (2) hypothesized developmental differences among other groups, (3) behavioral differences among subjects at different developmental levels, and (4) predicted changes in developmental level.

Differences among Pathological Groups. Validation studies have applied the scoring system to various subtypes of schizophrenics, brain damaged, neurotics, ulcer patients, and mental defectives.

Friedman (1952) studied the developmental functioning of catatonic and hebephrenic schizophrenics by comparing their developmental Rorschach scores with those of normal adults and children. The results of his study, which were consistent with theoretical expectations, led to the following conclusion:

> On the whole, the results would suggest that the perceptual functioning of the schizophrenic, in its structural aspects, is intimately related to that of the child. Its characteristics are those of a primitive globality, syncretism, lability, diffuseness, and rigidity. In the capacity for differentiation and hierarchic integration which marks the normal adult group, the schizophrenic group seems to suffer considerable impairment. Although there is this similarity to children, certain aspects of higher level functioning are identifiable. In terms of an interpretation in the light of regression, it would be possible that such aspects may be vestiges which point to the incompleteness of regression. Thus, the previous operation on a higher developmental level may not be completely erased (Friedman, 1952, pp. 93–94).

In a later study by Lebowitz (1963), paranoid schizophrenics similarly were found to obtain developmentally lower scores than normal adults.

Several studies have demonstrated the ability of the developmental scores to distinguish between different levels of schizophrenic regression. Siegel (1953) tested and confirmed the hypothesis that paranoid schizophrenics are less regressed than hebephrenic and catatonic schizophrenics. The paranoid schizophrenics were found to be functioning at a developmental level similar to 6- to 10-year-old children, while the level of functioning for the hebephrenic and catatonic group was closer to 3- to 5-year-old children.

Wilensky (1959a) found that closed-ward chronic schizophrenics functioned at a developmentally lower level than open-ward chronic schizophrenics. Becker (1956) classified a group of schizophrenics into "process" and "reactive" types by means of the Elgin Prognostic Scale (Wittman, 1941); the classification was based primarily on the nature of onset and the prepsychotic personality. Becker's finding that the process schizophrenics were more primitive and undifferentiated in their developmental functioning than reactive schizophrenics led him to conclude that these subgroups may actually represent two endpoints of a continuum of degree of personality organization. Although a replication of Becker's study by Judson and Katahn (1964) failed to confirm his findings, a comparison of the Elgin scores revealed that Judson and Katahn's group of schizophrenics as a whole were less severely disturbed. Other research has corroborated the fact that there is indeed a difference in developmental level between process and reactive schizophrenics (Fine and Zimet, 1959; Zimet and Fine, 1959).

Fowler (1957) has pointed out the importance of controlling for the prognostic or social adequacy variable in studying the developmental differences between schizophrenics and normals. Using the Phillips scale (Phillips, 1953) to summarize data on both past and present social-sexual adjustment, Fowler compared the developmental functioning of four groups: psychotics of high and of low social adequacy, and normals of high and of low social adequacy. His results indicate that while the per cent of developmentally low scores occur more often in individuals of lower social adequacy, these low scores *fail* to discriminate between normals and psychotics.[3] Fowler hypothesizes that the reason previous studies have found the developmentally low scores to discriminate between schizophrenics and normals is due to the fact that schizophrenics are typically of a lower social adequacy level than normals.

Following Werner's (1948) hypothesis that adults with brain damage tend to function at lower developmental levels, Peña (1953) compared the performance of brain-damaged adults with that of normal adults; this expectation was confirmed. Peña further reasoned that brain-damaged individuals should show a higher level of functioning than chronic schizophrenics, in that the pathology in the schizophrenic has developed over a relatively longer period of time. By comparing the developmental functioning of brain damaged with the functioning of hebephrenic and catatonic schizophrenics (Siegel, 1953) and children (Hemmendinger, 1953), Peña found that the brain-damaged subjects resembled 6-to 10-year-olds in the frequency of developmentally low W responses, while the chronic schizophrenics performed more like 3- to 5-year-olds.

Frank (1952) compared the performance of neurotics with normals, predicting that the neurotic group would obtain fewer developmentally high scores than the normals. Frank found that the neurotic group functioned developmentally at a level somewhere between normal adults and 10-year-old children; neurotics obtained fewer developmentally low D scores than 10-year-olds, but not as many + + and + scores as normals. Thus, in comparison to normals, neurotics are mainly deficient in their organizational capacities.

On the general assumption that individuals suffering from psychosomatic disorders are less mature than normal adults, Lebowitz (1963) compared hospitalized duodenal ulcer patients with nonpsychosomatic surgical patients.

[3] Fowler found that "integrative" scores *did* discriminate between normals and psychotics, but as these scores are from Phillips' developmental scoring system, this finding is discussed in Chapter 3.

Because of the possibility that the significantly lower I.Q. for the ulcer group may have accounted for Lebowitz's obtained significant difference in the developmental level (see pp. 52–54), the findings cannot be taken as a clear confirmation of her hypothesis.

In a study of the developmental functioning of adult mental defectives, Rosenblatt and Solomon (1954) tested three hypotheses: (1) mental defectives may be expected to function at a lower developmental level than normal adults; (2) due to the presence of early signs of future development, normal children should function at a higher level than defectives of comparable mental ages; and (3) because schizophrenics and organics may be expected to show vestiges of a once-obtained higher level of functioning, both of these groups should give more developmentally high scores than mental defectives. As the data on adults, children, and organics were obtained from the summary tables of studies by Friedman (1952), Hemmendinger (1953), and Peña (1953), respectively, Rosenblatt and Solomon were not able to make statistical comparisons between the performance of mental defectives and these other groups. By "inspection," however, all three of the hypotheses received confirmation.

The results of these studies comparing normals with schizophrenics, brain damaged, neurotics, and mental defectives, as well as studies in which various pathological groups are compared among themselves, all seem to indicate that Friedman's developmental scoring system can differentiate statistically among groups according to theoretical expectation. As far as the frequency of false positives and negatives which one might expect to encounter when the system is used clinically for differential diagnosis, no data yet have been collected to enable us to come to any definite conclusion.

Differences among Other Groups. Research has been conducted to compare developmentally the parents of disturbed children and adults, individuals having ideational orientations with those having acting-out orientations, social with solitary delinquents, and creative with noncreative music students.

As part of a larger study on the characteristics of parents of disturbed children and adults, Singer and Wynne (1963) found a significant overall difference in Rorschach developmental level among four groups of parents. Although no individual comparisons were carried out, the four groups—presented in order of decreasing level of maturity—were parents of acting-out neurotic children, parents of autistic children, parents of withdrawn neurotic children, and parents of adult schizophrenics.[4]

A study by Hurwitz (1954), one of a series of three dissertations at Clark University, was based on Werner's (1948) prediction that with increasing levels of development there should be a greater ability to delay motoric acting-out. Hurwitz confirmed this hypothesis, finding that hyperactive boys in particular were lower than hypoactive boys on the index of integration (+ + and + scores). Misch (1954) found that individuals

[4] A study by Lerner (1965), who also employed the developmental scoring system in the investigation of parents of disturbed individuals, is described on p. 50.

who express their aggression motorically (i.e., assaultive) function at a lower developmental level than those who express their aggression verbally, (i.e., threats of assault). Similarly, Kruger (1954) found that individuals who actually attempted suicide were developmentally lower than those who only threatened to commit suicide, and sexual deviants who acted out their impulses functioned at a lower developmental level than deviants who were only preoccupied with these sexual desires. Kruger also hypothesized that as the turning-in of aggression represents a more indirect approach to impulse expression, suicidal people should be developmentally higher than assaultive people; this hypothesis was confirmed.

Based on previous research, Kissel and Reisman (1963) predicted that "solitary" delinquents (i.e., those who commit crimes alone) were developmentally lower than "social" delinquents (i.e., those who commit crimes with others). The authors also hypothesized that because solitary delinquents typically manifest a greater variety of disturbance, they should represent more variable levels of development than social delinquents. Only this second hypothesis was confirmed.

Cooper (1961) tested the hypothesis that creative individuals possess the capacity for "regression in the service of the ego," and should consequently have a wider range of developmental levels of functioning than less creative individuals. Cooper compared two groups of music students who were rated as more or less creative by members of the faculty. Except for a greater number of Wm scores in the less creative group, the two groups were found to be essentially the same developmentally. It is possible to explain these negative results by the fact that Cooper's groups were relatively homogeneous with respect to creativity; the comparison was *not* between creative and noncreative individuals, but between music students who showed more or less creativity.

It appears, then, that the most consistent finding in this general area is that parents of schizophrenics and neurotics differ according to developmental level, and that individuals who express their conflicts ideationally are developmentally higher than those who act out their conflicts. The findings on the social nature of delinquency and the creativity of music students are at best inconclusive.

Differences at Different Developmental Levels. Studies have been conducted to determine how individuals functioning at varying developmental levels differ in their general behavioral characteristics, in their performance in particular situations, and in the way in which their parents resolve intrafamilial conflicts.

Levine (1960) attempted to relate level of development with different types of symptoms in psychotic patients. Although Levine hypothesized that patients at lower developmental levels should show more regressed symptoms (e.g., hallucinations), the results indicated that level of development showed only an inverse relationship to apathy, lack of motivation, and lack of goal directedness. A factor analysis (Levine and Cohen, 1962) of all the symptoms studied revealed that overall development level had low but significant correlations with "uncooperativeness" ($r = -.27$) and "apathy"

($r = -.32$). Becker (1959) similarly factor analyzed a variety of schizophrenic symptoms and found that developmental level loaded $-.46$ on the "schizophrenic withdrawal" factor and $-.64$ on the "reality distortion" factor. It might be noted here that when the relationship between type of symptom and developmental level is predicted from Werner's (1948) theory, the results are more clear cut than those of Levine (1960), Levine and Cohen (1962), and Becker (1959). Thus, studies have confirmed the expectation that people who express their conflicts ideationally are developmentally higher than those who act out their conflicts motorically (Hurwitz, 1954; Kruger, 1954; Misch, 1954). Research has also confirmed the prediction that in comparison with externally oriented behavior (i.e., assault, robbery), behavior or symptoms which represent the inward turning of impulses (e.g., suicide, self-blame) occur more often in people of higher developmental levels (Kruger, 1954; Zigler and Phillips, 1960).

Hunter, Schooler, and Spohn (1962) studied the interpersonal behavioral correlation of developmental level for a large group of male chronic schizophrenics. Based on ratings of the patients' ward behavior, the authors found low but significant correlations between overall developmental level and social interaction ($r = +.273$), "parasocial" (i.e., reading, writing, T.V. viewing) behavior ($r = +.340$), nonfunctional (i.e., self-manipulation, active movement, nonfunctional object manipulation) behavior ($r = -.313$), and "null" (i.e., sleep, no behavior) behavior ($r = -.292$). Using a similar type of patient population, Wilensky (1959a) reports a significant postive correlation ($r = .71$) between developmental level and social participation in a small-group problem-solving situation.

Using normal male adults as subjects, Lofchie (1955) predicted that individuals with higher developmental levels should perform better under distraction stress conditions (e.g., flashing lights, ringing bells, air blasts). The results indicated that subjects with higher index-of-integration scores functioned more effectively at a visual-motor task under these distraction conditions. As Lofchie has pointed out, the ability to function under these conditions is similar to what Witkin, Lewis, Hertzman, Machover, Meissner, and Wagner (1954) have called "field independence."

Based on the assumption that the severity of disorder among schizophrenics has its roots in the nature of the family's communication system, Lerner (1965) studied the interaction between parents of male schizophrenics who differed in their Rorschach developmental level. Although *DL* scores were not available for the normal subjects whose parents were also studied, previous research (Friedman, 1952; Lebowitz, 1963) would lead us to expect that they would score developmentally higher than the schizophrenics. The parents of the three groups (low *DL* schizophrenics, high *DL* schizophrenics, and normal controls) were presented with a series of family problem situations, and the manner of resolving the conflict was measured. Lerner's findings confirmed his expectation that developmentally more mature sons had parents who were more effective in their resolution of intrafamilial conflicts.

In general, studies in which developmental level has been related to various types of behavior and characteristics have found that individuals with higher levels of development are characterized by showing better interpersonal functioning, greater energy levels, a better ability to function under conditions of environmental distraction, and having parents who more adequately resolve intrafamilial conflicts.

Predicted Changes in Developmental Level. In addition to the predicted increase in developmental functioning in children of increasing age levels, one can also expect certain changes to occur at other ages as well, such as adolescence, and old age. Changes in developmental level may also be predicted as a function of different types of experimental manipulations, which Werner (1948) has called the "genetic experiment."

Wilson (1954) extended Hemmendinger's (1953) study on the progression of developmental levels in children by obtaining data on subjects between 6 and 17 years of age. Wilson hypothesized, however, that because of the stresses accompanying adolescence, there should be a temporary disruption in developmental level of functioning. Her results confirmed this prediction, in that developmental level was found to increase up until 12 and 13 years, but then dropped between ages 14 and 17. This decline was only temporary, as functioning was found to increase at adulthood. Similarly, Rochwarg (1954) predicted that because of the general decline in functioning accompanying old age, one should expect to find fewer developmentally high and more developmentally low scores. Using older (ages 68–91) and younger (23–45) male subjects, Rochwarg confirmed this hypothesis. As I.Q. and developmental level have been found to be positively related (Goldfried, 1962b), the higher vocabulary I.Q. scores which were found to be characteristic of the aged group probably resulted in a conservative estimate of decline of functioning.

Phillips and Framo (1954) have reported the results of dissertations by Framo (1952) and Freed (1952) on the *microgenetic* development of individual percepts. According to the microgenetic hypothesis, there is a developmental sequence in the evolution of any given percept; this sequence is believed to parallel the ontogenetic development of perception, in that it progresses from a global diffuseness to a greater articulation and finally to an integration of parts. To study the microgenetic development of individual percepts, Framo (1952) and Freed (1952) presented Rorschach blots tachistoscopically to normal and schizophrenic subjects, respectively. Four exposure speeds were used (.01, .10, 1.0, and 10.0 seconds), and different subjects were used at each presentation speed. When these Rorschachs were scored developmentally, the normal and schizophrenic subjects were both found to be functioning at low levels for the brief exposure times (i.e., presumably at the early stages in the development of the percept). With increased exposure times, normals showed an increase in developmentally high and decrease in developmentally low scores, whereas the schizophrenics lagged behind in the developmental sequence.

Based on the premise that sensory deprivation facilitates a weakening of the distinction between self and environment, Goldfried (1961) predicted that sensory-deprived subjects should function at lower developmental levels. This hypothesis failed to receive confirmation, probably because of the relatively brief (45 minutes) duration of deprivation.

Although relatively little research has been carried out to study predicted changes in developmental level, the use of the Friedman's developmental scoring of the Rorschach as a dependent variable merits future research energies.

Trait Validity

The research included in this section includes studies on the relationship between Rorschach developmental level and (1) measures of severity of disturbance, (2) intellectual functioning, and (3) other measures of developmental level.

RELATION TO MEASURES OF SEVERITY OF DISTURBANCE. The developmental scoring system has been found to be a good indicator of severity of pathology. Consequently, one would expect to find a relationship between the scoring system and other measures of disturbance. Of the research done in this area, one study (Becker, 1956) has obtained partially positive results, while two others (Goldfried, 1962a; Levine and Cohen, 1962) have failed to find any relationship at all.

Becker's (1956) study investigated the relationship between developmental level and the discrepancy between abstract ability and vocabulary scores. The rationale for the discrepancy score is based on the assumption that under conditions of psychological disturbance, abstract thinking becomes more readily impaired than vocabulary ability. Becker found developmental level and an abstract-minus-vocabulary score to be significantly related ($r = .60$) for male, but not for female schizophrenics ($r = -.21$).

Goldfried (1962a), in a study of the relationship between the MMPI and Rorschach developmental levels, classified MMPI records of psychiatric patients into "psychotic" and "neurotic" categories (Meehl and Dahlstrom, 1960). The results revealed no relationship between the Rorschach developmental level and the MMPI measures of severity of disturbance. Similarly, Levine and Cohen (1962) failed to find any relationship between developmental level and the MMPI "ego-strength" scale for a group of psychiatric subjects. Although one can speculate about the possibility that these neagtive results are due to the different levels of functioning measured by these two instruments (Goldfried, 1962a), more data on the relationship between the developmental scoring system and other indicators of disturbance are needed before a less speculative explanation is possible.

RELATION TO INTELLECTUAL FUNCTIONING. As the developmental level construct refers to the level of cognitive functioning at which an individual can operate, it would not be at all surprising to find the developmental scoring of the Rorschach to have some relationship to intellectual functioning. Ainsworth and Klopfer (1954) have speculated similarly that "vague, global perception reflects a relatively low level of capacity, and. . .the more refined and differentiated the perception the higher the level of intelligence" (p. 353).

Goldfried (1962b) confirmed the relationship between developmental level and I.Q. within a psychiatric population. Using both the Becker and the Wilensky methods of estimating overall developmental level, Goldfried found the two measures of developmental level correlated .39 ($p < .001$) and .44 ($p < .001$), respectively, with I.Q.

In the first of a set of studies investigating the cognitive and intellectual correlates of W responses, Blatt and Allison (1963) found that developmentally high W scores (W + + and W +)/R correlated .46 ($p < .01$) with problem-solving efficiency. In light of the fact that they used a small, homogeneous sample (26 male graduate students), this correlation is impressively high. In their second study, Allison and Blatt (1964) used neuropsychiatric patients who were selected to represent a wide range of intellectual functioning; the WAIS I.Q. scores varied from 60 to 140. Within this population, (W+ + and W +)/R correlated .57 ($p < .001$) with I.Q. Two additional significant correlations between W scores and I.Q. were obtained among the female subjects in their sample: − .41 ($p < .05$) for (Wa and Wv)/R and − .44 ($p < .05$) for Wm/R.

Friedman and Orgel (1964), using the protocols of the original validation samples (catatonic and hebephrenic schizophrenics, paranoid schizophrenics, brain damaged, neurotics, and normals), correlated various developmental scores with I.Q. Statistical significance was obtained only for the paranoid sample, where mature W scores correlated .41 ($p < .05$) and mature W and D scores, .38 ($p < .05$). It should be noted that for each of their samples, the I.Q. scores were based on estimates from various vocabulary tests, and that the range was relatively narrow (85–120). Friedman and Orgel added an additional group of patients with varying diagnoses, whose Wechsler–Bellevue or WAIS I.Q.s varied from 59 to 146. For this sample, low but significant correlations were found for (W + + and W +)/ total W ($r = .20$; $p < .05$) and (W + + and W + and D + + and D +)/ total W and D ($r = .22$; $p < .05$). When subjects obtaining I.Q. scores below 79 were eliminated, however, these correlations fell below significance.

Friedman and Orgel's findings prompted Kissel (1965) to investigate the relation between I.Q. and developmental level among patients in a child guidance clinic. The subjects ranged from 11 to 16 years of age, and varied between 80 and 124 in level of intellectual functioning. The fact that Kissel found a correlation of .42 ($p < .01$) between the Wilensky *DL* scoring and I.Q. is perhaps less interesting than his *inability* to achieve statistical significance by using the percentage scores utilized in Friedman and Orgel's study.

Although the bulk of the evidence would seem to point in the direction that Rorschach developmental level and I.Q. are indeed related, the limits of this relationship are not as clear as we might like. Such factors as I.Q. range, age of population, and developmental summary score may very well be important variables. Also, especially since I.Q. scores are comprised of different aspects of intellectual functioning, it would seem worthwhile to investigate the differential relationship between each of these different areas (e.g., abstract thinking, social comprehension, visual-motor coordination) and Rorschach developmental level.

Relation to Other Measures of Developmental Level. No research as yet has been carried out to determine the relationship between Friedman's developmental scoring of the Rorschach and other measures of developmental level. As developmental approaches have been taken in the scoring of auditory (Friedman, 1956), motoric (Friedman, 1958; Lebowitz, 1963), and word association tasks (Flavell, Draguns, Feinberg, and Budin, 1958), research relating these other developmental indicators to the Rorschach scoring system is clearly indicated.

OVERALL EVALUATION

More than simply a means of describing the developmental sequence, Werner's concept of developmental level provides us with an interesting and useful approach to the assessment of the structural adequacy of cognitive functioning in general. On the basis of the research findings described throughout the chapter, it is clear that Friedman's scoring of the Rorschach results in a good measure of the developmental level of functioning.

The scoring is based primarily on location scores, it is easy to learn, and can be applied quickly and reliably. Because the developmental-level construct relates to cognitive functioning, the developmental scoring of the Rorschach has very broad applications. Research with Friedman's developmental scoring has shown it to be successful in differentiating children at various age levels, mental defectives at different mental age levels, as well as normal adults from neurotics, aged, brain damaged, and schizophrenics. The developmental scoring system has also been found to differentiate among schizophrenics at different levels of disturbance as well as the parents of schizophrenics and neurotics. Further, taking males who vary in their Rorschach developmental level, one can differentiate their parents as to the way in which they resolve intrafamilial conflicts. The developmental scoring can distinguish successfully between individuals with ideational as compared with acting-out orientations to life, and also seems to bear some positive relation to intellectual functioning. Finally, Friedman's scoring system has been found to predict length of hospitalization in schizophrenics, social participation in chronic schizophrenics, and the ability to function under conditions of environmental distractions in normals.

The research failures with the developmental scoring have been comparatively few. In particular, studies on the social nature of delinquency, the degree of creativity among music students, the prediction of successful community placement of mental defectives, and the attempt to induce changes in developmental level as a function of brief sensory deprivation have yielded negative results.

The use of Friedman's scoring system for research purposes is more clearly indicated than its clinical use. Although several types of pathological and nonpathological groups can be significantly differentiated, the lack of information as to the overlap among these groups makes it difficult to estimate the value of the developmental scoring for diagnostic or predictive purposes in clinical usage. Some normative data are available, but these need to be improved upon by increasing the number of subjects, using females as well as males, noting the overlap among groups, and the empirical determination of whether or not separate norms are needed at different levels of total R.

Like psychoanalytic theory, the research on the developmental scoring system has concentrated mostly on males. Future research efforts should determine if the scoring can validly be applied for females as well. Some other potential research problems include the use of the developmental scoring for predicting success in therapy, as well as for distinguishing among normal subjects with different social participation skills. Attempts should also be made to relate the developmental scoring of the Rorschach with other measures of developmental functioning and severity of psychological disturbance and to investigate in further detail the relationship with intellectual, cognitive, and creative abilities. And finally, as it has been shown to be a valuable research tool, Friedman's scoring of the Rorschach should receive greater use as a dependent variable in studies attempting to induce experimental changes in developmental level of functioning.

Chapter 3

PHILLIPS' DEVELOPMENTAL LEVEL SCORING

This chapter deals with Phillips and his associates' (Phillips, Kaden, and Waldman, 1959) revision and extension of Friedman's (1952, 1953) developmental scoring system. After a brief statement of the assumption underlying the developmental level construct as employed by Phillips et al., the chapter describes the revised scoring system itself. Although practically no normative data are available, what little were obtainable are presented. A discussion of the reliability and validity of the scoring system is followed by an overall evaluation of the strengths and weaknesses of the system.

THEORETICAL BACKGROUND

The theoretical definition of the developmental-level construct used by Phillips and his associates is essentially the same as that used by Friedman (Werner, 1948, 1957). As indicated in Chapter 2, Werner's description of the developmental sequence is based on the *orthogenetic principle,* which implies that development "proceeds from a state of relative globality and lack of differentiation to a state of increasing differentiation, articulation, and hierarchic integration" (Werner, 1957, p. 126). While Werner's theory presumably describes only the sequence of development, its range of application extends to a surprisingly wide variety of problem areas (e.g., psychopathology, social adequacy, cognition, etc.). A more complete discussion of the developmental-level construct has been presented in Chapter 2.

Although Phillips et al. have drawn heavily on the orthogenetic principle, they have departed somewhat from Werner's theory in revising and extending Friedman's scoring system. Based on the findings that certain variables not included by pathological groups (e.g., movement responses and the degree of form dominance), Phillips et al. have included additional scoring categories within their system. Their revision has also omitted certain categories which appear in the Friedman system (e.g., + + and + scores), and replaced them with other scores (e.g., integration scores, which are differentiated on the basis of whether the integration involves movement, spatial position, color, etc.).

While Friedman made use of location scores only in attempting to parallel Werner's structural approach to developmental theory, Phillips and his colleagues have made certain changes in the hope that their revised system would improve upon the validity and clinical utility of the developmental scoring of the Rorschach. It would probably be safe to conclude that although most of the assumptions underlying the scoring procedures outlined by Phillips et al. are tied to Werner's theory of development, the revisions which have been made have as their base the past experimental findings with the Rorschach in general.

PHILLIPS' DEVELOPMENTAL SCORING SYSTEM

The revised developmental scoring system contains rules for scoring *four* general aspects of Rorschach performance. They are as follows:

I. Adequacy and Specificity of Form
   A. Mediocre
   B. Minus
   C. Vague
   D. Amorphous
II. Determinants Used in Combination
   A. Form dominance
   B. Form subordination and absence
III. The Perception of Activity—Movement Responses
   A. M
   B. FM
   C. m
IV. Organization of Blot Elements
   A. Adequate organization
      1. Functional integration
      2. Collective integration
      3. Positional integration
      4. Structural integration
   B. Inadequate organization
      1. Fabulized combination
      2. Contamination
      3. Confabulation

Before presenting the scoring criteria for the specific developmental indices, the following are some general rules regarding when determinants may be scored, and when a response should be scored *twice*.[1]

[1] Except for minor changes in wording and organization, most of the revised scoring system criteria are reprinted from *Journal of Genetic Psychology,* **94**, 273–282 (1959) by permission of the publishers and authors.

General Rules for Scoring

1. *Score* determinants which are developed in the *inquiry* but which modify the original percept. An example is as follows:

Free Assoc.	*Inquiry*	*Scoring*
Card I: Bat (W)	A black bat and it's flying	W C'F.FM+ A P

2. *Score* a response *twice* if *either* of the two following criteria are met:
   (a) There are at least two scorable, *nonidentical* contents which occur in the *free association.* An example is as follows:

Free Assoc.	*Scoring*
Card VIII: Two animals (D1)[2] climbing over some rocks	W FM+ A P D F+ Ls

   (b) If one of the contents introduced in the *inquiry* is of *minus* form level. An example is as follows:

Free Assoc.	*Inquiry*	*Scoring*
Card VIII: Two caterpillars (D1)	Crawling over some shrubbery	W FM− A D F+ Ls

3. *Do not* score a response twice if *either* of the two following criteria are met:
   (a) A new percept which does not modify the original percept is developed in the *inquiry.* An example is as follows:

Free Assoc.	*Inquiry*	*Scoring*
Card VIII: Two animals (D1)	They're climbing over some rocks	W FM+ A P

   (b) Two or more contents occur in the *free association* but one of the contents meets *all* of the following three criteria:

   1. It occupies approximately *less than one-fourth* of the figure percept.
   2. It contains *only form* as a determinant.
   3. It falls into the class of *mediocre* response.

   An example is as follows:

Free Assoc.	*Scoring*
Card III: Two men (D1) stirring a pot (D7)	D M+ H P

I. Scoring Criteria for Adequacy and Specificity of Form

The scoring symbols referring to the *mediocre* (m), *minus* (−), *vague* (v); or *amorphous* (a) form quality are used as location subheadings (e.g., Wm, Dm, Ddm, W−, D−, Dd−, etc.).

[2] The numbering of details follows that given by Beck (1949, 1961).

A. Mediocre (m). "Mediocre" is scored when *all* four of the following criteria are met:

1. There is a scorable single content including those responses given in plural form, for example, "animals." (For restrictions on this definition, see also "integrative" responses, pp. 63–64.)
2. The content has a specific structural requirement. (See "vague" responses, pp. 59–60.)
3. The response is of adequate form level (F+).
4. The response does not cross color (including white space) boundaries. (See "structural integrative" responses, pp. 66–67.)

The majority of responses will probably be scored in the "mediocre" category, for this includes all of the easily achieved, common W, D, and Dd responses.

Some examples of the *mediocre* response are as follows:

	Free Assoc.	*Inquiry*	*Scoring*
Card I:	Bat (W)	It's black	Wm FC'+ A P
Card III:	Red bowtie (D3)	The color and the shape	Dm CF+ Pr P
Card VII:	A harbor (W)	The curved shape	Wm F+ Ls

B. Minus (−). "Minus" is scored when *both* of the following criteria are met:

1. There is a scorable single content including those responses given in plural form, for example, "animals." (For restrictions on this definition, see also "fabulized combination" and "contamination," pp. 67–68.)
2. The response is of inadequate form level (F−).

Some examples of *minus* responses are as follows:

	Free Assoc.	*Inquiry*	*Scoring*
Card II:	Insect (W)	Shape	W− F− A
Card VIII:	Caterpillar (D1)	Shape and multicolored	D− FC− A
Card IX:	Teeth (Dd 21)	Shape	Dd− F− Hd

C. Vague (v). "Vague" is scored when *both* of the following criteria are met:

1. The content must be F+.
2. The content must *not* imply a specific structural requirement. Thus, since "harbor" implies a U-shaped structure, it is scored *mediocre,* and *not vague*. The response "water" has no such specific structure requirements and is therefore scored as *vague*.[3]

[3] Phillips and Smith (1953, pp. 321–376) have ordered all contents by class along a continuum of specificity. By making reference to these classes, one can judge any response according to the specificity criterion for inclusion in the "vague" category. Almost all contents in the first three classes of the Phillips–Smith system are scored "vague."

Some examples of the *vague* response are as follows:

	Free Assoc.	*Inquiry*	*Scoring*
Card I:	Clouds (W)	Shape	Wv F+ Cl
Card II:	Explosion (D3)	General outline	Dv F+ Expl.

In addition, such contents as "shrubbery," "stain," "map" (unelaborated), "land," "smoke" (noncolumnar), and "rocks" are scored *vague,* as well as primitive organisms such as "amoeba." Anatomy contents cover the entire range of the specificity continuum, and thus must be judged individually. The following anatomy contents, however, if unelaborated, are scored *vague*: "medical chart," "inside of body," "X ray."

D. AMORPHOUS (A). "Amorphous" is scored when *both* of the following criteria are met:

1. The percept falls into the class of "vague" responses.
2. Any of the following is given as the only determinant: C, C′, c, V, m.

Some examples of the *amorphous* response are as follows:

	Free Assoc.	*Inquiry*	*Scoring*
Card II:	Blood (D3)	The color red	Da C Bl
Card IV:	Something disintegrating (W)		Wa m Ab

II. Scoring Criteria for Determinants Used in Combination

Usually, the basis for scoring "form dominance," "form subordination," or "form absence" in color, achromatic color, texture, or vista responses is dependent on the inquiry.

The use of color or achromatic color to *locate* percepts does *not* influence scoring. Examples of responses where color is *not* scored: "The red part—could be a butterfly," "The green part looks like an insect," "The darker grey part looks like a cloud."

A. FORM DOMINANCE (FX). Form is scored as *dominant* if the subject does *any* of the following:

1. In the *inquiry* mentions color, achromatic color, texture, or vista *spontaneously* subsequent to details, giving emphasis to shape. Examples are as follows:

	Free Assoc.	*Inquiry*	*Scoring*
Card I:	Bat (W)	Shape, it's black	Wm FC′+ A P
Card III:	Butterfly (D3)	Wings and body, it's red	Dm FC+ A
Card VII:	Clouds (W)	General formation, it's fluffy	Wv Fc+ Cl
Card IX:	Chasm (Ds8)	Shape, seen from high up	Dm FV+ Ls

2. In the *inquiry* mentions color, achromatic color, texture, or vista only

on question. Examples are as follows:

	Free Assoc.	*Inquiry*	*Scoring*
Card I:	Bat (W)	Wings and body (?)—it's black	Wm FC′+ A P
Card III:	Butterfly (D3)	The shape (?)—it's red	Dm FC+ A
Card VII:	Clouds (W)	Shape of clouds (?)—also fluffy	Wv Fc+ Cl
Card IX:	Chasm (Ds8)	Shape (?)—looking at it from high	Dm FV+ Ls

3. In the *free association only* uses color, achromatic color, texture, or vista to modify a percept which falls in the class of *mediocre* responses (see p. 59). Examples are as follows:

	Free Assoc.	*Inquiry*	*Scoring*
Card I:	Distant bird (W)	Outline	Wm Fc+ A
Card II:	Red butterfly (D3)	Shape	Dm FC+ A P
Card V:	Black bat (W)	The shape	Wm FC′+ A P
Card VIII:	Furry animals (D1)	Head, body, legs	Dm Fc+ A P

B. Form Subordination and Absence (XF and X).

1. Form is scored subordinate (XF), if the subject does *any* of the following:
   (a) In the *inquiry,* color, achromatic color, texture, or vista is *given primacy.* Examples are as follows:

	Free Assoc.	*Inquiry*	*Scoring*
Card III:	Bow tie (D3)	Red bow tie	Dm CF+ Pr P
Card VI:	Bear skin (D1)	It's furry like a skin	Dm cF+ Ad P

   (b) In the *inquiry,* color, achromatic color, texture, or vista is *mentioned first.* Examples are as follows:

	Free Assoc.	*Inquiry*	*Scoring*
Card II:	Cave (D6)	The distance and general shape	Dm VF+ Ls
Card IV:	Clouds (W)	The darkness and the outline	Wv C′F+ Cl

   (c) In the *inquiry,* color, achromatic color, texture, or vista *only* is used to define a percept which falls into the class of "mediocre" responses. Examples are as follows:

	Free Assoc.	*Inquiry*	*Scoring*
Card I:	Bat (W)	Because it's black like a bat	Wm C′F+ A P
Card IV:	Gorilla (W)	It's all hairy	Wm cF+ A P

   (d) In the *free association only,* color, achromatic color, texture, or vista is used to modify a percept which falls in the class of "vague" responses. Examples are as follows:

	Free Assoc.	*Inquiry*	*Scoring*
Card IV:	Black thunderclouds (W)	Outline	Wv C'F+ Cl
Card VI:	Distant mountain (D1)	Jagged shape	Dv VF+ Ls
Card IX:	Colored paint (W)	Arrangement	Wv CF+ Art

2. If *no form* (X) is verbalized and the content falls into the class of "vague" responses, the rules for scoring *amorphous* responses presented on p. 60 are followed. Examples are as follows:

	Free Assoc.	*Inquiry*	*Scoring*
Card I:	I get the impression of being high up (W)	Just the impression of depth	Wa V Abst
Card II:	Blood (D3)	The color red	Da C Bl

III. Scoring Criteria for the Perception of Activity—Movement Responses

A. Human Movement (M). M is scored when *either* of the following two criteria are met:

1. Movement is perceived in *human content.* Movement includes, *in addition* to more overt activity:
   (a) Postural references or any verbalized kinesthetic strain, for example, "standing," "leaning," "bent," "twisted."
   (b) Part body postural referents, such as "pointing," looking."
2. Movement that is *uniquely human* is perceived in animal content, for example, "dogs gossiping," "lions dancing."

Do not score M if verbalizations of activity (primarily gestural) are associated with descriptions of inner states or functions, such as "angry," "brooding." M is *not* scored *unless* such verbalizations are accompanied by descriptions of bodily activity outlined in criteria 1 and 2 above.

B. Animal Movement (FM). FM is scored for those responses *not* scored as M in which movement is perceived in animal content, for example, "cats running," "rabbit jumping."

C. Inanimate Movement (m). m is scored for action in *either* of the following:

1. Inanimate objects, for example, "volcano erupting," "top spinning," "rocks falling down."
2. Natural or abstract forces, for example, "something falling apart,"

"power radiating from the center," "something hanging from the edge."

Do not score m for *either* of the following:

1. Expressive descriptions of parts of living creatures, for example, "grotesque faces," "threatening images."
2. Ambiguous dynamic terms, for example, "stretched out," "spread out," "attached."

IV. Scoring Criteria for the Organization of Blot Elements

A. ADEQUATE ORGANIZATION. The "integration" score (i) represents the adequate organization of the blot elements. Specifically, this scoring reflects the *appropriate organization* (i.e., not fabulized combination, confabulation, or contamination) of two or more *adequately perceived* blot elements (i.e., not F-) into a unified response. This includes the organization of *any* of the following: (a) two or more "mediocre" elements, (b) two or more "vague" elements, (c) a "mediocre" and a "vague" element, or (d) the combination of a "mediocre" or "vague" element with an "amorphous" element.

"Integration" may be *scored* when:

1. The elements in the responses are either identical or nonidentical contents.
2. The *basis for integration* is developed in the inquiry only, and modifies the original percept. An example is as follows:

	Free Assoc.	*Inquiry*	*Scoring*
Card III:	Two men (D1)	They're dancing together	Di M+ H P

3. A *new percept* is developed in the inquiry for which a relationship is established to the "basic" percept. Neither the additional percept per se nor the determinants associated with the additional percept is scored. An example is as follows:

	Free Assoc.	*Inquiry*	*Scoring*
Card VIII:	Two animals (D1)	Climbing a green mountain (D8)	Di FM+ A P

4. A relationship is established between an adequate percept on the blot and an imaginal object *not seen* on the blot itself. An example is as follows:

	Free Assoc.	*Inquiry*	*Scoring*
Card IV:	A monster (W)	Looking for a victim	Di M+ (H)

"Integration" is *not scored* when additional content (e.g., clothing) occupies all or part of the *same area* used for the original percept. Examples are as follows:

Free Assoc.		*Inquiry*	*Scoring*
Card III:	Two people (D1)	They have black tuxedoes on	Dm FC′+ H, Cg P
Card III:	Two people (D1)	They're wearing high-heeled shoes	Dm F+ H, Cg P

Note: Integrative scoring can be assigned only *once* in any given response, even if integration is determined by more than one of the four ways described below. However, the numerical functional integrative score described below will always be given when it occurs.

1. Functional Integration (i^f). Functional integration is based upon an interaction between two or more conceptually independent subunits, that is, *movement* of at least one object in relation to at least one other object.

Functional integration is scored when *both* of the following criteria are met:

(a) The criteria for "integration" as discussed above are satisfied.
(b) The response contains M, FM, or m as a determinant. Examples are as follows:

Free Assoc.		*Scoring*
Card III:	Two people holding something (D1)	Di^f M+ H P
Card VI:	A plant (D3) coming through the soil (D1)	Wi^f Fm+ Bt
Card VIII:	Two beavers (D1) climbing a mountain (D2 and D8)	Wi^f FM+ A P

Quantitative Scoring of Functional Integration. Functional integration responses are given weighted scores of 4, 2, 1, or 0, depending upon the type of movement on which the integration is based. The following are the criteria for each quantitative level:

Score 4—Active human content. A weighted score of 4 is given to a functional integrative response in which *both* of the following criteria are met:

(a) An M response in *human* content.
(b) The movement is *active*. Such verbs as "fighting," "walking," "grasping," "climbing," "pushing," and the like are included in the class of active verbs. Where movement is not stated in verb form, the full score of 4 is given to the appropriate *noun,* for example, "two dancers," "two fighters," and so on.

Examples of functional integrative responses given a score of 4 are "two figures dancing," "men lifting up some object," "a man riding on horseback," and so on.

Score 2—Active animal content. A weighted score of 2 is given to a functional integrative response which meets *any* of the following criteria:

(a) An FM response, such as "two bears climbing a hill," "two dogs sniffing each other," and so on.
(b) M in animal content, such as "two bears talking to each other," "two dogs gossiping," and so on.
(c) M in anatomy content, such as "two skeletons dancing."
(d) M in active human-like, that is, (H) content, such as "two marionettes dancing."
(e) Representations of action, such as, "a scene from *Night on Bald Mountain*," "devil insects having a festival," and so on.

Score 1—Passive or static movement. A weighted score of 1 is given to a functional integrative response where movement (either human or animal) is passive or static. Examples of movement included in this category are *any* of the following:

(a) Verbs connoting *passive receptive attitudes,* such as, "drinking," "sucking," "warming hands over fire," "cooking."
(b) Verbs implying *static movement,* such as "sitting," "facing," "looking," "starting," "holding," "touching," "standing."
(c) *Stopped motion* verbs, such as "about to," "trying to," "going to," "getting ready to," "engaged in."
(d) *Flector verbs,* such as "bending," "leaning," "sleeping," "bending down," "stooping," "bowing."

Score 0—Body part or inanimate movement. A weighted score of 0 is given to a functional integrative response which falls into *either* of the following categories:

(a) Responses where the movement occurs in *part body* (Hd or Ad) content, such as "two heads, looks like they're arguing," "women looking at each other, just from the bust up."
(b) Responses in which the movement is *inanimate,* such as "water over rocks."

Note on assigning weighted scores: In instances where a given functional integration response meets the criteria of *more than* one score level, the *first verb* mentioned determines the weighted score. Examples are as follows:

Two men facing each other, talking.	Score 1
Two men talking, facing each other.	Score 4

2. *Collective Integration* (i^c). Collective integration is scored when an overall *grouping* is actively imposed on the blot, either in the free

association or inquiry. The essential feature is evidence of a conceptualizing, classifying process as distinct from one of sheer enumeration. If the form level of the class term is F+, an "integrative" scoring is given, even though specific enumeration may involve F− elements.

Some of the *key words* which are indicative of collective integration are

(a) "group," "garden," "pair," and "collection." Examples are as follows:

	Free Assoc.	*Scoring*
Card IV:	Pair of boots (D6)	Di^{c} F+ Cg
Card VII:	Group of islands (W)	Wi^{c} F+ Ge
Card VIII:	Flower garden (W)	Wi^{c} F+ Bt
Card X:	Ocean scene (W)	Wi^{c} F+ Na

(b) "bust of," "emblem with," "coat of arms with," "ornament of," and "statue of." Examples are as follows:

	Free Assoc.	*Scoring*
Card II:	Emblem with two bears (D1)	Di^{c} F+ Embl.
Card VII:	Statue of two dogs (D1)	Di^{c} F+ (A)

Do not score collective integration when only enumeration is given, for example, "lots of. . . ," "a few. . . ," "couple of. . . ," "two. . . ," "picture of. . . ," "drawing of. . . ." The word "bunch" may or may not be integrative, depending on context, for example, "bunch of kids" (no); "bunch of grapes" (yes).

3. Positional Integration (i^{p}). Positional integration is scored when there is a *spatial relationship* between the elements perceived. Examples are as follows

	Free Assoc.	*Scoring*
Card II:	Two dogs, nose to nose, barking (D6)	Di^{p} FM+ A P
Card VI:	Totem pole set on a rock (W)	Wi^{p} F+ Ay
		Dv F+ Ls
Card X:	A limb with bugs on it (D11)	Di^{p} F+ Bt
		Dm F+ A

Note: "Two people sitting across from each other" is scored *positional* integration; integration is based on the spatial relation "across." "Two people leaning against a post" is scored *functional* integration; integration here is based on the movement "leaning."

4. Structural Integration (i^{s}). For responses scored structural integration, a single content is arrived at by unifying two or more colored areas, including the use of white space for its form characteristics. The essence of this category is *color-boundary crossing.* Examples of W responses (Wi^{s}) are as follows

Card II:	"volcano," "butterfly," "clowns"
Card VIII:	"flower," "fountain," "boat"
Card IX:	"fountain," "gladiola bulb"

Examples of structural integration involving D areas (Di^s) are as follows:

Card II:	"man" (lateral half)
Card VIII:	"tree" (D8)
Card IX:	"mushroom from atom bomb" (D9)

Do not score structural integration in the following two instances:

(a) The single content which falls into the *vague* category, even though it crosses color boundaries, continues to be scored "vague," for example, Card VIII: "design" (W); Card IX: "map" (W); Card X: "explosion" (W).

(b) One of the colors:
  (1) Occupies substantially all of the area required for a percept,
  (2) Occupies only a relatively small area, and
  (3) Is not explicitly referred to by the subject.

For example, Card X: "lion" (D2) is *not* scored integrative; however, for "fried egg," where the yolk (Dd33) is pointed out, integrative *is* scored.

B. Inadequate Organization. Scores reflecting the inadequate organization of the blot include the *fabulized combination, contamination,* and *confabulation* categories.

1. Fabulized Combination (fab). Fabulized combination is scored when *both* of the following criteria are met:

(a) Responses in which two or more areas, separately interpreted, are combined on the basis of spatial relationship in a way which does not reasonably occur in nature.

(b) Such a combination is not explained nor is it reasonably rationalized in a spontaneous fashion, that is, without questioning by examiner.

Note: Rules for "double scoring" (see p. 58) apply to fabulized combinations. In addition:

(a) The *fabulized combination* score is given to the percept which occurs *first* in the free association.

(b) Scoring for fabulized combination does *not* influence the scoring of form level of the individual percepts.

Examples of fabulized combinations are as follows:

	Free Assoc.	*Scoring*
Card V:	Looks like a mule with wings (W)	Wfab F− A
		Dm F+ Ad
Card VII:	Couple of baby lambs in the clouds dancing (W)	Wfab FM− A
		Dv F+ Cl
Card X:	Couple of strange little green birds (D12)	Dfab FC.M− A
	standing on some organ of the body (D1)	Dv F+ An

Do not score fabulized combination when there is an *adequate rationalization.* Examples which are *not* fabulized combinations are as follows

	Free Assoc.	*Scoring*
Card I:	Or it could be a person with butterfly wings in a dance recital (W)	Wi M+ H, Rc Dm F+ Ad, Cg

Comment: "In a dance recital" rationalizes the response.

	Free Assoc.	*Inquiry*	*Scoring*
Card VII:	Some kind of nymphs dancing on the top of a cloud	Nymphs are supposed to perform the supernatural	Wi M+ (H) Dv cF.C'F+ Cl

Comment: The content "nymphs" serves to rationalize the response.

2. *Contamination (contam).* Contamination is scored when two independent responses to the *same area* are fused into a single percept.

Notes: Since a contamination involves two percepts, the response is scored *twice.* Further,

(a) The *contamination* score is given to the percept which occurs *first* in the free association.

(b) Scoring for contamination does *not* influence the scoring of form level of the independent percepts.

Examples of contamination are as follows

	Free Assoc.	*Scoring*
Card IV:	Front of a bug—the front of an ox—the front of a bug-ox	Wcontam F− A W− F− A

Comment: F− is scored for both responses because both "bug" and "ox," if given independently, would warrant F− scoring.

	Free Assoc.	*Inquiry*	*Scoring*
Card VIII:	Flag in the sky (D5)	Flag because of the form, and sky because of the color	Dcontam F+ Obj Da C Na
Card IX:	Looks like grass, also looks like a rabbit—a grassy rabbit (D1)	Grass because it looks like tall grass and it's green; shape of a rabbit	Dcontam CF+ Bt D− F− A

3. *Confabulation (DW, DdW, DD, DdD).* Confabulation is scored when *both* of the following criteria are met:

(a) The interpretation of an area determines the interpretation of other areas.

(b) The content developed is *not* a minor elaboration of the initiating percept.

Note: Scoring for *confabulation* does *not* influence the scoring of form level.

There are *two types* of *confabulated* responses. These are as follows:

(a) A response to a larger area which is determined by the response to a smaller one. Examples are as follows:

	Free Assoc.	*Inquiry*	*Scoring*
Card IV:	A human body —a female body (W)	Woman's sexual organs (D3) and if so, then whole thing would pertain to a woman's body	DW F— An, Sex
Card VI:	Cat (W)	Because of the whiskers (Dd26)	DdW F— A

(b) A response in which the content given to a detail is given also to a larger blot area. An example is as follows:

	Free Assoc.	*Inquiry*	*Scoring*
Card VI:	Bird (W)	Because of the top part (D3) is a bird	DW F— A

Interpretive Significance of the Developmental Indices

Adequacy and Specificity of Form

As the scoring indices representing the adequacy and specificity of form are essentially the same as those in Friedman's system, the reader is referred to Chapter 2 (pp. 27–31) for a discussion of their interpretive significance. It might be noted here that in studies by Phillips and his associates, one of these scores (D-) has been found to be related to a type of "decontextualization" ability (Brooks and Phillips, 1958; Lipton, Kaden, and Phillips, 1958). Specifically, D- responses have shown to be negatively related to the ability to keep competing response tendencies independent in a variety of cognitive tasks; the fewer number of D- responses, the better the ability to "decontextualize" oneself from such conditions of cognitive distraction.

Determinants Used in Combination

The developmental scores involving determinants used in combination (form dominance, subordination, or absence) are believed to reflect the ability to exercise control over one's impulses, a characteristic associated with higher levels of development. Studies have shown that the emphasis of form dominance (FX) over form subordination and absence (XF + X) is more typical of individuals who threaten assault than those who actually act out assaultively (Misch, 1954), who threaten suicide rather than actually attempt it (Kruger, 1954), and those who are preoccupied with sexually deviant thoughts as opposed to those who act out these deviant impulses (Kruger, 1954). The prominence of FX over XF + X has also been found to be more characteristic of underactive as compared to overactive boys. Further, whereas the emphasis on form-dominant responses increases with age in underactive boys, the increase does not occur with boys who are overactive (Hurwitz, 1954). The FX response has also been found to occur more often in normals than in schizophrenics (Friedman, 1960; Hersch, 1962), and the XF + X more often in schizophrenics than normals (Friedman, 1960). In a comparison of more and less creative music students, Cooper (1961) found more creative students to have a greater number of XF + X scores, and fewer FX scores. This last finding was not confirmed by Hersch (1962), who found no significant difference between artists and normal controls on either of these two scores.

Perception of Activity

Responses involving the perception of activity (movement responses M, FM, and m) presumably reflect one's general level of ideational activity —a characteristic which varies directly with level of development. Further, the empathic experience of motion (particularly human movement) is believed to be vicariously related to actual bodily movement (Werner, 1945); the more the ideational activity, the less the likelihood of physical acting out. Research evidence has indicated that M responses are more characteristic of hypoactive than hyperactive boys; whereas M responses increase with age for hypoactive boys, this increase is not as evident for hyperactive boys (Hurwitz, 1954). M responses have also been found to occur more often in individuals who threaten assaultive behavior than those who actually act out assaultively (Misch, 1954).

Futher evidence for the developmentally high nature of M responses comes from a study by Hersch (1962), which found that artists obtained more M scores than normals, and normals more than schizophrenics. The frequency of M has also been found to relate positively to successful post-hospital adjustment for married male psychiatric patients (Kaden and Lipton, 1960). In the area of cognitive functioning, M has been shown to be positively related to the ability to articulate a figure from a more complex background (Lipton, Kaden, and Phillips, 1958).

Relatively little research evidence is available for the developmental nature of FM and m responses. One study (Kruger, 1954) has compared several groups on an index of total movement, which takes into account *all* types of movement. By giving a plus score for two or more M, two or more FM, and one or more m, Kruger found that this total index was higher for individuals who threatened rather than attempted suicide, for sexual deviants who were preoccupied with their impulses as opposed to those who acted upon them, and for those people who turned their aggression inward (suicidal) as compared with those who directed their aggression toward others (assaultive).

Organization of Blot Elements

ADEQUATE ORGANIZATION. The adequate organization of the blot elements—the integrative responses—represents the highest developmental level of functioning. In many respects, the integrative scores resemble the + + and + scores described in Chapter 2. In the revised scoring system, however, integrative responses are classified separately according to whether the basis for integration is functional, collective, positional, or structural. Typically, research using the revised developmental scoring has compared groups on the basis of the functional integration (Fi) score. Although scores representing *total* integration or integration in W or D areas are sometimes used in research, no data are available on the specific interpretive significance of the collective, positional, or structural integration scores.

The Fi score, because of both the organizational and ideational capacities it reflects, may be viewed as the highest developmental index in the revised scoring system. This score not only indicates a high level of cognitive ability, but also the capacity for mature interpersonal relations. As the Fi response usually involves the interaction of two or more people or animals, one may speculate about its symbolic reflection of social participation. On a more empirical level, however, the Fi response has been found to relate positively to mature marital interaction (Kaden, 1958), participation in social organizations (Jordan and Phillips, 1959), and post-hospital adjustment in married male schizophrenics (Kaden and Lipton, 1960). Despite these findings, Friedman (1960) was unable to distinguish between schizophrenics and normals on the basis of this score. In the area of cognitive functioning, Fi responses are positively related to the ability to articulate a figure from a more complex ground (Lipton et al., 1958). Eisdorfer (1960) has also found that with the loss in hearing accompanying old age, there is a decrease in the ability to produce Fi responses.

The weighting of the Fi score, which depends on the enrgy level and type of movement used for the integration of blot elements, has received little research attention. Studies typically have investigated the discriminatory power of the functional integration or movement scores, but not the joint weighting of the two. The only study reporting the use of the weighted score is one by Friedman (1960), who was unable to differentiate between normals and chronic schizophrenics on the basis of this score. Further research is needed to determine whether this aspect of the revised developmental scoring is worth retaining.

INADEQUATE ORGANIZATION. The fabulized combination, contamination, and confabulation scores, which represent the inadequate organization of the blot, may be interpreted as representing some of the developmentally lowest levels of functioning. The theoretical rationale for the primitive nature of these scores is described in Chapter 2 (p. 31). Although relatively rare, these scores have been found to occur more often in the records of children and regressed schizophrenics (Friedman, 1952). When used together as an index of primitive thought (IPT), these developmentally low scores are found more often in protocols of assaultive individuals than in the records of those who merely threaten assault (Misch, 1954).

Interscorer Reliability

Although the revised developmental scoring system makes use of many of the indices from Friedman's system, an independent evaluation of the interscorer reliability of the revised scoring is needed. This separate evaluation is warranted not only because of the new scores added to the system, but also because of the more complex criteria used in scoring those indices retained from Friedman's system. In light of the greater number of categories and the more elaborate criteria for the revised developmental scoring, it is considerably more difficult to learn and apply this system as compared with Friedman's approach. However, it is possible that these more painfully elaborate rules, because they can help to resolve problems in scoring difficult responses, may serve to increase the interscorer reliability. As the interscorer agreement for Friedman's system is over 90%, chances are that the reliability for the revised system is not much higher.

There is little in the way of actual data on the interscorer reliability of the revised system. Kruger (1954), Misch (1954), and Hurwitz (1954) made use of the developmental scoring during a transitional period, when Phillips was in the process of revising Friedman's system. During this time, the "revised" system consisted of only the addition of M, FX, XF, and X scores to Friedman's basic approach. The per cent of interscorer agreement for this transitional system was 96.8 (Kruger, 1954), 93.4 (Misch, 1954), and 95.7 (Hurwitz, 1954); each value represents agreement between two judges. A later study using the revised system as it is in its present form, but one in which M, FX, XF, and X were not scored, found 91.0% agreement between two judges (Nickel, 1957). Although "integration" was scored in Nickel's study, no distinction was made as to the specific type of integration.

Actual evidence for the interscorer reliability of the revised developmental scoring system as a whole is lacking. However, if one had to best-guess as to its reliability level, it would probably be safe to say that it was "high."

Summary Scores

The scores in the revised developmental scoring system have been summarized according to their absolute frequency of occurrence, their percentage relative to total R, and their weighting as to level of development reflected.

Absolute Scores

Several studies using the revised scoring system have made direct use of the absolute number of each of the developmental indices in a protocol. This summation of scores has been carried out for individual scores as well as scores which summarize a more general type of response; only the scores of the latter type will be described here.

The integration scores have been summarized by the total number of integrative responses in the record (Ti), the functional integrative responses (Fi), and the number of integrative responses in the W and D locations

(Wi and Di). As genetically high W and D scores each reflect different aspects of mature functioning (see Chapter 2, pp. 27–28), it would probably be best to use Wi and Di separately in the clinical and research applications of the system.

Form dominance (FX) is used to summarize the sum of FC, FC′, Fc, and FV responses in the protocol. Similarly, form subordination and absence (XF + X) is computed by totaling all the CF, C, C′F, C′, cF, c, VF, and V responses. The FX and XF + X scores may be used separately, or they may be combined further into a unitary score (Fx) representing the overall influence of form in the record. This overall score can be computed by Fx = FX − (XF + X). If the resulting value of Fx is zero or greater, the dominance of form is indicated; if the value of Fx has a minus sign, form subordination is reflected. For research purposes, constants may be added to Fx to eliminate working with negative numbers. To achieve a more refined Fx measure, one may assign weights to each of the responses before totaling them and arriving at the FX, XF, and X values. Following the weighting system traditionally used for color (Beck, 1949), FX responses are multiplied by 0.5, while XF and X responses are multiplied by 1.0 and 1.5, respectively.

Percentage Scores

Adequate and Organized Responses (AO%). This developmentally high value is the ratio of all responses of both adequate form level and organization to the total number of responses. The score may be computed by the following formula:

$$\text{AO\%} = \frac{\text{mediocre} + \text{integrative responses}}{\text{total R}} \times 100$$

Where interest is in only the most developmentally mature responses, mediocre responses may be omitted from the computation.

Inadequate and Unorganized Responses (IU%). Responses of inadequate form quality and organization, representing developmentally low levels of functioning, may be calculated as follows:

$$\text{IU\%} = \frac{\text{minus} + \text{vague} + \text{amorphous} + \text{fabulized combination} + \text{contamination} + \text{confabulation responses}}{\text{total R}} \times 100$$

Vague responses are sometimes omitted, as these represent a more intermediate level of functioning.

Index of Primitive Thought (IPT). This index is used to reflect an even more primitive level of functioning than the IU index. Only responses of inadequate organization are included in IPT, as follows:

$$\text{IPT} = \frac{\text{fabulized combinations} + \text{contaminations} + \text{confabulations}}{\text{total R}} \times 100$$

Weighted Indices

In our discussion in Chapter 2 of single, overall measures of developmental level, it was pointed out that because it masks information as to the patterning of scores comprising the total score, this type of index was not particularly useful clinically. Further, such indices are of limited research value in studies where the difference between groups may be too subtle to be detected by this overall measure. These considerations should be kept in mind in applying any of the following three indices: the composite index (CI), the genetic score (GS), and the determinant score (DS).

Composite Index (CI). This overall measure of developmental level was originally formulated by Lane (1955), and, because of the way in which the value is computed, can be used for research purposes only. The computation of the CI involves the following three steps: (1) The distributions of each of the several developmental scores or summary scores (e.g., AO%, Ti, IU%, etc.) for all subjects in a study are divided into quartiles. (2) Weights of 4, 3, 2, or 1 are assigned to the score values in each of the four quarters of the several distributions, so that the 4 weighting corresponds to the developmentally higher, and the 1 weighting to the developmentally lower direction. For example, subjects whose AO% or Ti score fell within the fourth quarter (i.e. 76–100 percentile) of the distribution would receive a rank of 4 for that particular index or score; a rank of 1 would be assigned to scores in the first quarter (i.e. 0–25 percentile). In order for subjects to receive a rank of 4 for IU%, on the other hand, their IU% value would have to have fallen in the *first* quarter of the distribution. (3) The sum of the ranks obtained by each subject for each of the several scores is computed, and this represents the final CI score. Thus, the higher the CI score, the developmentally higher the level of functioning.

Genetic Score (GS). The genetic score (GS) involves the weighting of form level and organizational quality on a 25-point scale (Grace, 1956). Each of the values refers to a particular type of response in a given location area; Table 3.1 indicates the weighting assigned to each response. To arrive at the final GS, the mean weighting for each of the 10 cards is first computed, and then all 10 values are averaged. The values of GS theoretically can range from 1 to 25, with 1 representing the lowest and 25 the highest level of developmental functioning possible; in actual practice, GS values rarely fall outside a range of 11–23.

Determinant Score (DS). The determinant score (DS), as formulated by Grace (1956), is designed to complement the GS value in summarizing a protocol, in that the DS involves the weighting of form dominance and movement. The DS weights (see Table 3.2) are applied only to responses receiving a GS weight of 20 or more—that is, mediocre or integrative responses. Responses involving multiple determinants (i.e., blends) may receive more than one weighting, provided that the aditional determinants fall within a *different* category. For example, the scoring Dm FC.Fc+ Na would receive DS weights of 3 and 2 (see Table 3.2), coresponding to the two different determinant categories represented in this scoring ("color"

TABLE 3.1
Weighting of Responses Used in the Computation of the Genetic Score (GS)

Response	*Weighting*
Contamination	
W	1
D	2
Dd	3
Fabulized Combination	
W	4
D	5
Dd	6
Confabulation	
W	7
D	8
Dd	9
Minus	
W	10
D	11
Dd	12
Rejection	13
Amorphous	
W	14
D	15
Dd	16
Vague	
W	17
D	18
Dd	19
Mediocre	
Dd	20
D	21
W	22
Integrative	
Dd	23
D	24
W	25

TABLE 3.2
Weighting of Responses Used in the Computation of the Determinant Score (DS)

Response	*Weighting*
Movement	
M	5
FM	3
m	1
Color	
FC	3
CF	1
Texture, Achromatic Color, and Vista	
Fc, FC′, FV	2
cF, C′F, VF	1

and "texture, achromatic color, and vista"). Scorings such as Wm M.m+ H or Di FC.CF+ Bt would each receive only one weighting, as the additional determinants comprising the blend in both instances are from the same category ("movement" and "color," respectively). In instances such as these, where the multiple determinants occur in the same category, the single weighting assigned represents the determinant with the *higher* ranking. Thus, according to Table 3.2, the weighting for M.m+ would be 5; for FC.CF+, the weight would be 3.

The total DS value is arrived at by totaling the values for all responses and dividing by the total number of ranks assigned. Accordingly, the higher DS values represent developmentally higher levels of functioning.

NORMATIVE DATA

Normative data on the revised developmental scores are practically nonexistent. With the exception of some data on summary scores (AO% and IU%) for normals and schizophrenics (Fowler, 1957), there are no data available which can be used for clinical purposes. The norms available for Friedman's original system may be applied to those scores retained in the revised developmental scoring; these data are presented in Table 2.4. As far as data on those individual scores added to the revised system are concerned, nothing is yet available. Grace (1956) has complied some norms for the revised scoring system, but these are based on the overall genetic score (GS) and determinant score (DS), which are not particularly useful in the clinical application of the system.

The data which are available, however humble they may be, are presented here together with a description of the sample on which they were based.

Nature of the Sample

The sample used for these normative data consists of normal male adults and hospitalized male schizophrenics. These two groups are further subdivided according to their level of social adequacy, as measured by the Phillips scale (Phillips, 1953). Social adequacy, which is based on case-history information concerning past and present social-sexual adjustment, has frequently been used as a prognostic indicator. When the social-adequacy concept is applied to the schizophrenic group, it can be viewed as an index of premorbid adjustment, and consequently may be used to classify patients into "process" and "reactive" categories. Thus, the "high social adequacy" schizophrenics described in Table 3.3 refer to "reactive" schizophrenics, while the "low social adequacy" schizophrenics refer to "process" schizophrenics. It may be noted further that the I.Q. scores for the normal and schizophrenic groups as indicated in Table 3.3 were based on estimates from vocabulary ability.

TABLE 3.3

Characteristics of Sample for Normative Data on the Revised Developmental Scoring System

					Age		I.Q.		Years of Education	
Group	*Sex*	*Color*	*N*	*Mean*	*Median*	*Range*	*Median*	*Range*	*Median*	*Range*
Normal Adults										
High Social Adequacy[a]	Male	White	20	34.0	34.0	25–44	100	85–125	10	7–17
Low Social Adequacy	Male	White	20	35.6	36.0	25–48	99	85–123	8	6–12
Schizophrenics										
High Social Adequacy	Male	White	20	33.1	32.0	26–46	101	88–138	10	7–16
Low Social Adequacy	Male	White	20	32.9	33.0	26–42	100	87–125	9	6–13

[a] Social adequacy was determined by the Phillips scale (Phillips, 1953), which makes use of data on past and present social-sexual adjustment.

Data on Developmental Summary Scores

Bearing in mind the restrictions on the sample (a small number of white males), see Table 3.4 for data on adequate and organized responses (AO%) and inadequate and unorganized responses (IU%) for the normal and schizophrenic groups. The computation of these two summary scores differs slightly from the method described in the section above on summary scores in that mediocre responses were omitted from the AO%, and Dd scores were not included in the computation of both AO% and IU%.

The AO% scores presented in Table 3.4 were found to be significantly greater for the normal than for the schizophrenic group, regardless of social adequacy level. The IU% scores, on the other hand, were found to be significantly higher for individuals of low social adequacy, whether they were normal or schizophrenic (Fowler, 1957). Although no data are available on the per cent of overlap between groups, an inspection of the ranges in Table 3.4 leads one to expect that the clinical use of these values alone to differentiate normals from schizophrenics would probably result in a large proportion of diagnostic errors. Perhaps AO% and IU% computed for W and D locations separately would prove to be more efficient diagnostic scores, as has been noted for Friedman's system in Chapter 2.

A good deal more normative data are needed for the revised developmental scoring system. Norms are needed for each of the individual indices, as well as summary scores across a variety of samples which include data on the percentage of overlap between groups. Further, as Podell and Phillips (1959) have found that the absolute frequency of such scores as Di, D −, FX, XF + X, Dv, Fi, M, and IPT were correlated with total number of responses within two separate samples of normal subjects, normative data on these scores should be computed for different levels of R.

TABLE 3.4
Mean, Median, and Range of Modified AO% and IU% for Normals and Schizophrenics

	Adequate and Organized Responses (AO%)[a]			Inadequate and Unorganized Responses (IU%)[b]		
Group	*Mean*	*Median*	*Range*	*Mean*	*Median*	*Range*
Normal Adults						
High Social Adequacy	18.9	19.2	0.0–47.0	24.5	21.7	10.0–50.0
Low Social Adequacy	15.4	14.3	0.0–54.6	36.6	36.0	0.0–63.2
Schizophrenics						
High Social Adequacy	11.3	8.4	0.0–33.3	32.8	32.4	9.1–53.8
Low Social Adequacy	11.3	10.0	0.0–31.3	41.6	37.5	13.3–72.7

[a] The method of computing AO% differs from that described on p. 73; the data in this table were based on the following formula: AO% = (W + D integrative responses/all W + D) × 100. Thus, mediocre responses and Dd scores were omitted.

[b] The method of computing IU% differs from that described on p. 73 only in that Dd scores were excluded. Thus, the data in this table were computed by IU% = (W + D minus + vague + amorphous + fabulized combination + contamination + confabulation responses/all W + D) × 100.

RELIABILITY

The discussion of the reliability of the revised developmental scoring will be very brief, as no research as yet has been conducted to estimate the stability of this measure over time. Studies of the test-retest reliability of this scoring approach may be considered to be relevant, especially as many of the revised developmental indices reflect presumably stable interpersonal and social competency characteristics (see section on validity, below). Consequently, research providing stability coefficients, as well as estimates of change in absolute level of scores, is clearly needed.

VALIDITY

The large majority of validity studies on the revised developmental scoring system are of the construct type. Only two studies resembling concurrent validity (Grace, 1956; Hurwitz, 1954), and one of the predictive type (Kaden and Lipton, 1960) have been reported in the literature. Further, in contrast to the validity research on Friedman's scoring system described in Chapter 2, more research has been carried out on the cognitive correlates of the revised developmental scores (Brooks and Phillips, 1958; Feffer, 1959; Lipton et al., 1958; Podell and Phillips, 1959; Smith and Phillips, 1959).

Criterion-Related Validity

Concurrent Validity

The research on the concurrent validity of the revised scoring system has studied the relationship between the developmental scores and age. Hurwitz (1954) found that for a group of 50 hyperactive boys, M and form dominance increased between ages 3 and 12. Similarly, Grace (1956) found that with 30 children between the ages of 2 and 10, estimates of developmental level increased with age. The correlations between age and developmental level indices reported by Grace are as follows: for genetic score (GS), $r = .57$ ($p < .01$); for determinant score (DS), $r = .55$ ($p < .01$), and for a combined GS and DS index, $r = .76$ ($p < .001$). However, neither DS nor GS was found to differ significantly between a group of 5–10-year-olds and normal adults. Whether this is a limitation of the particular summary scores used, or of the scoring system itself, needs to be studied further. Thus, the general question of whether or not the revised developmental scores parallel development with age remains partially open to further investigation.

Predictive Validity

Strictly speaking, predictive validity is not appropriate for the evaluation of the developmental scoring, as the use of a predictive criterion group to represent developmental level would depart too much from the theoretical meaning of the construct. However, one study has been included in this section, primarily to demonstrate the predictive ability of the scoring system.

Although the criterion group in Kaden and Lipton's (1960) predictive study does not depict the developmental level construct per se, some of the underlying characteristics defining the group are undoubtedly related to level of development. Kaden and Lipton were interested in using M and Fi as prognostic indicators of post-hospital adjustment in first-admission, married male schizophrenics. A small group of patients was divided on the basis of their "successful" (N = 11) and "unsuccessful" (N = 9) adjustment. "Success" was defined as (1) the ability to remain out of the hospital on an extended visit for at least one year, and (2) the ability to maintain employment for six months of that year; the "unsuccessful" group was composed of those patients who failed to meet one or both of the two criteria for success. Although the two adjustment groups did not differ as to age, I.Q., education, or length of hospitalization, M and Fi were both found to occur significantly more often in the successful adjustment group.

Using the median of the combined distributions from the successful and unsuccessful adjustment groups as the cutoff score, one may estimate the amount of overlap between groups for both M and Fi. For M, there were no false positives and 25% false negatives; for Fi, there were 5% false positives and 20% false negatives. These estimates should not be taken as accurate reflections of the amount of overlap to be expected in actual clinical usage, as the number of cases on which these values are based is quite small. However, the relative absence of false positives suggests strongly that when M or Fi is present in a record (above some yet undetermined cutoff point), one can be fairly safe in estimating that the patient *has* the ability to function eventually outside a hospital setting. The relative infrequency of these scores, on the other hand, does *not* necessarily imply that this ability is absent. This use of the developmental scores as predictive indices shows promise, and unquestionably warrants further investigation.

Construct Validity

The evaluation of the nomological construct validity of the revised developmental scoring system includes research on (1) hypothesized developmental differences among pathological groups, (2) hypothesized developmental differences among other groups, (3) differences in social adequacy among groups of different developmental levels: (4) predicted changes in developmental level, and (5) the hypothesized internal structure of the scoring system itself.

Nomological Validity

Differences among Pathological Groups. Research has been conducted to study the ability of the revised developmental scoring system to distinguish between male schizophrenics and normals, schizophrenics and their wives, schizophrenics at different levels of disturbance, and between normals and sexual deviants.

The results of research have shown that overall estimates of developmental level can distinguish between normal adults and schizophrenics, where the developmental functioning of schizophrenics was found to fall somewhere between the functioning of a group of 2-to-5, and a group of 5-to-10-year-olds (Grace, 1956). Normal adults were found to produce more integrative responses than schizophrenics in some studies (Fowler, 1957; Hersch, 1962), but not in others (Friedman, 1960). More consistent findings were obtained in the case of form-dominance measures, which were found to be more characteristic of normals than schizophrenics (Friedman, 1960; Hersch, 1962). M was also found to occur more often in normals than schizophrenics (Hersch, 1962), while the converse was true for the index of primitive thought (IPT).

When the revised developmental scoring has been used to distinguish between schizophrenics differing as to severity of disturbance, mixed results have occurred. Grace (1956) was unable to find any difference among paranoid, hebephrenic, or simple schizophrenics on either genetic or determinant summary scores. Fowler (1957), on the other hand, found that low social adequacy or "process" schizophrenics obtained more developmentally immature scores than high social adequacy or "reactive" schizophrenics. Fowler's analysis included mostly indices from Friedman's system; movement, Fi, and form-dominance indices were not used in the comparisons. Consequently, the use of the revised system to make finer discriminations among pathological groups has not yet been demonstrated.

A study by Kaden and Lipton (1962), comparing the developmental functioning of male schizophrenics with the functioning of their wives, has produced results which are somewhat difficult to interpret. Presumably expecting that there should be some discrepancies between the functioning of the schizophrenic and his wife, Kaden and Lipton found no difference on any of those indices studied—Fi, M, Wi, FX, XF + X, W−, and IPT. This study had no control group, making it difficult to interpret these findings. Kaden and Lipton report impressionistically that, in their past use of the scoring system, they have found that normals typically obtain more Fi scores than were obtained by the subjects in their study; the implication is that *both* the schizophrenic and his wife function at lower developmental levels than normal couples.

Sjostedt and Hurwitz (1959) hypothesized that because of the pregenital orientation of sexual deviants, these pathological groups should function at developmentally lower levels than normals. Taking into consideration the fact that 20 statistical comparisons were made, the single significant finding that male homosexuals and exhibitionists as a group produced more FC responses than normals may be interpreted as a chance occurrence. Although one might have predicted that sexual deviants and normals would differ on an estimate of level of *psychosexual* development, there is little reason to hypothesize any difference in the *structural* aspects of their cognitive functioning levels as defined by Werner (1948, 1957).

In general, research on the ability of the revised developmental scoring system to distinguish among pathological groups has not been nearly as extensive or successful as it has for Friedman's system. Those studies which have been done in this area seem to indicate that while schizophrenics can generally be differentiated from normals on the basis of the revised system, the developmental differences found among schizophrenics at different levels of severity of pathology are not as clear cut.

Differences among Other Groups. The revised developmental indices have been used to study the developmental differences between ideationally and motorically oriented individuals, between creative and uncreative music students, and between artists and "normals."

Hurwitz (1954) tested Werner's (1948) hypothesis that an inverse relationship exists between motoric acting out and ideational activity. Using M as an ideational index, Hurwitz found a greater incidence of ideational activity in hypoactive as compared with hyperactive boys. In line with the expectation that the ability to delay motor behavior is a developmentally advanced characteristic, a relatively greater frequency of form-dominant responses were found to characterize the hypoactive group. Similarly, Misch (1954) found that overtly assaultive males obtained fewer M and form-dominant scores, but a higher index of primitive thought (IPT) than individuals who made only threats of assault. A study of the relation between developmental level and impulse control in suicidal and sexually deviant groups has also confirmed the hypothesized relationship (Kruger, 1954). That is, Kruger found that in comparison to individuals who attempted suicide or acted out their sexually deviant impulses, those who threatened suicide or who were only preoccupied with their deviant thought gave significantly more form-dominant and combined movement (M, FM, and m) responses.

On the basis of Kris' hypothesis that creative individuals possess the capacity for "regression in the service of the ego," Cooper (1961) predicted that the cognitive functioning of creative people would be characterized by both developmentally primitive and mature aspects. In a developmental comparison between more and less creative music students, the creative students were found to have more XF + X scores, while the less creative student had more FX scores. The greater incidence of FX scores in the less creative group went counter to Cooper's prediction that this score would reflect the control over regression which is presumably characteristic of more creative individuals. Hersch (1962) compared more extreme groups (successful artists and normal adults) on the revised developmental indices. Unlike Cooper, Hersch found that the creative subjects have more M responses than normals, although no difference was found between the relative frequency of FX + X responses. Hersch also found that the greater frequency of FX and IPT for the artist group was significant at the 0.10 level (one-tailed test). The findings of Cooper and Hersch are much too tenuous to conclude that the revised developmental indices have confirmed Werner's hypothesis that "a person's capacity for creativity presupposes mobility in terms of regression and progression" (Werner, 1957, p. 145).[4]

[4] It may be of interest to note that the addition of a "physiognomic" score in Hersch's study yielded positive results. A "physiognomic" score was assigned to those responses in which life-like characteristics were attributed to the blot itself, e.g., the blot looks "happy" or "sad." Hersch found that while normals and schizophrenics could not be distinguished on the basis of this type of score, the artists obtained significantly more physiognomic scores than either normals or schizophrenics.

The general findings of research in which the revised developmental indices were used to differentiate among various nonpathological groups indicate that the scoring system can distinguish successfully between ideationally and motorically oriented individuals. When the scoring system is used to study creativity, it is considerably more limited.

Developmental Level and Social Adequacy. Several attempts have been made to relate the revised developmental scoring to adequacy of social functioning. The underlying premise for these studies has been that the developmentally mature individual has a greater stability and flexibility in his dealings with the environment (Werner, 1948). Consequently, the developmentally higher the individual's level of functioning, the greater his social effectiveness, where effectiveness is determined by such factors as interpersonal, marital, sexual, occupational, and educational adjustment (Phillips, 1953; Phillips and Cowitz, 1953).

Studies have generally confirmed this hypothesized positive relationship between general developmental level and social effectiveness in adult males (Fowler, 1957; Grace, 1956; Lane, 1955). Fowler (1957) suggests additionally that it is the absence of developmentally low responses that is particularly indicative of socially effective behavior. Using a group of adolescent males, Smith and Phillips (1959) found no consistent relationship between developmental level and social effectiveness.

In a study relating separate aspects of social effectiveness to developmental level, Jordon and Phillips (1959) report that the presence of Fi scores is positively associated with participation in social organizations. Similarly, Kaden (1958) found functional integration scores in married men to be positively related to the type of marital interaction in which both parties shared in the decision making.

An interesting approach in relating socially adequate behavior with developmental level has been taken by Prague (cited in Phillips, 1959). She classified behavior according to Maslow's notion of hierarchy of needs, in such a way that behavior at the lower end of the hierarchy was considered to be motivated by physical needs, while behavior at the higher end was viewed as fulfilling the need for self-actualization. According to Phillips' description, Prague found that the prominence of behavior motivated by hierarchically lower needs was related to a high incidence of developmentally low scores, whereas behavior motivated by more mature needs was related to developmentally high scores.

The research evidence, then, seems clear that the revised developmental scoring system is a useful indicator of the effectiveness and maturity of one's functioning in the area of social and interpersonal relations.

Predicted Changes in Developmental Level. Changes in developmental level of functioning have been studied under both natural and experimental conditions.

Although Wilson's (1954) study of the developmental changes accompanying adolescence made use of Friedman's scoring system, her findings with the index of primitive thought (IPT) are relevant here. Whereas she found evidence of temporary regression on the basis of Friedman's developmental location scores during ages 14–17, no change was noted for the IPT. The IPT occurred only rarely in her sample, perhaps indicating the relative lack of severity of the temporary regression during adolescence. Eisdorfer (1960) was similarly unable to find any increase in IPT associated with hearing or visual decrement in old age, although Fi scores were found to occur with a significantly greater frequency in the aged who experienced no hearing loss.

Nickel (1957) set up an experimental situation to test the hypothesis that developmental level of functioning would decrease under conditions of stress. After the induction of "stress" (i.e., the intellectual achievement of subjects was criticized and their attempts to please the experimenter were thwarted), subjects showed a significant decrement in AO% and increase in IU%. The increase in IU% was largely a function of the increment in D− responses.

While the use of the revised developmental scoring system to detect changes in functioning shows some promise, relatively few of the revised scores have been used in the analyses. Further, research in a wider variety of problem areas is needed before a more complete evaluation can be made of the system's value as an indicator of changes.

Internal Structure of the Scoring System. Podell and Phillips (1959) have intercorrelated and factor analyzed the revised developmental indices for two groups of normal males. The three general factors that have emerged correspond favorably with the theoretical description of the three stages in the developmental sequence, namely, an initial globality, an articulation of parts, and finally a reintegration and organization (Werner, 1948, 1957). The "globality" factor found by Podell and Phillips was represented by W−, Wv, XF + X, and IPT. At the intermediate developmental level—"varied productivity"—there were positive loadings for R, Di, FX, and a negative loading for D−. The third factor, "accuracy and human movement," represents the highest level of functioning; on this factor, Wi, Fi, and M were positively loaded, while D−% had a negative loading.[5]

Trait Validity

In the evaluation of the trait validity of the revised scoring, the relationship to (1) other measures of developmental level, (2) I.Q. scores, and (3) other cognitive tasks are discussed.

[5] With the exception of D−%, the intercorrelation and factor analysis of the indices were based on the absolute frequency and not the percentage values of the scores. Because of this, the results of this study on the interrelationship of those scores adopted from the original developmental scoring system should *not* be used in the evaluation of Friedman's system. In Friedman's developmental scoring, the indices are represented by percentage scores (e.g., Wv% = Wv/all W), and not the absolute frequency of the score. The likelihood of different results emerging from a factor analysis using percentage scores is confirmed by Podell and Phillips' finding that D− and D−% had loadings on different factors.

Relationship to Other Developmental Level Measures. Some attempts have been made to relate the revised developmental scoring system to the developmental ordering of a variety of cognitive tasks.

Brooks and Phillips (1958) related individual developmental indices to performance on cognitive tasks presumably reflecting Werner's (1948) paired-opposite continua of "rigid-flexible," "diffuse-articulate," and "syncretic-discrete." Similarly, Podell and Phillips (1959) investigated the relationship between the three levels of development as measured by the Rorschach scoring and seven clusters of cognitive tasks arranged according to developmental level. The results of both these studies failed to provide anything resembling a clearcut confirmation of these hypothesized relationships. As this may have been due to the inadequacy of the revised scoring system or the poor sampling of cognitive tasks, further research relating the Rorschach scoring to the developmental scoring of other cognitive tasks (Flavell et al., 1958; Friedman, 1956, 1958) is recommended.

Relationship to I.Q. In line with theoretical expectation, the revised developmental scoring of the Rorschach has been found to be related partially to level of intellectual functioning. Lane (1955) noted that vocabulary test estimates of I.Q. were positively related to the composite index (CI) measure of developmental level, and Smith and Phillips (1959) found "trends" ($p < .10$) to suggest that integrative and movement responses were related to I.Q. for a group of adolescent boys.

Relationship to Cognitive Tasks. Research has been done to relate individual as well as overall developmental indices to several different aspects of cognitive functioning. The findings of these studies, however, have not always proved consistent with theoretical expectation.

In the first of a series of three studies on the cognitive significance of the developmental indices, Brooks and Phillips (1958) found several contradictory results. For example, some indices were found to be related to cognitive tasks which, according to theory, they should *not* have been. Other developmental scores showed *both* positive and negative relationships to a variety of tasks, presumably reflecting similar aspects of functioning. The only consistent finding was with respect to D−, which was negatively related to type of flexibility in which the reorganization of the external environment is called for.

Lipton, Kaden, and Phillips (1958) attempted to unravel the confusing findings of Brooks and Phillips by classifying tasks according to the type of "decontextualization" ability required. Decontextualization, which bears a striking resemblance to field independence (Witkin et al., 1954), is defined as "the process whereby an element is separated from the totality in which it is embedded" (Lipton et al., 1958, p. 291). The two types of decontextualization tasks described by Lipton et al. are termed the "articulation" and "independence" tasks. The articulation task, in which the individual must articulate a figure from a complex ground (e.g., Gottschaldt figures), is interpreted as being more complex cognitively than the independence type, where the subject is required to keep two competing response tendencies independent while working on the task (e.g., the Stroop color-word test). Confirming this hypothesis that the articulation task is more complex cognitively, Lipton et al. found M and Fi to be positively related to articulation ability. Although independence ability was found to be negatively related to developmentally lower scores, the greater heterogeneity of the independence tasks made for less clear-cut results; only D− and D−% were found to bear negative relationships to the ability to keep competing responses independent.

Podell and Phillips (1959) related three levels of developmental indices (obtained by factor analysis) to seven types of cognitive tasks, which were arranged according to developmental level. The only predicted relationship that was confirmed was between the developmentally lower Rorschach and cognitive task levels. Specifically, "globality" on the Rorschach was found to correlate with lability ($r = .35$; $p < .05$) and simple repetitive ability ($r = .27$; $p < .10$). The developmentally intermediate Rorschach level ("varied productivity") correlated with cognitive abilities that were reliably rated by judges as reflecting the most developmentally *advanced* of the seven tasks. Thus, "varied productivity" was related to the ability to work with unstructured tasks ($r = .40$; $p < .05$), to separate elements from complex backgronds ($r = .40$; $p < .05$), and to solve tasks according to self-developed principles ($r = .35$; $p < .05$). The highest Rorschach index of development ("accuracy and human movement") was found to correlate with the ability to separate elements from complex backgrounds ($r = .44$; $p < .01$), with verbal organization ($r = .30$; $p < .10$), with verbal fluency ($r = .33$; $p < .10$), and with lability ($r = .34$; $p < .10$). Both verbal fluency and lability had been rated by judges as reflecting developmentally *low* levels of functioning.

A slightly different aspect of cognitive function was studied by Feffer (1959), who was interested in relating developmental level to role-playing ability. Feffer hypothesized that role-playing ability, because it reflects an internal cognitive restructuring of the environment, is indicative of a developmentally higher level of functioning. Based on a measure of role-playing ability derived from stories told from different points of view, Feffer found overall developmental level to be higher for those subjects who possessed the ability to take the role of the other. This finding agrees nicely with the postitive relationships found between developmental level and adequacy of social and interpersonal functioning (Fowler, 1957; Grace, 1956; Jordon and Phillips, 1959; Kaden, 1958; Lane, 1955; Prague, cited in Phillips, 1959).

The general evaluation of the cognitive significance of the revised indices is mixed. Many of the predicted cognitive correlates of the developmental scores failed to receive confirmation; in addition, several relationships which ran counter to theoretical expectation were found. The only consistent and theoretically interpretable findings have been that M and Fi responses are indicative of the ability to articulate a simple figure from a complex background, that D− responses correspond to the difficulty in maintaining independence between competing responses in cognitive functioning, and that global and developmentally low scores (W−, Wv, XF +

X, and IPT taken as a group) reflect lability in functioning. And finally, an overall estimate of developmental level of functioning has been found to be positively related to the capacity to carry out the internal cognitive restructuring required in assuming the role of the other.

OVERALL EVALUATION

The revised developmental scoring system differs from Friedman's system primarily in the addition of the developmental use of determinants. As the revised scoring uses more than just location scores, it does not parallel the purely structural aspects of Werner's developmental theory of cognitive functioning as well as Friedman's approach does. Further, because more aspects of a response are scored and more elaborate scoring criteria have been established, the revised developmental scoring takes longer to learn and to apply than does Friedman's system. One may question whether some of the distinctions added to the scoring are warranted (e.g., classification of integration into structural, positional, and collective categories), particularly as neither a theoretical description nor empirical evidence is available for the interpretive significance of the scores.

In addition to the structure of the system itself, the revised developmental scoring does not match up to Friedman's approach on empirical grounds. This is true not only because relatively less validity research has been conducted on the revised system, but also because of the less consistent findings of the research that has been done. The progression of the revised developmental scores with age has not been as firmly established as it has for Friedman's system. Although the revised scoring can differentiate between normals and schizophrenics, it is questionable whether the revised scoring system can differentiate more finely among pathological groups varying in severity of disturbance. When the revised developmental scoring system has been related to performance on cognitive tasks reflecting different developmental levels of functioning, only a few of the predicted relationships have been confirmed. Further, like the validity research on Friedman's scoring, most of the research on the revised scoring system is limited by its use of male subjects only.

The revised scoring system *has* been shown to be successful in distinguishing between individuals with ideational, as compared with motoric, orientations to impulse expression. Some of the revised indices show promise in the prediction of post-hospital adjustment. Overall level of development, as measured by the revised scoring system, has also been found to relate positively with the ability to assume the role of the other. In line with this last finding, the revised scoring has proven to be particularly successful in assessing adequacy of social functioning; the developmentally higher the level of functioning as measured by the Rorschach, the greater the ability to adjust flexibly and adequately to the demands of one's social environment.

In appraising the clinical usefulness of the revised scoring, consideration should be given to the availability of normative data and to the indication of overlap that may be expected to occur between groups. As there is little available data on norms or extent of overlap, a more complete evaluation of the clinical application of the scoring system must await future research. In establishing norms on the frequency of individual scores, data should be obtained for different levels of total R for those scores which have been found to correlate with R (Di, D−, FX, XF + X, Dv, Fi, M, and IPT).

One final question might be raised at this point, namely, which of the two developmental scoring systems is "better." In comparing the various advantages and disadvantages of the two systems, it would appear that the Friedman approach is preferable. Although Phillips and his associates originally maintained that their revision and elaboration might provide a more refined discrimination among clinically relevant groups, the empirical findings accumulated to date have not shown this to be the case. The failure of the Phillips system to improve upon the discriminating power of Friedman's approach, when taken together with the added complexity involved in learning and in applying this more elaborate scoring, leads us to conclude that the "cost" of using the revised developmental scoring does not appear to be worth the "payoff."

Chapter 4

ELIZUR'S HOSTILITY SCORING

Practicing clinicians and researchers alike have shown considerable interest in the use of the "hostility" construct. Describing an individual's level of hostility not only offers information about the person himself, but also implies something about the impact he is likely to have on others. In light of the fairly widespread interest in hostility, it is not at all surprising to find that attempts have been made to use the Rorschach as a measure of this characteristic.

The most popular approach in the use of the Rorschach as a measure of hostility has focused on the content rather than the formal aspects of the response. Although a number of different systems have been devised for the scoring of hostile content (Arnaud, 1959; DeVos, 1952; Elizur, 1949; Finney, 1955; Fisher and Hinds, 1951; Hafner and Kaplan, 1960; Murstein, 1958; Pattie, 1954; Towbin, 1959), this chapter will cover only Elizur's (1949) system. Elizur's scoring for hostility has been used more often than any of the other approaches and, by and large, these other scorings represent modifications or elaborations of Elizur's system.

The chapter begins with a definition of the "hostility" construct which the Elizur scoring purports to measure. The scoring system is outlined next, and this is followed by a presentation of some of the available normative data. After a discussion of reliability and validity studies, the chapter concludes with an overall evaluation of the use of the Rorschach for measuring hostility.

DEFINITION OF THE CONSTRUCT

Buss (1961) makes a distinction between *aggression, anger,* and *hostility. Aggression,* according to Buss, refers to an instrumental response of a punishing nature; this aggressive response may be either physical or verbal, and may be direct or indirect. *Anger* is viewed as an emotional state, presumably having some drive properties. Buss describes *hostility* as the more long-term, negative attitude or frame of reference which is taken toward people or things. Although somewhat different from each other, these three conceptualizations clearly refer to closely related aspects of behavior.

In his description of what the content scoring of the Rorschach purports to measure, Elizur (1949) uses the term *hostility* to refer to "feelings of resentment and enmity, which are often repressed in our culture but almost inevitably show up in the individual's distorted attitudes toward people, either being too antagonistic or too submissive" (p. 248). Thus, although Elizur's use of the term "hostility" in part encompasses drive or motivational properties (cf. Buss' concept of anger) as well as actual instrumental reactions (cf. Buss' concept of aggression), the "hostility" revealed in the Rorschach responses refers more to the fairly stable negative attitude with which the person views his world (cf. Buss' concept of hostility). To use the "trait-state" distinction typically made with respect to the concept of anxiety (Spielberger, 1966), one may view the Elizur scoring system as attempting to assess a more generalized "trait" of hostility, rather than a more or less transitory "state" of the individual at any given time.

It might be noted that in considering hostility as a personality characteristic of the individual, no theoretical stand is taken here as to whether the origins of this trait are instinctual (Freud, 1955) or reactive (Bandura and Walters, 1959; Dollard, Doob, Miller, Mowrer, and Sears, 1939). In addition, no claim is made for the use of the hostility scoring system as a means of assessing the *form* which the instrumental act of aggression might take. A greater number of hostile responses on the Rorschach may be interpreted only as reflecting a more intense hostile attitude or feeling. The *way* in which this hostility is expressed (i.e., overt or covert, direct or indirect, inward or outward, etc.) would depend additionally upon the particular characteristic style of the individual in expressing himself.

HOSTILITY SCORING SYSTEM

Elizur's approach to the scoring of content for hostility can be learned very easily. Similarly, the actual process of scoring a protocol according to this system should take only about five minutes.

As the scoring does not make use of either the location or the determinants of the response, the usual careful inquiry is not needed. Consequently, if the Rorschach is used in a research project as a measure of hostility, the total administration time should run only about 15 minutes. Together with the fact that relatively little experience with the Rorschach is needed in the administration (and scoring) of the test for this purpose, the saving in administration time makes the hostility scoring system an attractive research tool.

At times, however, a minimal sort of inquiry may be needed. This is the case only for the clarification of the more ambiguous responses. Thus, by inquiring (i.e., "tell me more about it") into a response such as "two girls staring at each other," a hostile elaboration of "they're arguing" might conceivably be elicited. Such hostile elaborations elicited in the inquiry *are scored.*

The criteria for Elizur's hostility scoring system are outlined below, together with some sample responses.

Scoring Criteria

The scoring for hostility is based solely on the content of the response, with no attention paid to either card or location. Each response may be characterized as reflecting one of three levels of hostility. Responses in which hostility is *obviously* expressed are scored *H*. If hostility is expressed *less obviously,* or if it is expressed *symbolically,* the response is scored *h*. Those responses in which there is *no indication* of hostility remain unscored. The general categories of responses, arranged according to decreasing level of hostility, are (1) expressive behavior, (2) emotions and attitudes expressed or implied, (3) objects of aggression, (4) symbolic responses, (5) double connotation, and (6) unscorable or "neutral" responses.

I. Expressive Behavior

SCORE *H*. If hostility is associated in any way with the *behavior* of the figure in the percept. Included here is not only aggressive behavior, but the *results* of aggressive activity as well.

Examples of such *H* responses are as follows:

Animals fighting
Butterfly who got its wing torn
Killed animal
People arguing
Squashed bug
Wolf devouring its prey

II. Emotions and Attitudes Expressed or Implied

SCORE *H*. If the emotions and attitudes of contempt, hatred, dislike, criticism, derogation, and so on are clearly reflected in the response. The hostile attitude may be on the part of the *subject* giving the response (e.g., "the kind of man I hate"), or may be attributed to the object in the *percept* (e.g., "a cruel man"). The feeling or attitude of hostility or derogation may also be *implied* in the response (e.g., "stupid face").

Examples of such *H* responses are as follows:

Angry face
Cruel man
Stupid-looking animal
Type of animal I hate
Ugly figure
Quarrelsome person

SCORE *h*. If the hostile attitude or feeling is expressed or implied to a *lesser* extent than that indicated above.

Examples of such *h* responses are as follows:

Beggars
Brute
Freaks
Frowning people
Gossiping woman
Silly-looking man

III. Objects of Aggression

SCORE *H:* If the response contains an object which is *typically* used for aggressive purposes. However, a response such as "H bomb," because of the overpowering element of anxiety, is *not* given a full score of *H*.

Examples of such *H* responses are as follows:

Arrow	Cannon
Blackjack	Gun
Bullet	Jet fighter

SCORE *h:* If the response involves an object which, though typically used in other ways, may *also* be employed for aggressive purposes.

Examples of such *h* responses are as follows:

Hammer	Scissors
Knife	Teeth
Pliers	Vise

IV. Symbolic Responses

SCORE *h:* If the response reflects hostility and the like *symbolically;* this type of response is scored conservatively.

Examples of such *h* responses are as follows:

Feeling of conflict	Symbolizes fighting
Red represents anger	War mask

V. Double Connotation

SCORE *h:* If *both* hostility and anxiety are clearly reflected in the response, or if it is not clear cut which of the two is involved. See Chapter 5 for a complete description of the criteria used in scoring anxiety responses.

Examples of such *h* responses are as follows:

Frightened animal about to attack	Mouse caught in a trap
Headless man	Person being grabbed from behind
Man being hanged	Policeman

VI. Unscorable or "Neutral" Responses

Do not score: If in both its unelaborated or elaborated form, the response contains *no* indication of hostility as determined by any of the above criteria.

Examples of responses which are "neutral" regarding hostility are as follows:

Animal skin	Fish
Bears	Map
Butterfly	Rocks
Dangerous place	Tree
Dead leaf	X ray

Interscorer Reliability

In light of the simple, straightforward scoring criteria described above, it is not at all surprising to find that the interscorer agreement on total hostility level is high (Cummings, 1954; Elizur, 1949; Forsyth, 1959; Sanders and Cleveland, 1953; Siegel, 1956; Smith and Coleman, 1956).

Using eight graduate students who had only a brief period of training in the use of the scoring system, Elizur (1949) found the average correlation between scorers to be .82. When Elizur's own scoring of these protocols was compared with the average scoring of the eight students, a correlation of .93 was obtained. Forsyth (1959) compared his own scoring with the scoring of two raters having *even less* experienec than graduate students—namely *wives* of graduate students. Forsyth's results were quite favorable, in that the two reliability coefficients were .94 and .91.

In studies where the reliability estimates were based on the scoring of more experienced raters, the correlations between two scorers were .98 (Sanders and Cleveland, 1953), .92 (Cummings, 1954), and .78 (Siegel, 1956). Using criteria very much the same as Elizur's, Smith and Coleman (1956) obtained an intraclass correlation of .90 for three scorers.

One study was conducted to estimate the *intrascorer* reliability with the system (Forsyth, 1959). After a one-month interval, Forsyth rescored the same group of records and achieved near-perfect agreement ($r = .99$) between the two scorings.

Based on the results of the studies cited above, it is safe to conclude that the interscorer agreement for Elizur's hostility is good—the average correlation coefficient being somewhere in the neighborhood of .90.

Summary Scores

In summarizing the level of hostility in any given protocol, no separate summary scores are obtained for the five different scorable categories described above. Instead, a single, overall score is arrived at to represent level of hostility, irrespective of the way in which this hostility might have been indicated. This hostility level (HL) score is obtained simply by (a) assigning a weight of 2 to those responses scored *H,* and 1 to responses given an *h* score, and (b) totaling all the weights in the protocol.

Although not suggested by Elizur, it would appear to be fruitful to add some sort of a "bonus" weight for those hostile responses which are *minus* in form level. The reasoning behind this is that the lack of conformity to the stimulus demands of the blot is probably determined in large part by the intensity of the hostility underlying the response. Thus, minus responses scored *H* could be given a weight of 3 instead of 2, and *h* responses of minus form quality could be assigned a value of 2 rather than 1.

In trying to estimate the possible effect that the total number of responses in a record might have on the obtained *HL* score, one runs into a conflicting set of research findings (Goodstein, 1954; Goodstein and Goldberger, 1955; Gorlow, Zimet, and Fine, 1952; Grauer, 1953; Lit, 1956; Sanders and Cleveland, 1953; Stotsky, 1952; Wolf, 1957). A detailed discussion of the relationship between *HL* and R is presented on pp. 97–98. Because it is likely that some sort of relationship *does* exist between *HL* and R (the exact nature of which is still unclear), it is advisable that at least some consideration of total R be taken into account in arriving at an overall estimate of hostility level. Consequently, rather than simply totaling the weighted values in arriving at an *HL* score, it would be preferable to compute an *HL%* (i.e., *HL*/R). Although this does not completely eliminate the effect of R, it nonetheless reduces it (Sanders and Cleveland, 1953).

NORMATIVE DATA

Although no systematic attempts have been made to collect normative data for Elizur's hostility scoring system, several studies have reported means and standard deviations for their subject populations (Cummings, 1954; Elizur, 1949; Gorlow et al., 1952; Murstein, 1956; Siegel, 1956). Because of size and nonrepresentativeness of samples, as well as several other factors, these data are "normative" only in the very loosest sense of the word.

Nature of the Samples

Data are available for normal and neurotic adults (Elizur, 1949), college students and outpatients (Siegel, 1956), hostile and friendly college students with varying degrees of insight into their attitudes (Murstein, 1956), delinquent and nondelinquent adolescents (Gorlow et al., 1952), and nail-biting children (Cummings, 1954). A more complete description of these samples is presented in Table 4.1.

The records for neurotic adults that were used in Elizur's (1949) study were selected from hospital files. The criteria for selection were (1) the Rorschach had to have been given after the diagnosis was made, (2) the total R had to be at least 20, and (3) the I.Q. had to be greater than 85. Of the 22 patients selected, two were diagnosed as character disorders; the remainder represented the full variety of psychoneurotic disorders. The normal adults in Elizur's study were matched with the neurotic group on the basis of sex, age, and intelligence.

The 60 male clinic patients in Siegel's (1956) sample were selected from among veterans who were applying for treatment at a V.A. mental hygiene clinic. The college students were attending the University of Buffalo.

The subjects in Murstein's (1956) study consisted of college fraternity members who had been rated as being either friendly or hostile by other members of their fraternity. The extent to which the individual's rating of himself coincided with the group's rating of him was used to determine amount of "insight." Concerning the Rorschach, Murstein instructed the subjects to give three responses per card; for the possible effect of this procedure, see the discussion on the effect of total R (p. 97).

The delinquent adolescents (Gorlow et al., 1952), who were randomly chosen from court records, consisted of individuals who had committed "antisocial" acts. The nondelinquent subjects were selected from schools

TABLE 4.1
Characteristics of the Normative Data Sample

		Sex		Age			I.Q.		Years of Education	
Group	*N*	*Male*	*Female*	*Mean*	*S.D.*	*Range*	*Mean*	*S.D.*	*Mean*	*S.D.*
Normal Adults (Elizur, 1949)	22	—[a]	—	34.0	8.1	—[a]	103.6	9.9	—	—
Neurotic Adults (Elizur, 1949)	22	—	—	33.8	9.3	—	101.4	12.6	—	—
Clinic Patients (Siegel, 1956)	60	60	0	29.0	5.7	—	111.0	12.0	11.0	2.3
College Students (Siegel, 1956)	60	60	0	19.0	2.1	—	—	—	13.5	1.0
Fraternity Members (Murstein, 1956)										
Hostile—Insightful	20	20	0	—	—	—	—	—	—	—
Hostile—Noninsightful	20	20	0	—	—	—	—	—	—	—
Friendly—Insightful	20	20	0	—	—	—	—	—	—	—
Friendly—Noninsightful	20	20	0	—	—	—	—	—	—	—
Delinquent Adolescents (Gorlow et al., 1952)	13	10	3	12.3	0.5	—	88.0[b]	10.5[b]	—	—
Nondelinquent Adolescents (Gorlow et al., 1952)	13	10	3	12.2	0.5	—	87.0[b]	7.0[b]	—	—
Nail-biting Children (Cummings, 1954)	70	35	35	—	—	10–14	103.6	—	11.0[c]	—

[a] A dash (—) indicates that these data were not available.
[b] Estimates based on the Wechsler–Bellevue I vocabulary scores reported by Gorlow et al. (1952).
[c] Approximation of years of education for both parents.

having children with socio-economic backgrounds similar to those in the delinquent group.

The group of nail biters described by Cummings (1954) were selected from grade school children for whom it was evident that—to one degree or another—they tended to bite their nails.

The I.Q. scores reported in Table 4.1 were based on the Wechsler–Bellevue (neurotic adults), a short form of the Wechsler–Bellevue (normal adults and clinic patients), the Wechsler–Bellevue vocabulary test (delinquent and nondelinquent adolescents), and a short form of the California Test of Mental Maturity (nail biters).

Data on Hostility Scores

The data on hostility level (*HL*)—that is, the total weighted number of hostile responses—for each of the groups described above are outlined in Table 4.2. Data were available only for *HL*, and not for *HL%* (i.e., *HL*/R). From an inspection of Table 4.2, it is evident that the available norms on hostility level present some confusion. For example, the *HL* scores for the fraternity members in Murstein's (1956) sample are considerably higher than the scores for Siegel's (1956) college students. Whether this discrepancy is due to fraternity membership, the fact that Murstein's subjects were required to give three responses per card, regional differences (Murstein used college students in Texas, whereas Siegel used Buffalo students), or a host of other variables, cannot be readily determined.

Actually, the need for normative data on hostility level does *not* involve an extension of, or an improvement over, those norms which exist at present. It is highly unlikely that the hostility scoring will ever prove to be very useful clinically in the diagnosis of "neurosis," "delinquency," "normality,"

TABLE 4.2
Means and Standard Deviations of Hostility Level (*HL*) for Each of the Samples

	Hostility Level (*HL*)	
Group	*Mean*	*S.D.*
Normal Adults	1.30	1.80
Neurotic Adults	5.60	4.50
Clinic Patients	3.90	3.74
College Students	2.63	2.52
Fraternity Members		
Hostile—Insightful	7.40	4.02
Hostile—Noninsightful	5.15	3.85
Friendly—Insightful	5.55	2.28
Friendly—Noninsightful	4.95	3.35
Delinquent Adolescents	10.00	5.42
Nondelinquent Adolescents	4.00	1.39
Nail-biting Children	11.93	6.33

or the like. We know little about a person if, on the basis of norms, we can conclude that he is "as hostile as a neurotic." The way in which the scoring system *can* be of most use clinically is in the straighforward assessment of *hostility level,* as it has been defined earlier in this chapter. As a representative sample of "normal" subjects will vary in the extent to which they are hostile, normative data on such a sample per se are of little use. Instead, the norms which *are* needed for the hostility scoring are those presenting data on individuals who, on the basis of extensive observation and ratings, have been found to vary in their level of hostility. As the *HL* score presumably reflects only *level* of hostility—*regardless of the way in which this hostility is expressed*—the observations and ratings of subjects should be carried out on this variable alone.[1] In the final analysis, it is only by relating norms on the hostility scoring with this external reference point that Elizur's system can be used clinically.

The Problem of Overlap. Although the data presented in Table 4.2 appear sufficient for us to make rough estimates as to the amount of overlap among these various groups, we are faced with some real limitations. To begin with, the number of cases on which these data were based varies considerably. Thus, while the norms for nail biters were compiled from 70 cases, the data on the two groups of adolescents were based on Ns of only 13. Because of the small N for most of these groups, not much confidence may be placed in the adequacy of these data as working norms. Further, the testing situation in some cases (e.g., Murstein's data) was altered, in that subjects were required to give a certain number of responses per card. But perhaps the most important limitation of all is in regard to the point made above. That is, in order to make use of hostility norms in clinical work, the data must be tied to groups which are clearly known to vary according to degree of hostility.

In setting up norms of this type and then estimating the amount of overlap which occurs among individuals who have been rated at different hostility levels, it is important that these data be based on a sample representing the full range of hostility levels. The use of a restricted sample in the rating of subjects would undoubtedly result in a good deal of overlap on the Rorschach hostility scores. The amount of overlap which may be expected in a maximally variable sample remains a crucial—and as yet unanswered—question for future investigation.

Norms for Different Levels of R. In evaluating a content scoring of the Rorschach such as Elizur's, it is particularly important to consider the possible effect that the number of responses has on the final score. At first, it seems likely that the more responses given by a subject, the greater the possibility that at least *some* of them will reflect hostility. Yet, as is shown below, the problem is not that clear cut.

The results of studies on the relationship between Rorschach hostility level and total R have been consistently confusing. Several studies have noted

[1] This approach to the rating of hostility was employed by Haskell (1961). As part of a larger study, Haskell made use of therapists' ratings of the extent to which their patients were hostile, regardless of the mode or obviousness of expression.

significant differences between groups in *HL without any differences* in R. Thus, Goodstein and Goldberger (1955) found high-manifest anxiety subjects to have greater *HL* scores than low-manifest anxiety subjects, Stotsky (1952) found *HL* to be greater for remitting than nonremitting schizophrenics, Wolf (1957) obtained significantly high HL scores for acting-out as compared with nonacting-out patients, and Lit (1956) found that college students on probation had higher *HL* scores than dean's list students. In all of these studies, the groups compared failed to differ in total R. Although these findings seem to imply that *HL* and R are not related, the results of still other studies point to a different conclusion (Goodstein, 1954; Gorlow et al., 1952; Grauer, 1953; Sanders and Cleveland, 1953). In fact, these other studies are confusing not only because they offer evidence that a significant relationship *does* exist between *HL* and R, but also because they point to some contradiction as to the *direction* of this relationship. On the one hand, Sanders and Cleveland (1953) found that for a large group of college students (N = 270), the correlation between *HL* and R reached + .67 ($p < .001$)[2]; similarly, Grauer (1953) found unimproved schizophrenics to have both a higher *HL%* and total R than improved schizophrenics. Goodstein (1954) and Gorlow et al. (1952), on the other hand, have obtained evidence which suggests that *HL* and R are *not positively,* but *negatively* related. Using the Rorschach hostility scores of 57 college students, Goodstein obtained a low but significant negative correlation with R ($r = -.25$; $p < .05$). Gorlow et al. also found that adolescent delinquents obtained significantly *higher HL* scores, but significantly *fewer* responses than nondelinquents.

The results of these studies seem to have exhausted most possibilities—namely, that the relationship between *HL* and R is *nonexistent, positive,* or *negative.* A possible explanation—based more on speculation than data—for what seems like a very frustrating paradox is that the relationship between *HL* and R is *curvilinear* (i.e., U-shaped). That is, some individuals, because of their high level of hostility, may be reluctant to give the examiner what he wants—responses. Because of the intrinsic hostile nature of these people, however, the *HL* achieved in their records can still be relatively high. On the other hand, one would also expect to find a high *HL* score in those protocols containing many responses, in that there is a greater probability that some of the responses will be hostile in nature. Consequently, it is conceivable that the nature of the obtained relationship between *HL* and R in any given study depends upon the particular distribution of R for that sample.

The use of *HL%* instead of *HL* can, at least to some extent, eliminate the effect of R on the overall estimate of hostility (see footnote 2, below). To the extent to which this hypothesized U-shaped relationship exists, it would probably be more appropriate to collect separate norms for three levels of total R: low (i.e., below 15), medium (i.e., 15–40), and high (i.e., above 40).

[2] When *HL%* (i.e., *HL*/R) and R were correlated, the value of r was considerably lower ($r = .20$), but still significant ($p < .01$).

RELIABILITY

According to the definition of the construct as outlined in the beginning of this chapter, hostility level may be expected to be a fairly stable characteristic of the individual. Before describing the research findings relevant to the stability of *HL* over time, brief mention might be made of the internal consistency of the Rorschach hostility scores.

Internal Consistency

The only study on the internal consistency of the Elizur hostility scoring system has been done by Elizur (1949) himself. He divided the protocols of 30 normal volunteers into odd and even responses, and obtained a corrected correlation of 0.75. Lest this value be interpreted at face value, it should be pointed out that this correlation is apt to be spuriously high as a function of the preponderance of nonhostile responses which typify most records. This issue is more of academic interest than anything else, as the determination of the split-half reliability of this particular scoring system has little value in its evaluation. The question of stability over time, on the other hand, is more crucial.

Stability

Two studies have been carried out, which, only in the very loosest sense, may be classified as dealing with the test-retest reliability of Elizur's scoring system (Epstein, Nelson, and Tanofsky, 1957; Lucas, 1961).

Epstein et al. (1957) group-administered 10 different 10-set "homemade" inkblots to a small, homogeneous group of subjects—16 college students who had volunteered for the study. Although the Rorschach blots themselves were not used, the homemade blots were scored for hostility according to Elizur's criteria. The subjects were tested twice a week for five weeks with a different set being administered each time. Based on reliability coefficients obtained from an analysis of variance, Epstein et al. (1957) estimated the stability across all 10 sets to be .30 ($p < .001$). In addition, no difference in mean *HL* was found across administrations.

In Lucas' (1961) study, the sample consisted of 28 9-year-olds (17 boys and 11 girls) who were given the Rorschach twice, with an interval of eight weeks between administrations. Inasmuch as these subjects comprised the control group in part of a larger study, Lucas did not obtain test-retest correlations. What she did compare, however, was the difference in mean *HL* between the two administrations. The results turned out to be quite embarrassing, in that there was a significant increase ($p < .01$) in *HL* between the testings. Lucas attributes this finding to the possibility that the 9-year-olds felt more at ease during the second administration (as a function of greater familiarity), and consequently were less reluctant to express whatever hostility they felt. Although Lucas does not suggest it, a third Rorschach administration might have been a good way of testing this interpretation of her results.

The studies of Epstein et al. (1957) and Lucas (1961), although relevant to the test-retest reliability of the hostility scoring of the Rorschach, offer only minimal information for the evaluation of the system's stability. What still remains needed is research on the test-retest reliability (as well as changes in mean *HL*) with a larger and more heterogeneous group of subjects.

VALIDITY

Because of the ease with which a Rorschach protocol may be scored for hostility, several studies have included Elizur's scoring in addition to the more conventional ways of analyzing the record. In general, this "shotgun" approach has resulted in a good deal of validity research on the hostility scoring system. In some instances, however, this added scoring for hostility appears to have been thrown in with little attention to its relevance to the problem being studied. Thus, in this section, the reader may occasionally find arbitrary studies, such as the use of the hostility scoring to predict the course of illness for pulmonary tuberculosis patients (Cohen, 1954).

The studies relevant to the criterion and construct validity of Elizur's scoring for hostility are described below. Included here also are some studies which have made use of scoring systems differing slightly from Elizur's, but similar enough to have clear implications for the validity of Elizur's approach.

Criterion-Related Validity

Concurrent Validity

The concurrent validity of the hostility scoring system may be estimated from (1) research in which the criterion groups were based on the past history of aggressive behavior, and (2) research which has used behavioral rating scales for the criterion measure.

Acts of Aggression. In a study by Gorlow et al. (1952), the Rorschach records of 13 adolescent delinquents were compared with those of 13 nondelinquents matched on the basis of age, I.Q., and socio-economic background. The delinquents were randomly selected from court files on the basis of the "antisocial" acts which they had committed. The results indicated that, despite the lower total R, the delinquents obtained significantly higher *HL* scores.

Using a random sample from the files of a V.A. neuropsychiatric hospital Wolf (1957) divided subjects (most of whom were diagnosed as schizophrenic) into a group of 20 who had, and a group of 17 who had not, acted out aggressively. Aggressive acting out was determined by both case history data and current progress notes. Wolf's findings were in accord with his prediction, in that acting-out patients had significantly higher hostility scores on the Rorschach ($p < .005$). Similarly, Towbin (1959) compared the records of hospitalized male schizophrenics who were classified as being "aggressive" and "nonaggressive." The classification was based on ward notes: aggressive patients were those who, within a given four-month period, had committed two or more acts of assault; nonaggressive patients had shown no assaultive or self-directed aggressive behavior during the four-month period. Although Towbin based the hostility scoring on Elizur's criteria, separate analyses were made for aggressive content, objects of aggression, derogatory percepts, and derogatory remarks about the testing procedure itself. Except for the frequency of aggressive content, the aggressive patients showed significantly more of each of the three other hostile indicators in the Rorschach records. In one final study comparing the Rorschachs of schizophrenics, Haskell (1961) failed to find any differences in Rorschach hostility level between patients who had previously acted out aggressively (physically or verbally) and those who had not.

In summary, despite the fact that the Elizur scoring for hostility was not designed as a diagnostic indicator for aggressive acting out, level of hostility on the Rorschach has generally been found to be related to overt acts of aggression—at least when the comparison is made between fairly distinct groups. However, these positive findings have been indicated on a group basis only, and no data are available as to the clinical or idiographic application of the Rorschach for the diagnosis of aggressive acting out.

RATINGS OF HOSTILITY. As part of his original validation of the hostility scoring system, Elizur (1949) interviewed 20 volunteers to obtain information in the areas of submissiveness, dependency, anxiety, and hostility. Although he had no estimate of the accuracy of notes taken during the interview, Elizur obtained high interjudge agreement on the submissiveness, dependency, anxiety, and hostility ratings which were based on these notes. The results indicated that the only significant correlation with *HL* was the rating for hostility, where the correlation was .60 ($p < .01$); the nonsignificant correlations with the other rated personality characteristics were .22 for submissiveness, − .16 for anxiety, and − .04 for dependency.

Buss, Fisher, and Simmons (1962) related the Rorschach *HL* with the rating of aggressive behavior of psychiatric patients. The ratings of the patients' behavior (i.e., assaultiveness, irritability, negativism, resentment, suspicion, verbal aggression, etc.) were obtained from three sources: psychiatrists, psychologists, and close relatives. The psychiatrists made their ratings on the basis of case-history information and an interview with the patient. The ratings of the psychologists were based on test data (presumably non-Rorschach data) and the patients' behavior during the testing. On the basis of data obtained from interviews with relatives, three judges were able to make reliable hostility ratings for each patient. Although no estimate of reliability of rating within the group of psychiatrists or psychologists was possible, the rating of patients for the two groups of judges correlated fairly well with each other. The findings of this study failed to yield significant correlations between *HL* and any of the three sets of ratings.

Smith and Coleman (1956) studied the relationship between Rorschach hostility level (as indicated by scoring criteria quite similar to those of

Elizur) and the behavioral manifestations of hostility in a group of 9- to 15-year-old boys attending a remedial reading class. The authors predicted a curvilinear relationship between hostility level and overt aggressiveness, in that a very high hostility score on the Rorschach was interpreted as implying that the subject would probably have difficulty in expressing this drive behaviorally. When the children in the medium range were compared with the rest of the children (i.e., those having the highest and lowest hostility scores), the former group was found to have been rated by teachers as showing significantly more physical aggression, verbal aggression, and quarrelsomeness. However, this curvilinear relationship was not actually demonstrated, in that Smith and Coleman made no comparison of the behavioral ratings for subjects at the three points on the continuum—low, intermediate, and high. Although Smith and Coleman's interpretation of the curvilinear relationship is a tenable one, it is also possible that their findings were solely a function of the relatively low ratings given to the subjects who showed few signs of hostility on the Rorschach. A later study by Coleman (1967) made use of peer ratings of aggressiveness among a group of normal boys (ages 10 to 13 years). The findings of this study, which were analyzed independently within four separate classroom settings, revealed high positive correlations between *HL* and aggressiveness (ranging from .62 to .67) for three of the four replications.

Using a content scoring system quite similar to Elizur's, Haskell (1961) failed to find any relationship between nurses' behavioral ratings of 38 schizophrenics and the patients' Rorschach hostility level scores; the ratings, which showed good interjudge reliability, were based on observations of the verbal and physical aggression of the patients during a five-day period. Interestingly enough, Haskell's findings were more encouraging when he made use of ratings by the *therapists* of these same 38 patients. The therapists rated their patients on (1) the extent to which they had expressed aggressive feelings (either directly or indirectly), and (2) the degree to which hostility was one of their major conflict areas. The obtained contingency coefficient between Rorschach hostility level and ratings on (1) was .30 ($p < .05$); for ratings on (1) and (2) combined, the coefficient was found to be slightly higher—.39 ($p < .01$). It might be noted that although the nurses' and therapists' ratings showed a low but significant relationship to each other, the therapists' hostility ratings had no relationship with the patients' past history of overt physical or verbal aggressiveness.

Similarly, Walker (1951) employed therapists' ratings for his criterion measure, and similarly obtained favorable results; the ratings were made as to general level of hostility, regardless of the mode of expression. Using essentially the same scoring criteria as Elizur, but assigning weightings between 0 and 4 instead of 0 and 2, Walker found Rorschach hostility level to be related significantly to the ratings of therapists (as estimated from the phi coefficient, Pearson $r = .78$).

The general findings with the use of ratings of hostility as the criterion measure seem to indicate that when these ratings are based on either interviews specifically designed to elicit information about hostility (Elizur, 1949), the behavior of the individual during therapy sessions (Haskell, 1961; Walker, 1951), or peer ratings of aggressiveness among boys (Coleman,

1967), then the validity of the Rorschach hostility scoring is confirmed. Ratings which are obtained from less intensive interviews (Buss et al., 1962), or which refer to only the more obvious indications of aggression (Haskell, 1961), have generally failed to show any relationship to the Rorschach score. Even though Rorschach hostility level has shown to be related to the more careful and subtle ratings, no data are available as to the amount of overlap existing between subjects who were rated at different levels of hostility. However, judging from the correlations obtained by Elizur (1949), Coleman (1967), and Walker (1951)[3]—ranging from .60 to .78—the clinical use of the Rorschach as a measure of general hostility level would seem to show considerable promise.

Predictive Validity

The criterion measures used in those studies relevant to the predictive validity of Elizur's hostility scoring have been either (1) the overt expression of aggression or (2) the course of a particular illness. The appropriateness of this second type of criterion is dubious, as its relevance to the hostility criterion is unclear. Actually, this research on prognostic indicators for the course of illness has made use of a number of measures, with Rorschach hostility level being thrown in as an easily obtainable additional score.

Overt Aggression. Gluck (1955) selected 30 neuropsychiatric patients in an army hospital and placed them in a stress situation designed to provoke hostile feelings; the hostility was estimated by means of judges' ratings. Using the hostility-level scores from Rorschachs obtained during earlier routine testing, Gluck was unable to predict the patients' expression of hostility in the experimental situation. An obvious shortcoming in this study is that no estimate was made of the patients' abilities to control or hide their feelings, which is a crucial variable in almost any study attempting to predict overt impulse expression—let alone a study conducted in a psychiatric army hospital!

In a study by Rader (1957), the problem of differences in impulse control was dealt with indirectly—by the nature of the sample, as well as the situation in which the aggression was to be observed. Rader used a sample of 38 male prison inmates who, as evidenced by the fact that they were in prison, may be said to have had generally poor control over their aggressive impulses. Further, the situation within which the aggressive behavior was rated was a relatively permissive one—namely, group therapy sessions. Each inmate was rated on a hostility dimension by the group therapist; there were several groups, some of which had co-therapists. The ratings on each subject were based on a total of approximately 8 to 10 sessions, and took into account a variety of direct and indirect verbal expressions of aggression (e.g., attacking the prison and the staff, dominating the sessions, disregarding the feelings of others, etc.). The *intrajudge* rating of reliability from session to session was generally high (in the .90s), although the available *interjudge* coefficients ranged between .35 and .89.

[3] The contingency coefficient used by Haskell (1961) does not provide an adequate estimate of *strength* of relationship and is therefore not appropriate to the point being made here.

Despite this deficiency in the criterion measure, Rader found that the per cent of aggressive responses on the Rorschach correlated positively with the ratings of the therapists ($r = .39$, $p < .05$).

Course of Illness. The Elizur hostility scoring has been used to predict length of hospitalization for schizophrenics (Grauer, 1953; Stotsky, 1952), and, of all things, course of illness in pulmonary tuberculosis patients (Cohen, 1954). Although the theoretical relevance of hostility level as a prognostic indicator in these studies is not very clear, brief mention might be made here of their findings.

Grauer (1953) compared 18 "improved" (i.e., discharged) and 18 "unimproved" (i.e., long-term treatment) paranoid schizophrenics on the hostility-level scores which were obtained during the early period of hospitalization. The length of hospitalization, although not specified by Grauer, was twice as long for the "unimproved" group; both groups were matched for age, I.Q., and years of education. The results of this study indicated that the discharged group had a significantly lower *HL%* than the more long-term group. Directly conflicting results were obtained by Stotsky (1952), who found remitting schizophrenics to have *higher HL* scores upon admission as compared with nonremitting schizophrenics. The remitting group was composed of patients who had been hospitalized for less than two years—the average length of hospitalization being six months—and had remained out of the hospital for more than six months. The patients in the nonremitting group were hospitalized for more than two years; the average length of hospitalization for this group was 35 months. The two groups did not differ as to age, education level, or marital status, although the remitting schizophrenics did have a significantly higher I.Q. It seems unlikely, though, that Stotsky's conflicting findings were a function of the difference in intelligence, especially as Elizur (1949) found I.Q. and *HL* to be unrelated. The need for an explanation of Grauer's and Stotsky's contradictory findings is more academic than practical, as it is difficult to see any particularly strong theoretical reason to use *HL* as a prognostic indicator for length of hospitalization.

Certainly, an even less appropriate use of the hostility scoring is to predict the recovery of tuberculosis patients (Cohen, 1954); this study was of the "shotgun" variety referred to earlier in that hostility was investigated along with a number of other easily scored variables. Hence, it is not too much of a blow to the validity of the scoring system that Cohen was unable to find any relationship between *HL* and course of illness in pulmonary patients.

The research findings on the predictive validity of the hostility scoring are quite meager. Any attempt to predict overt aggression by means of the Elizur scoring alone neglects the important variable of impulse *control*. Rader (1957) was able to circumvent this problem by using a group of subjects who were homogeneously low in their ability to control their impulses, as well as by predicting to a criterion situation in which impulse expression was permitted. However, it is unlikely that the Rorschach hostility score *alone* can be used successfully to predict how members of a more heterogeneous group of subjects are going to behave in more typical life situations. What is needed in addition is an estimate of the *extent to which,* and the *way in which* the individual generally expresses his impulses. Perhaps hostility-level scores could be used together with Rorschach developmental level scores (see Chapters 2 and 3), the latter of which have been shown to be useful in differentiating individuals with acting-out orientations from those having ideational orientations to impulse expression (Hurwitz, 1954; Kruger, 1954; Misch, 1954). Even if such measures of both impulse level and control ability do prove fruitful in prediction studies, estimates of overlap and efficiency relative to base rates would still be needed if this predictive use of Rorschach *HL* is to be used clinically.

Construct Validity

In the following discussion of the construct validity of the Elizur scoring system, nomological and trait validity studies will be discussed separately.

Nomological Validity

This section includes those research attempts made (1) to relate *HL* to behavioral characteristics or symptoms which presumably are indirect reflections of hostility, (2) to study the relationship between insight and level of hostility, and (3) to induce changes in *HL* experimentally.

Relation to Behavioral Characteristics and Symptoms Reflecting Hostility. The symptoms and behavioral characteristics to which *HL* has been related include nail biting, teeth grinding, neurodermatitis, coronary disease, neurosis, and academic probation.

Using 70 male and female nail biters between the ages of 10 and 14, Cummings (1954) rated the children as to the severity of the nail biting; the index used proved to be quite a reliable one. Confirming the assumption that nail biting, at least in part, indirectly reflects hostility, Cummings obtained a .34 ($p < .01$) correlation between *HL* and nail biting. It should be noted that *only* nail biters were used in this study; had children with no nail-biting habits been included in the sample, the sample would have been less attenuated and correlation might have been even higher.

Vernallis (1955) hypothesized that if teeth grinding in part reflects the hostile tendencies on the part of the individual, this behavior pattern should be positively related to *HL*. Using college students as subjects, Vernallis compared 40 teeth grinders with 40 controls matched for age, sex, I.Q., and education level; teeth grinding was determnied by means of a questionnaire. The results of the study proved to be quite favorable, in that a biserial correlation of .57 ($p < .01$) was found between teeth grinding and *HL*.

Cleveland and Fisher (1956) report, although only in part, the results of a study in which they set out to test the hypothesis that neurodermatitis is a manifestation of "repressed aggression." The underlying premise was that the skin trouble takes the place of the expression of hostile feelings; consequently, this group should have lower *HL* scores. Although the authors indicate that the neurodermatitis patients were compared with control patients having industrial skin lesions, the mean *HL* is reported for the former group only ($\bar{X} = 2.5$). Unfortunately, scoring the Rorschachs for hostility was an afterthought in this study, and was carried out after records from the control group were no longer available. However, from the relatively low mean *HL* score of 2.5 obtained by the experimental group (see Table 4.2), Cleveland and Fisher seem to feel that their findings offer some confirmation for their hypothesis.[4]

As part of a larger study to determine some of the personality characteristics associated with coronary disease, Cleveland and Johnson (1962) report some findings for *HL*. Although they propose no rationale for using *HL* scores in this study (other than the fact that the Rorschach protocols were available and could be readily scored), it is possible to speculate that coronary disease is more likely to occur in people who are fairly active, assertive, and independent. Thus, when acute myocardial infraction patients were compared to a matched group of noncoronary patients, the coronary group was found to have significantly higher *HL* scores.

The hypothesis that neurotics are more hostile than normals, as tested by Elizur (1949), seems to come more from general clinical observation than from any specific theoretical prediction. Elizur selected 22 diagnosed neurotics from hospital files and compared them with a group of normal subjects matched on the basis of sex, age, and I.Q. The neurotic subjects had been diagnosed as such before the Rorschach was administered and, except for two character disorders, the group was composed of patients representing the range of typical psychoneurotic classifications. Elizur's findings confirmed his expectation, in that the neurotic group obtained a significantly higher *HL*. In addition, the neurotics were also found to be significantly more variable in their *HL* scores than the normal controls.

Lit (1956) compared 40 college students on probation with a matched group of 40 dean's list students, the assumption being that these probational students were more disturbed (angry young men and women?) and consequently should show more indications of hostility. The two groups were matched not only as to their sex, age, and class level, but also on the basis of their scholastic aptitude. Using a scoring system practically identical to Elizur's Lit found more indications of hostility for the probation students. Although these results are in line with Lit's hypothesis, it still remains possible that the hostility of the probation students might have been a function of *having been placed on probation*. This alternate interpretation could have been easily tested if preprobational Rorschach protocols were available. Further, the comparison of probational students with non-dean's list students would have been preferable, inasmuch as Lit's findings could conceivably have reflected the relatively nonhostile nature of dean's list students, and not the hostility of students on probation.

All in all, the results of construct validity studies in which the hostility

[4] In a cross-validation study, where the hostility scores were obtained from the Holtzman Ink Blot Test, Cleveland found significantly lower scores for dermatitis cases than for controls (Personal communication, December 23, 1963).

scoring system has been related to hypothesized manifestations of hostility (particularly nail biting, teeth grinding, neurosis, and coronary disease) have been quite favorable. Further research along these same lines (e.g., bed wetting) not only would be valuable in filling out the construct validity of Elizur's scoring system, but would also aid in the more complete understanding of the various behavioral manifestations themselves.

HL AS A FUNCTION OF INSIGHT. In a study by Murstein (1956), it was hypothesized that in situations in which there is no strong threat to the individual (i.e., the typical Rorschach administration), hostile people with insight will project more hostility on the Rorschach than will hostile individuals who lack insight. The theoretical basis for this hypothesis is not at all clear, and Murstein never really justifies the reasoning behind this prediction. In any event, the use of the Elizur scoring for hostility failed to confirm the hypothesis. Using discrepancy measures between the individual's self-ratings and his friends' ratings of him on the dimensions of hostility and friendliness, Murstein found that hostile-insightful subjects had significantly higher *HL* scores than friendly-noninsightful; the *HL* scores of hostile-insightful subjects were higher than both hostile-noninsightful and friendly-insightful subjects, but the difference failed to reach statistical significance.

INDUCTION OF CHANGES IN *HL*. According to Elizur's definition of the construct his scoring system purports to measure, hostility is conceived of as being a relatively long-term, stable attitude or approach to the world (i.e., trait rather than state). It would seem, then, that simple experimental attempts to modify *HL* would not prove too successful. Nevertheless, a variety of studies have concerned themselves with ways in which changes in *HL* might be brought about, either by experimentally induced "frustrations," changes in the nature of the blots themselves, or variations in the subject's perception of the examiner.

Kates and Schwartz (1958) studied the effect of "self-esteem" stress on change in *HL*. By means of a counterbalanced design using the Rorschach and the Behn–Rorschach, the authors informed a small group of college females just before the second test was administered (one to two weeks later) about the negative personality characteristics revealed in the first test they had taken. No significant difference in *HL* was revealed for this group, or for a control group who were merely subjected to the two testings. Lucas (1961), using a group of 9-year-olds, employed a similar approach in her attempt to induce changes in *HL*. She administered the Rorschach twice, and just before the second testing some eight weeks later, deprecated the children and told them they had done poorly on some task. As was the case with Kates and Schwartz, however, no change in *HL* was obtained.

In a study on the influence of color and shading on *HL* scores, Forsyth (1959) administered a different set of "Rorschach" cards to each of three groups. All three sets were the same insofar as the shape of the blots was concerned. One set consisted of the standard blots, the second of achromatic blots, and the third set of a "silhouette" of the blots (in which shading was eliminated). A comparison of the mean *HL* scores among the three sets revealed no significant difference.

Towbin (1959) predicted that hospitalized patients would produce fewer hostile responses on the Rorschach if they perceived the examiner as having more power and status. Using male schizophrenics of average intelligence, Towbin induced high and low "power" sets by telling the patients that the examiner was (or was not) in a position to make administrative decisions about them. The "status" set was produced by varying the information told to patients regarding the examiner's position in the hospital hierarchy. The presence of hostility in the Rorschach (as defined by a system based on Elizur's method) was found to be unrelated to either of these two experimental conditions. As Towbin also reports some findings which cast into doubt the effectiveness of the experimental sets for some of the subjects, these negative findings do not imply unequivocally that hostility level on the Rorschach is independent of the subject's perception of the examiner. In fact, the evidence outlined below (Sanders and Cleveland, 1953) suggests that the personality characteristics of the examiner may indeed influence the subject's obtained *HL* score.

Sanders and Cleveland (1953), in a most interesting approach to the study of variations in *HL* scores, had each of nine graduate students administer the Rorschach to 30 undergraduates. The graduate students, who had volunteered to take part in the experiment, had relatively little experience in administering the Rorschach, although they had taken the test themselves. The undergraduate subjects were all males who had volunteered to be tested with the understanding that the results of the protocol would be discussed with them afterwards. On the basis of adjective check lists filled out by the subjects about their examiners after they were tested, each examiner was classified as to his *overt hostility*; the *HL* score obtained from the examiner's own Rorschach protocol was used to determine his level of *covert hostility*. The examiners were also rated as to their *overt-anxiety* level by subjects, as well as *covert-anxiety* level from a scoring of their Rorschachs (see Chapter 5). Sanders and Cleveland then made four sets of comparisons: The Rorschach hostility scores of subjects tested by the three *most* (1) overtly hostile, (2) covertly hostile, (3) overtly anxious, and (4) covertly anxious examiners, respectively. The findings indicated that the more *overtly hostile* examiners elicited significantly *lower HL* scores from subjects, while the more *covertly hostile* examiners obtained *higher HL* scores from their subjects. Further, it was found that *covertly* anxious examiners evoked higher *HL* scores from their subjects.

The most obvious and general implication of Sanders and Cleveland's findings is that a person's Rorschach hostility level is, at least in part, a function of the personality characteristics of the examiner. Specifically, the results imply that the more openly hostile examiner will tend to *suppress* the subject's expression of hostility on the Rorschach, whereas the more covertly hostile (and anxious) examiner will *facilitate* this expression of hostility. This generalization, however, should be accepted with caution. First of all, the mean *HL* and standard deviation for all of the undergraduate subjects in the study were 6.9 and 6.1, respectively—both of which are relatively high (see Table 4.2). Further, the general instructions given to potential subjects were somewhat unique, in that they were told that the results of the testing would be discussed with them if they volunteered for the experiment. Insofar as these subjects approached the testing situation with the expectation that they were going to learn more about themselves personally, they did not constitute a representative sample of subjects typically tested with the Rorschach. Exactly how this different set may have influenced the specific findings of Sanders and Cleveland is not clear. In the light of their higher *HL* scores, one may speculate that the subjects tended to be more open, in anticipation of finding out more about themselves.[5] In addition, the extent to which the *examiners* themselves constituted a representative, and hence generalizable sample may also be called into question. Sanders and Cleveland's conclusions on the effects of examiners are based on a very small and atypical sample of examiners. The groups of most and least hostile or anxious examiners had an N of only *three* each, none of whom had much training or experience in Rorschach administration.[6]

Finally, quite apart from the methodological shortcomings, one is faced with somewhat of a paradoxical "double bind" in trying to use Sanders and Cleveland's results to evaluate the validity of the hostility scoring system. The authors conclude that examiners with higher *covert* levels of hostility (as indicated by their own *HL* scores) tend to elicit higher *HL* scores from their subjects. Thus, the Elizur hostility scores for *examiners* are assumed to be "accurate" (i.e., uninfluenced by the hostility or anxiety of the testers who administered the Rorschach *to them*), whereas the scores for the *subjects* in the study are taken as being contaminated by the personality characteristics of the examiners. There appears to be some "bootstrap" reasoning in this conclusion.

In general, most of the studies which have attempted to alter *HL* experimentally have yielded negative findings. Although these results are consistent with the defined characteristics of the hostility-level construct—namely, that it refers to a fairly stable attitude on the part of the individual—the negative results in these studies may reflect methodological limitations and not the stability of the *HL* score. For example, there is some question as to how effective the experimental treatment was in Towbin's (1959) study. Making the conclusion that there is no "true" difference or change upon failing to reject the null hypothesis is typically a risky step.

The positive results of Sanders and Cleveland's (1953) study on the effect of the examiner's own hostility and anxiety on the *HL* scores of his subjects raises some serious questions concerning the validity of the Elizur hostility scoring for *certain types of testing situations.* At the most simplistic level, Sanders and Cleveland's findings indicate the following: When normal volunteers who expect to learn of the results of the testing are given the Rorschach by a relatively small and inexperienced group of examiners (of an unspecified level of hostility and anxiety), the *HL* obtained by subjects

5 It is interesting to note that Elizur (1949), in one part of his study, selected volunteers in much the same way as Sanders and Cleveland and similarly found relatively higher scores for these subjects.

6 For a more complete discussion of this general issue of sampling, see Hammond (1954).

is in part determined by certain personality characteristics of these examiners. Because of the somewhat unique sampling of both subjects and examiners, it is difficult to legitimately generalize these findings to the typical Rorschach testing situation. On the other hand, the likelihood that these examiner influences occur in the more typical clinical interaction *should not be ruled out* because of the limitations of Sanders and Cleveland's findings. The obvious implication is that a replication along these lines should be carried out with a more representative sampling of not only *subjects* who typically take the Rorschach, but also of *examiners* who usually administer it as well.

Trait Validity

The research on the trait validity of Elizur's hostility scoring of the Rorschach described in this section involves studies on the relationship between *HL* and (1) self-ratings of hostility, (2) other measures of hostility, and (3) nonhostility measures.

Relation to Self-Ratings. The original, as well as the most extensive, study of the relationship between *HL* and self-ratings was conducted by Elizur (1949). Using a group of 30 college volunteers (15 males and 15 females), Elizur had his subjects fill out a fairly subtle "questionnaire" as well as a set of "self-rating" scales. The questionnaire consisted of 55 hostility- and anxiety-related questions which the subject had to rate on a nine-point scale, indicating the extent to which the question applied to him. The areas covered in the questionnaire included hostility, submissiveness, aloofness, ideas of reference, depression, anxiety, and dependency. The so-called "self-rating" measure focused on the extent to which the subjects felt a need to *control* their hostile feelings, their tendency to succumb, and their feelings of depression, anxiety, and dependency. Hence, both the questionnaire and self-ratings contained personality characteristics which theoretically *should* and *should not* be related to level of hostility (cf. Campbell and Fiske's (1959) multitrait-multimethod approach to test validation).

The results of Elizur's study are presented in Table 4.3. The hostility-related personality characteristics obtained from the questionnaire and self-ratings are on the left side of the table, and the anxiety-related characteristics are directly below; at the bottom are those characteristics presumably reflecting *both* hostility and anxiety. Elizur's findings are quite impressive. As can be seen in Table 4.3, practically all of the hostile characteristics (direct and indirect) on the left correlated significantly with *HL,* whereas none of the anxiety characteristics were significantly related. Those characteristics believed to reflect *both* hostility and anxiety were all found to be significantly correlated with *HL*. Further, if the results of an interview with 20 of these subjects are taken as a criterion measure, the Rorschach proves to be *more accurate than either type of self-report.* That is, the correlation between *HL* and the interview estimates of hostility was .60 ($p < .01$), whereas the self-rating and questionnaire measures correlated only .46 ($p < .05$) and .39 (ns), respectively, with the interview.

Walker (1951) attempted to relate the results of a hostility questionnaire to hostility level on the Rorschach. Walker's questionnaire was more

TABLE 4.3
Correlations Between *HL* and Various Personality Characteristics of 30 Normal Volunteers as Determined by Questionnaires and Self-Ratings (after Elizur, 1949)

Hostility Characteristics	*Correlation with HL*
Questionnaire on Hostility	
Self-blame	.44[a]
Subject Regarded as Good Natured	.27
Subject Was "Goody-Goody" Child	.53[b]
Subject Believes That People Are Hostile	.55[b]
Subject Believes That People Are Selfish	.21
All Items Combined	.74[b]
Self-ratings on Control of Hostility Toward Others	
Friends	.15
Members of the Family	.38[a]
Minority Groups	.37[a]
All Items Combined	.45[a]
Questionnaire on Submissiveness	.64[b]
Self-ratings on Control of Tendency to Succumb	.31
Questionnaire on Aloofness	.43[a]
Anxiety Characteristics	*Correlation with HL*
Questionnaire on Anxiety	
Fears and Phobias	.23
Lack of Self-confidence	.28
Both Items Combined	.31
Self-ratings on Control of Anxiety	
Fear	.17
Worry	.05
General Shyness	.14
Sexual Shyness	.26
Feelings of Inferiority	.09
All Items Combined	.19
Questionnaire on Dependency	.19
Self-ratings on Control of Dependency Wishes	.17
Characteristics Reflecting both Hostility and Anxiety	*Correlation with HL*
Questionnaire on Ideas of Reference	.48[b]
Questionnaire on Depression	.44[a]
Self-ratings on Control of Depressive Moods	.41[a]

[a] Significant at the .05 level.
[b] Significant at the .01 level

direct than Elizur's; the study also differed from Elizur's in that Walker used neuropsychiatric patients (neurotics and psychotics) instead of normal subjects. Perhaps because of the nature of the hostility questionnaire and sample used, Walker failed to obtain any significant relationship between the questionnaire and Rorschach estimates of hostility level.

Relation to Other Hostility Measures. The Elizur system of scoring the Rorschach for hostility has been related to other Rorschach hostility scoring systems, TAT and MAPS measures of hostility, hostility inventories, and estimates of hostility from sentence-construction methods.

In noting studies where the Elizur hostility scoring has been related to other Rorschach hostility measures, it should be kept in mind that most of these other scoring systems have been based on Elizur's approach. Because these later approaches use many of Elizur's criteria, it would indeed be surprising if they *did not* correlate with Elizur's system. Murstein (1956), using his own scoring (which scales responses from 0 to 7), obtained a .84 correlation with a sample of 80 college males. Buss et al. (1962) scored the Rorschachs of 96 psychiatric patients according to Elizur's and DeVos' (1952) method, and found the two systems correlated to .74.

Using a multiple-choice form of the TAT (hostility, anxiety, achievement, and blandness), Goodstein (1954) was *unable* to find any relationship between this measure of hostility and the *HL* scores obtained from the group Rorschach protocols of 57 college students. Similarly, Buss et al. (1962) attempted to relate a multiple-choice form of the TAT with the Elizur scoring of the Rorschach. For a group of male psychiatric patients, a nonsignificant correlation of .18 was obtained. However, for female patients, the two measures correlated $-.40$ ($p < .01$). On the basis of these studies alone, it is difficult to come to any conclusion on the relationship between the Rorschach and TAT as measures of hostility. The multiple-choice approaches to the TAT used in these studies did not control for the influence of social desirability, and the alternatives chosen may not have reflected the type of response which would have been given by the usual method. On the other hand, Walker (1951), who used the MAPS rather than the TAT, scored the actual stories for hostility according to a system described by Fine (1948). The results of Walker's study were quite favorable, in that he obtained a Pearson r (estimated from phi) of .73 between the two measures.

The findings from studies on the relationship between *HL* and hostility inventory scores have generally been negative. Siegel (1956), using the MMPI for his item pool, devised a manifest hostility scale (MHS); however, no significant relationship was found between *HL* and MHS scores for male college students or outpatients. Buss et al. (1962) used the Buss–Durkee hostility inventory and found an r of only .10 for male (ns) but a .41 correlation ($p < .01$) for female patients.

Buss et al. (1962) also employed a sentence-construction approach to the assessment of hostility. These authors provided psychiatric patients with scrambled sentences, where the task consisted of eliminating one word and contructing a sentence. For example, "take arm his break" could be made into a hostile or nonhostile sentence, depending on the word omitted. Buss and his associates also asked subjects to construct sentences, using one of two words indicated on 3×5 cards; each card contained a hostile and a neutral word. The Rorschach *HL* was found to be unrelated to the scores obtained by either of these sentence techniques.

The general findings on the relationship of *HL* to other measures of hostility indicate that the Elizur scoring correlates highly with other Rorschach hostility scorings, as well as with a thematic analysis of fantasy material (MAPS). Paper-and-pencil measures of hostility (including a multiple-choice TAT) seem to be measuring something different. With these direct and fairly obvious paper-and-pencil measures, it is highly likely that the subject's choice will be influenced by what he feels the socially desirable or acceptable response to be. Consequently, the failure of the Elizur scoring system to relate to these other measures cannot be construed as pointing to the invalidity of the Rorschach approach.

RELATION TO NONHOSTILITY MEASURES. The Elizur hostility scoring has been related to anxiety measures, the F scale, and I.Q.

The question of whether or not measures of hostility and anxiety theoretically *should* be related is somewhat complex. Although one clearly may be anxious about his hostile feelings toward others, anxiety frequently occurs for a multitude of other reasons as well. Similarly, an individual's hostile feelings may or may not create anxiety for him. Consequently, depending on the nature and heterogeneity of the sample, there should be some inconsistency in the empirically obtained relationships between hostility and anxiety.

From the empirical viewpoint, the findings regarding the relationship between *HL* and measures of anxiety have gone along with this anticipated inconsistency. Goodstein (1954), using the group Rorschach responses of 57 college students, failed to find any significant relationship between *HL* and Rorschach anxiety level (*AL*). Similarly, the relationship between *HL* and scores on the Taylor Manifest Anxiety Scale (MAS) was found to be nonsignificant ($r = -.20$); with the number of responses of the Rorschach partialed out, however, the resulting correlation of $-.26$ between *HL* and MAS scores reached significance at the .05 level (Goodstein, 1954). For a group of nail-biting children, no significant relationship was found between *HL* and *AL* (Cummings, 1954).

When the relationship between hostility and anxiety has been studied in a large or fairly heterogeneous sample, or when subjects consisted of only those at the extremes of the anxiety distribution, more positive findings have resulted. Thus, Sanders and Cleveland (1953) found that for 270 college males, *HL* and *AL* correlated .52. Elizur (1949) found that when he pooled the protocols of 30 college volunteers, 22 neurotics, and 22 matched controls, a significant correlation was obtained between *HL* and *AL* ($r = .27$; $p < .05$). From a pool of 139 psychiatric patients for whom Rorschach protocols and MAS scores were available, Goodstein and Goldberger (1955) compared the *HL* scores of 16 high-anxiety with 16 low-anxiety subjects. According to expectation, the high-anxiety group had significantly greater *HL* scores.

Siegel (1956) studied the relationship between *HL* and authoritarianism. He administered the Rorschach and the F scale to both a psychiatric and college-student population, and divided each of the two samples into high, medium, and low F scale scores. The only significant finding was that patients with low F scores had significantly higher *HL*s than patients with high F scores. Because of the very marked effects of response style and social desirability on F scores, these essentially negative findings may be attributed to the fact that the F scale is measuring something other than authoritarianism.

Theoretically, no relationship between hostility level (as we have defined it) and I.Q. is expected to exist. Elizur (1949) offers some minimal evidence on this relationship by failing to obtain any significant correlations between I.Q. and *HL within* a small sample of neurotics (N = 22) and of normals (N = 22). Because of the size and the homogeneity of these samples, this study should be taken only as being "suggestive" of the lack of the relationship between *HL* and I.Q.

OVERALL EVALUATION

Elizur's system of scoring of the Rorschach for hostility level (*HL*) is based solely on the content of the response. The "hostility" construct itself, which the system purports to measure, refers to the individual's general, and presumably stable, negative attitudes and feelings toward the world around him. The scoring attempts to measure only the general *level* of hostility, and *not the way* in which this feeling or attitude might be expressed behaviorally. Consequently, two individuals may obtain similar *HL* scores and yet manifest their hostility differently; one person may act out his aggression physically, while the other may express his hostile feelings verbally. In this regard, it would seem fruitful to make a joint use of *HL* and Rorschach developmental level (see Chapters 2 and 3), the latter of which has proved to be useful in assessing the manner in which individuals typically handle their impulses.

The Elizur scoring system itself is easy to learn and apply. Responses are simply classified into three categories: obvious, less obvious, or no indications of hostility. The actual scoring of a record may be done within a relatively short period of time, and with a high degree of reliability; the interscorer reliability is in the neighborhood of .90. The precise effect of the total R on the obtained *HL* score has not yet been clearly established. It seems probable that the relationship between *HL* and R is not a direct but a curvilinear one—U-shaped. Thus, the subject who is resistive and obtains a low R may show signs of hostility on those few responses which he does give, whereas the person with a high R may give several hostile responses on the basis of chance. The evidence for this curvilinear relationship is only indirect, and the effect of R on *HL* needs to be studied further.

Although one would expect that an individual's characteristic hostility level is a fairly stable trait, there is no good research evidence on the test-retest reliability of *HL*. Some studies have shown, however, that experimentally induced frustrations, as well as the elimination of color or shading on the blot, do little to influence *HL*. Some evidence pointing to the possible influence of the examiner's own personality characteristics (hostility and anxiety) on the *HL* score elicited from the subject has raised a serious question. And although the results of the study which raised this question were limited by a nonrepresentative sampling of subjects and examiners, the question of examiner influence on *HL* remains one very much in need of further research.

Most of the validity studies on Elizur's system have turned out quite well. Individuals who in the past have been known to have acted out aggressively are typically found to have higher *HL* scores than those who have no acting-out history. When careful estimates of *level* of hostility (regardless of mode of expression) have been used as criterion measures—based on peer ratings, ratings of therapists, or estimates based on interviews specifically designed to assess hostility level—the correlation with *HL* has proven to be relatively high. The predictive validity of the Elizur hostility scoring, on the other hand, has not fared nearly as well. The *HL* score cannot be used as a good prognostic indicator of course of illness in schizophrenics. Further, as a means of predicting whether or not someone is likely to act out aggressively, the hostility scoring system in itself seems to have little utility. This is not surprising, inasmuch as the score purports to reflect degree of hostility, and not style of expression. The use of some measure reflecting the *way* in which an individual expresses his feelings, *in addition* to *HL* scores, would most likely result in a more accurate estimate of acting out potential.

Rorschach hostility level has been found to be related to a variety of behavioral characteristics and symptoms which presumably are indirect manifestations of hostility. Thus, the severity of nail biting in children and teeth grinding in adults has been found to be positively related to *HL*. The *HL* scores of coronary patients and neurotics have been shown to be higher than the scores of normal controls. College students on probation obtain higher *HL* scores than a comparable group of dean's list students. More tentative findings indicate that neurodermatitis patients, who are presumably expressing their hostility somatically, show less hostility on the Rorschach than individuals with nonpsychosomatic skin disturbances. When normal subjects have rated themselves as to a number of hostility-related and anxiety-related personality characteristics, *HL* has been found to correlate only with those traits reflecting hostility. Further, when the subjects' own self-ratings for hostility and *HL* scores have each been related to an interviewer's estimate of the subjects' hostility, *HL* has been shown to have a higher correlation with this criterion measure than have the self-ratings.

The research findings on the relationship between *HL* and other measures of hostility indicate that the Elizur system correlates highly with other Rorschach hostility-scoring systems. This is not very surprising, as these other systems make use of many of Elizur's scoring criteria. Studies on the relationship between *HL* and hostility scores obtained from multiple-choice forms of the TAT point to the fact that these two approaches are not measuring the same variable. However, when the estimate of hostility is obtained from the subject's own story and not from his selection from the available alternatives, then the fantasy (MAPS) estimate of hostility correlates well with *HL* scores. In general, research evidence has shown that *HL* scores have little relationship to paper-and-pencil measures of hostility.

In estimating the usefulness of the Elizur hostility scoring system in clinical practice, we nautrally must take into account the question of norms. The available data which may be considered as even indirectly serving as norms leave much to be desired. Aside from the methodological problems which exist (e.g., unrepresentative sample, small Ns, etc.), the *type* of groups on which data have been collected to date cannot be of much use in clinical evaluation. Take, for example, the potential usefulness of normative data on neurotic subjects. It is highly unlikely that the strong point of the *HL* score will ever be in its ability to diagnose neurosis; it also makes little sense to use this type of normative data to say that a given individual is "as hostile as a neurotic." Validity studies have indicated, on the other hand, that *HL* seems to be a good indicant of level of hostility, and it is therein that the need for norms exists. In fact, it is only by establishing *HL* norms for each different rated level of hostility (based on therapists' ratings, intensive interviews, careful observations, etc.), and noting the amount of overlap in *HL* scores among these various independently rated levels, that the Elizur hostility scoring can be put to its best use clinically.

Chapter 5

ELIZUR'S ANXIETY SCORING

Anxiety probably represents one of the most important concepts currently used in the explanation of human behavior. Anxiety is believed to be related not only to psychopathological conditions, but also to so-called "normal" behavior. Because of the intensely unpleasant psychological and physiological characteristics of anxiety, individuals will react or behave in various ways in order to diminish this emotional state. Should the anxiety reach too high a level, a disruption of the individual's ability to function ensues.

The Rorschach anxiety scoring to be presented and evaluated in this chapter was formulated by Elizur (1949). Similar to Elizur's scoring system for hostility described in Chapter 4, his anxiety scoring of the Rorschach is based on the content, rather than on the formal elements of the response. Although there are some minor variations on Elizur's scoring criteria (Arnaud, 1959; DeVos, 1952), his system has been the most popular by far. After a more explicit definition of the construct of anxiety, then, this chapter outlines and evaluates Elizur's anxiety scoring of the Rorschach.

DEFINITION OF THE CONSTRUCT

In "Inhibitions, Symptoms and Anxiety," Freud (1959) presented his revised description of the anxiety construct. At the most general level, Freud indicated that anxiety may be viewed as the individual's affective response to

Chapter 5 is an extended version of "The assessment of anxiety by means of the Rorschach," by Marvin R. Goldfried, published in the *Journal of Projective Techniques and Personality Assessment,* 1966, *30,* 364–380; and reprinted with permission of author and publisher.

a state of "danger." More specifically, the potential danger to the individual may stem from his own unacceptable impulses (*neurotic* anxiety), the fear of punishment from one's conscience (*moral* anxiety), or some actual physical threat from the external environment (*real* anxiety). These different conceptualizations of anxiety are more typically referred to as simply *anxiety, guilt,* and *fear,* respectively.

Elizur's definition of the construct his system purports to measure falls more in line with what is usually termed "anxiety" rather than "fear" or "guilt." Although he says little explicitly about the origins of the emotional condition, Elizur implies that this condition of high drive or arousal has an internal rather than an external basis. Further, the conceptualization of anxiety reflected in the scoring system refers to *experienced* anxiety, rather than "unconscious anxiety"—that is, the anxiety which has been successfully reduced or avoided by means of defensive maneuvers. Still further, the anxiety level indicated by Elizur's content scoring may be viewed as reflecting more of a relatively *general personality characteristic* of the individual, rather than the transitory reaction to a stressful situation (cf. Spielberger, 1966).

Lazarus (1966) has noted that although theorists differ in their conceptualizations of the origins of anxiety, there is general agreement that anxiety represents both a response—to a conflict or some personally unpleasant situation—and a signal of or cue for danger. A further point of agreement is that anxiety is typically viewed as *"a drive in that it is capable of motivating instrumental behaviors such as avoidance or escape which reduce the fear"* (Lazarus, 1966, p. 72). Given a certain level of anxiety, however, individuals will vary in the specific way in which this tension is manifested. Thus, Elizur (1949) has noted: "*Anxiety* is thought of as an inner state of insecurity which may take one or more of the following forms: fears, phobias, lack of self-confidence, extreme shyness, ideas of reference and marked sensitivity" (p. 248). In addition to the way in which the anxiety is expressed, people with comparable levels of anxiety will also differ as to the defenses they typically use to reduce or eliminate the state of tension.

As was the case in the definition of the "hostility-level" construct presented in Chapter 4, the anxiety presumably revealed in the Rorschach content scoring refers only to *level of anxiety,* and not to the way in which it is expressed or reduced. In order to assess these latter characteristics, the individual's personality style and preferred defensive behaviors must be considered.

ANXIETY SCORING SYSTEM

As in the case of Elizur's scoring for hostility described in Chapter 4, the anxiety scoring system can be learned and used without much difficulty. In fact, the general format of the scoring systems for hostility and anxiety are similar.

In scoring a protocol for anxiety, only the content of the response is used—with no regard for card, location, or determinants. Although an inquiry may be called for in order to score certain responses, the type of questioning required need not be of the more traditional type. Thus, to a response of "a large animal" given in the free association, the simple question of the "tell-me-more-about-it" variety might result in an elaboration such as: "It's very frightening looking." Regardless of whether the anxiety is revealed in the free association or in the inquiry, the response is still scored according to the same criteria.

Elizur's specific criteria used in scoring a protocol for anxiety, as well as some sample responses, are described below.

Scoring Criteria

As already noted above, the content of the response, regardless of its location, is scored for degree of anxiety manifested. If anxiety is "expressed obviously and explicitly" in the response, a score of *A* is assigned. If anxiety is expressed less obviously, or if it is expressed clearly but symbolically, the response is given a score of *a*. If no anxiety at all is reflected, the response is considered "neutral" and consequently remains unscored. Six general types of responses, arranged roughly according to decreasing level of anxiety reflected in them, include (1) expressive behavior, (2) emotions and attitudes expressed or implied, (3) cultural stereotypes of fear, (4) symbolic responses, (5) double connotation, and (6) unscorable or "neutral" responses.

I. Expressive Behavior

SCORE *A*. If anxiety is associated in any way with the *behavior* of the figure perceived.

Examples of such *A* responses are as follows:

Animal retreating
Girl running away
Man being charged by a bull
Person hanging onto a cliff
Rabbit running away
Woman huddled over in fear

II. Emotions and Attitudes Expressed or Implied

SCORE *A*. If the response clearly reflects the emotions or attitudes of fear, unpleasantness, sorrow, pity, and so on. The feeling or attitude may be related to the *subject* himself (e.g., "It's the kind of bug that scares me") or to an object in the *percept* (e.g., "a frightened animal"). Further, the feeling or attitude may be *implied,* such as in the response "a dangerous place."

Examples of such *A* responses are as follows:

Dangerous cliff
Darkness and gloom
Frightened animal
Nervous man
Scared cat
Weeping child

SCORE *a*. If anxiety is expressed or implied in the feeling and attitudes, but to a *lesser extent* than that indicated above.

Examples of such *a* responses are as follows:

Man with a cornered look	Unpleasant animal
Sad child	Whimpering dog
Timid person	Worrisome-looking cliff

III. Cultural Stereotypes of Fear

SCORE *A*. If the response generally *connotes fear* in our society. Scoring of this type of response should be done cautiously.

Examples of such *A* responses are as follows[1]:

Atomic explosion	Haunted house
Blood	Human skull or skeleton
Corpse	Smoke
Fire	Snake
Ghosts	Vampire
Graveyard	Witch

SCORE *a*. If the connotation involves more a *"moderate degree of unpleasantness"* than actual fear. As is the case with the *A* responses in this general category, scoring for cultural stereotypes should be done conservatively.

Examples of such *a* responses are as follows:

Altar	Jack-o'-lantern
Cobweb	Mosquito
Church	Spiders
Firecracker	Storm clouds
Idol	Volcano

IV. Symbolic Responses

SCORE *a*. If the response reflects fear or anxiety, but in symbolic form. As is the case with cultural stereotypes, symbolic responses should be scored conservatively.

Examples of such *a* responses are as follows:

Animals balancing on a rock	Cancerous tumor
Black signifies death	Dead leaves
Bottomless pit	Diseased lung

V. Double Connotation

SCORE *a*. If the response clearly reflects *both* anxiety and hostility, or if it is not clear as to which of the two emotions is involved. For a fuller description of the criteria for hostility scorings, see Chapter 4.

[1] One of Elizur's examples under this category is "bat." Inasmuch as this response is so strongly "pulled" by Cards I and V, only the nonpopular "bats" would seem to warrant a score of *A*.

Examples of such *a* responses are as follows:

Frightened animal about to attack	Mouse caught in a trap
Headless man	Person being grabbed from behind
Man being hanged	Policeman

VI. Unscorable or "Neutral" Responses

Do not score: If the response, in both its elaborated or unelaborated form, reflects *no anxiety* as determined by any of the above criteria.

Examples of "neutral" responses with respect to anxiety are as follows:

Animal skin	Helmet
Bears	Map
Beggar	Rocks
Butterfly	Tree
Hammer	X ray

Interscorer Reliability

Just as the scoring criteria for Rorschach anxiety level parallel the hostility scoring system outlined in Chapter 4, so is there a comparably high interscorer agreement for this system as well (Cummings, 1954; Elizur, 1949; Forsyth, 1959; Mogar, 1962; Sanders and Cleveland, 1953).

In studies comparing the reliability between two scorers, the obtained correlations have been found to be .99 (Sanders and Cleveland, 1953), .94 (Cummings, 1954), .95 and .90 (Forsyth, 1959), and an intraclass r of .81 (Mogar, 1962). The reliability coefficients reported by Forsyth (1959) were between his own scoring and the scorings of graduate students' wives, demonstrating the relative ease with which the criteria may be applied. Elizur (1949) similarly compared the reliability among eight inexperienced scorers and found an average correlation of .77. A comparison of Elizur's own scoring with the average scoring of these eight judges yielded a correlation of .89.

Brief note might be taken of Forsyth's (1959) finding regarding the *intrascorer* reliability. With a one-month interval, Forsyth found a .98 correlation between his two sets of scores.

It is clear, then, that even with only a minimal amount of experience with the criteria, one can use Elizur's anxiety scoring of the Rorschach with a fairly high degree of reliability.

Summary Scores

Although there are five separate categories under which responses may be scored for anxiety, these different classifications are used simply to facilitate the process of scoring and are not taken into account in summarizing the protocol. Rather, an overall anxiety level (hereafter referred to as *AL*) score is arrived at by counting up the weighted number of anxiety-related responses in the record. More specifically, *AL* is computed by first assigning a weight of 2 to all those responses scored as *A*, and a weight of 1 to those responses scored *a; AL* simply represents the total of all the weights.

The scoring system depends only upon the content of the response, and Elizur has made no provision for differentially scoring anxiety-related responses which do, and which *do not* agree with the form demands of the blot. Inasmuch as minus responses presumably reflect a distortion produced by some relatively strong inner state or characteristic of the individual, it would seem appropriate to utilize this reasoning in scoring for anxiety. An additional weighting for anxiety-related responses of minus form level can involve just that—namely, an *additional weight of one point* assigned to minus responses scored *A* and *a*.[2]

As is the case with most other approaches to the Rorschach, there is the likelihood that the summary scores will mean very different things for protocols of different lengths. This is "the-effect-of-R" issue which continues to haunt us in the interpretation of Rorschach scores. With respect to the anxiety scoring, the findings regarding the effect of total R on *AL* are somewhat equivocal (Goodstein, 1954; Gorlow, Zimet, and Fine, 1952; Grauer, 1953; Page, 1957; Sanders and Cleveland, 1953; Stewart, 1950; Westrope, 1953); the evidence seems to point in the direction of a *positive relationship* between the two. A more complete description of the findings of these studies is presented below. In line with our discussion of how to summarize a protocol, it is recommended that at least some minimal attempt be made to account for total R. Thus, instead of using *AL* as a final score, it would be profitable to make use of *AL%* (i.e., *AL*/R) instead.

NORMATIVE DATA

The only data which can be even remotely construed as normative are those means and standard deviations reported in connection with various research reports (Cummings, 1954; Elizur, 1949; Gorlow et al., 1952; Stewart, 1950; Westrope, 1953; Zimet and Brackbill, 1956). The samples on which these scores were based suffer from such limitations as nonrepresentativeness, smallness of N, and insufficient background information; however, these are the only data that are available to date.

Nature of the Samples

Rorschach *AL* scores have been obtained for normal adults, college students at the extremes of the distribution on the Taylor Manifest Anxiety Scale, neurotic adults, psychotic adults, personality disorders, clinic patients, delinquent and nondelinquent adolescents, and nail-biting children. The available characteristics of the subjects in these samples are indicated in Table 5.1.

The normal adults were selected by Elizur (1949) so as to be com-

[2] The suggestion to assign added weight to minus responses was also made in connection with the content scoring for hostility (Chapter 4).

TABLE 5.1
Characteristics of Normative Data Sample

Group	N	Sex		Age			I.Q.		Years of Education	
		Male	*Female*	*Mean*	*S.D.*	*Range*	*Mean*	*S.D.*	*Mean*	*S.D.*
Normal Adults (Elizur, 1949)	22	—[a]	—	34.0	8.1	—	103.6	9.9	—	—
College Students (Westrope, 1953)										
High Anxiety	24	12	12	—	—	—	—	—	—	—
Low Anxiety	24	12	12	—	—	—	—	—	—	—
Neurotic Adults (Elizur, 1949)	22	—	—	33.8	9.3	—	101.4	12.6	—	—
Neurotic Adults (Zimet and Brackbill, 1956)	32	32	0	—	—	—	—	—	—	—
Psychotic Adults (Zimet and Brackbill, 1956)	32	32	0	—	—	—	—	—	—	—
Personality Disorders (Zimet and Brackbill, 1956)	33	33	0	—	—	—	—	—	—	—
Clinic Patients (Stewart, 1950)	112	112	0	28	—	19–47	—	—	—	—
Delinquent Adolescents (Gorlow et al., 1952)	13	10	3	12.3	0.5	—	88.0[b]	10.5[b]	—	—
Nondelinquent Adolescents (Gorlow et al., 1952)	13	10	3	12.2	0.5	—	87.0[b]	7.0[b]	—	—
Nail-biting Children (Cummings, 1954)	70	35	35	—	—	10–14	103.6	—	11.0[c]	—

[a] A dash (—) indicates that these data were not available.
[b] I.Q. estimates based on the Wechsler–Bellevue I vocabulary scores which were reported by Gorlow et al. (1952).
[c] Approximation of years of education for both parents.

parable to his group of neurotic adults on the basis of age, sex, and I.Q. Although the I.Q. scores for the normal subjects were based on a short form of the Wechsler–Bellevue, full-scale Wechsler–Bellevues were available for the neurotic group. The data on neurotic subjects were obtained from hospital files and were selected on the basis of the three following criteria: (1) the Rorschach must have been given subsequent to the diagnostic decision, (2) the total number of responses on the Rorschach could not have been below 20, and (3) the full-scale I.Q. could not have been below 85. With the exception of two patients diagnosed as character disorders, the subjects in this group represented the full range of neurotic diagnostic categories.

The two groups of college students in Westrope's (1953) sample were selected from a larger pool of introductory psychology students on the basis of their scores on the Taylor Manifest Anxiety Scale (MAS). The group of high anxiety subjects was composed of 12 males and 12 females whose MAS scores were in the upper 20% of the distribution (i.e., a score of 22 or higher). The low anxiety subjects had a similarly equal number of males and females, and were selected from those students whose MAS scores fell in the lower 20% (i.e., a score of 7 or lower). Westrope presents no additional data on the subjects used in the study.

Except for diagnostic classification, no other background information was presented by Zimet and Brackbill (1956) in their description of the male hospital patients comprising the neurotic, psychotic, and personality disorder samples. The 32 neurotic adults included the following classification: 14 anxiety reaction, 10 hysterics, 5 undifferentiated, and 3 others. The group of 32 psychotic patients was composed of schizophrenics of the following subcategories: 18 paranoid, 12 undifferentiated, and 2 simple. Zimet and Brackbill's sample of 33 personality disorders include 12 passive-aggressive personalities, 8 psychopaths, 7 cases of emotional instability, and 6 personality-pattern disturbances. No indication is given by the authors as to the reliability of these diagnoses.

Stewart's (1950) sample was selected from patients attending a V.A. mental hygiene clinic. In addition to having taken the Rorschach, all patients had to have been subsequently seen in therapy for at least eight sessions. The sample was comprised of patients whose diagnoses varied from "near normal" to "psychotic." A more precise indication of the diagnostic composition of the clinic's population is offered by Futterman, Kirkner, and Meyer (1947), who point out that about two-thirds of the cases were neurotic. Futterman et al. further mention that the patients attending this clinic had attained a higher educational level than is usually found in the general population.

The group of delinquent adolescents (Gorlow et al., 1952) were selected at random from court records on the basis of their having committed "antisocial" acts. The delinquent sample was matched with a group of non-delinquents on the basis of sex (10 males and 3 females in each group), age, I.Q. (Wechsler–Bellevue vocabulary scores), and socio-economic background.

The grade-school children in the nail-biting group were selected on the basis of clear indications they bit their nails to some degree or another. The mean I.Q. reported in Table 5.1 is based on the results of the short form of the California Test of Mental Maturity.

Data on Anxiety Scores

The available data on *AL* for the several samples described above are indicated in Table 5.2.

There is a marked discrepancy in Table 5.2 between the data for Elizur's (1949) and for Zimet and Brackbill's (1956) samples of neurotic adults. Because of the insufficient background information available on these two samples, it is not evident what the possible reasons for these inconsistent findings might be.

Some very weak hints of a developmental trend seem to be present for the samples of normal subjects, with *AL* scores decreasing from the nondelinquent adolescents, to the college students, and finally to the normal adults. Although these findings are admittedly only "suggestive," it does appear consistent with the notion that maturity brings with it more security and less anxiety. A more precise developmental study with *AL* is certainly worthwhile, and if differences *are* in fact found among different age levels, the need for separate age norms would be indicated.

Although these data may serve to give some rough idea of *AL* scores for a variety of populations, the clinical utility of this information is unfortunately limited. As was similarly pointed out in Chapter 4 in the case of Rorschach hostility scores, the most profitable clinical value of a score such as *AL* does not rest in its ability to make differential diagnoses. Even

TABLE 5.2
Means and Standard Deviations of Anxiety Level (*AL*) for Each of the Samples

	Anxiety Level (*AL*)	
Group	*Mean*	*S.D.*
Normal Adults	5.20	2.7
College Students		
High Anxiety	9.88	5.4
Low Anxiety	6.42	4.0
Neurotic Adults (Elizur, 1949)	12.50	3.1
Neurotic Adults (Zimet and Brackbill, 1956)	6.70	4.0
Psychotic Adults	6.70	4.0
Personality Disorders	6.90	4.0
Clinic Patients	7.80	3.7
Delinquent Adolescents	11.38	2.7
Nondelinquent Adolescents	8.15	4.2
Nail-biting Children	11.93	5.4

though a patient's anxiety level may be taken into account in arriving at a diagnostic decision, various other symptoms and characteristics must be considered as well. The use of Rorschach *AL* scores in clinical practice should be purely descriptive rather than diagnostic; that is, the score in itself should be used only to indicate *the extent to which a patient is anxious.*[3] Inferences concerning diagnostic and other decisions obviously will be made from the patient's level of anxiety. However, in order to take this descriptive approach and assess a patient's anxiety level, there is the need for normative *AL* data *not on different diagnostic groups, but rather on individuals at varying, independently rated levels of anxiety.* The ratings obviously must be consistent with the definition of the anxiety construct underlying the *AL* score, and should involve criterion groups which fully sample subjects at the varying degrees of anxiety. With the availability of *AL* norms for individuals at each of several different carefully rated levels of anxiety, the estimates of overlap among the different rated criterion levels would provide the needed information on the precision of this scoring for the individual case.

NORMS FOR DIFFERENT LEVELS OF R. Several studies have found that, at least in the case of college students, the longer the Rorschach protocol, the higher the *AL* score obtained. The significant positive correlations reported between total R and *AL* have been .64 (Sanders and Cleveland, 1953), .50 (Westrope, 1953), and .25 (Goodstein, 1954). On the other hand, Stewart (1950) found that although *AL* and therapists' ratings were positively related, there was no difference in R between those rated high and those rated as low in anxiety. Page (1957), who found no relationship between frequency of daydreams and *AL* for college females, did find a higher R for the more frequent daydreamers. While Stewart's and Page's results offer some weak evidence that *AL* and R are not necessarily related, there are still other findings which suggest that *AL* is *inversely* related to R. Thus, Gorlow et al. (1952) report that while delinquent adolescents obtained significantly higher *AL* scores than nondelinquents, the total R for the delinquents was *lower.* Similarly, Grauer (1953) indicates that although good-prognosis schizophrenics had a higher *AL%* than poor-prognosis schizophrenics, the good-prognosis group obtained fewer R.

Despite these somewhat conflicting findings, the positive correlations obtained by Sanders and Cleveland (1953), Westrope (1953), and Goodstein (1954)—which provide a more direct test of the relationship between *AL* and R than do the other studies—seem to be enough of an indication that high *AL* scores will be obtained in longer Rorschach records. The effect of R can in part be controlled for by the use of *AL%* instead of *AL* scores, requesting subjects to give a fixed number of responses to each card, deciding to score only the first responses to each card, or classifying indi-

[3] The authors readily acknowledge the need in clinical practice for information about the *situations* which elicit the anxiety. The fact that this information is not readily obtainable from the Rorschach, together with some of the implications of the clinical utility of the measure, is discussed at some length in Chapter 13.

viduals into high and low total R before comparing groups. In addition, it is recommended that the normative data collected on subjects at the several rated levels of anxiety be dichotomized in addition according to high vs. low total R.

RELIABILITY

The definition of anxiety, as it relates to what the Elizur scoring purports to measure, implies more of a long-term personality characteristic than it does a transitory emotional state. Consequently, studies on the stability of *AL* scores over time are clearly in order. On the other hand, estimates of internal consistency, because of the inequality of "items" (i.e., cards), are less appropriate in the evaluation of the system.[4]

As yet, there has been no good, direct test of the stability of *AL* scores over time. Although there are a couple of studies which suggest that stability of scores does exist, the evidence is not strong enough to be very convincing (Epstein, Nelson, and Tanofsky, 1957; Lucas, 1961).

Epstein et al. (1957) gave a small group of 16 college students (eight males and eight females) 10 different sets of homemade inkblots. Each different 10-blot set was group-administered over a period of five weeks, with two sets given per week. The responses were scored according to Elizur's anxiety criteria, and a reliability coefficient was derived from an analysis of variance of these scores. Across all 10 sets, the obtained coefficient was .26 ($p < .001$). Further, the mean *AL* scores among the 10 administrations were not found to differ significantly from each other.

As part of a study to test the effects of frustration on hostile Rorschach responses, Lucas (1961) additionally scored the protocols for *AL*. There was an eight-week interval between the two Rorschach administrations for both experimental and control groups—subjects in the former group being depreciated by the experimenter prior to the second testing. Lucas used 9-year-olds as subjects, with an N of 28 in each of the two groups. The results indicated no change in *AL* for subjects in either of the two conditions. Inasmuch as the two Rorschach administrations were carried out to test the results of a specific experimental manipulation, the relationship between the scores in the two testings was not reported in terms of correlation coefficients.

As mentioned above, the evidence regarding the stability of *AL* scores is at best suggestive. Epstein et al. (1957) used a small, homogeneous group, did not use the actual Rorschach cards, and group-administered the tests. Lucas' (1961) sample was similarly small and homogeneous, and no estimate of degree of relationship is provided for the two administrations. Consequently, the need to demonstrate the stability of *AL* scores over time continues to exist.

[4] Forsyth (1959) has found that anxiety responses occur most often on Cards I and IV, and least often on Cards III and VII. The only actual report of internal consistency is by Elizur (1949); for a group of 30 normal subjects, he found a corrected correlation of .48 between odd and even *responses.*

VALIDITY

Despite the fact that criterion-related validity research—particularly concurrent validity—is completely appropriate in the evaluation of Elizur's anxiety scoring, the large majority of studies are related to the construct validity of the system. This may be due largely to the fact that the content scoring for anxiety, because of the ease with which it can be done, is typically included in studies along with a number of other (Rorschach and non-Rorschach) indices. Consequently, the relationship between *AL* and the experimental groups may not be a direct one—as it would be in the case of a criterion-validity study. The relevance of anxiety to the particular group may instead have to be inferred from theory, thereby placing the study into the construct-validity classification.

After a brief discussion of the available criterion-related validity studies, we shall describe the evidence for the construct validity of the system.

Criterion-Related Validity

It seems clear enough how, perhaps by means of ratings, concurrent criterion groups can be formed to represent varying degrees of anxiety. It is less clear how to go about setting up a criterion group about which *AL* scores can be used to make some prediction—at least if the criterion group must reflect level of anxiety. In fact, the scoring system itself purports to measure how anxious a person is, *not* how anxious he will be. The only research which might remotely qualify for the evaluation of the system's predictive validity are those studies in which the criterion measure is only *indirectly* related to level of anxiety (e.g., course of hospitalization). There is some obvious overlap here with construct validation, and two of the studies which are relevant to both predictive and construct research (Grauer, 1953; Stotsky, 1952) will be discussed under the two validity headings.

Concurrent Validity

The only two studies which are related to the concurrent validity of the system (Elizur, 1949; Stewart, 1950) have both made use of *ratings* in the definition of the criterion groups.

Elizur (1949) interviewed 20 volunteer college students for the purpose of obtaining information regarding anxiety, hostility, dependency, and submissiveness. As Elizur was the only interviewer in this study, the only possible reliability check was on the ratings made from the interview notes; the interjudge reliability for the ratings on each of the four variables was found to be good. Elizur reports that between *AL* and the interview ratings of anxiety, the obtained correlation was .71 ($p < .01$). Considering the size and homogeneity of the group, this finding is quite impressive. Rorschach *AL* was also found to be significantly related to ratings of hostility ($r = .46$, $p < .05$), but not dependency ($r = .23$) or submissiveness ($r = .07$).

Using 112 male patients in a V.A. mental hygiene clinic, Stewart (1950) obtained therapists' ratings of anxiety. The ratings, which were done after the patient had at least eight therapy sessions, were made on the basis of the therapists' observations of verbalized anxiety, anxious behavior, and anxiety-related symptoms. The therapists were predominantly experienced psychiatrists, psychologists, or social workers; no estimate of intrarater or interrater reliability was reported. The obtained relationship between *AL* and a median split of therapists' ratings of anxiety (i.e., high vs. low) was expressed by a phi coefficient of .25 ($p < .01$); from this value, the estimated Pearson r was .39.

In sum, the findings of Elizur (1949) and Stewart (1950) are quite favorable in supporting the concurrent validity of the Rorschach as a measure of anxiety. Further work along these lines is clearly called for, however, especially in light of our discussion above regarding the type of norms which are needed for the clinical application of this system (see p. 126).

Predictive Validity

The Elizur scoring for anxiety has been used to predict length of hospitalization for schizophrenics (Grauer, 1953; Stotsky, 1952), success in psychotherapy (Gallagher, 1954), and—because it was included along with a number of other Rorschach scores—course of illness in tuberculosis patients (Cohen, 1954).

Based on the hypothesis that the higher the level of anxiety in schizophrenics, the greater the likelihood that they are still struggling with their conflicts, Grauer (1953) compared the pretreatment *AL* scores of 18 "improved" and 18 "unimproved" paranoid schizophrenics. Improvement was defined by whether or not the patient remained in the hospital after a series of shock treatments. Although Grauer does not indicate the exact length of hospitalization for the two groups, he does point out that the unimproved group had been transferred to long-term treatment and had been hospitalized twice as long as the improved group. The two groups of patients, all of whom were male, were matched on the basis of age, I.Q., and years of education. Grauer's findings were consistent with his hypothesis, in that the improved group had a significantly higher *AL%*. In a similar study by Stotsky (1952), the admission *AL* scores of remitting schizophrenics were greater than the scores of nonremitting schizophrenics, although the difference failed to reach statistical significance (p between .10 and .20).

Gallagher (1954) attempted to use *AL* as a prognostic indicator for psychotherapy. He compared the pretherapy scores of 15 most successful cases, 15 least successful, and 34 dropouts (after one or two sessions). The subjects were all college students at a university clinic, and the therapist was a graduate student with a client-centered orientation. "Success" was determined by ratings of the therapist, client, and the difference in emotional tone between the first and last session. The median number of sessions for the two groups of remainers was between five and six. The results of the study failed to indicate any difference in *AL* among the three groups.

Cohen (1954), who attempted to use a number of Rorschach scores to predict the course of illness in pulmonary tuberculosis patients, found *AL* to be unrelated to prognosis.

Although some evidence does exist that Elizur's scoring for anxiety has some possibility of estimating length of hospitalization in schizophrenics—at least on a group basis—the prognostic utility of the system per se is of necessity limited. Level of anxiety is only one of the many factors which need to be considered in assessing prognosis. The more appropriate use of *AL* in either its research or clinical application is as a *concurrent measure,* and any predictions made about a subject's future status will have to be inferred from not only currently existing anxiety level, but from whatever other variables might be relevant to that particular type of prediction.

Construct Validity

As mentioned earlier, the majority of validity studies on Elizur's anxiety scoring system are of the construct type. For a few of these studies (e.g., Gorlow et al., 1952; Page, 1957) the precise reason for hypothesizing differences in *AL* between groups is vague, possibly because *AL* was used as just one of a number of measures on which differences were sought.

Nomological Validity

The research on the nomological validity of the anxiety content scoring includes studies involving (1) the relationship between *AL* and symptoms or characteristics believed to be a reflection of anxiety, (2) attempts to bring about change in *AL,* and (3) the prediction of differential performance between groups obtaining different *AL* scores.

RELATION TO SYMPTOMS OR CHARACTERISTICS REFLECTING ANXIETY. Although not all clearly reflect the presence of anxiety, the symptoms and behavioral characteristics to which Rorschach *AL* has been related are as follows: nail biting, teeth grinding, neurosis, psychosis, personality disorders, coronary diseases, delinquency, daydreaming, and academic probation.

Based on the hypothesis that nail biting is at least in part a reflection of anxiety, (Cummings, 1954) tested a group of 70 nail-biting children between the ages of 10 and 14 years. Although it was clearly indicated that they all tended to bite their nails, the children varied as to the severity of nail biting. The obtained correlation between *AL* and severity of nail biting turned out to be low but significant ($r = .28, p < .05$). This correlation might have been somewhat suppressed in that it was based on a relatively homogeneous population (all nail biters); had non-nail biters been used as well, a stronger relationship might have been obtained.

Vernallis (1955) hypothesized that teeth grinders should obtain higher *AL* scores than normal controls, in that this symptomatic behavior was in part indicative of anxiety and tension. Based on a questionnaire distributed to a pool of college students, two groups were formed: 40 teeth grinders and 40 matched controls. Although low, the resulting biserial r with *AL* proved to be statistically significant ($r = .29\ p < .05$).

A comparison between 22 neurotics and 22 normal controls (matched for age, sex, and I.Q.) carried out by Elizur (1949) revealed, as per expectation, that the neurotic subjects obtained significantly higher *AL* scores. Zimet and Brackbill (1956) also studied the relationship of anxiety to diagnosis, but instead chose to test the null hypothesis. Specifically, they predicted that, contrary to traditional notions of diagnosis, psychotics, neurotics, and character disorders would show no difference in Rorschach anxiety level. The obtained *AL* scores for the three groups were practically identical, although considerably lower than the *AL* for the neurotics in Elizur's study (see Table 5.2). Aside from the description on p. 124 of the specific diagnostic categories within each of Zimet and Brackbill's three groups, little else about the sample which might shed light on these discrepancies is reported (e.g., acuteness of disorder, length of hospitalization, etc.). In a replication and extension of the study, Ullmann and Hunrichs (1958) did find that character disorders had higher scores than either neurotics or psychotics, but even more interesting, that neurotics and psychotics who were referred for testing tended to be more anxious than neurotics and psychotics who were tested routinely.

In a study carried out by Cleveland and Johnson (1962), the hypothesis tested was that coronary patients may be characterized as being under a state of chronic tension. In a comparison of hospitalized acute myocardial infarction patients with matched noncoronary patients about to undergo surgery for various other physical disorders, the authors were successful in confirming their prediction.

Although it is not completely evident that adolescent delinquents should necessarily be more anxious than nondelinquents, Gorlow et al. (1952) compared the Rorschach records of 13 delinquents randomly chosen from court files with a group of 13 matched controls. Despite the small N, as well as the fact that the nondelinquents gave more responses on the Rorschach, the delinquent group obtained a significantly higher *AL*.

From a larger pool of college females, Page (1957) selected a group of 20 high and 20 low scorers on a scale measuring the frequency of daydreams. Using the *AL* scores obtained from a group Rorschach, Page found that the higher scores obtained for the more frequent daydreamers failed to reach statistical significance ($p < .10$). It would seem unlikely, however, that daydreaming per se should be related to anxiety level. Instead, one would expect that the particular *content* of the daydreams should bear some relationship to *AL*. For example, higher anxiety scores may be anticipated for those whose daydreams are phobic in nature. A follow up of Page's study, classifying daydreams (or even ordinary dreams) according to content, would provide a more relevant test of the system's construct validity.

Based on the assumption that academic difficulty in college is in part a function of emotional problems, Lit (1956) attempted to relate Rorschach anxiety level to academic achievement. The anxiety scores of probation students failed to differ significantly from the scores obtained by a group of dean's list students matched on the basis of age, sex, class, and scholastic aptitude. An obvious difficulty with this study is that only the two extremes were compared, both of which might be composed of students who are very anxious—although for different reasons. The inclusion of a group of "average" students would have provided a better test of the hypothesis.

Although the results of studies described above are not uniformly favorable to the validity of Elizur's scoring for anxiety, not all of these studies have provided good tests of the system's construct validity; the legitimacy of the hypothesis in many of these studies may be called into question.

The negative results obtained by comparing probational students with dean's list students and frequent daydreamers with infrequent daydreamers are not too surprising, in that there is no good theoretical reason for expecting these groups to differ. Even though adolescent delinquents were in fact found to have higher *AL* scores than nondelinquents, the reasons for this predicted difference are not completely evident. In considering the study by Zimet and Brackbill (1956), which compared psychotics, neurotics, and personality disorders, it is not very clear whether the evidence can be said to be *for* or *against* the validity of Elizur's system. On the one hand, the authors have actually *confirmed* their hypothesis that the three groups would not differ in their *AL* scores. On the other hand—apart from the fact that their test of the null hypothesis is questionable methodologically—Zimet and Brackbill acknowledge that their hypothesis was contrary to traditional expectation. Depending on whose hypothesis one is willing to accept—Zimet and Brackbill's or traditional—the results of the study may be taken as contributing either favorably or unfavorably to the construct validity of the scoring system. The finding of Ullmann and Hunrichs (1958) that patients referred for testing—presumably because of complications regarding status or diagnosis—obtain higher *AL* scores than those patients who are tested routinely, however, may be interpreted as offering some support for the anxiety scoring.

The hypothesis that nail biting is a behavioral manifestation of anxiety is considerably clearer, and has been confirmed with the use of Rorschach *AL* scores. The view of teeth grinding as a manifestation of anxiety has similarly been successfully tested by means of the Rorschach. Further, the relatively well-accepted hypotheses that neurotics tend to be more anxious than normals, and that coronary patients are more tense than noncoronary patients, have been borne out with the scoring system.

It would appear, then, that for those studies which have provided a poor or ambiguous test of the construct validity of the anxiety scoring, the results have been negative. However, for those studies in which the symptoms or behavioral characteristics investigated have a clearer theoretical relationship to the construct of anxiety, the findings have reflected more favorably on the validity of the scoring system.

Induction of Changes in *AL*. Several attempts have been made to induce changes—a decrement as well as an increment—in the subject's anxiety level on the Rorschach. The specific approaches have involved carbon dioxide treatment, examiner differences, experimentally induced "frustration stress," and the elimination of color and shading in the blots.

Lebo, Toal, and Brick (1960) selected a group of 24 male prisoners from those inmates who were referred to the prison psychiatrist; the predominant symptom in all cases had been anxiety. The experimental group consisted of 12 patients who were given carbon dioxide treatment; the number of treatments ranged from 14 to 22, with a mean of 19.2. The control group was matched on the basis of age, I.Q., and length of institutionalization. Although Lebo et al. mention that the interval between the two administrations of the Rorschach was the same for both groups, the actual time between the two testings is not specified. Using a one-tailed test, a significant ($p < .05$) decrease in *AL*% was found for the experimental group between the two administrations. The pre-post difference for the control group was not significant with a two-tailed test, but would have been significant at the .05 level had a one-tailed test been used as well. The controversy concerning the appropriateness of one-tailed tests notwithstanding (Eysenck, 1960; Goldfried, 1959), it is clear that the decrement in the experimental group cannot be attributed legitimately to the carbon dioxide treatment. In light of other findings (Kates and Schwartz, 1958; Lucas, 1961) indicating no change in pre-post *AL* for control subjects, it does not seem likely that the decrement in the control subjects of Lebo et al.—which admittedly reached significance only with a one-tailed test—was simply a function of the time between the two administrations. Perhaps something akin to the "Hawthorne effect" was operating in the study by Lebo et al., whereby the anxiety level of the patients was somewhat alleviated by the attention they received (i.e., having been referred to the prison psychiatrist and given the Rorschach). This interpretation is admittedly speculative.

Sanders and Cleveland (1953) studied the effect of the examiners' own anxiety and hostility level on the Rorschach *AL* scores of subjects. Nine graduate students were themselves given the Rorschach, after which they each administered it to 30 undergraduates. Each of the 270 undergraduates was asked to rate his examiner at the end of the testing with regard to his anxiety and hostility; these ratings were used as estimates of the examiners' *overt* levels of anxiety and hostility. The examiners' *covert* levels of anxiety and hostility were based on their own Rorschach *AL* and *HL*[5] scores, respectively. The results of this study indicated that the subjects' *AL* scores were not related to either the level of anxiety or hostility (overt and covert) of the examiner. These findings in themselves cannot be taken as conclusive evidence against the effect of the examiner's personality characteristics on the subject's obtained *AL* score, especially in light of some of the shortcomings of this study, which were mentioned in connection with the evaluation of Elizur's hostility scoring system (e.g., an adequate sampling of subjects and examiners was not used). For a more complete discussion of the difficulties inherent in this study, the reader is referred to Chapter 4, pp. 108–110.

As part of a study to test the effect of frustration on Rorschach hostility level, Lucas (1961) scored the protocols of two groups of 9-year-olds for *AL* as well. Neither the group which was frustrated (failure on a task and depreciation by the examiner) nor the control group showed any change in *AL* between the two Rorschach testings. Kates and Schwartz (1958) used two small groups of college students in a similar study, presenting the "stress" to the experimental group by means of written descrip-

[5] See Chapter 4.

tions of their poor adjustment; this negative description was said to have been based on their initial testing. The Rorschach and the Behn–Rorschach administrations were counterbalanced within both groups, with a one- to two-week interval between testings. The findings revealed no change in *AL* for either the experimental or control group. Although the purpose of the study presumably was to increase *AL* as a function of this "self-esteem stress," one might also have predicted a *decrease* in *AL* for the experimental group; inasmuch as these subjects had done poorly during the first testing, this was a chance for them to look healthier. The temptation to use these findings as evidence against situational influences (either "stress" or "faking good") on obtained *AL* scores should be tempered somewhat by the fact that only 12 subjects were used in each of the two groups.

Forsyth (1959) was interested in studying the effect of color and shading on *AL,* and made use of three different sets of Rorschach cards, each of which was administered to separate groups of 30 subjects each. In addition to the standard set, Forsyth used achromatic (no color) and silhouette (no shading) sets; these two experimental sets of cards were exactly the same as the Rorschach blots, except for the variables of color and shading, respectively. The results indicated that neither color nor shading influenced the *AL* scores obtained.

According to our earlier conceptualization of what *AL* purports to reflect, "anxiety" was defined as the general characteristic of insecurity which was more of a personality "trait" than a reaction to some specific stressful situation (i.e., "state"). Consequently, attempts to induce changes in *AL* by means of some short-term, experimental manipulations should not prove to be very successful. As described above, the studies which attempted to alter *AL* by means of carbon dioxide treatment, variations in the examiner's anxiety and hostility levels, mild "stress" in the form of personal depreciation, and variations in the color and shading of the blots have all yielded negative results. As the inability to bring about changes in *AL* might have been a function of methodological weaknesses in the studies, the interpretation of these findings as providing evidence for the stability of the *AL* score should be made with caution.

DIFFERENTIAL PERFORMANCE BETWEEN GROUPS AT DIFFERENT ANXIETY LEVELS. Rorschach *AL* has been used to predict recovery among schizophrenics and to estimate performance decrement under stress. Although the studies by Grauer and Stotsky have already been discussed in connection with the predictive validity of the system, they will again be mentioned here briefly because of their relevance to construct validity.

Grauer (1953) hypothesized that the presence of anxiety in hospitalized schizophrenics was a reflection of their continuing struggle with their conflicts; hence, these patients should have a better prognosis than patients for whom less anxiety is present. This hypothesis was confirmed, in that discharged paranoid schizophrenics showed a significantly higher admission *AL%* than long-term patients. Stotsky (1952) also found remitting schizophrenics to have had higher *AL* scores upon admission than nonremitting schizophrenics, although the obtained difference only "approached" statistical significance (p between .10 and .20).

Westrope (1953) set out to determine whether or not *AL* reflected the extent to which a performance decrement would occur under conditions of stress. Specifically, she hypothesized that in comparison to subjects obtaining lower *AL* scores, subjects with higher scores would show greater impairment in their digit symbol performance as a function of stress; the obtained nonsignificant Pearson *r* of .15 between *AL* and performance decrement failed to confirm this hypothesis. Although the hypothesis seems fair enough —more insecure individuals are more easily affected by stress—there is some doubt that the test of it was adequate. The experimental induction of "stress" seems to have been sufficient, in that subjects were told that their performance on some earlier task had been poor, that they were being observed by psychologists, and that they could expect shock at almost any time. The deficiency in the study was with respect to the subjects used. In line with the primary purpose of her study, Westrope originally selected 24 high- and 24 low-anxiety scorers on the Taylor Manifest Anxiety Scale. Inasmuch as she found that the Taylor scores in her sample were not related to *AL scores,*[6] however, the group of 48 subjects did not actually include those individuals who obtained scores at the extremes of an *AL* distribution. In fact, relative to the findings reported in other studies, the mean *AL* was somewhat *high* for even the low Taylor scorers (see Table 5.2). Had subjects constituting the high and low points on the *AL* distribution been used, rather than the more homogeneous sample that actually was used, the findings of the study might have been different.

Trait Validity

This section will cover those studies in which Rorschach *AL* has been related to (1) self-ratings of anxiety, (2) other anxiety measures, and (3) nonanxiety measures.

Relation to Self-Ratings. The only attempt to relate *AL* to self-ratings was carried out by Elizur (1949), who had a group of 30 volunteers complete a self-administered "questionnaire" and a set of "self-ratings." In the questionnaire, subjects were asked to rate themselves on 55 items, which were either directly or indirectly related to personality characteristics indicative of anxiety, hostility, or both. For the self-ratings, the emphasis was on the subjects' felt *need to control* their anxiety-related feelings, dependency wishes, depressive moods, tendencies to succumb, and feelings of hostility toward others.

The correlations between *AL* and the data from both the questionnaire and self-ratings are indicated in Table 5.3. The left side of the table depicts the results for the anxiety-related characteristics, directly below shows the findings for the hostility-related characteristics, and the bottom presents the relationship between *AL* and those characteristics believed to reflect both anxiety and hostility. With the exception of general shyness, all anxiety-related characteristics were found to correlate significantly with *AL*. Similarly, Rorschach *AL* correlated with all those characteristics pre-

[6] See pp. 137–138 for a more full discussion of the relationship between *AL* and the Taylor scale.

TABLE 5.3
Correlations Between *AL* and Various Personality Characteristics of 30 Normal Volunteers as Determined by Questionnaires and Self-Ratings (after Elizur, 1949)

Anxiety Characteristics	*Correlation with AL*
Questionnaire on Anxiety	
Fears and Phobias	.58[a]
Lack of Self-confidence	.39[b]
Both Items Combined	.61[a]
Self-ratings on Control of Anxiety	
Fear	.39[b]
Worry	.42[b]
General Shyness	.17
Sexual Shyness	.46[a]
Feelings of Inferiority	.52[a]
All Items Combined	.52[a]
Questionnaire on Dependency	.57[a]
Self-ratings on Control of Dependency Wishes	.73[a]
Hostility Characteristics	*Correlation with AL*
Questionnaire on Hostility	
Self-blame	.19
Subject Regarded as Good Natured	−.29
Subject Was a "Goody-Goody" Child	−.06
Subject Believes That People Are Hostile	.22
Subject Believes That People Are Selffish	.06
All Items Combined	−.02
Self-ratings on Control of Hostility Toward Others	
Friends	.18
Members of the Family	.03
Minority Groups	.15
All Items Combined	.16
Questionnaire on Submissiveness	.33
Self-ratings on Control of Tendency to Succumb	.05
Questionnaire on Aloofness	.31
Characteristics Reflecting both Anxiety and Hostility	*Correlation with AL*
Questionnaire on Ideas of Reference	.50[a]
Questionnaire on Depression	.54[a]
Self-rating on Control of Depressive Moods	.50[a]

[a] Significant at the .01 level.
[b] Significant at the .05 level.

sumably reflecting both anxiety and hostility. In line with Campbell and Fiske's (1959) notion of a multitrait-multimethod approach to validation (i.e., a test should not only correlate with those traits it purports to measure, but should also *fail* to correlate with characteristics it does *not* purport to measure), none of the correlations with the hostility-related characteristics proved to be significant.

There is one further finding in support of the scoring system. In light of the high correlations with self-report measures, it might be argued that—despite the validity of the Rorschach as a measure of anxiety—these self-administered techniques are the more efficient and economical measures to use. After all, why should one bother to administer and score a Rorschach if the subject himself is willing to give you the information upon request? However, if one is willing to accept detailed interviews with 20 of these same subjects as an appropriate criterion, then the Rorschach turns out to be a better estimate of anxiety than the paper-and-pencil measures (Elizur, 1949). The correlation between *AL* and the interview ratings of anxiety was found to be .71 ($p < .01$), while the respective self-rating and questionnaire correlations of .36 and .38 failed to reach statistical significance.

RELATION TO OTHER ANXIETY MEASURES. A number of attempts have been made to relate Rorschach *AL* to other measures of anxiety. The most frequent attempt by far has been the study of the relationship between *AL* and the Taylor Manifest Anxiety Scale. Other anxiety measures to which *AL* has been related have been based on other MMPI scores, the multiple-choice TAT, and the Draw-A-Person.

Among psychiatric patients, Goodstein and Goldberger (1955) found that in comparison to 16 subjects who achieved a low score on the Taylor Manifest Anxiety Scale (MAS), 16 high scorers obtained a higher *AL%* ($p < .04$ with a one-tailed test); the two groups did not differ in total R. On the other hand, Mogar (1962), who used 123 patients at all MAS levels, found a nonsignificant correlation of .07 with *AL%*. For college students, the findings are somewhat conflicting, although largely negative. Goodstein (1954) obtained a correlation of .38 ($p < .01$) between *AL* and MAS for a group of 57 college students; even with total R partialed out, the r remained significant ($r = .36$, $p < .01$). Westrope (1953), who used 24 high- and 24 low-MAS subjects, found a significant difference in the predicted direction until she partialed out total R; with the control for R, the difference could only be interpreted as a chance fluctuation. Other studies (Forsyth, 1959; Kates and Schwartz, 1958) similarly failed to obtain any relationship between *AL* and MAS.

On theoretical grounds, one cannot find any good reason why *AL* and MAS should *not* be related. Sarason (1960) and Kimble and Posnick (1967) have pointed out that the type of "anxiety" that the MAS purports to measure refers to neurotic tendencies, general maladjustment, and self-dissatisfaction—which is quite similar to the trait conception of anxiety we have presented in connection with Rorschach *AL*. One may argue, however, that what is revealed by the MAS are these obvious and clearcut manifestations of anxiety which the subject is willing to admit upon direct questioning. The anxiety being measured by the Rorschach, on the other hand, although within the subject's conscious awareness, is manifested indirectly and more subtly, and is not as easily confounded by conscious control and social desirability factors. This interpretation is admittedly hypothetical, but one which is open to empirical verification.

Zimet and Brackbill (1956) correlated *AL* with estimates of anxiety obtained from the MMPI. They found that for a group of 97 psychiatric patients, the relationship between *AL* and both Welsh's anxiety index and Pt (uncorrected for K) was low but significant (*r* of .25 and .21, respectively). Within a smaller group of normal subjects (N = 30), however, Forsyth (1959) failed to obtain any relationship to Welsh's A scale on the MMPI.

Using a multiple-choice TAT with anxiety, hostility, achievement, and blandness as the four alternatives, Goodstein (1954) found no relationship to the *AL* scores achieved by a group of college students.

The only attempt to relate Rorschach *AL* to a measure of anxiety obtained from another projective test (a multiple-choice TAT would not really qualify as being a projective method in the usual sense) has been Mogar's (1962) study with the Draw-A-Person (DAP). Mogar employed the 12 reliably scored DAP indices of anxiety formulated by Hoyt and Baron (1959) and related each index to the *AL* scores of 123 psychiatric patients. Of the point biserial correlations obtained for the 12 dichotomous DAP indices, three were significant at the .01 level ($r = -.31$ for reinforcement, $r = .26$ for smallness of size, and $r = .24$ for overestimation of head size relative to figure), one at the .05 level ($r = .18$ for omissions), and one at the .10 level ($r = .14$ for hair shading). Rorschach *AL* did not relate to the DAP indices of placement, type of line (faint), shading, erasing, size of head, body area out of proportion, and size 1:2.

With the exception of anxiety estimated from the DAP, measures of anxiety obtained from the MAS, MMPI, and multiple-choice TAT do not seem to be related to Rorschach *AL*. As these paper-and-pencil measures of anxiety are probably more susceptible to faking and social desirability influences, "set" studies with the Rorschach—that is, effects of conscious dissimulation on obtained *AL*—are needed to determine whether or not these failures to obtain consistencies between measures are in fact a function of the subject's conscious control. The relative absence of attempts to relate Rorschach *AL* to other projective measures of anxiety (e.g., TAT) is somewhat surprising, and studies of this type are clearly needed in order to establish the trait validity of the Elizur anxiety scoring system.

RELATION TO NONANXIETY MEASURES. The only two nonanxiety measures to which *AL* has been related have been Rorschach hostility level and I.Q.

The precise hypothetical relationship between anxiety and hostility is not at all clear. Although certain people are undoubtedly made anxious by their hostile feelings, others are not (cf. Rosenwald, 1961). Conversely, it is possible for a person to be anxious for reasons which have little or nothing to do with hostility. The findings of studies relating Rorschach *AL* and Rorschach hostility level (*HL*) have been found to differ, depending upon the composition of the sample. For a group of 270 college students who volunteered for testing, Sanders and Cleveland (1953) found a .52 correlation between *AL* and Rorschach *HL*. Although Elizur (1949) failed to obtain significant correlations between *AL* and *HL* within groups of, respectively, normal volunteers, neurotics, and matched controls, the correlation for the three groups combined reached a significant value of .27 ($p < .05$). For a group of 70 nail-biting children (Cummings, 1954) and 57 college students (Goodstein, 1954), the correlations were virtually zero ($r = .04$ and $.07$, respectively).

No relationship was found between I.Q. and *AL* within a sample of 22 neurotics and 22 normals (Elizur, 1949). Unfortunately, the size and homogeneity of these two groups do not provide a fair test of the correlation between *AL* and I.Q.

OVERALL EVALUATION

The concept of anxiety, as it is reflected in Elizur's scoring of the Rorschach, refers to an experienced, more or less long-term personality characteristic of an individual (i.e., trait anxiety), rather than a relatively transitory reaction to a stressful situation (i.e., state anxiety). Further, our discussion of the construct has referred only to the degree or level of anxiety, and not to the way in which it is expressed or reduced; to assess how an individual will cope with his anxiety, information regarding his defensive style is needed.

The general format of the Elizur scoring for anxiety level (*AL*) is much like the scoring for Rorschach hostility level outlined in Chapter 4. Thus, only the content of the response is used, regardless of card or location. The scoring criteria, which are easily learned and reliably applied, are based on the degree or obviousness of the anxiety revealed in the response. Because *AL* has been found to correlate with R—the longer the protocol, the higher the *AL*—the score used to summarize a protocol should more appropriately be expressed as a proportion to total R (i.e., *AL*/R).

Inasmuch as the type of anxiety which the Elizur scoring purports to measure is more of a relatively stable personality trait, some indication of the test-retest reliability of *AL* is quite in order. Unfortunately, no really good assessment of the stability of *AL* over time has been made as yet. Although the stability of *AL* remains an open question, it might be noted here that a number of experimental manipulations (e.g., self-esteem "stress") have failed to bring about any change in *AL*.

A good deal of research related to the validity of the scoring system has been carried out. Possibly because the scoring of a record for *AL* can be accomplished quite easily, the hypotheses in some of the construct-validity research are not as clearly relevant to the concept of anxiety as they might be. For most of those studies in which the test of validity seems appropriate, however, the findings have been shown to be favorable. Thus, Rorschach *AL* has been found to be positively related to ratings of anxiety (based on interviews or therapy sessions), nail biting in children, and teeth grinding in adults. *AL* scores have been noted to be high in the case of neurotics, adolescent delinquents, coronary patients, and psychiatric patients who present diagnostic problems. Further, in contrast to nonremitting schizophrenics, the admission *AL* scores of remitting schizophrenics have been found to be greater. Rorschach *AL*, on the other hand, has shown little or no relationship to frequency of daydreaming, academic probation, or differential diagnosis among psychotics, neurotics, and character disorders.

In addition, the evidence has been unfavorable for the prognostic use of *AL* as an indicator of success in therapy for college students, or recovery from illness for tuberculosis patients.

Anxiety level has correlated well with normal subjects' self-ratings of characteristics believed to be related to anxiety, but not of those characteristics reflecting only hostility. In addition, using an interviewer's estimate of anxiety as the criterion measure, *AL* proved to be a better measure than did self-ratings. The existing evidence on the relationship between *AL* and Rorschach hostility level is not clear cut, with much depending on the heterogeneity of the group on which the test has been made. The only test of the relationship between *AL* and anxiety estimates from other projective tests has been carried out with the Draw-A-Person; the results of this study were found to be favorable. Further studies relating Rorschach *AL* to various other projective measures are needed. The attempts to relate *AL* to a paper-and-pencil measure of anxiety, such as the Taylor Manifest Anxiety Scale, and to a multiple-choice form of the TAT, indicate that these other instruments are not measuring the same thing. One may assume that these discrepant findings are due to the greater "fakability" of the paper-and-pencil measures, a hypothesis which can be tested by comparing the effect of instructional set (to fake "good" or "bad") on Rorschach *AL* relative to these other anxiety measures.

Normative data on *AL,* essential for the clinical application of the scoring system, is quite minimal. The available data are based on the means and standard deviations reported in connection with various research findings; no actual normative studies have been conducted. As the presence of anxiety per se does not necessarily imply a given diagnosis, it would appear that the need is not so much for data on different diagnostic groups as it is for individuals at different, carefully rated levels of anxiety. However, the correlations of .71 and .39 which have already been reported between *AL* and judge's ratings of anxiety would suggest that a fair amount of overlap among these differently rated anxiety levels may be expected. Even if Rorschach *AL* should be shown to lack the precision needed for idiographic application—an issue that is discussed in Chapter 13—its value as a research measure of anxiety would nonetheless remain.

Chapter 6

BODY-IMAGE BOUNDARY SCORING

The concept of body image has found a significant place in the formulations about personality both by theorists who emphasize the importance of early experience and by those who stress the impact of the current situation. Whether the discussion centers about the infant trying to separate himself from the external world and learning what is part of him and what belongs to others, or whether it is concerned with the existential immediacy of current situations, body image is of crucial importance.

Fisher and Cleveland (1958b) have devised a system for scoring the Rorschach in a manner they feel sheds light on the individual's body image. Particularly, the system attempts to describe the body boundaries according to whether they are "firm" and "substantial," or, on the other hand, "weak" and easily "penetrable." This chapter describes the scoring system, presents normative data and some limited information about reliability, and then discusses a large number of validity studies which the system has generated.

BODY-IMAGE BOUNDARY CONSTRUCT

Fisher and Cleveland's interest in the body-image boundary dimension began with their study of the personality of patients with rheumatoid arthritis (Fisher and Cleveland, 1955). At that time, they noted that the Rorschach responses of these patients were characterized by a number of unusual references to the boundary qualities of the percepts. From these observations they developed a scoring system for the Barrier quality of Rorschach responses. Initially this Barrier quality seemed to have been somewhat negative, in that the implication was that these patients were rigid both in their personality patterns and in their conception of their body.

However, this negative implication very quickly dropped out and theorizing about the high Barrier person has become quite positive. The theoretical system sees an individual's body image as being a reflection of the type of object relations he has been able to establish. That is, people with high Barrier scores are seen as having formed substantial images of their own bodies and as being capable of dealing with others from this locus of a firm, well-integrated self-image. Being secure within their own home base, so to speak, they are able to deal with people and situations in a commanding, well-integrated, and effective manner. Conversely, those individuals with lowered Barrier scores are seen as having infirm, easily penetrable body images, and, as a result, deal with others from this weakened position.

The physical referent for an individual's conception of his body-image boundary is not clearly specified, but it is seen as usually being identified with his body wall. However, exceptions to this location at the body wall can be cited in the cases of individuals in early stages of development or acting under a variety of pathological syndromes. Since the individual's body image corresponds only roughly to the body wall, and since it includes a number of explicit and implicit attitudes, it is not seen as being consistently related to any physical characteristics of the individual. It is stable after it has become developed and not easily changeable despite changes in the physical appearance of the individual.

Although the concept is developed in body terms, it seems more clearly to be a theory of personality development rather than a theory of body development, in that the role of the body is seen as important only in the way it mirrors significant developmental experiences. Thus, although the concept arose from the study of physically ill individuals, a number of hypotheses were tested with patients with psychosomatic disorders, and a number of studies have concerned body images of the subjects directly, the later developments in the theorizing having almost served to take the body out of body image; at some points, it is difficult to distinguish between body boundaries and ego boundaries, or between body image and self-concept.

Although the theorizing about the individual has left the body far in the background, there also has been a tendency to collect physiological data and to relate particular patterns of physiological responsivity to the body-image boundary concept. A rather elaborate theory of physiological reactivity has been stated by Fisher and Cleveland (1957). They hypothesize that individuals with clear and definite body-image boundaries are predominantly reactive in the outer body layers and less reactive within the body interior; on the other hand, those individuals who are characterized by more weak and indefinite boundaries exhibit the converse pattern (with reactivity being particularly high in the body interior and much less pronounced at the body exterior). The body exterior in this theory includes the skin, the striate musculature, and the vascular components of these two systems; the body interior, on the other hand, includes all of the internal viscera. Although this division is not one of a common or easily recognizable differentiation of the nervous system, it does serve to distinguish roughly between those areas which are under voluntary and conscious control, and those which are more clearly within the realm of involuntary response. Hence, individuals who have more firm and definite body-image boundaries are more capable of responding voluntarily and mastering a situation, whereas those of more indefinite boundaries are more passive recipients of stimulation, with their predominant response being involuntary and interior. There have been a number of studies which have tested this particular theory, and there also have been a number of studies with a variety of psychosomatic patients which have stemmed from the hypothesis that excitation is centered in the body exterior for the person with firm body boundaries, and in the body interior for persons with weak body boundaries.

Aside from the physical and physiological characteristics of the person with well-developed body boundaries, there also is a personality constellation which Fisher and Cleveland have identified with such an individual. This model sees the person with well-developed boundaries as being self-steering; that is, the definiteness of his boundaries is presumed to be directly related to his ability to function as an independent person, with clear and definite standards and goals. He approaches tasks in a forceful manner, is not easily frustrated, and expresses himself through actively dealing with the environment in an attempt to make it conform to his own wishes. The person of less clearly defined body boundaries is seen as possessing the opposite of these characteristics in that he is more passive, more easily suggestible, and more easily frustrated. Rather than attacking the environment and making it conform to his wishes, he is more likely to allow the environment to shape him and to be passive in the face of external stimulation.

The concepts which have been defined above are related principally to a single score—the Barrier score—in the Fisher–Cleveland scoring system. There is also a second score, the Penetration of Boundary score, a dimension that was initially conceptualized as reflecting the personal vulnerability the individual might feel. Theoretically, this dimension was seen as being the opposite of the Barrier dimension and predictably should have been highly negatively correlated with the Barrier dimension. This has not proven to be so, and most of the research and most of the theorizing have centered upon the Barrier concept, with the Penetration of Boundary concept having been dropped by the wayside.

THE BODY-IMAGE BOUNDARY SCORING SYSTEM

There are two basic scores which are arrived at in the body-image boundary scoring system. One score is called the *Barrier* score, reflecting responses which focus on the definiteness of the structure or surface qualities of the percept. The second score is called the *Penetration of Boundary* score, and emphasizes the weakness, lack of substance, and penetrability of the percept's boundaries. These scores are derived exclusively from the content of the responses, independent of whether that content is elicited in the free association or in the inquiry.

Fisher and Cleveland's specific criteria for scoring for Barrier and Penetration of Boundary are described below.[1]

Scoring Criteria

Barrier Score

There are a number of different categories in which responses may qualify for a Barrier score. They are as follows:

1. ARTICLES OF CLOTHING. The Barrier score is also applied if the articles of clothing are worn by animals and birds. If the clothing is being worn by a person, however, it is scored only if it is unusual in its covering or decorative function. Note the examples of clothing being worn by humans that are scored as Barrier responses:

Woman in a high-necked dress	Imp with a cap that has a tassel on it
Person in a fancy costume	People with mittens or gloves
Woman in a long nightdress	People with hoods
Man with a crown	Feet with fancy red socks
Man in coat with a lace collar	Man with a cook's hat
Man in a robe	Man with chaps

Man with a high collar

The popular boots on Card IV, and the bowtie on Card III are not scored as clothing because of the frequency with which they are given.

Examples of clothing being worn which are *not scored:*

Woman in a dress　　Man with a hot

Man with a coat on

2. ANIMALS WITH DISTINCTIVE OR UNUSUAL SKINS. The response is scored only if more than the head of the animal is given. This category of response was included on the assumption that concern with animals having unusual, valued, specially marked, or specially protective skins represents a focus on some aspect of the substantiality of covering surfaces. The following is a complete list of such animals:

Alligator	Fox	Lynx	Prairie dog	Skunk
Badger	Goat	Mink	Rhinoceros	Tiger
Beaver	Hippo	Mole	Scorpion	Walrus
Bobcat	Hyena	Mountain goat	Sea lion	Weasel
Chameleon	Leopard	Peacock	Seal	Wildcat
Coyote	Lion	Penguin	Sheep or lamb	Wolverine
Crocodile	Lizard	Porcupine	Siamese cat	Zebra

[1] Except for minor changes in wording and organization, the scoring criteria are reprinted from *Body Image and Personality* by Seymour Fisher and Sidney E. Cleveland, Copyright © 1958, by Litton Educational Publishing, Inc., by permission of Van Nostrand Reinhold Company.

Any animal skin (except "bearskin" on Card IV) may be considered Barrier if unusual emphasis is placed on the *textured, fuzzy, mottled,* or *striped* character of the surface. Examples include "fuzzy skin," "skin with spots," "skin with stripes."

Included in this general covering category are *all shelled creatures except crabs and lobsters.* "Crabs" and "lobsters" are excluded because of their frequency of occurrence. Lobsters and crabs are scored only in the unusual instances in which the shell alone is seen. Examples of shelled creatures:

Snail
Mussel
Shrimp
Clam
Turtle

3. Enclosed Openings in the Earth. Examples include:

Valley
Ravine
Mine shaft
Well
Canal

4. Unusual Animal Containers. Examples include:

Bloated cat
Pregnant woman
Kangaroo
Udder

5. Overhanging or Protective Surfaces. Examples include:

Umbrella
Awning
Dome
Shield

6. Armored or Protectively Walled Things. Examples include:

Tank
Battleship
Rocket ship in space
Armored car
Man in armor

7. Covered, Surrounded, or Concealed Things. Examples include:

Bowl overgrown by a plant
House surrounded by smoke
Log covered by moss
Person behind a tree
Man covered with a blanket
Person hidden by something
Someone peeking out from behind a stone
Donkey with load covering his back
Person caught between two stones

8. Objects Having Unusual Containerlike Shapes or Properties. Examples include:

Bagpipes
Throne
Ferris wheel
Chair

9. Do Not Score Masks or Buildings. There are, however, a few exceptional instances in which unique structures are scored. The following are the exceptions:

Quonset hut	Tent
Igloo	Arch
Fort	

10. Do Not Score Instruments Which Grasp or Hold. Examples include:

Pliers	Tongs
Tweezers	

11. Additional General Examples of Barrier Responses.

Basket	Cove	Lake surrounded by land
Bay	Curtain	Land surrounded by water
Bell	Dancer with veil	Mountain covered with snow
Book	Frosting on cake	Net
Book ends	Fuzzy poodle	Pot
Bottle	Globe	River
Bubble	Harbor	Screen
Cage	Headdress	Spoon
Candleholder	Hedge along a walk	Urn
Cave	Helmet	Wall
Cocoon	Inlet	Wallpaper
	Wig	

Penetration of Boundary Score

An individual's feeling that his body exterior is of little protective value and can be easily penetrated is believed to be expressed in his Rorschach responses in three general ways:

1. In terms of images that involve the *penetration, disruption, or wearing away of the outer surfaces of things.* The following Rorschach responses are illustrations of such images: "bullet penerating flesh," "shell of a turtle that has been broken open," "squashed bug," "badly worn-away animal skin."
2. In terms of images that emphasize *modes or channels* for getting into the interior of things or for passing from the interior to the exterior. Some examples are "vagina," "anus," "open mouth," "an entrance," "doorway."
3. In terms of images that involve the surfaces of things as being *easily permeable or fragile.* The following are examples: "soft ball of cotton candy," "fleecy fluffy cloud," "mud that you can step through."

The following is an enumeration of the more specific subcategories of Penetration of Boundary responses:

1. Mouth Being Opened or Being Used for Intake or Expulsion. Examples include:

- Dog eating
- Dog yawning
- Man sticking tongue out
- Man vomiting
- Boy spitting
- Person with mouth open
- Animal drinking

Do *not* score references to use of the mouth for singing or talking.

2. Evading, Bypassing, or Penetrating through the Exterior of an Object and Getting to the Interior. Examples include:

- X-ray picture
- Body as seen through a fluoroscope
- Cross section of an organ
- Body cut open
- Inside of the body
- Autopsy

3. Body Wall Being Broken, Fractured, Injured, and Damaged. Examples include:

- Mashed bug
- Wounded man
- Person bleeding
- Wound
- Man stabbed
- Man's skin stripped off

Do *not* score instances in which simple loss of a body member has occurred (e.g., amputation, head cut off) unless there is a description of concomitant bleeding.

Another subvariety of this category includes responses involving some kind of degeneration of surfaces. Examples include:

- Withering skin
- Diseased skin
- Withered leaf
- Deteriorating flesh

4. Openings in the Earth That Have No Set Boundaries or from Which Things Are Being Expelled. Examples include:

- Bottomless abyss
- Fountain shooting up
- Geyser spurting out of ground
- Oil gusher coming in

5. All Openings. Examples include:

- Anus
- Birth canal
- Doorway
- Entrance
- Looking into the throat
- Nostril
- Rectum
- Vagina
- Window

6. Things Which Are Insubstantial and without Palpable Boundaries. Examples include:

- Cotton candy
- Ghost
- Shadow
- Soft mud

7. Transparencies. Examples include:

Can see through the dress
Transparent window

8. Further General Examples of Penetration of Boundary Responses Include:

Animal chewing on a tree	Bat with holes
Broken-up butterfly	Torn fur coat
Jigsaw not put together	Frayed wings
Doorway	Deteriorated wings
Fish with meat taken off	Grasshopper pecking at something
Broken body	Harbor entrance

Man defecating

Any single response can be scored only once as Barrier and once as Penetration even though it might qualify under a number of different subcategories. However, any response may be scored *both* as Barrier and as Penetration of Boundary. Responses such as "man with broken armor," "bombed battleship," and "broken bottles" contain both references to unusual protective or containing properties which would qualify them as Barrier responses, and also references to disrupted boundaries which would qualify them as Penetration responses.

Summary Scores

In summarizing any given Rorschach record, the total number of responses falling into each of the Barrier and Penetration categories is compiled. Each response is given a value of 1, and the final Barrier (*B*) and Penetration (*P*) are arrived at by simply totaling the number of responses in each of the two categories, respectively.

It should be noted that this system is presented in an abbreviated and slightly different form in the original monograph (Fisher and Cleveland, 1955), and that earlier scoring system provided the basis for many early studies. In the earlier report, *B* was scored for images referring to containers, enclosed spaces, and hard boundary surfaces, and also where the percept involved covering over or concealment of one thing by another. *P* was scored according to the same criteria in both reports, but the earlier version is described in less detail.

An approach to constructing a content-analysis index similar to *P* has been presented by Cassell (1964). He refers to his index as a body interior awareness index and recognizes it as having the same properties as were originally intended for *P*. A body interior score is given for each Rorschach response which contains a reference to the interior of the body, to openings in the body interior, or to breaks in the body surface. This represents a modification of *P* scoring by eliminating responses which reflect body boundary indefiniteness and adding references to internal organs. Cassell gave a group Rorschach with total R set at 25 to a group of 185 undergraduate students and scored the protocols for both *B* and body interior awareness dimensions. On the body interior measure, low-*B Ss* scored higher than high-*B Ss* ($p < .001$). No correlation is given between the two measures, but it would appear from these data that the correlation would be high and negative. Cassell claims that the two indices are independent, but with response total limited and no double scoring allowed, a negative correlation may be built in. Aside from this original study by Cassell, there is no evidence that his body interior awareness index has been used. It would seem initially that this would be worth some investigation, and could be scored in studies where *P* might originally have been scored, and might prove, upon further investigation, to be a valuable complement to *B* scoring.

THE EFFECT OF R. There is a very clear relationship between both *B* and *P* and the number of responses given in the Rorschach record. As might be expected, *Ss* producing more responses tend to produce more *B*, and also more *P*. Although there are no other relationships between *P* and other Rorschach variables, the situation is somewhat complicated in the case of *B*. Fisher and Cleveland indicate that when R is not controlled, high-*B Ss* exceed low-*B Ss* in R and in number of shading responses, while low-*B Ss* have a higher F+%. Because of this, a number of different methods have been suggested for controlling R.

The principal method which has been applied is to ask the subjects to give a fixed number of responses to each card. This system has been used so that the fixed number of responses can be either 24 or 25. The *Ss* are told to give three responses to Cards I, II, III, and VIII, and two responses to each of the other cards if 24 responses are desired or, for 25 responses, to give three responses to Cards I, II, III, VIII, and X, and two responses to the other cards.

When Rorschachs have already been given in the usual fashion, an alternative approach for equating R is to eliminate from study all records with less than 15 responses, and to reduce all records with more than 25 responses to 25. The procedure for reduction is to use the first three responses on Cards I–V, and the first two responses on Cards VI–X. If there is a shortage of responses on any card, the first additional response on the next card is taken into account. If the shortage is on Card X, there is no specific suggestion given, but we would presume that you would then take the last additional response from the preceding card.

A final approach to the problem of R is not to control for R but to ignore R as long as there is no significant difference in R between the groups. This procedure seems least preferable, because differences in R may not be statistically significant and yet may be sufficiently large to promote significant differences in *B* or *P*.

The second system, in which responses are reduced to a set number, seems most preferable because it utilizes the standard Rorschach procedure and does not artificially suggest to the *S* how many responses should be given. However, it is clear that there is a difficulty in comparability across studies if different investigators express preferences for different methods of controlling R.

When R is controlled, there are no differences in W, F+%, color total, shading total, or M between high-*P* and low-*P* *S*s. However, there are some differences which remain between high-*B* and low-*B* Ss; high-*B* Ss exceed low-*B* *S*s in number of W responses, and low-*B* exceed high-*B* in F+%, even when R is controlled. Mednick (1959) has criticized the entire scoring system because it does not properly take into account the covariation of *B* with W, and many of the personality characteristics which have been suggested for the high-*B* individual have also been suggested for the high-W individual. Landau (1960) has reported no significant correlation between *P* and W%, M%, or F+%, and no significant correlation between *B* and W%, but has reported a significant correlation between *B* and M% (r = .34), and also between *B* and F+% (r = .35). Similarly, Shipman, Oken, Goldstein, Grinker, and Heath (1964) have reported a correlation between *B* and M that is in the .60s. The point that Mednick has made about the covariation of *B* with W is equally serious if the covariation exists with M, as these two studies would seem to suggest. Descriptions of the high-W and the high-M individual on the Rorschach also stress their self-steering behavior, and if *B* is to contribute something beyond the usual personality characteristics assigned to the high-W and high-M individual, it must be demonstrated that these characteristics exist after the covariation with W and M have been accounted for.

THE RELATION BETWEEN *B* AND *P*. The relation between *B* and *P* was initially hypothesized as being high and negative. Information directly comparing these two scores has been presented by Fisher and Cleveland (1956b, 1958b), Landau (1960), Jaskar and Reed (1963), and Compton (1964). These investigators present a total of 12 correlations between the two variables computed from a variety of different samples. The correlations range in value between −.14 and .58, with only three reaching significance, and these all being positive correlations. Since both *B* and *P* have demonstrated to be correlated with R, it is not entirely surprising that correlations between the two should occasionally reach significance. It would seem from a perusal of these data that the relationship between *B* and *P* is clearly not

TABLE 6.1
Correlations between *B* and *P*

Study	*N*	*Group*	*Correlation*
Fisher and Cleveland (1956b)	83	Students	−.12
Fisher and Cleveland (1958b)	25	Dermatitis Patients	.52[a]
Fisher and Cleveland (1958b)	25	Arthritis Patients	.25
Fisher and Cleveland (1958b)	22	Burn Patients	.33
Fisher and Cleveland (1958b)	20	Ulcerative Colitis Patients	.58[a]
Fisher and Cleveland (1958b)	30	Students	.51[a]
Fisher and Cleveland (1958b)	60	Students	.02
Landau (1960	40	Paraplegics	.06
Jaskar and Reed (1963)	30	Psychiatric Patients	.04
Jaskar and Reed (1963)	30	Hospital Employees	−.14
Compton (1964)	30	Psychiatric Patients	.15

[a] $p < .01$.

negative, and might be orthogonal. Table 6.1 presents the various correlations that have been obtained between these two variables.

Interscorer Reliability

A great deal of evidence has been presented concerning the interscorer reliability of the body-image boundary scoring system (Blatt, 1963; Compton, 1964; Daston and McConnell, 1962; Eigenbrode and Shipman, 1960; Fisher and Cleveland, 1955, 1958b; Jaskar and Reed, 1963; Landau, 1960; Masson, 1963; Ramer, 1963; Sieracki, 1963).

The *P* score has obtained both the lowest ($r = .61$; Daston and McConnell, 1962) and the highest ($r = .99$; Fisher and Cleveland, 1958b) interscorer reliability coefficients. The general trend of the correlations for both *B* and *P* is in the high .80s and low .90s, and indicates that scoring can be accomplished with highly satisfactory interscorer reliability.

A potential problem has been noted by Daston and McConnell, who found a reliability of .61 for the Penetration score; after they discussed their approach to scoring, their reliability was raised to .79 with a second set of records. The difficulty was that one scorer had been scoring such things as frank anatomy responses, which are specifically excluded by the scoring system and yet which seem to have the quality of penetration about them. Fisher and Cleveland (1955), who indicated 76% agreement on *B* scoring and 63% agreement on *P* scoring, caution that it is necessary for the scorers to be motivated in order for them to be able to use the system effectively.

If the minimal requirement of motivation and strict adherence to the criteria is followed, there should be no difficulty in achieving adequate

TABLE 6.2
Interscorer Reliability for Barrier and Penetration Scoring

Study	*N*	*Barrier*	*Penetration*
Blatt (1963)	8 Records	75% Agreement	—[a]
Compton (1964)	—	"Few Differences"	"Few Differences"
Daston and McConnell (1962)	40 Records	.84	.61
Daston and McConnell (1962)	48 Records	.84	.79
Eigenbrode and Shipman (1960)	10 Records	.84	—
Fisher and Cleveland (1955)	12 Records	76% Agreement	63% Agreement
Fisher and Cleveland (1958b)	20 Records	.82, .82, .91, .97, .97	.83, .87, .91, .94, .99
Jaskar and Reed (1963)	60 Records	.83	.78
Landau (1960)	—	.97	.92
Masson (1963)	200 Responses	95.5% Agreement	—
Ramer (1963)	96 Records	.81, .90, .96	—
Sieracki (1963)	—	.89, .94, .95	—

[a] A dash (—) indicates that these data were not available.

reliability. Table 6.2, which summarizes all of the data relevant to inter-scorer reliability, indicates that the scoring criteria may be used with a fair degree of accuracy.

NORMATIVE DATA

One of the major difficulties in properly presenting normative data on the body-boundary scoring system is that it has been used in situations where there was variation in the blots used as stimuli (Rorschach and Holtzman), in the method of administration (individual and group), and in the number of responses given (unrestricted and fixed).

In this chapter we shall deal only with studies in which the Rorschach blots themselves have been used and eliminate from consideration all studies using the Holtzman blots as stimuli, or those employing some multiple-choice response format, as has been attempted by Fisher and Cleveland (1958b) and Fish (1960). Both individual and group approaches will be considered.

Nature of the Sample

The majority of the studies from which normative data are available have utilized a student population. This has been true of the work of Cassell (1964), Cassell and Fisher (1963), Fisher (1964), Fisher and Cleveland (1958b), Fisher and Fisher (1964), Masson (1963), and Ramer (1963). These studies include data from over 1000 male and 1000 female college students, with a median age slightly above 20.

In addition to data on students, norms are also available on patients with varying forms of physical ailments. Blatt (1963) studied patients with essential hypertension, ulcerative colitis, or atopic eczema. These patients were described as nonpsychiatric patients, of at least average intelligence, and free from any disease other than the specified psychosomatic illness. The duration of illness did not exceed eight years for either the hypertension or colitis group, but did for the eczema group, where onset might have been in infancy, but these patients had been symptom free for a period until at most eight years prior to her study.

Cleveland and Johnson (1962) studied a group of coronary patients and a group of presurgery patients. The coronary patients were all hospitalized following an acute, myocardial infarction, were all less than 40 years of age, and, in the case of half the patients, it was their first hospitalization for cardiac difficulty; the remaining half had their initial myocardial infarction from four months to five years earlier. The presurgery patients who manifested a variety of different illnesses were tested on the day prior to major surgery.

Fisher (1959b) selected 40 aged *S*s from 27 middle-class families; he also selected a control group of 32 younger *S*s taken from the same families. These younger *S*s were either grown-up children or in-laws of the aged *S*s.

Fisher and Cleveland (1955), in the study in which the scoring system was initially proposed, studied patients with stomach disturbances, ulcerative colitis, rheumatoid arthritis, neurodermatitis, and conversion hysteria. These patients all had approximately 10 or 11 years of education and were equated across that dimension. It is interesting to note that the conversion hysteria subgroup, contrary to expectations from the literature, was composed predominantly of males. In their book (1958b), Fisher and Cleveland also report norms from an additional group of arthritic patients taken from a study by Mueller and Lefkovits (1956).

Orbach and Tallent (1965) report the results of Rorschachs administered to 31 patients who were seeking assistance in the management of their colostomies. These patients were part of an initial group of 48 patients, but 17 patients withdrew because of their growing resistance to participation in the investigation. The group was composed of predominantly European Jewish patients, most of whom had been foreign born and had no more than elementary-school education. All had lived with the colostomy from 5 to 10 years without recurrence of cancer.

Sieracki (1963) studied a group of V.A. patients with visible and with nonvisible permanent physical disabilities, matched for age, education, and time since onset of the disability. The patients with visible physical disabilities all had some disability of ambulation and were predominantly paraplegics or amputees. The patients with nonvisible physical disabilities were predominantly patients with tuberculosis.

Ware, Fisher, and Cleveland (1957) studied a group of patients hospitalized in a poliomyelitis respiratory center. The group included all types of poliomyelitis cases, with a wide range of severity of disability, although there was a predominance of severe cases. The patients had a median education of 13 years, and a median Wechsler verbal I.Q. of 114.

There have been some, but remarkably few, studies which have applied the body-boundary scoring system to the records of psychiatric patients. Fisher and Cleveland (1958b) report data from one such study comparing the records of normals, neurotics, undifferentiated schizophrenics and paranoids. All the groups were roughly comparable with respect to age, education, and socio-economic status, and the hospitalized groups were comparable with respect to length of hospitalization. The normal *S*s were taken from the protocols collected by Beck in his original normative study of the Rorschach (Beck et al, 1950). The neurotic patients were all men hospitalized at the Houston V.A. hospital with a diagnosis of psychoneurosis, anxiety reaction. This diagnosis had been made on the basis of the presence of generalized anxiety, revealed in such symptoms as tension, insomnia, and restlessness, and the absence of other specific neurotic symptoms such as conversion reaction, tics, compulsions, and obsessions. The undifferentiated schizophrenic group was composed of patients at a state hospital who had been diagnosed on the basis of symptoms indicative of a psychosis such as disorientation, hallucinations, flattened affect, and delusions, and the absence of specific signs such as catatonic stupor or well-systematized delusions. The paranoid group was also composed of state-hospital patients who had been diagnosed as schizophrenia, paranoid type. In each case, there was some delusional pattern, although the degree of systematization varied.

Jaskar and Reed (1963) compared the Rorschach protocols of hospitalized and nonhospitalized females. The hospitalized patients were consecutive admissions to a state psychiatric hospital, with the exclusion of organics or patients who had recently been on electroconvulsive shock therapy. The nonhospitalized women were consecutive applicants for employment at the same state hospital. The two groups did not differ in age, education, intelligence, number of children, or marital status. They did differ on the MMPI F scale, but the direction of the difference is not indicated in the report.

Shipman et al. (1964) studied a group of depressive patients. These patients, who were predominantly neurotic, were chosen on the basis of an acute illness in which intense depression was the major component. None of the patients had received electric shock therapy or had significant abnormalities in physical examination.

Some information on the Rorschach protocols of a variety of cultural groups is reported by Fisher and Cleveland (1958b). By rescoring protocols obtained by DeVos (1954), they were able to present the records of a number of native-village Japanese, Issei, or Japanese-born Americans, and Nisei, or American-born Japanese. By rescoring a number of records accumulated by Kaplan (1956) they present the records of the Bhil group of India, the Navajo and Zuni Indians of the southwest United States, the Tuscarora Indians of the northeast United States, a group of Hindus of India, and a group of Haitians. In order to deal with differences in median R among the various cultures, records were extracted from each available cultural sample in a manner that would allow matching of R across groups. The extent to which this selection procedure might have distorted the representativeness of the sample is unknown. Miner and DeVos (1960) have presented the records of two groups of Algerian Arabs. One group is composed of urban Arabs who lived in Algiers or some French city for over 20 years. The other group was composed of oasis Arabs, nine of whom had never had any city contact, and 11 of whom had visited Algiers but had not remained there for longer than six months. All of these *S*s had been born on an oasis with the exception of two, and in these cases, their parents had been born on an oasis.

The final set of normative data presented is in Fisher and Cleveland (1958b) and presents the records of a variety of different occupational groups. The great majority of these records were collected initially by Roe (1951, 1952b, 1953) and were rescored by Fisher and Cleveland.

Data on Body-Image Boundary Scores

One difficulty in evaluating the Fisher–Cleveland approach is that the scoring system presented in the 1955 monograph and the scoring system presented in the 1958 book are somewhat different from each other. The difference would lead one to suspect that both *B* and *P* would be higher if the system outlined in the book were used than if the one used in the monograph were utilized, since much more detailed criteria are present in the book. An examination of the norms, which are presented in Table 6.3, confirms this hypothesis. The table, aside from indicating some characteristics of the sample, also lists whether the Rorschach was administered individually or in groups, and, if reported, the median R. In those cases where it is clear that the monograph and not the book scoring system was employed, information to that effect is noted in the table. However, there are a number of cases where it is impossible, due to the brevity of the report, to ascertain which scoring system was used. It would be a reasonable guess, judging from the norms, that a great majority of the data presented in the Fisher and Cleveland book was scored by the Fisher and Cleveland monograph method, and the normative data presented in the book were inappropriate to the scoring system presented therein.

In the book, Fisher and Cleveland state that there are no differences in *B* or *P* as a function of method of administration or sex of the *S*. Their *S*s had a median *B* of 4 and a median *P* of 2. A more accurate normative statement might be derived from a study by Fisher (1964) in which almost 700 students were tested. Testing was by group administration, with R set at 25. It indicated that the median *B* was 6 for males and 7 for females, and that the median *P* was 3 for males and 2 for females; these sex differences were statistically significant. This study by Fisher is the only one in which significant sex differences are reported, and the significance of the difference is probably due, in large measure, to the size of the sample. Where sample size is under 100, no sex differences have been noted.

It appears that when the Rorschach is administered individually and the sample is composed of individuals other than college students, median *B* is somewhat lower than the 6 or 7 obtained in group administration to students. It cannot be determined whether the reduction is due to the difference in the sample or in the method of administration. The issue of variation of body-image boundary scores among samples has been the subject of a number of construct-validity studies, as will be reported later in the chapter .

Some developmental data are also reported by Fisher and Cleveland (1958b). It is not clear whether these records were scored according to the old or the new system, but it does seem that fewer *B* can be expected from children and early adolescents, without a great deal of variation through this period.

A great majority of validity studies with the body-image boundary scoring system have taken the approach of dividing *S*s at the median into high- and low-*B* groups, and then comparing the two. It is apparent from studying the table of norms that this is a most unreliable approach to studying characteristics of high- and low-*B* *S*s, since the median can differ as a function of method of administration, sex, constitution of the sample, and R. *S*s classified as high *B* in one study may well have been classified low *B* in another study. Thus, it would seem preferable either to study more extreme groups rather than breaking at the median, so that more stability of classification could be anticipated, or, since most of the studies were correlational, to report product moment correlations throughout the entire range of scores rather than to artificially dichotomize at an unstable median and then perform chi squares.

TABLE 6.3

Study	Group	N	Sex		Median Age	Rorschach Administration	Median R	Barrier		Penetration	
			M	F				Median	Range	Median	Range
Fisher and Cleveland (1958b)	Students	18	18	0	—[a]	Individual	23	2	—	—	—
Fisher and Cleveland (1958b)	Students	23	23	0	—	Individual	21	2	—	—	—
Ramer (1963)	Students	96	0	96	—	Group	25	5.82 (6.31[b])	0–15	—	—
Cassell (1964)	Students	115	115	0	—	Group	25	6	0–13	—	—
Cassell and Fisher (1963)	Students	55	55	0	20	Group	25	6	0–13	3	0–8
Fisher (1964)	Students	274	274	0	21	Group	25	6	0–16	3	0–12
Fisher (1964)	Students	50	50	0	20	Group	25	6	2–13	—	—
Fisher (1964)	Students	109	109	0	22	Group	25	6	0–14	—	—
Fisher (1964)	Students	49	49	0	21	Group	25	5	2–12	—	—
Cassell (1964)	Students	70	0	70	—	Group	25	6	0–14	—	—
Cassell and Fisher (1963)	Students	45	0	45	20	Group	25	6	0–14	3	0–7
Fisher (1964)	Students	290	0	290	21	Group	25	7	1–18	2	0–12
Fisher (1964)	Students	42	0	42	20	Group	25	7	2–18	—	—
Fisher (1964)	Students	112	0	112	22	Group	25	7	0–15	—	—
Fisher (1964)	Students	74	0	74	21	Group	25	6	2–15	—	—
Masson (1963)	Students	100	41	59	22.04[b]	Group	20	3.40 (3.55[b])	1.90[c]	—	—
Fisher and Fisher (1964)	Students	118	46	72	20	Group	25	5	—	—	—
Fisher and Fisher (1964)	Students	79	50	29	20	Group	25	6	—	—	—
Fisher and Fisher (1964)	Students	46	19	27	20	Group	25	6	—	—	—
Fisher and Fisher (1964)	Students	64	50	14	20	Group	25	6	—	—	—

Fisher and Fisher (1964)	Students	51	35	16	20	Group	25	6	—	—	—
Fisher and Fisher (1964)	Students	48	8	40	20	Group	25	5	—	—	—
Fisher and Fisher (1964)	Students	20	3	17	20	Group	25	7	—	—	—
Fisher and Cleveland (1958b)	Students	ca. 180	—	—	—	Group	24	4	—	2	—
Fisher and Cleveland (1958b)	Normal Children	46	46	0	5–7[d]	Individual	12	1	0–6	—	—
Fisher and Cleveland (1958b)	Normal Children	52	0	52	5–7[d]	Individual	12	2	0–7	—	—
Fisher and Cleveland (1958b)	Normal Children	37	37	0	8–10[d]	Individual	15	2	0–5	—	—
Fisher and Cleveland (1958b)	Normal Children	35	0	35	8–10[d]	Individual	14	2	0–5	—	—
Fisher and Cleveland (1958b)	Normal Children	40	40	0	10–13[d]	Individual	16	2	1–6	—	—
Fisher and Cleveland (1958b)	Normal Children	42	0	42	10–13[d]	Individual	16	1	0–7	—	—
Fisher and Cleveland (1958b)	Normal Children	30	30	0	10–13[d]	Individual	25	2	0–6	—	—
Fisher and Cleveland (1958b)	Normal Children	30	0	30	10–13[d]	Individual	25	2	0–7	—	—
Fisher and Cleveland (1958b)	Normal Adults	50	30	20	—	Individual	20[b]	3	0–6	1	0–5
Fisher and Cleveland (1958b)	Normal Adults	21	21	0	—	Individual	22	2	—	—	—
Jaskar and Reed (1963)	Hospital Employees	30	0	30	—	Individual	25	4.10[b]	1.64[c]	2.80[b]	1.92[c]

[a] A dash (—) indicates that these data were not available.
[b] Mean.
[c] Standard deviation.
[d] Range.
[e] Scored by system described in Fisher and Cleveland (1955).

TABLE 6.3 (cont.)

Study	Group	*N*	Sex *M*	Sex *F*	*Median Age*	*Rorschach Administration*	*Median R*	Barrier *Median*	Barrier *Range*	Penetration *Median*	Penetration *Range*
Fisher (1959b)	Family of Aged	32	10	22	36	Individual	20	5	—	2	—
Fisher (1959b)	Aged	40	14	26	67	Individual	18	5	—	1	—
Fisher and Cleveland (1958b)	Eminent Psychologists	9	—	—	—	Individual	25	6	—	—	—
Fisher and Cleveland (1958b)	Noneminent Psychologists	40	—	—	—	Group	25	5	—	—	—
Fisher and Cleveland (1958b)	Eminent Anthro-pologists	9	—	—	—	Individual	25	5	—	—	—
Fisher and Cleveland (1958b)	Noneminent Anthro-pologists	16	—	—	—	Group	25	5	—	—	—
Fisher and Cleveland (1958b)	Eminent Artists	20	—	—	—	Individual	25	4	—	—	—
Fisher and Cleveland (1958b)	Eminent Physicists	15	—	—	—	Individual	25	3	—	—	—
Fisher and Cleveland (1958b)	Noneminent Physicists	34	—	—	—	Group	25	4	—	—	—
Fisher and Cleveland (1958b)	Eminent Biologists	12	—	—	—	Individual	22	3	—	—	—
Fisher and Cleveland (1958b)	Noneminent Biologists	40	—	—	—	Group	25	4	—	—	—
Fisher and Cleveland (1958b)	Eminent Mathemati-cians and Chemists	17	—	—	—	Individual	25	3	—	—	—
Fisher and Cleveland (1955)	Rheumatoid Arthritis Patients	25	25	0	31.8[b]	Individual	17	4[e]	0–8[e]	1[e]	0–6[e]
Fisher and Cleveland (1958b)	Arthritis Patients	28	28	0	—	Individual	17	4	—	1	—
Fisher and Cleveland	Neurodermatitis	25	25	0	34.0[b]	Individual	21	4[e]	0–15[e]	2[e]	0–7[e]

Blatt (1963)	Atopic Eczema Patients	16	—	—	23–50[d]	Individual	—	1.8[e]	0–6[e]	1.3[e]	0–5[e]
Fisher and Cleveland (1955)	Stomach Disturbance Patients	25	25	0	31.7[b]	Individual	22	1[e]	0–3[e]	5[e]	1–9[e]
Fisher and Cleveland (1955)	Ulcerative Colitis Patients	20	0	20	33.5[b]	Individual	16	1[e]	0–5[e]	3[e]	0–11[e]
Blatt (1963)	Ulcerative Colitis Patients	16	—	—	23–50[d]	Individual	—	2.3[e]	0–5[e]	1.5[e]	0–3[e]
Orbach and Tallent (1965)	Colostomy Patients	31	18	13	60[b]	Individual	—	0.80[b]	0.9[c]	3.00[b]	3.2[c]
Blatt (1963)	Essential Hypertension Patients	16	—	—	23–50[d]	Individual	—	0.5[e]	0–2[e]	0.3[e]	0–3[e]
Cleveland and Johnson (1962)	Coronary Patients	25	25	0	35.3[b]	Individual	—	4.2	0–9	4.4	0–9
Cleveland and Johnson (1962)	Presurgery Patients	25	25	0	35[b]	Individual	—	4.0	0–9	1.9	0–4
Ware et al. (1957)	Poliomyelitis Patients	56	29	27	26	Individual	25	3[e]	0–8[e]	—	—
Sieracki (1963)	Visible Physical Disability	25	25	0	20.55[d]	Individual	25	5.48[b]	2.48[c]	—	—
Sieracki (1963)	Nonvisible Physical Disability	25	25	0	20.55[d]	Individual	25	5.36[b]	2.62[c]	—	—
Fisher and Cleveland (1955)	Conversion Hysteria Patients	20	14	6	30.0[b]	Individual	20	5[e]	1–15[e]	2[e]	0–7[e]
Fisher and Cleveland (1958b)	Neurotics	40	40	0	—	Individual	19.7[b]	3	0–9	2	0–5
Fisher and Cleveland (1958b)	Undifferentiated Schizophrenics	40	30	10	—	Individual	18.5[b]	2	0–6	4	0–9
Fisher and Cleveland (1958b)	Paranoids	40	28	12	—	Individual	19.1[b]	2	0–10	3	0–10
Shipman et al. (1964) (1964)	Depressives	15	7	8	30.7[b]	Individual	—	4.5[b]	3.8[c]	—	—

TABLE 6.3 (cont.)

Study	Group	N	Sex M	Sex F	Median Age	Rorschach Administration	Median R	Barrier Median	Barrier Range	Penetration Median	Penetration Range
Jaskar and Reed (1963)	Psychiatric Patients	30	0	30	—	Individual	25	4.73[b]	2.41[c]	2.70[b]	2.15[c]
Fisher and Cleveland (1958b)	Japanese Villagers	16	16	0	—	Individual	13	2	—	—	—
Fisher and Cleveland (1958b)	Japanese Villagers	21	0	21	—	Individual	13	2	—	—	—
Fisher and Cleveland (1958b)	Issei	26	26	0	—	Individual	18	1	—	—	—
Fisher and Cleveland (1958b)	Issei	24	0	24	—	Individual	16	1	—	—	—
Fisher and Cleveland (1958b)	Nisei	25	25	0	—	Individual	25	3	—	—	—
Fisher and Cleveland (1958b)	Nisei	25	0	25	—	Individual	25	4	—	—	—
Fisher and Cleveland (1958b)	Bhils	21	21	0	—	Individual	18	4	—	—	—
Fisher and Cleveland (1958b)	Navajos	24	24	0	—	Individual	19	3	—	—	—
Fisher and Cleveland (1958b)	Zunis	28	28	0	—	Individual	19	3	—	—	—
Fisher and Cleveland (1958b)	Tuscaroras	23	23	0	—	Individual	18	3	—	—	—
Fisher and Cleveland (1958b)	Hindus	24	24	0	—	Individual	19	2	—	—	—
Fisher and Cleveland (1958b)	Haitians	21	14	7	—	Individual	20	2	—	—	—
Miner and DeVos (1960)	Urban Arabs	28	28	0	36.7[b]	Individual	—	2.8[b]	—	—	—
Miner and DeVos (1960)	Oasis Arabs	20	20	0	35.6[b]	Individual	—	2.1[b]	—	—	—

The *B-P* score has been reported only in two studies. One is that of Cassell and Fisher (1963) and the other is a study by Fisher (1964). From these studies, it can be indicated that the median *B-P* score of males is approximately 2, and ranges between −5 and +13, while the median *B-P* score of females is 4 and also ranges between −5 and +13.

RELIABILITY

The body-image boundary of an individual is conceptualized as a stable characteristic which, despite many situational and physical changes in the individual, remains essentially unchanged. For this reason, assessment of the stability of the scoring system is appropriate as a measure of reliability and, in a sense, as a measure of construct validity. There have not been any studies of the internal consistency of the system and it does not seem as though such an approach would have meaning, since the items are not intended to be equivalent.

Stability

There have been only two studies which have reported data pertinent to an assessment of the stability of the body-image boundary scoring system. The first was a study by Cleveland (1960), which involved essentially a reanalysis of data published by R. Fisher (1958b). Fisher administered the Rorschach to 50 psychotic women, 25 of whom had had a gynecological exam before the first testing. After a five-day period, the Rorschach was readministered. No differences were found in *B* or *P* between the groups of women. Combining the groups, the test-retest reliability of *B* was .65, and of *P* was .89. Cleveland pointed out that *B* had an unusually limited range in this particular sample and this might have contributed to the low estimate of its reliability.

The major evidence which has been presented concerning the stability of the scoring system appears in a study by Daston and McConnell (1962). They administered the Rorschach individually to 20 male veterans who were hospitalized with physical disorders, but free of any psychiatric disorders. After an interval of two months, the Rorschach was readministered by the same examiner. In order to deal with the effect of differential R level between the two records, *B* and *P* scores from the longer record of the pair were reduced in accordance with the ratio of the two response totals. All protocols were scored by two raters. One rater found test-retest correlations for *B* to be .90, and for *P* to be .82. The second rater obtained similar reliability figures of .88 and .79, respectively. The records were also sent to Fisher and Cleveland, who scored the records in an unspecified manner that was intended to minimize the effects of differential response productivity on a card-by-card basis. By doing this, they arrived at a test-retest correlation of .93 for *B* and .90 for *P*.

A *t* test between the means of *B* and *P* in Daston and McConnell's test-retest study found that all differences were insignificant. However, the decline in *P* did approach statistical significance. The authors interpret this as showing the sensitivity of *P* to minimal changes; this same theme of the sensitivity of *P* to minimal changes is repeated in some studies on the effects of therapy. The distinction between the sensitivity of an index responding to minimal situational changes and the unreliability of an index is not clear unless the changes can be predicted before the experiment is completed. Without further independent evidence of the reliability of *P*, the alternative suggestion that the index is not sufficiently reliable seems to be the more parsimonious.

Despite some differences in mean *P* over time, the test-retest correlations for both indices are all in an acceptable range. The evidence indicates that an individual's relative position within a distribution of scores is reasonably reliable, at least over a two-month period.

VALIDITY

There are a number of general problems which seem to run through the majority of the validity studies. Rather than repeat the same comments when reviewing each of the studies, these general issues will be dealt with at this point.

First, there seems to be an inordinate number of one-tailed tests, which appear in the literature as attempts to validate the body-image boundary concept. Aside from the usual questions about the appropriateness of using one-tailed tests during early stages of hypothesis testing, there are some examples which make it clear that one-tailed tests are being used as a method of manipulating statistics. As an example, after reviewing a study by Davis (1960), Fisher and Cleveland state "the difference. . . is significantly (.05 – .01) in the direction opposite to that predicted. The reason for this reversal of results. . . is not at all clear" (1958b, p. 334). They then go on to speculate about possible reasons for this reversal. The fact that this tactic of "switching tails" inflates one's probability level has been noted in the past (Goldfried, 1959). Hence, in our evaluation of the validity research, all probabilities will be restated as though two-tailed tests had been performed. In some cases, this will lead to conclusions different from those in the published study.

A second problem, which crops up continually, is an inappropriate attribution of causality following an examination of data within a correlational framework. Thus, after examining the Rorschachs of Roe's *S*s (1951, 1952b, 1953) and noting some relationship between *B* and profession, Fisher and Cleveland conclude: "It would appear that an individual's boundary characteristics may exert an influence on the degree to which he directs his interests and activities toward people as contrasted to things and abstractions" (1958b, p. 169). The only appropriate conclusion from the demonstrated correlation would be to note the consistency between an individual's boundary characteristics and his occupation. Again, rather than repeat this criticism throughout the rest of this chapter, more speculative conclusions about causality will simply be avoided, accepting the likelihood, once more, that the evaluation of the findings of some studies in the review will not always agree with the conclusions drawn in the original paper itself.

A final problem of some generality is the method of treating the results. By far the most common approach to data analysis involves the use of the median test. This test is employed by dichotomizing the distribution of boundary scores at the median, and then drawing conclusions about the characteristics of high- and low-*B* or -*P* individuals. While this approach is usually appropriate, it does not seem to be the best way of handling these data. Particularly since the norms have fluctuated, the classification as to high and low *B* or *P* may differ markedly from study to study, and failures to replicate may be based on performing the median split at a different point in the distribution. For future workers it would be recommended that a statistic which uses the entire distribution, such as a correlation coefficient, would be a better choice of test and would lead to conclusions that might prove to have more generality.

Criterion-Related Validity

It is difficult to assess the criterion-related validity of the body-image boundary scores because it is unclear as to what would be an appropriate criterion. The body-image barrier is a construct, and cannot be measured directly. As a result, the great majority of validation work most properly should be classified under the rubric of construct validity.

Measures of concurrent validity presuppose the existence of an acceptable means of classifying people into appropriate groups. There is no such method applicable to classification along the body-image boundary dimension and techniques using parallel measuring instruments, due to the equally hypothetical validity of those instruments, are more properly thought of as appropriate to trait-validity studies.

Although one cannot readily conceive of a criterion for body-image boundary, the measure itself has been used for predictive purposes. However, since no study has allowed sufficient time to pass to qualify as predictive in any meaningful sense, and, in any case, what is being predicted is related to the scoring system in a hypothetical rather than a direct way, these studies will also be considered in the construct-validity section.

Construct Validity

The studies described in this section can be broken down into studies of nomological validity—which predominate in the literature—investigating a number of hypotheses which can be drawn from the conceptualization of the body-image boundary scoring system, and studies of trait validity, which relate the scoring system to a number of relevant measures.

Nomological Validity

The studies classified under nomological validity fall into a number of different categories: (1) relationship to physical illnesses (whether or not they are psychosomatic), (2) relationship to physiological indices, (3) relationship to self-steering behavior, (4) relationship to a variety of other personality dimensions, (5) relationship to psychopathology, and (6) relationship to cultural characteristics.

Relationship to Physical Illnesses. Physical illnesses studied include both diseases considered to have extensive psychosomatic components, and illnesses of a more exclusively physical etiology.

The initial study, which gave rise to the body-image boundary scoring system, was one which contrasted psychosomatic illnesses of an exterior and interior site. Fisher and Cleveland (1955) studied differences in Rorschach responses of patients with interior psychosomatic symptoms (stomach disturbance, ulcerative colitis), and those of psychosomatic disturbances with an external site (rheumatoid arthritis, neurodermatitis, conversion hysteria). Using the preliminary version of the scoring system, each group of patients with exterior symptoms was compared with each group of patients with interior symptoms on both *B* and *P*. On *B*, every comparison produced a significant chi square value, with patients with exterior symptoms attaining the higher scores. The smallest chi square values were obtained when the comparisons involved the group with colitis. The patients with stomach disturbances had significantly higher *P* scores than any of the patients with exterior symptoms, although the chi square values were of a smaller magnitude than was true with *B*. None of the comparisons involving the group with colitis were found to be significant.

The records of five arthritic patients and five patients with stomach disturbances were then submitted to three psychologists who were instructed in body-image scoring and asked to classify the records according to the group of origin of the patients. Two were able to make the classification perfectly, and one did it with only one reversal. Since instruction in the body-image criteria was given to the psychologists, it is difficult to see this design, which appears in a number of other studies, as more than a crude replication of the more precise and objective application of the body-image scores to the records.

In an attempt to show that the distinctiveness of the responses of the exterior group was not due to the presence of an exterior symptom, but rather to the psychosomatic onset of that symptom, control groups with similar symptomatology of more clearly physical origin were selected. Arthritis patients were compared with patients suffering back pain and neurodermatitis patients were compared with patients who had skin damage. The results indicated that each of the appropriate psychosomatic groups had higher *B* scores than did their controls. No information is given about *P* for these comparisons. These findings are taken as evidence that it is not the presence of an external symptom that elevates *B*, but rather the body image which produces the exterior psychosomatic symptom. The impact of the evidence is somewhat weakened when one considers that the duration of the symptom was longer in the case of each of the exterior groups than in its control—by one year for the arthritis and back-pain groups, and nine years for the dermatitis and skin-damage groups. However, no relationship was found between duration of symptom and *B* scores within the arthritis or dermatitis groups (or within the conversion group); no information is given as to differences in *P,* differences in the control groups, or differences in any other interior group.

An examination of median *B* and *P* scores makes it appear as though the exterior psychosomatic patients have scores characteristic of the normative group, and the significant differences are produced by interior patients, who have higher *P* and lower *B* scores than would be expected from these data. It was this original study by Fisher and Cleveland which led to the great attention given to the body-image boundary scoring system, and which has been taken as presenting evidence showing differences in the body boundary between patients whose psychosomatic disorder is exterior, as opposed to those whose disorder has an internal location.

Because of the importance of the study, there have been a number of attempts to replicate various portions of it. Two studies have compared patients with arthritis with patients having some internal psychosomatic disturbance. Williams (1962) compared rheumatoid arthritis patients with peptic ulcer patients and found no differences in *B,* but differences in *P,* with the ulcer patients exceeding the arthritic patients, as would be predicted. There is some difficulty in interpreting these data, as half of the ulcer patients were medicated, and no information is given about the possible effect of phenobarbital on either *B* or *P.* Cleveland, Reitman, and Brewer (1964), working with 10-year-olds, compared patients suffering from juvenile rheumatoid arthritis with asthmatic patients. As predicted, arthritic patients had significantly higher *B* than did the asthmatics, but there were no differences in *P.* Although there were some inconsistencies in these two replications, they generally support the initial finding that arthritis patients have different patterns of body-image boundary scores than do patients with internal psychosomatic illnesses.

Patients with skin problems have been studied with less success. Eigenbrode and Shipman (1960) compared a group of patients with skin disorders, most of whom had atopic eczema, with patients of internal disorders, most of whom had ulcers. The authors were not able to find significant differences in *B,* and do not report any comparison of *P.* Brown (1959) compared contact dermatitis patients with a control group and found no significant differences in either *B* or *P.* There was no indication that the controls had been exposed to the allergens producing the contact dermatitis (usually poison ivy), so this negative result is not seen as particularly decisive. Blatt (1963) compared patients with an exterior symptom (atopic eczema), an interior symptom (ulcerative colitis), and an intermediate symptom (essential hypertension). Using the 1955 version of the scoring system, she compared each group with every other group on both *B* and *P.* The only significant result found was that colitis patients exceeded hypertension patients on *B,* a finding which would not have been predicted if hypertension were considered an intermediate disorder. It might be argued that hypertension is clearly an interior disorder, but the significant differences between the groups would still not have been predicted. Blatt indicates that there were no differences among the groups in R, but she does not give the number; an examination of the medians would make it appear as though the scores for all groups were unusually low. If this is because of a limited

R, it would not be seen as decisive, since records of this sort are more typically discarded.

The evidence presented above concerning patients with psychosomatic disorders seems somewhat varied. There have been a number of surprising and consistent differences found among some groups of patients, particularly when comparisons involved arthritics. There have also been a number of consistent failures to replicate, particularly with colitis patients and patients with skin disorders. Perhaps the varied type of origin possible for dermatitis would explain inconsistent findings with that particular disorder. A decisive replication of the initial Fisher and Cleveland study using the current version of the scoring system seems to be very much in need.

A number of studies have also been performed using body-image boundary scores with patients of more traditional physical illnesses. One of these studies also followed the exterior vs. interior model. Fisher and Cleveland (1956c) studied patients with cancer of either an external or internal location. In an initial study, they obtained the records of six patients with an external melanoma, and 11 with cancer of the cervix, and attempted to sort them (blindly) into external and internal categories. They were able to classify them with only two misidentifications, but did not specify the cues they utilized in making the classification. These results are significant, but when one considers that the built-in base rates are closer to 67% than 50%, they are somewhat less spectacular than might appear at first glance.

The more elaborate study reported in this same paper involves the records of patients with a variety of exterior cancers (a great majority were breast cancer cases) and patients with interior cancers (a great majority had cancer of the cervix). The two groups differed significantly in the predicted direction, with the exterior group having higher *B* and lower *P*. In order to anticipate the criticism that these differences might be based on a realistic attention to a symptom of external or internal location, the records of the interior group were compared with a control group, composed of patients who had had colostomies because of cancer and had lived with the colostomy for a period of 10 years. There were no differences between this group and the interior group on *P*. Results with *B* are not reported. This is interpreted by Fisher and Cleveland as demonstrating that the presence of interior symptoms over a long period of time does not increase *P*. It is clear that here, as in many other instances, a longitudinal study would be necessary to provide a more direct test of whether the body-image scores are antecedent or consequent to the illness.

One other attempted study of patients with colostomies is reported by Orbach and Tallent (1965). Their colostomy patients were given a Rorschach as part of a battery in a large-scale study of that particular group, and their scores are compared with the general norms in the Fisher and Cleveland book. The results indicate that the colostomy group had significantly lower *B* but no differences in *P*. Since R is not taken into account, and their group was foreign born, undereducated, and older than most groups that have been studied, comparison of their scores with the normative group of entirely different characteristics seems to be without much meaning.

McConnell and Daston (1961) examined pre- and postdelivery Rorschachs of a number of multiparous women in an attempt to examine body-image change during pregnancy. There were no differences in pre- and postdelivery *B*, but there was a significant increase in *P*. Since there was almost a significant decrease in *P* in the reliability study, and there was no control group with which to compare these women, it does not seem as though any interpretation would be justifiable, although one is made. The women in the study were divided as to whether their attitudes toward pregnancy were positive or negative, with the division forced into a seemingly artificial 50–50 grouping. These ratings were made with adequate reliability and a comparison of the women with positive attitudes and those with negative attitudes showed no significant differences in *P*, but differences that closely approached significance in *B*; the women rated as having positive attitudes had higher *B* scores. No relationship was shown between either body-image boundary score and semantic differential rating of "my body at the moment" taken both pre- and postdelivery. The authors suggest that this is because the semantic differential is a conscious measure and the body-image boundary score is an unconscious measure. This distinction, however, has not been applied in other studies using conscious measures that have shown correlations with the body-image boundary scoring system.

Cleveland and Johnson (1962) studied the personality patterns of young males with coronary disease. They compared their coronary patients with a comparable group of presurgery patients, so that *S*s in both groups were experiencing a life-endangering situation. Although there were no differences in *B*, the presurgery patients had significantly lower *P*. Other tests administered in this study were interpreted as showing that the coronary patients maintained conscious high self-esteem, which might be reflected in B, but that this was accompanied by a good deal of unconscious anxiety, which might be reflected in *P*. These interpretations, of course, are highly speculative.

Sieracki (1963) examined Rorschach protocols of patients with visible and nonvisible physical disabilities. There were no differences in *B* between the two groups. However, when the groups were divided as to their attitude toward the disability on the basis of the Berger Sentence Completion Test, the high-*B* patients were found to have a significantly more positive attitude toward their disability than did the low-*B* patients, whether the disability was visible or nonvisible.

In a study of a somewhat different slant, Masson (1963) investigated attitudes toward visible disabilities in a group of students who, themselves, were nondisabled. Correlations between *B* and a measure of attitudes toward visibly disabled persons taken from the Granofsky Pictures Test were all nonsignificant. However, the instructions to the *S*s that the experiment was about the feelings of nondisabled persons toward the disabled may have primed social desirability stereotypes and distorted the expression of real attitudes on the Pictures Test. The stories told to pictures of disabled persons were scored on the discomfort relief quotient (DRQ) and, after eliminating all *S*s who expressed anxiety in their stories to neutral pictures, the high-*B S*s were found to have a lower DRQ than did the low-*B S*s.

Ware et al. (1957) studied the adjustment of patients with poliomyelitis. Based on the composite opinions of professional staff, patients were divided into "satisfactory" and "unsatisfactory" categories. A chi square was performed and the overall result was significant ($p \leq .05$), indicating that high-*B* patients were more likely to have made a satisfactory adjustment to their illness than were low-*B* patients. Subanalyses demonstrated that this effect was not a function of either physical involvement or duration of illness. Although this is consistent with the meaning of the *B* score, in that those individuals who possess a more satisfactory, well-defined body image are better able to adjust to some trauma to that body, it should be pointed out that the initial Rorschachs were taken after the onset of poliomyelitis. Hence, it is not clear whether both the retention of a well-defined body image and adequate adjustment were responses to the disability, or whether the body images of the well-adjusted patients were more well defined before the onset of the illness. The time between the initial testing and the evaluation of adequacy of adjustment is not given, so that it is difficult to identify the extent to which this is a predictive study. In any case, the overlapping scores between the satisfactory and unsatisfactory adjustment patients are too great to allow for much predictive efficiency.

Landau (1960) studied the response to treatment, as measured by a sentence completion test and a psychosocial rating scale, of 40 recently injured male paraplegics. The patients in her study were tested once shortly after admission to a rehabilitation program, and again several months later. It would appear that the maximum time which might have elapsed between the administration of the Rorschach and the administration of the criterion tests was nine weeks. *B* was significantly correlated with each of the criterion measures in the .50s ($p < .01$) and *P* produced negligible and insignificant correlations with all criteria. When an overall adjustment measure was correlated with all of the potential predictors in the study (the Secord Homonym Test and the Secord–Jourard Body Cathexis Test were also administered) *B* was the major contributor to the correlation ($r = .55$, with .63 being the maximum R reached) and *P* did not add anything to the multiple correlation. It may be of some parenthetic interest to note that a correlation employing F+%, W%, and M% as predictors produced a multiple correlation of .51 with the overall adjustment measure, as compared to the correlation of .55 with *B*. However, it should also be added that none of the Rorschach variables taken alone correlate nearly as well with the overall adjustment measure as did *B*.

In summary, there is some evidence that there are differences in the body-image boundary patterns of individuals whose illness is exterior and those whose illness is interior, whether the etiology of the illness is psychosomatic or physical. However, the two most comprehensive studies demonstrating this difference (Fisher and Cleveland, 1955, 1956c) both utilized the preliminary form of the body-image boundary scoring system. It would be of some importance to replicate this study using the current version of the scoring system.

The other findings of importance from this group of studies all indicate the greater ability of high-*B Ss* to adjust to their illness. *P,* in the studies in which it was employed, did not prove to be significantly related to the criteria. This leads to the suggestion that further exploration be done using *B* as a predictor, with particular emphasis on situations such as response to a rehabilitation program for an individual with a physical illness, which are congruent with the conception of the body-image dimension. It does not seem as though further exploration of *P* as a predictor would prove very fruitful. This possible personality characteristic of the *B* group will be dealt with in more detail in sections which are concerned specifically with the self-steering characteristics of high-*B Ss*, their personality characteristics, and their relationship to psychopathology.

Relationship to Physiological Indices. Studies investigating the relationships between body-image boundary scores and physiological indices are usually tests of hypotheses derived from Fisher and Cleveland's (1957) theory of physiological reactivity. This theory is closely tied to the observations reported in the study of patients with psychosomatic symptoms. Based on the observations that patients with exterior symptoms differed from patients with interior symptoms, they hypothesized that high-*B Ss* would be characterized by greater reactivity on physiological indices of exterior dimensions, while low-*B Ss* would be characterized by greater reactivity on internal physiological indices.

A number of reanalyses of physiological studies are presented in Fisher and Cleveland (1958b). The first of these is a reanalysis of a study by Haber (1954) of tactile sensitivity in amputees. In this study, *B* was shown to correlate significantly with light-touch threshold on the intact limb. This was the only significant correlation of six that were performed. A reanalysis of a study by Herring (1956) investigating physiological responsivity during surgery showed that there was no correlation between *B* and maximum heart rate during surgery, but that there were significant correlations between *B* and both the minimum heart rate during surgery and basal metabolism. It would have been predicted that *B* would correlate negatively with both maximum and minimum heart rate, since heart rate is an internal measure. The absence of the correlation with maximum heart rate was not consistent with this hypothesis, but the correlation with the minimum heart rate was. No explanation is offered for the correlation with basal metabolism. Funkenstein, King, and Drolette (1954) studied response to frustration in a laboratory situation. Barrier scores were compared with three measures of interior reactivity, one measure of exterior reactivity, and systolic and diastolic blood pressure, which are considered somewhat intermediate. Of the six correlations, the only significant one was with pulse rate and, as predicted, low-*B Ss* tended to have higher pulse rates. Finally, a study of EEG patterns conducted by Travis and Bennett (1953) was reexamined by Fisher and Cleveland. The per cent time alpha, considered by some investigators to be a correlate of passivity, was found to be negatively correlated with *B*. Since a decrease in alpha is seen as a preparatory response, these results may have more to do with differences in the situational response than to any enduring personality characteristics.

All of these findings are consistent with the Fisher and Cleveland hypotheses, but none provide particularly strong evidence, as they were all studies intended for some other purpose. The most consistent finding throughout these studies is the tendency for cardiac rate, which is presumed to be an avenue of expression in low-*B* *S*s, to confirm predictions from the theory.

In a study that was designed to be a test of the hypothesis of exterior versus interior reactivity, Fisher (1959a) related *B* to heart rate and number of galvanic skin responses of a specified amplitude. Measurements were taken during an anxiety phase in which the experimenter was aloof and noncommunicative and various noises in the background served to disturb *S*s, and also during a rest period which followed reassurance. There were no significant correlations between *B* and either physiological index during the rest period, but during the anxiety phase, *B* correlated positively with the galvanic skin response measure (.46) and negatively with heart rate (−.51). These results, showing greater exterior reactivity for high-*B* *S*s and greater interior reactivity for low-*B* *S*s, were exactly as predicted. Fisher explains the presence of positive results during the anxiety phase, but not during the rest phase, as due to the uncontrolled nature of the rest period and the more standard meaning of the anxiety period.

In a study that was specifically designed to provide an extensive test of the exterior-interior hypothesis, Davis (1960) related *B* to three measures of exterior reactivity (electromyogram, galvanic skin response, peripheral resistance), three measures of interior reactivity (pulse rate, stroke volume, cardiac output), and three exploratory measures (systolic, diastolic, and mean blood pressure). Measurements were taken during an initial rest period and following a stress period, and all measures were transformed to standard scores to promote comparability. The only one of the nine measures to show a relationship to *B* during the prestress period was the electromyogram, a measure on which high-*B* *S*s exceeded low-*B* *S*s, as predicted. The prestress and poststress measures were combined to develop a series of autonomic lability scores, a measure of responsiveness independent of base level. Six of the nine autonomic lability scores were significantly related to *B*. High-*B* *S*s exceeded low-*B* *S*s on electromyogram scores and low-*B* *S*s exceeded high-*B* *S*s on pulse rate, stroke volume, cardiac output, systolic blood pressure, and mean blood pressure. Specific hypotheses were made for four of these six measures and differences were consistent with the hypotheses in every case. Separate rank orderings of the six interior or exterior physiological measures for the high- and low-*B* *S*s were made according to relative order of responsivity, and rank order correlations were performed. Correlations during the prestress period were −1.00, during the poststress period were −.86, and for autonomic lability scores were −.83 ($p \leq .05$). High-*B* *S*s were most reactive on electromyogram and least on pulse rate for all conditions. Low-*B* *S*s were most reactive on pulse rate twice and least on electromyogram during all three measures. The Davis study seems to indicate that responses to stress are primarily exterior for high-*B* *S*s, and primarily interior for low-*B* *S*s. The prestress data here, as in the previous Fisher study, do not indicate any basis for claiming a predisposition toward such reactivity.

Williams (1962), in a study which combined both interest in the psychosomatic groups and physiological indices, measured muscle activity, heart rate, and GSR of peptic ulcer and rheumatoid arthritis patients in a rest-stress-recovery paradigm. After dropping data from subjects taking phenobarbital, *B* was compared with the physiological indices. Of 12 comparisons made, significant relationships were shown only with two. High-*B* *S*s had higher muscle activity during stress, and low-*B* *S*s had higher heart rates during stress. These results, both in terms of the specific physiological index and the significance during stress only, are consistent with the previous studies.

Shipman et al. (1964) included the Rorschach in a large battery of tests given in an investigation of some personality characteristics associated with muscle tension. Muscle tension was reported from seven different muscles in each of four sessions. Three of these sessions were arousing in different ways (which were not significantly different) and a fourth was a neutral rest session. Overall muscle tension level correlated with *B* on three of the four readings, with the highest value being .83. The individual muscles which showed the highest correlation with *B* were the biceps, quadriceps, and the trapezius. The highest correlation reported here was .86 between the biceps during a neutral interview and *B*. A general conclusion was that high overall muscle tension seemed to be associated with high emotional stability, high Rorschach M, and high Rorschach *B*. The association of muscle tension with *B* is consistent with previous examinations of this index.

Cassell and Fisher (1963) studied the relationship between body-image boundary and the response of *S*s to an intradermal injection of histamine phosphate. This typically leads to a local dilation of the capillaries and wheal formation, which is followed by a localized erythema; this is known as the histamine-flair reaction. It was predicted that the flair reaction would be greater in high-*B* *S*s due to their propensity to exterior body response. Both the size and the color of the flair were measured (reliably), and these measurements were correlated with the previously obtained Rorschach scores. For males, none of the obtained correlations were significant. For females, *B* correlated significantly with both the color and the size of the flair reaction (.42 and .31), but *P* did not correlate with either measurement. *B-P* was also employed in the study, and it correlated significantly in females with the color of the flair (.31), but not with the size. For 51 of the male *S*s data were also collected on the duration of the flair, and these scores were significantly related to the *B-P* index. No convincing explanation is offered as to why results should have been positive with females, but not with males. One possibility that has been suggested, since only one concentration of histamine was used, is a difference in male and female threshold for the histamine-flair response, but this is not likely since both the color and the size of the reaction did not differ significantly between the male and the female groups.

Finally, Armstrong (1964) related body-image boundary characteristics to conditioning of both galvanic skin response and heart rate. The experiment had a rest-pretraining-conditioning-extinction sequence, with a pseudo-conditioning paradigm employed. The measurement employed for both galvanic skin response and heart rate was the response to the conditioned stimulus minus the response to the control stimulus, with both scores corrected for basal resistance. Galvanic skin response conditioning occurred in both the high-*B* group ($p \leq .05$) and the low-*B* group ($p \leq .10$). There were no significant differences between the two groups. Heart rate conditioning occurred in the low-*B* group ($p \leq .05$), but not in the high-*B* group. A trend analysis of the heart rate conditioning data showed a tendency ($p \leq .10$) for the low-*B* group to exceed the high-*B* group, and this trend reached significance during the last third of the trials. When just the last third of the trials were considered, an analysis of variance showed a significant *B* X conditioning interaction ($p \leq .01$). High-*B* *S*s exceeded low-*B* *S*s on galvanic skin response and low-*B* *S*s exceeded high-*B* *S*s on heart rate conditioning. For high-*B* *S*s, galvanic skin response conditioning was greater than heart rate conditioning, but there were no differences between the two for low-*B* *S*s. There were no significant results in examining extinction trials. Since the *S*s began the procedure with similar responses to both the conditioned stimulus and the control stimulus, and eventually the response to the control stimulus dropped out, Armstrong interprets these results as being due to selective adaptation and suggests that this mechanism must be considered along with reactivity in understanding the relationship between body image and physiological response.

In summary, there has been a consistent series of findings that demonstrate the greater physiological reactivity of high-*B* *S*s on *exterior* indices and low-*B* *S*s on *interior* indices. Because of multiple comparisons, there have also been a number of negative results, but there has been some consistency among the indices. Positive results are seen most clearly when the exterior index is muscle tension and the interior index is heart rate. Somewhat equivocal results have been shown when the exterior index is galvanic skin response. Positive results appear most clearly when the *S* is experiencing stress, and are not seen nearly as sharply during resting periods. It would seem that differential physiological reactivity and adaptation may be present, but it remains to be demonstrated that there are differences in resting-level values of the physiological indices. Taking the physiological results in combination with the psychosomatic results, there seems to be an indication that the body-image measurements, or more precisely, *B,* is related to an external-internal body dichotomy.

Relationship to Self-Steering Behavior. The majority of the studies which attempt to delineate a series of consistent personality characteristics of the high-*B* individual can be grouped under the rubric of "self-steering behavior." With one minor exception, all of these studies were reported in Fisher and Cleveland (1958b) and most, if not all, seem to have been based on the preliminary version of the body-image boundary scoring system. Self-steering behavior is a construct that is applicable to an individual who is an independent person with definite standards and goals and forceful, striving ways of approaching tasks. His preferred approach to problems is an active one in which he attempts to make aspects of the environment conform to his own desires and standards. A number of hypotheses were generated by this construct and the research reported attempts to see the extent to which these behaviors were more likely to appear in high-*B* than in low-*B* individuals. There were seven specific hypotheses tested, each one involving the relationship between *B* and a particular aspect of self-steering behavior.

The first aspect of self-steering behavior to be considered was *level of goal setting*. Fisher and Cleveland (1956b) administered the Rorschach and five TAT cards, which were scored for level of aspiration, definiteness of attitude toward parents, and deceptiveness. No reliability was indicated for the TAT scoring. High-*B Ss* received higher scores than low-*B Ss* on all three dimensions. In a cross-validational study, both level of aspiration and definiteness of attitude toward parents were upheld. High-*P Ss* also showed higher levels of aspiration than did low-*P Ss*, but there were no significant differences between the *P* groups on the other dimensions, and this relationship was not cross validated. In a subsequent study by Appleby (1956) following a similar design, none of the relationships reported in the initial study were cross validated ($p \geq .05$). Fisher and Cleveland (1958b) report one additional study in which high-*B Ss* were significantly higher than low-*B Ss* in number of aspiration themes produced on the TAT. Neither Fisher and Cleveland nor Appleby found significant relationships between *B* and McClelland's achievement motive. In reanalyzing data collected by Kelly and Fiske (1951), a curvilinear relationship was found between *B* and need achievement. Since the curvilinearity was determined after the fact and is unique to this set of data, the possibility must be considered that the relationship was generated by chance. However, if there indeed is a possibility of *B* being related to some criterion in a curvilinear fashion, this is a relationship which would not be discovered in the usual median test approach and suggests a further reason, besides those already mentioned, why such an approach does not do justice to the data. Other studies reported by Fisher and Cleveland (1958b) indicate that there were no significant relationships among *B*, overachievement, and underachievement, although the findings were in the predicted direction. *B* was related to students' choice of writing a paper for extra credit in order to earn a higher grade and to instructors' ranking of their independence, but not to instructors' ratings of the extent to which they set goals of high achievement for themselves. The great majority of the studies relating *B* to various measures of goal setting are in the predicted direction, but there is some question about their statistical significance and ability to be cross validated.

A second area of self-steering behavior is *need for task completion*. Fisher and Cleveland (1956a), reanalyzing data collected by Jourard (1954) and using the preliminary scoring system, related *B* to the Zeigarnik effect. Thirty small tasks were attempted by the *Ss*, half of which were completed and half were not, with instructions determining whether or not the task could be completed. An index expressing the percentage of incomplete tasks recalled was not related to *B* on an initial recall, but was related to it at a second recall, with high-*B Ss* showing a greater tendency to recall incomplete tasks than did low-*B Ss*.

The dimension of *suggestibility* was approached by reanalyzing data collected by Steisel (1952). High-*B Ss* were found to be less suggestible on both an ink blot suggestion test and a postural sway test than were low-*B Ss*.

Ability to *express anger outwardly* when frustrated was approached through reanalysis of the data collected by Funkenstein, King, and Drolette (1954). It was found that high-*B* individuals predominated in the group that was able to express their anger outwardly against the experimenter, while low-*B Ss* predominated in the group that directed their anger inward in a self-blaming fashion.

Orientation toward *self-gratification* was approached by asking *Ss* two projective questions, one of which inquired about how they would spend their time if they only had one month left to live, and the other asking how they would spend an unlimited amount of money. High-*B Ss* gave significantly ($p < .05$) more self-gratifying replies to the first question, and more ($p < .10$) self-gratifying replies to the second question.

A more elaborate approach was taken in studying the mode of *reaction to stress situations.* In a reanalysis of a study by Fisher (1950), *Ss* were allowed to succeed and then caused to fail very badly on a hand-steadiness aspiration task. Before each trial, *S* was asked to estimate what scores he expected to achieve and following the trial was given an arbitrary score which constituted feedback of success or failure. It was hypothesized that *Ss* who could deal realistically with stress would reduce their estimates of future performance as they met with continuous failure. High-*B Ss* did make such a reduction as compared to low-*B* Ss, demonstrating what was considered a more realistic adjustment to stressful failure. However, one wonders whether this may not have some implication for the previously hypothesized differences in level of aspiration between high- and low-*B Ss*. Performance on the Wechsler-Bellevue Digit Symbol under rest and stress conditions was compared by reanalyzing data from two different studies in which opposite results had been obtained. In one study, better adjusted *Ss* showed greater decrement under stress than did more poorly adjusted *Ss*, and in the other study, they showed less decrement. Performance of the high-*B Ss* was consistent with the performance of the better adjusted *Ss* in both studies. As a last bit of evidence cited to support the contention that high-*B Ss* respond to stress more adequately than do low-*B Ss*, the study by Ware et al. (1957) with polio patients showed that high-*B Ss* were more likely to adjust to their illness. The sum of these studies points consistently to the ability of high-*B Ss* to respond to stress with a more realistic, adequate method of coping than low-*B Ss*.

A final dimension of the self-steering construct which was investigated was *perceptual stability*. This involved a determination of the relationship between *B* and the field-dependent/field-independent continuum. Two separate reanalyses reported by Fisher and Cleveland show that there were no relationships between the two continua. In addition, Appleby (1956) found no relationship between *B* and the rod-and-frame test. All three analyses agree that *B* is not related to the field-dependency/field-independency continuum.

In summary, it would appear that *B* is related to a number of personality characteristics which, for want of a better label, may be called self-steering behavior. The most adequately investigated dimension of this construct, with the most consistent results, involves the individual's ability to respond to a stressful situation. Something along this line was also indicated in a number of the predictive studies and it does appear that the high-*B S* is capable of more mature behavior than the low-*B S*. It would be of critical importance to demonstrate these findings with the current scoring system in use, and with covariation with Rorschach variables such as W and M, which are also seen as being associated with maturity and adequacy of behavior, accounted for.

Relationship to a Variety of Personality Dimensions. A number of studies which have related *B* to some personality dimensions seem to have been generated in a more or less "shotgun" approach, as opposed to the more theory-oriented predictions generated by the self-steering construct. These will be grouped in what seems to be a somewhat meaningful fashion and the implications will be explored.

The first set of studies deals with the relationship between *B* and a variety of overt behaviors. Fisher and Cleveland (1958b) report on the relationship between *B* and sociometric nominations on two separate occasions. Of 17 possible variables, only one successfully differentiated high- and low-*B S*s on an initial administration of the sociometric questionnaire. This question asked for the nomination of individuals who most want a warm, friendly group. On the second administration, when the *S*s had an opportunity to know each other better, there were significant differences on three of the 17 items. These items were the warm, friendly group item, nominations for the members most accepted by the group, and individuals who operate independently of the process analyst. On each item, high-*B S*s received more nominations than low-*B S*s.

Cleveland and Fisher (1957) report on a study in which six groups were involved. Three were constructed so as to be composed of high-*B S*s, and three so as to be composed of low-*B S*s. The groups were given the task of making up two stories and then discussing the criteria for success in our culture. Judges were given pairs of stories and discussion material, one of which came from a high-*B* group and one from a low-*B* group, and were asked to judge which was more concerned with aspiration and achievement, and which was more concerned with the philosophy of humanitarianism. The high-*B S*s were judged as being more concerned with aspiration and achievement, and more concerned with the philosophy of humanitarianism, but this is limited by the use of only three pairs of groups. Ramer (1963) reported a more elaborate study in which *S*s were seen in groups, were led to believe that they were working with only one partner in the group, with, in fact, each working on his own with the experimenter delivering bogus notes. The *S*s were asked to construct a story and were given an opportunity to discuss by notes their story with their presumed partner. High-*B* *S*s exceeded low-*B* *S*s in both number of messages sent and in number of units of communication included in the messages. The analysis of the qualitative features of these messages was generally unsuccessful, partially because of the unreliability of the Bales scoring system, as applied in this study. Fisher (1964a) had 10 experienced interviewers interview a large number of *S*s in an unstructured, freely interacting situation, and then make judgments as to communicativeness, insightfulness, and identity resolution. No judgments were given as to the reliability of the interviewer ratings, and each of the three dimensions was intercorrelated with each other dimension at highly significant levels. Almost 40% of the *S*s were rated unusually easy to communicate with, a finding which might cast some doubt upon the adequacy of the rating scale. High-*B* *S*s were rated as significantly easier to communicate with, and had significantly higher scores on an average of the three ratings. They also had higher, but not significantly so, scores on the other two dimensions. Each of these studies seems to indicate that in a behavioral situation, either individual or small group, the high-*B S* will make greater efforts at communication than will the low-*B S*. This finding, too, can be considered consistent with the self-steering construct.

A number of studies have implications for the developmental growth and sex linkage of *B*. Fisher and Cleveland (1958b) report a study in which there seemed to be little difference in *B* produced by children in the age range from 5 to 17, although their median *B* production appears to be lower than would be expected from an adult, and seems to be based on the preliminary scoring system. Within these age ranges, sex differences are identified at the 5–7-year-old level, at which time girls exceed boys, and at the 10–13-year level, at which time boys exceed girls. While these results are interpreted as mirroring differences in certainty over life goals and role standards at these points of socialization, they may also be an artifact of an analysis which used a median *B* score based on the 5–17 range in each of the subanalyses. If the median had been determined from the group in which the analysis was being performed, one might question whether or not these same sex differences would have appeared. Fisher and Fisher (1959) report no sex differences in the 5–12-year range and differences favoring girls in the 13–17-year range. In the earlier study there were no sex differences reported in the 13–17-year range. Fisher and Fisher (1964), with a large group of college students, report no sex differences in *B*. Fisher (1964b), also with college students, reports that females produce more *B* responses than males.

Finally, Fisher (1959b), comparing a sample of aged *S*s with younger controls drawn from the same families as the aged group report no differences in either *B* or *P* between the two groups, and this is interpreted as being an indication that *B* and *P* reflect long-term personality dispositions. However, Fisher and Cleveland (1958b), in a study of body-image similarities among family members, compared *B* of various pairs of family members. Data were collected from fathers, mothers, adolescent children, and younger children, and most of the possible pairs were investigated. No relationships exceeded chance levels. This raises a question about the appropriateness of the use of a control group from the same family. If this question is to be answered, it is clear that a long-range study would be needed.

It would seem as though the developmental differences reported may very well have been a function of method of administration, R, and situational characteristics. Studies employing small numbers of *S*s generally do not report sex differences, but when a large number of *S*s are tested, the superiority of the females on the *B* dimension may begin to appear. However, it is questionable whether this statistically significant sex difference is of any practical significance.

The one attempt to relate *B* to occupation was in the reanalysis of data collected by Roe (1951, 1952b, 1953). *S*s from the disciplines of psychology, anthropology, art, physics, biology, and mathematics-chemistry were compared with each other. It was found that psychologists had higher *B* scores than physicists or biologists, and that psychologists and anthropologists combined had higher *B* scores than physicists and biologists combined. There are so many possible comparisons that could have been made among disciplines, particularly when combination groupings are employed, that it is difficult to attribute these findings to anything other than chance.

Fisher and Cleveland (1958a) compared *B* with responses to TAT-type pictures scored for need for sex, and a questionnaire asking for the day of last orgasm, frequency of orgasm, and present sex drive. High-*B* *S*s exceeded low-*B* *S*s in TAT need for sex and in day of last orgasm; the other comparisons were not significant. This was interpreted as an indication that the high-*B* *S* had greater freedom to enter into intimate relationships. Since neither correlate was shown to be related to satisfactory sexual experience, this conclusion was somewhat questionable.

Compton (1964) correlated *B* and *P* with responses on a clothing fabric and design preference test, and the *S*s' weight-to-height ratio among a group of hospitalized chronic psychiatric patients. It was found that *B* correlated positively with the weight-to-height ratio and negatively with preference for saturated color and for strong figure-ground contrasts. *P* correlated positively with preference for warm colors and for large patterns. While some speculative interpretations of these results were offered, there is so little known about the test with which the *B* and *P* scores were correlated, that it is difficult to place a great deal of faith in any interpretation.

Finally, Wertheimer and Bachelis (1966) correlated *B* and *P* scores with the Farnsworth–Muncell 100 Hue Test of Color Discrimination and found a significant positive correlation with *B*, but none with *P*. This was interpreted as showing that *B* was a measure of cognitive differentiation. This employment of *B* as a cognitive rather than a body-image variable is somewhat unique.

The studies reported in this section, generated as they were in an unstructured and a theoretical fashion, provide very little independent information. Those few significant correlations which are reported and cannot be attributed to chance expectancies in a large correlational study may be interpreted as being consistent with the self-steering construct advanced initially by Fisher and Cleveland. As such, some of the same problems about covariation with other Rorschach variables have been raised but not satisfactorily solved to date.

Relationship to Psychopathology. Surprisingly few studies have investigated *B* scores of psychiatric patients. Some of these have utilized the comparison among diagnostic groups design and others a pre-post design in which the effect of hospitalization upon body-image boundary scores was investigated.

Fisher and Cleveland (1958b) report a study in which *B* and *P* of normals, neurotics, undifferentiated schizophrenics, and paranoid schizophrenics were compared. *B* scores of neurotics exceeded those of undifferentiated schizophrenics and paranoid schizophrenics, and *B* scores of the combined normal and neurotic group exceeded those of the combined schizophrenic groups. *P* scores of normals and neurotics, either singly or combined, were less than those of the two schizophrenic groups, again, either singly or combined. A study reported by Jaskar and Reed (1963) paired a group of hospitalized females with applicants for employment at the state hospital in which the *S*s were confined, and found no differences between the two groups in either *B* or *P*. These two studies are the only ones which compare intact groups and they disagree somewhat in their findings. Due to the paucity of evidence, it seems most reasonable to conclude that this is still an open question. Fisher, Boyd, Walker and Sheer (1959) attempted to compare the Rorschach protocols of parents of schizophrenics, neurotics, and normals. However, the large differences in R among these groups led to the exclusion of so many records that no significant differences were found.

Fisher and Cleveland (1958b) report a small study in which pre-post records were obtained from patients in psychotherapy. The modal pattern in patients rated as improved was a higher *B* and a lower *P* upon retest.

These authors also studied the records of 23 group-therapy patients being seen in private practice. These records had been obtained prior to treatment. After an unspecified length of time, the therapist was asked to select the two patients in each of his groups who ranked highest and the two who ranked lowest on a group-activity dimension, which was based on the degree to which a patient took the lead in getting the group to deal with personal problems, and a humanitarianism dimension, which referred to the degree of interest and concern demonstrated for the feelings of other group members. There was a significant relationship between *B* and group activity, but not between *B* and humanitarianism. The small number of *S*s and the highly subjective nature of the criterion make these results seem quite tentative. The high-*B* patient, secure in his base of operations (his well-defined body), was more able to participate in the group therapy proceedings than was the low-*B* patient.

Cleveland (1960) reported a reanalysis of a Rorschach study by Goldman (1960), where acutely ill and hospitalized schizophrenics were rated on admission and discharge on an unspecified 11-item scale. Thirty-three of the 45 patients were classified as improved, with 14 of these being classified as markedly improved. In both the improved and markedly improved patients, there were significant declines in *P*. In the markedly improved group, there was a significant increase in *B*. No significant changes occurred on *P* scores for the unimproved patients or on *B* scores for the improved or unimproved patients. The use of *P* as an index of change has some precedent in prediction studies, and is a very difficult index to utilize because of its reported change in a test-retest reliability study. The comparisons made do not indicate whether the changes in the improved patients were significantly more than the changes in the unimproved patients, but just report on changes within each group. It is possible that a great portion of *P* change can be attributed to unreliability. This criticism is not applicable to *B*. However, this is one of the few instances in which changes in *B* consistent with environmental and situational changes have been reported. It has been more traditional to speak of *B* as a very stable, long-term personality characteristic, and as being unaffected by a number of traumatic physical experiences, such as colostomy. It would be interesting, on replication with a larger number of patients and a more well-known method of defining improvement, to see if, in fact, *B* was as responsive to the changes brought about by hospitalization. These results might be a function of the acute illness of the patients and the subsequent dramatic change that might occur.

RELATIONSHIP TO CULTURAL CHARACTERISTICS. The studies in this section also fall into two groups; one of these compares existent cultural groupings, and the other compares the effects of cultural change on *B*.

Fisher and Cleveland (1958b) report a comparison among a large number of cultural groups whose Rorschach records were obtained from Kaplan (1956). The groups involved were Bhils of India, Hindus from India, Haitians, and Navajo, Zuni, and Tuscarora Indians of the United States. These groups were compared to a number of U.S. samples as well. In order to equate for R, selections were made within each set of records and it is quite possible that a number of cultures were distorted in order to select records from the needed response range. Of the 36 possible comparisons among the groups, only four were significant and each of these recorded a difference between one of the cultural groups and the American sample. Especially since the American sample had an unusually low R, the meaning of this study is not at all clear.

Fisher and Cleveland (1958b) also examined differences in the Rorschach protocols of Japanese village men and women, as well as Issei and Nisei men and women. Unfortunately, it was impossible to compare across the three cultural groups because of wide differences in median R. Within each group, the only sex differences shown were for the Nisei men and women, with the women having slightly higher *B* scores. Again, the median test demonstrating the significant difference was based upon the median of the entire group rather than the subgroup within which the comparison was performed, and so the reality of the difference is somewhat questionable.

Miner and DeVos (1960) studied the Rorschach records of a group of Arabs, some of whom had been born and remained on an oasis, and others of whom had moved from the oasis into an urban area. The study was intended to show the effect of French urban culture on personality. Urban *S*s had significantly higher *B* than did oasis *S*s. The Rorschach was given through interpreters and no information is given about R. In general, there are so many uncontrolled, but plausible differences between the two groups of *S*s (e.g., *S*s choosing to move from the oasis may have been more "self-steering" originally) that it is difficult to attribute a slight difference in *B* to the impact of French urban culture.

Cultural change is not the most appropriate area for the application of *B*. Differences among cultural groups and differences within a single group as a result of a cultural change may be so multiple as to make the interpretation of one isolated difference somewhat questionable. If this work is to be done at all, it should be clear that the only appropriate design is longitudinal. If there is some self-selection as to who is exposed to a cultural change and who is not, as was true in the study of the urban and oasis Arabs, the cross-sectional design may serve to obscure those differences which led to the differentiation of the groups, rather than to identify those changes which are a result of the differentiation.

In summary, there are two major types of studies which have fallen within the construct-validity category. One group of studies has reference to the physical and physiological properties of the individual, and seems much more related to the original conception of the body-image construct. A second group of studies is more focused on the personality characteristics of those individuals who obtain high-*B* scores, and this development seems very much an afterthought to the initial conceptualization of the construct. Studies within the first category have, for the most part, been reasonably successful. In psychosomatic illnesses, physical illnesses, and physiological indices, there have been differences between high-*B* and low-*B* *S*s which have been identified in a reasonably reliable, if not altogether consistent, manner. These changes have, for the most part, been with *B* and not with *P*, and they have been congruent with an external-internal dimension. High-*B* scorers are more responsive on external physiological indices and seem more likely to develop external physical symptoms, either physical or psychosomatic. On the other hand, low-*B* scorers seem more responsive on internal physiological indices and more prone to internal illnesses.

The personality studies seem to indicate that the high-*B* *S* is more self-steering than the low-*B* *S*, but these data are not entirely clear. Some important replication studies have failed and there is a very real problem of possible covariation with other Rorschach variables. This covariation would seem to have less impact on the physical studies, but there too, it would be wise to investigate the possibility. It appears as though the direction for future research in this area would favor use of *B* rather than *P*.

Trait Validity

Studies which are classifiable as trait-validity studies on the body boundaries scoring can be placed into three major groupings: (1) relationship to measures of the same construct, (2) relationship to measures of intelligence and verbal productivity, and (3) relationship to various other measures.

RELATIONSHIP TO MEASURES OF THE SAME CONSTRUCT. The Secord Homonym Test (Secord, 1953) is a word-association test that includes a large number of stimulus words that can elicit associations to either a body part or a nonbody meaning; e.g., "colon" and "graft." Fisher and Cleveland (1958b) report a significant difference between high- and low-*B* *S*s in number of bodily associations. Jourard and Secord (1955) have also developed a Body Cathexis Scale, in which *S*s rate the positiveness of their feelings about various body parts. Landau (1960) and Jaskar and Reed (1963), using correlational techniques, report no significant relationship between either *B* or *P* and responses to either the Secord Homonym Test or the Body Cathexis Scale.

Fisher and Cleveland have developed a Barrier scoring which may be applied to the drawing of a house. The details of the scoring as outlined by Fisher and Cleveland (1958b), are based on the facade. The authors have demonstrated a relationship between the Rorschach and Draw-A-House high-*B* groups in one sample, but in another sample the relationship could be obtained only after the elimination of a large portion of the sample, including all males. Similarly, Appleby (1956) failed to confirm the relationship between the Rorschach and Draw-A-House scorings.

Fisher and Cleveland (1958b) report a number of different attempts to correlate *B* with other measures of similar constructs. In one study, *S*s were told to place a check after the words "heart," "muscle," "stomach," or "skin," each time he noticed a sensation in any of the areas. *S*s made these observations for a period of three minutes. The number of skin sensations was unrelated to *B* and dropped from analysis, so that further analyses reported a contrast between one exterior (muscle) and two interior (heart, stomach) measures. Even with this after-the-fact manipulation of the variables to be compared, no relationships of reported body associations to *B* reached statistical significance ($p < .05$).

In a later study, and the largest study of the relationships between *B* and patterns of body perception, Fisher and Fisher (1964) compared *B* with four separate indices devised to measure body perception. In the first test, *S*s were given a piece of paper with four body sectors (skin, stomach, muscle, heart) listed. They were told to place a check next to each one each time a prominent body sensation occurred. The final score on this measure (as well as each of the three other measurements described below) was made up of the number of exterior responses minus the number of interior responses. The test was given to two samples and in both samples the rho correlation between *B* and body sensations was .33 ($p < .01$). The correlation between *B* and the total number of associations was not significant. In the second test, 30 different experiences or feelings were listed and the *S* was instructed, for each item listed, to check one of the four body areas where the main sensation occurred the last time the *S* had such a feeling or experience. Two separate samples were used, and although the relationship to *B* was not significant in the first sample, a correlation of .47 ($p < .01$) was obtained in the second. For the third test, *S*s were asked to swallow a pill which they were told was harmless but had a variety of side effects; the pill was, in fact, a placebo. After a brief period of time, *S*s were asked to respond to a 16-item checklist (which included four items for each of the four body areas) and to indicate which symptoms they experienced as a result of taking the pill. Correlations between *B* and the exterior-minus-interior score were significant and positive in the male group, but not in the female group. In the fourth test, *S*s were shown a list of 20 phrases, drawn equally from the four clusters, and placed in random order, allowed to study it for a minute, and then given a five-minute recall period in which they were asked to list all the phrases they could remember. This test was given to two samples and in both, correlations between *B* and exterior-minus-interior scores were positive and significant.

Performance on the Projection Movement Sequence, a test in which a variety of scenes reflecting the movement of powdered black iron filings controlled by two hand magnets, is presented to *S*s who are asked to tell stories to them, was compared with *B*. The number of dissolution fantasies, phrased in body terms, was found to be negatively related to *B*. Dissolution of inanimate objects was specifically excluded from consideration on the Projection Movement Sequence, but inanimate objects are scorable for both *B* and *P* responses on the Rorschach. It is not clear as to whether the significant result might have been a function of this apparent inconsistency and an after-the-fact decision to exclude the inanimate dissolution fantasies.

B was also compared to the phantom limb phenomenon (Fisher and Cleveland, 1958b). *S*s were asked to draw their perception of their phantom limb relative to the stump. *S*s who experienced a phantom limb external to their stump were more likely to have low *B* than *S*s who perceived the phantom limb as inside the stump. Consistent with this last finding, it was hypothesized that high-*B* *S*s have a greater capacity to rebuild a realistic body boundary after a physical trauma.

A sentence-completion test with stems concerning the skin was devised and scored as to number of completions which reflected body vulnerability (Fisher and Cleveland, 1958b). High-*B* *S*s gave a significantly smaller number of sentence completions with body-vulnerability connotations than low-*B* *S*s. Fisher and Cleveland (1958b) also collected a set of dreams from *S*s and these dreams were rated as to the definiteness or vagueness of boundaries within the dream. This was then related in turn to *B*, and while results fell in the predicted direction, they they did not reach statistical significance. Finally, a chance relationship was discovered between body-image scores and Sheldon's somatotype scores.

Fisher and Cleveland (1956b) administered a symptom checklist which contained seven exterior and seven interior symptoms. It was found that high-*B* *S*s checked significantly more exterior body symptoms than did the low-*B* *S*s, but there were no differences between the groups in number of interior body symptoms checked. There were also no significant differences in the relationship between body symptoms and *P*. Appleby (1956) replicated this study, but could not cross validate the findings. In addition, he also administered a psychosomatic experience blank and did not find any significant relationships between it and *B*.

Fisher (1964b) gave a body-prominence test along with the Rorschach. This asked the *S*s to list a number of things that they were aware of at the present moment, and the score assigned was the number of references to their body. This test was given on three different occasions, and *B* was correlated with the sum of body references given on all three testings. It was given to four separate samples and did not correlate in any of the samples with *B* scores of males, but did correlate, in each of the samples, with *B* scores of females. The conclusion is drawn that awareness of one's body is related to *B* in women, but not in men, and that this difference is due to the different cultural implications of the body for men and women, since women, more than men, are encouraged to be conscious of their physical appearance in our society.

The general pattern of relationships between *B* and other measures of similar constructs has been mixed, inconsistent, and, for the most part, negative. This is not entirely surprising, in that a large number of the tests were specially designed and had no proven validity. One notable exception is the study by Fisher and Fisher (1964) in which *B* showed a consistent series of positive relationships to a set of specially designed tests and experiments, all of which were again chosen to reflect the exterior-interior dimension, which *B* has been reasonably successful in doing.

Relationship to Measures of Intelligence and Verbal Productivity. Three studies have investigated the relationship between *B* and intelligence. Appleby (1956) compared *B* with the Wonderlic Personnel Test, which was used as a measure of intelligence, and found no relationship in a sample of college students. Fisher and Cleveland (1958b), reanalyzing data collected from graduate students by Kelly and Fiske (1951), found no relationships between *B* and Miller Analogies scores. Ware et al. (1957), in a group of polio patients, found no significant difference in Wechsler–Bellevue I.Q. between high- and low-*B* *S*s. All the studies agree in the lack of relationship between intelligence and *B*, but all the studies dealt with samples of unusually bright *S*s, and in at least two of the studies we can expect that the correlations were performed over a restricted range.

Appleby (1956) compared *B* with number of words used in the total Rorschach protocol and found significant differences between high- and low-*B* *S*s along this dimension in both an original and a cross-validation sample. However, Fisher and Cleveland (1958b) report two subsequent studies comparing *B* and *P* scores with Rorschach protocol word count, and no significant relationships were demonstrated. They further demonstrated that 69% of all *B* scores and 30% of all *P* scores were based on single words, and no more than four words were needed for either *B* or *P* responses. In one further study, *B* and *P* scores were compared to a "language facility" test—which was a multiple-choice vocabulary test, and so might have closer relationship to intelligence than to verbal productivity—as no significant relationships were found with what, again, was a very bright and homogeneous group of professionals in the mental health field.

The evidence that has been presented would seem to indicate that body-boundary scores are not influenced by intelligence and verbal facility. However, there is still some need to establish this discriminant validity in a more heterogeneous and less intellectually gifted sample.

RELATIONSHIP TO VARIOUS OTHER MEASURES. Fisher and Fisher (1959) compared *B* with an aniseikonic lens comparison of the left and right sides of the body, a puppet representation of the right and left sides of the body as being masculine or feminine, and a galvanic skin response measure of right-left reactivity. Among *S*s between the ages of 5 and 12, there were no significant relationships with any of the measures. For *S*s between 13 and 17, left-reactive galvanic skin response *S*s had higher *B* scores than did right-reactive or no-gradient *S*s. There were no significant relationships with either the puppet or the aniseikonic measure. Fisher (1960) used these same measures as well as measures of autokinetic effects and some sex-role identification figure drawings. The only significant result which is reported is between *P* and galvanic skin response directionality, and this was based on the female group and not significant in the male group. Jaskar and Reed (1963) administered a drawing-completion test which was a measure of masculinity-feminity and found that it did not relate to either *B* or *P*. These findings are all so unclear, both as to the pattern of correlation with the body-image scores and the meaning of the variables being correlated, that they add little information to our knowledge of the body-image scoring system.

Two studies have compared body-image scoring with measures of manifest anxiety. Sieracki (1963) found a nonsignificant correlation between *B* and anxiety scores on the IPAT, and Shipman et al. (1964) found a significant negative correlation ($r = -.61$) between *B* and the Taylor Manifest Anxiety Scale. There were also two investigations of the relationship between *B* and the F scale by Fisher and Cleveland (1956b) and Appleby (1956). In neither of the studies were significant relationships found.

A number of studies have compared *B* with scores on personality inventories. Fisher and Cleveland (1958b), reporting on the reanalysis of the Kelly and Fiske (1951) study, compare B with scores on the Allport–Vernon Study of Values and the Strong Vocational Interest blank. No correlations with the Allport–Vernon reach the .05 level of significance. On the Strong, the low-*B* group exceeds the high-*B* group in the group scales for professional and quantitative science interests. The high-*B* group exceeds the low-*B* group in the group scale reflecting interest in sales and the individual sales manager scale. In the second study reported by Fisher and Cleveland, the *B* score is related to the Morris–Jones Ways to Live Measure, the Allport–Vernon Study of Values, and the Thurstone Interest Schedule. None of the comparisons was significant beyond chance levels. The second study reported by Fisher and Cleveland indicates that there is no significant relationship between *B* and self-concept as expressed by the Bill's Index of Adjustment and Values. Appleby (1956) related *B* to scores on the Allport–Vernon Study of Values, the Thurstone Interest Schedule, the Edwards Personal Preference Schedule, and the Sheer Self-concept Test. Of the 50 correlations performed, only six were significant in the total sample. However, five of these showed a large number of significant correlations among themselves, and there were a great many correlations performed, so there is some question as to whether or not these results may be accounted for on the basis of chance. Sieracki (1963) compared *B* with Kuder Preference Record scores on the computational, persuasive, scientific, and social service scales and found no significant differences between high- and low-*B* groups. The results of these "shot-gun" attempts have not been very productive, and there do not seem to be any significant patterns that have emerged from these studies.

A potentially more important series of correlations, because of the implications for relationships with intelligence and verbal facility, was between *B* and social class. Landau (1960) found a significant correlation of .35 between *B* and social class; the correlation between *P* and social class was nonsignificant. Masson (1963) failed to obtain any relation between college students' *B* scores and the social position of their fathers. However, since college students are clearly class-mobile, the meaning of this correlation is not clear.

In summary, then, the trait-validity studies seem to reinforce the ability of the body-image Barrier scores to distinguish between interior and exterior aspects of body responding. Some discrimination is established between these scores and measures of intelligence. It would be of value to investigate further relationships with variables such as intelligence, verbal productivity, and social class in samples of greater heterogeneity.

OVERALL EVALUATION

The body-image boundary scoring system was originally derived from a clinical hunch of Fisher and Cleveland after a study of the personality characteristics of arthritis patients. It was seen as having implications for the definiteness of the body image of the patients, and initial studies reflected the origin of the body-image concept. It has later been expanded to include a personality type seen as being characteristic of a high-*B* individual.

The scoring criteria have been based on clinical judgment, and no attempt was made to assess the contribution of the various scoring subcategories to the validity of the overall system. Eigenbrode and Shipman (1960) have criticized the scoring on precisely these grounds. Cassell (1964) has revised the *P* scoring and produced an index, while based equally on clinical judgment, which seems to be more in line with the original expectation of Fisher and Cleveland for the *P* dimension.

The research findings with respect to *P* have generally been disappointing. It has not related to *B* in the hypothesized ways, and has often been ignored in more recent studies. Where it has been used, findings have often failed to confirm the hypotheses.

Findings surrounding the use of *B* have been much more encouraging. *B* has generally been successful when it has been applied in studies which contrast exterior and interior modes of responding, whether this contrast is on physical symptoms, physiological responses, or psychological tests. When *B* has been related to personality characteristics, it has been reasonably successful only in the case of self-steering behavior, and here the results are somewhat clouded by a possible artifact. Covariation with other Rorschach variables which are also seen to be related to self-steering behavior must be ruled out before the independent value of *B* can be established.

All of the relationships which have been investigated have been based on dichotomization at a median, which has varied between 3 and 6. The use of this high vs. low dichotomy, as well as the large amount of overlap obtained in the research, would suggest that, except in extreme cases, the *B* score has little clinical value for idiographic decisions. Equal problems are posed for research, since the failure to replicate can often be traced to the use of varying median scores, resulting in the failure of the high-*B* groups to be constituted of individuals with similar scores.

A major problem involved in research with the body-image boundary scoring system has been the liberty which the various investigators have taken with the types of stimuli, administration, and response total employed. Rorschach and Holtzman plates, group and individual administrations, and prescribed and free response totals have been used in the several validation studies. There has been no adequate demonstration of equivalence across these various methods. It would have been possible to write a large number of reviews, each for a different subgroup of approaches, and this perhaps would have found more consistency among the various research findings. There is a notation in a dissertation by Conquest (1963) that Fisher, in a personal communication, has recommended the use of the Holtzman blots rather than the Rorschach blots because one response per card makes response total comparable, under easy control, and allows the presentation of a wider range of stimuli. This advice has not been taken by Fisher, whose own studies reflect the continued use of the Rorschach blots; Cleveland's more recent work has employed the Holtzman blots. Without a great deal of further work with both sets of stimuli, it does not seem reasonable to make an a priori judgment between the two.

A great deal of potential research with the body-image boundary scores suggests itself. A good deal of this research is basic methodological work that might have been performed at a much earlier stage. The relationship between the Rorschach and the Holtzman blots, between group and individual administration, between fixed and free response totals, all must be investigated. The relationships of each of the subcategories of *B* and *P* scores ought to be related to a meaningful construct; this might help to refine the scoring system itself. In the light of the validity research, it would seem that the most appropriate construct would involve an ability to discriminate between exterior and interior response. Further work might be done with Cassell's revision of *P* scoring as it has been largely untested and does relate in a meaningful way to *B,* while Fisher and Cleveland's *P* has been tested and found wanting. In many of these studies it would be important to investigate the extent to which traditional Rorschach scores (e.g., W and M) are able to predict the findings; in studies investigating personality variables, such an approach is particularly important. The relationship between the body-image boundary scoring system and the effectiveness of therapy has been only barely approached. One method which has promise, but which is not sufficiently developed, is the use of *B* as a predictive device in suggesting who may and who may not be more responsive to treatment. This seems true of both psychiatric and physical complaints. Finally, a longitudinal study of *B* would be of great value. It is somewhat confusing to read in one study that the failure to find differences between groups is a tribute to the stability of *B,* and in another study that differences between groups are a tribute to the sensitivity of *B.* There have been difficulties in using *P* over time because it is not clear as to just how much change might be expected in a control group. A longitudinal study would help to establish the stability of the body-image boundary scores, to provide a foundation for studies of change, and to make it possible to use the scoring system for predictive purposes.

Chapter 7

HOMOSEXUAL SIGNS

Homosexuality, a practice which has been in existence since the beginning of recorded history, has been condemned by our society on social, religious, and legal grounds. In fact, because of the "taboo" quality associated with the very topic itself, attempts at research in the area often prove to be quite difficult (Hooker, 1963).

According to the figures in the Kinsey report, it is estimated that one out of every three men in this country has had at least one homosexual experience beyond adolescence (Kinsey, Pomeroy, and Martin, 1948). Quite apart from the possibly inflated nature of the Kinsey figures, this estimate cannot be taken to mean that one third of our male population are "homosexuals." The whole issue of what constitutes homosexuality involves more problems than one might initially suspect; some of these difficulties will be discussed below.

The early reports on the assessment of male homosexuality by means of the Rorschach left much to be desired (Bergmann, 1945; Due and Wright, 1945; Lindner, 1946). The evidence for the so-called homosexual signs described by these authors consisted primarily of their clinical, "seat-of-the-pants" experience with the Rorschach. It was really not until Wheeler (1949) collated and tested these several signs experimentally that any actual data as to their validity started to become available. Despite the fact that Rorschach signs for male homosexuality have appeared more recently in other sources (e.g. Piotrowski, 1957; Schafer, 1954; Ulett, 1950), and that some attempts have been made to develop signs for the diagnosis of homosexuality in females (Armon, 1960; Fromm and Elonen, 1951),

Chapter 7 is an extended version of "On the diagnosis of homosexuality from the Rorschach," by Marvin R. Goldfried, published in the *Journal of Consulting Psychology,* 1966, vol. 30, pp. 338–49. Copyright © 1966 by the American Psychological Association, and reproduced by permission.

most of the research efforts have focused on those indices outlined by Wheeler. This chapter will deal primarily with the description and evaluation of Wheeler's signs for homosexuality.

DEFINITION OF HOMOSEXUALITY

As mentioned earlier, the problem of defining homosexuality appears at first to be fairly straightforward. To state simply that homosexuality refers to a condition whereby sexual gratification comes from relations with members of the same sex, however, has only minimal clinical significance; some of the reasons for the limitations of this simplistic definition are noted below.

While it is typical for people to have had homosexual experiences during their early years, the persistence of this behavior in adulthood is considered to be perverse. Further, it is often maintained that an adult's homosexual behavior reflects more than just a sexual problem—namely, that it is indicative of a more general psychological maladjustment. Hooker (1957) has challenged this notion that the homosexual is a more generally disturbed individual, and has suggested instead that "homosexuality is symptomatic of pathology, but that the pathology is confined to one sector of behavior, namely, the sexual" (p. 30). Hooker bases her viewpoint on test data collected from a group of seemingly well-adjusted homosexuals who were living in the community. Inasmuch as there are many homosexuals who are severely disturbed in their nonsexual areas of functioning as well, Hooker's conclusion seems to be a bit overstated. A more appropriate conclusion would appear to be that while some homosexuals are maladjusted, others are not. Even without reference to the hypothesis that homosexuality is an indication of a greater disturbance, one can make a good case for the viewpoint that the homosexual tends to be more maladjusted for no other reason than—at least within our society—he is more likely to be sexually frustrated than the person who seeks heterosexual gratification. Further, in comparison to the nonhomosexual, the sexual gratification that the homosexual *does* obtain is more likely to be accompanied by feelings of guilt and shame.

How much do we know about a person when we categorize him as a "homosexual"? Here, too, we may quote Hooker (1957), who has hypothesized the following: "Homosexuality as a clinical entity does not exist. Its forms are as varied as are those of heterosexuality" (p. 30). A homosexual may be active or passive in the role he adopts, he may seek out relations with many other men or he may prefer a more stable "marriage," and he may receive a good deal of pleasure in his sexual relations or may be impotent.

To complicate matters still further, the label "homosexuality" tends to be used as a broad category under which are included individuals who act out their homosexuality, people who are troubled by their homosexual thoughts, and those who are not completely aware of their homosexual tendencies but nonetheless are made anxious by them. In this regard, Wheeler (1949) indicated some of the reasons why he chose not to use the history of overt homosexual activities in defining his criterion group:

1. Single or even multiple homosexual acts are relatively frequent in the essentially "normal" heterosexual individual, especially under what might be described as extenuating circumstances.
2. Overt homosexual acts may not be performed by those individuals who have a strong desire for them but fear their implications.
3. Cultural pressures are such that a statement of either the desires or the acts is difficult to elicit regardless of whether or not the individual conceives of them as homosexual (p. 111).

Instead of using only overt homosexuals for his criterion group, Wheeler also included those individuals whose homosexuality was considered to be latent (i.e., suppressed or repressed tendencies). In fact, only four of the 60 subjects in his "homosexual" group could reliably be said to have been overt homosexuals.

Rather than viewing homosexuality as referring to an actual entity, it is probably more accurate to speak of "homosexual tendencies," a characteristic which all individuals possess, but to varying degrees. With this view of homosexuality as a construct rather than a directly observable criterion, the implication for the Rorschach signs for homosexuality is that they may be more easily evaluated by means of the construct rather than criterion-validity type of study. This point will be discussed again later in the chapter.

HOMOSEXUAL SIGNS

Based on the writings of Bergmann (1945), Due and Wright (1945), and Lindner (1945), as well as general clinical experience, Wheeler compiled a list of 20 signs presumably indicative of homosexuality. The signs are based on the content of the response; some of the scored responses must be given to specific blot areas (see Signs 1–14), but others may occur anywhere in the record (see Signs 15–20).

The face validity of some of the signs—or more accurately, the underlying rationale for the signs—is fairly obvious. For other signs, however, the justification seems to be more of a far-fetched rationalization than a rationale. In the final analysis, however, the utility of any given sign rests on its empirical and not its theoretical relevance.

Although the scoring criteria of all 20 signs are outlined below, the reader should be cautioned that *not all 20 have been shown to be empirically valid.* In the section following the description of the signs, some attempt will be made to assess their differential validity. The interscorer reliability will then be discussed, and the method by which the protocol may be summarized will be noted.

Scoring Criteria

SIGN 1. Card I (W or W̸): A mask, human face, or animal face.

The rationale behind this is based on the hypothesized relationship between homosexuality and paranoia; the unreal and persecutory aspects of the environment are reflected in this sign.

Examples of such responses are as follows:

"Fox's face"
"Man's face"
"Theatrical mask"

SIGN 2. Card I (lower center D): The torso of a male or a muscular female.

The rationale of confused identity, which underlies this sign, is fairly clear.

Examples of such responses are as follows:

"Japanese man"
"Male dancer"
"Oriental priest"
"Woman athlete"

SIGN 3. Card II (lower center D): A crab or a crab-like animal.

The assumption here is that a blot area which presumably resembles the female genital is seen as being threatening and tactually unappealing.

Examples of such responses are as follows:

"Crawfish"
"Crustacean of some sort"
"Deep-sea crab"
"Lobster—it's been cooked"

SIGN 4. Card III (W or W̸): A human response, but with sex confusion.

The rationale here is the same as for Sign 2; namely, confusion of sexual identity.

Examples of such responses are as follows:

"Half-man, half-woman"
"Man with breasts"
"Woman, but she has a penis"

SIGN 5. Card III (W or W̸): A human response, but with sex uncertain.

The uncertainty of the sexual identification of the figures presumably reflects conflict in this area.

Examples of such responses are as follows:

"Could be men or women"
"Figures—can't tell the sex"
"Two sexless people"

SIGN 6. Card III (W or W̸): An animal or animal-like (i.e., dehumanized) response.

By "dehumanizing" what is typically perceived as human figures, the subject avoids having to make any commitment regarding the sex of the figures.

Examples of such responses are as follows:

"Birds"
"Featherless chickens"
"Gorillas"
"Ostrich-like natives"

SIGN 7. Card IV (W or W̸): A contorted, monstrous, or threatening human or animal.

The rationale stated by Wheeler (1949) for this sign is not altogether clear: "feminine (passive) identification with male figure seen as threatening, etc." (p. 104). It would seem more reasonable instead to accept a rationale simply on the basis of the subject's difficulty in identifying with the masculine figure.

Examples of such responses are as follows:

"Baboon ready to pounce"
"Gruesome giant, seen from below"
"Horrid beast"
"Man looking back through his legs"

SIGN 8. Card V (W, W̸, or center D): A human or humanized animal.

Wheeler acknowledges that the rationale for this sign, which involves the humanization of a figure typically seen as an animal, is not terribly clear. Davids, Joelson, and McArthur (1956) have suggested that this type of response may reflect "a confusion of role and sexual identity, or even of body image, as a source of anxiety" (p. 171).

Examples of such responses are as follows:

"Bugs Bunny"
"Dancer"
"Peter Rabbit"
"Woman dressed as a bat"

SIGN 9. Card VI (center or top D): An object implying some sort of cleavage.

The assumption underlying this sign is that for the homosexual, sexuality is associated with aggressive and destructive overtones.

Examples of such responses are as follows:

"Oil well, drilling"
"Path of a projectile"
"Ship with foaming wake"

SIGN 10. Card VII (W, W̸, or top D): A depreciated female figure.

The homosexual's derogatory attitude toward women is believed to underlie this type of response.

Examples of such responses are as follows:

"Old bags"
"Old maids gossiping"
"Silly-looking witches"
"Women—yakety-yak"

SIGN 11. Card VIII (lateral D): An animal with incongruous parts or several incongruous animals.

According to Wheeler, the confused perception of the anatomy of animals reflected in this type of response may be viewed as an extension of the rationale for Sign 2—namely, confused identity.

Examples of such responses are as follows:

"Bear with rat's head"
"Rat or lion or something"
"Sheep with the skin of a leopard"

SIGN 12. Card IX (upper lateral D): A dehumanized human figure.

The avoidance of sexual specification by dehumanizing the figure (see Sign 6), as well as depreciation, is the stated underlying rationale for this sign.

Examples of such responses are as follows:

"Caricature of men"
"Ghosts"
"Gremlins"
"Monsters with guns for arms"

SIGN 13. Card X (top center D): An animal attacking or fighting over the central object.

According to Wheeler, the attack of this phallic-like object—which may reflect a masturbatory fear or may even be a sexual goal in itself—is the rationale for the inclusion of this type of response. Surprisingly enough, Wheeler does not point out directly that fear of castration may be reflected in this sign.

Examples of such responses are as follows:

"Beavers gnawing a tree"
"Beetles fighting over a stick"
"Creatures devouring their prey"

SIGN 14. Card X (pink—all or upper half—plus center blue): A human figure with the blue having to do with orality.

The rationale presented by Wheeler—"Preoccupation with oral (pregenital) stimulation"—seems far-fetched, especially since the relevancy to homosexuality per se is not at all clear.

Examples of such responses are as follows:

"Children blowing bubbles"
"Irishmen with growth on lips"
"Men smoking a pipe"
"People drinking through straws"

SIGN 15. Any card: Human or animal oral detail responses.

The reasoning behind this sign simply refers to the oral preoccupation, with possible implications of sexual gratification; the implications for homosexuality are not specified or altogether clear.

Examples of such responses are as follows:

"Decayed teeth"
"Full lips"
"Open mouth showing tonsils"
"Tongues sticking out"

SIGN 16. Any card: Human or animal anal detail, or references to such.

The emphasis on anality, with possible relationship to sexual gratification, is presumed to reflect homosexual tendencies.

Examples of such responses are as follows:[1]

"Buttocks"
"Dog defecating"
"Rectum"
"Woman with a large ass"

SIGN 17. Any card: Humans or animals seen as "back-to-back."

According to Wheeler, this type of response reflects the "Bizarre anatomical relationships between two like people or animals" (p. 105) which is indicative of homosexual activity. Actually, this sign appears to be more of an extension of Sign 16 than anything else.

Examples of such responses are as follows:

"Dancers with backs together"
"Men with their backs pressed against each other"
"Two sheep back-to-back"

SIGN 18. Any card: A human object or act having to do with religion.

The rationale for this sign is based on the hypothesized relationship between paranoia and homosexuality, the former presumably being re-

[1] Davids, Joelson, and McArthur (1956) have found that "rear-view" responses are indicative of homosexuality. In light of their findings, Sign 16 might be extended to include such responses as: "a person with his back to you," "women doing the can-can," as well as other similar responses.

flected in this religious preoccupation. Wheeler further suggests that the presence of religious objects or acts may also be indicative of guilt feelings.

Examples of such responses are as follows:

"Altar"
"Cathedral"
"Man praying"
"Priest's cross"

SIGN 19. Any card: Male or female genitalia.

The preoccupation with sexuality, according to Wheeler, may conceivably be a function of unfulfilled gratification.

Examples of such responses are as follows:

"Penis"
"Testicles"
"Vagina"
"Woman's private parts"

SIGN 20. Any card: Feminine clothing.

The rationale for this sign (i.e., "Feminine identification") is fairly clear cut.

Examples of such responses are as follows:

"Hair ribbon"
"Nylon stockings"
"Panties"
"Woman's fur coat"

Validity of Individual Signs

Based on the studies which report data relevant to the validity of the individual signs (Aronson, 1952; Davids et al., 1956; DeLuca, 1966; Fein, 1950; Ferracuti and Rizzo, 1956, 1958; Machover, Puzzo, Machover, and Plumeau, 1959; Nitsche, Robinson, and Parsons, 1956; Reitzell, 1949; Wheeler, 1949), it is possible to come to some very general conclusions concerning the relative merits of the 20 indices. From these findings, it is somewhat easier to point to those signs which have consistently *failed* to hold up under empirical test than it is to conclude which signs have generally proven to be *valid*. While a few signs have fared relatively well, most indices are either of ambiguous validity (i.e., the findings are not consistent from study to study) or are clearly poor.

The 20 signs may be classified into three general categories: (1) *Unquestionably poor:* These signs have consistently failed to obtain statistical significance, either because of the infrequency of their occurrence or their inherent invalidity. (2) *Ambiguous validity:* The indices in this category have shown to be valid in some studies, but not in others. (3) *Probably*

TABLE 7.1
Summary Statement of the Validity of the Individual Homosexual Signs

Sign Number	*Probably Good*	*Ambiguous Validity*	*Unquestionably Poor*
1			X
2		X	
3			X
4			X
5			X
6		X	
7	X		
8	X		
9			X
10	X		
11		X	
12		X	
13		X	
14			X
15		X	
16	X		
17	X		
18		X	
19		X	
20	X		

good: The research evidence for these signs, although somewhat inconsistent, seems to point to their validity. The signs that fall into each of the three classifications—which in themselves are admittedly somewhat arbitrary and subjective—are presented in Table 7.1.

No single sign can ever really be expected to be pathognomic of homosexuality. The question then becomes how many signs need to be present before some statement concerning homosexuality can be made. It is certainly possible that a number of signs categorized in Table 7.1 as being of "ambiguous validity," when used as a group, can serve as a valid measure of homosexuality. Unfortunately, all the studies on the Wheeler indices which have compared groups on more than a single sign have used *all* of the signs—including those which are unquestionably poor. Additional research, or perhaps simply a reanalysis of findings of these previous studies, should be done in order to determine whether there is an improvement in discriminatory ability with the *exclusion* of signs 1, 3, 4, 5, 9, and 14. In any case, *it is recommended that these six "unquestionably poor" signs be discarded in any future clinical or research work with the homosexual indices.*

Interscorer Reliability

From the description of the criteria for the 20 signs, as well as from an inspection of the sample responses, it would appear that most of the signs could be scored with a fair degree of reliability. There are nevertheless a few indices which are somewhat vague as to their scoring criteria. In the case of Sign 10, for example, there is room for variation in determining what constitutes a "derogatory" attitude toward women. The scoring criteria are not spelled out as well as they might be in this instance.

The "findings" reported in the research literature on the interscorer reliability can easily leave one with a feeling of frustration. For the most part, the reliability among scorers has been reported in qualitative rather than quantitative language. Thus, Hooker (1958) has concluded that "there is *considerable* room for subjectivity in scoring" (p. 36).[2] Grauer (1954), on the other hand, has pointed out: "Differences in scoring between two psychologists were *slight* and were easily reconciled after a conference on discrepant points" (p. 459). To complicate matters further, Meketon, Griffith, Taylor, and Wiedeman (1962) first report that "*considerable* subjective judgment does seem to be required in scoring," but that with discussion and further references to the scoring criteria, "the judges moved *closer and closer* to being of *one mind* as to the signs in later records" (p. 283).

The only study in which there is an actual numerical estimate of interscorer reliability was done by Davids et al. (1956). They report that two judges were in agreement in their scoring of 83% of the responses. In the case of the total number of signs in each record, the obtained coefficient was .92.

It would seem, then, that while there is some room for variation in the scoring of certain (as yet unspecified) signs, a reliable statement can be made concerning the total number of indices which appear in a given protocol.

Summary Scores

According to Wheeler, a record may be summarized by a simple tabulation of the number of signs which appear in it. Signs 1–14, which refer to specific cards and blot locations, obviously can occur only once in a given protocol. Inasmuch as Signs 15–20 can conceivably appear on any card and in any location, the question arises as to whether or not a given sign should be tallied into the summary score if it occurs more than once in a record. Meketon et al. (1962) have noted that from a close analysis of Wheeler's (1949) data, it would appear that each sign was counted only once for any given record; Wheeler has confirmed the fact that this was the approach he had taken.[3] Most studies subsequent to Wheeler's, however, have counted a sign no matter how often it occurred in a protocol. There is nothing inherently wrong with this latter approach. In fact, it is probably a more appropriate method in that it is in better accord with the common notion that the greater frequency of a theme on a projective test is more indicative of the personality characteristic presumably reflected in this theme.

There is only one caution which should be pointed out in regard to the multiple tabulation of a given sign within a protocol. If a study is being

2 Italics in this and subsequent quotations concerning scorer reliability are ours.
3 Personal communication, January 1965.

conducted to determine the relative efficiency with which each of the 20 signs is able to differentiate between groups, it would be best to tally each score on a dichotomous, present/absent basis. The reasoning behind this is based largely on statistical grounds, so that in a sign-by-sign comparison of groups there is no confounding of *number of records* in which the sign occurs with frequency of occurrence *within individual records.*

Independent of the issue of single or multiple tabulation of signs is the question of whether or not the summary score itself should consist of a simple counting of signs. It is probably best to deal with this question by means of a discussion of the effect of productivity on the final score.

THE EFFECT OF R. In summarizing a record by simply counting the total number of signs, it is easy to see where the total number of responses in that record has to be taken into account. Despite some very tangential and weak evidence that R is unrelated to the number of signs produced—Davids et al. (1956) note that the three homosexuals with the longest protocols had fewer than the average number of signs for the entire homosexual group—there is strong research evidence indicating that total R and the number of homosexual signs produced are positively related. Specifically, Aronson (1952) found the following correlation coefficients between R and the number of signs for the three groups of 30 *S*s each: delusional psychotics, $r = .646$ ($p < .01$); nondelusional psychotics, $r = .537$ ($p < .01$); normals, $r = .303$ (ns). The relatively low correlation obtained for the normals was probably a function of the infrequency with which the homosexual signs appeared in that particular group ($\bar{X} = 1.10$, S.D. = 1.10). When Aronson pooled all three groups and computed the correlation, the obtained value was .675 ($p < .001$), indicating a very marked effect of total R on the final summary score.

The ways in which various researchers have attempted to cope with this effect of R have been either to base the scoring on only the first response given to each card, or to make use of the ratio of signs to total R. Wheeler (1949) had originally noted that the use of percentage scores might prove to be better than a simple counting of signs. His argument against using percentage scores does not, at least to the authors, seem to be very convincing. He states: "The major objection to this was that it would complicate any future application of the signs to individual records in the practical clinic situation and would make occurrence in a testing-the-limits procedure doubly difficult to evaluate" (pp. 116–117).

Rather than summarizing the protocol by the simple tabulation of homosexual signs, it is recommended that the per cent of signs relative to total R be used. There is some evidence to indicate that the percentage score, at least in part, accounts for the effect of R. Thus, the significant difference in number of signs between two groups of homosexuals—which seems to have been due to differences in R—disappeared when the groups were compared on the basis of percentage scores (Yamahiro and Griffith, 1960). An inspection of Table 7.3, p. 203, will illustrate further the way in which percentage score accounts for variations in total R.

NORMATIVE DATA

As is the case with most special scorings of the Rorschach, normative data on the homosexual signs have been a by-product of the various studies with the signs. Hence, the samples on which these data are available tend to be relatively small and often unique to certain types of environmental situations.

Nature of the Samples

From the studies in which the data were reported, norms are available on overt homosexuals living in the community, homosexuals attending a clinic, homosexuals in prison, female homosexuals, delusional and nondelusional psychotics, paranoid schizophrenics, neurotics, alcoholics, and normals. The characteristics of these several samples are outlined in Table 7.2. As can be seen in the table, relatively little in the way of demographic material was available on some of the samples, particularly those subjects used in the studies by Davids et al. (1956) and Meketon et al. (1962).

To supplement the data in Table 7.2, some additional relevant information on the subjects in these various studies might be noted. Hooker's (1958) sample of overt homosexuals was contacted through the auspices of the Mattachine Society—an organization whose purpose is to bring about a better acceptance of homosexuality by society. The homosexuals were selected from those volunteers who appeared to be fairly well-adjusted and had no history of ever having been in therapy. As can be seen in Table 7.2, their intellectual and educational levels were higher than those of the general population. Except for a few heterosexual experiences on the part of three subjects, the sample was comprised of individuals who were exclusively homosexual.

The subjects in Yamahiro and Griffith's (1960) study were all living in the community at the time of the testing. Following an incident in which two children were sexually assaulted, local legislative pressures began to move in the direction of having all sexual deviates hospitalized. Consequently, the police picked up all known sexual deviates; the homosexuals in Yamahiro and Griffith's sample were among those apprehended by the police. Although six of the 22 homosexuals had a previous record of sexual misconduct, the group also included some respected members of the community. As can be seen from Table 7.2, the group as a whole was above average in intellectual ability. The context within which this group of homosexuals was tested was a unique one, particularly since they faced possible hospitalization.

Davids et al. (1956) obtained their group of homosexuals from college students applying for help at a University Clinic. The subjects, who had problems revolving around their homosexual practices, approached the testing with the knowledge that the clinic was aware of their homosexuality.

TABLE 7.2
Characteristics of the Sample

Group	*Sex*	*N*	Age *Mean*	Age *S.D.*	Age *Range*	I.Q. *Mean*	I.Q. *S.D.*	I.Q. *Range*	Years of Education *Mean*	Years of Education *S.D.*	Years of Education *Range*
Homosexuals in Community (Hooker, 1958)	Male	30	34.5	—[a]	25–50	115.4	—	91–135	13.9	—	9–18
Homosexuals in Community (Yamahiro and Griffith, 1960)	Male	22	31.3	—	16–58	110.0	12.9	—	—	—	—
Homosexuals in University Clinic (Davids et al., 1956)	Male	20	—[b]	—	—	—	—	—[c]	—	—	—
Homosexuals in Prison (Ferracuti and Rizzo, 1956)	Male	20	—	—	22–49	—	—	—	—	—	—
Female Homosexuals in Prison (Ferracuti and Rizzo, 1958)	Female	20	—	—	16–40	—	—	—	—	—	—
Delusional Psychotics (Aronson, 1952)	Male	30	30.8	4.58	—	11.27[d]	2.24	—	10.9	3.10	—
Delusional Psychotics (Meketon et al., 1962)	Male	42	—	—	—	—	—	—	—	—	—
Paranoid Schizophrenics (Meketon et al., 1962)	Male	50	—	—	—	—	—	—	—	—	—
Paranoid Schizophrenics (Grauer, 1954)	Male	31	28.0	—	—	100	—	—	10.0	—	—
Nondelusional Psychotics (Aronson, 1952)	Male	30	29.0	4.49	—	10.97[d]	1.94	—	11.1	2.26	—
Neurotics (Davids et al., 1956)	Male	20	—[b]	—	—	—	—	—[c]	—	—	—
Neurotics (Meketon et al., 1962)	Male	52	—	—	—	—	—	—	—	—	—
Alcoholics (Meketon et al., 1962)	Male	45	—	—	—	—	—	—	—	—	—
Heterosexuals in Prison (Ferracuti and Rizzo, 1956)	Male	20	—	—	24–50	—	—	—	—	—	—
Female Heterosexuals in Prison (Ferracuti and Rizzo, 1958)	Female	20	—	—	16–40	—	—	—	—	—	—
Normals (Hooker, 1958)	Male	30	36.6	—	27–48	116.2	—	94–133	14.3	—	11–18
Normals (Aronson, 1952)	Male	30	26.9	3.50	—	11.57[d]	1.63	—	10.9	1.53	—
Normals (Davids et al., 1956)	Male	20	—[b]	—	—	—	—	—[c]	—	—	—

[a] A dash (—) indicates that these data were not available.
[b] The subjects were obtained from a university, so it is safe to assume they were primarily of "college age."
[c] The authors report that the subjects ranged from high average to superior intelligence.
[d] Wechsler–Bellevue weighted vocabulary scores.

Their range of intellectual functioning was from high average to superior; the socio-economic status of the group similarly was higher than average.

Neither of the two homosexual groups tested by Ferracuti and Rizzo (1956, 1958) were English speaking; each group being prisoners in their own native country, the male homosexuals were Italian and the females were Puerto Rican.[4] The males, whose homosexual behavior had been observed during the time they were in prison, had been arrested for homicide (N = 16), attempted homicide (N = 2), and rape (N = 2). Similarly, the overt homosexuality of the female group was not known prior to their arrest, but was based on the observation of their behavior while they were in prison. Both groups were tested after it was known that they had engaged in homosexual activities.

The delusional psychotics (Aronson, 1952), although comprised mostly of male paranoid schizophrenics in a V.A. Hospital, were classified as such on the basis of ratings. Using case history data, subjects were reliably rated on a seven-point scale (from 0 to 6) on the extent to which delusions were present in their symptomatology. Only patients with a rating of 4 or more were included in this group; the mean rating for the group was 4.9. The religious affiliation of the patients was representative of that of the general population. Occupationally, the group was comprised of mostly unskilled or semiskilled workers. At the time of the testing, the average length of hospitalization for the group was less than six months. Although little demographic data are presented by Meketon et al. (1962), their delusional psychotics were obtained from V.A. hospital files by means of Aronson's rating scale method.

The protocols of paranoid schizophrenics, obtained by Meketon et al. (1962) from V.A. hospital files, were selected for only those patients on whom there was an unambiguous diagnosis (i.e., no change in diagnosis over time and agreement between team diagnosis and psychologist's opinion). Beyond this information, little else is reported about the composition of this group. The paranoid schizophrenics in Grauer's (1954) sample similarly consisted of male V.A. hospital patients on whom there was good agreement as to final diagnosis.

The group of nondelusional psychotics was comprised of V.A. patients who, on the basis of the same rating system used to form the delusional group, had received a score of 2 or less; the average rating for the group was 0.63 (Aronson, 1952). The diagnostic subcategories of schizophrenia represented by the nondelusional group were as follows: 18 undifferentiated, five mixed, three simple, two catatonic, one hebephrenic, and one schizophrenic reaction. As was the case with Aronson's delusional group, patients in the nondelusional sample were representative with respect to religion, were primarily unskilled or semiskilled, and on the average had been hospitalized for less than six months.

Davids' et al. (1956) neurotic subjects consisted of male college students who had applied for treatment at a university clinic. The diagnostic

[4] The authors would like to thank Burton G. Andreas and Martin Stone for their help in the translation of the 1956 and 1958 articles, respectively.

classifications represented in this sample included anxiety states, obsessive-compulsives, hysterics, and depressives. Intellectually, the group was at least high average; the socio-economic status of the group also tended to be high.

The Rorschach records of the neurotics in Meketon's et al. (1962) sample were randomly selected from the files of a V.A. hospital. The major stipulation for the inclusion of a patient in this group was that his diagnosis had to have remained consistent throughout the course of hospitalization. This same criterion was employed in the formation of the alcoholic group, which was obtained from the files of the same hospital.

The heterosexual prisoners in Ferracuti and Rizzo's two studies (1956, 1958) were comparable to the homosexual prisoners described above. That is, the males were Italians who had been arrested for homicide (N = 11), attempted homicide (N = 3), or rape (N = 6), and had manifested no homosexual behavior during their imprisonment. The female prisoners, who had not been observed to be homosexual while in prison, were Puerto Ricans who had been matched with their homosexual counterparts on the basis of age, reason for conviction, and length of stay in prison.

Hooker's (1958) group of normal subjects, which consisted of volunteers obtained through various community organizations, were matched with her homosexual group on the basis of age, I.Q., and years of education. The normal subjects were fairly well adjusted, were not in therapy, and, except for three who had had one homosexual experience after adolescence, were all exclusively heterosexual. As part of the agreement made in arranging to obtain these subjects, they were informed that the purpose of the testing was to make comparisons between heterosexual and homosexual men.

The normal subjects tested by Aronson (1952) were selected from several community organizations, with the stipulation that they be white, World War II veterans, under 40 years of age, with less than 12 years of education, and no previous psychiatric history. Information as to the prevalence of homosexual activity within this group was not available, although Aronson points out that 26 of the 30 subjects were married; this, of course, serves as only indirect evidence of the exclusive heterosexuality of this group.

The normals tested by Davids et al. (1956) were male college students who were above average in I.Q. and socio-economic status. They had all volunteered to be tested in what they were told was an ongoing research project dealing with personality evaluation.

Data on Homosexual Signs

The normative data on Wheeler's homosexual signs, which are summarized in Table 7.3, are based on the tabulation of all 20 signs. In light of the fact that six of these 20 signs have not proven to be valid, the norms in Table 7.3 should be interpreted with caution. Although both the number and the percentage of signs are presented in the table, the positive effect of total R would indicate that the percentage of signs is the more appropriate score to use. Both scores have been presented whenever possible, primarily

TABLE 7.3
Means and Standard Deviations for Number of Homosexual Signs, Percentage Signs, and Total R[a]

Group	Number of Signs		Percentage Signs[b]		Total R	
	Mean	*S.D.*	*Mean*	*S.D.*	*Mean*	*S.D.*
Homosexuals in Community (Hooker, 1958)	6.03	5.75	15.45	10.14	37.7	17.39
Homosexuals in Community (Yamahiro and Griffith, 1960)	2.30	1.75	12.10	8.64	22.1	12.45
Homosexuals in University Clinic (Davids et al., 1956)	5.20	2.59	9.30	4.74	67.9	43.13
Homosexuals in Prison (Ferracuti and Rizzo, 1956)	2.35	1.98	—[c]	—	14.6	2.48
Female Homosexuals in Prison (Ferracuti and Rizzo, 1958)	3.05	2.56	—	—	16.7	4.91
Delusional Psychotics (Aronson, 1952)	7.10[d]	4.21[d]	22.90[d]	12.30[d]	33.9	19.92
Delusional Psychotics (Meketon et al., 1962)	—	—	11.40	11.10	—	—
Paranoid Schizophrenics (Meketon et al., 1962)	—	—	11.60	9.50	—	—
Paranoid Schizophrenics (Grauer, 1954)	3.07[d]	3.14[d]	15.70[d]	11.10[d]	—	—
Nondelusional Psychotics (Aronson, 1952)	1.90[d]	1.96[d]	8.50[d]	7.50[d]	22.2	9.20
Neurotics (Davids et al., 1956)	2.30	2.32	5.30	5.53	45.0	28.25
Neurotics (Meketon et al., 1962)	—	—	8.80	7.20	—	—
Alcoholics (Meketon et al., 1962)	—	—	10.00	8.30	—	—
Heterosexuals in Prison (Ferracuti and Rizzo, 1956)	0.07	0.71	—	—	14.9	4.46
Female Heterosexuals in Prison (Ferracuti and Rizzo, 1958)	0.95	1.07	—	—	13.9	3.81
Normals (Hooker, 1958)	3.40	2.91	8.80	5.53	32.9	14.97
Normals (Aronson, 1952)	1.10[d]	1.10[d]	4.90[d]	5.40[d]	22.0	5.08
Normals (Davids et al., 1956)	2.80	1.38	6.30	4.19	50.6	19.63

[a] The data reflect the tabulation procedure whereby signs 15–20 were tallied for as many times as they appeared in a protocol.
[b] Percentage signs = number signs/total R.
[c] A dash (—) indicates that these data were not available.
[d] In addition to Wheeler's 20 signs, Aronson and Grauer used a sign (household furnishings) suggested by Reitzell (1949). Inasmuch as the data for Aronson's and Grauer's groups were based on 21 signs, the norms for these samples are slightly inflated.

to illustrate the limitations inherent in the simple tabulation of number of signs.

The Problem of Overlap. An inspection of the data on the percentage of signs reveals that a good deal of overlap exists among the various groups. In addition to the fact that nondiscriminating signs have been included in the final scores, it is possible that some overlap exists as a function of the nature of the subjects themselves. That is, if Wheeler's signs are indicative of homosexual tendencies present in everyone to varying degrees, and not simply the fact that a person engages in overt homosexual behavior, then overlap between the groups should be expected. Wheeler himself used the variable of homosexual tendencies (overt, suppressed, repressed, and absent) in studying the validity of the signs. Unfortunately, he did not present either the number or percentage of signs obtained for these groups. If one agrees that the more practical application of the Rorschach is not so much as a measure of overt homosexuality, but rather as a means of assessing the strength of homosexual tendencies, then the type of norms which are called for should be more appropriate to this latter purpose. As yet, no such norms are available.

RELIABILITY

Most of us would agree that homosexuality is a characteristic that is very resistant to change. In evaluating any measure of homosexuality, it is thus quite reasonable to expect that the scores obtaind by this measure will be stable over a period of time. With respect to Wheeler's homosexual indices, research evidence on the test-retest reliability is most conspicuously absent.

VALIDITY

Although the concurrent validity approach would seem at first to be the more appropriate method for evaluating the Rorschach homosexual signs, a closer inspection of the meaning of "homosexuality" indicates that this is not necessarily so. In fact, if one accepts the definition of homosexuality as being more of a continuous variable than a diagnostic entity, construct validity becomes an equally relevant method to use in an evaluation of the system. As it turns out, the research done with the signs reflect both the criterion and the construct approaches to validity.

Criterion Validity

In a consideration of the criterion validity of Wheeler's indices, the reference should be made more specifically to concurrent criterion groups rather than to groups about which one makes some prediction. The one study which is tangentially relevant to the predictive value of the signs, however, will be noted briefly before the concurrent validity is discussed.

Predictive Validity

In a study by Grauer (1954), discharge from the hospital rather than homosexuality was used to define the criterion group. Based on the assumption that latent homosexuality is considered "an unfavorable sign by psychotherapists," Grauer compared a group of continuously hospitalized with another group of discharged paranoid schizophrenics on the basis of the homosexual signs revealed in their pretreatment Rorschachs. Grauer neglects to point out that the poor prognosis typically associated with homosexuality refers to the unlikelihood that the homosexuality will be modified, and not to the patient's status regarding hospitalization; there is an equivocation here on the term "prognosis." Grauer's failure to find the homosexual signs related to discharge from the hospital, consequently, should not come as too much of a surprise.

Concurrent Validity

In addition to the use of overt homosexuals in defining the criterion group, research on the concurrent validity of the homosexual indices has also defined the criterion by means of ratings of homosexual tendencies in individuals. With the exception of a couple of studies (Davids et al., 1956; Hooker, 1958), most of the research described in this section is seriously limited on methodological and statistical grounds. These shortcomings will be noted in the discussion of the various studies below.

Overt Homosexuality as the Criterion Measure. One of the earliest studies with Wheeler's signs involved a comparison of homosexuals, hysterics, and alcoholics (Reitzell, 1949). The Rorschach records of the 26 homosexuals (two of whom were females) used in this study were obtained from clinic files; most of the subjects in this group had been arrested for their homosexual activity. The protocols for the group of hysterics (21 females and five males) came from Reitzell's own files as well as those of local psychiatrists. The alcoholics (20 males and six females), who were all tested by Reitzell, included both chronic and periodic drinkers. Inasmuch as some theorists might maintain that alcoholics suffer from relatively strong underlying homosexual conflicts, it is not quite clear why this group was compared to the homosexuals.[5] In comparing these three groups on the Rorschach, Reitzell added two signs to Wheeler's list of 20: (a) household furnishings (e.g., lamp), and (b) eyes, given as a separate response.

Aside from any relatively minor methodological shortcomings which may exist in Reitzell's study (e.g., confounding of sex with diagnosis), the results themselves are difficult to interpret on other grounds. Reitzell reports the following: Out of a total of 504 responses, the homosexual group gave 71 signs; out of 744 responses, the group of hysterics obtained 64 homosexual signs; and for the alcoholic subjects, 51 out of their 568 responses were judged to be indicative of homosexuality. Although the

[5] In Table 7.3, it will be noted that the percentage of signs for Meketon's et al. (1962) group of alcoholics is relatively high.

homosexual group appears to have given relatively more signs, the confounding of intra- and intersubject scores to comprise the totals for each of the three groups does not allow for any conclusion as to the statistical significance of these differences. Reitzell does report that when the homosexual group is compared with the other two combined, the obtained coefficient of association (Q) is +.39. Unfortunately, there are no probability levels given for Q itself (Yule, 1924), so statistical significance must be determined separately by means of chi square; Reitzell does not provide the data to make this possible. Some data provided in her paper do allow us to conclude, however, that the two signs she added to Wheeler's list of 20 failed to discriminate among the groups.

In a set of parallel studies by Ferracuti and Rizzo (1956, 1958), the Rorschachs of prisoners who had engaged in homosexual practice with other prisoners were compared with the records of those who had never manifested any behavior indicative of homosexuality. In their first study with male prisoners in Italy, Ferracuti and Rizzo report that the difference in mean number of signs between the two groups failed to reach statistical significance. When the groups were compared by means of chi square (e.g., 0 to 1 versus 2 or more signs), however, the difference was highly significant ($p < .001$). In the second study, the female overt homosexuals and controls—who were prisoners in Puerto Rico—were found to differ significantly in the number of signs, regardless of the statistical method of analysis. In the case of both these studies, however, a closer inspection of the data reveals that the statistical significance was primarily due to the differences between the groups for sign 19—male or female genitalia. Thus, their findings are not as strikingly favorable for the Wheeler indices as a whole as they might at first appear.

Nitsche, Robinson, and Parsons (1956) compared two small groups (19 cases in each group) of male clinic patients: those convicted of homosexual behavior and those patients—most of whom were court referrals—whose problems were not related to homosexuality. Nitsche et al. made their comparison on the basis of 12 of the signs suggested by Chapman and Reese (1953), Due and Wright (1945), Fein (1950), and Ulett (1950); many of these signs are similar to Wheeler's. Although the homosexual group revealed relatively more signs (4.2 vs. 2.7), the difference failed to reach statistical significance.

Fein (1950), who also used a set of homosexual signs which had some similarity to Wheeler's, studied three groups of male college students: nine who were referred because of their homosexual problems, 10 whose main complaint was personal inadequacy, and 24 who were normal. Fein's conclusion that her particular signs discriminated among groups was based solely on "inspection." In the opinion of the present writers, her findings are of minimal value.

Based on the research described thus far, there is no real evidence for deciding one way or another about concurrent validity. The studies have either been poorly designed, the statistical analyses have been unclear or completely nonexistent, or the sample has been small or somewhat unique. The only appropriately designed and analyzed studies carried out in this particular area have been those by Davids et al. (1956) and Hooker (1958).

Davids et al. (1956) compared three groups of male college students on the basis of the Wheeler indices: 20 overt homosexuals who had applied for treatment in a university clinic, 20 neurotics who were being seen at the same clinic, and 20 normal students who volunteered for testing. All groups were found to be comparable with respect to literary and aesthetic interests. Although the group of homosexuals obtained significantly more ($p < .01$) Wheeler signs than either the neurotics or normals, their total number of responses also tended to be higher. When the three groups were compared on the basis of per cent of signs, however, the scores for the homosexual group were still found to be significantly greater than either the neurotic or the normal group ($p < .05$); the neurotics and normals failed to differ from each other on the basis of either number or percentage of signs. An additional, qualitative finding by Davids et al. was that the homosexual subjects tended to be more ego-involved in the testing and more sensitive in their responses to the cards. As will be seen below, this qualitative finding was also noted by Hooker (1958).

As part of a larger project on male homosexuality, Hooker (1958) tested 30 homosexuals and 30 matched controls. The homosexuals were all living in the community, were not being seen in any type of therapy, and generally seemed to be fairly well-adjusted individuals. The control subjects, with the exception of three who had one postadolescent homosexual experience, were all exclusively heterosexual. Because of the arrangements made in obtaining the normal volunteers from various community organizations, they had to be told the purpose of the study. The possibility that this may have affected the Rorschach performance of these subjects is somewhat substantiated by the relatively high percentage of signs obtained by this particular group of normal subjects (see Table 7.3).

The comparison of Hooker's two groups revealed that when matching is not taken into account statistically, no difference was found. With the use of a t test for correlated means, or a simple sign test, the findings indicate a significantly greater per cent of signs for the homosexual group ($p < .005$ and .001 for the t test and sign test, respectively). Hooker, as Davids et al. (1956), additionally notes that, on a qualitative basis, the records of the homosexual group seem to have been characterized by a sensitive, delicate-like style (e.g., "an elegant gopher," "ethereal cherubs," etc.). It might be worthwhile to pursue this qualitative finding further in future research.

An additional study by Yamahiro and Griffith (1960) might be mentioned briefly before concluding this section. They also tested a group of homosexuals living in the community, and report a comparison of their results with the performance of the homosexuals in Davids' et al. (1956) study. The authors failed to obtain any difference in per cent of Wheeler's signs between the two groups of homosexuals.

The above findings of the more adequately designed and analyzed studies would seem to indicate that Wheeler's signs can significantly differentiate a group of homosexuals from a group of nonhomosexuals—whether they be normal or neurotic. The overlap between these groups, however, has been found to be large. One likely reason for this overlap undoubtedly rests in the grossness of the set of signs. At least six of the signs included in Davids' et al. and Wheeler's comparisons (signs 1, 3, 4, 5, 9, 14) have in the past been found to be completely invalid. Another possible source of overlap lies in the nature of the groups compared. That is, to the extent that those subjects comprising the normal and neurotic groups[6] possessed underlying homosexual tendencies, the differences between groups would tend to be on the conservative side—with the end result being statistical overlap. Until some actual research is done on the overlap due to the six invalid signs, as well as to the latent homosexual tendencies present in certain groups, the diagnostic efficiency of the Rorschach per se as a measure of homosexuality will remain an open issue.

Ratings of Homosexual Tendencies. Wheeler (1949), who was one of the first to investigate the effectiveness of the Rorschach as a measure of homosexuality, has been the only researcher to test the signs against ratings of homosexual tendencies, rather than overt homosexual behavior. Using 100 male patients who were being seen in therapy at a V.A. mental hygiene clinic, Wheeler classified the subjects on the basis of the therapists' judgment that homosexuality was *absent, repressed, suppressed,* or *overt.* All patients in the sample had taken a Rorschach upon admission to the clinic; the therapists' ratings were obtained after the patient had been seen for at least eight sessions. The 25 therapists consisted of eight psychiatrists, eight psychologists, and nine social workers, who either had the appropriate training or were about to complete it.

Of the 100 patients rated, only four were considered to be overt homosexuals. For purposes of statistical analysis, Wheeler included the records of these four subjects together with those of the 13 patients whose homosexual tendencies were believed to be suppressed, as well as with those of the 43 whose homosexuality was rated as being repressed. Thus, only 40 out of 100 patients were believed to have shown no indication of homosexual tendencies during their therapeutic contacts. Inasmuch as the questionnaire completed by the therapists included a number of specific items concerning the patients' characteristics, Wheeler was able to present the following overall picture of the criterion group:

> If the therapist's impression of the patient was such that he described him as homosexual, whether repressed, suppressed, or overt, then he also tended to feel that there was a lack of "warmth" in current heterosexual relationships of the patient and that he identified with his mother, at the

[6] Davids' et al. (1956) group of neurotics was in part made up of obsessive-compulsive neurotics, who have been found by Vetter (1955) to possess more homosexual tendencies—as measured by Wheeler's signs—than either undifferentiated neurotics or normals.

> same time that he verbalized hostility toward her; also the therapist was likely to believe that the patient did not possess an exclusively masculine appearance and manner or, in other words, that he was somewhat effeminate (Wheeler, 1949, p. 115).

In addition, those patients included in this "homosexual" group were more likely to have revealed during the course of therapy that they had had at least homosexual experience at one time or another, that they had masturbated at some time during their life, and at one time had been restricted to an all-male environment (e.g., boarding school). Although it is certainly possible that the "nonhomosexual" patients also had these experiences, they were not as likely to have *revealed* this information in therapy.

Considering Wheeler's comparatively unique and sophisticated approach in testing the validity of the homosexual signs, his analysis of the data leaves one with a feeling of frustration. In comparing the criterion with the control group, Wheeler dichotomized the frequency of signs between 2 and 3 (i.e., 0 to 2 vs. 3 or more) and computed the relationship between the signs and groups by means of Yule's Q—the coefficient of association (Yule, 1924). The coefficient of association, an infrequently used statistic whose limits are -1.00 to $+1.00$, does not in itself reveal anything about the significance of a relationship; to do this, the data must first be analyzed by means of chi square. Consequently, Wheeler's report that a Q value of $+.42$ was obtained between the likelihood of patients being included in the criterion group and the likelihood of giving three or more homosexual signs on the Rorschach, is frustratingly incomplete. An even higher Q ($+.50$) was obtained when the dichotomy was made between 0 to 3 vs. 4 or more signs, but here again no mention is made of the corresponding chi square value or level of statistical significance.

Perhaps one of the more interesting of Wheeler's findings—as well as one which allows for some inference about statistical significance—is that the relationship between homosexual signs and therapists' ratings showed variation among different therapists. That is, those therapists who had been in therapy themselves obtained a Q of $+.59$ between ratings of homosexual tendencies and frequency of signs, whereas the Q for the therapists never having been in therapy was only $+.22$; the difference between these two values is significant at the .05 level. When the therapists were divided into those five who were *mostly likely* and those five who were *least likely* to be able to detect homosexual tendencies in patients—the division being made by the chief of the clinic, based on his knowledge of these therapists—the resulting Q scores $+.54$ and $-.20$, respectively, differed significantly at the .05 level. The most noticeable of all differences among therapists, however, was based on professional affiliation. The three groups of therapists obtained the following values of Q: psychiatrists, $+.90$; psychologists, $+.28$; and social workers, $+.01$. The degree of association obtained by psychiatrists was significantly greater than that reached by either psychologists or social workers ($p < .01$); the Q value for psychologists was not significantly greater than that obtained by social workers.

The overall findings of Wheeler's study are not as clear cut as one might hope them to be. The only really firm conclusion which may be drawn from the study is that the relationship between the homosexual signs on the Rorschach and therapists' ratings of homosexual tendencies will vary, depending upon the therapists training, his ability to detect these tendencies, and his own personal course of therapy. There is clearly a temptation to view this conclusion as reflecting the validity of the homosexual signs, and perhaps it is being overly conservative to say that it does not. Nevertheless, nowhere in Wheeler's study is there any sound statistical basis for concluding that the relationship between the homosexual indices and the likelihood of being included in the criterion group does, or does not, exceed chance expectation.

Construct Validity

Possibly because of the relative ease with which a homosexual criterion group can be formulated, relatively little work has been done on the construct validity of the Wheeler indices. As has been suggested earlier in this chapter, however, the more relevant clinical and theoretical conceptualization of homosexuality is as a continuous variable and not as a dichotomous entity. Once we conceive of homosexuality as a trait along which individuals vary, the construct validity approach to the homosexual signs emerges as an area with many interesting possibilities—some of which will be noted below. The directions in which future research might head are discussed below within the context of both the nomological and trait validity of the signs.

Nomological Validity

The research on this aspect of construct validity has involved primarily the comparison of various psychopathological groups believed to vary in their underlying homosexual tendencies. Specifically, the Wheeler signs have been used to test (1) the popular psychoanalytic hypothesis that homosexual conflicts are responsible for the existence of paranoid delusions, and (2) the less wide-spread notion that obsessive-compulsive neurotics and peptic ulcer patients can be characterized as having strong latent homosexual tendencies.

Homosexual Signs and Paranoid Delusions. Freud has maintained that a homosexual conflict lies at the root of all paranoid delusions. To cite the most common example, delusions of persecution are said to evolve from the basic homosexual desire ("I love him") which is first inverted ("I hate him") and then projected outward ("He hates me"). The Rorschach homosexual signs have been used by Aronson (1952), Grauer (1954), and Meketon et al. (1962) in testing the psychoanalytic hypothesis directly, and by Chapman and Reese (1953) in a less direct test of the theory.

Aronson (1952) compared the frequency of the Wheeler indices among three groups: 30 delusional schizophrenics, 30 nondelusional schizophrenics, and 30 normals. The schizophrenic subjects, who were all male patients in a V.A. hospital, were assigned to the two groups on the basis of their delusional symptomatology. Applying a 0–6 rating scale to case-history data, Aronson was able to obtain two reliably rated extreme groups; the average rating for the delusional schizophrenics was 4.9, whereas the average for the nondelusional group was 0.63. As it turned out, the delusional group was composed primarily of patients diagnosed as paranoid schizophrenics while no one in the nondelusional group had this diagnosis. With the exception of the fact that the normal subjects were somewhat younger than the delusional patients, all three groups were comparable as to age, I.Q., and education.

The results of Aronson's study turned out positively, in that the per cent of homosexual signs obtained by the delusional psychotics was significantly greater than that given by either the nondelusional psychotic or the normal group ($p < .001$). The finding that the nondelusional psychotics obtained a significantly ($p < .05$) higher percentage score than the normals was due primarily to the fact that the psychotics gave more male and female genital responses (sign 19). Were this sign to be omitted from the tally, the scores obtained by the normals and nondelusional psychotics would not have differed significantly.

Grauer (1954) attempted to replicate Aronson's findings by scoring the Rorschach protocols of paranoid schizophrenics for homosexuality; the sample was composed of only those patients on whom the diagnosis was unequivocal. Grauer compared the scores obtained by his sample with those in Aronson's study, but reported the statistical findings for only one of these comparisons: his group of paranoid schizophrenics vs. Aronson's group of nondelusional schizophrenics. Although the delusional patients obtained a higher per cent of signs, the t value of 1.71 failed to reach statistical significance (p between .05 and .10).

Still another replication of Aronson's study was carried out by Meketon et al. (1962). In their study, they found that diagnosed paranoid schizophrenics gave significantly higher percentage scores than neurotics ($p < .05$ with a one-tailed test). Similarly, when the group of paranoid schizophrenics was pooled with another group of patients for whom delusions of persecution was the primary symptom, and their protocols were compared with those of neurotics and alcoholics, the one-tailed t test revealed the paranoid/delusional group to have a higher percentage of homosexual signs ($p < .05$).

A study by Chapman and Reese (1953) might be mentioned here, in that it bears indirectly on the psychoanalytic explanation of paranoid thinking. Based on the hypothesis that homosexuality may be conceptualized as representing some point between schizophrenia and normality—that is, the homosexual's gratification is neither totally narcissistic nor is it heterosexual—Chapman and Reese compared the Rorschach records of six schizophrenics (three of whom were paranoid) with those obtained from six normals. The results indicated that the schizophrenics obtained significantly more homosexual signs. These findings can probably be interpreted in a number of ways, only one of which is consistent with the psychoanalytic theory of paranoia.

Although the replications of Aronson's original study have not turned up with as striking results, they nevertheless have offered support for the existence of some sort of positive relationship between the Wheeler indices and delusional thinking. According to the overall findings on this relationship, it is probably safe to conclude that while homosexual concerns may pervade some delusions, not all paranoid thinking can be explained by this hypothesis.

HOMOSEXUAL SIGNS AND OTHER DISORDERS. The Wheeler homosexual indices have been used as one of several measures in studies on the underlying characteristics of obsessive-compulsive neurotics (Vetter, 1955) and peptic ulcer patients (Marquis, Sinnett, and Winter, 1952).

On the basis of psychoanalytic theory, Vetter (1955) tested the hypothesis that "conflicts between male and female identifications constitutes the focal conflict in obsession-compulsion" (p. 50). The Rorschach records of three groups of 30 males each were compared: obsessive-compulsive neurotics, undifferentiated neurotics, and normals. The group of obsessive-compulsives was composed of patients being seen at a university clinic. All patients in the group displayed clear-cut obsessive-compulsive symptoms, as well as formal Rorschach signs believed to be indicative of obsessive-compulsive neurotics (Kates, 1950b). The undifferentiated neurotic group, who were patients at the same university clinic, consisted primarily of hysterics. The third group was made up of college students who volunteered to be tested. All three groups were comparable as to age and years of education. Using Wheeler's signs 1–14 only, Vetter found the obsessive-compulsive group obtained the highest per cent of signs, the undifferentiated group was next, and the normal group had the lowest; the differences among the three groups were significant at the .01 level. The fact that the undifferentiated neurotics obtained more signs than the normals suggests either that the Wheeler signs in part reflect more general (sexual) conflicts, or that homosexual problems are involved among these undifferentiated neurotics as well. Empirical evidence for deciding which of these two possibilities is more likely is not yet available.

Using the Wheeler indices as one of their measures, Marquis et al. (1952) set out to investigate the "ulcer personality." The theoretical reasoning behind their study is not too clear, except perhaps that the oral-passive conflicts believed to be associated with peptic ulcers conceivably could be interpreted as reflecting homosexual tendencies. This hypothetical relationship between homosexuality and ulcers is admittedly far from very clear. In any event, the comparison of peptic ulcer patients with a matched group of patients with other psychosomatic disorders revealed that those patients suffering from ulcers gave significantly more homosexual signs ($p < .05$).

The findings of those studies relevant to the construct validity of the homosexual signs have generally been favorable. Considering homosexuality as a continuous personality variable rather than a dichotomous entity, there are a number of other possible approaches which may be taken in filling out the construct validity of the Wheeler indices. For example, one might expect to find Rorschach differences between men whose profession is "masculine" (e.g., engineering) as compared with men whose profession is more "feminine" in nature (e.g., interior decorating). Further, it could be predicted that individuals who give more homosexual signs would have difficulty in functioning in situations which tend to evoke homosexual tendencies—such as army barracks and the like. Research which could be done to test these as well as a host of other hypotheses would not only serve to offer evidence for the construct validity of the homosexual signs, but would also add to our understanding of homosexuality as well.

Trait Validity

With the exception of a single study in which an attempt was made to relate the Wheeler indices with TAT signs of homosexuality (Davids et al., 1956), no work at all has been carried out on the trait validity of the Rorschach homosexual signs. The reasons for the lack of research in this area of validity are not at all clear; to speculate about possible reasons for the void would be out of place here. What *is* more relevant to our task here would be to suggest some directions which research relevant to the trait validity of the signs might take. This will be done after the one existing trait validity study (Davids et al., 1956) is described.

As part of the investigation described earlier on the ability of the Wheeler indices to differentiate overt homosexuals from neurotics and normals, Davids et al. (1956) additionally tested the relationship between the Rorschach and TAT signs of homosexuality within each of these three groups. The 10 TAT homosexual signs, which had never before been actually validated empirically, were obtained from an unpublished survey by Lindzey, Tejessy, Davids, and Heinemann (1952).[7] As was also noted earlier in this chapter in the case of the Wheeler indices, the set of 10 TAT indices may include some invalid signs which serve only to provide error variance to the scoring. Thus, some signs (e.g., sexual references) will undoubtedly occur primarily as a function of the card itself (e.g., 13 MF), and consequently may be expected to be present in the records of normal subjects (cf. Goldfried and Zax, 1965). Despite the relative crudeness of both the Rorschach and TAT signs, Davids et al. found a correlation between the two of $+.52$ ($p < .05$) within the group of 20 homosexuals. Within the groups of 20 normal and 20 neurotic subjects, however, the nonsignificant correlations were $+.05$ and $-.09$, respectively. It may be, then, that the crudeness of one or both systems is such that the more subtle differences in latent homosexuality cannot be detected with any degree of accuracy.

[7] The 10 TAT signs, which were found to be reliably scored, were as follows: (1) Card 9 makes *S* uncomfortable. (2) *S* reports that the people in Card 10 have no real affection for each other. (3) Card 12 elicits a hypnotism theme. (4) The hero in Card 18 is being attacked from or pulled to the rear. Unlike signs 1–4, signs 5–10 may be elicited by any card: (5) Inappropriate identification. (6) Recurrent identification shift. (7) Inappropriate identification of sex and figure. (8) Hostility toward marriage and opposite sex. (9) Theme of women killed by men. (10) Sexual references.

Should future research reveal that it is the Wheeler indices which cannot accurately detect latent homosexual tendencies, the practical usefulness of the Rorschach as a measure of homosexuality would become limited indeed.

In order to round out the evidence on the trait validity of the Wheeler indices, certain questions must become the focus of future research. Perhaps two of the most crucial of these questions are the following: (1) Does the Wheeler scoring system measure homosexual tendencies, or does it detect a more general sexual maladjustment? (2) If the signs *do* measure homosexuality only, can they reveal those tendencies which the subject could (or would) not reveal without the test? None of the research studies already done have been designed to deal with these issues; until each of these questions can be answered, both the clinical and research utility of the Rorschach scoring for homosexuality will be uncertain.

OVERALL EVALUATION

Instead of conceptualizing homosexuality as a well-defined diagnostic category, it is theoretically more appropriate to refer to the construct of homosexual tendencies—that is, personality characteristics which individuals possess, but to varying degrees. The view of homosexuality as an entity seems in part based on the ability to make the dichotomy between overt homosexuals and individuals for whom homosexual behavior is not apparent. It is clear, however, that other variables (e.g., guilt, social sanction, etc.) may serve to determine whether or not a person will express his homosexual tendencies overtly. The use of the Rorschach as a measure of homosexuality, therefore, would do better to describe these tendencies within the person, rather than attempt to indicate whether these tendencies would be acted upon. The additional use of some measure of mode of expression—such as the developmental scoring of the Rorschach—may be of assistance in serving this latter function.

Wheeler's scoring of the Rorschach for homosexuality, which has received most of the research attention, involves the content of the response only. There are 20 signs in all—some that are specific to certain cards and areas, but others that can be applied wherever they may occur in a record. Based on the research findings of Wheeler and of others, however, it is safe to say that six of these 20 signs are unquestionably poor. Another six signs have held up fairly well under empirical test, while the remaining eight are of "ambiguous validity." Despite this evidence, the validity research with the system has typically included *all 20 signs,* including those which contribute nothing but error variance.

The scoring criteria in Wheeler's approach are fairly straightforward. The evidence on interscorer reliability indicates that while the agreement in the scoring of specific responses is only fair, there is good reliability in determining the total number of signs which may be said to characterize the protocol as a whole. Wheeler's suggestion that the summary score need be expressed only by the absolute number of signs in a record must be reevaluated in light of the positive relationship which exists between total number of responses and number of homosexual signs; a better summary score would involve instead the ratio of signs to total number of responses. A careful literature search has revealed that no test has been made of the stability of a subject's score over time.

The normative data on the homosexual signs, which are available primarily as a by-product of validity research with the system, indicate that the overlap among several groups is great. The presence of overlap may be a function of the inclusion of the six unquestionably poor signs in the tabulations, the presence of homosexual tendencies in the nonovert homosexual subjects, and/or the more general weakness of the Rorschach as a measure of homosexual tendencies. In order to determine more precisely which of these three possibilities is most correct, it is suggested that normative data be obtained on subjects varying as to the strength of their homosexual tendencies, using only those indices which have held up under empirical test.

Inasmuch as the validity research with the Wheeler indices has been based on the inclusion of some invalid signs, the positive findings which have been found should be interpreted as representing a conservative estimate of the difference between groups. Apart from this inclusion of invalid indices, it is unfortunate that a good deal of the validity research remains uninterpretable on other grounds. Either because of poor experimental design, statistical confounding, or the use of statistics with no available probability levels, it is difficult to use some of the findings to evaluate the status of the scoring system. The results of the interpretable studies, however, have typically been favorable. Thus, research has indicated that overt homosexuals can be distinguished from individuals who show no indication of homosexuality. Research findings have also indicated that delusional psychotics typically show more Wheeler signs than nondelusional psychotics, thereby offering support for the psychoanalytic theory of paranoia. In addition, obsessive-compulsive neurotics have been shown to have more homosexual tendencies than undifferentiated neurotics, and peptic ulcer patients more than other psychosomatic patients. Wheeler, who compared latent and overt homosexuals with individuals for whom homosexuality was not present, reports a positive relationship between the presence of these homosexual tendencies and the presence of the Rorschach signs. Unfortunately, Wheeler expresses this relationship by means of the Yule's *Q*, for which there are no known probability levels. One of Wheeler's more interesting findings, however, is that there were individual differences in the therapists' ratings of homosexual tendencies. Specifically, the relationship between the Wheeler signs and psychiatrists' ratings was significantly greater than the relationship obtained for either psychologists or social workers.

Additional possibilities for construct validity research with the Wheeler indices could relate the Rorschach performance to such variables as masculine vs. feminine choice of profession, ability to function in all-male situations, as well as other studies along these lines. Also, some research is needed to eliminate the possibility that the Wheeler indices may be measuring *general* sexual disturbance or deviancy, rather than homosexuality in particular.

From a more general viewpoint, it can be maintained that the only real justification for a Rorschach measure of homosexuality is in those instances where the individual is unwilling or unable to reveal this information to the clinician directly. In addition, one can probably legitimately question the need for a measure of homosexuality in clinical practice merely to determine the sexual orientation of the patient. Rather, the value of a Rorschach measure of homosexuality more appropriately lies in its ability to detect those individuals for whom homosexual thoughts or behavior present a problem. Although no data currently available which are relative to any of these questions, any complete assessment of the Rorschach scoring for homosexuality must, at least in part, be based on these considerations.

Chapter 8

SUICIDE INDICATORS

Man's attempt to take his own life is not new. In fact, it is quite likely that the practice of suicide has been in existence almost as long as natural death itself (Zilboorg, 1936). Relative to other causes of death, however, the actual incidence of suicide is relatively infrequent. Given 10,000 randomly selected individuals living in the United States each year, about *one* of these will voluntarily take his life (Farberow and Shneidman, 1961; Pokorny, 1964; Shneidman and Farberow, 1957).

Despite the relative infrequency of successful suicides, efforts to devise means of detecting suicidal individuals need little justification. The various attempts which have been made to detect and prevent suicidal attempts have been based on the belief that the suicidal person does, in some direct or indirect way, forewarn others of his intention. These communications on the part of the suicidal person may even be viewed as a covert way of asking to be stopped—the so-called "cry for help." The question which concerns us in this chapter is whether or not the Rorschach can be used as one of the ways of detecting communications or characteristics of potentially suicidal individuals.

WHAT CONSTITUTES SUICIDE?

The definition of "suicide" or perhaps more appropriately, the classification of "suicidal behavior," is an intriguing but complicated undertaking (cf. Neuringer, 1962). Even if we restrict our meaning of suicide—so that it deals only with behavior related to the actual cessation of one's life and not the chronic, self-destructive tendencies which may be viewed as suicidal in nature—we still encounter a number of different behaviors which we might call "suicidal." The categories which typically have been used in classifying suicidal behavior include *serious and intentional suicides, suicidal gestures, threats of suicide,* and *suicidal ideation.*

Serious and intentional suicides refer to those incidents which most people tend to think of when they think of suicide. Hence, this type of suicidal behavior usually involves some effective means of self-destruction, such as taking lethal dosages of drugs, cutting one's wrists, hanging, shooting, and so forth. Unless somebody is able to intervene in time, the suicidal individual is typically successful in taking his own life.

Suicidal gestures are basically manipulative in nature. The suicidal attempt is designed to get attention, sympathy, and help from others. The attempt is typically quite feeble, and often carried out in such a way that some other person is likely to be on hand. There always remains the possibility, of course, that the individual making this gesture may be successful "accidentally" and take his own life.

Although *threats of suicide* refer to the individual's open acknowledgement of his intention to make a suicidal attempt, this threat—as well as any actual attempt which may follow—may be a gesture used for manipulative purposes, or it may indicate the person's serious intention to do away with himself. *Suicidal ideation,* as in the case of threats of suicide, may encompass a wide variety of behavior, ranging from the ruminations which can allow one to predict a serious suicidal attempt to the fleeting thought of suicide which occurs to most people at one time or another during their lifetimes. Consequently, unless suicidal ideation as well as threats of suicide are further classified as to their seriousness, the use of these last two classifications can be misleading. The same holds true for the often-used categories of "successful" and "attempted" suicide, each of which may encompass both serious as well as manipulative behavior.

Although the above-mentioned categories may have a certain amount of usefulness in the classification of suicidal behavior, the utility of a classificatory system in this area should be viewed in light of the very transitory and conflicted nature of serious suicidal intentions. As Shneidman (1963) has noted "...most individuals who are acutely suicidal are so for only a relatively short period and that, even during the time they are suicidal, they are extremely ambivalent about living and dying" (p. 42). In addition, there is also some reason to believe that the very attempt at suicide has a "cathartic" effect (Farberow, 1950; Rosen, Halles, and Simon, 1954; Shneidman & Farberow, 1957), in that the individual, after his attempt at suicide —assuming he is still alive—is less upset emotionally then he was prior to the act.

In light of the transitory characteristics of the seriously suicidal person, it would not seem appropriate to make use of the Rorschach to describe the "suicidal personality" per se. Instead, the more appropriate use to which the Rorschach might be put would be to provide us with the more or less short-lived danger signs or clues to assist us in detecting and preventing the serious suicidal attempt from occurring.

One brief word about theory before concluding this discussion. The theoretical explanations of suicide have been varied, and include such hypotheses as the introjection of a love object and the subsequent turning in of hostility, the desire to rejoin a deceased loved one, the atonement for feelings of guilt, the desire to "leave the field," as well as a variety of other reasons (Appelbaum, 1963; Farberow and Shneidman, 1961; Shneidman and Farberow, 1957). To describe in detail the various theoretical speculations on suicide would go beyond the scope of this chapter. Some of the signs to be described have had no foundation in theory, but were derived on a purely empirical basis. In those cases where the suicide indicators were derived from theory, the underlying rationale will be noted in conjunction with the description of the signs.

SUICIDE INDICATORS

There have been more than a dozen different suggestions of Rorschach signs or configurations which presumably reflect suicidal potential. These proposed indicators, each having received some but not a great deal of research attention, are described and evaluated in the sections which follow. Those indicators which have been suggestd but which have not received any empirical test (e.g., Ulett, Martin, and McBride, 1950) will not be dealt with at all in the description and evaluation.

The several suicide indicators which have been presented by different writers have consisted of (1) signs or configurations based totally on the *formal scoring* of the protocol (Appelbaum and Holzman, 1962; Beck, 1945; Kruger, 1954; Martin, 1951; Piotrowski, 1950; Rabin, 1946), (2) specific *content* believed to reflect suicidal tendencies (Costello, 1958; Grasilneck, 1954; Fleischer, 1957; Lindner, 1946; Sapolsky, 1963), or (3) indicators which take into account *both formal and content* elements of the protocol (Hertz, 1948, 1949; White and Schreiber, 1952).

In the initial presentation of the different suicide indicators which follows, the reader should be cautioned that each of these suggested systems is simply *described* as the originator has suggested it. Although any available information on interscorer reliability and cutoff scores is noted for each approach, the evaluation of the validity of these indicators is taken up later in the chapter.

Indicators Based on Formal Scoring

Beck's Configurations

In conjunction with his interpretation of a particular Rorschach protocol, Beck (1945) has speculated about the characteristics of the suicidal individual:

> An oppressive anxiety, strenuous inner conflict projected in a neurotic structure of compulsive form, and much mulling over...of deeply personal life experiences—when all this emerges in an individual of most superior intelligence...the pattern is always ominous with threat of suicide (p. 326).

Based on this statement, both Sakheim (1955) and Fleischer (1957) have outlined five suicide indicators which they believe to reflect Beck's clinical speculation. These indicators are as follows:

1. *Oppressive anxiety.* The primary criteria for this sign is the presence of shading shock and/or the subject's preoccupation with shading.
2. *Neurotic structure.* The configuration of scores believed to reflect neurotic structure include low R, M, and F%, high A% and At, as well as rejection trends.
3. *Strenuous inner conflict.* Among the many possible indicators of this tendency are color shock, low C, P failure, blocked M, flexor and extensor M combined, m, and so forth.
4. *Mulling over.* This characteristic is defined by the presence of four or more M responses in the record.
5. *Shading shock on Card IV.* The typical indicators of shock include rejection of the card, delayed reaction time, F− responses, unusually low R, and so on.

Although there are no data available on interscorer reliability, it is clear that a good deal of subjectivity is involved in determining the presence of an indicator. In effect, subjective judgment enters at three points: (1) the scoring of the protocol per se, (2) the determination of what constitutes the relative presence or absence of the several scores within each configuration (e.g., "high" M, "low" C, etc.), and (3) the number of items required to make the decision that a configuration is "present" in the record. Despite Sakheim's (1955) suggestion that the mean scores for Beck's et al. (1950) normal sample be used to divide "high" from "low," and that at least one-half of the items must be present before a configuration is said to exist, it is unlikely that the interscorer agreement will ever be very good.

With respect to the optional cutoff score, Fleischer (1957) has found that the presence of *any four or more* of Beck's five signs was best able to differentiate among individuals who actually committed suicide, those who attempted it unsuccessfully, those who threatened suicide, and those with no indications of suicidal behavior at all. The overlap among these four groups is presented later in this chapter in conjunction with the discussion of normative data.

Martin's Checklist

In an unpublished dissertation carried out at the University of Kentucky, Martin (1951) empirically derived a checklist consisting of 16 signs which significantly differentiated ($p < .10$) those neuropsychiatric patients who had made serious attempts on their lives from patients who displayed no suicidal behavior at all. Although Martin was able to cross-validate the overall checklist successfully, there were certain individual signs which did not hold up well in his and in subsequent studies with the list. Nevertheless, all 16 of these signs have been employed in subsequent research, together with a seventeenth which Martin had found to differentiate between groups. From the findings of studies dealing with the utility of individual signs (Daston and Sakheim, 1960; Martin, 1951; Weiner, 1961a), it is possible to determine which signs have and which have not held up well under test. In the presentation of Martin's 17 signs—many of which are, by the way, overlapping—some indication is made as to the ability of each sign to differentiate between groups. Those signs which typically have been found to differentiate have been given a double asterisk (**), those which show a less-consistent history of individual validity will be noted by means of a single asterisk (*), while signs which have typically failed under three cross validations will have no asterisk.

Martin's checklist, together with an indication of the validity of each individual sign, is as follows:

1. Number of D responses is either less than 6 or more than 20.
*2. D% is either less than 60 or more than 79
**3. Number of CF responses is either 1 or 2.
4. Total number of color responses is greater than 1.
**5. Weighted sum C is greater than 1.0 but less than 3.5.
**6. C and/or CF responses appear first on Cards VIII, IX, or X.
**7. C and/or CF responses appear in the protocol, but sum Y and sum T is 0.
8. Number of FV and VF responses is less than 1.
9. Sum Y is less than 1.
**10. Sum Y and sum T are less than 1.
11. Difference between M and sum C is less than 1.5.
12. Total number of H and Hd responses is greater than 6.
13. Number of content categories is either less than 6 or more than 13.
14. Ratio of responses on VIII, IX, and X to total R is greater than 29%.
15. Number of P responses is either less than 3 or more than 6.
*16. Number of P responses is less than 3, and F+% is greater than 60.
*17. Average time of first response to each card is less than 27 seconds.

Apart from minor errors in computation, one would assume the interscorer reliability associated with the use of Martin's checklist to be near perfect. Given a scored protocol, there is virtually no subjectivity involved in determining whether or not a given sign is present. Indeed, except for 90% agreement on sign 10, Daston and Sakheim (1960) report their interscorer reliability to be "close to perfect." The interscorer reliability for the checklist, however, must additionally be considered in light of the findings which indicate that in the typical scoring of Rorschach protocols, interjudge agreement has varied between 83 and 93% (Hertz, 1938; Neuringer, McEvoy, and Schlesinger, 1965; Pratt, 1951; Ramzy and Pickard, 1949).

Inasmuch as the number of signs in a record has been found to be unrelated to total R (Daston and Sakheim, 1960; Martin, 1951; Weiner, 1961a), a simple tally of signs would yield an appropriate summary score. Although Martin as well as Daston and Sakheim are in agreement that the most efficient cutoff score has been shown to be seven or more signs, this issue is nonetheless open to debate. Granted that this score enables one to predict most accurately, it nevertheless results in a fair degree of overlap (see Table 8.3).

Piotrowski's Signs

In his *Rorschach Compendium,* Piotrowski (1950) hypothesizes about suicidal indicators as follows:

> Numerous c′ [i.e., dark shading] with a very inferior F+%, many W, and a powerful sum C may point to suicidal tendencies: in such a case the aggressive activity is turned against the individual himself (p. 73).

Piotrowski's speculation has been cast into four signs by both Fleischer (1957) and Sakheim (1955), who then tested them empirically. The signs are as follows:

1. The presence of two or more shading responses.
2. Beck's F+% is less than 70.
3. The per cent of W responses is greater than 30.
4. The "powerful sum C" has been interpreted differently by Fleischer and Sakheim:
   (a) Fleischer: The sum C is greater than 2.5.
   (b) Sakheim: The number of CF + C responses exceeds the number of FC responses.

In the findings of both Fleischer and Sakheim, the use of three or more signs, as well as the presence of all four signs, failed to distinguish between groups. It appears that this particular pattern of signs occurs infrequently in the records of both suicidal and nonsuicidal patients.

Rabin's Shock Indicator

On the basis of the case study of a psychiatric patient who murdered his wife and subsequently committed suicide, Rabin (1946) has hypothesized that the joint appearance of shading shock and color shock in a Rorschach protocol is indicative of suicidal potential. These signs are believed to indicate the individual's deep state of depression and anxiety, as well as the inability to deal effectively with his emotions. Rabin further suggests that the complete absence of shading as a determinant is also a poor sign, in that it reflects the inability to gain some release by the open expression of dysphoric feelings.

The phenomenon of "shock" can be determined by a number of criteria, all of which indicate the subject's disrupted response processes. Thus, the presence of such factors as card rejection, delayed reaction time, poor form quality, reduction in number of responses, disturbed succession, as well as other similar indicators, would lead one to infer that the subject has been "shocked" by the dark or colorful nature of the card. Clearly, the determination of shock in a protocol can be highly subjective in certain borderline cases. The present writers know of no actual studies which have focused on the reliability of judging the presence of color and/or shading shock.

Appelbaum and Holzman's Color-Shading Sign

The color-shading response—which involves the presence of shading as a determinant in a colored blot area—has been suggested by Appelbaum and Holzman (1962) as a useful diagnostic indicator of suicidal potential. The interpretative significance behind this particular score is believed to be the "heightened sensitivity to affect" presumably characteristic of the suicidal individual (Appelbaum, 1963). A further elaboration of the presumed theoretical significance of color shading is provided by Appelbaum and Colson (1968).

The scoring of a response for color shading is done in much the same way as the scoring for almost any determinant. Using the symbol (C) to stand for color shading, we can see where the scoring of FC(C) would be applied to the following example:

> Card VIII, lower center: "It's the shape and color of an iris; the insides look velvety because of the shading."

In scoring a response with the (C) determinant, the color and shading typically must be mentioned in the free association or inquiry, with the exception of those instances where it is clear that shading is being used in a colored area. Thus, the response "soiled wallpaper" to the mottled green area on Card IX would receive scoring of (C)F.

Appelbaum and Holzman note that the diagnostic significance exists regardless of the content or the form dominance of the response. A later finding by Neuringer, McEvoy, and Schlesinger (1965) would suggest that the added stipulation of a *minus form level* is needed for the valid application of the sign. Although no research has been done relative to the reliability of scoring for color shading, determining the presence of (C) in a record seems to be relatively unambiguous.

In a sense, the color-shading response is considered as a pathognomic sign. Thus, the determination of suicidal potential is made on the basis of color shading being *present* or *absent* in the test protocol. Appelbaum and Holzman found that the multiple occurrence of color shading was not differentially associated with suicidal potential; this finding was later replicated by Appelbaum and Colson (1968). Low but significant point biserial correlations of +.31 (Appelbaum and Holzman, 1962) and +.41 (Appelbaum and Colson, 1968) have been found to exist between color shading and total R, although R alone did not differentiate between groups.

Kruger's Developmental Scoring

In the process of testing an hypothesis from Werner's (1948) theory of development—specifically, that less immediate and direct forms of tension reduction are associated with higher developmental levels of functioning—Kruger (1954) found certain scoring indices which differentiated between threatened and attempted suicidal individuals.

The scoring indices used by Kruger were taken from both Friedman's and Phillips' developmental scoring systems (see Chapters 2 and 3, respectively). In particular, Kruger found that in those cases where there is a question of suicidal potential, a higher score on two developmental scores—namely, the index of integration and the form-dominance score—is indicative of a threat rather than a serious attempt at suicide. These scores are computed as follows:

1. INDEX OF INTEGRATION. Using the scoring criteria outlined in Chapter 2, the index of integration is computed as follows:

$$\text{Index of Integration} = \frac{(W{+}{+}) + (W{+}) + (D{+}{+}) + (D{+})}{\text{all }(W{+}D)} \times 100$$

2. FORM DOMINANCE. The dominance of form to such determinants as color, shading, texture, and vista is determined by the following formula:

$$\text{Form dominance} = FX - (XF + X)$$

The symbol FX refers to the total weighted number of FC, FY, FT, and FV in the record, while XF and X similarly refer to the total weighted number of responses where form is subordinate and absent, respectively. The particular weight given to each response depends upon the degree to which form is present, so the form-dominant (FX) responses are each multiplied by 0.5, the form-subordinate (XF) responses by 1.0, and the responses lacking form (X) by 1.5. The interscorer reliability for these developmental indices is quite high. Kruger reports that the per cent agreement between herself and another scorer was 96.8.

The only suggested cutoff score noted by Kruger for the index of integration was based on the common median for both groups; the median was 22.0. Although this cutoff score allows for a significant differentiation between groups, it also results in a good deal of overlap. With respect to the form-dominance score, Kruger was able to achieve a fairly high degree of accuracy by using only the sign of the final value. Thus, a potentially suicidal person whose score had a minus sign (indicating a relatively high incidence of form subordination and absence in the record) would be more likely to make a serious overt attempt on his life. On the other hand, the suicidal risk whose score is *zero* or has a *plus* sign (reflecting form dominance) is more apt to engage in threats rather than actual serious attempts. The question of overlap and actual clinical prediction with these two scores will be discussed further on in the chapter.

Content Indicators

Lindner's "Suicide Card" Responses

In his well-known discussion of the interpretive significance of various types of content, Lindner (1946) has hypothesized that Card IV may be viewed as the "suicide card," where the presence of at least one response reflecting depression and decay is indicative of suicidal tendencies. The pathognomic responses to this card include content such as "decaying tooth," "black smoke," "burned and charred piece of wood," and "something rotten." Although no actual reliability data are available, the scoring is straightforward enough for one to expect a high degree of interscorer agreement.

Morbid Content

The significance of morbid content as a suicide indicator has been suggested by a number of researchers (Fleischer, 1957; Hertz, 1948; Sakheim, 1955; White and Schreiber, 1952). The variety of possible responses which may be classified in the "morbid" category is actully quite large, and includes all responses—regardless of card—which connote death, depression, sickness, or destruction. There have been no published estimates of the interscorer reliability in judging whether a response should be considered morbid in nature. Although some responses can certainly be scored quite easily (e.g., "diseased lung"), others may prove to be more difficult (e.g., "a little girl who cut her finger"). In addition, most writers who have suggested the importance of morbid content have failed to indicate the number of such responses which need to be present before the diagnostic sign is said to exist. The one exception here has been in the work of Fleischer (1957), who has suggested that one morbid response may be considered indicative of suicidal tendencies, but only if the morbidity is clearly implied.

Crasilneck's Direction of Aggression

On the assumption that suicide involves self-directed aggression, Crasilneck (1954) has attempted to distinguish among three expressions of aggression for the purpose of studying suicidal potential: aggression against self, aggression toward others, and aggression by others. Although this classification may be legitimate enough, the assumptions underlying Crasilneck's scoring criteria are tenuous. He suggests that aggression which is turned against self is seen by content reflecting inanimate death and mutilation, that aggression toward others is symbolized by open fighting, explosions, and the subject's criticisms of the test, and that aggression seen as being inflicted by others is signified by animate death responses. Inasmuch as none of these categories proved to be useful on empirical test, the inappropriateness of the criteria, as well as the lack of data on interscorer reliability, remain academic issues.

Sapolsky's Symbolic Content

Sapolsky (1963) has suggested that if a subject offers a response to the dark middle bottom area (i.e., Beck's D6) in Card VII, there is the likelihood that "suicidal ideation" (whether it be attempt, threat, or thought) exists for this person. His reasoning behind this hypothesis, although clearly debatable on a number of counts, is as follows: Psychoanalytic speculation has it that one of the motivating forces underlying suicidal behavior is the wish to return to the womb; since Card VII is the "mother card," and the lower middle D area to this card symbolizes the womb, *any response* given to this location is indicative of covert return-to-the-womb fantasies. Thus, a response to this blot area, whether it consists of "vagina" or "man in a top hat and overcoat," is suggested by Sapolsky as a pathognomic indicator of suicidal potential.

Costello's Content

On a pure and simple empirical basis, Costello (1958) attempted to determine the content of those responses which were found to occur with a differential frequency in suicidal and nonsuicidal psychiatric patients. Perhaps the best way to describe his findings is by means of Table 8.1. The only items which differentiated among the two groups at the .05 level or better were winged animal in flight (FM) to Card V, human response to Card V, map to Card VII, and deer's head to Card IX. There is the strong likelihood that these findings, which were never cross validated, would fail to hold up under further test.

TABLE 8.1
The Frequency of Certain Responses for Suicidal and Nonsuicidal Patients

		Group	
Card	*Response*	*Suicidal (N = 30)*	*Nonsuicidal (N = 30)*
I	Map (W)	12	6
III	Human in Vigorous Action	6	12
III	Human in Passive Posture	13	6
III	Marionettes	2	8
IV	Tree (W)	2	8
V	Winged Animal	7	14
V	Winged Animal in Flight (FM)	20	10
V	Human Response (D or W)	0	8
VI	Animal Response (Top D)	4	10
VI	Object (Top D)	10	5
VII	Map (W or D)	9	2
VII	Response to Dark and Light (Bottom)	5	10
VIII	Tree (Top D)	3	9
IX	Deer's Head	0	8
IX	Man's Head (Bottom Pink)	9	4
X	Plan (W)	11	5
X	Rabbit's Head	3	8

Content and Formal Indicators Combined

Hertz's Configurations

In one of the earliest attempts made to study the possible suicide indicators on the Rorschach, Hertz (1948, 1949) devised a set of 14 suicidal configurations, eliminating four of these after they failed to discriminate between groups. Her original configurations consisted of the following 14 characteristics revealed in the Rorschach performance: (1) neurotic structure, (2) deep anxiety, (3) depressed states, (4) constriction, (5) active conflict, (6) obsessive-compulsive personality components, (7) hysterical features, (8) ideational symptomatology, (9) agitation phenomena, (10) resignation trends, (11) sudden and/or inappropriate emotional outbursts, (12) withdrawal from the world, (13) paranoid tendencies, and (14) chaotic sexuality. With even a casual perusal of these configurations, the reader will notice that some of these indicators are overlapping, while others tend to be mutually exclusive. The nonindependence of the configurations may be seen even more clearly by an inspection of the scoring criteria outlined below.

As already mentioned, Hertz dropped four of the configurations from her list—obsessive-compulsive personality components, hysterical features, paranoid tendencies, and chaotic sexuality, to be specific. Aside from the theoretical inappropriateness of these characteristics as indicators of suicidal trends, these configurations failed to hold up under test. Hertz's final list of 10 configurations, together with some indication of the component parts within each configuration (Hertz 1948, 1949), is as follows[1]:

1. *Neurotic structure.* This characteristic is indicated by means of low R, M, FC, and F%, the presence of m and shading disturbance, rejection trends, overvalent connotations in the content, and "behavior pointing to insecurity and strain."
2. *Deep anxiety.* Evidence for this tendency consists of the excessive use of shading and/or the presence of shading shock.
3. *Depressed states.* The manifestations of a depressed state in a record include reflections, low R, W, M, and C, high F, slow reaction time, narrow content range, as well as observable "behavior manifestations of sadness, anxiety, and dejection."
4. *Constriction.* A protocol is said to be constricted if R, M, C, and 0 are low, F%, P, and Dr are high, several indications of control are evident, the range of content is narrow, and the subject shows a general evasiveness in his behavior mannerisms.
5. *Active conflict and deep inner struggle.* This quality is indicated by low M and C, unbalanced M:C ratio, color shock, m, S, flexor and extensor M combined, blocked M, M in Dr and Hd, P failure, midline details, preoccupation with symmetry, content reflecting or symbolizing conflict.
6. *Ideational symptomatology.* According to Hertz (1949), the presence of ideational symptomatology in a record is indicated primarily by the nature of the content. Specifically, she states that ideational symptomatology is implied by:

> . . . content which reflects peculiar, eccentric thinking, fixed ideas, phobias, obsessions, compulsions and delusions, especially where content is dysphoric and depressed in nature. Pathological content frequently includes evidence

[1] Note that configurations 1, 2, and 5 in particular are virtually identical to Beck's indicators *neurotic structure, oppressive anxiety,* and *strenuous inner conflict,* respectively.

> of special bodily preoccupation, sex fears, homosexual fantasies, ideas of insufficiency and incompleteness, castration anxiety, ideas of persecution, of influence and of reference, abnormal religious absorption, delusions of sin and guilt, morbid fatalistic ideas, and the like (pp. 47–48).

As if this configuration were not already difficult enough to determine, Hertz points out that ideational symptomatology is additionally indicated by the presence of M−, O−, F−, color, and shading.

7. *Agitation.* The indications of agitation include high F −, O −, Dr, S, and perseveration, low M, C, A, P, and shading, self-references, and manifestations of restlessness in the subject's behavior.
8. *Resignation trends.* In addition to the subject's behavioral signs of listlessness, indifference, and dejection, this configuration is also seen by flexor M, low C, many shading responses, absence of S, and narrow content.
9. *Sudden and/or inappropriate emotional outbursts.* Hertz (1949) simply states that this tendency is indicated by "sudden, spasmodic and unexpected color in a record" (p. 48).
10. *Withdrawal from the world.* This characteristic is reflected by slow reaction time, the absence of FC, low P, H, and % OB[2], high F−, spaces used to indicate holes, the presence of O−, as well as a lack of feeling tone on the part of the subject.

As already noted in connection with the description of Beck's configurations, the possible sources of disagreement in scoring may enter at each of three given points: (1) during the actual scoring of the record for location, determinants, and content; (2) in decoding what constitutes "high" or "low" scores, certain types of content, various behavioral manifestations, as well as other signs which are included within a configuration; and (3) in finally arriving at some decision as to whether or not each of the 10 configurations is present or absent. Hertz says little to help the would-be scorer in using her configurations. On the contrary, her suggestion seems to do little but add even more unreliability to the scoring. She notes:

> In identifying a configuration, it must be emphasized, not all patterns listed had to appear in a record. The examiner had to determine from the entire picture whether or not there was sufficient evidence to conclude that a specific configuration should be recorded. The final determination was of course subjective and in the last analysis depended upon the skill, the training and the intuitive sense of the examiner (Hertz, 1949, p. 48).

Although no actual data on interscorer reliability have ever been published, researchers who have used Hertz's configurations report having had a

[2] According to Hertz, % OB "refers to the sum of responses containing inanimate objects in relation to the total number of responses given. These would include all responses where content involves nature and artificial objects" [Personal communication, October 1965]. Thus, everything but animal, human, and anatomy responses are used in arriving at this score.

difficult time in the application of her criteria (Fisher, 1951; Sakheim, 1955). In the hope of clarifying the criteria for judging the presence of a configuration, Sakheim indicates he had made "liberal use" of the norms published by Beck et al. (1950) in order to determine the cutoff points for the various "highs" and "lows" within each configuration. Further, he suggests that one may conclude that a configuration is present if at least one-half of all signs, or one-third of "the most valid" signs, exist in the record. Despite Sakheim's attempt at objectification, one would predict that unreliability in scoring for Hertz's configurations continues to loom large.

The cutoff score suggested by Hertz in depicting a protocol as indicating suicidal potential is the presence of five or more configurations. Although this cutoff point does detect a fair percentage of true positives, it also yields a large number of false positives (see Table 8.3). By setting the cutoff point at five or more configurations, the number of false positives are reduced, but so are the true positives. This general problem of overlap will be discussed later on in the chapter.

White and Schreiber's Indicators

Just for the record, we might mention the suicide indicators suggested by White and Schreiber (1952). In an overly optimistic article on the ability of the Rorschach to diagnose "suicidal risks," they propose the joint use of content and formal indicators of suicide. Specifically, they recommend that the content include those negatively toned responses which imply death, sickness, mutilation, anatomy, fear, falling, darkness, cloudiness, aggression, passivity, restlessness, and the like. They indicate that the formal scoring should be used to assess the level of reality contact, the degree of tension and anxiety, the relationship between energy and feelings, and the control indicated in the record. White and Schreiber make their scoring system virtually impossible to evaluate as to interjudge agreement and cutoff score when they conclude that the formal and content aspects of the record must be combined "clinically" to determine whether or not a suicidal risk is present.

METHODOLOGICAL PROBLEMS

Before attempting to present any of the actual research findings on the Rorschach suicidal indicators, it might be worthwhile if we first discussed some of the methodological problems which typically have been associated with these studies. In our discussion, we shall not deal with issues such as vagueness of scoring criteria or naivete of experimental design, but instead focus our attention on those problems which are more or less associated with the area of suicide prediction itself (cf. Cutter, Jorgensen, and Farberow, 1968; Neuringer, 1964). Included within this section, then, will be a discussion of the criterion selection process, the interval between testing and the event, the problem of whether or not the testing occurred before or after the act, and the complicating factor of base rates.

Criterion Selection

In our discussion in the earlier part of the chapter, we pointed out that there were a number of ways of defining "suicidal behavior." Although some of these definitions encompass fairly homogeneous types of behavior (e.g., serious and intentional suicides), other conceptualizations of suicidal behavior are far too broad to have any theoretical or practical significance (e.g., suicidal attempts).

Despite the apparently obvious fact that much of the behavior which gets classified under a given "suicidal" category may be only remotely related, a good deal of research in this area has involved criterion groups composed of "successful and attempted suicides," "attempted suicides," and "attempted, threatened, and contemplated suicides." The actual meaning of the classification can also interact with the sex variable, in that suicidal attempts on the part of females reflect attention-getting gestures more often than they do in males.

Time Interval between Testing and Suicidal Behavior

It is generally agreed that serious suicidal behavior—whatever particular form it may take—is set off by some sort of crisis, and that the actual suicidal danger exists for a relatively short period of time. Consequently, any attempt to devise or validate suicide indicators on the Rorschach should be done only with those protocols obtained during this critical period.

In much of the suicide research with the Rorschach, the time interval has been as much as one year before the attempted or successful suicide, and as long as three months after an unsuccessful attempt. In a fair number of studies, no mention of the time interval is given at all.

There seems to be no easy way to solve the practical problem of obtaining Rorschach protocols on individuals shortly before they make an attempt at suicide. Clearly, to be able to note when an individual is about to make an attempt on his life would obviate the need for the Rorschach as a diagnostic predictor. Consequently, the research literature in this area often involves the use of "stale," and perhaps no longer appropriate Rorschach protocols.

Testing before or after the Event

For obvious reasons, the variable of testing before or after the suicidal behavior does not exist for successful suicides; only the time interval is a relevant problem. In the case of unsuccessful attempts, threats, and ideation, on the other hand, the point at which the testing takes place *is* a relevant problem. This is most true in the case of suicide attempts, which seem to provide some sort of cathartic effect, leaving the individual less disturbed than those people prior to their successful suicide or those who merely threaten suicide. (Farberow, 1950; Rosen, Halles, and Simon 1954; Shneidman and Farberow, 1957). In several of the studies to be discussed in this chapter, the subjects constituting the "suicide attempt" group consisted of some individuals tested before, but others after the attempt. In the large majority of instances, however, the testing of unsuccessful suicide attempts occurred after the incident, thereby minimizing the likelihood of obtaining valid suicide indicators in the protocol.

The Problem of Base Rates

One of the most seriously limiting problems in the entire area of suicide detection and research lies, ironically enough, with the relative infrequency with which suicides occur. Despite the undeniable importance of this base-rate problem, virtually all studies dealing with suicide indicators on the Rorschach have managed to ignore the issue completely.

The problem of base rates in clinical prediction becomes of more and more crucial consideration as the likelihood of occurrence or nonoccurrence of the event departs more from a 50–50 split. In the case of suicides, the incidence of occurrence to nonoccurrence in this country is 0.01% to 99.99% respectively (Farberow and Shneidman, 1961; Pokorny, 1964; Shneidman and Farberow, 1957). In the use of the Rorschach as a predictor of suicide, however, it is safe to say that its primary application would be in the case of neuropsychiatric patients. Although it has been estimated that the incidence of suicide among psychiatric patients ranges anywhere from four to 17 times greater than that in normals, this would simply change the occurrence/nonoccurrence ratio to some point between 0.04–99.96 and 0.17–99.83 (Dublin, 1963; Pokorny, 1964; Temoche, Pugh, and MacMahon, 1964). What this means in practical terms is that even though studies may point to the fact that a suicide indicator results in only a small proportion of overlap, the application of the percentage of false positives to the actual nonoccurrence of suicide creates too much overlap to make it practical. Consider, for example, a sample of 1000 patients, only 1.7 of whom at the most are likely to commit suicide each year. Although the prognostic indicator which picks up 90% of these suicidal patients will successfully detect about 1.5 of them, a 10% rate of false positives which are also detected by the instrument turns out to be approximately 100 patients in number!

In discussing this very problem of base rates in suicide detection, Rosen (1954) has noted that one approach in narrowing the occurrence/nonoccurrence gap is by means of those variables which have been found to be associated with suicide. As we have already seen, one of the ways of making the base rates a little more equitable is by first classifying the individual as a psychiatric patient. It might also be noted that the suicide rate is even higher for ex-patients during the first six months period following their discharge from the hospital (Pokorny, 1964; Temoche et al., 1964). In addition, it has been found that the suicide rate is notably greater in the case of those patients for whom depression is a primary symptom (Pokorny, 1964). Other demographic variables which have been found to be related to the incidence of suicide include such factors as age, sex, and marital status (Dublin, 1963). Litman and Farberow (1961) have made the following helpful generalizations on the basis of their findings:

> At all ages, suicidal communications from males arouse more concern than similar communications from females, and, in general, the older the person, the more serious is the self-destructive potential. Moreover, the danger increases with age much more for males than for females (pp. 49–50).

If we add to the above-mentioned demographic variables such situational factors as a loss of a loved one, the development of a serious and chronic illness, or other similar crises in an individual's life, the problem of base rates in suicide detection can be reduced measurably.

NORMATIVE DATA

In this section, an attempt will be made to present those data which have been collected in conjunction with the validity studies on the several suicide indicators described earlier in the chapter. With the exception of the approaches suggested by Costello (1958), Crasilneck (1954), and White and Schreiber (1952), some data have been found for each of the various indicators. In a number of instances, the same subjects were used to generate data for more than one set of indicators; this may be seen more clearly from an inspection of Tables 8.2 and 8.3.

Nature of the Samples

Comparatively little can be presented in the way of a demographic description of the subjects on whom normative data are available. Whatever information is available as to number, sex, age, I.Q., and years of education may be seen by the summary in Table 8.2. Any further description of the nature of these samples is best presented in the order in which they are listed in Table 8.2.

Successful Suicides. The subjects in these samples were all taken from psychiatric hospitals. Fleischer (1957) reports that over one-half of his subjects had received a diagnosis of psychosis, and had been tested one year or less prior to their suicide. Daston and Sakheim (1960) obtained their protocols from a variety of hospitals, but report no information as to the diagnostic classifications of these patients. They did indicate, however, that the Rorschach had been administered "shortly" or "months" prior to death. Appelbaum and Holzman's (1962) sample was composed of approximately equal numbers of patients receiving a neurotic, psychotic, and character-disorder diagnosis. The authors fail to report how soon before death those suicide cases were tested.

Successful and Attempted Suicides. The data collected by Neuringer et. al. (1965) on this extremely heterogeneous group of women include protocols obtained from seven actual suicides carried out by psychiatric patients; the Rorschachs had been obtained between three months to one year prior to the time of death. The remainder of the sample was composed of 14 women tested at the Los Angeles Suicide Prevention Center. The

Rorschach was administered to these subjects within a month (and in most cases within one week) after their attempt on their lives; Neuringer et al. do not specify the seriousness of these attempts. Sakheim's (1955) sample consisted of psychiatric patients (diagnosed as primarily psychotic and neurotic) who had all made serious attempts on their lives. Although the lives of most of these patients had been saved by the unexpected intervention of some other person, seven were successful in taking their own lives. Sakheim reports that 30 of the patients had received the Rorschach within an average of two months after their attempt, while 10 had been tested within the average of six months prior to their suicidal attempt.

Attempted Suicides. The subjects in Fleischer's (1957) group were obtained primarily from the county psychiatric hospital and consisted mostly of diagnosed psychotics. They had been given the Rorschach one month or less after their attempts, which varied as to seriousness of intent. Martin (1951) reports that the psychiatric patients in his group had all made quite serious attempts on their lives, by methods such as shooting, cutting of the throat or wrists, stabbing, and the like. Eleven of these subjects were tested prior to their attempt, but 25 were tested afterwards; no information is given as to the time interval involved. Weiner's (1961a) sample was comprised of psychiatric patients who were tested in a hospital setting or in an outpatient clinic. The suicidal attempts were considered to be serious, and had occurred prior to the administration of the Rorschach. The attempts made by the psychiatric patients in Appelbaum and Holzman's (1962) sample undoubtedly varied as to seriousness, especially since better than half of the subjects had been diagnosed as character disorders. A later sample reported by Appelbaum and Colson (1968) was selected from a group of hospitalized patients, for whom it was determined that the attempted suicide was more than a gesture. All the testing for these last two groups was done after the attempt had been made, the time interval of which is not specified by the authors. Kruger (1954) reports that her sample was obtained from various psychiatric hospitals and clinics, and included primarily neurotic patients who had made serious attempts on their lives; the actual time of the testing is not specified. The psychiatric patients constituting both Costello's (1958) and Fisher's (1951) groups all were tested after they had made their suicidal attempts. Fisher had additionally noted that the subjects were diagnosed as schizophrenics, and had been given the Rorschach approximately three months after their attempt.

Attempted, Threatened, and Contemplated Suicides. Psychiatric patients were used in the case of all three samples in this classification. Sapolsky (1963) and Cooper, Bernstein, and Hart (1965) placed subjects in this category if they had threatened or attempted suicide prior to hospitalization and/or attempted or thought of suicide during the course of their hospitalization. Hertz (1949), who obtained her cases from files of private psychiatric hospitals, V.A. hospitals, clinics, and other sources, similarly grouped patients on the basis of showing indications of suicidal talk or ideas, as well as actual attempts. In all three samples, neither the degree of seriousness nor the point at which the testing occurred is specified.

TABLE 8.2
Characteristics of the Samples

		Sex		Age			I.Q.[a]			Years of Education		
Group	*N*	*Male*	*Female*	*Mean*	*Median*	*Range*	*Mean*	*Median*	*Range*	*Mean*	*Median*	*Range*
Successful Suicides (Fleischer, 1957)	25	18	7	—[b]	27.0	20–60	—	106.0	84–136	—	12.0	7–16
Successful Suicides (Daston and Sakheim, 1960)	36	36	0	—	—	—	—	—	—	—	—	—
Successful Suicides (Appelbaum and Holzman, 1962)	30	13	17	33.0	—	—	120.0	—	—	—	—	—
Successful and Attempted Suicides (Neuringer et al., 1965)	21	0	21	—	—	—	—	—	—	—	—	—
Successful and Attempted Suicides (Sakheim, 1955)	40	12	28	33.0	—	16–59	105.5	—	79–141	10.0	—	—
Attempted Suicides (Fleischer, 1957)	25	6	19	—	25.5	15–47	—	104.0	76–132	—	12.0	8–16
Attempted Suicides (Martin, 1951)	36	36	0	—	31.8	20–56	—	—	—	—	Between 10 and 12	—
Attempted Suicides (Weiner, 1961a)	24	9	15	30.0	—	16–55	—	—	—	—	—	—
Attempted Suicides (Appelbaum and Holzman, 1962)	39	7	32	32.0	—	—	119.0	—	—	—	—	—
Attempted Suicides (Appelbaum and Colson, 1968)	42	7	35	32.0	—	—	118.0	—	—	—	—	—
Attempted Suicides (Kruger, 1954)	16	8	8	—	31.5	17–56	—	113.0[c]	84–140[c]	—	11.0	6–16
Attempted Suicides (Costello, 1963)	30	15	15	35.5	—	14–72	—	—	—	—	—	—
Attempted Suicides (Fisher, 1951)	20	17	3	—	29.5	18–41	—	106.0[d]	99–119[d]	—	—	—
Attempted, Threatened, and Contemplated Suicides (Sapolsky, 1963)	28	10	18	31.1	—	17–62	—	—	—	—	—	—

Attempted, Threatened, and Contemplated Suicides (Cooper et al., 1965)	41	—	—	—	—	—	—	—	—	—	—	—
Attempted, Threatened, and Contemplated Suicides (Hertz, 1949)	70	—	—	—	—	—	—	—	—	—	—	—
Attempted and Contemplated Suicides (Broida, 1954)	20	20	0	28.6	—	20–44	—	—	—	10.7	—	4–15
Threatened Suicides (Fleischer, 1957)	25	7	18	—	28.0	18–55	—	101.0	75–117	—	12.0	7–16
Threatened Suicides (Kruger, 1954)	15	9	6	—	34.0	25–53	—	111.0[c]	79–144[c]	—	10.0	7–16
Nonsuicidal NP Patients (Fleischer, 1957)	25	10	15	—	25.5	18–50	—	101.0	72–120	—	12.0	8–16
Nonsuicidal NP Patients (Martin, 1951)	36	36	0	—	31.3	21–54	—	—	—	—	Between 10 and 12	—
Nonsuicidal NP Patients (Weiner, 1961a)	63	—	—	—	—	—	—	—	—	—	—	—
Nonsuicidal NP Patients (Neuringer et al., 1965)	15	0	15	—	—	—	—	—	—	—	—	—
Nonsuicidal NP Patients (Sakheim, 1955)	40	12	28	35.0	—	14–58	106.7	—	81–136	10.0	—	—
Nonsuicidal NP Patients (Appelbaum and Holzman, 1962)	96	56	40	35.0	—	—	117.0	—	—	—	—	—
Nonsuicidal NP Patients (Appelbaum and Colson, 1968)	35	22	13	35.0	—	—	115.0	—	—	—	—	—
Nonsuicidal NP Patients (Broida, 1954)	20	20	0	28.3	—	22–42	—	—	—	10.9	—	8–14

[a] Unless otherwise indicated, all I.Q. scores are based on the Full-Scale Wechsler–Bellevue.
[b] A dash (—) indicates that these data were not available.
[c] The I.Q. was either based on the Wechsler–Bellevue or estimated from the Stanford–Binet Vocabulary Score.
[d] I.Q. estimated from Wechsler–Bellevue Vocabulary Score.
[e] In all probability, these subjects were bright normal or better.

TABLE 8.2 (cont.)

Group	*N*	Sex		Age			I.Q.[a]			Years of Education		
		Male	*Female*	*Mean*	*Median*	*Range*	*Mean*	*Median*	*Range*	*Mean*	*Median*	*Range*
Nonsuicidal NP Patients (Costello, 1958)	30	15	15	35.4	—	14–70	—	—	—	—	—	—
Nonsuicidal NP Patients (Sapolsky, 1963)	28	10	18	30.3	—	14–60	—	—	—	—	—	—
Nonsuicidal NP Patients (Cooper et al., 1965)	65	—	—	—	—	—	—	—	—	—	—	—
Nonsuicidal NP Patients (Fisher, 1951)	20	13	7	—	33.0	23–44	—	109.0[d]	91–134[d]	—	—	—
Nonsuicidal NP Patients (Hertz, 1949)	108	—	—	—	—	—	—	—	—	—	—	—
Nonsuicidal Criminal Offenders (Neuringer et al., 1965)	13	0	13	—	—	—	—	—	—	—	—	—
Nonsuicidal Thyroid Subjects (Appelbaum and Holzman, 1962)	52	0	52	34.0	—	—	115.0	—	—	—	—	—
Nonsuicidal Normals (Neuringer et al., 1965)	8	0	8	—	—	—	—	—	—	—	—	—
Nonsuicidal Highway Patrolmen (Appelbaum and Holzman, 1962)	53	53	0	35.0	—	—	116.0	—	—	—	—	—
Nonsuicidal Psychiatric Residents (Appelbaum and Holzman, 1962)	50	48	2	29.0	—	—	129.0	—	—	—	—	—
Nonsuicidal College Students (Appelbaum and Holzman, 1962)	20	0	20	—	—	19–21	—[e]	—	—	—	—	—

[a] Unless otherwise indicated, all I.Q. scores are based on the Full-Scale Wechsler–Bellevue.
[b] A dash (—) indicates that these data were not available.
[c] The I.Q. was either based on the Wechsler–Bellevue or estimated from the Stanford–Binet Vocabulary Score.
[d] I.Q. estimated from Wechsler–Bellevue Vocabulary Score.
[e] In all probability, these subjects were bright normal or better.

Attempted and Contemplated Suicides. Broida (1954) reports that the patients in his sample, practically all of whom were diagnosed schizophrenics, were obtained from a "suicide ward." Half of the patients in the sample had made an attempt on their lives, while the other half were extremely depressed individuals who had continually verbalized their desire to commit suicide. Broida implies that all patients were suicidal at the time of the testing.

Threatened Suicides. Using hospitalized patients who were primarily diagnosed as being psychotic, Fleischer (1957) obtained Rorschach protocols on those individuals who had, either verbally or in writing, made a threat to take their lives; the Rorschach testing took place one month or less after this threat was made. Using mostly neurotics who were either hospitalized or being seen in an outpatient clinic, Kruger (1954) obtained the protocols of those patients who had made nonserious suicidal threats or clearly manipulative suicidal gestures. Kruger does not indicate the point in time at which the Rorschach was administered.

Nonsuicidal (N.P.) Patients. With the exception of the data collected by Hertz (1949) and Weiner (1961a), the subjects in all samples consisted of psychiatric patients who were hospitalized at the time of the testing. Hertz obtained protocols from outpatient clinics as well as hospitalized patients, as did Weiner. In the case of all subjects in these samples, there were no indications of suicidal ideas, threats, or attempts.

Other Nonsuicidal Samples. The data on female criminal offenders were obtained by Neuringer et al. (1965) from the files of a prison, and did not include any individuals who showed any marked signs of disturbance or indications of suicidal tendencies. Neuringer et al. simply note about their small group of normal subjects that they were obtained as part of a research project on normal behavior. In Appelbaum and Holzman's (1962) sample of female thyroid subjects, only 15 showed indications of thyroid disfunction; the remaining 37 subjects had served as controls in a study on personality characteristics of thyroid patients. The data on highway patrolmen referred to by Appelbaum and Holzman were obtained from the protocols collected by Rapaport, Gill, and Schafer (1946). At the time Appelbaum and Holzman rescored these records, none of these patrolmen had yet made an attempt on his life. The sample of psychiatric residents was composed of a group of those individuals who had been tested routinely in conjunction with their admission to the Menninger School of Psychiatry. Appelbaum and Holzman say little about the female college students except that they had been tested as part of a project on cognitive functioning.

Data on Suicidal Indicators

Whatever data have been found to be available on the various suicide indicators are summarized in Table 8.3. The inspection of this table reveals that in the case of most of these suicide indicators, a fair amount of overlap between groups exists.

The Problem of Overlap. As noted earlier in this chapter, the percentage of false positives becomes a crucial issue in the evaluation of a suicide indicator, in that the nonsuicidal group in any population is far greater in number than the suicidal group; hence, even the relatively small percentage of false positives results in a large absolute number of incorrectly detected cases. To use "morbid mood" as an example, we note that despite the fact that Fleischer (1957) found 100% of the successful suicides to give one or more such responses, 32% of the nonsuicidal patients—which would be translated into an absolute number of patients far greater than those who commit suicide—are also classified as being suicidal by means of this indicator.

The use of the form-dominance score (Kruger, 1954) has been shown to be useful in differentiating between suicidal patients who make an overt attempt on their lives and those who merely threaten to do so. It should be noted that this index can be applied only *after* it has been determined that the individual is a "suicide risk." In essense, the form-dominance score—and to a lesser extent the index of integration—is helpful in determining the manner in which suicidal tendencies will be expressed. Since the incidence rates for threat vs. attempt do not radically depart from the 50–50 split—as does the suicidal vs. nonsuicidal comparison—the diagnostic efficiency of the form-dominance score represents a considerable improvement over base rates.

In looking over Table 8.3 to find which indicators are successful in detecting a fair percentage of successful suicides, and which additionally show a minimal percentage of false positives among the nonsuicidal groups, we note that most of the approaches are seriously limited in their predictive ability. Relative to the other indicators, it appears that four or more of Beck's configurations, and to a lesser extent, six or more of Hertz's configurations seem to have fared somewhat better. Thus, Fleischer (1957) was able to detect 80% of the successful suicides using Beck's configurations, with no false positives whatsoever. When Fleischer used Hertz's configurations, 88% of the successful suicides were correctly identified, again with no false positives being detected. Further evidence by Sakheim (1955) and Fisher (1951), however, indicates that from 10 to 25% false positives in a nonsuicidal population may be expected with Hertz's configurations.

In considering the problem of overlap between groups, Fleischer (1957) attempted to derive suicide indicators which would detect as many suicide cases as possible, but with the minimization of false positives. Using a pool of indicators composed of many of those signs and configurations discussed earlier in this chapter, Fleischer derived two sets of configurations, each of which minimized overlap between groups. His first set of configurations turned out to be a combination of those suggested by Hertz and Beck, and were (1) deep anxiety, (2) neurotic structure, (3) depressed states, (4) withdrawal, (5) sudden and/or inappropriate emotional outbursts, (6) resignation trends, (7) agitation, and (8) mulling over. Fleischer reports that the presence of any four of the first seven configurations, when they appear in a protocol in conjunction with the eighth, characterizes 88% of the successful suicides, 68% of the attempted suicides, 72% of threatened suicides, and 0% of nonsuicidal patients. The second set of derived con-

TABLE 8.3
Normative Data on Each of the Several Suicide Indicators

Beck's Configurations

Group	*% Showing Four or More Configurations*	*% Showing Three or More Configurations*
Successful Suicides (Fleischer, 1957)	80	92
Attempted Suicides (Fleischer, 1957)	28	60
Threatened Suicides (Fleischer, 1957)	44	68
Nonsuicidal NP Patients (Fleischer, 1957)	0	28

Martin's Checklist

Group	*Number of Signs Given*			*% Showing Seven or More Signs*	*% Showing Eight or More Signs*
	Mean	*S.D.*	*Median*		
Successful Suicides (Daston and Sakheim, 1960)	7.11	—[a]	7.33	64	47
Successful and Attempted Suicides (Neuringer et al., 1965)	8.30	2.00	—	—	—
Attempted Suicides (Martin, 1951)[b]	7.17	2.19	8.00	61	50
Attempted Suicides (Weiner, 1961a)	—	—	8.83	—	79
Nonsuicidal NP Patients (Weiner, 1961a)	—	—	7.04	—	41
Nonsuicidal NP Patients (Martin, 1951)	4.42	1.28	4.21	8	3
Nonsuicidal NP Patients (Neuringer et al., 1965)	8.40	2.10	—	—	—
Nonsuicidal Criminal Offenders (Neuringer et al., 1965)	8.40	1.80	—	—	—
Nonsuicidal Normals (Neuringer et al., 1965)	6.80	2.00	—	—	—

Piotrowski's Signs

Group	*% Showing Three or More Signs*	*% Showing All Four Signs*
Successful and Attempted Suicides (Sakheim, 1955)	17.5	0
Nonsuicidal NP Patients (Sakheim, 1955)	7.5	0

[a] A dash (—) indicates that these data were not available.
[b] The data on Martin's samples are based on only 16 signs, which may account in part for the relatively lower scores for his two groups.

Rabin's Shock Indicator

Group	*% Showing Sign*
Successful and Attempted Suicides (Sakheim, 1955)	47.5
Nonsuicidal NP Patients (Sakheim, 1955)	32.5

Appelbaum and Holzman's Color-Shading Sign

Group	*% Showing Sign*
Successful Suicides (Appelbaum and Holzman, 1962)	90
Successful and Attempted Suicides (Neuringer et al., 1965)	33
Attempted Suicides (Appelbaum and Holzman, 1962)	82
Attempted Suicides (Appelbaum and Colson, 1968)	88
Nonsuicidal NP Patients (Appelbaum and Holzman, 1962)	19
Nonsuicidal NP Patients (Appelbaum and Colson, 1968)	49
Nonsuicidal NP Patients (Neuringer et al., 1965)	27
Nonsuicidal Criminal Offenders (Neuringer et al., 1965)	0
Nonsuicidal Thyroid Subjects (Appelbaum and Holzman, 1962)	17
Nonsuicidal Normals (Neuringer et al., 1965)	75
Nonsuicidal Highway Patrolmen (Appelbaum and Holzman, 1962)	9
Nonsuicidal Psychiatric Residents (Appelbaum and Holzman, 1962)	24
Nonsuicidal College Students (Appelbaum and Holzman, 1962)	35

Kruger's Developmental Scoring

Group	*% With Low Index of Integration (Below 22.0)*	*% Showing Low Form Dominance ("Minus" Scores)*
Attempted Suicides (Kruger, 1954)	69	80
Threatened Suicides (Kruger, 1954)	27	15

Lindner's "Suicide Card" Responses

Group	*% Giving One or More "Suicidal Response"*
Successful and Attempted Suicides (Sakheim, 1955)	5
Successful and Attempted Suicides (Broida, 1954)	15
Nonsuicidal NP Patients (Sakheim, 1955)	5
Nonsuicidal NP Patients (Broida, 1954)	0

Morbid Mood

Group	*% Giving One or More Morbid Response*
Successful Suicides (Fleischer, 1957)	100
Attempted Suicides (Fleischer, 1957)	56
Threatened Suicides (Fleischer, 1957)	88
Nonsuicidal NP Patients (Fleischer, 1957)	32

Sapolsky's Symbolic Content

Group	*% Giving One or More Response to D6 on Card VII*
Attempted Suicides (Costello, 1958)	17
Attempted, Threatened, and Contemplated Suicides (Sapolsky, 1963)	68
Attempted, Threatened, and Contemplated Suicides (Cooper et al., 1965)	54
Nonsuicidal NP Patients (Costello, 1958)	33
Nonsuicidal NP Patients (Sapolsky, 1963)	23
Nonsuicidal NP Patients (Cooper et al., 1965)	48

Hertz's Configurations

Group	*% Showing Four or More Configurations*	*% Showing Five or More Configurations*	*% Showing Six or More Configurations*
Successful Suicides (Fleischer, 1957)	96	—	88
Attempted Suicides (Fleischer, 1957)	68	—	24
Successful and Attempted Suicides (Sakheim, 1955)	—	88	60
Attempted Suicides (Fisher, 1951)	—	75	45
Attempted, Threatened, and Contemplated Suicides (Hertz, 1949)	—	83	—
Threatened Suicides (Fleischer, 1957)	88	—	40
Nonsuicidal NP Patients (Fleischer, 1957)	24	—	0
Nonsuicidal NP Patients (Sakheim, 1955)	—	28	10
Nonsuicidal NP Patients (Fisher, 1951)	—	80	25
Nonsuicidal NP Patients (Hertz, 1949)	—	16	—

figurations were based totally on Hertz's indicators, and consisted of (1) neurotic structure, (2) deep anxiety, (3) depressed states, (4) constriction, (5) active conflict and deep inner struggle, and (6) resignation trends; four or more of the configurations was used as the cutoff score. Fleischer notes that these configurations were derived so as to maximize the likelihood of detecting successful suicides. His findings indicate that 96% of the successful suicides are detected by this means, whereas only 28% of the attempts, 40% of the threats, and 0% of the controls constitute the false positive rate. Although the two sets of configurations suggested by Fleischer seem to offer a certain amount of promise, it must be remembered that they were derived empirically on one particular population, and have not as yet been cross validated. Considering the fact that nonsuicidal patients were not detected by these configurations, a cross validation of these indicators is unquestionably worthwhile.

RELIABILITY

No evidence has been reported on the stability of any of the above indicators over time. In the use of the Rorschach as an indicator of suicidal potential, however, the appropriateness of such reliability studies is questionable. Suicidal potential is such a transitory state that attempts to study stability over time will of necessity yield low correlations. In the evaluation of the various suicide indicators discussed in this chapter, therefore, the evaluative criterion of reliability will not be applied.

VALIDITY

In discussing the research evidence for the validity of the several suicide indicators described earlier in the chapter, separate considerations of the construct and criterion validities cannot easily be made. First of all, no studies at all bearing any relationship to the construct-validity format have been carried out with the indicators. This is not very surprising, inasmuch as interest in Rorschach suicide indicators rests more in the practical than in the theoretical realm. Even in the case of trait validity, which may simply involve the correlation of Rorschach suicide indices with other measures of suicidal potential, however, no research evidence is available.

The second, and perhaps more important reason for not discussing the research according to the various classifications of validity is that most of the studies do not fall clearly into either the concurrent or predictive categories. Thus, with the exception of those few studies which used successful suicides as the criterion group (Appelbaum and Holzman, 1962; Daston and Sakheim, 1956; Fleischer, 1957), the criterion groups in most of the investigations were composed of some subjects who were tested before, but others who were tested after the suicidal behavior had occurred. Although these studies may be said to constitute criterion-validity research, classifying them as being either of the concurrent or the predictive type is not feasible.

Instead of subclassifying the types of validity studies, as we have done in the case of the evaluation of other applications of the Rorschach, this section will simply describe the research evidence as it applies to each of the several suicide indicators outlined earlier in the chapter.

Indicators Based on Formal Scoring

Beck's Configurations

Sakheim (1955) compared a group of 40 suicidal psychiatric patients—33 of whom made serious attempts on their lives and seven of whom were successful—with a group of nonsuicidal controls matched on the basis of sex, age, educational level, and I.Q. Some of the suicidal patients were tested prior to their attempt, although most were tested afterwards. Sakheim compared the group on the basis of each of Beck's five configurations separately, obtaining statistically significant differences between the groups on the basis of the configurations "oppressive anxiety" and "shading shock on Card IV"; the differences were in the predicted direction, with the suicidal group showing those configurations more frequently than the control group. Although the frequency of the other three configurations ("neurotic structure," "strenuous inner conflict," "mulling over") was greater in the suicidal group, the differences failed to reach statistical significance.

Rather than comparing groups on each of the specific configurations, Fleischer (1957) used the presence of all five, any four, and any three signs as cutoff points. His four groups, consisting of 25 psychiatric patients each, were as follows: successful suicides, suicide attempts varying in degree of seriousness, suicide threats, and nonsuicidal controls. Except for the successful suicides, the suicidal groups were tested after the event occurred. The results indicate that with the use of a cutoff score of either three or more, or four or more configurations, the four groups could be significantly differentiated from each other ($p < .01$). In the case of both cutoff scores, the configurations occurred most often in the successful suicidal group and least often in the nonsuicidal controls.

Martin's Checklist

Martin (1951) applied his empirically derived checklist to the Rorschach protocols of two groups of male neuropsychiatric patients: those who had made serious attempts on their lives and nonsuicidal patients matched on the basis of age, I.Q., education, and diagnosis. Despite the fact that subsequent cross validations had revealed that nine of these 17 signs do not hold up (see p. 221), Martin found significantly more signs present in the suicidal than in the control group ($p < .001$). Since some of the 36 suicidal patients were tested before the attempt and others afterwards, Martin compared these two subgroups on the basis of the number of signs indicated; the findings failed to yield any difference in the number of signs yielded.

Using patients from both a hospital and a clinic setting, Weiner (1961a) compared the number of Martin signs occurring in the records of patients making serious suicidal attempts with those showing no suicidal tendencies. The results reveal a significantly larger number of signs ($p < .01$) present in the records of suicidal patients. Weiner further records that the variables of age, sex, and setting (hospital vs. clinic) bore no relationship to the number of signs given. He did find, however, that diagnosis *was* related to Martin's signs. Specifically, his results indicate that nonsuicidal neurotic patients gave fewer signs than did nonsuicidal psychotics or character disorders, the diagnosis being determined by either the intake committee (clinic patients) or the discharge diagnosis (hospitalized patients).

In an extension of Martin's original study, Daston and Sakheim (1960) applied the signs to a group of patients who had been successful in their suicide attempts. The Rorschach protocols on these patients were obtained "shortly" or "months" before the occurrence of suicide. Using Martin's attempted suicidal and nonsuicidal groups as points of comparison, Daston and Sakheim report that while the successful suicides do not differ from the serious attempters in the number of signs given, they do obtain significantly more than the nonsuicidal controls ($p <.01$).

Except for Weiner's study, positive results were obtained with samples which were composed of all male subjects. This prompted Neuringer et al. (1965) to test the validity of Martin's signs in the case of females. The four groups in Neuringer's et al. study consisted of 21 successful and attempted suicidal females, 21 nonsuicidal female V.A. patients, 13 nonsuicidal female criminal offenders, and eight nonsuicidal normal females. The results of the study failed to reveal any significant differences in the number of signs among the four groups. It would seem unlikely that the negative results were the function of the sex of the subjects, especially since Weiner found no relationship between sex and number of signs given. It is possible, however, that these negative findings might be due in part to the nature of the suicidal group, which consisted largely of attempters. Although Neuringer et al. do not specify the seriousness of these suicidal attempts, most previous research seems to indicate that attempts in females are more likely to be manipulative than serious. Another aspect of the composition of this suicidal group which differs from previous research with the signs is that the females making the suicidal attempt were not psychiatric patients, but instead people who were referred to the Los Angeles Suicide Prevention Center after the attempt had been detected.

In general, the weight of the research evidence with Martin's checklist seems to indicate—at least at the group level—the signs can successfully distinguish between suicidal and nonsuicidal patients.

Piotrowski's Signs

A test of the validity of Piotrowski's four signs was carried out by Sakheim (1955), who compared the Rorschach performance of a group of patients who had either made serious or successful attempts on their lives with a matched nonsuicidal control group. The results of Sakheim's study failed to reveal any evidence for the validity of Piotrowski's signs—either individually or as a group. A study by Fleischer (1957), in which the comparison was made between successful suicides, attempted suicides, threatened suicides, and nonsuicidal controls, similarly failed to yield any evidence to support the validity of the signs.

Rabin's Shock Indicator

Rabin's (1946) suggestion that suicidal potential was particularly indicated by the joint appearance of shading shock and color shock was tested empirically by Sakheim (1955) and Fleischer (1957). The results of both these investigations were found to be negative. Sakheim failed to obtain a difference between a group of attempted and successful suicidal patients and a group of nonsuicidal controls. Fleischer's comparison of successful suicides, attempted suicides, threatened suicides, and nonsuicidal controls on the basis of Rabin's shock indicator similarly yielded nonsignificant findings.

Appelbaum and Holzman's Color-Shading Sign

The use of the color-shading response as a suicide indicator has been studied empirically by Appelbaum and Holzman (1962), who were originally responsible for suggesting its application. They studied the presence of color-shading response within a variety of populations, including psychiatric patients who were successful in their suicide attempts, patients who made unsuccessful attempts, nonsuicidal psychiatric patients, highway patrolmen, nonsuicidal individuals serving as subjects in a thyroid study, psychiatric residents, and college students. Appelbaum and Holzman's findings indicate that the color-shading response was present beyond chance expectation within each of the two suicidal groups, and absent more often than might be expected by chance for each of the five nonsuicidal control groups. Further, a tally of the presence or absence of the color-shading response for the combined experimental vs. combined control groups yielded a chi square of 111.76, which is significant well beyond the .001 level. Further statistical analyses indicated that the single vs. the multiple occurrence of color shading within a protocol was not differentially associated with suicide. The authors also note that neither the form-dominance variable nor the morbidity of the content of color-shading responses was of any additional assistance in detecting suicidal tendencies. These findings were successfully replicated in a later study by Appelbaum and Colson (1968).

Of all those studies dealing with suicide indicators on the Rorschach, Appelbaum and Holzman's investigation is the only one which has presented some data relevant to the question of base rates. They report that over a three-year period, 28% of the 252 patients hospitalized at Menninger had either successfully or unsuccessfully made attempts on their lives. In computing the predictive efficiency of the color-shading response in this particular hospital population (cf. Pauker, 1962), one notes that the indicator is capable of correctly identifying 82% of all patients, thus misclassifying only 18%. In comparison to judging all patients in the hospital as nonsuicidal—which would misclassify the 28% who indeed are suicidal—

the use of the color-shading indicator represents an improvement of 10% over base rates.

In Neuringer et al.'s (1965) study, which has already been discussed in conjunction with Martin's checklist, a group of female suicidal patients (composed of actual as well as attempted suicides) were compared with a nonsuicidal patient control group, as well as with nonsuicidal criminal offenders and normal subjects. The findings do not corroborate those of Appelbaum and his associates, in that no significant differences were found among the four groups in the occurrence of the color-shading response.

There is one further point which should be noted in conjunction with the color-shading indicator. In discussing the significance of this particular type of response, Appelbaum and Holzman (1962) hypothesize that it reveals the individual's "searching, penetrating characteristics" as well as his "sensitivity to nuances of feeling." The data in Table 8.3 offer an interesting informal corroboration of this hypothesis. A fairly large percentage of psychiatric residents, nonsuicidal college students (female), and nonsuicidal normal females, all of whom may be expected to possess a relatively high degree of sensitivity to feelings, have at least one color-shading response in their Rorschach records. Conversely, the color-shading response is completely absent among the group of criminal offenders, and only infrequently present among the highway patrolmen. It may be appropriate, then, to view the presence of color-shading responses as being indicative of affective sensitivity, which may be seen as a necessary but not sufficient condition for suicide.

Kruger's Developmental Scoring

Kruger (1954) studied the relationship between Rorschach developmental level and the expression of suicidal tendencies. In particular, she obtained the protocols of patients who had made serious but unsuccessful attempts on their lives, and compared them with the records of patients who were simply preoccupied with thoughts of suicide or had made manipulative suicidal threats. The actual point at which the testing occurred is not specified by Kruger. The findings with both the index of integration and the form-dominance measure revealed that the nonacting-out groups were developmentally more mature than those who made actual attempts on their lives. One additional finding of Kruger's was that the suicidal group obtained a higher index of integration than a group of assaultive subjects, confirming the hypothesis that the inward expression of aggression is a more indirect and thereby more mature method of impulse expression.

In evaluating the utility of the developmental scores in predicting suicide, it should be emphasized that the relative absence of developmentally high scores in a record by no means implies suicidal tendencies. Rather, Kruger's study offers evidence for the fact that once suicidal tendencies become a question, the use of developmental scores can be of assistance in determining just how these tendencies will be expressed. More so than other indices, then, the developmental scores cannot be used in and of themselves in determining the potential for suicide.

Content Indicators

Lindner's "Suicide-Card" Responses

Although Lindner (1946) himself offered no empirical evidence on the validity of depressive and decay responses to Card IV, Broida (1954) and Sakheim (1955) have tested his suggestion in their research on the Rorschach's ability to detect suicidal tendencies. Broida found that in the comparison of psychiatric patients who were believed to be suicidal risks (because of previous attempts or frequent thoughts) with nonsuicidal controls, no significant difference was found between groups. Similarly, Sakheim obtained negative results in his comparison of attempted suicides with nonsuicidal patient controls. Aside from the inability of decay and depressive responses on Card IV to differentiate between suicidal and nonsuicidal patients, it might also be noted that this type of response occurs relatively infrequently in the records of patients in general.

Morbid Content

The only studies on the use of morbid content by itself as a means of predicting suicidal potential have been conducted by Sakheim (1955) and Fleischer (1957). Sakheim failed to obtain any significant difference between a group of attempted and successful suicidal patients and those who have no indication of suicidal potential. The presence of morbid content occurred in a little less than a third of the protocols within each of Sakheim's two groups. Fleischer, on the other hand, found that 100% of successful suicidal patients who had been given the Rorschach a year or less prior to their suicide gave at least one morbid response. Fleischer obtained statistical significance across his four comparison groups (successful suicides, attempted suicides, threatened suicides, and nonsuicidal controls), but with the presence of considerable overlap. As may be seen from Table 8.3, the relatively more frequent presence of morbid responses in those patients who had threatened but not made actual attempts at suicide, suggests that the overt suicidal attempt may serve to alleviate these dysphoric feelings. As a means of differentially predicting who will act on their suicidal impulses and who will merely make threats, the use of morbid content on the Rorschach is clearly limited. In this connection, the use of the developmental scores employed by Kruger in her study of the expression of suicidal tendencies might prove fruitful if used in conjunction with the presence of morbid responses.

Crasilneck's Direction of Aggression

Crasilneck (1954) attempted to use the content of the response to determine the means by which an individual would express his aggression—against himself, toward others, or from others. As has been noted earlier in this chapter, Crasilneck's scoring criteria seem arbitrary and somewhat tenuous. Possibly because his scoring does not accurately reveal direction of aggression, he was unable to obtain any significant differences between patients who made serious suicide attempts and those whose attempts seemed to be more attention seeking in nature.

Sapolsky's Symbolic Content

In his test of the assumption that responses to the dark middle bottom area of Card VII are indicative of suicidal ideation, Sapolsky (1963) obtained the records of 28 hospitalized patients who responded to this blot area as well as of 28 comparable patients who failed to respond to the area. Ratings of suicidal ideation were then obtained, which were defined as a threat or attempt at suicide prior to hospitalization and/or the attempt or thought of suicide during hospitalization. More than half of the subjects in both groups combined were classified as having had suicidal ideation, a fact which mitigates the utility of this type of criterion measure. In any event, Sapolsky was successful in obtaining a significant relationship between those patients who responded to this blot area and those who showed suicidal ideation. Sapolsky obtained comparable results in a replication of this study. Cooper et al. (1965) and Drake and Rusnak (1966), on the other hand, were not successful in their cross validation. Even with analyses within diagnostic classifications, Cooper et al. failed to obtain statistical significance. Some of the data published by Costello (1958) are also relevant to Sapolsky's suggested diagnostic indicator. Costello compared the content of responses from the records of attempted suicidal patients with those from nonsuicidal patients, which included those responses given to the dark middle bottom area of Card VII. Although Costello did not find any significant difference between the two groups for this particular response, what might be interpreted as a trend seemed to reveal that the *nonsuicidal* group responded more frequently to this blot area.

Apart from the practical limitations of Sapolsky's criterion measure, the other research evidence on this approach has failed to confirm validity of the method.

Costello's Content

Costello compared the frequency of different types of responses for a group of patients who had made a suicidal attempt and a group who had shown no indications of suicidal potential. Costello's results are presented in a somewhat unorthodox manner, in that he presents what he calls "common" and "typical" responses for each of the two groups. According to Costello, the "common" response is one which occurred for at least 25% of the group members, while a "typical" response is one which characterizes one group as opposed to another; a typical response is defined as one which is a common one in one group, but which occurs twice as often as it does in the other group.

As the result of Costello's tally of the content for each group, 17 responses qualified as being either "common" or "typical." Of these responses, which are presented in Table 8.1, only four may be considered to be statistically significant. Because of the size of the original pool of responses, it is likely that these differences have emerged by chance.

Content and Formal Indicators Combined

Hertz's Configurations

More so than any other of the suicide indicators discussed thus far, Hertz's suggested configurations have been subjected to a number of empirical investigations (Berk, 1949; Fisher, 1951; Fleischer, 1957; Hertz, 1949; Sakheim, 1955).

After eliminating four configurations described in her 1948 paper on suicide indicators, Hertz (1949) compared a group of suicidal patients with nonsuicidal controls. The Rorschach protocols were obtained from a variety of sources, with the suicidal criterion being defined primarily by the presence of some indication of a suicide attempt, threat, or idea in the patient's case history. Using five or more configurations as her cutoff point, Hertz found that she was able to differentiate between the two groups beyond the .001 level.

Sakheim (1955), who made an attempt to clarify Hertz's scoring procedure somewhat, compared the performance of attempted and successful suicide patients with a matched nonsuicidal group. With five or more configurations serving as a cutoff point, Sakheim obtained a phi coefficient of $+.58$ ($p < .01$); with six or more configurations as the cutoff, the tetrachoric correlation of $+.70$ similarly proved to be statistically significant. Fleischer (1957) made use of Sakheim's scoring clarifications, finding that six or more configurations, as well as four or more configurations, significantly differentiated among four groups of psychiatric patients—successful suicides, attempted suicides, threatened suicides, and controls.

Fisher (1951) compared patients who had made suicide attempts with those who had neither made overt attempts nor revealed any suicidal ideation. The results of this study failed to yield any positive evidence for the validity of Hertz's configurations. It might be noted, however, that Fisher admitted to having difficulty in using Hertz's criteria for the 10 configurations; he indicates that while he did in fact use Hertz's configurations, different criteria were employed in defining the configurations. It is quite possible that Fisher's failure to obtain positive findings may have been due to the different procedure by which he scored for the configurations.

Berk (1949) compared two groups of schizophrenic patients, both of which were comparable as to diagnosis, duration of illness, and educational level. The suicidal patients, who, on the basis of staff judgment, were believed to be suicidal at the time of the Rorschach testing, had a history of at least one attempt on their lives; the nonsuicidal patients were judged as being so by members of the staff. The results of the study proved to be nonsignificant. Berk notes that although the two groups had comparable diagnoses, the suicidal group was composed of more patients with a history of assaultive behavior, as well as homosexual acting out beyond adolescence. Just how these unique characteristics of the suicidal sample may have affected the results, however, is not clear.

Although some of the findings presented above are slightly conflicting, the bulk of evidence seems to point to the fact that Hertz's configurations are capable of significantly distinguishing between groups.

White and Schreiber's Indicators

From a methodological point of view, White and Schreiber's (1952) study on the diagnosis of "suicidal risks" by means of the Rorschach has very strong as well as very weak features. White and Schreiber took pains to use Rorschach protocols which were obtained immediately before or after the time when it was evident clinically that suicidal tendencies were present. Suicidal tendencies were defined by the authors as the actual occurrence of suicide, attempts at suicide, threats or suicidal ideation. From a pool of 1250 protocols obtained in a private psychiatric hospital, 105 were judged as "suicidal" in nature. As noted earlier in the chapter, White and Schreiber's joint use of content and formal indicators was carried out "clinically." Of the 105 suicidal protocols, 77.2% belonged to patients who had been placed in the criterion group. Of another group of 56 consecutive hospital admissions, the authors report that 59% of the suicidal risks were detected by means of their scoring approach, while 41% went undetected. White and Schreiber fail to present data on the percentage of false positives in this sample, but instead attempt to point out where the large percentage of false negatives was a function of the inaccurate placement of these patients in the suicidal category. In short, one may conclude that White and Schreiber's indicators are of little use in detecting suicidal behavior.

OVERALL EVALUATION

Although suicide occurs infrequently, attempts to predict and interfere with its happening need little justification. The actual definition of "suicidal behavior" varies, and can refer to serious and intentional suicides, suicidal gestures of a primarily manipulative nature, open threats of suicide, and suicidal ideation. Although the first two categories represent fairly homogeneous groupings of behavior, the suicidal threat and suicidal ideation categories can include individuals who vary considerably as to degree of seriousness. Several studies in this area have defined the criterion group according to whether the suicide was attempted or successful; like suicidal threats and ideation, however, attempts at suicide may be either serious or manipulative. The problem of determining a suicide criterion group is compounded further by the fact that suicidal tendencies refer to a transitory state. Research on individuals who at one time had shown suicidal tendencies may be using an inappropriate criterion group at the time of the study.

Over the years, more than a dozen different Rorschach signs or configurations have been suggested for possible use in the prediction of suicidal behavior. Some of these indicators make use of the formal scoring of the record, others of the content, and still others of a combination of the formal and content elements. After reviewing the research literature in this area, it is safe to conclude that most of the suicide indicators have failed to receive empirical support. Thus, the suicidal signs suggested by Piotrowski, Rabin, Lindner, Crasilneck, Costello, Sapolsky, and White and Schreiber have not even proved useful on a group basis. Despite the fact that Martin's checklist,

Hertz's configurations, Appelbaum and Holzman's color-shading response, and morbid mood responses have been found to differentiate significantly between groups, the large amount of overlap places a serious limitation on their clinical applications. Of all those suicide indicators suggested by different writers, Beck's configurations appear to result in the least amount of overlap. It might also be noted that once the existence of suicidal tendencies has been established, the use of the form-dominance score, as suggested by Kruger, becomes a valuable index in arriving at a decision about how these tendencies will be expressed (e.g., threats vs. attempts).

In reviewing the research literature on Rorschach suicide indicators, it becomes apparent that certain methodological problems are inherent in the area of suicide prediction per se. The definition of the suicide criterion often varies from study to study, with some criterion groups containing individuals whose suicidal behavior is only remotely similar. Those studies which define the criterion group by means of suicidal ideation or threats do not seem to be getting at the important issue. The more appropriate criterion group for which predictive indicators are needed is composed of those individuals who do not give open or obvious clues to their forthcoming suicide, but who do indeed take their lives. Because suicidal tendencies exist as more or less of a temporary state of the individual, rather than a personality trait or characteristic, the measuring instrument which is used to predict suicidal behavior must be administered at the time the suicidal risk exists. The use of "stale" Rorschach protocols is not at all appropriate for research in this area. An additional consideration regarding the time of the testing is whether or not the test is administered before or after the suicidal event. There is reason to believe that an unsuccessful suicide attempt serves as a catharsis, thereby making it difficult to validate suicide indicators from test protocols obtained after this unsuccessful attempt.

A final problem in the area of suicide prediction is that of base rates. Because of the relative infrequency with which suicide occurs, it is extremely difficult to improve over predictions made from base rates alone. In particular, the difficulty lies in the large number of false positives which are likely to emerge. Even with a predictive instrument which detects only a small percentage of false positives, this small percentage, when applied to the overwhelmingly large number of nonsuicidal cases in the population, is likely to result in the placement of far more subjects in the false positive than in the true positive category. A partial solution to the dilemma of base rates involves the use of demographic and situational variables which have been found to be associated with suicide to eliminate some of the false positives detected by the predictive device.

Because of the above-mentioned methodological problems associated with suicide prediction, rather than any inherent weakness in the diagnostic sensitivity of the Rorschach, we are not too optimistic about the validation of Rorschach indicators for the clinical prediction of suicide.

Chapter 9

NEUROTIC SIGNS

The search for neurotic signs represents a brief and inglorious chapter in Rorschach research. In the late 1930s American psychologists began to embrace the Rorschach as a tool for clinical diagnosis, and the advent of World War II created a pressing need for psychodiagnostic indices that could quickly identify probable emotional disturbance in military recruits and other wartime personnel. Spawned by these two influences, several Rorschach sign lists for scoring neurosis or maladjustment were born and flourished during the 1940s. By the mid-1950s these sign lists had all but disappeared from the literature, victims of their narrow-band approach to personality functioning and their resultant lack of clinical or research utility.

Yet the major neurotic and adjustment sign lists definitely merit inclusion in this book. Because they broke ground in quantifying clinical diagnosis, they generated a substantial amount of clinical investigative work; because they provided a projective and presumably sophisticated index of maladjustment, they significantly promoted the use of the Rorschach as a measuring instrument in personality research. The literature on neurotic signs is additionally important to review because it catalogs virtually the full range of methodological impasses and oversights that have plagued Rorschach research. Of these, one doomed this area of study from its inception—namely, that the criterion, neurosis, was not and never has been systematically defined, conceptually, phenomenologically, or in any other way.

The murkiness of neurosis as a psychological state needs to be kept in mind as various Rorschach sign lists for it are discussed in this chapter. On the conceptual level, there is no personality characteristic that can be propounded as uniquely neurotic. All of the traditional neurotic symptoms —anxiety, conversion, phobias, depression, and obsessive-compulsive phenomena—appear in psychotic as well as neurotic people, and all of the behavior patterns attributed to neurotics—immaturity, rigidity, low anxiety tolerance, mild distortions of reality, and the like—are as indicative of character disorder as of neurosis. Perhaps symptom neuroses and character disorders should both be considered neurotic behavior; however, there is no general agreement that such is the case, and the point here is not to resolve such complex classification issues but rather to highlight the nosological morass against which intrepid Rorschach investigators set out to develop, validate, and apply indices of neurosis.

Researchers in this area typically have attempted to bypass conceptual vagaries of classification by utilizing independently or previously recorded clinical diagnoses as the criterion for the presence of neurosis. Unfortunately, however, the reliability of psychiatric diagnoses has proved generally low, and available data suggest that neurotic disorders are among the least reliably diagnosed of traditional nosological categories (Sandifer, Pettus, and Quade, 1964; Schmidt and Fonda, 1956). Hence the attempt to develop broadly valid Rorschach indices of neurosis from clinical populations has been seriously handicapped by the inconsistency with which neurosis is diagnosed from one clinician to the next, from one time to the next, and from one clinical setting to another.

The impact of this criterion problem and of other methodological limitations has been apparent in the general failure of Rorschach sign lists for neurosis or maladjustment to achieve cross validation beyond the subject group or setting in which they were originally examined. To illustrate, this chapter will review the rise and fall of five major systems for scoring Rorschach indices of neurosis or maladjustment: the signs, respectively, of Miale and Harrower-Erickson, Munroe, Davidson, Muench, and Fisher.

FIVE SCORING SYSTEMS

The Miale and Harrower-Erickson, Munroe, Davidson, Muench, and Fisher Rorschach scoring systems for neurosis or maladjustment are overlapping but vary in their origin, complexity, and ease of scoring. This section will outline the development and scoring criteria of these five systems.

Miale/Harrower-Erickson Neurotic Signs (MHE)

Florence Miale and Molly Harrower-Erickson reported the first attempt to develop a Rorschach scoring system for neurosis in a 1940 paper (Miale and Harrower-Erickson, 1940). Their explicit goal was to identify Rorschach variables that would assist the clinical differentiation of psychoneurotic patients from patients with other forms of psychopathology, and they listed the following five structural personality characteristics as common to all cases of psychoneurosis:

1. Lack of inner stability.
2. An infantile adaptation.
3. Inability to adjust to the environment.

4. Excessive anxiety and tension.
5. Stereotypy and restriction of spontaneity, with an attempt to substitute conscious control for genuine adjustment.

In their actual research, however, Miale and Harrower-Erickson did not utilize subjects manifesting diverse forms of psychopathology, nor did they derive their Rorschach criteria for neurosis from their conception of neurotic personality structure, for example, considering what Rorschach scores might be indicative of an infantile adaptation. Rather, they searched empirically for Rorschach score differences between just two subject groups: 43 patients, aged 15–55, who had been diagnosed as psychoneurotic in clinical settings, and 20 "normal" individuals of comparable age and intelligence, from unspecified sources. From comparisons between these neurotic and presumably normal subjects they derived the following nine "neurotic signs," five or more of which in a record they regarded as strongly suggestive of neurotic disturbance:

1. $R < 25$.
2. $M < 2$.
3. $FM > M$.
4. $F\% \geq 50\%$.
5. Rejection of one or more cards.
6. $FC < 2$. Subsequently modified to be scored only when $FC < 1$ (Harrower-Erickson, 1942, 1943).
7. $A\% \geq 50\%$. Subsequently modified to be scored when either $A\%$ or $At\% \geq 50\%$ (Harrower-Erickson, 1942, 1943).
8. Color shock. Scored for rejection, delayed time to first response, or appearance of F − responses on colored cards.
9. Shading shock. Scored for rejection, delayed time to first response, or appearance of F − responses on Card IV or VI.

Munroe Inspection Technique (IT)

The Monroe Inspection Technique (IT) was developed by Ruth Munroe in 1940 to facilitate brief screening of Rorschach protocols for indices of maladjustment, and it was published initially as one of a series of papers devoted by the *Rorschach Research Exchange* to the utilization of the Rorschach method as a selective instrument for defense purposes (Munroe, 1941). The IT requires the examiner to note "important deviations from the usual" on a check list that embodies most of the major Rorschach scoring categories. For each category on which the subject deviates from the usual he receives one, two, or three checks, depending on the extent of his deviation. Munroe formulated her criteria for assigning checks on an a priori basis from the cumulative experience of Rorschach workers: "I have relied upon generally accepted judgments as to what constitutes clinically significant deviation in Rorschach performance..." (Munroe, 1944, p. 46).

Munroe (1941) initially utilized the IT to assign qualitative adjustment ratings to 101 young women, the 1940 freshmen class at Sarah Lawrence College, but she subsequently concluded that a simple tabulation of the number of checks for each protocol would yield a quantitative measure of adjustment adequately correlated with external criteria (Munroe, 1944, 1945b). The complete IT scoring system (Munroe, 1944, pp. 55–70) is extremely complex and involves a series of weights based on the length of the record and the interrelationships of various scoring categories. For purposes of general information and comparison with the other systems, it is relevant to list just the major points of "deviation" at which the IT system begins to assign checks:

1. T/R $> 60''$ or $< 30''$.
2. Rejection of one or more cards.
3. W% $> 60\%$ or $< 15\%$.
4. Dd% $> 10\%$.
5. S > 1.
6. Succession rigid, loose, or confused.
7. P < 4.
8. Original responses $> 50\%$.
9. At + Sex > 1.
10. Wide or narrow range of content, e.g., A% $> 60\%$.
11. F% $> 50\%$ or $< 15\%$.
12. Form quality vague, bizarre, or overly exacting.
13. Shading shock.
14. FK + Fc $> 50\%$, or Fc < 2.
15. cF + c > 1.
16. KF + K + kF + k > 1.
17. FC′ > 3 or C′F + C′ > 1.
18. M < 3 or $> 30\%$.
19. FM < 2, or FM:M $> 2{:}1$.
20. m > 1 or $> 10\%$.
21. M + FM + m $> 40\%$ or $< 10\%$.
22. Color shock.
23. FC < 2.
24. CF < 1, or CF:FC $\geq 2{:}1$.
25. C ≥ 1.
26. FC + CF + C < 3 or $> 30\%$.
27. (FC + CF + C) $>$ 2(M + FM + m), or (M + FM + m) $>$ 2(FC + CF + C).

Davidson Signs of Adjustment

Helen Davidson, influenced by the prior use of Rorschach sign lists by Miale and Harrower-Erickson and by Piotrowski, developed a "signs of adjustment" list as part of an extensive study of personality characteristics in bright children (Davidson, 1943). Her scoring criteria, like those of Munroe, were derived on an a priori basis from previous sign lists, clinical experience, and normative expectations. Although Davidson (1950) subsequently conceptualized good adjustment in terms of (1) inner stability and maturity, (2) rational control in emotional situations, and (3) rapport with the world outside, she did not attempt to relate her Rorschach signs to these personality variables.

Davidson (1943) initially scored 23 presumed signs of adjustment in the Rorschachs of 60 boys and 42 girls, aged 9–14, all of whom had measured IQs in excess of 120. She then discarded five signs that demonstrated a low biserial correlation with the total number of signs per record (below .23) and a sixth sign because it was present almost universally. The remaining list of 17 signs, because of its internal consistency, was taken by Davidson to yield a valid index of adjustment:

1. $M \geq FM$.
2. $M > 2$, including additionals.
3. Sum $C > Fc + c + C'$.
4. $F\% \leq 50\%$.
5. $Dd + S\% \leq 10\%$.
6. $P > 3$ and $< 30\%$.
7. $R > 20$.
8. $FC \geq CF$.
9. $FC > 1$.
10. $C < 1$.
11. VIII–X% of 40–60%.
12. $FK + Fc > 1$.
13. W:M of approximately 2:1.
14. $A\% \leq 50\%$.
15. No color shock.
16. No shading shock.
17. No rejections.

Muench Signs of Personal and Social Adjustment

In 1947 George Muench reported an assessment of the efficacy of nondirective therapy by means of the Rorschach and two other personality tests, the Kent–Rosanoff Word Association Test and the Bell Adjustment Inventory. His subjects were 12 clients who were administered these three measures prior to and immediately following a course of nondirective treatment. For his Rorschach variables in this study Muench selected 11 signs of "personal adjustment" and 11 signs of "social adjustment," all taken from previous work by Davidson, Hertz, and Klopfer and presumed to represent normal expectation.

Despite the fact that Muench's list represented a new and unique combination of previously suggested adjustment indices, he eschewed any interest in validating it in its own right:

> All of these patterns have been validated through clinical applications by the various Rorschach workers. It is not the purpose of this study to further validate the patterns described, but to accept the validation of various investigators (Muench, 1947, p. 16).

The shakiness of the prior validations on which Muench was content to rely will be elaborated subsequently in this chapter. The signs he chose for his list are the following:

Personal adjustment:

1. $M > 2$.
2. $M \geq FM$.
3. $W > 2$.
4. $F+/\text{sum } F \text{ undiff} \geq .70$. F undiff includes "all responses to form, whether or not the form is clear, and whether or not there is an admixture of color or movement."
5. $F+\% \geq 70\%$.
6. $H > Hd$.
7. $g \geq 10\%$. Based on weights of 0.5 for popular Ws, 1.5 for original Ws, and 1.0 for other Ws of good form.
8. $FCh > ChF + Ch$. Based on weights of 0.5 for FCh, 1.0 for ChF, and 1.5 for Ch.
9. $A\% \leq 50\%$.
10. Oligophrenic details absent.
11. $P > 4$.

Social adjustment:

1. $R > 19$.
2. $R+\% \geq 85\%$.
3. $FC > 1$.
4. $FC \geq CF + C$. Based on weights of 0.5 for FC, 1.0 for CF, and 1.5 for C.
5. $C < 1$.
6. VIII–X% of 40–60%.
7. $FC' + Fc > 1$.
8. $F{:}FC' + Fc \leq 2{:}1$.
9. No rejections.
10. $M + FC > CF + C$.
11. $H + A{:}Hd + Ad \geq 2{:}1$.

Fisher Degree of Total Maladjustment

Seymour Fisher developed a Rorschach index of total degree of maladjustment as one variable in an extensive study of patterns of personality rigidity and their determinants (Fisher, 1950). Like Munroe, Davidson, and Muench, Fisher established his scoring criteria on an a priori basis according to "a range of Rorschach signs which are clinically recognized as indicating various degrees of personal maladjustment. . ." (Fisher, 1950, p. 10). He made no effort to select, evaluate, or modify his scoring criteria on the basis of his subjects' performance, even though his samples were appropriate for examining the criterion validity of his index for identifying neurosis: (1) 20 normal women (occupational therapy students, student nurses, student social workers, and stenographers), aged 20–45; (2) 20 women diagnosed as conversion hysterics, aged 18–50; and (3) 20 women diagnosed as paranoid schizophrenics, aged 21–55.

In Fisher's system each relevant sign is given a weighted score determined from its relation to other Rorschach factors and from its presumed degree of significance for maladjustment (Fisher, 1950, pp. 45–47). As with Munroe's IT, the complete system is too detailed to reproduce here in full, and the following summary of its major criteria will suffice to indicate its flavor:

1. Dd% $\geq$ 18%.
2. W% > 30% or <15%.
3. Sequence confused.
4. M < 3.
5. M − $\geq$ 1.
6. C $\geq$ 1.
7. FC − $\geq$ 1.
8. FC < 1.
9. Color naming.
10. F +% < 65%.
11. R < 20.
12. T/1R > 24″.
13. Rejection of one or more cards.
14. Y $\geq$ 1.
15. S > 3.
16. P < 4.
17. Sex $\geq$ 1.
18. A% > 60% or <30%.
19. H < 2.
20. Hd:H $\geq$ 3:1.
21. Sex confusion.
22. Bizarre logic.
23. Perseveration.

Similarities Between the Systems

The above sign lists reflect numerous similarities between the Miale/Harrower-Erickson, Munroe, Davidson, Muench, and Fisher systems. To help the reader identify those Rorschach variables that have figured most prominently in attempts to measure neurosis or maladjustment, Table 9.1 indicates the scoring categories common to three or more of the systems. These common categories reveal close scoring congruence. With the exception of some disagreement on R (a subject with 21–24 responses would receive a score for neurosis from the MHE and a score for good adjustment from the Davidson and Muench systems), the scoring criteria for these common variables are virtually identical across the systems.

TABLE 9.1
Common Scoring Categories in Rorschach Indices of Neurosis or Adjustment

	Indices of Neurosis or Maladjustment			Indices of Adjustment	
Category	*Miale/Harrower-Erickson*	*Munroe*	*Fisher*	*Davidson*	*Muench*
R	<25	—	<20	>20	≥20
Dd%	—	>10%	>17%	≤10%	—
M	<2	<3	<3	>2	>2
M/FM	M < FM	M < ½FM	—	M ≥ FM	M ≥ FM
F%	>50%	>50%	—	20–50%	—
FC	<1	<2	<1	>1	>1
C	—	>0	>0	0	0
P	—	<4	<4	>3	>4
Color Shock	Present	Present	—	Absent	—
Shading Shock	Present	Present	—	Absent	—
Rejection	Present	Present	Present	Absent	Absent

Comment

It is important in concluding this introductory section to emphasize that none of the five Rorschach systems under discussion was born of a research strategy that maximized its chances for a long life. Generally there are two productive strategies for deriving potentially valid psychometric indices: (1) a conceptual strategy, in which scoring criteria are selected according to their apparent theoretical relationship to aspects of the variable being measured—for example, since low F+% reflects inaccurate perception and perceptual distortion is a prominent feature of schizophrenia, it seems reasonable to select low F+% as a likely Rorschach indicator of schizophrenia; and (2) an empirical strategy, in which repeated comparisons between relevant criterion groups are used to sift out test scores that consistently discriminate among them. The more carefully a set of diagnostic signs is derived from a conceptual framework or put through the rigors of empirical cross validation, the more likely it is to prove valid and useful in the hands of subsequent clinicians and researchers.

Miale and Harrower-Erickson approximated the empirical approach in selecting their neurotic signs, but by sampling only normal and neurotic subjects they left entirely open the possibility that the MHE list relates to psychological disturbance generally and has no specific import for neurosis. The other workers—Munroe, Davidson, Muench, and Fisher—relied primarily on clinical consensus in selecting their signs, without additionally testing their discrimatory capacity or relating them to conceptual criteria of neurosis or adjustment. Although clinical consensus is a valuable source of hypotheses, Cronbach (1949, p. 393) has clearly made the point that "among the propositions suggested by clinical work, some are certainly untrue, due to faulty observation, inadequate sampling, and errors of thinking." Thus, the methodology used to construct these five scoring systems minimized their prospects for being validated beyond the initial studies in which they were reported.

RELIABILITY

Although the reliability of the MHE, IT, Davidson, Muench, and Fisher systems for assessing nuerosis or maladjustment has not been explored extensively, some data are available concerning interscorer agreement for all but Fisher's list and concerning retest reliability for all five systems.

Interscorer Agreement

At first glance all five systems would appear to have some inherent handicaps with respect to interscorer agreement. The IT, Muench, and Fisher systems are long and complex, and the shorter MHE and Davidson systems include the highly subjective scores of color shock and shading shock. Regarding these two categories, many users of the MHE and Davidson signs have commented on the lack of objective, widely accepted criteria for color and shading shock (Ives, Grant, and Ranzoni, 1953; Ross, 1942), and others have modified the lists to exclude them (Davids and Talmadge, 1963; Jourard, 1954; Lessing, 1960; Rust and Ryan, 1953).

As a specific illustration of the problem with color shock, it is interesting to note that Brockway, Gleser, and Ulett (1954) and Horrall (1957) both question the utility of color shock as an index of maladjustment since it appeared in 98% and 89%, respectively, of their large samples of normal subjects; Corsini and Uehling (1954), in contrast, report only a 34% incidence of color shock among 50 normal subjects. Such inconsistent findings imply either that color shock has little if any relationship to maladjustment or that it cannot be scored reliably. In either case, color shock would appear to have minimal utility as a diagnostic indicator for neurosis.

Such scoring handicaps notwithstanding, the shorter MHE and Davidson systems consist primarily of simple, objective scores, and Munroe, Muench, and Fisher provide very detailed scoring instructions for their more complex systems. As might be expected, therefore, the few available data indicate fairly good interscorer agreement for them:

MHE. Haimowitz and Haimowitz (1952) scored a modified version of the MHE neurotic sign list for 56 psychotherapy patients and 15 normal controls. This modified system omitted some of the more objective MHE scores but retained color and shading shock and added scores for oligophrenic details and for confabulated responses, both of which involve somewhat subjective judgments. Two scorers independently evaluating 20 of the Haimowitz and Haimowitz records achieved percent agreements ranging from 93–100% over the 10 signs scored, with a mean percent agreement of 97.4.

IT. Kates (1950a) used the IT in a study of job satisfaction among 100 male clerical workers whose Rorschach records were scored independently by two examiners. Kates reports a correlation coefficient of .94 between the IT scores assigned by these examiners.

DAVIDSON. Two of the previously mentioned studies in which color shock and shading shock were omitted from the Davidson list report good interscorer agreement for the remaining 15 signs. Rust and Ryan (1953) utilized two independent scorers for the records of 100 male college students and found a product-moment correlation of .69 between the total scores they assigned. Concerning individual signs, only the score for $C < 1$ generated notable disagreement ($r = .18$), whereas 11 of the remaining 14 signs they scored had agreement coefficients ranging from .60 to 1.00. Davids and Talmadge (1963), in a study of fifty 27- to 56-year-old mothers of disturbed children, observed a 100% agreement between the scorings of 15 Davidson signs by two experienced psychologists.

MUENCH. Although no quantitative data on the interscorer reliability of the Muench system have been reported, some qualitative suggestion of good scoring agreement appears in a paper by Hamlin and Albee (1948). They tested a small sample of college students specifically to provide a control group for the 12 therapy patients used by Muench in his initial application of his system. Without indicating their raw data, Hamlin and Albee state that they had to discard two of the Muench signs because of difficulties in scoring them: F +/sum F undiff, and $g \geq 10\%$. The remaining 20 scores, as checked independently by two examiners, were retained by Hamlin and Albee; presumably their decision to retain these 20 signs indicates that they were able to score them reliably.

Retest Reliability

There is some evidence that the scoring systems for neurosis or maladjustment are reasonably stable over time and resistant to transient situational influence:

MHE. Haimowitz and Haimowitz (1952) retested their 15 control subjects, who received no treatment or other experimental manipulation, four months after the initial examination. The mean number of MHE signs for this group was 4.0 on the first testing and 3.9 on retesting, and there was no significant retest difference on any of the scoring factors. Furthermore, a number of control subjects who had experienced important life changes in the four-month interval (surgery, engagement, pregnancy, completing college) had similar test and retest profiles.

IT. Mills (1955a) administered the Rorschach to 21 abnormal psychology students and 22 history students at the beginning and end of a college semester. The mean IT scores for the psychology students were virtually identical over this five-month interval (14.8 and 14.6), and a decrease from 10.2 to 8.6 in the mean IT of the history students did not represent a statistically significant change. These data appear to indicate relative stability of the IT over time. However, it should be noted that the lack of a significant mean change indicates group stability only and does not reveal whether or not individual members of the group shifted in their relative positions around the mean. Without a correlation coefficient between the test and retest scores (Mills provides none), these data only suggest and do not confirm good retest reliability for the IT.

DAVIDSON. Davidson (1950) reports an unpublished study by Lorge and Davidson in which 46 bright (IQ above 120) and 50 dull (IQ of 71–100) children aged 9–12 were tested twice over a one-year interval. The bright children had a retest correlation of .64, but their mean Davidson index increased significantly, from 8.9 to 11.0 The dull children had almost identical mean adjustment scores on the first and second testings (7.8 and 7.9, respectively), but their retest coefficient was only .32.

Although the Davidson index thus failed to order the measured adjustment of the dull children consistently over the one-year interval, the implications of this finding for reliability cannot be judged adequately in the absence of information concerning actual changes in the relative adjustment of these youngsters that may have occurred during the year. The data for the bright children are even more difficult to interpret. These youngsters were consistently ordered by the Davidson list over time, but as a group they earned significantly higher adjustment on retest. To infer good retest reliability from these data it would be necessary to assume that bright 9- to 12-year-old children should be expected to achieve improved adjustment from one year to the next.

To the extent that (1) maturity is a central aspect of good adjustment and (2) the Davidson measures maturity, such an inference may be sound. However, Ives, Grant, and Ranzoni (1953), who retested a sample of normal youngsters at ages, 11, 13, 15, and 18, report a striking absence of change in the incidence of the Davidson signs between 11 and 18. Two of the signs—R more than 20 and M more than 2—became increasingly frequent in the records of these youngsters over time, but none of the other 15 signs demonstrated any consistent developmental trends.

Other cross-sectional data concerning possible relationships between maturity and Rorschach indices of adjustment will be discussed shortly. The available longitudinal data are insufficient to decide the question of whether the adjustment level of normal children as measured by the Davidson index should be expected to increase with age.

MUENCH. In the Hamlin and Albee (1948) study of Muench's adjustment signs, a no-treatment group of 16 college students was administered the Rorschach twice over a five-month interval. These subjects displayed no statistically significant retest changes in the Muench signs of personality adjustment. Interestingly, this no-treatment group was significantly improved in adjustment as measured by the Bell Adjustment Inventory over the same five-month interval. Hamlin and Albee present some supplementary evidence that the Bell was particularly sensitive to transient anxiety experienced by students at the beginning of their semester and diminishing over its course, whereas the Muench index was resistant to such situational influence and reliably sampled a relatively stable aspect of personality structure.

FISHER. Rhoda Fisher (1958) scored the Fisher index for two groups of women admitted to a state hospital who were tested twice over a five-day interval. The experimental group included 25 women who were tested immediately following a gynecological examination, which was presumed to constitute a disturbing and stressful experience, and retested five days later; for the control group, 25 women were tested and retested at a similar interval independent of any planned stressful experience.

Neither the experimental nor the control group in this study demonstrated a significant change in their mean Fisher index from test to retest. For the control group, this five-day interval may be too short to provide an adequate estimate of retest reliability for the index. However, from the data for the experimental group, Fisher infers that the measure is sufficiently indicative of enduring personality characteristics so as not to be significantly affected by stress arising out of temporary situational embarrassment and anxiety.

NORMATIVE DATA

Much of the research data on Rorschach signs of neurosis and adjustment are relevant both to the normative incidence of these signs in various subject groups and to their capacity for validly discriminating among these groups. This section will present normative data for the five scoring systems, and the next section will consider the implications of these data for the concurrent validity of the systems.

Because the published reports vary considerably in the amount of information they provide, the normative data presented below are sketchy. There is a particular dearth of description concerning the definition and selection of the subject samples, and the labels in the following tables are those used by the authors of the various studies.

MHE

Table 9.2 reports the available raw data for various subject groups on the Miale/Harrower-Erickson neurotic signs. Even without statistical analysis, several features of these data cast doubt on the MHE's capacity to

TABLE 9.2
Incidence Data for the Miale/Harrower-Erickson Neurotic Signs

		Sex		Age		Signs		
Study	*N*	*M*	*F*	*Range*	*Mean*	*Mean*	*Range*	*% with Five or More*
Miale and Harrower-Erickson, 1940								
Normals	20	—[a]	—	15–55	—	1.5	0–3	—
Neurotics	43	—	—	15–55	—	6.5	3–9	—
Ross, 1941a, 1941b								
Superior Normals	34	21	13	13–76	—	1.3	—	0
Soldiers	53	53	0	19–45	—	2.0	—	2
Somatic Illness without Neurotic Features	19	8	11	18–57	—	2.2	—	5
Somatic Illness with Neurotic Features	26	15	11	21–63	—	2.3	—	0
Neurotics	42	18	24	15–51	—	3.0	—	14
Psychotics	15	8	7	14–48	—	3.7	—	20
Epileptics	19	11	8	16–62	—	3.0	—	37
Cerebral Lesions	18	17	1	13–52	—	5.0	—	55
Subcortical Lesions	10	5	5	22–58	—	3.3	—	30
Schatia, 1941								
Asthmatics	40	32	8	14–76	36.7	5.2	1–9	62.5
Harrower-Erickson, 1942, 1943								
Normals	385	—	—	—	—	—	—	15
Neurotics	74	—	—	—	—	—	—	80

Hertzman and Margulies, 1943								
Junior-High School Students	60	60	0	—	13.8	5.1	—	—
College Students	62	62	0	—	19.3	3.1	—	—
Neff and Lidz, 1951								
Soldiers, AGCT above 110	32	32	0	19–37	25.0	—	—	34
Soldiers, AGCT 90–109	38	38	0	19–37	25.0	—	—	78
Soldiers, AGCT below 90	30	30	0	19–37	25.0	—	—	70
Haimowitz and Haimowitz, 1952								
Normals	15	—	—	25–45	—	4.0	—	—
Psychotherapy Patients	56	—	—	25–45	—	3.0	—	—
Ives, Grant, and Ranzoni, 1954								
Normal Adolescents	107	54	53	11	11	4.5	—	51
Normal Adolescents	112	63	59	13	13	4.0	—	31
Normal Adolescents	106	54	52	15	15	3.8	—	32
Normal Adolescents	114	70	76	18	18	3.9	—	36
Berkowitz and Levine, 1953								
Neurotics	25	25	0	—	—	5.0	—	72
Psychotics	25	25	0	—	—	4.8	—	60
Grauer, 1953								
Paranoid Schizophrenics	36	36	0	—	28.2	6.3	—	—
Cohen, 1954								
Tuberculosis Patients	45	45	0	—	27.7	3.4	—	—

[a] A dash (—) indicates that these data are not available.

identify neurotic disturbance in any consistent fashion:

1. Samples of normal adults have ranged from 1.5 to 4.0 in their mean MHE; the 4.0 mean for normals reported by Haimowitz and Haimowitz (1952) actually exceeds the mean of 3.0 observed in neurotic subjects by Ross (1941a, b).
2. The majority of the psychotic subjects studied by Berkowitz and Levine (1953) and the cerebral lesion group tested by Ross (1941a, b) demonstrated the number of signs critical for the diagnosis of neurosis (five or more)—60% and 55%, respectively.
3. Schatia (1941) found a high mean MHE (5.2) and a frequent incidence of five or more sgins (62.5%) in patients with asthma, an illness that usually involves psychosomatic determinants; yet Ross (1941a, b) reports a mean of only 2.3 signs among his somatically ill subjects with neurotic features, none of whom had five or more signs.
4. Neff and Lidz (1951) observed a relatively low incidence of five or more MHE signs among bright soldiers (34%), but a notably high incidence among soldiers of average or below average intelligence (78% and 70%, respectively). The possible relationship between the MHE and intelligence, to the detriment of its diagnostic utility, thus remains to be explored.
5. Finally, the normal adolescents studied by Ives et al. (1954) had MHE scores more similar to those of pathological than of normal adult samples. These data indicate the need to examine further a possible relationship of the MHE to age or developmental status.

IT

Table 9.3 summarizes normative incidence data for the quantitative scoring of the Munroe Inspection Technique. These findings suggest either that nonpatient adults in various lines of work vary considerably in their adjustment, or that the IT does not consistently measure adjustment. The mean IT scores for the various samples of college students range from 8.6 to 14.8, and the groups of nonpatient adults range from the 7.7 mean IT of the paleontologists (Roe, 1946c) to the 13.0 of the clerical workers (Kates, 1950a) and the 13.1 of the Haward and Marszalek (1958) unspecified normals. The mean IT scores of the two groups of identified neurotics studied by Kates (1950b)—11.2 and 10.0—fall midway in the observed range for normals.

Davidson

Incidence data for the Davidson signs of adjustment are reported in Table 9.4. More so than the previous two tables, Table 9.4 indicates some consistent findings in the expected direction, and it also includes further information on the relationship of adjustment indices to age:

1. As would be expected, the child guidance patients reported by Elkins (1958) and Lessing (1960) have lower adjustment means (6.6 and 7.0, respectively) than the nonpatient samples of children reported by Margulies (1942), Davidson (1943), and Elkins (1958). Unfortunately, Elkins and Lessing did not score the full list of signs (see footnotes for Table 9.4), and there is no way of assessing the precise influence of this procedural variation on the scores they obtained.
2. The Corsini and Uehling (1954) differentiation between prison guards (9.1) and prison inmates (8.2) is consistent with expectation. The relatively low adjustment mean of 7.9 for the clerical workers (Kates, 1950a) does not fit as well; yet this is the same group that demonstrated relatively high maladjustment on the IT (see Table 9.3).
3. Concerning the relationship between age and adjustment scores, the Davidson data do not bear out the suggestion from the MHE findings (see Table 9.2) that presumably normal adolescents and children will display poorer adjustment on the Rorschach than normal adults.

Muench

Table 9.5 lists the few incidence data available for the Muench signs of personal and social adjustment. The mean values indicate considerable overlap between groups that presumably should differ in adjustment. Some samples of identified patients have demonstrated fewer Muench signs, and others more Muench signs, than control groups of college students.

Fisher

Incidence data for the Fisher index of maladjustment are listed in Table 9.6. This table indicates the clearest expected separation of diagnostic groups of any of the five systems. The normal samples have a mean Fisher ranging from 32.1 (Thetford and DeVos, 1951) to 47.7 (Fine et al., 1955); neurotic subjects have received mean scores near 60 (Fisher, 1950; Thetford and DeVos, 1951); and schizophrenic samples have scored on the average in the mid-80s (Fisher, 1950; Thetford and DeVos, 1951).

VALIDITY

Criterion-Related Validity: Concurrent

As would be expected from the previous tables of normative incidence data, these five scoring systems for neurosis or maladjustment have as a group proved incapable of validly differentiating groups according to their diagnostic status or adjustment level. The possible utility of the Davidson suggested by Table 9.4 does not bear up under statistical analysis, and of these systems only the Fisher has demonstrated any reasonable degree of concurrent validity.

Most if not all of the studies reviewed below are subject to major

TABLE 9.3
Incidence Data for the Munroe Inspection Technique

		Sex		Age		Signs	
Study	*N*	*M*	*F*	*Range*	*Mean*	*Mean*	*Range*
Munroe, 1945							
High School and College Students	250	—[a]	—	—	—	—	2–16
Psychiatric Patients	100	—	—	—	—	—	14–26
Munroe, 1946							
College Students	80	0	80	—	—	9.0	2–17
Roe, 1946b							
Painters	20	20	0	38–68	51	10.3	3–18
Roe, 1946c							
Paleontologists	16	16	0	25–58	—	7.7	1–15
Paleontology Technicians	9	9	0	19–62	—	9.4	2–19
Roe, 1949							
Biologists	20	20	0	—	51.2	8.9	2–19
Kates, 1950a							
Clerical Workers	100	100	0	—	29.7	13.0	2–23
Kates, 1950b							
Anxiety Neurotics	25	25	0	—	—	11.2	—
Obsessive-Complusives	25	25	0	—	—	10.0	—

Kates, 1950c							
Policemen	25	25	0	—	32.8	11.9	—
Roe, 1951							
Physical Scientists	19	19	0	31–56	44.7	11.2	6–19
Physics Teachers	48	48	0	24–65	37.3	11.3	2–25
Montalto, 1951[b]							
Normal Children	57	—	—	6–7	6.9	12.8	3–23
Roe, 1952b							
Scientists	61	61	0	—	—	10.8	—
Faculty Members	382	382	0	—	—	10.1	—
Mills, 1955b							
Abnormal Psychology Students	21	—	—	—	—	14.8	8–36
History Students	22	—	—	—	—	10.2	6–16
Cooper, 1955							
College Freshmen	77	42	35	—	—	8.6	—
Horrall, 1957							
College Students	102	—	—	—	—	11.9	2–27
Haward and Marszalek, 1958							
Normals	100	—	—	—	—	13.1	—
Neurotics	100	—	—	—	—	14.2	—
Psychotics	100	—	—	—	—	17.0	—

[a] A dash (—) indicates that these data are not available.
[b] Scored for only 24 of 27 items.

TABLE 9.4
Incidence Data for the Davidson Signs of Adjustment

		Sex		Age		Signs	
Study	*N*	*M*	*F*	*Range*	*Mean*	*Mean*	*Range*
Margulies, 1942							
Successful Students	69	21	48	—[a]	13.8	9.3	—
Unsuccessful Students	38	32	6	—	13.8	7.2	—
Davidson, 1943							
Normal Children	102	60	42	9–14	11.5	10.3	7–17
Kates, 1950a[b]							
Clerical Workers	100	100	0	—	29.7	7.9	—
Ives, Grant, and Ranzoni, 1953							
Normal Adolescents	107	54	53	11	11	7.7	—
Normal Adolescents	112	63	59	13	13	8.4	—
Normal Adolescents	106	54	52	15	15	8.4	—
Normal Adolescents	114	70	76	18	18	8.1	—
Corsini and Uehling, 1954							
Prison Guards	50	50	0	21–45	—	9.1	—
Prison Inmates	50	50	0	21–45	—	8.2	—
Jourard, 1954							
Nursing Students	58	0	58	20–21	—	8.3	3–15
Elkins, 1958[c]							
Normal Children	40	27	13	8–10	9.3	7.1	—
Child Guidance Patients	40	27	13	8–10	9.1	6.6	—
Lessing, 1960[c]							
Child Guidance Patients	49	26	23	5–17	—	7.0	—
Davids and Talmadge, 1963[d]							
Mothers of Disturbed Children	50	0	50	27–50	35	7.3	—

[a] A dash (—) indicates that these data are not available.
[b] Scored for 16 of 17 signs.
[c] Scored for 13 signs.
[d] Scored for 15 signs.

TABLE 9.5
Incidence Data for Muench Signs of Adjustment

		Sex		Age		Signs	
Study	*N*	*M*	*F*	*Range*	*Mean*	*Mean*	*Range*
Muench, 1947							
Psychotherapy Patients	12	—[a]	—	—	—	12.4	—
Hamlin and Albee, 1948[b]							
College Students	16	—	—	—	—	11.1	—
Carr, 1949							
Psychotherapy Patients	9	—	—	—	—	12.0	—
Hamlin, Albee, and Leland, 1950[b]							
College Students	20	—	—	—	25.2	11.6	—
Psychiatric Patients	20	—	—	—	27.6	10.7	—
Hamlin, Berger, and Cummings, 1952[b]							
Psychotherapy Patients	20	20	0	—	—	10.5	—

[a] A dash (—) indicates that these data are not available.
[b] Scored for 20 of 22 signs.

TABLE 9.6
Incidence Data for Fisher Degree of Total Maladjustment

		Sex		Age		Signs	
Study	*N*	*M*	*F*	*Range*	*Mean*	*Mean*	*Range*
Fisher, 1950							
Normals	20	0	20	20–45	24	36.9	—[a]
Conversion Hysterics	20	0	20	18–50	35	59.7	—
Paranoid Schizophrenics	20	0	20	21–55	37	85.5	—
Neff and Glaser, 1954							
Vocational Counseling Clients	100	—	—	—	23.3	37.4	—
Fine, Fulkerson, and Phillips, 1955							
Normals	74	74	0	—	—	47.7	—
Rabinovitch, Kennard, and Fister, 1955							
Normals	50	23	27	—	22.6	38.8	—
Psychiatric Patients	64	31	33	—	23.9	48.4	—
Thetford and DeVos, 1951							
Normals	60	—	—	—	—	32.1	—
Neurotics	30	—	—	—	—	59.4	—
Schizophrenics	30	—	—	—	—	86.7	—
Fisher, 1958							
Psychiatric Patients	50	0	50	—	—	77.1	—

[a] A dash (—) indicates that these data are not available.

methodological criticisms, especially with regard to the selection and definition of the subject samples. However, the striking lack of significant findings that have emerged from them obviates any painstaking assessment of their design. It is appropriate to assume that at least some of the uncontrolled sources of error variance in a research study will act to inflate rather than attenuate the significance of the results. Given this fact, the predominantly sow's-ear data reviewed below seriously challenge whether any amount of improved research design in this area could generate a silk purse.

MHE

The early enthusiasm for the MHE sign list as an index of neurosis was based on only flimsy evidence of its concurrent validity, and subsequent findings provide little solace to its enthusiasts. Each of the original nine signs extracted by Miale and Harrower-Erickson from their comparisons between diagnosed neurotic patients and normal controls occurred with markedly greater frequency in the neurotics. However, because Miale and Harrower-Erickson did not apply any statistical treatment to their data, they had no assurance that even the large mean difference between their groups (6.5 signs among the neurotics, 1.5 among the normals) had arisen other than by chance.

The later reports of Harrower-Erickson (1942, 1943) emphasized (a) that all nine signs had occurred more frequently among accumulated samples of 74 neurotic and 385 normal subjects and (b) that since only 10% of subjects with four signs in their records but 39% of those with five signs were neurotic, the criterion of five or more signs was confirmed as appropriate for diagnosing neurosis. However, these reports still do not include any statistical analysis, and Harrower-Erickson does not comment on the fact that 61% of her records with five "neurotic" signs were given by her presumably normal controls, as were 53% of the 6-sign records, 26% of the 7-sign records, and 33% of the 8-sign records. Thus in these early studies the MHE picked up appreciable numbers of false positives, which came home to roost in later failures to validate the MHE as a neurotic indicator.

Three other early studies claiming concurrent validity for the MHE also omitted data necessary to document this claim. Schatia (1941, p. 158), in his study of 40 asthmatic patients, states without elaboration that "all patients found to be neurotic by the Rorschach gave the same impression clinically." Brussel, Grassi, and Melnicker (1942) report "good concurrence" between clinical and Rorschach MHE diagnoses of neurosis among 16 soldiers recovering from concussion, but they do not present any data to this effect. Bradway, Lion, and Corrigan (1946) state that a relatively frequent occurrence of five or more MHE signs (54%) among a group of promiscuous women they studied confirmed their impression that neurotic trends were frequent in this population, but they too fail to include raw data in support of their impression.

Those studies of the MHE in which appropriate data analysis has been undertaken have indicated consistently its inability to differentiate neurotic from other patient samples. Ross' (1941a) neurotic subjects had significantly ($p < .01$) more MHE signs than his superior normals, soldiers, and patients with somatic illness with or without neurotic features. However, his brain-damaged, psychotic, and epileptic subjects also demonstrated a significantly higher MHE score than these other groups and did not differ significantly from the neurotics—except for the cerebral lesion group, which had significantly more "neurotic" signs than the neurotics.

Regarding schizophrenic subjects, the additional studies by Berkowitz and Levine (1953) and Rieman (1953) found no significant difference between neurotic and schizophrenic subjects, whether hospitalized or ambulatory, on eight of the nine MHE signs. The ninth sign was shading shock, which was significantly ($p < .05$) more frequent among hospitalized schizophrenic than hospitalized neurotic patients. Thus, the one consistently differentiating sign in these two studies differentiated in the wrong direction.

These findings might be interpreted to indicate that, although the MHE cannot differentiate neurotic from other disturbed people, it does adequately separate patient from normal samples. However, in the Haimowitz and Haimowitz (1952) study the normal controls had a higher mean MHE (4.0) than the psychotherapy patients (3.0). Haimowitz and Haimowitz suggest that, within the given college population from which their normal and patient samples were drawn, those people who seek psychotherapy are likely to be somewhat less disturbed than those who do not come for help. This tortuous logic seems much less compelling than the simpler and more direct inference that the MHE cannot validly discriminate people in terms of adjustment, much less separate neurotic from other patient groups.

Finally relevant to this conclusion is a study by Barry, Blyth, and Albrecht (1952), in which they had 31 men who had completed or discontinued treatment at a V.A. mental hygiene clinic return to the clinic for an evaluation interview and Rorschach testing. Barry et al. found no significant correlation between MHE scores and independent interview ratings of adjustment for these men.

IT

In her initial studies of 348 Sarah Lawrence freshmen, Munroe (1945b) compared IT checklist scores with three external criteria for adjustment difficulty: (1) referral to the college psychiatrist; (2) requiring considerable amounts of faculty consultation; and (3) being designated as a "personality problem" by a faculty committee responsible for regular reviews of student records. She found that of students with six or less IT checks, only 23% had demonstrated one or more of these maladjustment criteria. The incidence of adjustment difficulties rose to 37% among students with 7–9 checks and to 84% for those with IT scores of 10 or more. The corrected contingency coefficient between adjustment and these IT scores was .62, significant beyond the .01 level.

Despite this promising beginning, four subsequent IT studies have yielded mixed data concerning its capacity to order people according to their adjustment and no support for its clinical diagnostic use. Holtzman (1952) had groups of 24 and 22 college males rank each member of their group, including themselves, on their adjustment. The rank-difference correlations between these adjustment rankings and the subjects' Rorschach IT scores were .33 and .49 for the two groups, respectively. Both correlations are significant at the .01 level, and, to the extent that peer ratings can be accepted as a criterion of adjustment, they support the concurrent validity of the IT for discriminating adjustment level among presumably normal subjects.

However, the data from Horrall's (1957) study of achieving and nonachieving college students and from Barry et al.'s (1952) work with former psychotherapy patients do not confirm this impression. Among Horrall's subjects 19 bright high-achieving students demonstrated significantly better overall adjustment (measured by the TAT) and significantly fewer psychological conflicts (as inferred from questionnaires) than 21 equally bright but low-achieving students. Yet the IT scores for the high- (11.3) and low-achieving (11.7) groups did not differ significantly. For Barry et al.'s group the rank-order correlation between IT scores and the independent interview ratings of adjustment failed to reach significance.

In the only other reported application of the IT to patient samples, Haward and Marszalek (1958) obtained mean IT scores of 13.1 from 100 adults who had never been psychiatric patients, 14.2 from 100 hospitalized neurotics, and 17.0 from 100 hospitalized psychotic subjects. Although these IT values fall in a direction consistent with increasing maladjustment, from normality through neurosis to psychotic disturbance, the differences obtained did not achieve statistical significance. Haward and Marszalek (1958, p. 484) conclude flatly that "the Munroe check list is an unsuitable instrument for use in psychiatric personality assessment," and there are no data to challenge the cogency of their conclusion.

Davidson

In an early application of the Davidson index Gair (1944) reported that a modified version of this scoring system corresponded well with teacher ratings of maturity in 29 highly intelligent (IQ above 134) 7-year-olds. However, Gair did not document her impression statistically, nor did she include sufficient data in her paper to allow any independent assessment of her conclusion. Those studies of the Davidson index in which adequate data are reported have consistently failed to yield any evidence of its concurrent validity for discriminating either among well and poorly adjusted nonpatient samples or between patient and nonpatient groups.

Ives et al. (1953) compared the Davidson scores and independent interview ratings of adjustment obtained from approximately 100 adolescents evaluated longitudinally at ages 11, 13, 15, and 18. The correlations between Davidson scores and interview ratings of adjustment were largely nonsignificant at all ages, and Ives et al. (1953, p. 56) conclude, "The sign lists do not hold up as indicators of adjustment or the lack of it. . . ." Similarly, Sipprelle (1955) found a correlation of only − .16 between Davidson scores and interview ratings of adjustment for 39 scientists.

Corsini and Uehling (1954) found no significant difference between the mean Davidson scores of 50 prison inmates who were considered by the prison psychiatrist to have serious emotional conflicts (8.24) and 50 prison guards who were "of undamaged reputation" and had given a good account of themselves on selection interviews (9.08). Corsini and Uehling also note that three of the 17 Davidson adjustment signs occurred more frequently in the relatively disturbed inmate group and only one of the remaining 14 signs—no rejections— discriminated significantly ($p < .05$) in the expected direction.

Brockway et al. (1954) also found little support for the individual Davidson signs as adjustment indicators. They chose a sample of 151 men who had no history of psychological disturbance and used a psychiatric interview to divide them into subsamples of 126 "well-adjusted normals" and 25 "maladjusted normals." Of the 17 Davidson adjustment signs, eight occurred in a larger percentage of maladjusted than adjusted subjects, that is, were reversed. Only one of the signs ($M \geq 2$) significantly ($p < .05$) differentiated between the groups in the expected direction.

Brockway et al. (1954) were almost equally unsuccessful in discriminating their adjusted normals from a group of 40 psychiatric patients with primarily anxiety symptoms. Four of the Davidson signs were reversed in this comparison, and only three ($M \geq 2$, $FK + FC \geq 2$, and VIII–X% of 40–60%) discriminated significantly in the expected direction.

Likewise, Elkins (1958) could not distinguish patient from nonpatient children with the Davidson, even though she modified the scale to make it more appropriate for her age group. Using a 13-sign list, she obtained a mean Davidson score of 6.6 for 40 child-guidance clinic patients averaging 9 years of age and a mean Davidson of 7.1 for a control group of 40 children described by their teachers as well-adjusted. Although these mean scores lie in the expected direction, the difference between them is not statistically significant.

Muench

The results of the only two studies clearly addressed to the concurrent validity of the Muench sign list are mixed. Hamlin et al. (1950) compared the following three subject groups for 20 of the 22 Muench signs: 20 presumably normal college students chosen randomly from psychology classes; 31 presumably "mildly maladjusted" subjects, a group composed of the psychotherapy patients previously studied by Muench (1947) and the college students with poor adjustment scores on the Bell Adjustment Inventory studied by Hamlin and Albee (1948); and 20 patients from a V.A. mental hygiene clinic, presumed to be "severely maladjusted." The mean Muench scores for these groups were 11.6, 11.1, and 10.7, respectively; although these scores fall in the expected direction, they do not differ significantly from each other.

Barry et al. (1952) used the Muench signs in their study of 31 male V.A. clinic patients who returned some time after completing treatment for reevaluation with interviews and Rorschach testing. The rank-order correlation between interview ratings of adjustment and the Muench adjustment signs for these men was .37, which is significant beyond the .05 level. However, Barry et al. failed to confirm this relationship when they compared the Muench signs on the original Rorschach testing with adjustment ratings based on the patients' initial clinic interviews. Although their retrospective data may have been less reliable than their current findings, these results at best stamp the concurrent validity of the Muench adjustment signs as uncertain.

Fisher

In contrast to the other four scoring systems, the Fisher adjustment index has consistently differentiated among normal, neurotic, and psychotic subjects. In the original Fisher (1950) study, his 20 normal women (occupational therapy students, student nurses, student social workers, and secretaries), 20 women diagnosed as conversion hysterics, and 20 paranoid schizophrenic women showed a progressive increase in mean maladjustment scores (36.9, 59.7, and 85.5, respectively), and all of the between-group differences were statistically significant.

The subsequent comparisons of identified groups by Thetford and DeVos (1951), Neff and Glaser (1954), and Rabinovitch et al. (1955) confirmed this discriminatory capacity of the Fisher index. The mean Fisher scores observed by Thetford and DeVos among 60 normal (32.1), 30 diagnosed neurotic (59.4), and 30 diagnosed schizophrenic (86.7) men and women parallel the Fisher (1950) data and differ significantly from each other at the .01 level or beyond.

Neff and Glaser divided their 100 vocational counseling clients, who had a mean Fisher of 37.4, into three subgroups: 50 essentially normal subjects, 41 who appeared to have neurotic difficulties, and 9 who gave evidence of psychotic disturbance. The mean Fisher scores for these subgroups were 28.3 for the normals, 44.0 for the neurotics, and 64.8 for the psychotics. Again, the values lie in the expected direction, and each differs significantly ($p < .01$) from the others. Finally, the Fisher index of 38.8 observed by Rabinovitch et al. among 50 normal subjects (secretaries, student nurses, and other hospital personnel with no criminal or psychiatric history) was significantly ($p < .02$) lower than the Fisher of 48.4 they obtained from 64 consecutive psychiatric admissions to the hospital where their study was done.

Criterion-Related Validity: Predictive

Only a handful of studies has examined the capacity of the Rorschach sign lists for neurosis or adjustment to predict behavior, and their implications barely scratch the surface. These studies have been limited primarily to predictions of academic performance and response to psychotherapy, their results have been unimpressive, and their appropriateness for assessing the clinical and research utility of the Rorschach is subject to question, as amplified below.

MHE

Three studies have examined the capacity of the MHE signs to predict response to treatment. Grauer's (1953) sample of paranoid schizophrenic V.A. hospital patients consisted of 18 who improved enough to be discharged from the hospital and 18 similar in age, intelligence, and education who remained unimproved and hospitalized. Grauer hypothesized that the improved patients would have demonstrated more pretreatment evidence of neurotic anxiety, as indicated by the MHE, than those who failed to improve. The mean MHE scores for the improved (7.0) and unimproved (5.6) groups tended in this hypothesized direction but did not differ significantly from each other.

Similarly, Haimowitz and Haimowitz (1952) compared pretreatment MHE scores associated with successful and less successful outcome in their sample of 56 psychotherapy patients. Like Grauer, they found a higher mean incidence of neurotic signs among the 18 most successful cases (3.3) than the 18 least successful (2.2), but they do not indicate any significance level for this difference.

Finally, Cohen (1954) divided his sample of turberculous patients into a group of 26 who responded well to medical treatment and 19 whose progress was less than had been expected. The mean MHE scores for these two groups (3.2 and 3.7, respectively) were not significantly different. It may be questioned whether the capacity to predict recovery from tuberculosis, or from paranoid schizophrenia, appropriately tests the validity of a Rorschach index of neurosis. Most of the studies mentioned in this section are subject to a similar criticism, which is elaborated on p. 280.

IT

The predictive validity of the IT has been assessed primarily in relation to academic performance. Munroe (1945) compared four levels of adjustment rating (from "adequately adjusted" to "severe problem") in 348 college freshmen girls with their academic standing (superior, satisfactory, low average, failing) at the end of their first year. The corrected contingency coefficient between the IT ratings and academic standing was .49, which is significant beyond the .01 level. Interestingly, the IT scores obtained from these girls on admission predicted their freshmen academic performance somewhat better than their ACE scores, which correlated .39 with their academic standing.

Schmiedler, Melson, and Bristol (1959) were similarly successful in predicting the overall four-year academic record of 633 college girls from adjustment ratings derived from their Rorschach IT at admission. Although Schmiedler et al. do not report their raw IT data, they indicate that good adjustment inferred from the IT was significantly related to receiving both academic and extracurricular honors, whereas IT indications of poor adjustment were significantly associated with subsequent withdrawal before graduation, being on probation, and seldom taking part in extracurricular activities.

Despite these impressive findings, two other studies have failed to document a predictive relationship between the IT and academic performance. Cooper (1955) administered the Rorschach and the Ohio State University Psychological Test (OSU) to 42 male and 35 female subjects as they entered college and compared these test scores with their grade-point averages at the end of their first, second, and third semesters. Whereas the

OSU correlated significantly with academic performance at all three points (coefficients of .54, .47, and .52), the correlations between IT score and grade-point average for the girls were only .03, .07, and − .07 at the end of the first, second, and third semesters, respectively, and for the boys, − .12, − .32, and − .41. Only the last of these values reaches significance at the .05 level.

Horrall's (1957) college student sample included groups of bright high-achieving (N = 19), bright low-achieving (N = 21), average high-achieving (N = 20), and average low-achieving (N = 19) subjects. Even with this control for ability, which was based on ACE scores, Horrall found no significant differences in admission IT scores between the bright high (11.3) and low (11.7) achievers or between the average high (12.9) and low (11.6) achievers.

Finally, one study has examined the capacity of the IT to predict response to psychotherapy. Harris and Christiansen (1946), assessing 53 patients who received brief psychotherapy because of their delayed convalescence from some physical disease or injury, were unable to differentiate the pretreatment IT scores of those who improved with psychotherapy from those who did not.

Davidson

The Davidson index has also been used to predict academic performance, but without success. Montalto (1946) found a correlation of −.002 between the Davidson scores and grade-point averages of 90 high school girls. In Rust and Ryan's (1953) sample of 100 Yale upperclassmen, 29 were identified as underachievers, 36 as normal achievers, and 35 as overachievers, and Rust and Ryan were unable to differentiate among them on the basis of their total Davidson adjustment scores.

In studies of response to treatment, the limited Davidson data available are inconsistent. Lessing (1960) compared the pretreatment Rorschach records of 29 children who were considered by their therapists to have improved during their visits to a child-guidance clinic with 20 youngsters who had not shown improvement. The mean Davidson values for these groups, derived from a modified 13-sign list, were 7.2 for the improved and 6.6 for the unimproved youngsters, which does not represent a significant difference.

Davids and Talmadge (1963), on the other hand, successfully predicted movement in social casework therapy from Davidson scores. In this study casework therapists rated 50 mothers of children undergoing residential psychiatric treatment for their progress during weekly interviews extending over a year or longer. The 28 mothers in this sample who were considered to have displayed movement had a mean Davidson of 9.0, whereas 22 mothers who had evidenced no movement had a significantly ($p < .001$) lower mean of 5.1.

It is interesting to note that the Lessing and the Davids and Talmadge studies imply that the better-adjusted subject will show more improvement, whereas the MHE studies of Grauer and of Haimowitz and Haimowitz suggest that the more neurotic subject will do better in treatment. These contrary findings could relate to the considerable differences between the subject populations of these two sets of studies. Nevertheless, given the number of scores common to the MHE and Davidson indices (see Table 9.1), these contrary data emphasize the inconsistency with which Rorschach scores for neurosis or adjustment have predicted response to treatment.

Muench

Although several studies with the Muench index involve some predictive elements, all of them relate more to construct than to predictive validity and are discussed in the next section.

Fisher

The one study concerned primarily with the predictive validity of the Fisher index is reported by Arnholter (1962), who administered the Rorschach to 35 unemployable adults in a sheltered workshop program for vocational rehabilitation. Follow-ups at three and six months following completion of the program indicated that 23 of the 35 trainees had become employed. The Fisher scores of these 23 successful trainees, obtained during the program, did not differ significantly from the scores of the 12 subjects who remained unemployed.

Comment

The above studies indicate at best a mixed success in predicting academic performance from these Rorschach scoring systems and no success in predicting response to psychotherapy. Such data usually lead to the conclusion either (1) that the designs of these various researches are flawed or (2) that the Rorschach has minimal utility as an assessment instrument. The first of these conclusions is irrelevant and the second unjustified. Both overlook the fact that studies of the type reviewed in this section are inappropriate to the psychometric evaluation of the Rorschach.

The Rorschach is intended to measure various aspects of personality structure and dynamics. If Rorschach variables happen to predict academic performance or response to psychotherapy, all well and good—but there is no reason why they should. Academic performance and response to psychotherapy are complex phenomena determined only in part by personality variables. Intellectual ability, motivation, quality of teaching, and many other factors unrelated to personal adjustment exert a significant influence on academic performance, and response to psychotherapy is as demonstrably affected by a patient's motivation and expectations, his therapist's genuineness and warmth, and the appropriateness of the particular treatment method employed as by the patient's degree of maladjustment or neurotic disturbance. To expect to predict a person's behavior in complex, multidetermined situations from knowledge of his personality structure and dynamics only is presumptuous; to assess the validity of Rorschach scales by examining their capacity to make such predictions is misguided; and to fault the test for failing to achieve predictions in such situations is unjustified.

Construct Validity

Studies of the construct validity of the five systems being discussed include several carefully designed efforts to conceptualize their relationship to other personality variables and numerous miscellaneous studies in which their capacity to measure adjustment has been assumed. This research is reviewed below.

MHE

Studies relevant to the construct validity of the MHE have consisted primarily of very modest attempts to assess differences in MHE scores in situations where adjustment differences might be presumed to exist. Thus Hertzman and Seitz (1942), in a study of response to simulated high altitude, found a higher mean MHE score among five subjects who could not complete the experiment because of psychological distress (5.4), and 13 subjects who were able to tolerate the high-altitude experience (3.8). To the extent that relatively maladjusted subjects would be expected to be more likely to break down in a stress situation, these findings would support the construct validity of the MHE. However, such an inference from the Hertzman and Seitz study is attenuated by (1) their small sample, (2) their failure to provide any statistical treatment of their data, and (3) the unexplored possibility that any number of nonneurotic factors may have contributed to the subjects' inability to complete the experiment.

The other available studies inspire even less confidence as adequate assessments of construct validity. Lisansky (1948) reports that 10 epileptic patients had a higher mean MHE (5.6) than 10 diabetics (4.4), and that this difference, significant at the .10 level, indicates a tendency for epileptics to respond to their sickness with more adjustment difficulties than diabetics. However, Lisansky does not provide any rationale for why epileptics should be expected to adjust less well than diabetics to their condition, nor does she allow for the possible influence of adjustment differences among her subjects prior to or independent of the onset of their physical ailment.

Osborne and Sanders (1950) report that among 15 patients with duodenal ulcer or functional gastrointestinal symptoms, in whom prominent neurotic personality features would be expected, 13 had five or more MHE signs. Unfortunately, Osborne and Sanders failed to include any control group to indicate the MHE scores they might have obtained from other subject groups in the setting where they did their study. Allison and Allison (1954) were unable to differentiate the pre- and posttest MHE scores of lobotomized and control patients and concluded that the MHE is insensitive to changes in adjustment. Yet such a conclusion can be justified only if significant effects of lobotomy on adjustment are otherwise demonstrated.

Two studies have explored age-related changes in MHE scores that might reflect its construct validity. Thus Hertzman and Margulies (1943), obtaining a mean MHE of 5.1 from 60 junior-high school boys and a mean MHE of only 3.1 neurotic signs from 62 male college students, concluded that the MHE measures the increasing maturity expected with increasing chronological age. However, Ives et al. (1953), using a longitudinal rather than cross-sectional design, found no consistent changes in MHE scores over the years 11–18 in a sample of 145 adolescents.

IT

In contrast to the largely inadequate MHE studies cited above, the IT literature includes five appropriately designed studies of its construct validity, that is, studies in which theoretically derived differential predictions of adjustment level were assessed in appropriately defined criterion groups. In the first of these studies Kates (1950b) pointed out that most conceptions of psychopathology would predict that patients with anxiety reaction, in which anxiety is diffuse, will manifest a greater degree of inner stress than persons with obsessive-compulsive disorder, in which anxiety is presumably bound by the obsessive-compulsive symptoms. If this is the case, and if the IT measures manifest psychological stress, Kates reasoned, anxiety hysterics should receive higher IT scores than obsessive-compulsive patients. In a study of 50 V.A. mental hygiene clinic patients he confirmed a significant ($p < .01$) difference in mean IT scores between 25 anxiety hysterics (11.2) and 25 obsessive-compulsive patients (10.0).

Kreinheder (1952), proceeding from the conceptually expected relationship between good adjustment and good reality contact, compared the IT scores of 30 adult subjects with their performance on six perceptual measures designed to assess conformance to normative standards of objective reality. The multiple R between the measures of reality contact and IT scores was .69, which confirmed the predicted relation between maladjustment as inferred from the IT and weak reality contact.

Chodorkoff (1954) and Mills (1955a) were similarly successful in achieving IT differentiations predicted from conceptual frameworks. Chodorkoff hypothesized a relationship between maladjustment, inaccurate self-description, and perceptual defense. Studying 30 male college students, he found a correlation of −.34 between IT scores and accurate self-description, as inferred from comparisons between self-descriptions and descriptions derived from a battery of tests; and a correlation of .29 between IT scores and perceptual defense, as indicated by difficulty in tachistocopic recognition of threatening words. Although these correlations fall somewhat short of significance, they do indicate the expected trends toward the interrelation of poor adjustment, inaccurate self-description, and perceptual defense.

Mills hypothesized that a course in abnormal psychology, because of the nature of its content, would be more likely than a history course to attract students with adjustment problems, who presumably expect the course to help them with their personal difficulties. He obtained a mean IT of 14.8 from 21 college students enrolled in an abnormal psychology course and a significantly ($p < .05$) smaller IT mean of 10.2 from 22 students in a history course. These findings confirm his hypothesis and lend additional construct validity to the IT as a measure of adjustment.

Finally, Holtzman (1952) achieved mixed results in a study involving a hypothesized relationship between good adjustment and leadership capacity. In one sample of 24 college men he obtained a significant rank-order correlation of .53 between IT scores and leadership as judged by the group's ranking of its members. However, a replication of this procedure with a second group of 22 college men yielded an insignificant correlation of .15 between adjustment as inferred from the IT and leadership as indicated by peer ratings.

Several additional studies in which the authors did not proceed from conceptually derived predictions of differential adjustment nevertheless bear on the construct validity of the IT. Roe (1946a), for example, found significant differences among the mean IT scores of three groups of painters, including five who were moderate drinkers (7.6), nine who were steady social drinkers (8.8), and six who were excessive drinkers (14.3). To the extent that increased drinking frequency can be presumed to represent increased adjustment difficulty, Roe's data support the construct validity of the IT. Similarly, in the previously mentioned Hertzman and Seitz (1942) study of high altitude simulation, those subjects who could not adapt to the experimental situation demonstrated a higher mean IT (9.2) than those who were able to tolerate it (6.5).

Kates (1950a, 1950c) reports two studies of the relationship between job satisfaction and adjustment. In the first study the IT scores of 100 clerical workers correlated only .02 with their satisfaction with their jobs, as inferred from questionnaire data. Kates appropriately concluded from this finding that either (1) job satisfaction is determined by variables other than psychological adjustment, or that (2) the IT, because it cannot distinguish between satisfied and dissatisfied workers, is invalid as an adjustment index.

In the second study Kates found a significant ($p < .05$) correlation of .47 between IT scores and job satisfaction among 25 policemen, which indicates that the *more maladjusted* policemen were *more satisfied* with their work. Although numerous rationales might be stretched to account for this finding (e.g., because of the nature of police work, only a maladjusted person could find satisfaction in it), the data contrast with the more common view that job dissatisfaction stems at least in part from individual maladjustment.

Three other studies without significant results can be interpreted as either having no bearing on the validity of the IT index or, if adjustment differences are presumed to be related to the independent variables of the study, as negating its construct validity. Allison and Allison (1954), in their pre- and posttesting of patients who underwent lobotomy, found no changes in IT scores and concluded that this index is as insensitive as the MHE to adjustment changes occurring following lobotomy.

Montalto (1952) compared the IT scores of four groups of children, aged 6–7, whose mothers had been rated as demonstrating one of the following four types of maternal behavior: ideologically democratic, restrictively cold, spontaneously democratic, and restrictively warm. She found no differences in mean IT among children of these four types of mothers and concluded that there is no demonstrated relationship between these types of maternal behavior and childhood adjustment; the alternative possibility would be that such a relationship exists but was not adequately measured by the IT in this study. In a similarly ambiguous study, Shah (1957) was unable to differentiate successful from unsuccessful missionary workers on the basis of their IT scores.

Finally, some miscellaneous studies have compared the IT with other test scores. Concerning other presumed measures of adjustment, the IT has proved unrelated to the Bernreuter Personality Inventory (Munroe, 1941) but significantly correlated (−.51) with the Basic Rorschach Score (BRS). Because of the many points of potential overlap between the IT and BRS scoring systems, however, this correlation between them is specious. More clearly suggestive of some construct validity for the IT are data reported by Munroe, Lewinson, and Waehner (1944), who rated the adjustment of 45 college women from the IT and independently from impressions of their spontaneous drawings. The adjustment ratings from the two techniques on a four-point scale yielded a significant ($p < .01$) degree of association between the two measures.

In two other studies with no obvious implications for adjustment, Andersen and Munroe (1948) found no IT differences between gifted painting students and promising students of composition and design, and Munroe (1946) observed no significant IT differences between students with better quantitative than linguistic skills, as measured by the ACE, and students with differential ability in the reverse direction.

Davidson

Two appropriately designed construct-validity studies of the Davidson index have been reported. In a field study of 217 Ojibwa Indians, Hallowell (1951) used the Rorschach to assess adaptation in three geographical areas representing different levels of acculturation with non-Indian society. Consistent with his conceptualized relationship between personal adjustment and rate of acculturation, he found significantly greater indications of maladjustment, as indicated by the Davidson, in the area where acculturation had proceeded most rapidly and a correspondingly greater incidence of signs of adjustment among Indians undergoing the slowest acculturation.

Jourard (1954) hypothesized a relationship between recall of completed or interrupted tasks and ego strength, and he predicted that subjects with greater ego strength, as measured in part by the Davidson, would recall interrupted tasks preponderantly, and conversely. In a study of 58 nursing students he found no significant relationship between Davidson scores and recall preferences, and he appropriately concluded that either his hypothesized relationship between ego strength and recall preference was incorrect, or that the Davidson is an inadequate measure of ego strength, or both.

In other studies of factors possibly associated with the Davidson, Kates (1950a) found an insignificant relationship of − .16 between the Davidson and job satisfaction among the 100 clerical workers he studied, and Davidson (1943) found no relationship between her measure and family income level in her initial sample of children. The correlation between the Davidson and the IT in the Kates study was − .76, and Davidson (1950) cites unpublished data of Roman and Liff indicating a rank-order correlation of

.92 between IT and Davidson adjustment ratings for a sample of college students. These relationships between the Davidson and IT must, of course, be interpreted in light of the number of scoring criteria they share in common (see Table 9.1).

Finally, it should be noted that Ives et al. (1953) found for the Davidson, as for the MHE, no significant changes with age among the adolescents they followed longitudinally between ages 11 and 18.

Muench

Four studies relevant to construct validity have examined change in the Muench signs in relation to independently assessed response to psychotherapy. In Muench's (1947) original study of 12 patients in nondirective therapy, he found that the four patients who were considered by their therapists to have progressed most successfully demonstrated on the average improvement on 12.0 of his 22 adjustment signs, whereas the eight less successfully treated patients improved on a mean of only 9.6 signs. Although this outcome lies in the predicted direction, its significance level reaches only .12.

None of the subsequent Muench validity studies have achieved favorable results. Carr (1949), using 20 of the signs in a study of nine patients undergoing nondirective therapy, found no differences in increment or decrement on the signs among those rated by their therapists as having made significant, moderate, or no improvement. Hamlin, Berger, and Cummings (1952) compared 12 improved with eight unimproved patients who had been treated in a V.A. clinic. The pre- and posttherapy Muench scores, based on 20 of the signs, indicated improved adjustment for both groups (from 9.8 to 11.2 for the improved, from 11.6 to 12.4 for the unimproved), and the increment in measured adjustment for the improved patients was not significantly greater than for the unimproved.

Finally, Peterson (1954) correlated a composite score for success in therapy, derived from multiple criteria independent of the Rorschach, with improvement-decrement scores for pre- and posttherapy Muench signs. Among his 42 psychotherapy patients, the correlation between success in therapy and improved adjustment as indicated by the full 22-item Muench list was .12, and for the 20-item list used by Carr and Hamlin et al. the correlation was .26. Neither correlation indicates a significant relationship.

Fisher

Three well-designed studies bearing on the construct validity of the Fisher index have yielded positive results. Fine et al. (1955) hypothesized that, within a normal population, an inverse relationship will exist between maladjustment and social effectiveness. Working with 74 nonpatient subjects, they utilized ratings derived from psychiatric interviews as their index of social effectiveness and the Fisher score to measure maladjustment. As measured by a median test, maladjustment inferred from the Fisher was significantly ($p < .001$) associated with interview indices of limited social effectiveness.

Fisher, Boyd, Walker, and Sheer (1959) designed a study based on the expectation that the likelihood of psychological disturbance in an individual relates directly to the extent of maladjustment in his parents. They administered the Rorschach to the mothers and fathers of three groups of subjects: 20 V.A. hospital patients diagnosed as schizophrenic; 20 V.A. hospital patients diagnosed as neurotic; and 20 male veterans who had never requested treatment for neurotic or psychotic symptoms. Fisher et al. report that, although the Fisher scores did not differentiate between the parents of neurotic and schizophrenic patients, both of these groups of parents demonstrated significantly ($p < .001$) higher Fisher scores than the parents of the control subjects.

DeVos (1955), like Hallowell, hypothesized that adjustment differences occur in association with expected difficulties in acculturation. He administered the Rorschach to 60 American-born Japanese Americans (Nisei), 30 American-born Japanese Americans who had been sent back to Japan for an extended period of time during childhood (Kibei), and 50 immigrant Japanese Americans (Issei). Consistently with expectation, these three groups of subjects had a progressively increasing mean Fisher: 45.7 for the Nisei, 56.2 for the Kibei, and 66.5 for the Issei. The Issei and the Nisei differed at the .01 level of significance, and the other two between-group differences achieved the .07 level of confidence.

Two other studies using the Fisher have been concerned with change in adjustment observed among unemployable adults receiving rehabilitation training in a sheltered workship. In Arnholter's (1962) previously mentioned study, initial and terminal Rorschachs revealed no changes in Fisher scores commensurate with supervisors' ratings of the trainees' progress during the 12-week workshop program. In a similar study Neff (1955) found a significant ($p < .05$) decrease in Fisher maladjustment scores among vocational rehabilitation trainees whose supervisors had rated them as having become employable, but no significant difference in the pre- and posttraining scores of those who did not evidence improved employability. Hence these findings indicate no change in Fisher scores where no change would be expected, but only mixed success in reflecting change where it might be expected to occur.

In one other peripheral mention of the Fisher and Hinds (1951) report that the index correlated significantly with deviations from normal patterns of controlling hostility observed among paranoid and suicidal schizophrenic subjects.

Comment

These studies of construct validity are generally more promising than the research on the concurrent and predictive validity of the sign lists for neurosis or maladjustment. The construct-oriented work on the MHE has been poorly designed, that on the Muench has been unproductive, and for the Davidson the cross-cultural work of Hallowell is the only real glimmer of light. However, the IT has yielded positive results in well-conceived studies relating adjustment to reality contact, accurate self-description, perceptual defense, leadership capacity, and other relevant variables, and the Fisher has similarly been linked to social effectiveness, degree of family disturbance, and rate of acculturation.

As has been mentioned at several points in this section, construct-validity studies with negative results are difficult to evaluate: there is no way of judging whether the hypothesized relationships or the measuring instruments are inadequate. Yet it may be significant that it has been the most carefully conceived studies of the IT and the Fisher that have produced the significant findings reviewed above. The implication that better research yields better data is difficult to ignore. On the other hand, the fact that the two systems with the most promising indications of construct validity are also the two most complex and difficult to score may indicate in part why their application to research studies has not been pursued beyond the early work reported here.

OVERALL EVALUATION

The five Rorschach scoring systems for neurosis or maladjustment reviewed in this chapter—Miale/Harrower-Erickson, Munroe, Davidson, Muench, and Fisher—have little to offer in the way of clinical or research applications. Although they can be reliably scored, the normative data concerning them are sketchy, their capacity to differentiate criterion groups is questionable, and their utility in predicting behavior is minimal. Only the Fisher index, and to a lesser extent the Munroe, has demonstrated some consistent capacity to separate people according to their degree of psychological disturbance and to reflect adjustment differences inferred from conceptual rationales. However, the clinical and research potential of the Fisher and Munroe have not been actively explored, perhaps as a consequence of their long and complex scoring systems.

In concluding this chapter, it is important to stress that the bleakness of this area of Rorschach application does not justify any derogation of the Rorschach as a clinical and research instrument. Rather, as presented in the introduction, the largely unproductive literature on Rorschach signs of neurosis and adjustment bears staunch witness to the limitations not of the test, but of inadequately conceived and inappropriately constructed test indices. Because "neurosis" is such a broad and imprecise concept, there are no adequate criteria against which Rorschach scores presuming to measure it can be compared; because these five indices were compiled largely from clinical consensus, rather than from conceptual analyses or empirical sifting of potential test indices, there was never any solid basis for expecting them to differentiate adjustment levels or predict behavior. The failure thus lies with the indices themselves, crippled by the methods used to construct them, rather than with the Rorschach in general.

Chapter 10

SCHIZOPHRENIC SIGNS

The initial development of the Rorschach test had as one of its goals the identification of serious pathology, and a substantial proportion of Hermann Rorschach's normative subject group consisted of schizophrenic patients. Thus, from the very beginning, the Rorschach was seen as an instrument with potential value for differential diagnosis. It might therefore be expected that highly refined approaches to the diagnosis of schizophrenia would have been developed by this time. There is indeed a voluminous literature concerning various aspects of applying the Rorschach to differential diagnosis in schizophrenia (see Weiner, 1966). However, an examination of the existing Rorschach scoring systems appropriate to the diagnosis of schizophrenia reveals a long history of concern, but only a recent movement toward an approach to differential diagnosis which may prove fruitful.

As with every other diagnostic problem, the earliest work with the Rorschach and schizophrenia was clinical. The first research efforts involved the perusal of Rorschach records of schizophrenic patients and relatively unsophisticated comparisons between schizophrenic and nonschizophrenic groups. The composition of both the schizophrenic and nonschizophrenic samples varied widely from study to study, and the variables investigated were usually chosen in a shotgun manner and consisted of exhaustive lists of scoring categories. The single most influential work of this type was the landmark study of Rapaport, Gill, and Schafer (1946), which will be reviewed in detail below. Although less comprehensive studies of this model followed the work of Rapaport, et al., the emphasis in Rorschach research on schizophrenia began to change from comparisons of individual signs in schizophrenic and nonschizophrenic groups to the development of systems intended to identify schizophrenia. In this chapter we shall be concerned primarily with these systems. Finally, in recent years, perhaps because no single scoring system captured the imagination of many clinicians or researchers, a more conceptual approach to diagnosis has emerged, which seems promising but cannot yet be thoroughly evaluated.

The first portion of this chapter will be devoted to a review of the study done at the Menninger Foundation and reported by Rapaport and his coworkers. Although this study does not investigate a sign system and is, therefore, not a typical concern of this book, it will be reviewed (1) because of its historical position as the major representative of a class of studies that initially dominated the field, (2) because of its enormous impact on clinical thought, and (3) because of its role as the conceptual basis of a number of sign systems which developed out of hypotheses it suggested. The various systems of Rorschach schizophrenic signs will be described next, with a full presentation of all systems which have appeared in more than one journal article. Because none of these systems has been studied extensively, the chapter will be organized according to the systems rather than according to their psychometric properties. Finally, the chapter will summarize some of the earlier experiences in this area, present some current approaches, and make some suggestions as to possible future directions for research with the Rorschach in the diagnosis of schizophrenia.

THE RAPAPORT STUDY

In the years just following World War II, David Rapaport, along with Merton Gill and Roy Schafer, published *Diagnostic Psychological Testing,* a monumental two-volume work that had been awaited eagerly by the community of clinical psychologists. The book, which dealt with a battery of tests including the Rorschach, drew widely disparate responses from readers with different backgrounds. For the clinician it was a remarkable presentation of clinical thought, and served as a text in many graduate courses. For the researcher it was an overly ambitious project suffering from a number of serious flaws, not the least of which was an inept handling of statistics that virtually invalidated any data analysis. The work has recently been reissued in a one-volume revision edited by Robert Holt (1968), who has totally eliminated the research data. This contribution can now be presented to the public as a brilliant example of how a clinician approaches test data, rather than as an attempt to make it appear as though this approach has been validated, and without the drawback of being accompanied by a totally inadequate semblance of supporting research. The clinician can now learn from the theoretical material without escaping the necessity of subjecting Rapaport's inferences to validation, since the false security provided by countless pages of deceptively impressive statistical tables has been removed. An examination of some of the pitfalls as well as the often neglected strengths of the Rapaport study should be instructive to future researchers.

The two major methodological problems of the study concerned the constitution of the comparison groups and the methods of data analysis. The total sample comprised a normal control group and almost 20 groups of patients with different diagnoses, nine of which represented subtypes of schizophrenia. These groups were of unequal size, and some of them were so small as to limit severely any generalization that could be drawn from them. For example, the paranoid-state group contained only four patients. Furthermore, the groups differed along critical demographic and constitutional dimensions. The control group was remarkably different from most of the patient groups in intelligence, education, and socio-economic class, and the patient groups differed among themselves in such key variables as age and sex. Many of these variables are likely to influence Rorschach results. Intelligence, for example, is closely related to Rorschach productivity, which in turn is related to most of the Rorschach scoring categories. Rorschach differences between two groups that differ in intelligence are therefore as likely to derive from intellectual as from diagnostic differences between them. Thus it is impossible to know whether many of the significant differences in the Rapaport study are associated with diagnostic categories, as they were interpreted to be, or are merely artifacts of inadequately controlled confounding variables.

To compound this difficult situation further, the statistical analysis performed on the Rapaport data could have been a model for Cronbach's (1949) classic paper on the shortcomings of Rorschach research. Comparisons on numerous variables strongly related to R were made between groups that differed in their response totals. An enormous number of statistical tests were performed without regard to the implications that multiple testing has for established probability levels. Specific comparisons were made and specific cutoff points chosen after an examination of the data, a technique which plays havoc with probability estimates and also relegates any findings to pilot data, which cannot yield generalizations until they have been cross validated. These multiple faults account for the castigation the work received from research-oriented reviewers. On the other hand, these reviewers were frequently guilty of ignoring the merits of Rapaport's theoretical formulations; instead, with peculiar logic, they seemed to imply that since the data were not adequate for testing the hypotheses, the hypotheses must have been wrong in the first place.

Whereas frequent attention is drawn to the limitations of Rapaport's subject sampling, the positive aspects of his patient groups are rarely cited. These patient groups represented a broad spectrum of psychopathology, rather than just a few distinct or extreme diagnostic categories. Within each category, and particularly for schizophrenia, numerous subgroups were identified, thereby minimizing the heterogeneity that often cancels out effects when gross nosological distinctions provide the independent variable. Furthermore, these subgroups were not constituted according to a general system of categorization, but rather according to an explicitly stated system based on experience with these particular patients; hence, if there had been meaningful results the extent of their generalizability would have been clear. Finally, assignment of patients to these meaningful and relatively homogeneous groups was determined from careful and intensive diagnostic procedures, so diagnostic reliability was probably quite high. These strengths do not begin to compensate for the flaws of the Rapaport project, but they do provide lessons in design for subsequent researchers, who should build upon these positive aspects of the study rather than discard it in toto.

It is a more difficult task to find some compensating strengths in Rapaport et al.'s approach to statistical analysis, and this is particularly disappointing because some problems could very easily have been avoided. Rapaport et al. had very clear ideas, based on conceptual bridges between their theory of psychopathology and their theory of Rorschach analysis, as to what might have been expected from the various groups. If they had set out to test these a priori hypotheses, rather than opting for the shotgun, a posteriori, approach that they used, they could have avoided the multiple statistical tests that cast suspicion on the probability values they report.

Any restatement of Rapaport's formulations would be inappropriate here for a number of reasons. The research findings have been sufficiently discredited that their restatement would be a misleading academic exercise. As for his potentially more valuable clinical hypotheses, the purpose of this book is not to restate diagnostic guidelines without the accompanying rationales and research support. To do so would be to offer a cookbook, and Rapaport was quite outspoken in his opposition to such approaches, which he referred to as "dream book" analysis. However, while we shall not formally restate any of Rapaport's findings, they will be referred to at points where they formed the conceptual basis for the development of a sign approach, and the frequency with which this has occurred is a final tribute to the ultimate heuristic influence of the book, whatever its research shortcomings may have been.

PIOTROWSKI'S ALPHA INDEX

The alpha index was designed by Piotrowski in order to identify early, mild, incipient, and pseudoneurotic forms of schizophrenia in cases where a clinical expression of the pathology was masked and indefinite. The system is based on Rorschach indices of energy capacity and energy control, and it attempts to identify a disproportion between these two variables. The alpha pattern, when it emerges, is presumed to reflect overcontrol, underactivity, and underproductivity. The various Rorschach signs included in the alpha index are as follows:

1. W—This is scored in the traditional way and includes both DW and WS, as well as W responses.
2. Sum C—This, too, is scored in the traditional manner, with 1.5 given for each C, 1.0 for each CF, and 0.5 for each FC response.
3. Sum c—This is scored similarly to Sum C, with 1.5 assigned for each c response, 1.0 for each Fc response, and 0.5 for each subordinate c response (eg., Mc, CFc).
4. c′ shock—This is scored if either Card IV or Card V is rejected, if the reaction time to Card IV is longer than to any other card, or

if the reaction time to Card IV is longer than the average reaction time to each of the cards and the first scorable response to that card was preceded by a shock comment like "This is difficult."

5. F +%—This score is based on the form level of all F, Fc, and Fc′ responses and, if there are less than 10 of these, FM responses as well. In arriving at the percentage, any plus-minus response counts as one-third of a plus response. No indication is given as to the system used to determine whether or not a response is of plus-form level.

In order to arrive at an alpha score, weights are assigned to various levels of W, Sum C, Sum c minus Sum C, the presence or absence of c′ shock, and the sign F+% < 70. These weights are presented in Table 10.1. It should be noted that the weights given are those presented most recently by Piotrowski and Berg (1955). In the original presentation by Piotrowski and Lewis (1950) all Sum c minus Sum C scores above 3.0 were given a weighted score of 3.

TABLE 10.1
Piotrowski's Alpha Score Weights

Weighted Score	*W*	*Sum C*	*Sum c − Sum C*	*c′ Shock*	*F + % < 70*
4	0		Above 4.0		
3	1	0	3.5–4.0		
2	2	0.5	2.5–3.0		
1	3–4	1.0–1.5	1.5–2.0	Present	Present
0	Above 4	2.0–2.5	0–1.0		
−1		3.0–4.0			
−2		Above 4.0			

The alpha index applies only in those situations where W < 7 and Sum c ≥ Sum C. Where these two conditions do not prevail, the alpha index is not to be scored and does not apply. It is also intended for use only with subjects who are 16 years of age or older.

If alpha is equal to 3 or more, this is taken as an indication that the subject is more severely disturbed than merely neurotic. No distinction can be made between the various psychotic possibilities, although it is suggested that clinical signs can differentiate between the preschizophrenic and the manic depressive. In order to make the distinction between the possibility of an early schizophrenic condition and the presence of organic brain damage, a number of supplementary signs are suggested, as follows:

1. Ind P (inductive perception)—3 points. This is scored when the patient proceeds from the detail to a larger percept (e.g., an eye, a head) or names a series of integral parts of an unnamed larger object (e.g., eye, nose, mouth).
2. Size—2 points. The patient uses a word pertaining to size (e.g., small, large).

3. Frgm (fragmentation)—2 points. The patient uses a word which suggests the process of producing fragments (e.g., separated from, cut off, incomplete).
4. EmJ (emotional judgment)—1 point. The patient makes an emotional comment about a response or a card (e.g., foolish, silly, funny, odd, nice). Since 2 or more points is suggestive of schizophrenia rather than organicity, the inclusion of EmJ is completely superfluous, because if it is the only sign in the record it is not enough to produce a schizophrenic protocol, and if any single other sign is present alone, that would be enough to call the protocol schizophrenic.

No data are available concerning interscorer reliability, the stability over time, or the relationship to R of the alpha index. General studies of Rorschach scoring reliability make it doubtful that this index would prove to have high interscorer reliability, since neither C nor c are among the more reliably scored determinants.

Three studies have compared the incidence of the alpha index in schizophrenic and control groups. Piotrowski and Lewis (1950) examined Rorschach protocols of 30 schizophrenics and 20 neurotics whose diagnoses were reconfirmed by a psychiatric interview at least three years after the initial administration of the Rorschach. In addition to these subjects with confirmed diagnoses, they also studied 70 schizophrenics, 20 neurotics, 10 manic depressives, and 30 organics whose diagnoses were not reexamined after time. For the group with confirmed diagnoses a critical score of 3 on the alpha index successfully identified 28 of the 30 schizophrenics and 19 of the 20 neurotics. In the group of schizophrenics and neurotics whose diagnoses were not rechecked its success was not as dramatic, but it still achieved close to an 80% correct diagnosis rate and clearly surpassed the base rates in the population. Approximately three-quarters of the manic depressives and organic subjects were identified as schizophrenic by the alpha index; however, use of the supplementary signs for distinguishing organics from the schizophrenics yielded a correct diagnosis for 27 of the 30 reconfirmed schizophrenics and 25 of the 30 organics. It should be indicated clearly that the cutoff scores for both the alpha index and the supplementary signs were established with this group and shrinkage would be expected upon cross validation.

In a follow-up study, Piotrowski and Berg (1955) used a similar approach, beginning with 100 schizophrenics and 45 neurotics whose diagnoses were reconfirmed on the basis of a psychiatric follow-up three years later. Of these patients only 55 of the schizophrenics and 15 of the neurotics met the requirements concerning W, Sum c, and Sum C. In this alpha-appropriate group 46 of the schizophrenics and 12 of the neurotics were correctly diagnosed. Despite some shrinkage from the initial study, this outcome is still quite favorable. The proportion of false positives is minimal (6%), even though the proportion of false negatives (47%) is rather high. Further analyses were done to see what effect a violation of the requirements would have upon the alpha index. Where only the requirement concerning Sum c and Sum C was met, most of the neurotics but only about half of the schizophrenics were correctly identified. Thus an alpha of 3 or greater, with only the Sum c and Sum C met, is still suggestive of schizophrenia, but a lower score cannot be used to eliminate the possibility.

Where only the requirement concerning W was met, very few of the subjects reached a score of 3 and there was no difference between groups in the proportion exceeding the cutoff score. These results suggest that the crucial requirement is the one concerning Sum c and Sum C, and that if this requirement is met, alpha will operate with very few false positives but a high rate of false negatives. The alpha index can therefore be highly useful in arriving at a diagnosis of schizophrenia, but not particularly effective in ruling the condition out. As noted in Chapter 11, incidentally, Piotrowski's organic signs appear to operate in a similar fashion.

The only other study using the alpha index was reported by Abrams (1964), whose subjects were 60 hospitalized schizophrenic women: 20 had been in the hospital for less than a year and had no previous hospitalizations, 20 had been in the hospital between two and six years, and 20 had been hospitalized over seven years, with an average of 13 years. Abrams attempted to extend the alpha index to all levels of chronicity in the belief that it was sensitive to a particular type of schizophrenic reaction rather than to an early phase of schizophrenia as had been suggested by Piotrowski. Only five patients in each of the three groups met both requirements for the use of alpha, and all 15 of these patients had alpha scores beyond the cutoff point. Although figures are given for distributions where only one of the requirements was met, these data are not particularly valuable since Abrams does not specify which of the requirements it was. However, when neither of the requirements was met, virtually none of these schizophrenic subjects reached the cutoff score.

Whereas Piotrowski and Berg's subjects had an average I.Q. in excess of 120, the average I.Q. of Abrams' subjects was below 100, and the average I.Q. of his subjects reaching the cutoff point was below 85. Hence the alpha index appears applicable across I.Q. levels. Abrams' data further confirm that the requirements for applying alpha are important, that the presence of alpha is a reasonable diagnostic index for schizophrenia, and that the absence of alpha cannot be taken as a contraindication of schizophrenic disturbance. Abrams finally suggests that alpha is equally applicable in later as well as in earlier stages of schizophrenia, but is only useful in diagnosing a specific form of schizophrenia in which the patient is inhibited, apathetic, withdrawn, underactive, and highly controlled.

As is true of all of the sign approaches to the Rorschach diagnosis of schizophrenia, there has not been sufficient work with the alpha index to reach any definitive conclusions about its potential effectiveness. Whether it is useful for early onset of schizophrenia or whether it is equally effective at all levels of chronicity has not been established. It is clear that the index is limited by being applicable to only the small percentage of patients who meet its requirements, and even where applicable, it can be taken as a clear diagnostic sign only when the cutoff score is reached. Yet an alpha score of 3 or greater, when the requirements for the index are met, has proven to be an effective diagnostic sign in each one of the three studies where it has been used, and it accordingly deserves further attention. Of primary importance would be attempts to establish its interscorer reliability.

THIESEN PATTERNS

These patterns were first developed by Thiesen (1952) from comparisons between 60 schizophrenic adults and Beck's (1949) normal control group of 157 gainfully employed adults. Thiesen examined combinations of 20 major Rorschach scoring variables in the two groups and used three criteria to select his patterns. The first criterion was that the pattern occur in more than 10% of the patient records. This criterion insured that the pattern would occur frequently enough to be of diagnostic utility. The second criterion was that the pattern be present in less than 2% of the control group. This criterion was intended to reduce the number of false positives identified by the pattern. The third criterion was that the incidence of the pattern significantly differentiate the group at the .01 level of significance. This criterion was actually redundant, since it would be guaranteed by the presence of the first two criteria. The following five patterns met each of the criteria and were identified as significantly differentiating schizophrenics and normals:

Pattern A—The presence of three or more anatomy responses and four or more sex responses. It was remarked that this pattern may not be diagnostic in selected populations, such as analysands and friends of the examiner.

Pattern B—F +% of less than 69 and a Z score of less than 8.0.

Pattern C—No FC or M responses and an A% of less than 40.

Pattern D—An F% of less than 69, an A% of less than 40, and fewer than five P responses.

Pattern E—One or more DW responses and no FC responses.

These patterns apply only to records where 10 or more responses have been given. The presence of one or more patterns in an individual's protocol is considered diagnostic of schizophrenia. The absence of any patterns cannot be considered to indicate normality, however, and Thiesen emphasizes that accurate judgments cannot be made from the absence of patterns.

None of the studies using the Thiesen patterns gives any indication as to either their interscorer or retest reliability. The interscorer reliability is probably reasonably good, since the patterns are based on Rorschach scores which themselves have been shown to be reasonably reliable. However, the lack of evidence for test-retest reliability cannot be supplemented by inferences from other work and remains an important area of omission.

In the original Thiesen study the schizophrenic group and the control group did not differ in number of responses given to the Rorschach. Furthermore, when the groups were divided into high and low R on the basis of the mean of the control group, the presence of one or more patterns discriminated similarly in the high and the low groups. Thus the utility of the patterns does not appear to depend upon R. As for their validity, each of the patterns significantly differentiated Thiesen's two groups. The presence of one or more patterns occurred in 48.3% of the schizophrenic patients and only 3.2% of the control subjects. Despite the promise of a system that correctly labeled half of the schizophrenics in the initial study while misidentifying only a handful of normals, cross-validating efforts have not proved successful.

Rubin and Lonstein (1953) compared 42 hospitalized male schizophrenics with the Beck normal control group. None of the Thiesen patterns occurred in more than 10% of their schizophrenic sample, which contradicts one of the criteria for identification of patterns, and only pattern D differentiated significantly between patients and controls. The presence of one or more patterns identified only 16.7% of the schizophrenics, which represents considerable shrinkage from the original study and sharply reduces the diagnostic significance of the patterns.

In one additional cross-validation study, Taulbee and Sisson (1954) compared 62 hospitalized male V.A. patients diagnosed as schizophrenic with 157 normals who differed from the Beck sample. These normal subjects were predominantly female and were significantly older than the schizophrenics being studied. There were no differences in the incidence of any of the Thiesen patterns between this control group and the Beck normals, and, as in the Rubin and Lonstein study, none of the patterns occurred in over 10% of the schizophrenic sample. Patterns A, C, and D did differentiate between the schizophrenics and the normals, but patterns B and E did not. Although Rubin and Lonstein confirmed the infrequency of the patterns in normal subjects—only 4.5% of the normals showed one or more of the patterns—they had a very low yield of true positives, with only 27.4% of the schizophrenics demonstrating one or more of the Thiesen patterns.

In summary, the Thiesen patterns are a set of score combinations that occur relatively infrequently in the Rorschachs of either normal or schizophrenic subjects. They are clearly more likely to appear in schizophrenic than in normal groups; because of their infrequency, however, they can rarely contribute to diagnostic decisions and accordingly have little utility. Some investigators have suggested that the failure to cross validate Thiesen's system demonstrates the limited value of the pattern approach to diagnosis. Although the above data indicate the limited success of one particular pattern approach, they certainly do not justify any general statement about all pattern approaches. They do clarify, however, that considerable shrinkage can occur from an initial to a cross-validational study of empirically derived test indices, and that extensive cross validation of any such system is essential in establishing its capacities and limits.

THE DELTA INDEX

The delta index, or the index of pathological thinking, was first introduced by Watkins and Stauffacher (1952). This index emerged from the work of Rapaport, and the scoring criteria are based largely on his discussion of

Rorschach signs of pathological thinking. Watkins and Stauffacher assign scores to responses that represent a pathological loss or increase of distance from the blot and are therefore considered indices of deviant or deteriorated thinking. The delta index is intended to measure the extent to which the patient's reality control is contaminated by the inroads of primary process, that is, unconscious, archaic, and primitive ideational content. The various types of response that contribute to delta scoring are presented in Table 10.2, and a more detailed understanding of the meaning of each of the categories can be obtained most directly from a reading of Rapaport's original work. Each response in a record is scored for the presence or absence of the various delta categories; if a response can be scored on more than one category, it is scored only for that category with the highest weight. Thus no single response can be given a delta score higher than 1.00. No scores are assigned to additional responses. The summary score

TABLE 10.2
Weights for the Delta Index

Type of Response	*Delta Value*
1. Fabulized responses	0.25
2. Fabulized combinations	
(a) Spontaneously corrected or recognized	0.25
(b) Not corrected or recognized	0.50
3. Confabulations	
(a) Extreme affect-loading or specificity	0.50
(b) Far-fetched elaboration	1.00
(c) DW	1.00
4. Contamination	1.00
5. Autistic logic	1.00
6. Peculiar verbalization	0.25
7. Queer verbalizations	
(a) Usual	0.50
(b) Extreme	1.00
8. Vagueness	0.25
9. Confusion	0.50
10. Incoherence	1.00
11. Overelaborate symbolism	
(a) Moderate	0.25
(b) Extreme	0.50
12. Relationship verbalization	
(a) Between two percepts (same or different cards)	0.25
(b) Within a series of cards	
(1) Corrected or recognized	0.25
(2) Not corrected or recognized	0.50
13. Absurd responses	1.00
14. Deterioration color	
(a) Pure color	1.00
(b) With form (CF)	0.50
15. Mangled or distorted concepts	0.25

consists of the sum of all of the delta weights assigned to the responses, divided by the number of responses in the protocol. The delta weights of Watkins and Stauffacher are based on their clinical experience, are considered tentative in the original presentation, and have been modified in a number of ways by later investigators.

A considerable amount of information is available about the interscorer reliability of the delta index. Such data are particularly crucial for delta, since it involves nonstandard scores that require a great deal of interpretation. Watkins and Stauffacher had two psychologists score the records of 25 normals, 25 neurotics, and 25 psychotics, and found wide differences in reliability among the groups. Interscorer reliability for the normals was .04, for the neurotics .47, and for the psychotics .91. For the normal protocols the two judges differed significantly in the mean of the delta ratings they assigned. Yet, when all 75 protocols were combined, the overall scoring reliability was .78, and the low reliability in the normal sample is largely a function of the distribution of delta within this group. The normals gave very few delta responses and showed little within-group variability, whereas in the psychotic group, for whom scoring agreement was very good, the mean delta was fairly high and the group's variability pronounced. Given the attenuating effect of a restricted range on correlation coefficients, the low coefficient for these normal subjects should not be interpreted to indicate any inherent unscorability of the delta system, especially in view of the good scoring data obtained from the more variable psychotic group.

Additional information about interscorer reliability has been presented by Powers and Hamlin (1955), who scored 15 protocols and found a reliability of .88 for the overall delta index. However, for 87 individual delta responses scored the two judges achieved only 60% agreement on the index value to be assigned, and it was seldom that a jointly scored response was assigned to exactly the same category by both judges. On the other hand, many of the inconsistencies in categorization of individual responses were masked by the fact that both alternatives carried the same delta value, and the disagreements were further submerged in calculating summary scores for the entire protocol.

Pope and Jensen (1957), evaluating 38 protocols contributed by 15 patients at various stages of insulin coma treatment, report similarly to Powers and Hamlin an overall scoring reliability of delta, calculated by the Hoyt method and by a partial rank-order correlation removing the number of responses, of .80 and .85, respectively. However, they also observed a low percentage of agreement on individual categories, such that the scoring reliability for some of the categories falls considerably short of the overall reliability for the system. Both Powers and Hamlin and Pope and Jensen suggest that the infrequent occurrence and unreliability of some of the individual categories warrant a modification of the index—specifically, dropping some of the infrequently used scales and combining others to produce a markedly shortened and simplified scale.

The initial evidence concerning the validity of the delta index was presented by Watkins and Stauffacher. Because of the previously mentioned difficulty with interscorer agreement, particularly in the normal group, they analyzed their data separately for each of the two raters. For one rater the normal, neurotic, and psychotic groups all differed significantly from each other in mean delta; for the other rater the normals and neurotics did not differ significantly from each other, but both differed significantly from the psychotics. With a cutoff point of 5% delta applied to the scores of the less accurate rater, all of the normals were correctly identified, 36% of the neurotics were false positives, and 60% of the psychotics were correctly identified. With a 10% cutoff point, which Watkins and Stauffacher recommend, all of the normals were correctly identified, only 8% of the neurotics were false positives, and 48% of the psychotics were correctly identified. The authors suggest that 5% is the highest the delta index should reach in nonpsychiatric cases, and 10% or higher is a reasonable criterion score for a positive indication of schizophrenia.

Powers and Hamlin (1955) used the delta index with 50 subjects divided equally among five groups: socially adjusted subjects, anxiety neurotics, latent schizophrenics, paranoid schizophrenics, and catatonic schizophrenics. These diagnoses were reached independent of Rorschach protocols and appear to have been carefully determined. However, the diagnostic procedures used are not clearly specified, nor is any information given concerning the age, sex, or hospital status of the various groups. An analysis of variance revealed significant differences among these five groups in their delta index scores; critical ratios computed from the data indicate further that the socially adjusted subjects received significantly lower scores than the neurotics, who in turn received significantly lower scores than each of the schizophrenic groups. The schizophrenic groups did not differ among themselves.

The cutoff score of 5% delta correctly identified all of Powers and Hamlin's schizophrenic subjects, but misidentified *all* of their neurotics and 60% of their normals. Thus the 5% score was clearly too low to be discriminating in their sample. A 10% cutoff score was successful in identifying 26 of their 30 schizophrenics while misidentifying only 5 of their 20 nonschizophrenics, which represents a false-negative rate of 21% and a false-positive rate of 16%. Being even more conservative, Powers and Hamlin suggest 20% as the criterion score for schizophrenia. A delta of 20% labeled 14 of their schizophrenics correctly without picking up any nonschizophrenics, which means a 44% false-negative rate with no false positives. Thus a considerable increase in the false-negative rate is necessary to eliminate the false positives, and the choice between the cutoff scores of 10% and 20% will accordingly vary with the relative importance of diagnosing true positives and true negatives in the particular assessment situation.

Pope and Jensen (1957) were the first authors to construct a modified delta index, which they did by scoring each response on a five-point pathology scale from 0.00 to 1.00 in steps of 0.25 units. Their subjects were 41 psychiatric patients, 15 of whom were receiving insulin coma treatment, 14 of whom were undergoing electroconvulsive shock treatment, and 12 of whom were experiencing routine hospital care. Pretreatment Rorschachs were administered shortly after hospital admission and within a week before therapy commenced, and the posttreatment Rorschachs were obtained approximately one week after the conclusion of therapy, which was about three months after the initial testing. Psychiatric ratings of clinical change were also available, although Pope and Jensen do not indicate the nature or the reliability of the rating scales used.

The pre- and posttreatment comparisons indicated a significant reduction in the delta index of all patients combined, and a reduction in those patients who were receiving routine hospital care. The two groups of patients receiving somatic therapies showed insignificant reductions in their delta index scores, and there was no significant relationship between improvement on the delta index and improvement on the psychiatric rating scales. The significantly decreased delta in patients receiving routine hospital care can be interpreted as providing construct validation for the index, whereas the insignificant trends in patients undergoing somatic therapy is somewhat ambiguous, depending upon one's expectations from such therapies and upon the factors that may be involved in selecting patients to receive them. The lack of relationship between delta and the psychiatric ratings is also difficult to interpret, since no information is available concerning the nature of the ratings.

Kataguchi (1959) also modified the delta index and included it in a larger battery of tests. His modifications included the dropping of a number of the delta categories (confusion, relationship, verbalization, absurd responses, vagueness), the addition of a category (perseveration), and the elimination of weighting distinctions within categories, such as fabulized combination. He found marked differences between schizophrenics and neurotics in their delta index score, using a Japanese sample of subjects. He also refers to data of Nagasaka that confirmed differences in delta index scores between schizophrenics, neurotics, and normals in a Japanese sample.

Quirk, Quarrington, Neiger, and Sleman (1962) also included the delta index in a larger battery of tests. The delta score significantly differentiated their groups of normal, neurotic, acute schizophrenic, and chronic schizophrenic subjects, and they report a 66.2% accuracy of schizophrenic-nonschizophrenic distinctions with a 20% criterion score. Insufficient detail is given to be more specific about the nature of Quirk et al.'s findings. It is interesting to note, however, that in another portion of their battery Quirk et al. use the presence of less than 15 responses as a sign, and they comment that the use of R in the denominator of the delta index score serves to increase delta when R is low and to decrease it when R is high. It may be, therefore, that unusually brief or long records require modified interpretations of delta, even beyond the effect of including R in the denominator for delta scores.

In summary, the delta index is a somewhat cumbersome scoring system that is difficult to score reliably in nonpsychotic subjects but has nevertheless produced some reasonably encouraging differentiations between schizophrenic subjects. It has unfortunately been unusual for any two authors to use the index in quite the same way, which limits the assessment that can be made of it. There is reason to expect that a modified delta index, made easier to use and score and more thoroughly explored for normative levels, could contribute to identifying groups of subjects with an elevated incidence of pathological thinking.

WEINER'S SIGNS

Weiner has presented two separate sets of Rorschach signs of schizophrenia, both developed largely on empirical grounds with theoretical rationales appended after the fact. The first of the signs is "color stress," which represents a minimal use of chromatic color without any use of achromatic color. Color stress excludes those subjects who either use color freely, thus presumably demonstrating primary reliance on repressive defenses, or who avoid the use of color, thereby indicating strong reliance on intellectual defenses. Although there are obvious exceptions, Weiner's reasoning is that subjects with color stress are manifesting one of the characteristic features of schizophrenic disturbance, namely, lack of a stable defensive system. The initial color stress signs were the following:

1. The presence of one or two CF responses.
2. Sum C between 1.5 and 3.0.
3. The presence of at least one CF or C response without any C′ responses.

Weiner (1961b) first used the presence of any two of these three signs as indicative of color stress and then subsequently (Weiner, 1964) added an additional criterion for the presence of pure C. Thus color stress is scored when either two of the above three indicators appear *or* when one or more C responses are included in the record. The inclusion of C is consistent with the rationale that the color stress index reflects unstable defenses and inconsistent resources for integrating affective experience.

The second sign presented by Weiner (1962) is "deviant tempo," which is based on the following Rorschach indicators:

1. More responses are given to Card V than to Card IV.
2. More responses are given to Card V than to Card VI.
3. More responses are given to Card IX than to Card VIII.
4. More responses are given to Card IX than to Card X.

The presence of any one of these four indicators of deviant tempo is considered suggestive of schizophrenia. These signs are based on normative expectancies for the relative distribution of responses over the cards. Since all of the comparisons involve successive cards, both of which are either chromatic or achromatic, the effect of color is minimized. The rationale for the deviant tempo sign is that deviations from normative response tempo are likely to reflect the kinds of disturbances in the rate and flow of associations that characterize schizophrenia.

There is one study (Weiner, 1956a) which indicates that the color stress and deviant tempo signs are unrelated, with a phi coefficient between them of only .07. It is suggested in this paper that, since the two signs are independent, they may combine to yield a powerful index of schizophrenia when both are present, whereas the presence of neither would tend to contradict schizophrenia and the presence of just one without the other would warrant suspended judgment.

No information is available concerning either the interscorer reliability or the test-retest reliability of any of Weiner's signs. Deviant tempo is based on number of responses, and should be a highly reliably scored sign. Color stress, on the other hand, is based on various color scores, and may represent somewhat more of a scoring problem. Weiner's studies also do not indicate the relationship of either index to response total, although many of his comparisons were based on groups with equal numbers of responses.

Orme (1964) did investigate each of the original three color stress scores and each of the four deviant tempo scores in a sample of schizophrenics divided according to the median R for the group. Of these seven signs, only one—deviant tempo sign 3—differentiated the group, with those above the median in response total also showing a higher incidence of that sign. Orme did not assess whether the high- and low-response groups differed in the overall frequency of either color stress or deviant tempo, but the data for the individual signs would appear to minimize the possible influence of R on interpretations of these two indices.

Attempts to validate Weiner's signs have all followed essentially the same paradigm. Reasonably large groups of schizophrenics have been compared with groups of nonschizophrenic patients equated for Rorschach productivity. The average age of the subjects has been in the middle to upper 20s and sex has been equated but not specified. In Weiner's (1961b) original cross-validating samples, which included 49 schizophrenic and 92 nonschizophrenic psychiatric patients, color stress without the C criterion yielded a percentage of accurate diagnoses ranging from 65 to 81%. However, although the false negatives in these samples were modest, at 13–18%, the false-positive rates ranged from 30 to 56%.

When C was subsequently added as a color stress criterion, the accuracy achieved in additional cross-validating samples ranged from 60 to 76% (Orme, 1966; Weiner, 1964, 1965a). Direct comparisons within a single sample indicated that use of the added C criterion for color stress increased accuracy, but only slightly (Weiner, 1964). In these studies the false-positive rates remained high at 32–42%, while the false negatives ranged from 11% to 41%. Thus an increase in false negative indications appears to have been the price of the slightly higher accuracy achieved with the inclusion of the C criterion.

In studies of the deviant tempo index the accuracy of schizophrenic-nonschizophrenic judgments has ranged between 67 and 72% (Weiner, 1962, 1965a), with 26–46% false positives and 20–30% false negatives.

When color stress and deviant tempo were examined jointly (Weiner, 1965a), 46% of the cases fell into the category of no decision, that is, one or the other sign was present. For the just over half of the subjects in this study who demonstrated either both or neither of the signs, the schizophrenic-nonschizophrenic indication was correct in 83% of the cases, with only 11% false positives and 21% false negatives. Since these encouraging results have emerged from just a single study of the combined color stress and deviant tempo indices, some replication is in order to confirm their potential for clinical application.

In other studies with portions of the Weiner signs, Orme (1966) and Klinger and Roth (1964) have demonstrated a lack of ability of single indicators of color stress or deviant tempo to differentiate between schizophrenic and nonschizophrenic groups. However, as Weiner (1965b) has pointed out, the signs were not meant to be used singly, but rather in certain specified combinations. Hence these particular failures to replicate do not necessarily negate the diagnostic potential of the overall patterns, particularly when used in combination.

In summary, the Weiner signs have shown a fair degree of accuracy and, when applied jointly, have yielded a low incidence of false positive indications and a modest number of false negatives. They are empirically derived, and have suffered from the shrinkage upon cross validation that besets many empirical systems. Had some theoretical rationale for them been developed beforehand, rather than after the fact, and had the scoring been derived from the rationale, the systems might have fared better upon replication. Somewhat the wiser for his encounter with empirical shrinkage, Weiner (1968) has more recently emphasized the value of the conceptual approach to deriving Rorschach indices of schizophrenia (see p. 387).

OVERALL EVALUATION

Kelley and Klopfer (1938), in a paper seldom known or recalled by contemporary clinicians, concluded a review of Rorschach use in schizophrenia with the following comments:

> It must first be strongly emphasized that there is no single definite Rorschach or personality picture typical of schizophrenia as a whole.... The Rorschach patterns of a group of patients all labeled "schizophrenia" may be tremendously varied.... It is too much to expect that any known method of investigation, if applied indiscriminately to all the members of this group, will ever show any definite results.... No one case will present all of the signs, and many will present only a few.

The issues of the heterogeneity of diagnostic groups and the unreliability of diagnostic judgments which have been raised in relation to other syndromes are particularly cogent in investigations of schizophrenia. The diagnosis of schizophrenia is at times so idiosyncratic that the critical determinant is nothing more than local custom. One hospital's schizophrenic is another hopital's character disorder. Within the gross category of schizophrenia, diagnostic unreliability is compounded by distinctions between such subcategories as acute, chronic, paranoid, borderline, incipient, and what-have-you schizophrenia, which are conceived differently from one setting to the next. The unreliability of the diagnosis of schizophrenia is matched only by the difficulty in arriving at a definitive diagnosis of nonschizophrenia for comparison purposes. This lack of precise and uniformly applied diagnostic criteria for schizophrenia significantly impedes efforts to develop and validate assessment procedures for separating schizophrenic and nonschizophrenic groups.

If the problems created by unreliability could be resolved by strict adherence to precise criteria, the heterogeneity issue would remain to be tackled. No single system can be expected to identify with equal success the many diverse patterns of behavior disturbance subsumed under the category of schizophrenia, and much of the psychometric research in schizophrenia compares a heterogeneously composed group of schizophrenics with an equally heterogeneous group of nonschizophrenics, including in various studies organic, nonschizophrenic psychotic, neurotic, and character-disordered patients as well as normal controls. Thus the search for an index of schizophrenia is bound to be unrewarding unless the investigator recognizes the limitations the situation places upon him. Just as there are multiple components of the diagnostic group, there must be multiple patterns utilized in arriving at a diagnosis. Each of the signs reviewed in this chapter is likely to be more useful in assessing some forms or aspects of schizophrenia than others, and research designs must allow for such variations to be recognized and studied.

The implications of research findings for clinical application of the Rorschach are often debated. It is clear that statistical significance does not automatically indicate clinical utility. Most of the systems reviewed in this chapter have yielded replicable differentiations between diagnostic groups, but often without sufficiently precise discriminations to justify their application to any single patient in a diagnostic situation. On the other hand, it should be noted that a lack of statistical significance does not necessarily preclude clinical utility. A system based on relatively infrequent signs may occur too infrequently in usually appropriate samples to allow any possibility of statistically significant differences. Yet such a rare sign may be pathognomic and thus of considerable diagnostic utility should it happen to appear. This type of utility can usually be identified by examining the false-positive and false-negative rates that a sign generates. A sign that produces a great many false negatives but virtually no false positives is likely to be one of the rare but pathognomic indicators.

False-positive and false-negative rates are intimately related to conditions within a local situation and may not be generalized to other circumstances. This fact, considered with the heterogeneity and unreliablity of diagnostic categories, suggests that each individual clinician should familiarize himself with local norms. Without a clear recognition of how the term schizophrenia is used in any particular local situation it is unlikely that any clinician can determine the applicability of his diagnostic approach in that situation. These various methodological issues are discussed in detail by Weiner (1966), who reviews more fully than is possible here the clinical application of the Rorschach in the differential diagnosis of schizophrenia.

The results of many of the studies reviewed in this chapter are instructive regarding the potential utility of an empirical approach. The Thiesen patterns, in particular, represent the fate that can befall an empirical system, specifically, that tremendous shrinkage can occur between an initial validation group and later cross-validation samples. This shrinkage is compounded when cross validation is attempted in different settings, since the basis for diagnosis may be different. Even within the same setting, shrinkage is likely when signs that have been validated initially on clearly defined and extreme groups of schizophrenics and nonschizophrenics are then applied to vaguely defined and borderline groups where the diagnosis is questionable. Such lack of generalization of the system from one situation to the next should be anticipated; the literature clearly reveals that clinical utility often does not support initial research enthusiasm.

Whereas the empirical method is thus limited in developing psychodiagnostic indices, Weiner (1968) has encouraged conceptual approaches to the Rorschach diagnosis of schizophrenia. The conceptual approach requires the investigator to specify the defining personality characteristics of the condition to be diagnosed before attempting to develop any set of Rorschach indicators. After conceptually clarifying the condition to be identified, the investigator can then determine what aspect of the Rorschach best reflects these characteristics. At this point the problem becomes an empirical one, and research will establish whether the investigator's conception of the syndrome and of the relevant Rorschach indicators was appropriate.

If the conceptualization is relatively close to behavior it would seem most likely that the Rorschach can be of use in identifying the syndrome. In the various modifications of the delta index, which was derived from Rapaport's conception of pathological thinking in schizophrenia, the Rorschach can be seen essentially as a structured-interview-eliciting products of the thought process. When these thought processes show the pathological and regressive aspects that Rapaport conceptualizes as part and parcel of schizophrenia, the diagnostic decision becomes clear. In this case the Rorschach is being used as a structured interview and schizophrenic thought provides a behavioral index that is linked with a theoretical conception. Unfortunately, the attempts to apply this method have been excessively laborious and unreliable, but this type of approach seems to be a relatively promising one.

Chapter 11

ORGANIC SIGNS

It is possible, but not necessary, to become involved in a metaphysical discussion of the mind-body problem and the implied dualism of a distinction between functional and organic illness. We can grant that there are physiological processes underlying all behavior and still recognize that a large number of behaviors which are considered pathological are also regarded as being functional in origin. Other symptoms, however, can be traced initially to an impairment in the central nervous system and are considered organic in origin. This distinction is of importance in that the approach to treatment should, in part, depend upon the proper identification of the cause of the difficulty.

There are two major ways in which the Rorschach has been used in studying patients with organic damage. One approach has been to use the Rorschach along with a large number of other psychometric devices to determine the manner in which the damage has affected adaptive behavior. In this case, the validity of the Rorschach is assumed, and conclusions are drawn about the effects of brain damage on the basis of comparisons between organic and control groups. The second approach has involved the attempt to isolate Rorschach signs which are uniquely characteristic of brain-damaged populations, so that these signs can be used in arriving at the diagnosis of organicity. This chapter will be concerned exclusively with investigations of the second type, and will present a number of different sets of signs as well as an evaluation of the evidence concerning the efficacy of these signs in diagnosing organicity.

METHODOLOGICAL PROBLEMS

The study of organic brain damage presents a number of methodological problems which might best be noted prior to our description and evaluation of the Rorschach signs. In this discussion we shall not be concerned with general problems of design (e.g., adequate sample size and use of control groups) which beset the literature in this area, but rather with problems which arise out of the peculiar nature of this syndrome.

To begin with, the popular term for the syndrome, organic brain damage, contains a redundancy, in that brain damage can hardly be other than organic. Birch and Diller (1959) have argued that a distinction should be made between *brain damage,* which is an anatomic occurrence, and *organicity,* which is possibly a behavioral consequence. Of necessity, the Rorschach can be expected to be sensitive only to organicity. Organicity is not, however, a necessary sequel to brain damage. Lesions can exist with no apparent sensory, motor, mental, or emotional symptoms, and lesions can produce sensory or motor symptoms without accompanying mental or emotional difficulties. Every case in which a lesion exists without a cognitive or emotional symptom—in other words, in which brain damage exists without organicity—will produce a false negative, in that it would be impossible for the Rorschach to detect the brain damage in the absence of organicity.

A common assumption in constructing organic signs is that brain damage produces a distinctive pattern of behavior, and that the signs will be sensitive to this pattern. This contains the implicit and erroneous assumption that brain damage is a unitary concept and will produce the same behavior, regardless of the cause, nature, or circumstances of the injury. Reitan (1962) has shown that differential psychological effects will be produced by different types of pathological brain involvement. Differences can be discerned as a function of the specificity of the lesion (diffuse, focal, focal and diffuse, bilaterally focal), its hemispheric and lobular localization, its character (static, slowly progressive, moderately progressive, rapidly progressive) and its cause (cerebrovascular accident, tumor, disease, trauma). Each lesion is likely to produce both general and specific effects, and signs constructed from a heterogeneous group of organics can be sensitive, at most, to the general effects. Reitan appropriately cautions not to draw positive conclusions from negative findings when the group is heterogeneous, since the manifold symptomatology produced by different lesions may serve to cancel out any effects which exist.

Smith (1962) has suggested a number of additional problems which contribute to the heterogeneity of many groups of organics. Different psychological effects are produced by brain damage as a function of the suddenness with which tissue is destroyed, the condition of the rest of the brain, and the initial and subsequent effects on surrounding tissue and the cerebrovascular system. This distinction between initial and subsequent effects also suggests that the age of the lesion is of importance, since deficits are not necessarily constant. One is reminded of Von Monakow's distinction between temporary symptoms, which are early and due to diaschisis, and residual symptoms, which are late and due to secondary degeneration. Smith also has pointed out that lobular localization is not sufficient, since the lobular division is a gross anatomical one and not a functional one, so that more specificity of localization would be helpful.

In this elaboration of the detail in which we should be able to describe the lesion, it is easy to forget that the lesion occurs within a human being, and that the characteristics of that human being play a large part in determining the reaction to the injury. It is often difficult to separate the components of the organic response which are caused by the injury from those attributable to a personality dysfunction in response to a traumatic experience. Brain damage may initiate a pathological process, but many additional variables are highly influential in determining the specific response which will be observed. These variables include the patient's age, his premorbid personality and ability level, and the supports and demands from the environment. All of these factors will contribute to the heterogeneity of responses seen to similar physical injuries.

The criteria for subject selection and information about the *S*s presented in a study by Chapman and Wolff (1959) can serve as a model for investigators in the field. In order to be selected, the *S* had to meet the following criteria: a portion of the cerebral hemisphere had been resected; the extent and site of tissue removed was specifiable and was exclusively cortical; the lesion was static; there was no significant disease other than the cerebral defect being studied; age between 18 and 60; no diffuse cerebral dysfunction; resections were not performed for intractable pain or for psychiatric problems; and there was no significant impairment of speech, language, or motility. While some of these criteria might be modified by investigators with different interests (e.g., subcortical lesions) their specificity is highly commendable. Further, a table was presented which gave, for each *S*, age, education, occupation, the time in months since the operation, the pathological diagnosis, and the site, size, and side of the lesion. With the addition of information about sex and intelligence, this would be a maximally comprehensive presentation of subject characteristics within the practical limitations of data collection.

Signs are usually developed by comparing a heterogeneous organic group with a control group and selecting responses which differentiate the groups. The problems involved in the use of a heterogeneous organic group have been discussed above. A number of additional problems arise in the selection of an appropriate control group. If the differences are to be attributed to the brain injury, it is essential that the groups be matched on all relevant dimensions. These include age, intelligence, education, sex, race, socio-economic class, and premorbid personality structure. Some variables, such as personality structure, are often uncontrolled because of practical considerations, and others, such as race, may be of little moment, but it is inexcusable to omit consideration of age and intelligence, which are easily obtainable and of vital importance. Nevertheless, not one of the major systems of Rorschach indicators has controlled for these or any other variables in the initial sign construction studies.

Although it is clear that the control group should be selected so as to be equated with the organic group on a number of critical parameters, there is a moot question as to the group from which the controls should be selected. The most frequently chosen sources are normals and schizophrenics. Differential diagnosis between organicity and schizophrenia, and particularly chronic process schizophrenia, has proven extremely difficult. The pattern of symptoms resulting from brain damage and identified as reflecting organicity does not seem to be uniquely related to brain damage, but rather seems to be a more general deteriorative process which also can be seen in schizophrenia. Without getting involved in the question as to the possible organic basis of schizophrenia, it is clear that the choice of schizophrenics as a comparison group will provide the most severe test for any set of Rorschach signs. The use of normals, particularly when age and intelligence are not controlled, provides the most lenient test. However, the most reasonable test is provided when a group of known organics is compared with a group of patients with neurological complaints of known functional origin. This parallels the type of situation in which the signs will be used clinically, so that the results are most likely to be of practical import.

This type of comparison suggests that it should be unequivocally demonstrable that the "organic" patients have some neurological involvement, and that the "control" patients do not. The evidence for the diagnosis of the organic patients is not often given, and it is rare that any precautions are taken to ensure that patients in the control group are free of any neurological disorder. While it is a gross violation of sound experimental design to ignore any attempt to demonstrate clearly that individuals are appropriately placed in their respective groups, such a demonstration would not be an easy one to make. Psychologists may envy the precision of medical diagnostic procedures, but any familiarity with such procedures makes it clear that they leave much to be desired. The neurological examination, which is most often used as a criterion, is a variable and subjective procedure of questionable reliability. Laboratory procedures, despite their quantitative nature, are of variable usefulness and produce a great many false negatives. For example, Fisher and Gonda (1955), in a study comparing a variety of neurological procedures to a final diagnosis based in part on these procedures (an approach which gives a great advantage to the procedures), found the diagnostic accuracy of neurological examinations, electroencephalograms, skull X rays, lumbar punctures, and pneumoencephalograms to range between 37.5% and 69.3%, in a population where the base rate of organics was 71.2%. The neurological examination produced the most false positives, 31%, and the skull X rays the most false negatives, 81%. Thus, it is clear that it is one thing to make a recommendation about how to constitute groups for a maximally useful study and quite another thing to implement that recommendation. The lack of dependable criteria has created a great deal of difficulty in an area where validity studies are almost exclusively of the criterion-related type.

Some problems of design which are not restricted to this area, but which seem to be unusually prevalent in studies of organicity, are lack of cross validation and ignoring of base rates. Each of the major sets of Rorschach signs was constructed from a single comparison, with no attempt to cross validate the signs, so that chance played a maximum role in the selection of the signs. In some cases, where cross validation by another investigator has been attempted, signs have not held up, but it is not clear whether this is due to the general weakness of the signs or to their inappropriateness for the criterion group used in the cross-validation study, which has often differed markedly from the one employed in the initial study. Again, the need for greater differentiation among organic groups and greater specificity of the sign systems is clear.

There are a number of reasons why the initial promise of many Rorschach sign systems has had to be tempered by clinical experience. Failure to cross validate is one, and failure to take base rates into account is another. However, even if these flaws were corrected, this problem would be likely to persist, since the signs are identified by comparing the most clear and pure extreme groups, and then applied for differential diagnosis among the most difficult, equivocal groups. If test construction and test application were more equivalent situations, test usefulness would surely be improved.

Finally, a comment about practical matters of test administration is in order. Many studies have drawn protocols from old clinic files, and then rescored them for the Rorschach signs. As many of the Rorschach signs are qualitative, a verbatim recording would be necessary for accurate scoring, and there is no indication that this is uniformly true. Further, both with old records and current records, where accurate transcriptions can be assumed, there is rarely any mention made of the scorer being unaware of the patient's diagnosis. The absence of blind scoring and the presence of seriously incomplete records both lead to inaccuracies of test findings, with resultant failures to replicate being easily understandable.

In summary, the major problems cluster around three factors. The first of these concerns the heterogeneity of the effects of brain damage, and calls attention to the need to separate groups according to the characters of the lesion and of the affected person. The second cluster concerns the control group, and highlights some problems in selecting a group so as to be equivalent to the organic group and clearly free from organic pathology. Finally, there are a number of questions raised by standard principles of test construction and methodology, of which the need for cross validation and attention to base rates rank as the most important.

ORGANIC SIGNS

A number of different sets of Rorschach signs have appeared in the literature over the years. In this section we shall present in detail the systems of Piotrowski, Hughes, and Dörken and Kral, as these seem to have had the most attention by other independent investigators. In addition, we shall also present, but in a more superficial fashion, the signs that have been suggested by Aita, Reitan, and Ruth, by Evans and Marmorston, by Ross and Ross, and by Hertz and Loehrke. Since these signs have rarely been used by investigators other than those who originally advanced them, and a good deal less is known about them, they will be presented in much less detail. Since many single signs are included in a number of different systems, a comprehensive discussion of interscorer reliability will be postponed until the next section.

THE PIOTROWSKI SIGNS. The first of the sets of Rorschach signs of organicity to be published, and the one which has consistently received the most attention by investigators, is the system suggested by Piotrowski (1937). Piotrowski clearly stated the theory behind his system when he wrote, "It is known, of course, that the so-called higher mental processes change in a rather uniform manner following an organic disturbance in the central nervous system, while the sensorimotor reactions show a great variety of change according to the location and size of the disturbance (p. 525)." Since the publication of Piotrowski's original paper, this assumption of uniform change has come into question.

Piotrowski's 10 signs are reported as having been "selected by us" with the method of selection unspecified in any detail. His initial article compares an organic and a nonorganic group, but this comparison does not seem to have been the basis of sign selection.

The 10 Piotrowski signs of brain damage are as follows:

1. *R*. Total responses in the Rorschach protocol are less than 15.
2. *T*. The average time per single response is more than 1 minute. This sign is assessed by dividing the amount of time it takes to administer the free association portion of the Rorschach by the number of responses in the protocol.
3. *M*. The number of human movement responses are equal to or less than 1.
4. *Color denomination, Cn*. A response is classified as Cn if it contains merely the name and description of a blotch and if it is considered by the patient as a satisfactory response. Examples of Cn are "This is red" and "These are four dots of red ink, two of green, and two of yellow." Examples of responses which would not be scored Cn are "What the heck is the red going through" and "The green is beyond me. Dear, I cannot say anything about it."
5. *F%*. The percentage of good form responses is below 70. Form responses are considered in the manner of Rorschach, so that all responses on a psychogram between M and C are scorable as form response. No suggestion is given as to the manner of determination as to whether a response is good or poor form.
6. *P%*. The percentage of popular responses is below 25. In a later paper (Piotrowski, 1940) it is suggested that this sign should not be computed if there are more than 25 responses in the protocol. Piotrowski does not suggest a list of popular responses, but indicates only that a popular response is one given by at least one-third of a group of normal subjects. Hughes (1950) suggests the use of Klopfer's list of populars for the determination of this sign.

7. *Repetition, Rpt.* Repetition or perserveration is scored when the same response is given to several inkblots. Usually the first response shows good form and the following responses show less good form than the original one did. Piotrowski did not specify the number of repetitions necessary for the scoring of this sign. Hughes (1950) suggests it be scored when the same response is given on three or more cards.
8. *Impotence, Imp.* This is scored when the response is given in spite of the patient's recognition that it is an inadequate response. Piotrowski states clearly that this does not occur in the absence of Rpt, although the normative section will show that this stricture has often been ignored. Examples of responses scored as Imp are "If that is a bat, it is a foolish one" and "A butterfly, perhaps. What is it really, Doctor?"
9. *Perplexity, Plx.* This is scored when the patient shows a distrust of his own ability and a quest for reassurance. Examples of responses scored as Plx are "Two dogs. I love dogs. I had a dog. It was a brown dog—no, he was yellow. What else can a dog be, Doctor?" and "A picture in symmetry. You know what that is, Doctor? I can't explain myself. Symmetry, two things on both sides. I give up."
10. *Automatic phrases, AP.* This is scored when the patient shows a frequent use of a pet phrase in an indiscriminate fashion. Piotrowski does not specify the quantitative dimension of "frequent," but Aita et al. (1947) suggest that for AP to be scored, it must occur in more than half of the cards. Examples of responses scored as AP are "It's some kind of work...it's good work...this is some work" and "I don't like it, it is not nice."

As a guide to scoring, Piotrowski later (1940) suggested that if there is any doubt as to whether or not a response is to be scored, it is better to leave out a sign than to score it.

If a record contains *at least five of the 10 signs,* it is considered to be a diagnostic sign of a marked personality change whose etiology rests in an organic disease process which involves the cerebral cortex. If a record contains less than five signs, this does not allow a positive conclusion. Thus, strictly speaking, it should be impossible, if Piotrowski's scoring rules were attended to, for this system to produce a false negative, as the only diagnostic decision which can be made is for the presence of organicity, and in the case of the lack of a positive sign of organicity, no diagnostic judgment should be made.

In a later paper, Piotrowski (1940) has recognized that the presence of signs depends upon the personality of the individual being tested and suggests that the more marked the personality deviation of the individual, the more likely he is to produce a record which contains five or more signs. Thus, he adds that a qualitative analysis of the record is necessary along with the computation of signs to arrive at any final diagnostic decision.

Although Piotrowski does specifically indicate that the signs taken by themselves are not sufficient for the diagnosis of organic brain damage, they have been employed in that fashion by many other investigators, and we shall evaluate the quantitative use of the signs independent of any possible accompanying qualitative use.

Hughes Signs. The Hughes signs (1948) were not based on any theoretical assumption about organicity, as were the Piotrowski signs, but rather on a factor analytic investigation. However, the same assumption of the uniformity of the effect of brain damage was implicit, since the organic patients whose records were included in the factor analysis constituted a highly heterogeneous group, composed of individuals with traumatic head injuries, cerebral arteriosclerosis, brain tumors, and cerebral syphilis. The records of 100 patients, of whom 32 were organic, 39 neurotic, and 29 schizophrenic, were scored for Piotrowski's signs, Miale and Harrower-Erickson's neurotic signs, and Klopfer's schizophrenic signs. Factor analysis was then performed, using Thursone's complete centroid method, and eight orthogonal factors were extracted. Factor one was labeled the organic factor and provided the basis for the Hughes signs, with the factor loadings determining the weights of the various signs.

The Hughes signs are as follows (the weight of each sign is indicated in parentheses):

1. $R < 15$ (+1).
2. $R < 25$ (+1).
3. $M \leq 1$ (+2).
4. Color naming (+1).
5. $FC \leq 1$ (+1).
6. Perserveration (+2).
7. Impotence (+3).
8. Perplexity (+3).
9. Automatic phrases (+3).
10. Color shock (−2).
11. Shading shock (−2).
12. $FM > M$ (−1).
13. Confused succession (−1).
14. Contamination (−1).

It is immediately apparent that seven of the 14 Hughes signs are identical to Piotrowski's signs. A number of Hughes' original contributions, such as color shock and shading shock, are not elaborated, so that, presumably, a subjective judgment by the examiner is necessary to determine the presence or absence of these signs.

The score on Hughes signs can range from −7 to +17. Hughes recommends that if a patient has a score of +7 or more, this be considered as a sign that he is "probably organic." A score between +3 and +6 indicates that he is "possibly organic," and a score below +3 indicates that he is "not organic." Thus, the Hughes system can produce both false positives and false negatives, as it will make a definitive diagnosis of both organicity and the absence of organicity.

DÖRKEN AND KRAL SIGNS. Dörken and Kral (1952) present a set of Rorschach signs which are different from the Piotrowski signs and the Hughes signs in that the presence of the Dörken and Kral signs is considered contraindicative of organicity, and the absence of these signs is considered to be pathognomic of organicity. The signs were chosen in an unspecified way, and weighted according to their incidence in a criterion population. The theoretical rationale logically suggests that since organicity is a deficit, it should be indicated by the absence of positive signs, rather than the presence of negative signs.

The Dörken and Kral signs are as follows (the weights are given in parentheses following each sign):

1. M + m > 2 (2).
2. k + K + FK > 0 (1).
3. Fc + FC > 2 (1).
4. R > 20 (2).
5. S > 0 (1).
The anatomy response to the central detail in the top third of Card VIII is not considered a space response for the purpose of this sign.
6. Total form level > +20.0 (2).
7. 0 + % > 15 (1).

In the scoring of each of the categories, Dörken and Kral suggest that the scoring system outlined by Klopfer be used.

With the exception of the sign indicating the importance of the number of responses, this list of signs is different from the lists proposed by Piotrowski and by Hughes. Although the rationale is markedly different, that is, a high score indicates adequate functioning rather than organicity, it should be clear that in many cases the signs are simply the opposite of those in other systems, so that a person is considered organic by Dörken and Kral if he does not possess the sign R > 20, but is considered organic by Piotrowski and by Hughes if he does possess the sign R < 15 or R < 25.

The score on the Dörken and Kral signs can range between 0 and 10. The authors suggest that a score between 0 and 2 indicates organicity, and a score between 3 and 10 excludes an organic diagnosis. Again, this allows for both false positives and false negatives, as a definitive diagnosis is suggested for scores at either side of the cutoff point.

AITA, REITAN, AND RUTH'S SIGNS. Aita, Reitan, and Ruth (1947) suggested a number of qualitative signs of organicity. These were not proposed as a formal sign system, so no points were assigned for the presence or absence of these characteristics in a record, and no cutoff point is suggested as indicative or contraindicative of organicity.

The signs they suggest are the following:

1. *Inflexibility (Iflx).* In his entire record, the *S* does not use any part of the figure in more than one association. This sign is not used if the *S* gave two unrelated associations to any single blot area, or gave a detail response and an unrelated whole response to any card. For example, if the *S* sees Card I as a bat, and the central detail as a women, this would *not* be scored Iflx.
2. *Consideration of blots as actual objects (ActObj).* This is scored when the patient introduces his responses with a phrase like, "This is a ———." If qualifying responses like, "looks like" or "might be" are used, ActObj is not scored.
3. *Concrete responses (CR).* This is scored if, throughout the record, *no responses* are scored which characterize a quality or attribute of the percept. For example, "two distinguished men" or "a Grecian urn" would *not* be scored CR.
4. *Unclear definition of response (Def).* This response can only be scored after a searching inquiry. It is scored when the *S* cannot specify the individual elements that comprise his response. For example, he may see a butterfly, but not be able to specify the head, wings, or body. If this occurs anywhere in the record, the sign is scored.
5. *Catastrophic reaction (Catas).* This is scored if there are any overt emotional displays, whether they be expressed in words, by groaning, and so on, that occur during the test administration.
6. *Edging (Edg).* This is scored if the patient holds the card at unusual angles, such as peering at it from a side view. If this occurs at least once at any time during the test administration, the sign is scored.
7. *Irrelevant comments (IC).* This is scored if the patient makes a comment which is not pertinent in any observable way to the testing situation. An example of an IC response is "What is that new doctor doing next door? Is he here to take the place of ———."
8. *Covers parts of cards (CvrCds).* This is scored if the subject covers part of the card while attempting to give a response.
9. *Withdrawal and reattack (WR).* This is scored when the patient removes his attention from the card, perhaps turning away from it, and then renews his scrutiny of the card.

EVANS AND MARMORSTON SIGNS. Evans and Marmorston (1963a, 1964) have developed a lengthy checklist which represents a compilation of a number of signs suggested by other investigators. They have used portions of this checklist in a continuing research project studying differences between patients with cerebral thrombosis and those with acute myocardial infarctions. The initial 46-item list includes Piotrowski's 10 signs, Aita et al.'s nine signs, and a number of signs suggested either formally or informally by other investigators. These other signs included (1) eight suggested by Baker (1956) (body-image concern, the use of personal experience to justify response, poor background-foreground discrimination, self-derogatory remarks, sharp details with poor whole organization, inappropriate combinations of separate concepts, poor recall of responses in inquiry, sexual disturbance), (2) four responses suggested by Hertz and Loehrke (1954) ($A\% \geq 75$, $CF > FC$ with sum $C < 3$, $Fc + c + k + K + FK = 0$, more than one card rejection), (3) six signs described by Ames, Learned, Metraux, and Walker (1954) (an F− response to a popular area, $H = 0$, content categories ≤ 3, A in upper IV shading, bird heads on III, certain that there is a right answer), and (4) nine responses suggested by their own work (repeating response description, content perserveration, $F\% > 70$, $Dd + Dr + S = 0$, says what the blot is not, blot of ink or dab of paint, pictures painted over or drawn, form level ≤ 10.0, average weighted form level < 1.0).

The 46-item checklist was assigned weights of 1 or 2, depending upon whether the items differentiated the two groups in an initial study (1963b), was reduced to 26 items on the basis of differentiation of the two groups at the .01 level in a later study (1964), and was still further reduced to 10 items in the 1964 study by eliminating items which significantly intercorrelated with other items. The final 10-item list consisted of (1) Plx, (2) $F + \% < 70$, (3) Iflx, (4) WR, (5) body-image concern, (6) poor recall during inquiry, (7) certain there is a right answer, (8) repeating response description, (9) $Dd + Dr + S = 0$, and (10) says what blot is not.

There are a number of different cutoff points suggested for the 46-item weighted list, depending upon which comparison is being made. No cutoff point is suggested for the 10-item list. Their work is quite comprehensive, but is not yet in a form that could be readily adopted for clinical use without a good deal of further work, since a variety of cutoff points have been suggested.

Ross and Ross Signs. Ross and Ross (1944) attempted to construct a set of Rorschach signs which would give scores simultaneously for organicity and neurosis. They began with a wide variety of signs suggested by other investigators (Rorschach, Oberholzer, Piotrowski, Miale and Harrower-Erikson) and compared groups of normals, neurotics, and organics. Item analysis, which was not cross validated, divided the signs into four categories: (1) signs common to neurotics and organics, (2) signs present in neurotics but not in organics, (3) signs present in organics but not in neurotics, (4) signs present in normals and neurotics but not in organics. Differential weights were assigned to the signs according to the magnitude of group differences. The categories were then combined to form two scores. An *instability* score, which was arrived at by summing the first and second categories and subtracting the third, and a *disability* score, which was obtained by summing the first and third categories and subtracting from it the second and fourth categories. Means are available for a variety of groups, and ranges of expectation may be obtained by taking the standard error into account, but no cutoff score is suggested by Ross and Ross. Theoretically, one would expect organics to have high disability scores, but there is no suggested point beyond which the score has reached a level pathognomic of organicity. Some investigators have used the Ross and Ross signs in cross-validational work, but they have used a variety of cutoff points, and have not described how they arrived at the particular cutoff point they employed.

HERTZ AND LOEHRKE SIGNS. Hertz and Loehrke (1955) compared responses from groups of patients with posttraumatic encephalopathy, paranoid schizophrenia, and anxiety neurosis in an attempt to develop a configurational rather than a sign approach. Thirty-four configurations were selected and comparisons were made among the groups. Twenty configurations differentiated the organics from both schizophrenics and neurotics. Interrater reliability for these configurations ranged between 66.7 and 100%, with a median figure of 85.4%. While this is satisfactory, the configurations appear to be quite complex and a question may be raised as to whether this reliability could be duplicated by less well-trained and well-motivated investigators. Using the presence of eight or more configurations as the cutoff point, Hertz and Loehrke presented figures attesting to the efficacy of this approach. Since neither the selection of the configurations nor the establishment of the cutoff point were cross validated, this estimate of efficacy can be seen as representing the upper limit for this approach. The same groups of patients were compared on the Piotrowski signs, and the advantage shown by the Hertz and Loehrke signs was only slight. The Hertz and Loehrke signs were accurate in 82% of diagnoses, while the Piotrowski signs were accurate in 72.7%; the base rate was 66.7%. The Hertz and Loehrke signs produced fewer false negatives but more false positives than did the Piotrowski signs. This minimal difference, when the Hertz and Loehrke signs are operating at maximum efficiency, and the greater complexity of these signs as compared to the Piotrowski signs, suggest that there would not be a great deal of profit in pursuing this approach further.

RELIABILITY

Reliability will be discussed before normative data in this chapter because of the difficulty in separating any discussion of normative data from a discussion of the validity of each of the separate sets of signs, and because virtually none of the studies provide only information about reliability as we have been discussing it. Rather, the major focus of this section will be on interscorer reliability.

There have been very few studies dealing with organic signs which have concerned themselves with even this aspect of reliability. The assumption seems to have been made that the quantitative, "objective" nature of the organic signs guarantees their interscorer reliability, and makes formal testing of that objectivity unnecessary.

One study which did concern itself with scorer reliability was reported by Hertz and Loehrke (1954). They scored 24 records independently for both Piotrowski and Hughes signs. Unfortunately, they give their results in the form of chi-square tables which indicate that the frequency of incidence of each sign is similar for both raters. However, since the frequency of incidence of the signs is distinctly different, these same findings may have been obtained even if the raters had scored two entirely different sets of records. Presented in this form, without comparisons of either specific scoring decisions or summed scores per record, the data do not allow us to conclude anything about the scorer reliability of either system.

A study devoted exclusively to the scorer reliability of the Piotrowski signs and the Hughes signs was that of Forer, Farberow, Meyer, and Tolman (1952). They assumed the reliability of the signs which are stated in terms of Klopfer scoring categories, and just tested the reliability of the Piotrowski signs *Imp, AP, Plx, Rpt,* and the Hughes signs contamination, color shock, and shading shock. They report interscorer reliability, both between independent scorers and between the same scorer on two different occasions. For the Piotrowski signs, the percentage of agreement, both between a scorer and himself and between a scorer and an independent judge, was consistently in the 80s, with the exception of one pair of scorers, whose agreement on *Rpt* was in the low 70s. For the Hughes signs, contamination is consistently reliable, with percentage of agreement in the 90s, while color shock is consistently unreliable, with agreement between a scorer and himself on two separate occasions of only 74.6%, and between pairs of independent scorers of about 60%. Shading shock is somewhat intermediate, with reasonable agreement between a scorer and himself, but agreement in the 70s between independent scorers. However, these signs are all relatively infrequent in occurrence, so the percentage of agreement is inflated by a tendency for a large number of agreements to be recorded over the judgment "absent." Despite this inflation, it is quite clear that the Hughes sign color shock is unreliable, the Hughes sign shading shock is of questionable reliability, and none of the signs, with the exception of the Hughes sign contamination, show impressive reliabilities.

Some additional reliability data are reported by Evans and Marmorston (1963a, 1963b, 1964). Using their 46-item list, they report that the correlation between two sets of judgments by the same scorer, separated by a six-month interval, was .97. The test-retest reliability of the 46-item list was recorded as .77. However, in a study in which this list was administered on two separate occasions to patients receiving a placebo, there was a significant increase in the signs of deterioration on the second testing. The patients were about 60 years of age and had recently had either a cerebral thrombosis or myocardial infarction, so the increase might correspond to actual deteriorative processes rather than provide testimony to the unreliability of the instrument. Interscorer reliability on their 10-item checklist was reported as .87, with the percentage of agreement on individual items ranging between 91% and 100%.

The interscorer reliabilities of the items on the Piotrowski, Hughes, and Dörken and Kral lists which are based exclusively on Klopfer scoring may be inferred from other studies which have indicated reasonable reliability for that scoring system. However, the items which do not involve

Klopfer scores, but rather involve subjective judgments, have not been demonstrated to be reliable, and there have not been any clear demonstrations of the test-retest reliability of any of the systems taken as a whole. It is rudimentary that demonstrations must be provided of both the interscorer agreement and the reliability over time for the entire system, since judgments are made on the basis of summed scores.

It is of particular concern that reliability data be provided, because validity studies have been contradictory. It is difficult to decide whether the contradictions among the validity studies are due to the extreme heterogeneity of the samples employed or to the basic scoring unreliability associated with the measuring instrument itself. There is some suspicion that a number of unreliable signs are included in both the Piotrowski and the Hughes lists, since they include signs which are based exclusively on the subjective judgment of the examiner. These signs are not presented in sufficient specificity to be certain that two examiners will score them in a similar manner. Thus, even if it had been demonstrated that interscorer reliability could be achieved between two scorers who had been trained to interpret the signs in a specific manner, it would still be necessary to demonstrate that untrained scorers, having nothing to go by other than the printed list of instructions, would interpret that list in a similar manner, and arrive at similar judgments about each protocol.

Although high reliability can be demonstrated between trained scorers using the Klopfer system (with the exception of the *M* sign), the Klopfer categories which are utilized in the various sets of signs are those which are most prone to fluctuation and are dependent upon the mode of administration of the Rorschach. It has been shown that R, for example, varies greatly between examiners, and this sign is present on every major list of signs. Additionally, time per response is dependent upon the writing speed of the examiner as much as on the responding speed of the *S*.

If the signs are to be used, either clinically or in research, it is necessary to demonstrate that the systems are reliable, and this demonstration has not been made adequately for either interscorer or test-retest reliability. A clinically meaningful approach to interscorer reliability would have to include independent administrations of the Rorschach, rather than the simple scoring of the same protocol by two separate observers, since so many of the signs may vary as a function of administrative practices. However, even the demonstration that the same record would be scored in a similar manner by two judges, having no training other than that provided by an existent manual, would be welcome at this point.

NORMATIVE DATA

The normative data that have been presented on the signs often have been presented as a portion of a validity study, and are difficult to separate from that study. The somewhat arbitrary decision that has been made about presentation is to include the data about incidence of individual signs in the normative data section, and to postpone a discussion about differences between the groups in incidence of either individual signs or summed signs until the validity section.

Nature of the Sample

Because of the overlap that has been mentioned between normative and validity data, the table describing characteristics of the various samples includes both normative and validity studies. These data are presented in Table 11.1 and describe the organic and control groups, the method of diagnosis used, and the variables on which the groups were equated.

Organic Groups

Many of the organic groups which were studied were highly heterogeneous and are reported in the table as either "mixed" or "unspecified." "Mixed" has been used to describe samples which contain patients of differing organic defects, but which specify the defects that have been studied. "Unspecified" has been used to describe those reports which merely indicate that a group of brain-damaged patients was studied.

Brackbill and Fine (1956) studied a mixed group of 28 organics, of whom 23 were paretics and the others were distributed among Korsakoff's syndrome, traumatic head injury, and brain tumor. Dörken and Kral (1952) studied 70 patients, of whom 20 were diagnosed senile dementia and 10 were diagnosed cortical injury, extrapyramidal hyperkinetic injury, diencephalic injury, extrapyramidal akinetic injury, and diffuse organic nonsenile injury. Gottlieb and Parsons (1960) used a highly heterogeneous group, of which the modal category was seizure patients, constituting five of the 20, and the other 15 were distributed among less frequent sources of brain injury. Hughes (1950) studied patients who were distributed among the categories of traumatic head injury, cerebral arteriosclerosis, brain tumor, and cerebral syphilis. Ross (1941a) included 18 patients with a variety of different cerebral lesions, 10 patients with a variety of different central nervous system lesions which were either subcortical or noncortical, and 19 patients with a diagnosis of epilepsy.

Neiger, Slemon, and Quirk (1962) studied 20 patients with epilepsy, half of whom had an accompanying psychotic reaction and half of whom were free from psychosis. Both groups of patients had been hospitalized for many years. Reitan (1954) studied 18 aphasic patients, as well as 18 patients with unspecified brain damage. The aphasic difficulties were diverse and not precisely specifiable, and, in some cases, the patients had recovered from their aphasic symptoms when they were tested. However, they were still classified as aphasic for the purposes of the study. Reitan (1955b) studied a group of 50 patients of unspecified brain damage, but postoperative testing was delayed until the maximal benefits from hospitalization were received and the patients were ready for discharge, so that the incidence of organic signs in these records was probably minimized.

Even where a homogeneous-appearing group of patients has been studied, the homogeneity often surrounds the *cause* of the injury rather than the *location* of the injury. Thus, diagnoses such as cerebral concussion, postconcussion syndrome, and posttraumatic encephalopathy all indicate that the patient had received, by one means or another, a blow to the head, but do not specify the type of injury that might have resulted from that blow. Other diagnoses, such as pathology rostral to the foramen magnum, are so all-inclusive as to give no specific information. Another set of diagnoses, such as diabetes mellitus, epilepsy, hemiplegia, and multiple sclerosis are specific syndromes which may be caused by, or result in, a variety of different cerebral malfunctions. Multiple sclerosis, in fact, is caused by sclerotic plaques which are randomly distributed throughout the central nervous system, so that there is no clear indication that there is any cortical involvement in a multiple sclerotic patient without some information about symptomatology.

The *method* of diagnosis of brain injury leaves almost as much to be desired as the specification of the diagnosis. In almost half the cases the manner of diagnosis is unspecified, and in a number of other cases it is specified only by terms such as "clinical diagnosis," which give very little information. While the neurological criterion is not totally satisfactory, the interpretation of the studies would be a good deal easier if there were some reason for confidence in the classification of the criterion groups. The difficulty with the use of an unspecified or general diagnostic technique for classification is demonstrated clearly by Eckhardt (1961), who studied admission data from a large number of state hospitals and showed that 11 of 14 southern states used functional diagnoses more often than organic diagnoses, while 29 of 31 northern states used organic diagnoses as often or more often than functional diagnoses! Apparently the diagnosis of brain disorder is no more reliable than the diagnosis of functional problems, and that procedure has long been held in disrepute.

The median sample size employed with the organic groups was under 30. The inadequacy of samples this small, particularly with groups so heterogeneous, hardly needs be mentioned. In addition, the Evans and Marmorston studies (1963a, 1963b, 1964, 1965), all of which employ a reasonable number of organic patients, are reports from a continuing research program, so the protocols of many patients are reported over and over again.

Control Group

A number of studies also employed mixed or unspecified control groups, and a few do not use controls at all. A much larger number of studies using no control group are in the literature, but most of these have not been reported, because of the great difficulty in interpreting data from such projects.

Dörken and Kral (1952) had a control group of 60, which included 20 patients with the diagnosis of schizophrenia and 10 each classified as manic depressive, psychoneurotic, normals of superior intelligence, and normals of average intelligence. Eckhardt's (1961) 679 nonorganic patients

TABLE 11.1
Sample Characteristics

Study	Organic Group	Sample Size	Method of Diagnosis
Aita, Reitan, and Ruth (1947)	Head Injury in Combat	60	Surgeon's Report, Neurological Exam., Pneumoencephalogram
Allison and Allison (1954)	Lobotomy for Psychosis	8	Operation
Birch and Diller (1959)	Hemiplegia	20	Unspecified
Brackbill and Fine (1956)	Mixed	28	Unspecified
Diers and Brown (1951)	Multiple Sclerosis	25	Unspecified
Dörken and Kral (1952)	Mixed	70	Unspecified
Eckhardt (1961)	Unspecified	71	Psychiatric Staff
Evans and Marmorston (1963a)	Cerebral Thrombosis	108	Neurological Exam., Lab. Tests
Evans and Marmorston (1963b)	Cerebral Thrombosis	51	Neurological Exam., Lab. Tests
Evans and Marmorston (1964)	Cerebral Thrombosis	139	Neurological Exam., Lab. Tests
Evans and Marmorston (1965)	Cerebral Thrombosis	32	Neurological Exam., Lab. Tests
Fisher, Gonda, and Little (1955)	Pathology Rostral to the Foramen Magnum	84	Medical History, Neurological Exam., Routine Lab. Procedures, Some Special Lab. Procedures
Gottlieb and Parsons (1960)	Mixed	20	Surgery or One Unequivocal Neurological Sign or Two Equivocal Neurological Signs
Hertz and Loehrke (1954)	Posttraumatic Encephalopathy	50	Neurological Exam., EEG, Pneumoencephalogram, Psychiatric Exam.
Hughes (1948)	Mixed	50	Clinical Diagnosis
Koff (1946)	Cerebral Concussion	75	Loss of Consciousness, Elevated Spinal Fluid Protein
Loveland (1961)	Epilepsy	25	Seizures, Abnormal EEG's
Neiger, Slemon, and Quirk (1962)	Epilepsy	20	Unspecified
Oltean (1952)	Diabetes Mellitus	20	Medical Diagnosis
Piotrowski (1937)	Unspecified	18	Unspecified
Reitan (1954)	Unspecified	18	Surgeon's Report
	Aphasia	18	Neurological Exam., Pneumoencephalogram
Reitan (1955a)	Unspecified	23	Unspecified
	Postconcussion syndrome	23	Unspecified
Reitan (1955b)	Unspecified	50	Unspecified
Ross (1941b)	Mixed	47	Unspecified

Control Group	*Sample Size*	*Method of Excluding Organicity*	*Variables on Which Groups were Equated*
Nonorganic Neurological Patients	100	Neurological Exam.	Sex, Time after Injury
Psychosis	8	None	Sex, Age, Education, Diagnosis, Treatment, Duration of Hospitalization, Duration of Illness, Amount of Shock
None	—	—	—
Process Schizophrenia, Reactive Schizophrenia	36 24	None	None
Nonneurologic Hospital Patients	11	Neurologic, Psychiatric, and Psychologic Measures	Intelligence
Mixed	60	None	None
Mixed	679	None	None
Acute Myocardial Infarction	96	Gross Neurological Exam.	Sex, Education, Socio-economic Class, Outpatient Status (groups differed on age and race)
Acute Myocardial Infarction	50	Gross Neurological Exam.	Socio-economic Class
Acute Myocardial Infarction	136	Gross Neurological Exam.	Outpatient Status, Time after Acute Stage of Illness, Education (groups differed on age, race, and sex)
Acute Myocardial Infarction	45	Gross Neurological Exam.	Unspecified
Neurologic Patient with No Pathology Rostral to the Foramen Magnum	34	Medical History, Neurological Exam., Routine Lab. Procedures, Some Special Lab. Procedures	Sex, Race
Nonorganic Neurological Referral	20	Medical Diagnosis	Age, Sex, Race, Education
Schizophrenia, Paranoid Anxiety Neurosis	50	None	Age, Sex, Race, Education, Occupation
Mixed	168	None	None
Gross Stress Reaction	110	Reduced Spinal Fluid Protein	None
Unspecified	25	None	Age, Intelligence, Education, Sex, Race, Socio-economic Status
Normal	80	None	None
Schizophrenia	40		
None	—	—	—
Mixed	15	None	None (groups differed in age)
Nonorganic Neurological Patients	18	Neurological Exam.	Intelligence, Education, Sex, Time after Injury
Unspecified	23	Neurological Exam.	Age, Education, Intelligence, Sex, Race, Time after Injury
Unspecified	50	Neurological Exam.	Race, Sex, Age, Education
Mixed	189	None	None

were distributed among the diagnostic categories mental deficiency, schizophrenic reaction, paranoid schizophrenia, psychotic disorder, psychoneurotic reaction, personality disorder, and normal. Hughes (1948) included 68 schizophrenic patients, 74 neurotic patients, four manic depressives, and 22 normal *S*s in his control group. Piotrowski (1937) had a control group of 15, which was composed of 10 patients with noncerebral disturbances of the central nervous system, and five patients diagnosed as conversion hysteria. Ross (1941a) included 42 neurotic patients, 26 patients with a somatic illness with neurotic features, 19 patients with a somatic illness free of neurotic features, 15 psychotic patients, 53 soldiers who were mostly of low intelligence and who presented management problems to the Army, and 34 superior normals.

The method by which it is concluded that a control patient is free from any organic deficit, and therefore is properly placed in this group, is far from adequate. In almost half of the studies there are no techniques mentioned by which organicity was excluded as a consideration from control patients. Of the remaining studies, the technique most often used is the "neurological exam," a technique which can have a wide variety of meanings and which, at its best, is subjective and unreliable. Only two studies indicate the use of a procedure other than the neurological examination for excluding organicity. One of these, Koff (1946), used a laboratory procedure, and took a reduction in spinal fluid protein as an indication of the absence of organicity. Fisher and Gonda (1955), using more lumbar puncture indices than just spinal fluid protein, found that this method produced 72% false negatives, so that it is not unreasonable to expect that a substantial proportion of the control group in the Koff study was composed of patients suffering from a cerebral concussion. The only report in which the control group was studied with the same care as that given to the organic group, so that the diagnosis of organicity could be specifically indicated in the one case and specifically excluded in the other, was that of Fisher, Gonda, and Little (1955). For the most part, their control patients received the same laboratory procedures and examinations as their organic group, so that one might feel a little more confident that *S*s were properly classified in that study.

The control groups used by Aita, Reitan, and Ruth (1947) and Reitan (1954) consisted of patients in a neurological-neurosurgical ward and included patients with head injuries, headaches, and convulsions. Patients were classified as control because a neurologist indicated that there was no organic cerebral alteration. It is difficult to see how such a conclusion could have been reached, and there is no information given as to the basis for that decision other than the judgment of the neurologist. It seems as though these studies are comparing degrees of severity of brain damage, rather than comparing the presence and absence of brain damage.

The most acceptable model for choice of control groups is provided by studies such as that of Fisher, Gonda, and Little (1955) and Gottlieb and Parsons (1960), although the latter study did not take sufficient measures to ensure the absence of organicity in their control group. These studies used a population of neurological referrals, who were then classified by methods of varying effectiveness into an organic and a nonorganic group. This type of discrimination among neurological referrals is exactly the type of discrimination for which it is most reasonable to expect that the organic signs will be called upon to make in a clinical situation, and the success or failure of the signs in such a situation has the most relevance for clinical practice.

Variables for Equating Groups

In almost half of the studies reported in which organic groups were compared with control groups, the groups were not equated on any variable. In a small number of studies, the groups were equated on both age and intelligence, which is an absolute minimum, but there were also a number of studies in which groups were compared despite the fact that they differed in age. This difference in the Evans and Marmorston studies was small but significant, while in the Piotrowski (1937) study, it was almost 18 years. In the light of evidence reviewed below, indicating that organic signs vary as a function of both age and intelligence, it is inexcusable for comparisons to be made without first ensuring that any differences are not a function of these irrelevant variables.

The Piotrowski signs is the only system for which data are presented in sufficient detail to allow the development of normative tables. Table 11.2 presents the data concerning the percentage of occurrence of the individual Piotrowski signs in brain-damaged samples, and Table 11.3 presents the percentage of occurrence in nonbrain-damaged samples. The significance of the difference between these sets of samples will be examined in the validity section.

The first impression gained from examining these tables is that there is a great deal of variability in the incidence of any of the signs in either of the groups. Part of the variability can be attributed to the variability of the groups themselves. Psychotic groups invariably have higher percentages of incidence of the signs than do nonpsychotic groups. The brain-damaged groups contain a wide variety of different syndromes, and this variety could contribute a good deal to the variability of the scores. In other cases, the unreliability of scoring may be implicated. For example, it is unusual that a sign such as *AP,* which appears so rarely in most studies, is reported present in 64% of the brain-damaged and 44% of the non-brain-damaged samples by Loveland (1961). The suspicion that *AP* is being scored differently in this study than in the other studies is quite strong. Similarly, in some studies the incidence of *Imp* is higher than the incidence of *Rpt,* despite Piotrowski's statement that *Imp* cannot be scored in the absence of *Rpt*! This discrepancy can be noted in the studies of Aita et al. (1947), Hertz and Loehrke (1954), and Oltean (1952). It is clear that these examiners must have been scoring *Imp* differently than in the manner suggested initially by Piotrowski.

One other observation from perusing the tables is that there are no signs which consistently appear in such an overwhelming proportion of the

TABLE 11.2
Per Cent of Occurrence of Piotrowski's Signs in Brain-Damaged Samples

	Sample Size												
Study	*N*	*M*	*F*	*R*	*T*	*M*	*Cn*	*F%*	*P%*	*Rpt*	*Imp*	*Plx*	*AP*
Aita, Reitan, and Ruth (1947)	60	60	0	—[a]	—	—	11.7	—	—	21.7	41.6	45.0	26.7
Birch and Diller (1959)	10	—	—	70.0	0.0	60.0	10.0	40.0	40.0	60.0	60.0	50.0	10.0
Brackbill and Fine (1956)	28	28	0	83.0	17.0	69.0	17.0	34.0	41.0	55.0	14.0	38.0	31.0
Evans and Marmorston (1964)	139	92	47	84.0[b]	34.0	66.0[b]	3.0	33.0	61.0	32.0	27.0	36.0	1.0
Hertz and Loehrke (1954)	50	50	0	34.0	26.0	58.0	20 0	34 0	46.0	20.0	26.0	26.0	16.0
Loveland (1961)	26	13	13	24.0	20.0	48.0	12.0	48.0	48.0	60.0	16.0	56.0	64.0
Neiger, Slemon, and Quirk (1962)	20	20	0	40.0	95.0	90.0	20.0	80.0	75.0	50.0	5.0	45.0	15.0
Oltean (1952)	20	—	—	55.0	35.0	75.0	50.0	100.0	55.0	30.0	40.0	65.0	60.0
Piotrowski (1937)	18	12	6	66.6	77.0	94.35	44.4	72.15	55.55	83.25	44.4	38.85	38.85
Ross (1941b)	47[c]	33	14	68.16	38.34	57.51	10.65	42.6	46.86	48.99	17.34	44.73	10.65

[a] A dash (—) indicates that data were not available.
[b] N = 82 (Evans and Marmorston, 1964).
[c] Includes patients with cerebral lesions, central nervous system lesions, and epilepsy.

TABLE 11.3

Per Cent of Occurrence of Piotrowski's Signs in Nonbrain-Damaged Samples

Study	Sample Size			R	T	M	Cn	F%	P%	Rpt	Imp	Plx	AP
	N	M	F										
Aita, Reitan, and Ruth (1947)	100	100	0	—[a]	—	—	3.0	—	—	11.0	9.0	15.0	12.0
Brackbill and Fine (1956)	36(P)[b]	36	0	61.0	33.0	78.0	17.0	22.0	22.0	39.0	19.0	33.0	17.0
Brackbill and Fine (1956)	24(P)	24	0	54.0	25.0	58.0	0.0	12.0	54.0	21.0	4.0	12.0	4.0
Evans and Marmorston (1964)	136	108	28	53.0[c]	17.0	51.0[c]	1.0	5.0	38.0	9.0	9.0	13.0	0.0
Hertz and Loehrke (1954)	50(P)	50	0	24.0	12.0	54.0	8.0	42.0	44.0	22.0	4.0	0.0	0.0
Hertz and Loehrke (1954)	50	50	0	14.0	10.0	52.0	10.0	12.0	20.0	2.0	2.0	2.0	2.0
Loveland (1961)	26	13	13	20.0	4.0	48.0	0.0	44.0	44.0	40.0	12.0	32.0	44.0
Neiger, Slemon, and Quirk (1962)	80	60	20	10.0	58.75	52.5	1.25	7.5	51.25	7.5	0.0	8.75	1.25
Neiger, Slemon, and Quirk (1962)	40(P)	20	20	75.0	62.5	90.0	12.5	65.0	67.5	15.0	2.5	15.0	10.0
Piotrowski (1937)	15	6	9	13.33	20.0	53.33	0.0	0.0	26.67	33.33	0.0	6.67	0.0
Ross (1941a)	15(P)	8	7	86.67	60.0	53.33	13.33	26.67	33.33	20.00	6.67	33.33	33.33
Ross (1941b)	174	115	59	54.72	23.37	52.44	1.71	11.40	43.89	5.70	1.14	15.39	3.42

[a] A dash (—) indicates that these data were not available.
[b] Sample contains all psychotic patients.
[c] N = 77 (Evans and Marmorston, 1964).

brain-damaged samples, or which appear so infrequently in the nonbrain-damaged samples while occuring with greater frequency in the brain-damaged groups, as to be considered clearly pathognomic of organicity. However, we shall postpone discussion of the comparative incidence of these signs until we discuss validity.

Relationship to R

The relationship of the sum of the organic signs to R, and the relationship of any single organic sign to R, is an important variable to study. This is particularly the case in that each of the major systems of signs includes a reduction in R as one of its signs. Despite this, information about the relationship of R to individual signs is sparse, and to total signs, is absent.

Evans and Marmorston (1964), using a cutoff point of 12 responses as an organic sign, found that this sign shared 10% variance with the Aita sign Iflx. It did not share as much variance with any of the other Aita signs, or any of the Piotrowski signs which were examined. All of the Piotrowski signs were compared with R except for *AP, Cn,* and *M*. All of the Aita signs were compared with R except for *Catas, Edg, IC,* and *CvrCds.*

Hughes (1950), in the course of his factor analysis of a large number of signs, compared R < 15, which is both a Piotrowski and a Hughes sign, and R < 25, which is a Hughes sign, with all of the other Piotrowski and Hughes signs. Considering the Piotrowski signs first, the correlation between R and the other signs exceeded .30 for *T* (.33), *M* (.45), *F%* (.34), and *AP* (.33). The results were less good when the Hughes signs were compared. First, as might be expected, R < 15 and R < 25 correlate .92. R < 15 correlated above .30 with M ≤ 1 (.45), FM > M (− .37), FC ≤ 1 (.92), automatic phrases (.33), and confused succession (− .60). R < 25 correlates more than .30 with M ≤ 1 (.48), FC ≤ 1 (.77), perserveration (.30), impotence (.37), perplexity (.34), automatic phrases (.60), and contamination (.30). However, the correlations were all performed by means of the tetrachoric method, and considering the small number of *S*s and the probable one-sided split in the distribution of the presence or absence of most of the signs, the use of the tetrachoric correlation is questionable.

The indications from these very limited findings are that the individual Piotrowski signs may not be too strongly related to R, while at least some of the Hughes signs are. There is no information on the Dörken and Kral signs, and there is no information for any of the systems as a whole.

VALIDITY

The great majority of the validity studies done with the Rorschach organic signs can be classified as criterion-related validity studies. There have been a small number of construct-validity studies reported, and these will be discussed in a separate section following a review of the criterion-related studies.

Criterion-Related Validity

Studies classifiable as criterion validity all follow the same basic paradigm:

A group of organic patients and a group of nonorganic patients are selected, with varying degrees of specificity of diagnosis and adequacy of classification. The Rorschach is administered to all patients in both groups, and the numbers of *S*s exceeding the cutoff point for organicity is counted for both groups. This is a paradigm which is more closely related to a concurrent than a predictive model, and, with the use of relatively pure groups of patients, is one whose relevance for clinical practice remains to be demonstrated.

The criterion-related validity studies can also be divided into those studies which focus on the validity of individual signs and those studies which concern themselves with the validity of systems. These two types of studies will be treated in separate sections. In many cases, studies will be discussed under a classification other than that which would have been intended by the author. Where adequate data were included in the report, reanalysis was done, so that many of the results reviewed below were not specifically included in the initial studies.

Validity of Individual Signs

The only systems in which sufficient data have been published to allow for an adequate test of the validity of individual signs in the system are those of Piotrowski and of Aita and his associates. Data comparing the incidence of the individual signs in these systems in brain-damaged and in control groups are presented in Table 11.4.

PIOTROWSKI'S SIGNS. Although a simple counting procedure is obviously not the most appropriate approach toward deciding which of the signs are effective and which are not, there are some clear patterns observable in Table 11.4. The great majority of signs significantly differentiate the brain-damaged and control groups about half the time, and fail in that differentiation about half the time. Since the probability of a differentiation by chance is 5 in 100, this is a good deal more than would be expected. The sign which is successful in the discrimination most often is *Imp,* and the signs which seem least effective are *M, P%,* and *Cn.* It is also clear that when the comparison is being made between an organic and a psychotic group, the differentiation is a great deal more difficult to make than if it is being made between an organic and a nonpsychotic control group.

Table 11.4 suggests that, with the possible exception of *M, P%,* and *Cn,* the individual Piotrowski signs are able to distinguish between a brain-

TABLE 11.4
Comparisons of Incidence of Signs in Brain-Damaged and Control Groups

	Sample Size						Piotrowski Signs									
	Brain-Damaged			Control												
Study	*N*	*M*	*F*	*N*	*M*	*F*	*R*	*T*	*M*	*Cn*	*F%*	*P%*	*Rpt*	*Imp*	*Plx*	*AP*
Aita, Reitan, and Ruth (1947)	60	60	0	100	100	0	—[a]	—	—	NS[b]	—	—	NS	Sig[c]	Sig	Sig
Brackbill and Fine (1956)	28	28	0	36(P)[d]	28	0	Sig	NS	NS	NS	NS	NS	NS	NS	NS	NS
Brackbill and Fine (1956)	28	28	0	24(P)	28	0	NS	NS	NS	Sig	NS	NS	Sig	NS	Sig	Sig
Evans and Marmorston (1964)	139	92	47	136	108	28	Sig[e]	Sig	Sig[e]	—	Sig	Sig	Sig	Sig	Sig	—
Hertz and Loehrke (1954)	50	50	0	50(P)	50	0	NS	NS	NS	NS	NS	NS	NS	Sig	Sig	Sig
Hertz and Loehrke (1954)	50	50	0	50	50	0	Sig	Sig	NS	NS	Sig	Sig	Sig	Sig	Sig	Sig
Loveland (1961)	26	13	13	26	13	13	NS	NS	NS	NS	NS	NS	NS	NS	NS	NS
Neiger, Slemon, and Quirk (1962)	20	20	0	40(P)	20	20	NS	Sig	NS	NS	NS	NS	Sig	NS	NS	NS
Neiger, Slemon, and Quirk (1962)	20	20	0	80	60	20	Sig	Sig	Sig	Sig	Sig	NS	Sig	NS	Sig	Sig
Piotrowski (1937)	18	12	6	15	6	9	Sig	Sig	NS	Sig	Sig	NS	Sig	Sig	NS	Sig
Reitan (1954)	18[f]	18	0	18	18	0	—	—	—	NS	—	—	NS	Sig	NS	NS
Reitan (1954)	18	18	0	18	18	0	—	—	—	NS	—	—	NS	Sig	NS	NS
Reitan (1955a)	23[g]	23	0	23	23	0	NS	NS	NS	NS	NS	NS	NS	NS	NS	NS
Reitan (1955a)	23	23	0	23	23	0	Sig	NS	NS	NS	NS	NS	NS	Sig	NS	NS
Reitan (1955b)	50	35	15	50	35	15	NS	Sig	NS	NS	Sig	NS	Sig	Sig	Sig	Sig
Ross (1941b)	47	33	14	189	123	66	NS	NS	NS	Sig	Sig	NS	Sig	Sig	Sig	NS

TABLE 11.4 (cont.)

	Sample Size						Aita et al. Signs								
	Brain-Damaged			Control											
Study	*N*	*M*	*F*	*N*	*M*	*F*	*IFlx*	*ActObj*	*CR*	*Def*	*Catas*	*Edg*	*IC*	*CvrCds*	*WR*
Aita, Reitan, and Ruth (1947)	60	60	0	100	100	0	Sig	Sig	Sig	Sig	Sig	Sig	Sig	Sig	NS
Evans and Marmorston (1964)	139	92	47	136	108	28	Sig	Sig	Sig	Sig	NS	—	—	—	Sig
Reitan (1954)	18[f]	18	0	18	18	0	Sig	Sig	Sig	Sig	Sig	Sig	Sig	NS	NS
Reitan (1954)	18	18	0	18	18	0	Sig	Sig	Sig	Sig	Sig	Sig	NS	NS	NS
Reitan (1955a)	23[g]	23	0	23	23	0	NS	NS	NS	NS	NS	NS	NS	NS	NS
Reitan (1955a)	23	23	0	23	23	0	NS	NS	Sig	Sig	Sig	NS	NS	NS	NS
Reitan (1955b)	50	35	15	50	35	15	Sig	NS	Sig	Sig	Sig	NS	NS	NS	Sig

[a] Insufficient information.
[b] $P > .05$.
[c] $P \leq .05$.
[d] Sample contains all psychotic patients.
[e] N = 82 and 77 (Evans and Marmorston, 1963a).
[f] Sample contains aphasic patients.
[g] Sample contains postconcussion patients.

damaged and a nonpsychotic group, and that no single sign is consistently able to distinguish between a brain-damaged and a psychotic group.

AITA ET AL. SIGNS. The Aita signs, too, show the ability to make the discrimination between a brain-damaged and a nonpsychotic control group. As can be seen from an inspection of Table 11.4, the majority of the signs can make this discrimination a majority of the time. Exceptions are with *IC, CvrCds,* and *WR,* which often fail in the discrimination. Unfortunately, there have been no comparisons between brain-damaged and psychotic groups using the Aita signs, so it is not clear whether they would be capable of making this more difficult but clinically relevant discrimination.

Validity of Systems

There is a great deal of information available relevant to the validity of the Piotrowski signs, a reasonable amount of information about the validity of the Hughes signs, much less on the Dörken and Kral signs, and almost no information—other than that provided by the initial studies—concerning any of the other systems. In this section we shall deal with the Piotrowski signs, the Hughes signs, and the Dörken and Kral signs in turn, and then devote a short section to the assorted information concerning the other systems.

The tables which summarize the information about the validity of the systems indicate the composition and size of the organic groups and the comparison groups. They also record the number of false positives and the number of false negatives in each study. These terms are used here to denote the percentage of people incorrectly diagnosed as organic (false positives) and the percentage of people incorrectly diagnosed as nonorganic (false negatives). There is also a column which records the call rate, or the percentage of patients in the study who were diagnosed as organic. The next-to-last column in the tables records the base-rate accuracy, which indicates the percentage of diagnoses which would have been correct if all of the patients were classified in the majority category. In some cases, this would have meant that all patients were diagnosed organic, and, in some cases that all were diagnosed nonorganic, and reference to the two sample-size columns will indicate which of the two decisions would have been made. It should be emphasized that the base rate refers to the sample rather than the population, for which it would be difficult to determine an accurate base rate. The final column indicates the system's accuracy, or the percentage of patients diagnosed correctly. For an evaluation of the system, the accuracy of the system might be compared with the accuracy of the base rate. However, this can be somewhat misleading, since it makes the assumption that diagnoses of organic and of nonorganic are equally important, and so the absolute number of correct decisions are to be maximized. Depending upon the population, one might seek to maximize either the number of organics who are detected or the number of nonorganics who are detected. For a more balanced evaluation, therefore, it is also necessary to attend to the false-positives and false-negatives columns.

PIOTROWSKI SIGNS. Information regarding the efficacy of the Piotrowski signs in separating organic groups from various comparison groups are recorded in Table 11.5. Although there is a column recording the number of false negatives, and the Piotrowski signs have often been criticized for producing too many false negatives, it should be remembered that technically the Piotrowski system does not produce any false negatives, because it never arrives at a definitive diagnosis of nonorganicity!

Again, it is unwise to assess the validity of a system by counting the number of times in which it has been successful and the number of times in which it has been unsuccessful. No study has been performed which can be characterized as a definitive one. However, some information of interest may be produced by noting patterns within the table. There are a number of cases in which the accuracy of the signs exceeds the accuracy of the base rates. This is particularly true in situations where the base rates are around 50–50. As the distribution between the groups becomes more extreme in either direction, the ability of the signs to equal the base rates in accuracy becomes more difficult. This principle is generally true with any psychometric technique, as compared with base rates. The call rate for Piotrowski's signs is generally low, and, as a result, there are a number of false negatives, or of organics who are not detected by this system. However, there are very few instances where the number of false positives is excessive, except where the organic group is being compared with a schizophrenic group, and, as Brackbill and Fine (1956) demonstrate, only where the comparison is with a process schizophrenic group rather than a reactive schizophrenic group.

It would appear as though the Piotrowski signs are sensitive to a general deteriorative process which can be found in both an organic group and a chronic schizophrenic group, and will have a good deal of difficulty discriminating between those populations. However, if one excludes process schizophrenics from the comparison group, the presence of five or more Piotrowski signs provides a fairly safe indication of the presence of an impairment which has its origin in cortical dysfunction. The clinical use of the Piotrowski signs could be recommended if one has evidence which contraindicates the presence of chronic schizophrenia, and if one is careful to interpret a positive result but to suspend judgment in the case of a negative result.

HUGHES SIGNS. The data relevant to the evaluation of the efficacy of the Hughes signs are presented in Table 11.6. Hughes indicates the possibility of the use of a cutoff point of + 7 or of + 3, with the former being a *definite* indication of organicity, and the latter being a *possible* indication of organicity. Table 11.6 records separately the efficacy of each of these cutoff points.

The data recorded by Hughes in his initial study are quite promising, but the cross-validation work has not substantiated the promise offered in the intial study. This is a finding which is often true. It is unusual, outside of the initial Hughes study, for the accuracy of the Hughes signs to be

TABLE 11.5
Efficacy of Piotrowski Signs in the Diagnosis of Organicity

Study	*Organic Group*	Sample Size *N*	*M*	*F*	*Comparison Group*
Brackbill and Fine (1956)	Mixed	28	28	0	Process Schizophrenia
Brackbill and Fine (1956)	Mixed	28	28	0	Reactive Schizophrenia
Brackbill and Fine (1956)	Mixed	28	28	0	Schizophrenia
Dörken and Kral (1952)	Mixed	70	—	—	Psychosis
Dörken and Kral (1952)	Mixed	70	—	—	Normal and Neurosis
Dörken and Kral (1952)	Mixed	70	—	—	Mixed
Eckhardt (1961)	Mixed	71	—	—	Psychosis
Eckhardt (1961)	Mixed	71	—	—	Normal and Neurosis
Eckhardt (1961)	Mixed	71	—	—	Mixed
Fisher, Gonda, and Little (1955)	Mixed	84	84	0	Nonorganic Neurological Complaint
Gottlieb and Parsons (1960)	Mixed	20	10	10	Nonorganic Neurological Referral
Hertz and Loehrke (1954)	Posttraumatic Encephalopathy	50	50	0	Paranoid Schizophrenia
Hertz and Loehrke (1954)	Posttraumatic Encephalopathy	50	50	0	Anxiety Neurosis
Hertz and Loehrke (1954)	Posttraumatic Encephalopathy	100	100	0	Mixed
Koff (1946)	Cerebral Concussion	75	75	0	Gross Stress Reaction
Loveland (1961)	Epilepsy	26	13	13	Normal
Neiger, Slemon, and Quirk (1962)	Epilepsy	20	20	0	Schizophrenia
Neiger, Slemon, and Quirk (1962)	Epilepsy	20	20	0	Normal
Neiger, Slemon, and Quirk (1962)	Epilepsy	20	20	0	Mixed
Piotrowski (1937)	Mixed	18	12	6	Mixed
Ross (1941b)	Mixed	47	33	14	Mixed

[a] Percentage of patients diagnosed as organic.
[b] Accuracy if all patients were diagnosed in the majority category (see sample-size column).
[c] Percentage of patients diagnosed correctly.
[d] All numerical scores are percentages.

substantially better than the base-rate accuracy. In general, the pattern of the Hughes signs follows the pattern of the Piotrowski signs, in that the call rate is low, the number of false positives is not excessive, but the number of false negatives is quite large. In comparing the two cutoff points suggested by Hughes, it is clear that the cutoff point of + 7 is far superior to the cutoff point of + 3, in that it consistently produces a great many fewer false positives at the expense of very few additional false negatives, and is almost always more accurate in terms of percentage of total correct decisions made.

TABLE 11.5 (cont.)

Sample Size							
N	*M*	*F*	*False Positives*	*False Negatives*	*Call Rate*[a]	*Base-Rate Accuracy*[b]	*Signs Accuracy*[c]
36	36	0	56.5[d]	43.9	35.9	56.2	51.6
24	24	0	16.7	45.0	23.1	53.8	61.5
60	60	0	60.0	28.6	28.4	68.2	62.5
30	—	—	25.5	66.0	47.0	70.0	53.0
30	—	—	0.0	53.8	35.0	70.0	65.0
60	—	—	20.0	50.0	36.2	53.8	63.8
328	—	—	81.0	17.1	36.8	82.2	59.4
279	—	—	46.2	14.4	14.9	79.7	80.9
607	—	—	83.6	8.5	25.2	89.5	72.6
34	34	0	5.9	61.9	28.8	71.2	54.2
20	10	10	0.0	35.5	22.5	50.0	72.5
50	50	0	23.5	44.6	17.0	50.0	59.0
50	50	0	0.0	42.5	13.0	50.0	63.0
100	50	0	23.5	27.8	11.3	66.7	72.7
110	110	0	23.6	7.3	48.1	59.5	84.9
26	13	13	28.6	41.7	28.0	50.0	62.0
40	20	20	54.5	18.5	55.0	66.7	61.7
80	60	20	11.8	6.0	17.0	80.0	93.0
120	80	40	57.1	4.8	25.0	85.7	82.1
15	6	9	0.0	6.3	51.5	54.5	97.0
189	123	66	35.5	13.2	13.1	84.3	83.9

In studies which have used both the Piotrowski and the Hughes signs (Hertz and Loehrke, 1954; Fisher, Gonda, and Little, 1955), the Piotrowski signs seem to have slightly the better of it. They are more accurate, produce fewer false positives and also fewer false negatives. The difference is not great, but is consistently on the side of the Piotrowski signs. The great overlap between the two sets of signs probably accounts for the closeness in performance, and the additional signs introduced by Hughes in non-cross-validated work do not contribute a great deal to the diagnostic procedure.

TABLE 11.6
Efficacy of the Hughes Signs and Dörken and Kral Signs in the Diagnosis of Organicity

Study	*System*	*Organic Group*	Sample Size *N*	*M*	*F*	*Comparison Group*
Diers and Brown (1951)	Hughes (7)[d]	Multiple Sclerosis	25	25	0	Mixed
	Hughes (3)[f]	Multiple Sclerosis	25	25	0	Mixed
Fisher, Gonda, and Little (1955)	Hughes (7)	Mixed	84	84	0	Nonorganic Neurological Complaint
Hertz and Loehrke (1954)	Hughes (7)	Posttraumatic Encephalopathy	50	50	0	Paranoid Schizophrenia
	Hughes (3)	Posttraumatic Encephalopathy	50	50	0	Paranoid Schizophrenia
	Hughes (7)	Posttraumatic Encephalopathy	50	50	0	Anxiety Neurosis
	Hughes (3)	Posttraumatic Encephalopathy	50	50	0	Anxiety Neurosis
	Hughes (7)	Posttraumatic Encephalopathy	50	50	0	Mixed
	Hughes (3)	Posttraumatic Encephalopathy	50	50	0	Mixed
Hughes (1950)	Hughes (7)	Mixed	50	—	—	Schizophrenia
	Hughes (3)	Mixed	50	—	—	Schizophrenia
	Hughes (7)	Mixed	50	—	—	Normal and Neurosis
	Hughes (3)	Mixed	50	—	—	Normal and Neurosis
	Hughes (7)	Mixed	50	—	—	Mixed
	Hughes (3)	Mixed	50	—	—	Mixed
Dörken and Kral (1952)	Dörken and Kral	Mixed	70	—	—	Psychosis
	Dörken and Kral	Mixed	70	—	—	Normal and Neurosis
	Dörken and Kral	Mixed	70	—	—	Mixed
Fisher, Gonda, and Little (1955)	Dörken and Kral	Mixed	84	84	0	Nonorganic Neurological Complaint

[a] Percentage of patients diagnosed as organic.
[b] Accuracy if all patients were diagnosed in the majority category (see sample-size column).
[c] Percentage of patients diagnosed correctly.
[d] Cutoff point of +7.
[e] All numerical scores are percentages.
[f] Cutoff point of +3.

Dörken and Kral Signs. Data relevant to the evaluation of the Dörken and Kral signs are also presented in Table 11.6. Unfortunately, there has only been one study (Fisher, Gonda, and Little, 1955) which reported data about the Dörken and Kral system other than the initial study. The initial study was not cross validated, and so the promising results reported must be regarded with some reservation.

TABLE 11.6 (cont.)

Sample Size							
N	*M*	*F*	*False Positives*	*False Negatives*	*Call Rate*[a]	*Base-Rate Accuracy*[b]	*Signs Accuracy*[c]
11	11	0	25.0[e]	68.8	11.1	69.4	36.1
11	11	0	50.0	88.9	50.0	69.4	30.6
34	34	0	8.8	63.1	28.8	71.2	52.5
50	50	0	0.0	48.5	3.0	50.0	53.0
50	50	0	36.7	44.3	30.0	50.0	58.0
50	50	0	0.0	48.5	3.0	50.0	53.0
50	50	0	36.7	44.3	30.0	50.0	58.0
100	100	0	0.0	32.0	2.0	66.7	68.7
100	100	0	53.7	28.4	27.3	66.7	64.7
68	—	—	2.4	11.8	35.6	57.6	91.5
68	—	—	28.4	3.9	56.8	57.6	82.2
100	—	—	0.0	8.6	28.1	66.7	93.8
100	—	—	20.0	2.3	41.1	66.7	90.4
164	—	—	2.4	5.2	19.6	76.6	95.3
164	—	—	39.2	1.5	36.9	76.6	84.6
30	—	—	12.2	19.2	74.0	70.0	86.0
30	—	—	1.5	14.7	66.0	70.0	94.0
60	—	—	16.7	7.1	57.8	53.8	88.5
34	34	0	26.3	57.9	83.9	71.2	68.6

The Fisher, Gonda, and Little (1955) study, which compared all three systems, seems to favor the Piotrowski system and to place the Dörken and Kral system in the least effective role. This is true even though the Dörken and Kral system had the highest percentage of accuracy of the three systems studied. This accuracy was due to the preponderance of organics in the sample, and the tendency of the Dörken and Kral system to produce a diagnosis of organicity. Even in their initial study, it is clear that the Dörken and Kral system has a much higher call rate than either the Piotrowski or the Hughes system, and this call rate produces a great many more false positives without appreciably reducing the number of false negatives. While it would be of interest for this system to be studied further, the data that are available indicate that its tendency to diagnose organic too often would contraindicate its use in most clinical settings.

OTHER SYSTEMS. Neither the systems of Aita et al. or Ross and Ross provide a cutoff point, and so it is impossible to evaluate them in the same manner as we have evaluated the Piotrowski, Hughes, and Dörken and Kral systems.

Evans and Marmorston have presented a series of studies, but there has been a great deal of overlap in the patients employed in each of their studies, and no researchers other than themselves have used their cutoff point. The cutoff point, in fact, has varied greatly, depending upon the particular data used. At its best—where chance features of the distribution are maximized—the Evans and Marmorston signs do not seem to improve greatly on the success enjoyed by the Piotrowski signs. It would be of interest if these signs were to be employed by other investigators and compared directly with the other systems, and if stable cutoff points could be suggested. However, in the absence of such information, these signs do not seem ready for adoption in a clinical setting.

Hertz and Loehrke devised a system of configurations, but these, too, have not been used in any subsequent research. As has been indicated previously, this is a highly complicated system, and in the initial study, which maximized chance features of the distribution, it did not show sufficient superiority to the Piotrowski signs to justify its adoption for clinical use.

Construct Validity

There have been scattered studies which can appropriately be classified under the rubric of construct validity. These include studies of (1) pre-post changes, (2) relationships with intelligence, (3) relationships with age, (4) item analyses of the systems, and (5) miscellaneous studies.

Pre-Post Changes

The basic design of a pre-post study involves the administration of the Rorschach, the introduction of some treatment, and a second administration of the Rorschach. Differences in the incidence of signs between the two administrations are related to the impact of the treatment. A control group is usually included to rule out the possibility that changes might occur in the absence of a treatment.

Allison and Allison (1954) used the Dörken and Kral signs in a study of the effect of transorbital lobotomies. Sixteen psychotic patients were selected, and matched in eight pairs on a large number of relevant variables. The Rorschach was administered one month prior to the lobotomy and one month following the lobotomy. The changes in the number of Dörken and Kral signs did not reach statistical significance, but did tend to show an increase in the protocols of the operated group. Part of the difficulty in having the signs register the induced cortical damage caused by the lobotomy might lie in the very small sample size, which drastically reduced the power of the statistical procedures. Another problem might lie in the fact that seven of the eight pairs of patients had received extensive electroshock therapy, and so there might have been an already existent organic syndrome, upon which the operation was superimposed. Finally, the use of chronic hospitalized psychotic patients suggests that the preoperation protocols may already have had an organic component, so that it would be difficult for additional organicity to be registered.

Evans and Marmorston (1963b) studied the effects of premarin therapy by randomly dividing groups of cerebral thrombosis and myocardial infarction patients and administering premarin, an estrogen compound used to retard atherosclerosis, to half and a placebo to half. The Rorschach was readministered after a 6-to-16 month interval, during which time the patient had received either premarin or the placebo regularly. The protocols were scored on the Evans and Marmorston 46-item checklist. Greater change occurred in the protocols of the premarin patients than in the placebo patients in both the cerebral thrombosis and the myocardial infarction groups.

In a second study, Evans and Marmorston (1965) employed the same design, but used their 26-item scale in a replication of the previous study. In this study there were no significant differences between the premarin and the placebo groups, although the difference in the cerebral thrombosis group approached significance. When data from the two studies were combined, the premarin patients showed greater change than the placebo patients in the cerebral thrombosis group and in the two groups combined, but not in the myocardial infarction group taken alone.

Grauer (1953) selected 18 improved paranoid schizophrenics and 18 unimproved paranoid schizophrenics, and compared their Rorschach protocols. There were no differences in Piotrowski signs between the groups. Grauer had expected a difference on the grounds that there would be an organic component in those paranoid schizophrenics who did not show improvement. Aside from the questionable nature of this hypothesis, it is of interest to note that the criterion for improvement was discharge from the hospital, and seven of the 18 patients who were classified as improved had had previous episodes of hospitalization.

The most clear-cut and appropriate usage of the organic signs in a pre-post construct-validity design has been in the Evans and Marmorston studies, and in those studies this technique has shown some promise. Where the hypothesis under investigation is questionable, or the *S*s selected are such as to attenuate possible results, the findings have been less positive.

Relationships with Intelligence

Diers and Brown (1951) investigated the relationship of intelligence to the Hughes signs in the protocols of 15 high-intelligence multiple sclerotics, 10 low-intelligence mutiple sclerotics, and 11 low-intelligence controls. Not one of the high-intelligence multiple sclerotics received a Hughes score over + 7 and 14 of the 15 received scores under + 3. Most of the low-intelligence patients, whether they were multiple sclerotics or controls, received scores between + 3 and + 6, indicating possible organicity, and there were no differences in the distribution of scores btween those two groups. Some question may be raised about whether or not the multiple sclerotics, in fact, had cortical involvement, because insufficient information is given about their symptomatology. However, a correlation between the Hughes signs and intelligence was .46 ($p < .01$), and this indicates that there is a clear relationship between the two variables, and that it is more likely that a person of low intelligence will receive a Hughes score in the organic range than a person of high intelligence.

Evans and Marmorston (1963a) correlated their 46-item checklist with a number of additional test scores. The correlation of their checklist with WAIS vocabulary score was .39 ($p < .001$), and with a modified Goodenough scoring of the Draw-A-Person was − .45 ($p < .001$). These findings, too, support the negative relationship between organic signs and intelligence.

Saslow and Shipman (1957) correlated the Dörken and Kral signs with the Wechsler–Bellevue I.Q. in a group of 108 nonorganic women, and found a correlation of .52 ($p < .01$). Since the Dörken and Kral signs are directionally different from the Hughes and the Evans and Marmorston signs, this finding, too, supports the relationship between low intelligence and high incidence of organic indicants. In a personal communication, Saslow (1965) has reported that the correlation between Full Scale WISC I.Q. at age 11 and Dörken and Kral Rorschach signs at age 17 was above .50.

Ross and Ross (1944) correlated their disability rating with scores on the Binet vocabulary scale and a digit-span task, and found a significant negative correlation in both cases.

All the information which has been reported on the relationship between the organic signs and intelligence has consistently indicated significant negative correlation. It is clear that any study which fails to match groups on intelligence is introducing a gross artifact. It also seems reasonable that norms should be scaled in relationship to intelligence, so that varying cutoff points would be operative at varying levels of intelligence.

Relationships with Age

Evans and Marmorston (1963b), in the course of the premarin studies, related their 46-item checklist to age and found there was no significant correlation. However, in their 1964 study they found that the signs on their 10-item list were more prevalent in the records of their older *S*s (60–80) than their younger *S*s (40–59).

Piotrowski (1940) reports on the incidence of his signs as a function of age. Although there is not a great deal of information given about the nature of the *S*s who were tested, he reports that there is a steady increase with age in the percentage of patients tested who had five or more signs in their records. This range is from 42% in the below-12 age group to 89% in the above-50 age group.

There is not very much information available on the relationship of age to organic signs. Chesrow, Woseika, and Reinitz (1949), on the basis of questionable data, conclude that the Piotrowski signs are not related to normal aging, and Ames, Learned, Metraux, and Walker (1954) disagree without citing any specific data. While more information is clearly needed, the little evidence that is available does suggest that the incidence of signs increases in old age, and that investigators would be wise to provide matching on age as well as intelligence.

Results of Item Analyses

Hughes (1950) included all the Piotrowski signs in a factor analysis and constructed his system on the basis of the results of that computation. All of the Piotrowski signs except *T, P,* and *F%* loaded on the organic factor; the one exception, *p,* was used regardless of R, which is contrary to Piotrowski's scoring recommendation. Five of the signs, *M, Rpt, Imp, Plx,* and *AP,* had their highest loading on the organic factor, and these were the only signs in the Hughes system to receive a weight of more than 1. Weights were assigned on the basis of strength of factor loading.

Ross and Ross (1944) included some of the Piotrowski signs in an item analysis which divided a large group of signs into a number of categories, one of which represented signs which appeared in organic protocols, but not in neurotic or normal protocols. All of the Piotrowski signs which were included in this study (*Rpt, P%, Imp, Plx, Cn,* and *AP*), were placed in this organic differentiating category.

The item analyses which have been performed, therefore, agree that most of the individual Piotrowski signs do cluster in the records of patients with impairments due to organic dysfunction.

Miscellaneous Studies

Evans and Marmorston (1963a) are the only investigators to report a correlation between a Rorschach system and some other psychological approach to the measurement of organicity. They found that their 46-item list correlated significantly ($p < .001$) with Raven's Colored Progressive Matrices (.42), Wells and Ruesch's Proverbs (.52), and the Olin–Reznikoff Modification of the Pascall–Suttell scoring of the Bender–Gestalt (.41).

Evans and Marmorston (1964) also report that there are differences on their 10-item checklist between Negroes and Whites, with Negro cerebral thrombosis patients receiving higher scores than White cerebral thrombosis patients; this led them to introduce a correction for race into their scoring system. There is some question, however, as to whether this racial difference would have been maintained if there had been adequate control for other factors, such as age, education, and intelligence. The racial variable might have to be considered, but the evidence concerning this variable is not unequivocal.

Birch and Diller (1959) distinguish between two types of lesions which may result from anatomic damage to the brain. One type, the subtractive lesion, produces no active interference with cerebral functioning, and the amount of loss is proportionate to the amount of tissue destroyed, with organicity not a necessary sequel to the lesion. The second type, an active and additive lesion, produces effects beyond those of tissue loss, and interferes with continued functioning of intact tissue. They separated two groups of patients, one of which had subtractive lesions, and found that the Piotrowski signs were effective in diagnosing patients with the active lesions, but not in the diagnosis of patients with subtractive lesions. The correlation between the number of Piotrowski signs in a record and the number of medical signs of additive disturbance was .77. However, since Birch and Diller do not give any information about either the locus or the extent of the anatomic injuries in their two groups, the results are somewhat equivocal about their theory. The study does show that the Piotrowski signs are more sensitive in more serious disturbances, and that the presence of a positive indication with the Piotrowski signs is associated with organicity, while the absence of such signs in the protocol does not mean the absence of organicity.

Nadel (1938) compared patients with damage to the frontal lobes with patients with brain damage not affecting the frontal lobes and found that the Piotrowski signs were present for two-thirds of patients with frontal-lobe injury and for no patients with nonfrontal-lobe injury. However, there is an indication that the length of illness was almost twice as long in the patients with frontal-lobe injury, and so the interpretation of this study in terms of the locus of injury is somewhat equivocal.

These miscellaneous studies are each unique in their concern and equivocal in their findings, so that no consistent conclusions can be drawn.

OVERALL EVALUATION

In a review of some psychological tests of brain damage written some years back, Yates (1954), in summarizing the material concerning the Rorschach, concluded:

"That the Rorschach offers distinct promise in this problem cannot be denied; that it has been shown to be a satisfactory test of brain damage is open to question" (p. 732). Research in the intervening years has not contributed any data that would justify a modification of that statement. There is still a large question concerning the value of the Rorschach in the diagnosis of organicity, and there is every indication that the question will remain open as long as the same basic research design, with the same methodological problems, continues to be employed. An adequate definition of the nature of the organic involvement of the criterion group is usually absent, and the careful exclusion of organic involvement in the control group is ignored even more often. There have been no serious attempts to deal with the question of the reliability of any of the systems. The relationship of the signs to critical subject characteristics, such as age and intelligence, has barely been approached. The relationship of the signs to characteristics of the lesion has not been investigated. A great deal of research remains to be done in all of these areas if we are to reach a stage where a definitive statement can be made about the efficacy of the Rorschach in the diagnosis of organicity.

The relationship between the organic signs and neurological involvement follows a distribution described by J. Fisher (1959) as a "twisted-pear" distribution. This term is used to describe a situation in which the relationship between the predictor and the criterion assumes a nonlinear, heteroscedastic configuration. When this partial curvilinearity exists, the predictor becomes decreasingly predictive of the criterion as the scores increase from "poor" to "good." The measure is much more accurate at predicting maladaptive than adaptive behavior. This is clearly true of the relationship between the Rorschach signs and organicity, and has led to a series of studies in which the number of false positives are well within acceptable limits, but there are a great many false negatives produced.

Of all of the major systems, that of Dörken and Kral has the highest call rate, so it produces the most false positives. Unfortunately, it does this while continuing to produce the usual number of false negatives, and for this reason does not seem to be a particularly fruitful technique.

The Hughes signs are much more effective by using a cutoff point of +7 rather than +3. The Hughes signs overlap greatly with the Piotrowski signs, and it is difficult to see where the additional signs included in the Hughes list produce an appreciable advantage over the Piotrowski list.

The Piotrowski signs have been the subject of the most intensive research analysis and, despite a myriad of criticisms, seem to be the most effective of the existing techniques. As long as the other techniques are not clearly superior to the Piotrowski signs, and they are not, we would recommend that the Piotrowski signs be adopted, since it is possible to know more about the parameters of that set of signs than any of the less intensively investigated systems. The Piotrowski system clearly has some flaws, such as the inability to differentiate brain damage from chronic schizophrenia, but this is not likely to interfere with its use in a clinical setting, where it is unlikely that a chronic schizophrenic would be referred for a possible organic diagnosis. It is likely to be used most effectively on a neurological or medical ward where chronic schizophrenia is an unlikely diagnostic possibility, and the presence of a pathognomic number of Piotrowski signs should provide a clear indication of cortical dysfunction. A major drawback in its usefulness is the number of cases in which no diagnostic judgment could be reached. It is important to underline that *the absence of five Piotrowski signs does not contraindicate a diagnosis of brain damage,* but the presence of five or more, in a population where chronic schizophrenia is not a likely possibility, does provide a strong suggestion of the presence of brain damage. The areas in which the Piotrowski signs would be clinically effective are not clearly defined because of the lack of research on the relationship between the signs and age, intelligence, and lesion characteristics. The development of a carefully detailed scoring manual would help promote reliability of scoring and generalizability across research studies.

The most effective of the Piotrowski signs are those which might also be elicited by many other psychometric techniques. Perplexity, impotence, perserveration, and automatic phrases are manners of dealing with a stimulus situation rather than unique Rorschach variables, such as color denomination, reduced movement, and percent of popular responses, which are much less successful signs. Aside from substantiating the value of Piotrowski's signs as Rorchach indicators, research indicating the success of the several signs can be generalized to the interview situation and other tests, thereby providing general guidelines in the evaluation of the brain-damaged patient.

It is clear that if there is going to be any real progress in the area of organic signs, it will come about only through a clear departure from the past research paradigm. To begin with, it is necessary that investigators discard a unitary concept of brain damage and the consequent attempt to develop a general set of signs, for a more sophisticated delineation of organicity, and for multiple sets of relevant signs and norms. Reitan (1962) has suggested that "It is naive to hope that a single differential score index will reflect consistent findings over a range of variables as broad as that represented by brain damage of varying duration, type, localization, premorbid characteristics, and so on" (p. 427). The most appropriate approach to the development of meaningful organic signs would be through the isolation of groups of patients who were homogeneous as to lesion characteristics, and who were separated on critical dimensions such as age and intelligence. Adequate norms should be developed for these homogeneous subgroups of patients and cross-validated cutoff points suggested. These cutoff points should be based on comparisons, insofar as possible, with groups of patients having similar neurological complaints, but clear contraindications of brain damage. It is more important to minimize false positives in this neurological population than among chronic schizophrenics, because subsequent treatment is more likely to depend upon diagnosis. It also seems more feasible to reduce the number of false positives than to reduce the number of false negatives, judging from the performance of the typical sets of signs. The Rorschach, if it is included in an effective test battery, can make a substantial contribution despite the presence of a large number of false negatives. The reliability of sets of signs should be determined carefully and based on a detailed manual rather than the training of a limited number of judges, so that cross-investigator comparability of data could be ensured. Thus, if we are to reach the stage where we can say that the Rorschach offers something other than promise, and can justify our use of the instrument on the basis of clear research evidence, it would seem necessary to discard methodologically inadequate paradigms and to develop a completely fresh approach to the problem area.

Chapter 12

THERAPY PROGNOSIS

One of the most serious problems facing clinical psychology today is the fact that the need for therapeutic assistance exceeds by far the availability of trained professionals. In an attempt to alleviate this manpower shortage, more and more attention has been given in recent years to such approaches as the training of subprofessionals, more extensive use of consultation, as well as the institution of large-scale prevention programs. Although it is hoped that these approaches will help to alleviate the case-load pressures being experienced in hospitals and clinics, it is unlikely that they will ever eliminate the need for individual therapy. In the actual clinical situation, where the number of patients requiring treatment far exceeds the therapeutic time available, the need to estimate who is most likely to benefit from therapy will continue for some time to come. It is toward the goal of evaluating the prognostic use of the Rorschach that this chapter is directed.

DEFINITION OF PROGNOSIS

In describing an individual's prognosis for therapy, we often make the unwarranted assumption that therapy is both an effective and clearly delineated process. Thus, once we determine that the patient possesses certain characteristics—as determined by the Rorschach or any other means—it is assumed that the treatment we offer him is more likely to be successful. It is clear, however, that therapeutic approaches may differ widely, and that the effectiveness of each of these has to be determined empirically. From this point of view, we would appear to be somewhat premature in our attempts to develop and validate prognostic measures. The only justification one may offer for our current attempts at measuring prognosis for therapy is the very real and practical need which exists in the clinical situation. Clinicians find themselves in need of some measure of patient characteristics which, regardless of the specific therapeutic approach applied, indicate a greater likelihood of improvement. This approach to prognosis is admittedly global, and hopefully represents only an interim step in the refinement of our assessment procedures.[1]

Several writers have made an attempt to define those characteristics of the patient which would indicate a favorable prognosis for therapy. In particular, the concept "ego-strength" has been used by Barron (1953b), Klopfer, Kirkner, Wisham, and Baker (1951), as well as several others, to refer to the potential of the patient to benefit from treatment. Mindful of the fact that "ego-strength" is often fraught with surplus meaning, we may define this potential more operationally as the individual's ability to adjust to difficult situations. This adjustment ability clearly has its origins in previous learning and developmental experiences, although the specific nature of these antecedents may be unknown at present.

In many respects, the evaluation of prognosis for therapy is tantamount to an assessment of the individual's level of psychological adjustment. The underlying assumption here is that indications of the person's general coping ability can be useful in estimating the likelihood that he will benefit from therapy. Although it is difficult to take issue with validity of this assumption, it does lead one to the unfortunate conclusion that those who are capable of benefiting from most forms of therapy consist of individuals who need it the least. This is clearly implied in Strupp's (1962) review of therapy research, where he concludes:

> Patients considered good prognostic risks are described as young, attractive, well educated, members of the upper middle class, possessing a high degree of ego-strength, some anxiety which impels them to seek help, no seriously disabling neurotic symptoms, relative absence of deep characterological distortions and strong secondary gains, a willingness to talk about their difficulties, an ability to communicate well, some skill in the social-vocational area, and a value system relatively congruent with that of the therapist's (pp. 470–471).

In the process of defining the personality characteristics associated with prognosis for therapy, we find ourselves faced with the problem of establishing an adequate measure of improvement. Before noting some of the approaches which have been taken in the measurement of therapy outcome, it might be relevant to note that our present consideration of prognosis involves the prediction of improvement rather than continuation in therapy. Although the personality variables which predict continuation and improvement are undoubtedly related, the real concern in the clinical setting is not so much to estimate who is likely to remain in treatment as it is to predict who is more apt to *benefit* from it. Hence, research on prognosis as used

[1] With respect to behavior modification techniques, Goldfried and Pomeranz (1968) have taken an initial step in outlining the role of assessment in the selection of the appropriate treatment goals and therapeutic procedures.

in this chapter will involve only those attempts to utilize the *improvement* criterion.[2]

Although the research literature reflects the use of a wide variety of improvement measures, the three general approaches which have been taken in the measurement of success in therapy include (1) observations and ratings of change within the therapy session, as obtained by the therapist, the patient, or other professional staff, (2) data from various personality measures, and (3) behavioral data, such as specific behavioral changes (e.g., elimination of fears, compulsive rituals, etc.), as well as more general changes in daily living (e.g., job improvement, change in home life, etc.). In many respects the research on the prognostic use of the Rorschach represents a fair sample of therapy research in general, in that each of these approaches to measuring outcome has been utilized. Despite the practical difficulties in obtaining a representative sample of a patient's behavior, however, we would agree with Zax and Klein (1960), who have emphasized the need for outcome measures based on extratherapy behavioral changes. In the research to be described in this chapter, an attempt will be made to describe more fully the specific outcome criteria employed.

PROGNOSTIC INDICATORS

Most of the studies using the Rorschach to predict success in therapy have employed the Prognostic Rating Scale (PRS), devised by Klopfer and his associates (Klopfer, Kirkner, Wisham, and Baker, 1951). Several other writers have described the use of the Rorschach as a prognostic indicator of therapy outcome, but much of this work has been unsystematic. Following a brief description of some of these other prognostic attempts with the Rorschach (e.g., Harris and Christiansen, 1946), the chapter will outline and evaluate Klopfer's PRS.

Miscellaneous Prognostic Indices

Apart from the PRS, relatively little work has been done to devise Rorschach indicators to predict success in therapy. Most of the isolated studies which were carried out were done some years back, and typically yielded negative results. So as to give the reader some familiarity with this other work, some of the research will be briefly outlined.

The first published research paper on the use of the Rorschach to predict success in therapy was carried out by Harris and Christiansen (1946). From a larger pool of nonpsychiatric patients whose recovery from a physical disorder was prolonged, a group of 53 patients appearing to have "therapeu-

[2] The reader interested in the use of the Rorschach to predict continuation in therapy is referred to Affleck and Mednick (1959), Auld and Eron (1953), Gibby, Stotsky, Miller, and Hiler (1953), Gibby, Stotsky, Hiler, and Miller (1954), Kotkov and Meadow (1952, 1953), Rogers, Knauss, and Hammond (1951), and Taulbee (1958, 1961). One fairly consistent finding among several of these studies is that the single best indicator of continuation is total R.

tic possibilities" were selected for brief, psychoanalytically oriented therapy (5–45 sessions). At the end of treatment, each patient was rated by the training psychiatrist as to whether or not he had been a "good" or "poor" prognostic risk; the rating was based on a number of different factors including ward behavior, behavior in therapy, and a host of other unspecified variables. Although the authors did not find the two groups to differ significantly on any of the usual Rorschach scores, they suggest a weighting system based on the frequency with which certain scores seem to occur in each of the two groups. Thus, negative weights were given to those Rorschach scores which occurred more often in the "poor" group, and positive weights to those scores which occurred more often in the "good" group. The resulting prognostic signs were as follows: (1) +2 for M, FM, Anat-Sex, (2) +1.5 for FK, (3) +1 for FC, C, and C′, (4) −0.5 for F, (5) −1 for K, F−, and Reject, (6) −2 for c and FC, and (7) −2.5 for CF.

Although Harris and Christiansen did not cross validate their prognostic signs, further research on the method was followed up by Barron (1953a) and Rogers and Hammond (1953). Barron applied the Harris–Christiansen signs to a group of neurotic clinic patients who were seen in therapy once a week for a period of six months. Improvement was based on the difference between pre- and posttreatment ratings derived from case materials and presentations, information regarding the patients' subjective expression of well-being, the disappearance of symptoms, and general improvement in interpersonal relations; the judges who defined improvement showed an interrater reliability of .91. The relationship between the Harris–Christiansen Rorschach score and improvement in therapy was not nearly as high; in fact, the obtained correlation was .00.

A further attempt to cross validate Harris and Christiansen's signs was made by Rogers and Hammond (1953). They used a randomly selected group of patients who had been seen in therapy at a V.A. mental hygiene clinic for five sessions or more. The rating of improvement was carried out at the end of treatment by the therapist and the senior consulting psychiatrist; the authors do not specify the specific criteria used for these ratings. Like Barron, Rogers and Hammond failed to obtain a significant difference in the Harris–Christiansen signs between the improved and unimproved groups. They additionally compared the two groups on 99 different individual Rorschach signs (e.g., total R, D%, FC greater than CF, etc.), and also found negative results. Rogers and Hammond go on to suggest their own set of rules for predicting improvement. The method for applying these rules to given protocols is not at all clear, and since there has been no follow-up research carried out on this system, we shall not bother to describe them here.

Filmer-Bennett (1952) attempted to derive a set of prognostic signs which would predict improvement for both psychotic and nonpsychotic patients. Using a small group of patients who had undergone psychotherapy, shock therapy, or a combination of the two during their hospitalization, Filmer-Bennett classified them into improved and unimproved groups on the basis of their social and occupational adjustment subsequent to release from hospital. The two groups were compared on the basis of 60 signs, only nine of which differentiated at the .20 level or better. These nine signs, however, failed to hold up upon cross validation. Filmer-Bennett's conclusion that there still may be certain Rorschach patterns which can successfully predict outcome but are "discernible only to the highly skilled clinician" is what prompted him to carry out one more study in the area (Filmer-Bennett, 1955). In this second study he obtained the protocols of improved and unimproved cases, and presented them to 12 clinicians who were either ABEPP or who were qualified to take the diplomate exam. Their global judgments of prognosis failed to exceed chance expectancy.

Roberts (1954) selected 11 signs obtained from previous reports and scored the records of 51 primarily neurotic patients who had been seen in therapy at a V.A. mental hygiene clinic. The improvement criterion was comprised of the pooled ratings of an experienced psychologist, psychiatrist, and social worker who made their judgments on the basis of work adjustment, presence of symptoms, and pathological attitudes as revealed in the therapy notes; there was a high degree of reliability among the three raters. Of the 11 signs studied, a statistically significant difference was obtained only for one sign reflecting color responses. Specifically, she found that if [FC − (CF + C)] is equal to or greater than zero, then prognosis is poor. Inasmuch as this sign differentiated between the two groups at only the .02 level, the amount of overlap which probably existed would mitigate against its use as a prognostic indicator. To our knowledge, this sign has never been followed up in any subsequent research.

One final study might be noted before concluding this section. This was one conducted by Davids and Talmadge (1964), who were interested in constructing a measure to predict movement in psychiatric casework. The authors selected the mothers of 50 children who were about to enter a residential treatment center. These mothers were seen in weekly casework sessions for a period of a year, and then evaluated according to the Hunt–Kogan movement scale (Hunt and Kogan, 1950) in order to determine therapeutic progress. Twenty-eight mothers were placed in the movement group, and the remainder in the nonmovement category. On the basis of their findings, Davids and Talmadge devised a composite score, involving the weighting of different Rorschach scores according to the frequency of their occurrence in the two sets of records. Although their scoring system obviously distinguished between the movement and nonmovement groups (the system itself was *derived* from the patterning of scores in these records), no cross validation has as yet been reported in the literature. For a detailed description of the signs, the reader is referred to the original article.

In general, the scattered, hit-and-miss research carried out to devise new systems for predicting outcome in psychotherapy has not gotten very far. Some of the earlier reviews pointing to the inadequacy of the Rorschach as a prognostic indicator of success in therapy (e.g., Windle, 1952) used the above-mentioned studies as the sample of research in this area. The more recent reviews (e.g., Butler and Fiske, 1955; Fulkerson and Barry, 1961) which have evaluated the research on Klopfer's PRS, however, have been more optimistic. Hence, the remainder of this chapter focuses on a description and evaluation of the PRS as a means of predicting therapeutic success.

Klopfer's PRS Scoring Criteria

Before describing the actual scoring criteria for the PRS, it should be noted that the scale makes use of all scores appearing in a record, whether they are main scores appearing in the free association period, or additional scores given during the inquiry. Specific ratings are assigned to six different types of scores appearing in a record: human movement responses, animal movement responses, inanimate movement responses, shading responses, color responses, and form-level scores. The rationale for the scale, the interscorer reliability, and the overall summary score used will be described after the specific rating criteria have been outlined.[3] The criteria for the PRS—which are applied to protocols scored according to the system outlined by Klopfer, Ainsworth, Klopfer, and Holt (1954)—are as follows:

A. Human Movement Responses

Each M response is rated according to the three criteria below; then the *average* of these three ratings is assigned to that response.

Criteria	*Rating*
1. Amount of movement in space, described or implied	
a. Increasing living space (e.g., dancing, running, talking together, pointing)	1
b. Decreasing living space (e.g., bowing, kneeling, crying, crouching, and all Hd responses)	½
c. Merely alive (e.g., sleeping, lying down, sitting, balancing)	0
2. Freedom in seeing movement:	
a. Spontaneously sees action	1
b. Uses intermediary means of representing movement (e.g., picture of someone walking)	½
c. Reluctantly given in inquiry or follows from the logic of the situation	0
3. Cultural distance	
a. Real people of immediate cultural milieu	1
b. Culturally distant real people; culturally popular fantasy figures; and figures whose clothing or equipment practically conceals their human form (e.g., Ubangis, Mickey Mouse, Superman, diver in diving suit)	½
c. Unusual fantasy or culturally and/or historically extremely distant figures (e.g., Neanderthal men)	1

The average ratings of all the M responses are added algebraically, counting each M− response −1. The resulting raw score is converted into a weighted score by this table:

[3] Except for minor stylistic changes, the scoring criteria for the PRS are reprinted from the *Journal of Projective Techniques,* 1951, *15,* 426–428, by permission of the publisher and authors.

M Raw Score	*Weighted Score*
5–10.9	3
3–4.9 or 11–15.9	2
1–2.9 or 16–20.0	1
Less than 1 or more than 20.0	0
Less than 0 (any minus score)	−1

B. Animal Movement Responses

Each FM is rated according to the three criteria below and then the *average* of these three ratings is assigned to that response. The criteria parallel those which are used to rate M responses.

Criteria	*Rating*
1. Amount of movement in space	
a. Increasing living space (e.g., running, jumping, growling at each other)	1
b. Decreasing living space (e.g., crouching, stooping, bending over)	½
c. Merely alive (e.g., sleeping, lying down, sitting, standing)	0
2. Freedom in seeing movement	
a. Spontaneously sees action	1
b. Uses intermediary means of representing movement (e.g., picture of an animal flying or climbing, totem animal)	½
c. Reluctantly given in inquiry or follows only from the logic of the situation	0
3. Cultural distance	
a. Existing animals common to the culture (e.g., dog, bear, cat, crab, elephant, lion, spider, cat, monkey)	1
b. Existing rare animals, common extinct animals, or culturally popular fantasy animals (e.g., octopus, dinosaur, Mickey Mouse)	½
c. Unusual fantasy or culturally extremely distant animals (e.g., Pegasus, Push-me-pull-me, Cerberus, amoeba)	0

The average rating of all the FM responses are added algebraically, counting each FM− response −1. The resulting score is converted into a weighted score by this table:

FM Raw Score	*Weighted Score*
2 or more	1
1–1.9 or if raw score FM is twice raw score M or more	0
0–0.9	−1
Less than 0 (any minus score)	−2

C. Inanimate Movement Responses

Each m response is rated according to one of the criteria below.

Criteria	*Rating*
1. Natural and mechanical forces	
a. Counter gravity (e.g., explosion, rocket, mechanical motion, geyser, volcano)	1
b. Due to gravity (e.g., falling, rock poised precariously)	½

Criteria	*Rating*
2. Abstract forces	
a. Expressions projected onto inanimate objects (e.g., pumpkin with devilish expression)	1
b. Repulsion or attraction (e.g., this keeps two people apart or brings them together; this is the center from which all power emanates)	$\frac{1}{2}$
c. Dissipation (e.g., Card VIII, lower D, melting ice cream; Card IX, deteriorating mess)	0

The ratings of all the m responses are added algebraically, counting each Fm− as −1. The m raw score is then converted into a weighted score by this table:

m Raw Score	*Weighted Score*
3–5.9	2
1–2.9 or 6–10.0	1
0–0.9 or more than 10.0	0
Less than 0 (any minus score)	−1

D. Shading Responses

Each shading item is rated according to the weightings below. The individual ratings are added algebraically. The total thus obtained is multiplied by 3 and divided by the total number of shading entries. This is done regardless of whether these entries are ratings for single responses or for characteristics of the total record. This figure is then used as the total weighted score for shading responses.

Responses	*Rating*
Fc (warm, soft, or transparent)	1
FK	1
Fc denial	$\frac{1}{2}$
Fc (cold or hard)	$-\frac{1}{2}$
K, KF	0
Fc (shading used as color)	$-\frac{1}{2}$
Fk, kF, k	$-\frac{1}{2}$
cF	$-\frac{1}{2}$
Fc−	−1
FK−	−1
Fc (diseased organ)	−1
c	−1
Characteristics of total record:	
Shading evasion	$-\frac{1}{2}$
Shading insensitivity	−1

E. Color Responses

Each color item is rated according to the weightings below. The individual ratings are added algebraically. The total thus obtained is multiplied by 3 and divided by the total number of color ratings. The figure is then used as the total weighted score for color responses.

Responses	*Rating*
FC (color is important, essential and meaningful part of the concept)	1
CF (explosive or passive)	½
C_{des}	½
Color denial	½
C_{sym} (euphoric)	½
Unscorable color remarks expressing discomfort (e.g., Card II: that red doesn't mean anything)	½
F—C (forced, overeasy, bland)	0
F/C, C/F	0
C_{sym} (dysphoric)	−½
Color in diseased organ	−½
CF (explosive, but given without any sign of affect)	−½
FC−	−1
CF−	−1
C, C_n	−1
Color contamination	−1

F. Form Level

Each response is rated for form level in the usual manner. Then the *average* form-level rating is used as a weighted score except for the following modifications:

1. The occurrence of any "weakening" specifications anywhere in the record (i.e., specifications where 0.5 is subtracted from the form-level ratings of any response) reduces the weighted form-level rating for the *entire record* by 0.5.
2. The existence of discrepancies between the lowest form-level rating for any response in a record, provided it is a minus score, and the highest form-level rating for any response in the same record of at least 3.0, reduces the weighted form-level rating for the same record by 1.0.
3. These two may be cumulative in the same record. That is, where both occur in a record, 1.5 is subtracted from the average form-level rating.

Rationale Underlying the PRS

The underlying rationale for the six components of the PRS has been described in detail by Klopfer (1954). The reason for using certain scores is based on hypotheses about the interpretive significance of these scores, general clinical experience in using the test, and only some experimental evidence. Hence, Klopfer points out that human movement responses reflect the individual's inner stability and self-acceptance. Similarly, the quality and quantity of animal movement responses is said to be indicative of the manner in which the person handles his impulse expression. The type of inanimate movement responses is believed to reflect the individual's awareness of internal conflict. Klopfer additionally maintains that inasmuch as prognosis for therapy is related to an individual's acceptance of his need for affection, a certain emotional responsivity to the environment, and an adequate level of reality testing, the use of shading responses, color responses, and form-level rating, respectively, are important components in the PRS.

In reading Klopfer's detailed description of the rationale, it becomes evident that much of the thinking underlying the PRS is both speculative and vague. The speculative nature of the reasoning is evident in such statements as "...deficiencies in shading reactions have more serious implications for prognosis and adjustment than deficiencies in color reactions; the former seems to reflect serious disturbances in the *capacity* for warm interpersonal relations, while the latter appears to point toward disturbances in the *mechanics* of interpersonal relations" (Klopfer, 1954, p. 583). Klopfer's vagueness lies primarily in his attempt to delineate those characteristics which make for good "ego-strength." However speculative or vague the underlying assumptions may be, the validity and practical utility of the PRS depends, in the final analysis, on the empirical test of the measure itself.

Interscorer Reliability

An inspection of the scoring criteria for the PRS reveals that although certain mechanical procedures in the scoring are cumbersome, the criteria per se are relatively clear cut. One would expect little disagreement, for example, on the distinction between inanimate movement responses which are due to gravity (e.g., falling object), and those responses which reflect counter-gravity movement (e.g., rocket). The cumbrous aspect of the scoring involves the manner in which the ratings themselves are applied to the responses. In the case of human movement responses, for example, the procedure involves the following: (1) All human movement responses are rated on the basis of each of the three criteria, (2) the average of the three ratings for each response is computed, (3) the average ratings for all movement responses are then added algebraically, (4) the total rating arrived at for all movement responses is converted into the weighted score, and (5) the weighted movement score is finally added to the five other component weighted scores to form the final prognostic score. Apart from any error which might take place in the mathematical computation, however, it would seem that these are more likely to result in scorer fatigue than in unreliability!

The research evidence on the interscorer reliability of the PRS comes from only a few sources. Sheehan, Frederick, Rosevear, and Spiegelman (1954), using a sample of records scored by two judges, found an agreement of 71–88%. Adams and Cooper (1962) report that their reliability check between two judges yielded correlations which ranged from .93 to 1.00; these correlations reflect both the agreement between the computation of the final prognostic score and the scores assigned to each of the six component parts of the scale. Similarly, Endicott and Endicott (1963) report what may be considered a respectable interscorer reliability coefficient; they found that the final scores obtained by two independent raters correlated .86.

From the little research evidence available on interscorer reliability, it seems fairly clear that the PRS may be applied to a *scored* protocol with a good deal of agreement. The studies which would provide data on interscorer agreement, however, do not give any estimate of unreliability which might be involved in the initial scoring of the protocol. Thus, in order to obtain a more accurate picture of interscorer reliability, data are needed on the extent to which two or more scorers, given the same set of unscored protocols, are able to arrive at a similar PRS.

Summary Score

According to the original description of the scale by Klopfer et al. (1951), the final prognostic score may be arrived at by simply *totalling* the weighted scores assigned to each of the six component parts. With respect to the weightings themselves, it should be noted that while the particular weights described by Klopfer et al. had been based on clinical judgment, an empirical attempt at refining these weights by means of multiple regression techniques did not at all improve the predictive efficiency of the total score (Kirkner, Wisham, and Giedt, 1953). Although a number of attempts have been made to utilize each of these six component parts of the scale as separate prognostic indicators (Cartwright, 1958; Endicott and Endicott, 1964; Kirkner et al., 1953; Mindess, 1953; Seidel, 1960; Sheehan et al., 1954), there are inconsistent findings regarding the relative effectiveness of each of these subscores as used separately.

As has been the case with so many other measures in psychology, the popularity of a test usually prompts someone to develop a "short form." Such has been the case with the PRS (Cartwright, 1958). In computing her "strength score," only the weighted scores for human movement, color, and form level were used by Cartwright, with the final score being composed of the sum of the two highest weighted scores. The research carried out with this short form has not as yet provided us with enough information about its effectiveness as a prognostic indicator, let alone its efficiency relative to the usual summary score.

Despite the fact that there have been varied attempts to experiment with different approaches to the weighting of the six components of the PRS, the use of the individual components separately, and the development of a short form, it appears that the most appropriate method of obtaining the final PRS score continues to be the simple summation of the six weighted subscores.

While we would agree with the method of computing the final PRS score as suggested by Klopfer et al. (1951), we would question their suggested cutoff scores. The reasons for the disagreement are discussed in detail in the section of the chapter which deals with normative data (particularly pp. 359–361).

THE EFFECT OF R. Although there has been no direct empirical test of the relationship between total R and PRS scores, indirect evidence would suggest that some sort of relationship might exist. Bloom (1956), in conjunction with his interest in the possibility of obtaining prognostic indicators in underproductive protocols, found that although PRS scores obtained from normally productive protocols were positively associated with treatment history, PRS scores obtained from underproductive records (10 or fewer responses and one card rejection) had no relation to treatment history. Further indirect evidence for a possible relation between PRS and total R comes from two studies by Endicott and Endicott (1963, 1964). Using two separate patient populations, they found that total R was significantly related to improvement; the point biserial *r*s, each of which was significant at the .05 level, were .32 and .41, respectively.

In none of the research on the PRS carried out to date has there been an attempt to partial out the effects of R, or to study directly the relationship between R and PRS scores. Only one study (Sheehan et al., 1954) has provided evidence that PRS scores were able to discriminate successfully between a group of improved and unimproved patients, whereas total R could not. In the majority of studies dealing with the validation of the PRS, however, the possible confounding effects of R are not known. Any possible conclusions which may be drawn regarding the validity of PRS consequently must be tempered by the possibility of these being a function of R.

NORMATIVE DATA

Although there has been no systematic attempt to collect normative data on the PRS, some information relative to norms may be obtained by reanalyzing some of the data obtained from validation studies.

Nature of the Samples

In comparison with information available on most other applications of the Rorschach, the groups on which PRS data are available have been small and inadequately described. In most of the studies, the description of the sample refers to the entire group studied, with no separate distinction being made between patients who did and did not show improvement. In fact, with respect to the data themselves, several authors report normative data for the entire sample only, rather than for improved and unimproved patients separately. In those instances where the original scores themselves were also reported, we recomputed the data to provide separate norms for improved and unimproved subjects. We were able to obtain data on the PRS for the following groups: patients in a university counseling center, stutterers attending a clinic, patients in a psychology clinic, hospitalized neuropsychiatric patients, retarded children, and student nurses (see Table 12.1).

In describing her sample, Cartwright (1958) indicates that these self-referred patients were typical of those attending the University of Chicago Counseling Center. The only additional information of any relevance is that they were seen in therapy for an average of 26 sessions, with a range of 6–77. No separate descriptions of the improved and unimproved subgroups is offered.

The stutterers described by Sheehan et al. (1954) were all attending

TABLE 12.1
Characteristics of the Samples

Group	N	Sex		Age			I.Q.		Years of Education		
		M	*F*	*Mean*	*S.D.*	*Range*	*Mean*	*Range*	*Mean*	*S.D.*	*Range*
Patients in University Counseling Center (Cartwright, 1958)	13	8	5	26.4	—[a]	18–37	—	—	—	—	—
Stutterers in Clinic (Sheehan et al., 1954)	35	29	6	—[b]	—	17–54	—	—	—	—	—
Clinic Patients (Endicott and Endicott, 1964)	21	4	17	28.0[c]	—	18–45[c]	—	—	12.0[c]	—	8–16[c]
Clinic Patients (Endicott and Endicott, 1963)	40	5	35	27.9	6.30	—	—	—	11.5	1.23	—
Clinic Patients (Rockberger, 1953)	36	36	0	32.0	—	25–40	113.4	90–130	10.7	—	8–18
NP Patients (Kirkner et al., 1953)	40	38	2	30.0	—	19–59	—	—	—	—	—
Retarded Children (Johnson, 1953)	21	—	—	13.0[c]	—	9.5–16[c]	(low 70s)		—	—	—
Student Nurses (Mindess, 1957)	68	0	68	18.5	—	17–29	113.0	96–133	(Nursing School)		
Patients in University Counseling Center (Schulman, 1963)	20	20	0	24.0	—	17–34	—	—	—	—	—
NP Patients (Adams and Cooper, 1962)	36	36	0	38.0	7.80	28–56	—	—	9.6	3.40	3–18
Foster-Home Adolescents, Separated Early (Greenberg, 1969)	20	20	0	—	—	12–17	—	83–126	—	—	—
Foster-Home Adolescents, Separated Late (Greenberg, 1969)	20	20	0	—	—	12–17	—	86–120	—	—	—
Own-Home Adolescents (Greenberg, 1969)	20	20	0	—	—	12–17	—	85–134	—	—	—

[a] A dash (—) indicates that these data were not available.
[b] The authors mention that most of the patients were under 25 years of age.
[c] These figures are estimates based on the author's description of the sample.

the UCLA Psychological and Speech Clinic. The therapy consisted of a combination of speech therapy and psychotherapy which focused on any anxieties which might contribute to the stuttering; the therapy was administered in both individual and group settings. The outcome rating of improvement was determined by combined therapists' ratings; the authors offer no separate description of the improved and unimproved samples.

The clinic patients studied by Endicott and Endicott (1963, 1964) consisted of the dependents of armed forces personnel, and in some instances, the personnel themselves. The patients in one group (Endicott and Endicott, 1964) were seen once a week in psychoanalytically oriented therapy, while those in the other (Endicott and Endicott, 1963) were placed on the waiting list as part of a larger research project. Judgments regarding improvement were made for each of these groups six months later on the basis of an interviewer's rating of behavior and symptom change. Although the authors offer no separate description for the improved and unimproved patients who were treated, they do provide information regarding the comparability of the improved and unimproved subjects placed on the waiting list. In particular, they note that the two subgroups were not significantly different regarding age, sex, or duration of symptoms; it was found, however, that the improved group had a significantly higher level of education (12.1 years as compared with 11.1 years).

The clinic patients described by Rockberger (1953) were all attending a V.A. mental hygiene clinic, and were in individual therapy from anywhere between six and 41 months. Twenty-three of the patients were diagnosed as ambulatory schizophrenics and the remaining 13 as neurotics. The measurement of improvement was determined by a personality and symptom checklist which was completed by the individual therapist. Rockberger reports that the improved and unimproved group did not differ significantly on the variables of age, education, I.Q., or time in therapy (which was 5.6 months for each of the two groups). No mention is made regarding the comparability of diagnosis for the two groups. The likelihood that the two groups were *not* comparable regarding diagnosis is great, especially since Rockberger reports in the same study that the schizophrenic patients scored significantly lower on the PRS than did the neurotics. In general, the reader should be cautioned that although Rockberger's sample is described as consisting of "clinic patients," there is a good deal of heterogeneity represented here.

The information available on the samples studied by Kirkner et al. (1953) is minimal. They report that the protocols were taken from the hospital files, and consisted of the records of those patients who had been accepted for therapy. Thirty-eight of the patients were diagnosed as neurotic, and only two as psychotic.

The subjects in Johnson's (1953) sample were taken from a training school for mentally and educationally retarded children. These children were selected for special study after having been referred for treatment because of behavioral or academic problems. Most of them had been in the residential setting for more than two years, and were functioning intellectually in the low 70s as indicated by the Stanford–Binet.

The 68 student nurses studied by Mindess (1957) were originally obtained from a pool of 80 girls who had just entered nursing training; 12 students dropped out of training shortly after beginning school, and were consequently discarded from the sample. The training setting consisted of a Canadian Catholic hospital, and all but two of the student nurses were Catholic. Most of the students composing this sample came from upper middle-class homes.

Schulman (1963) offers little in the way of additional information regarding his sample, except perhaps that the patients were rated by their therapists as having a moderate degree of disturbance.

The NP patients studied by Adams and Cooper (1962) were all hospitalized in a V.A. general medical and surgical hospital. The patients carried a variety of diagnoses, although only about one-quarter of them were considered to be psychotic.

Greenberg (1969) indicates that all adolescents in his three groups had been equated for age, socio-economic status, and I.Q. The foster-home adolescents who had an "early" separation left their parents sometime between eight months and three years of age, whereas the "late" separation group were placed in foster homes when they were between four and nine years. The "own-home" adolescents, on the other hand, had never left their natural parents.

Data on PRS

From an inspection of the data presented in Table 12.2, it is evident that the establishment of norms on the basis of "improvement" or "nonimprovement" alone is not adequate. For example, research has shown that the PRS will vary as a function of diagnosis (Mindess, 1953; Rockberger, 1953; Seidel, 1960). Thus, the original suggestion by Klopfer et al. (1951) that specific ranges of PRS scores may *generally* be associated with specific prognostic statements is no longer valid. In their original article, Klopfer et al. had tentatively suggested that the following meanings be attributed to different ranges of the final score (Klopfer et al., 1951, p. 428):

Range	*Group*	*Meaning*
17 to 13	I	The person is almost able to help himself. A very promising case that just needs a little help.
13 to 7	II	Not quite as capable as the above case to work out his problems himself, but with some help is likely to do pretty well.
6 to 2	III	Better than 50–50 chances; any treatment will be of some help.
1 to −2	IV	50–50 chances.
−3 to −6	V	A difficult case that may be helped somewhat, but is generally a poor treatment prospect.
−7 to −12	VI	A hopeless case.

Apart from the naive and seemingly arbitrary "meaning" assigned to each of the six levels, we seriously question the clinical utility of the six

TABLE 12.2

Mean, Standard Deviation, and Range of Prognostic Rating Scale (PRS) Scores for Improved and Unimproved Patients and Total Sample

Group	Improved			Unimproved		
	Mean	*S.D.*	*Range*	*Mean*	*S.D.*	*Range*
Patients in University Counseling Center (Cartwright, 1958)	7.33	2.59	3.0–11.4	4.54	2.30	1.7–7.3
Stutterers in Clinic (Sheehan et al., 1954)	7.24	—[a]	—	4.67	—	—
Clinic Patients (Endicott and Endicott, 1964)	6.58	2.35	—	4.30	2.49	—
Clinic Patients (Endicott and Endicott, 1963)	5.92	1.62	—	3.96	2.75	—
Clinic Patients (Rockberger, 1953)	5.20	2.23	1.7–10.2	0.60	0.73	−0.4–3.1
NP Patients (Kirkner et al., 1953)	6.90	2.46	1.5–10.5	3.38	2.27	−0.60–8.1
Retarded Children (Johnson, 1953)	2.61	2.50	−2.5–7.6	−0.40	1.37	−2.0–1.4

Group	Total Sample		
	Mean	*S.D.*	*Range*
Student Nurses (Mindess, 1957)	6.25	2.58	0.2–11.7
Patients in University Counseling Center (Schulman, 1963)	3.78	1.62	1.3–7.3
NP Patients (Adams and Cooper, 1962)	1.54	2.69	−4.5–6.5
Foster-Home Adolescents, Separated Early (Greenberg, 1969)	2.34	—	−2.87–9.34
Foster-Home Adolescents, Separated Late (Greenberg, 1969)	2.37	—	−1.36–7.26
Own-Home Adolescents (Greenberg, 1969)	4.72	—	−1.50–9.82

[a] A dash (—) indicates that these data were not available.

levels themselves. To begin with, the ranges included within Groups I, V, and VI simply do not occur in clinical practice (see Table 12.2). In addition, the cutoff point one sets in deciding whom to treat and whom not to treat will clearly differ as a function of patient population, availability of therapeutic time, and base rates for recovery. From many points of view, then, the interpretations of final PRS scores as described by Klopfer et al. simply do not make sense.

On the assumption that most clinical settings may be characterized as having many more patients to treat than therapy hours available, it would seem appropriate to set the cutoff point for the PRS high enough to eliminate as many false positives as possible. If virtually all patients seen in therapy by this method are those having good prognosis—even though a fair proportion of good-prognosis patients never get seen—the practical utility of the PRS could receive some justification.[4]

There is some research evidence to indicate that the appropriate cutoff score will vary depending upon the nature of the patient population. Johnson (1953), for example, used a PRS score of 2 or greater as her cutoff point for a group of retarded children. She found that this score was able to eliminate all false positives, and yet include 73% of those cases who were subsequently rated as having improved. Rockberger (1953), who used the cutoff score of 2.4 among a group of psychiatric patients (most of whom were diagnosed as schizophrenic), was able to identify correctly 90% of the improved patients, but also found that 17% of the patients who scored above this cutoff point were rated as having been unimproved. In reanalyzing Rockberger's data, we found the cutoff score of 4 would completely eliminate all false positives, and yet accurately select 71% of the patients who subsequently improved. Still another cutoff point may be set for the sample described by Kirkner et al. (1953). In reanalyzing their data obtained from V.A. patients (most of whom were diagnosed as neurotic), a cutoff point of 5 seems to be most appropriate. Using this score, 81% of the improved patients are detected, with a false positive rate of only 9%. For a group of stutterers, Sheehan et al. (1954) used an even higher cutoff point (6.27) which apparently was still not high enough; this cutoff point detected 24% false positives. Sheehan et al. do not present their original data, so it was not possible for us to determine which would have been the more appropriate cutoff score to use.

Although it is evident that the appropriate cutoff score will vary from population to population, the scores described above are offered only as a tentative suggestion of what may be appropriate for different patient populations. More normative data are needed, particularly those including information on the efficiency of different cutoff points in different patient populations.

[4] We by no means wish to imply that the PRS should be the *only criterion* for deciding who should or should not be seen in therapy. Depending on the setting, other variables (e.g., the consequences to the patient if he is not seen by anyone) may play a significant role prior to any application of the PRS score.

RELIABILITY

For some reason which is not immediately apparent, there have been no studies carried out to investigate the stability of PRS scores over time. One would assume that inasmuch as the underlying characteristic measured by the PRS—whether it be termed ego-strength, adjustment potential, or whatever—is relatively stable over time, test-retest studies on the reliability of the system are in order.

VALIDITY

In contrast to the complete absence of reliability studies, a fair amount of validity research is available for the PRS. In reviewing the literature, it is not at all surprising to note that most of the work is related to the predictive validity of the system; after all, this is what the scale is all about. There is some construct validity research available, but not nearly enough to give us a complete understanding of the theoretical significance of the PRS score.

Criterion-Related Validity

Although there has been a good deal of predictive validity research done on the PRS, no work at all has been carried out on concurrent validity. In fact, it is difficult to imagine just how one would go about establishing a concurrent criterion group for the system. The PRS has been designed as a prognostic measure, and the most appropriate evaluation of its validity would seem to rest in the predictive area.

Predictive Validity

The research on the predictive validity of the PRS may best be classified according to the outcome criteria which were used. These outcome measures have included (1) observations or ratings of changes in overt behavior, (2) therapists' observations of behavior within the therapy session, (3) some combination of overt behavior change and therapists' ratings, and (4) changes on various personality tests and self-ratings.

CHANGES IN OVERT BEHAVIOR. The use of behavioral criteria has involved observations of behavior change in adult patients and in children, speech improvement among stutterers, and recovery and release from hospital for schizophrenic patients.

Rockberger (1953) studied a group of 36 male patients who were seen in individual therapy in a mental hygiene clinic; the therapist had been either an experienced psychologist, psychiatrist, or social worker. The determination of improvement was done by means of a 32-item personality and symptom rating scale completed by the therapist at the termination of treatment, which on the average occurred after 15.6 months; in addition to arriving at a total change score for each patient, the rating scale data were used to dichotomize the sample into improved and unimproved groups. Rockberger's findings are impressive. He obtained a Pearson r of .57 ($p <$ .001) between pretherapy PRS scores and improvement ratings. Partialing out the effect of I.Q. and educational level only served to increase the correlation to .60 and .64, respectively. The improved/unimproved dichotomy, when correlated with PRS scores revealed a point biserial r of .70 ($p < .001$). As noted earlier in the chapter, a reanalysis of Rockberger's data reveals that the use of a PRS cutoff score of 4 or greater completely eliminated the false-positive rate. Rockberger's findings would be very encouraging if it were not for one serious limitation in the study. Although he did demonstrate that the improved and unimproved groups did not differ significantly in age, I.Q., educational level, or time in therapy, Rockberger failed to compare the two groups with respect to diagnosis. Of the 36 patients in Rockberger's study, 23 were diagnosed as ambulatory schizophrenic, and the remaining 13 as neurotic. In fact, an additional finding reported by Rockberger is that a comparison between schizophrenic and neurotic patients on the basis of PRS scores yielded a point biserial r of .52 ($p < .01$), reflecting a higher score for the neurotic group. Rockberger says nothing about the comparability of his improved and unimproved groups with respect to diagnosis. Because of the possible confounding of improvement with diagnosis, this study cannot be taken as an adequate demonstration of the prognostic effectiveness of the PRS.

Endicott and Endicott (1964) used the PRS to predict improvement with psychoanalytically oriented therapy administered in an outpatient clinic for a group of 21 patients. The patients were seen once a week, and evaluated after a period of six months by an independent interviewer using a behavior and symptom change rating scale (Miles, Barrabee, and Finesinger, 1951). Of the total sample studied, 11 were judged to be "improved" and 10 "unimproved." Although the authors report that the improved patients had a significantly higher PRS than the unimproved group (point biserial $r = .43$; $p < .05$), they also report that total R was also significantly related to improvement (point biserial $r = .41$; $p < .05$). Endicott and Endicott do not report what the relationship was between PRS and improvement when total R is partialed out.

In order to find out whether there might be a differential remission rate for subjects having different PRS scores, Endicott and Endicott (1963) studied a group of 40 patients who had been placed on a clinic waiting list as part of a research project. These subjects were interviewed six months later and, on the basis of the symptom and behavior change scale taken from Miles et al. (1951), they dichotomized their entire sample into improved and unimproved subgroups. These subgroups did not differ on the basis of age, sex, or duration of symptoms; the improved subjects, however, had reached a higher educational level. It is of considerable interest that the results demonstrated that despite the fact that none of the subjects had been seen in therapy, the improved group had significantly higher PRS than the unimproved group (point biserial $r = .38$; $p < .05$). Consistent with their previous finding, however, Endicott and Endicott also report that total R alone was positively related to improvement (point biserial $r = .32$;

$p < .05$). The entire issue as to whether or not these subjects were truly "untreated" (they had two prewait interviews plus a testing session) relates to the intriguing question of the extent to which "placebo" factors contribute to the treatment process, a topic which goes well beyond the scope of this chapter.[5]

Novick (1962) tested the effectiveness of the PRS in predicting behavior change among "mildly disturbed" children in therapy. All subjects in the study were boys between the ages of 8 and 10 years of age. Using a cutoff score of 2 on the PRS, Novick was able to form two groups, each containing 22 subjects: a *high* (mean = 4.04, with a range of 2.1 to 7.5) and a *low* PRS group (mean = − 1.84, with a range of − 3.8 to − 0.1). The two groups were equated on the basis of age, I.Q., and degree of disturbance. Novick does not describe the type of therapy that was offered, noting only that it was carried out by three experienced therapists. The outcome criteria consisted of a behavior rating scale which was completed jointly by a clinic staff member and the parent, and covered such behaviors as a child's interest in school, frequency of temper tantrums, eating problems, and other related behavior problems. Although no behavior change was noted for either of the two groups after 10 therapy sessions, significant findings were revealed at the end of 20 sessions; the high PRS group showed a significant decrease in maladaptive behaviors, whereas the low PRS group showed no change.

Sheehan et al. (1954) were interested in using the PRS to predict change in stuttering for a group of 35 students receiving a combination of speech therapy and psychotherapy. Each subject was seen both individually and in groups, where particular focus was placed on those anxiety-provoking situations which might precipitate stuttering. Using a combined rating of speech improvement obtained from the three therapists involved in the treatment, Sheehan et al. failed to obtain any significant relation between these ratings and PRS scores.

In a study of the use of the PRS to predict hospital release and recovery, Seidel (1960) obtained a pool of 100 records from the file of St. Elizabeth's Hospital. All patients in this original pool were white, male schizophrenics between the ages of 20 and 50 who had been given the Rorschach within four months after admission. These patients were then classified into two categories: those hospitalized for three years or more, and those who had been released from the hospital within three years with a psychiatric evaluation of having "recovered." Thirty-one patients met the criterion for the hospitalized group, and 32 for the released and recovered group. Seidel does not describe the nature of the treatment for either of the two groups. Her results indicate that there is a low but significantly positive relationship between PRS scores and release from the hospital (point biserial $r = .40$; $p < .01$). In interpreting these findings, it is important to note that the two groups differed on the Phillips scale (Phillips, 1953), in that the released and recovered group had a more favorable premorbid social and

[5] For an interesting discussion of the role of the placebo effects in therapy, see Frank (1961) and Rosenthal and Frank (1956); for a more humorous account of the same topic, see Borgatta (1959).

sexual history. The fact that the more easily administered Phillips scale can predict release from the hospital as readily as the PRS would lead us to question the practical utility of the Rorschach for this purpose. Indeed, this is a question which is relevant to the utility of the PRS in predicting success in therapy as well, and will be considered at greater length at the end of this chapter.

Although the research on the effectiveness of the PRS in predicting overt behavior change has typically yielded positive results, these findings tend to be confounded with such uncontrolled variables as diagnosis, total R, and premorbid history—variables which also result in positive findings when used alone.

Observations of Behavior within Therapy. In the validation of the PRS, the research using the patients' behavior during therapy to determine outcome has made use of the therapists' rating of success or improvement, the nature of the treatment history, and the patients' ability to free associate.

For a group of 13 people being seen in client-centered therapy at the University of Chicago Counseling Center, Cartwright (1958) obtained counselors' ratings of "success" at the end of treatment. The outcome measure used was a nine-point scale devised by Seeman (1954), which is based on such factors as the amount of self-exploration displayed by the client during the sessions, the relationship to the counselor, and other similar process variables. Although the "success" and "failure" groups were small (eight and five subjects, respectively), Cartwright did obtain a positive relationship between counselors' ratings and PRS scores (tau $= .52$; $p < .03$). No information is given regarding the equivalency of the two groups with respect to total R or other non-Rorschach variables.

In the study with stutterers already cited in the previous section, Sheehan et al. (1954) also made use of therapists' ratings of change as an outcome measure. It may be recalled that each stutterer seen in the clinic was involved in both individual and group therapy, with three therapists having contact with each patient. On the basis of observed personality changes in patients, each therapist rated each patient on a four-point scale, with the final rating being determined by the average of these three independent judgments. A comparison of the most and least improved patients revealed a significantly higher PRS score for the improved group. The authors also make a point of noting that the two groups did not differ with respect to total R.

Kirkner et al. (1953) used a sample of 40 hospitalized V.A. patients who were seen in treatment by 20 different therapists—mostly advanced clinical psychology trainees. In judging whether the patient was improved or unimproved, the authors made use of the closing therapy notes to determine whether or not the goals for treatment had been met. Despite the crudity of this entire study, Kirkner et al. obtained positive results. They found a phi coefficient of .67 ($p < .01$) between pretreatment PRS scores and treatment outcome. As we have found with so many other studies in this area, the authors make no mention of the comparability of the improved and unimproved groups on other variables.

In an attempt to study the effectiveness of the PRS in predicting success in therapy for clinic patients, Mindess (1953) obtained therapists' ratings at the termination of treatment regarding the patients' pre- and posttherapy adjustment. In correlating PRS scores with therapists' ratings of posttherapy adjustment at the end of the six months of treatment, Mindess obtained a Pearson r of .81 ($p < .001$). An inspection of the scattergram revealed that 10 schizophrenics obtained the 10 lowest PRS scores. In order to create a more homogeneous sample, Mindess eliminated the scores of these patients. With the remaining total of 70 nonschizophrenic clinic patients, the correlation between PRS and adjustment ratings at the end of treatment was slightly lower but still significant ($r = .66$; $p < .001$). One additional finding in Mindess' study is of considerable interest. He found that the therapists' rating of the patients' level of adjustment prior to treatment, and the rating of adjustment at the end of treatment correlated .59 for this nonschizophrenic sample ($p < .001$). Although this pretherapy adjustment rating may have been influenced by other variables (e.g., the therapist's posttherapy adjustment rating obtained at the same time, or his contact with the patient during therapy), these findings offer some weak support for the possibility that an equally valid prognostic judgment might have been made from non-Rorschach data.

As part of a study on the use of unproductive protocols in predicting success in treatment, Bloom (1956) divided V.A. mental hygiene clinic patients into two categories: those showing good treatment history (behavior change, continuation in treatment, or termination by mutual decision of therapist and patient), and poor treatment history (no improvement and premature termination); the information for categorizing patients into these two groups was based on treatment notes and discussions with the therapist. Although Bloom was unable to find any relationship between PRS scores and treatment history for patients who had underproductive Rorschachs (fewer than 10 responses plus one rejection), he did find that for those patients with normally productive protocols (30 or more responses with no rejections), the PRS scores were significantly higher for the good treatment group. No information is provided regarding the equivalency of the good and poor treatment groups on other variables.

A study by Bordin (1966) on the relationship between PRS scores and free association revealed essentially negative results. Bordin used two groups of male college students who were asked to free associate for a 30-minute period; the free association behavior was rated according to motional involvement, spontaneity, and freedom of expression. For his first sample, PRS correlated significantly with only spontaneity (tau $= .22$; $p < .05$). In the second sample, the tau of .11 between PRS and spontaneity fell short of statistical significance.

As we have seen in the case of predictive validity studies for the PRS utilizing overt behavior change, the research predicting changes observed within the treatment setting itself have typically yielded positive findings. These positive findings, however, may very well be confounded by other variables which might just as easily have been used to differentiate patients into good and poor prognostic risks. One study in this section (Mindess,

1953) offers some indirect evidence that a therapist's rating of a patient prior to therapy might be just as useful in predicting change as PRS scores; this possibility should be explored more directly.

Overt Behavior Changes and Observations within Therapy. There has been one study with the PRS where the outcome criterion was determined by both observations of overt extratherapy behavior and judgments made from behavior during the therapy sessions themselves (Johnson, 1953). Johnson used the PRS to predict progress in play therapy for a group of retarded children. The improvement criterion was based on the therapists' observations of such factors as insight and working through, but also on the teacher's and supervisor's judgment of symptom and social change in these children. The results turned out to be positive, in that pretreatment PRS scores were found to be significantly related to this combined measure of improvement.

Changes in Personality Test Scores. There has been only one PRS validity study which has used personality test scores as an outcome measure (Fiske, Cartwright, and Kirtner, 1964). The study was part of a larger investigation of prognostic indicators and outcome criteria, and the change scores used were based on factor scores obtained from a factor analysis of a variety of different measures (e.g., MMPI, TAT, Sentence Completion, Q-Sorts, etc.). The subjects consisted of individuals (college students and members of the local community) who had been seen in client-centered therapy within a counseling center; the number of sessions ranged from three to 191, with a median of 26. The level of experience for the 30 different therapists used in the study covered a wide range (one to 24 years), and about one-third of the clients were seen by first-year psychology interns. The final results of the study were disappointing; none of the correlations between PRS scores and the posttherapy change scores proved to be significant. It should also be noted, however, that not many of the other predictive indicators fared much better. The authors speculate about the possible reasons for their negative results (e.g., nature of the client sample, experience level of the therapists, etc.), but never really arrive at any satisfactory explanation of their findings.

Construct Validity

Although the PRS was originally designed as a predictive instrument, there have been a number of studies offering some data on the construct validity of the measure. These construct-validity studies will be discussed separately under the subheadings of nomological and trait validity.

Nomological Validity

Assuming that PRS scores reflect an individual's level of "ego-strength" or adjustment potential, a number of hypotheses may be generated and tested by means of the PRS. The nomological validity studies have involved (1) the use of PRS scores to predict adjustment to new and difficult situations, (2) the relation between PRS and various populations, or (3) attempts to induce changes in PRS scores.

ADJUSTMENT TO NEW SITUATIONS. There have been three studies carried out which reflect the assumption that PRS scores, a measure of adjustment potential, should be related to the effectiveness with which an individual is able to adjust to a new and difficult situation—nurse's training, college teaching, and psychotherapy.

Mindess (1957) made use of the PRS to predict success in nurse's training. For a group of 68 student nurses at a Canadian Catholic hospital, he obtained measures of success at the end of one year of training by means of (1) grades, (2) ward supervisors' ratings (dependability, care of patient, relationship with peers, etc.), and (3) grades and ratings combined. His findings reveal that there indeed was a low, but significant positive relationship between PRS scores and success in training. The correlation between PRS scores and grades was .28 ($p < .05$). Although the correlation of .14 with supervisors' ratings did not reach statistical significance, PRS and the combined criterion of grades and ratings correlated .41 ($p < .01$). Mindess also found that with a multiple correlation for PRS and I.Q., the correlation with the combined criterion measure was increased to .59 ($p < .01$).

In association with a program to train teachers at a junior college, Brawer and Cohen (1966) made use of PRS scores to predict subjects' adaptability to this new setting. Ratings of the adjustment of each of the 20 interns to the role of college teacher were carried out by both the director of the training program and the interns' supervisors. The program director's rating was based on his observation of the interns' performance in seminars they had taken with him; the correlation of .35 between his ratings and PRS scores failed to reach statistical significance. The supervisors' ratings, which were based on observations of on-the-job performance, correlated .39 ($p < .10$) with PRS scores.

Sheehan et al. (1954), in their study involving the treatment of stutterers with speech therapy and psychotherapy, were also interested in finding whether PRS scores had any relation to the likelihood that patients would continue treatment. Of the 35 stutterers seen in treatment, 30 continued and five terminated prematurely. Sheehan et al. found that the pretreatment PRS scores were significantly higher for those who continued in treatment than for those who dropped out.

The attempts to demonstrate the use of PRS scores in predicting adjustment to new and difficult situations, although not overwhelmingly positive, are nonetheless encouraging enough to warrant further research along these lines. It is suggested, however, that rather than continue to predict performance in global situations where the exact nature of the stress is unspecified (e.g., college teaching), research be carried out to predict stress tolerance in more specific and experimentally controlled situations, such as visual-motor performance accompanied by stress, stressful social situations, and unstructured situations.

RELATIONSHIP TO VARIOUS POPULATIONS. An interpretation of the PRS as reflecting an individual's ability to tolerate stress easily leads one to question the relationship it might have to severity of disturbance. As part of his larger study of the prognostic use of the PRS, Rockberger (1953) subdivided his sample of 36 clinic patients into 23 ambulatory schizophrenics and 13 neurotics. His obtained point biserial r of .52 ($p < .01$) between diagnosis and PRS revealed significantly lower scores for the schizophrenic group; similar findings have also been noted by Mindess (1953). Seidel (1960) compared PRS scores among a group of hospitalized male schizophrenics and found that those receiving a diagnosis of paranoid schizophrenia obtained significantly higher scores than patients diagnosed as catatonic, hebephrenic, simple, undifferentiated, and schizoaffective.

Greenberg (1969) made use of the PRS in his investigation of the relationship between psychological adjustment and maternal deprivation. Although he found no difference in the PRS scores between male adolescents who were separated from their parents before the age of three years from those who were placed in foster homes after four years of age, each of these groups was found to have significantly lower scores when compared with adolescents who were raised by their natural parents.

Although the evidence indicating that there is a relationship between PRS and various diagnostic groups in a sense offers construct validity for the system, it also has certain practical implications for the use of the measure. These implications will be discussed at the end of the chapter.

Changes in PRS Scores. The few studies which have been carried out to induce change in PRS scores have typically predicted an improvement as a function of either therapy or some relevant experimental manipulation (i.e., sensory deprivation with psychiatric patients).

Sheehan et al. (1954), in conjunction with their study already cited a number of times earlier in the chapter, were able to retest 26 of the 35 stutterers treated in the clinic; five patients from the original group dropped out of treatment, and four were not available for testing. The authors failed to find any significant change between the pre- and posttherapy PRS scores. It should be noted, however, that the patients retested included those individuals rated as unimproved as well as those judged to have improved as a function of the treatment.

Johnson (1953) focused more directly on changes in PRS scores as a function of successful treatment, and not simply treatment per se. For a group of retarded children undergoing play therapy, she obtained post-PRS scores at the termination of treatment which, on the average, lasted two years. Her results indicate that success in treatment, as determined by both the therapists' judgment and observations of symptom and social change, was positively related to increase in PRS scores ($p < .02$).

Cooper, Adams, and Gibby (1962) note that clinical observations seem to indicate that psychiatric patients who have undergone sensory deprivation show increased desires for social contacts and psychotherapy. Consequently, an increase in PRS scores was predicted. Using Cartwright's (1958) short form of the PRS, the authors retested a group of male psychiatric patients the day after they had undergone six hours of sensory deprivation and found a significant increase. Adams (1964) later reported a replication of this study, using a control group not exposed to sensory deprivation, and failed to find any change in PRS scores.

In general, the evidence on changes in PRS scores seems to indicate that change is possible as a function of successful treatment or some effective experimental manipulation. In the light of these available findings, it might even seem appropriate to consider the use of PRS scores as an outcome, as well as a predictive measure.

Trait Validity

Relative to the other validity research on the PRS, little has been done to investigate trait validity. The research that is available has focused on relating the PRS to other prognostic indicators (such as the Phillips scale and the MMPI) as well as the correlation of PRS scores with such variables as I.Q. and education.

RELATION TO OTHER PROGNOSTIC MEASURES. Seidel (1960) reports a study where she correlated Phillips' case-history prognostic rating scale (Phillips, 1953) with the PRS for a group of 63 male schizophrenics. Using only Section I of the Phillips scale, which focuses specifically on premorbid social and sexual history, she found a low but significant correlation of .30 for her sample ($p < .05$).

Although the Phillips scale and the PRS do, at least to some extent, seem to be measuring the same thing, this does not appear to be the case with Barron's ego-strength (Es) scale on the MMPI (Barron, 1953b). Endicott and Endicott (1964) report nonsignificant correlations of .22 and .12 between the PRS and Es scores for treated and untreated clinic patients, respectively. Although PRS scores did correlate positively with improvement for each of these two samples, Es scores did not. Similarly, Adams and Cooper (1962) obtained a nonsignificant correlation of .13 between PRS and Es for a group of psychiatric patients. Using the same sample of patients, Adams, Cooper, and Carrera (1963) report a further analysis of the PRS and MMPI scores in general. By and large, they found nonsignificant correlations between the MMPI clinical scales and PRS scores. Although the authors go through elaborate steps to make the results look better than they actually are, the relationship between PRS and the MMPI scales generally seem to reflect little more than chance association.

Williams, Monder, and Rychlak (1967) compared PRS scores with independent ratings of prognosis carried out by psychiatrists and social workers. All patients were being seen in a child-guidance clinic, and were rated after having gone through the usual intake procedure. Although PRS was found to correlate positively with psychiatrists' ratings, the correlations with the social workers' failed to reach statistical significance. Williams et al. explain these findings by noting that inasmuch as the psychiatrists had seen the child as well as the parents—the social workers' contacts had been limited to the parents—they had more information on which to base their prognostic ratings.

RELATION TO OTHER VARIABLES. The remaining correlational research on the PRS has involved the variables of I.Q. and education, both of which have typically been cited as being significant factors in determining prognosis.

The two studies which have focused on the relationship between PRS and I.Q. have yielded conflicting results. Rockberger (1953), using a sample of 36 male clinic patients at a V.A. mental hygiene clinic reports a positive correlation of .51 ($p < .01$). Mindess (1957), on the other hand, for a group of 68 female student nurses, obtained a nonsignificant correlation of .10. The discrepant findings do not appear to be due to any difference in the range of PRS or I.Q. scores for the two groups, but instead may be a function of such variables as level of disturbance, sex, age, socio-economic background, or any of a number of other unmeasured variables.

OVERALL EVALUATION

The underlying construct reflected in the therapy prognostic use of the Rorschach may be called, for want of a better term, ego-strength or adjustment potential. Although the origin of this personality characteristic is probably a function of previous learning experiences, the actual definition is most often made in terms of consequent events, such as success in therapy. Thus, we find that the problem of defining prognosis is inextricably tied to the definition of therapeutic "success." Although the most preferable criterion for improvement would appear to be the observation of extra-therapy changes in overt behavior, observed changes in the therapy sessions themselves, as well as changes in test scores, have appeared in the Rorschach literature.

Apart from the research carried out by Klopfer and his associates on the use of the Rorschach to predict success in therapy, only a few other writers have attempted to devise prognostic signs. Most typically, these other systems either have not been cross validated or have failed to hold up under further testing. By way of contrast, the research on Klopfer's Prognostic Rating Scale (PRS) has been more systematic and encouraging.

The PRS scoring system is comprised of six component parts: human movement, animal movement, inanimate movement, shading responses, color responses, and form-level rating. Responses reflecting each of these six areas are assigned weights, and all the weights are tallied into a final prognostic score. Although the criteria are clear enough, some of the mechanical aspects of the weighting and computation tend to be cumbersome. Nonetheless, the application of these criteria result in relatively good interscorer reliability. No data are available on the test-retest reliability of the system of PRS scores. Klopfer and his associates have suggested the use of specific cutoff scores, but subsequent research findings suggest that, depending upon diagnosis, the most efficient (i.e., resulting in the smallest false-positive rate) cutoff score will vary. Further normative data are needed which would indicate the most appropriate score to use for varying patient populations.

The research on the predictive validity of the PRS has typically turned out to be positive. PRS scores are able to predict overt behavior change for clinic as well as hospital patient populations. There is also some evidence which suggests that PRS scores can predict changes which may be due to "spontaneous remission" as well. Despite these encouraging findings, the research suffers from the existence of confounding variables—such as diagnosis, premorbid history, and total R—each of which can successfully predict changes *independent* of PRS scores. Predictive validity research has also been shown to be positive in those studies where observed changes within the therapy session have served as the criterion measure; but here, too, our conclusions about the validity of the system must be tempered by the presence of other confounding variables. What little research has been done to use PRS scores to predict personality test score changes has yielded negative results.

The research findings on the construct validity of the PRS measure have, by and large, been favorable. Those studies which have used PRS scores to predict adjustment to new and difficult situations (e.g., nurses training, college teaching, and continuation in psychotherapy) have met with some success. We suggest that studies along these lines be continued, extending the work to the use of more experimentally controlled stress situations. Construct-validity research has also found that PRS scores are negatively related to severity of disturbance, positively related to good premorbid social history and sexual adequacy, and to educational level, and significantly lower for adolescents who had been separated from their natural parents. The research on the relationship between PRS and I.Q. scores is conflicting; research relating the measure to MMPI scores has consistently yielded negative results.

The construct-validity research findings leave us with a curious paradox. On the one hand, the results provide us with some support for the validity of the PRS as a predictive measure. On the other hand, the very fact that the PRS is related to such variables as diagnosis, premorbid history, and possibly I.Q.—variables which in and of themselves are important prognostic indicators—points to the practical limitation involved in the prognostic use of tests. If more easily obtainable demographic and other nontest data are as valid as test findings, then the use of test scores such as the PRS is clearly limited. In order to establish the practical utility of the Rorschach in predicting success in therapy, then it must be demonstrated empirically that it can contribute to efficient prediction when other relevant nontest variables have been controlled. Research is also needed to determine whether or not the PRS scores are able to predict change as a function of therapy, or simply the likelihood of change per se; that is, further therapy research with the system should include the necessary control groups.

One final comment on the use of Rorschach PRS scores. Although the measure may turn out to be useful to predict change as a function of the more traditional, insight-oriented therapies, it may turn out to be too global a measure to use for predicting success in the application of behavioral techniques (e.g., systematic desensitization, assertive training, reinforcement procedures, etc.). In the case of behavior modification procedures, where the areas for change are more specifically delineated, the relevant prognostic indicators are likely to vary depending upon the problem in question and the specific technique employed. The concept of ego strength may be just too global a characteristic to use in these instances.

Chapter 13

OVERALL EVALUATION AND IMPLICATIONS FOR THE FUTURE

This final chapter summarizes briefly the substantive findings from Chapters 2–12 concerning clinical and research applications of the Rorschach and then elaborates the following two major implications of current knowledge for further work with the test: First, there are numerous methodological considerations that have frequently been overlooked by Rorschach researchers and that must guide future attempts to assess the reliability and validity of Rorschach indices; second, there are a variety of practical considerations that affect the utility of Rorschach indices and that must be carefully weighed in future decisions to apply them.

REVIEW OF FINDINGS

Friedman's Developmental Level Scoring

Friedman's developmental level (*DL*) is an easily learned, reliably scored index based on aspects of location choice. *DL* scores have demonstrated good validity for a variety of personality measurements. This index can differentiate children at different chronological age levels, mental defectives at different mental age levels, and schizophrenics at different levels of disturbance, and it is also capable of discriminating neurotic, brain-damaged, and schizophrenic adults from normal adults. *DL* scores can also distinguish ideational from action-oriented individuals, and they can predict length of hospitalization and social participation in schizophrenics and resistance to distraction in normal adults.

Friedman's *DL* scoring therefore has considerable applicability, although its demonstrated strengths to date lie primarily in research. Its capacity for separating groups with sufficient freedom from overlap to justify clinical application to individuals has not yet been adequately assessed. Further research with the index is necessary to specify the precision of the distinctions it can make and also to determine its validity for female subjects, since virtually all of the work with it has been done with males.

Phillips' Developmental Level Scoring

Phillips' *DL* is an extension of Friedman's *DL* to include determinant as well as location-choice scoring for developmental level. Although the Phillips index was initially proposed as a revision and presumably an improvement of Friedman's *DL* scoring, it has to date yielded fewer consistent empirical findings than the Friedman index. The Phillips scores do not progress with age as clearly as the Friedman scores, nor have they successfully predicted performance on cognitive tasks that reflect different levels of functioning.

On the positive side, Phillips' *DL* has proved capable of distinguishing between ideationally and motorically oriented people, of predicting post-hospital adjustment in some psychiatric patients, and of assessing adequacy of social functioning in normal adults. Like the Friedman *DL,* however, the Phillips *DL* has seldom been applied to female subjects and has not yet demonstrated sufficient discriminatory precision to justify clinical use. The apparent inability of the Phillips index to improve on the discriminations achieved with Friedman's *DL* scoring, considered in light of the additional time necessary to learn and apply the more complex Phillips system, argues against replacing Friedman's *DL* scoring with it.

Elizur's Hostility Scoring

Elizur's scoring for hostility level (*HL*) is based on Rorschach content, is easy to learn and apply, and can be scored with a high degree of reliability. However, although *HL* scores are intended to indicate presumably stable characterological levels of hostility for which test-retest studies would provide an appropriate reliability index, adequate studies of this kind have not yet been done. There is additionally some indication that *HL* scores may be particularly sensitive to examiner influence, and this possibly confounding factor has not been fully explored.

Nevertheless, *HL* scoring has demonstrated some good concurrent and construct validity. *HL* scores correlate highly with interview estimates of hostility level based on interview measures, peer ratings, and therapist ratings of hostility level, and they also relate well to a variety of behavioral characteristics and symptoms that are presumed to reflect underlying hostility. Rorschach *HL* scores are furthermore correlated with certain other fantasy estimates of hostility level, although they do not appear to measure the same variable sampled by most paper-and-pencil tests of hostility.

Because *HL* scoring measures underlying dispositions rather than the manner in which they may be expressed, it has little capacity to predict aggressive behavior. For this reason, and because there are few normative *HL* data for diverse groups, *HL* scoring has limited clinical utility. For research purposes, however, it does appear to provide a good indication of characterological level of hostility.

Elizur's Anxiety Scoring

Elizur's scoring for anxiety level (*AL*), in common with *HL* scoring, is an easily learned, reliably scorable index based on response content. *AL* scores measure the characterological, underlying levels of anxiety, rather than situational anxiety or the manner in which anxiety is expressed. Nevertheless, as is the case for *HL* scoring, appropriate test-retest assessments of its reliability have not been carried out. Furthermore, in common with *HL, AL* lacks demonstrable predictive capacity but appears to have good concurrent and construct validity.

AL scores are positively related to independent ratings of anxiety level and are notably high among people with diagnosed psychological disturbances, who would be expected to have high levels of underlying anxiety. Rorschach *AL* furthermore correlates well with anxiety level as inferred from other projective tests, although it does not appear to measure the same variable sampled by most paper-and-pencil tests of anxiety.

AL scoring has not proved capable of discriminating among people with different types of psychopathology, and, like *HL* scoring, has not yet demonstrated sufficiently precise distinctions between subject groups to suggest potential for clinical use. Its major applications appear to be in research studies, for which it can provide a reasonably valid estimate of trait anxiety level.

Body-Image Boundary Scoring

The body-image boundary scoring developed by Fisher and Cleveland consists of content indices for Barrier (*B*) and Penetration (*P*) scores. *B* scores are presumed to represent a positive assertion of body-boundary definiteness, whereas *P* scores are intended to reflect feelings that the body exterior is easily penetrable and of little protective value. Both indices can be scored with a reasonably good degree of interscorer agreement.

Research with *P* scores has generally failed to demonstrate their utility or their relationship to the construct of body-boundary permeability. Studies of the *B* index, on the other hand, have yielded considerable evidence for the construct validity of body-boundary scoring. High *B* scores differentiate people with exterior physical or psychosomatic illnesses from people with interior symptom foci, and they also distinguish people who show greater physiological reactivity on exterior measures from those who are more responsive on internal body measures. High *B* scores are also significantly associated with a variety of indices of personality strength and resiliency, including ability to adapt to physical illness, general capacity to cope with stress, and relatively mature behavior in such self-steering situations as goal setting, task perseverance, resistance to suggestibility, and the outward expression of anger.

Research in this area has been complicated by alternate use of the

Rorschach and Holtzman inkblots to derive the boundary scores and by variations in the median value used to separate high-*B* from low-*B* subjects, and the measure has not demonstrated clinical value for idiographic decisions. Nevertheless, the available data clearly support research applications of *B* scores and suggest that further work with this index has good potential for sharpening its discriminatory power and broadening its applicability.

Homosexual Signs

Research attention to Rorschach signs of homosexuality has focused primarily on Wheeler's signs, which consist of 20 content scores that yield an overall index of homosexual tendencies. Although good interscorer agreement has been achieved for the Wheeler index, validity studies have tended to confirm only six of the 20 component signs as good indicators of homosexual tendencies. Of the 14 remaining signs, eight are of ambiguous validity and six are unquestionably poor. Despite being handicapped by the inclusion of these invalid signs, the Wheeler index has proved capable of distinguishing overt homosexuals from individuals who show no indications of homosexuality, delusional from nondelusional psychotics, and obsessive-compulsive from undifferentiated neurotics. Further research utilizing only those Wheeler signs known to have individual validity might well establish further the discriminatory power of the index.

Whatever its potential for identifying homosexual tendencies, whether for clinical or research purposes, the utility of the Wheeler index will depend on the availability of this information from readier sources, such as asking the subject. If he can simply state whether or not he is homosexual, the time necessary to obtain the Wheeler signs would not be justified, whatever their accuracy. Thus the merit of this index will lie in its as yet undetermined capacity to detect those individuals in whom underlying or otherwise unsuspected homosexual concerns are exerting a significant influence.

Suicide Indications

Of the many different Rorschach signs or configurations that have been suggested for possible use in the prediction of suicidal behavior, none has received consistent empirical support. Only a few of the suggested systems—Beck's configurations, Martin's checklist, Hertz' configurations, Appelbaum and Holzman's color-shading responses, and morbid mood responses—have been found to differentiate significantly between suicidal and nonsuicidal groups, and of these only Beck's configurations begin to approach the precision necessary for clinical application. If the presence of suicidal tendencies has already been established, however, Kruger's form-dominance score can validly predict whether individuals are likely to express their tendencies through actual attempts or merely through ideation and threats.

These primarily negative findings appear related more to the numerous methodological problems of research on suicidal behavior than to any inherent diagnostic insensitivity of the Rorschach. Criteria for suicide threats, gestures, and attempts have not been uniformly specified, important differences between transient suicidal ideation and actual suicide have not been carefully delineated, and many efforts to develop predictive indices have utilized data collected from subjects following rather than prior to suicidal behavior. Additionally, the very low base rates for suicide in most populations makes it difficult for any measuring instrument to achieve sufficient utility to justify its application. Further efforts to develop and validate Rorschach indices for suicide prediction are unlikely to succeed unless these methodological challenges can be met.

Neurotic Signs

As in the case of suicide indications, the major Rorschach systems for assessing neurosis or adjustment—Miale / Harrower-Erickson, Munroe, Davidson, Muench, and Fisher—have provided few consistent distinctions between individuals or groups. Although these various indices can be reliably and fairly easily computed from Rorschach summary scores, their capacity to relate to neurosis or adjustment is compromised by the unreliability of the criteria—like suicide, neither neurosis nor adjustment has ever been uniformly defined for clinical or research purposes.

On the positive side, the Fisher index and, to a lesser extent, the Munroe index do appear able to separate groups according to their degree of psychological disturbance. However, the normative data for these systems are insufficient to determine their suitability for individual application in clinical settings. Furthermore, the potential utility of all five systems for neurosis or adjustment is limited by the fact that each was constructed primarily from clinical impressions rather than from empirical sifting of potential signs with appropriate subject samples or from any conceptual relation to neurosis. Thus, in contrast to many of the suicide indications, these systems for neurosis or adjustment are unlikely to demonstrate clinically useful validity no matter how carefully they are studied.

Schizophrenic Signs

Despite the long history of attention to the Rorschach diagnosis of schizophrenia and the voluminous literature in this area, relatively little effort has been devoted to the development and psychometric assessment of Rorschach systems for identifying this disturbance. Four systems have been the subject of multiple journal articles—Piotrowski's alpha index, the Thiesen patterns, the delta index of Watkins and Stauffacher, and Weiner's signs for color stress and deviant tempo. Of these, only the delta index has been examined for reliability, and its interscorer agreement has thus far proved adequate only for subjects with some diagnosed extent of psychological disturbance.

The alpha index is applicable to only a small percent of subjects and gives no meaningful information when it is low. When it does emerge, however, a critical score on the index has proved consistently indicative of some form of schizophrenic disturbance. The Thiesen patterns appear to occur more frequently in the records of schizophrenic than of normal subjects. However, they are so infrequent in the records of either group as to have minimal utility for either clinical or research applications. The delta index is cumbersome to use, but has proved reasonably capable of differentiating schizophrenic from normal and neurotic subjects. Weiner's color-stress and deviant-tempo indices, when used together, yield fairly accurate differentiations between schizophrenics and nonschizophrenic psychiatric patients, with a particularly low incidence of false-positive indications of schizophrenia. However, the cross-validating studies of Weiner's indices reveal enough empirical shrinkage to warrant caution in their clinical application until further studies have been done.

Thus, all of these indices, with the possible exception of the Theisen patterns, have yielded some encouraging results but have not been assessed sufficiently to delineate their precise capacities and limitations. Further work in this area must meet the methodological challenge posed by the heterogeneity of schizophrenic conditions, the enormous variations in the ways in which this diagnostic label is applied, and the importance of integrating Rorschach diagnostic indices into conceptual frameworks relevant to the nature of schizophrenia.

Organic Signs

No definitive statement can be made as yet about the efficacy of the Rorschach in the diagnosis of organicity, primarily because the research on organic signs has characteristically failed to provide either an adequate definition of the nature of the organic involvement in the experimental group or careful exclusion of organicity in the controls. Studies in this area have furthermore consistently failed to consider the relationship of organic signs to such critical subject variables as age, intelligence, and size, locus, and duration of the lesion.

The most widely studied Rorschach system for organicity is the Piotrowski signs, which are frequently criticized but have nevertheless demonstrated greater clinical efficacy than any of the other existing systems. The Piotrowski signs cannot clearly differentiate brain damage from chronic schizophrenia, and they have the limitation of yielding a high rate of false-negative indications. However, in a general medical or neurological setting in which chronic schizophrenia is an unlikely diagnostic possibility, a critical score on the Piotrowski index constitutes a strong suggestion of cerebral dysfunction. Although further information is needed concerning the specific diagnostic implications of the Piotrowski signs for subjects of different age and intelligence levels and with different types of lesions, available data justify further development of this index for clinical applications.

Therapy Prognosis

The most systematic and encouraging Rorschach research on therapy prognosis has emerged from Klopfer's prognostic rating scale (PRS), which can be reliably scored and has demonstrated good predictive and construct validity. PRS scores can predict overt behavior change for clinic and hospital patients, due either to treatment or "spontaneous remission," and they also indicate individual capacity to adjust to new and difficult situations.

PRS has proved negatively related to severity of disturbance and positively correlated with educational level and with a premorbid history of social and sexual adequacy.

However, because PRS is significantly related to such variables as degree of disturbance and premorbid history, which by themselves can predict response to therapy, its practical utility may be limited. As in determining whether or not homosexuality is present, the ready availability of nontest data adequate to make the necessary distinctions diminishes the utility of psychodiagnostic testing. Additional data are also needed to identify whether PRS can predict response to forms of therapy other than traditional insight-oriented approaches, which have been involved in most of the research with it. Nevertheless, these considerations should not obscure the generally positive results of assessment work with this index.

Comment

As the reader will have noted, the substantive findings presented in this book and summarized above pertain to the Rorschach as an independent psychometric instrument and do not reflect its potential utility either as part of a test battery or as a tool in the hands of skilled clinicians. It is important in concluding this section to comment on and justify these areas of omission.

Regarding the test battery, the value of the Rorschach in actual clinical and research practice frequently lies in providing support for inferences derived from other kinds of data or in allowing comparisons with other tests. Thus a critical number of Piotrowski's organic signs may combine with indices of cognitive deficit on perceptual-motor tasks to yield a particularly strong suggestion of brain dysfunction, and the combination of a disordered Rorschach performance with fairly well-retained cognitive functioning on more structured tests may be crucial for identifying early or incipient forms of schizophrenia (see Weiner, 1966, Chapter 15).

Granting the usual superiority of a carefully selected test battery over reliance on any single test, it is still essential that each component of the battery have some demonstrable capacity for contributing to the assessment process. Each test must to some extent be able to stand on its own; although a good test battery should be able to improve on the diagnostic validity of its individual components, no battery composed of invalid tests can be expected to provide meaningful or useful personality assessments. For this reason the current presentation has focused on the individual reliability and validity of the most widely used Rorschach indices, independent of their potential participation in a test battery.

Concerning attention to global judgments derived from the Rorschach rather than to the discriminatory capacity of Rorschach scores, a strong argument has been made that the true test of a psychodiagnostic instrument is what it can be made to do in the hands of a skilled examiner (see Hunt, 1959; Hunt and Jones, 1962). From this point of view, efforts to assess the reliability and validity of diagnostic techniques should define the clinician as the measuring instrument and assess the utility of his judgments. When the clinician is viewed as the instrument and his judgments constitute the independent variables in assessment studies, the data obtained indicate both the general utility of the clinical psychodiagnostic process and the nature and possible origin of differences between examiners in the skill with which they can make diagnostic judgments.

However, the study of global Rorschach judgments has serious limitations as an approach to assessing and developing the psychometric adequacy of the Rorschach. For one thing, the skilled examiner can communicate and pass on his gifts only if he is able to specify the particular features of the Rorschach that he utilizes in making his demonstrably sound judgments —whether location choice, determinants, content, verbalizations, or various combinations and configurations of these basic variables. Assessment studies of global judgments may validate the clinician as a good diagnostician and may suggest the kinds of training, experience, or orientation that are associated with good capacity for deriving valid clinical judgments from the Rorschach; however, unless the clinicians indicate their method, such studies yield no communicable information about the strengths and weaknesses of Rorschach variables.

Furthermore, if the clinician cannot specify how he is using the Rorschach to arrive at his judgements, it is difficult to rule out the possibility that he is deriving clues primarily from his general interaction with the subject around the Rorschach, rather than from Rorschach data per se. In such a case the Rorschach will not be contributing much more to clinical decision making than could be realized from any nonspecific task or topic around which the examiner and subject interacted, and the validity of the clinician's judgments will have few implications for the validity of the Rorschach. Assessment of the Rorschach through study of global judgments derived from it must ultimately be concerned with the particular Rorschach variables that participated in the global judgments, and the previous chapters have accordingly focused on the reliability and validity of specific Rorschach indices.

Finally, some comments are in order concerning the overall tenor of the findings reviewed above. Many of the Rorschach indices surveyed have demonstrated sufficient validity to justify their use for research purposes. For the most part, however, the suitability of these indices for clinical use has not been adequately explored, and many of the chapters conclude with suggestions for kinds of further resarch necessary to delineate the full potential of Rorschach applications. Yet critics of the Rorschach method have been known to denigrate such suggestions on the grounds that any 50-year-old technique which must still be defended in terms of its potential is a candidate for the wastebasket.

Such assertions fallaciously presume that all research designs are created equal. It cannot be denied that the majority of the studies in the Rorschach literature have yielded negative or ambiguous results, and a superficial appraisal of these data could easily lead clinicians and researchers to despair of pursuing Rorschach applications. However, as reiterated in the various chapters of this book, Rorschach research is flagrantly riddled with methodological blunders and oversights that exclude much of it from serious consideration. Furthermore, the likelihood of outcomes favorable to Rorschach indices seems directly related to the care with which assessment studies have been designed, and impressive positive data have emerged from studies in which appropriately derived Rorschach indices have been assessed with appropriate samples against appropriate criteria and with appropriate requirements for making concurrent or predictive judgments.

These data affirm the potential of the Rorschach method for some uses, and no accumulation of negative findings from inadequate research diminishes this potential, whatever the span of years it covers. The student of the Rorschach needs to focus his attention on that small portion of the research that satisfies minimal methodological standards and concern himself with further studies that avoid at least the most obvious pitfalls of design. The next section outlines the major methodological considerations that need to be incorporated in studies of the reliability and validity of Rorschach indices.

METHODOLOGICAL CONSIDERATIONS

A number of methodological considerations in assessing Rorschach applications were introduced in Chapter 1 and have been touched on in Chapters 2–12. It is now appropriate to review these considerations and elaborate their implications for designing adequate studies of the reliability, criterion-related validity, and construct validity of Rorschach indices. Although this discussion will focus primarily on Rorschach scores, the points to be made relate generally to the psychometric adequacy of projective techniques and of psychodiagnosis in general. For further reading on these broader issues, the reader is referred to contributions by Holt (1970), MacFarlane and Tuddenham (1951), and Weiner (1966, Chapter 19), and to the volumes of McReynolds (1968), Rabin (1968), and Zubin, Eron, and Schumer 1965).

Reliability

Two major components of psychometric reliability are (1) the extent to which judges can agree on the scores they derive from a test and (2) the extent to which these scores accurately measure the variables they are intended to measure. Regarding interjudge agreement, the preceding chapters have reviewed available data for various Rorschach indices and found them for the most part favorable. As pointed out in Chapter 8, however, the apparently good scoring reliability for those indices based on Rorschach summary scores may be deceptive. Good interscorer agreement for such measures as Friedman's developmental level (*DL*) and Elizur's hostility level (*HL*) assures scoring reliability, since *DL* and *HL* are scored directly from Rorschach responses. However, this assurance does not apply to such indices as Piotrowski's organic signs or Martin's suicide checklist, which are determined from previously assigned summary scores rather than from individual responses. Judges who can agree on whether the number of M that has been scored for a record does or does not meet the Piotrowski criterion for organicity (M < 2) might not agree on the number of Ms they would score for the record if each were to begin with the raw data.

There is in fact good reason to expect that Rorschach examiners who fully comprehend and concur on the criteria for an index based on summary scores may differ in the summary scores they assign to individual protocols. Exner (1969) has recently demonstrated that there really is no "Rorschach" but rather at least five "Rorschach systems," and that examiners committed to different major systems (Beck, Hertz, Klopfer, Piotrowski, and Rapaport–Schafer) have difficulty agreeing on the scoring even for such a basic element as M.

Because there are different approaches to the scoring of Rorschach protocols, investigators must be circumspect in utilizing previously scored records to study interscorer agreement on clinical or research indices based on summary scores. It may be possible to establish that all of the records used for the study were initially scored within the same frame of reference and can be presumed to reflct reliable determination of summary scores. If such a fortunate circumstance does not obtain, the records should be rescored according to some preselected and carefully specified system before any attempt is made to assess the scoring reliability of an index calculated from summary scores. The literature suggests that much of the unreliability of Rorschach scoring can be eliminated by adequate pretraining and supervised experience with a specific system (Zubin, Eron, and Schumer, 1965, p. 185).

It is additionally necessary to recognize that a Rorschach index which can be reliably scored by one group of investigators and their trainees may not fare as well in the hands of others. The simpler and more explicit the criteria for a Rorschach index, the more likely it is that examiners working only from a written description will be able to score it reliably. However, the more complex the criteria, the greater is the possibility that implicit guidelines shared only by the original investigators and their students influence its scoring, and furthermore, that examiners working only from a manual will encounter ambiguities they cannot resolve without imposing guidelines of their own.

Studies of scoring reliability for Rorschach indices therefore need to be pursued beyond a single setting or group of investigators. Only if good interjudge agreement is achieved by a number of independently functioning clinicians and researchers, each working just from a written description of scoring criteria, can the index be presumed to have sufficient scoring reliability to justify its broad application.

As for accuracy of measurement, a test index can be considered reliable to the extent that it is free from systematic sources of error variance. Accuracy of measurement is traditionally judged from the stability of test scores across split-half, parallel form, or test-retest assessments. The higher the reliability coefficient demonstrated in such assessments, the freer the test can be presumed to be from extraneous influences that decrease accuracy of measurement.

As noted in Chapter 1, the Rorschach does not lend itself easily to split-half reliability studies, nor is there any satisfactory parallel form for the test. Rorschach reliability studies must therefore focus on retest methods, which must be carefully employed. A brief retest interval is likely to yield a spurious reliability estimate, since Rorschach retesting involves considerable memory and practice effects. Yet, for Rorschach indices that measure expected charges over time, retest intervals long enough to minimize memory and practice effects may produce low correlations that underestimate reliability.

In terms of methodology, then, it is important that retest reliability studies be designed with adequate attention to circumstances that should or should not be expected to transcend the stability of test scores. When the variable being assessed is presumed to be consistent over time, as in the case of characterological levels of anxiety (see Chapter 4) and hostility (see Chapter 5), a retest assessment of a Rorschach index intended to measure it can yield meaningful information concerning the reliability of the index. If the status of the variable is expected to change over time, as it is for level of perceptual organization in children (see Chapter 2), then a retest assessment of Rorschach indices for it becomes an indication of criterion-related validity for the index. If nothing is known of expected change or stability for the variable, then retesting with a Rorschach index contributes no information about either the reliability or validity of the index. In designing retest reliability studies, then, it is essential to identify and focus on variables that can be presumed to remain constant over a period long enough to ensure that memory and practice effects will not yield spurious reliability estimates.

Criterion-Related Validity: Concurrent

In Chapter 1 it was pointed out that criterion-related validity research demands explicit and precise definitions of criterion measures. Much of the Rorschach research on concurrent validity, especially in the area of clinical diagnosis, has been handicapped by inadequate delineation of the criterion groups. When the concurrent validity of Rorschach diagnostic indices is inferred from comparisons between subjects with different clinical diagnoses, as it often is, any diagnostic unreliability will limit the validity coefficient that can be obtained for the Rorschach indices. Thus the known unreliability of many psychiatric diagnoses poses a major methodological problem for Rorschach research.

There are several ways of contending with this problem. First, investigators can avoid defining their subject groups merely according to recorded clinical diagnoses and instead select their subjects on the basis of preestablished, explicit diagnostic guidelines. Clinical judges trained in specific selection criteria can avoid much of the variability observed among clinicians who record diagnostic labels in clinical settings, and such a procedure also provides other investigators with an explicit statement of how neurotics or schizophrenics or organics have been defined for a particular research study. If clinicians and researchers cannot agree on definitions of neurosis or schizophrenia or organicity, they can at least specify the criteria they use in selecting neurotic, schizophrenic, and organic subjects for their study, and the criteria can be more substantive than merely "50 each of diagnosed neurotics, schizophrenics, and organics were chosen for this investigation."

Secondly, investigators can avoid relying on gross nosological categories in the face of considerable information concerning the heterogeneity of diagnostic groups. Neurotic subjects may display primarily ideational or primarily hysterical defensive styles, the nature of schizophrenic disturbance varies significantly in relation to the acuteness or chronicity of the disorder and whether it is paranoid or nonparanoid in form, and patients with organic brain disease differ considerably in the extent, locus, and duration of their lesions. Adequate concurrent validity studies of the Rorschach require that such meaningful subcategories of clinical diagnosis be incorporated in the research methodology.

A final and more challenging problem relates to the fact that people with a similar psychological disturbance may vary considerably in their reaction to it. Of two people with brain dysfunction, for example, one may react to his perceived loss of function with marked manifest depression, while the other, utilizing denial, does not. A Rorschach index for organicity that contains several scores sensitive to manifest depression will do much better in discriminating the first kind of organic patient from a normal control group than it will in distinguishing the second. However, neither the relative success with the depressed organic patient nor the relative failure with the nondepressed one would accurately indicate the capacity of the Rorschach index to identify organicity as distinct from an individual's reaction to it.

This distinction between an event and the reaction to it is particularly relevant to suicide research, as mentioned in Chapter 8. Because studies in this area generally use postsuicide attempters as subjects, it is difficult to determine to what extent the obtained Rorschach data reflect the presuicidal personality dynamics that contributed to the attempt or rather postattempt changes in mood or attitudes.

Thus the timing of the Rorschach administration is crucial to an effective test of personality differences between suicidal and nonsuicidal persons or any two groups who have behaved differently. The sooner following an event or onset of a condition that the Rorschach is applied, the less is the likelihood that long-term adjustments or reactions will obscure the condition or disposition being assessed. Ideally, the measure should precede the event, as in the administration of Rorschach adjustment measures to a large sample of students at the beginning of a semester to allow later comparisons of adjustment level between those who achieve and those who fail (see Chapter 9).

Criterion-Related Validity: Predictive

Studies of predictive validity, in common with concurrent validity research, demand above all precise and appropriate criterion definition. Many studies purporting to assess the predictive validity of Rorschach indices, because they have attempted predictions of highly complex, multidetermined, and poorly demarcated behaviors, have yielded unnecessarily discouraging results. It is easy to lose sight of the fact that negative findings are significant only when they emerge from research that adequately tests the instruments or hypotheses under investigation.

The potential pitfalls in criterion definition for predictive validity studies of the Rorschach are particularly clear in relation to therapy prognosis (see Chapter 12). Considerable attention has been devoted to the general problem of defining appropriate outcome indices for clinical and research studies of psychotherapy, and no final or generally accepted resolution of this thorny question has as yet been achieved. Accordingly, the Rorschach investigator who selects for study and publishes data on subjects defined simply as "improved" or "unimproved" does a disservice to the Rorschach and to his colleagues. If he provides finer shades of improvement ("slightly improved," "significantly improved") and indicates that improvement was rated by the subjects' therapists or by a group of independent raters who reviewed the relevant clinical records, he still has not met the standards for adequate research design. Rather, his challenge is to determine as carefully as he can what his behavioral criteria are for calling someone "improved" or "unimproved" and to explicate these criteria in his report. Only such careful delineation and explication of criteria can offer any promise for the replication of research findings.

Whereas a clear specification of behavior variables will facilitate attempts to predict them, their complexity may still prevent any single index from predicting them adequately. Thus even a reliably definable and conceptually meaningful set of behavioral criteria may not be predictable from Rorschach indices or any other personality test index if the behavior is multiply determined by a number of interpersonal and environmental sources of variance (see Mischel, 1968). This is the problem of unmeasured variables noted in Chapter 1.

For example, the prognosis for a schizophrenic patient about to be discharged from a hospital will depend not only on the current status of his personality resources but also on such factors as the nature of the work or family responsibilities he will be expected to resume, the tolerance of the people in his immediate environment for continued manifestations of his disturbance, and the availability of continued outpatient treatment following discharge. Given these manifold influences on his post-hospital adjustment, it is unjustified to expect that a measure of personality will, by itself, predict his long-range course. In conjunction with other relevant variables, Rorschach indices of personality structure and dynamics may account for part of the variance that can accurately predict a complex outcome, just as a pliers, a screwdriver, and a wrench may all be needed to repair a faulty piece of machinery. One does not throw away the pliers because it cannot do the job alone.

Yet the Rorschach has frequently been asked to do the job alone, and many aspersions on its validity can be traced to studies in which it was asked to achieve such overly ambitious goals as the prediction of suicidal behavior, academic performance, and success in a variety of training and work situations. In designing predictive validity studies of the

Rorschach, the investigator needs to ask whether the criterion behavior can be predicted from personality structure and dynamics alone. If so, then his data may provide a meaningful validity assessment; if not, he needs first to determine what other independent variables are relevant to the behavior and then to include them along with the Rorschach in his predictive effort; and if he cannot answer the question at all, then he needs further study of the criterion behavior itself before he tests Rorschach indices against it.

Investigators furthermore need to recognize that some Rorschach indices by their nature have little relevance to predicting behavior, and for these indices prediction even to a criterion entirely determined by personality variance is an inappropriate validity assessment. In discussions of the Elizur indices for hostility and anxiety (Chapters 4 and 5), for example, it was pointed out that these indices measure a characterological level of underlying hostility and anxiety but do not sample the manner in which the individual expresses these affects. Of two people with similar amounts of hostility as measured by Elizur's *HL,* one may be ideationally oriented and express his hostility through sarcastic speech, while the other is action oriented and expresses his hostility in physically aggressive behavior toward others. Prediction of behavior for these two people from their personality structure and dynamics would require a combination of information from the Elizur about hostility level with other knowledge about defensive style.

Other indices have been derived in a manner that limits their ability to do many of the predictive jobs expected of them. This problem arises most commonly when Rorschach investigators use test indices apparent in people following some event to predict the occurrence of that event in a new sample. Predictive efforts based on postdictively validated indices may fail not only because of the previously mentioned differences that may obtain between the precursors of an event and the reactions to it, but also because there may be qualitative differences between what are presumed to be merely quantitative points along a single behavioral continuum.

For example, there is reason to believe that people who actually kill themselves differ in their personality make-up from people who make suicide threats, gestures, or attempts. Hence, a Rorschach index derived from studies of suicide attempters, even if should happen to predict suicide attempts in subsequent samples, cannot be expected necessarily to contribute to the prediction of actual suicide. Similarly, students of average or above average ability who do poorly in school but still manage to maintain passing grades may have significantly different personality dynamics from equally able students who underachieve to the point of failure. Accordingly, Rorschach scores found to differentiate between achieving and underachieving students, all of whom are still in school, may not validly predict the likelihood of student failure.

Studies of predictive validity must accordingly be designed in light of the facts (1) that personality features observed following an event may differ from those which determined its occurence and (2) that personality characteristics sufficient to produce tendencies toward a specific behavior may not be qualitatively identical to those which are necessary to precipitate full manifestation of the behavior. In designing predictive validity studies, therefore, investigators must be certain that the behavior they are asking the Rorschach to predict is truly comparable to the criterion behavior from which the supposed predictive index was derived. Without such certainty there cannot be an adequate assessment of the predictive validity of Rorschach indices.

Construct Validity

Assessments of construct validity, because they incorporate aspects of concurrent and predictive validity studies, require precise definitions of subject groups and of the characteristics to be sampled among them. In addition, however, adequate studies of construct validity require the predicted behavior to have a clear theoretical relationship to the criteria used for subject selection.

As illustrated in Chapter 5, for example, Rorschach anxiety-level (*AL*) scores are presumed to differentiate among people according to their characterological levels of anxiety, and nail biting is conceived in part as a behavioral manifestation of anxiety; hence, severity of nail biting should be significantly associated with extent of anxiety as measured by *AL,* and confirmation of this association demonstrated the construct validity of the *AL* index. On the other hand, the fact that Munroe's inspection technique (*IT*) has significantly predicted academic performance in several studies and failed to do so in other studies provides little information either for or against the construct validity of the *IT* as an adjustment index (see Chapter 9). Although maladjustment may contribute to academic ineptness, any theoretical relationship between them is much less compelling than the conceptual bridge between anxiety and nail biting.

Thus the methodological task in construct-validity studies of personality measures is to formulate theoretical relationships that appropriately link the personality characteristics being measured with the behavior being predicted. The previous chapters have repeatedly observed that the more clearly studies of Rorschach indices have involved such conceptual bridges between the independent and dependent variables, the more favorably the findings have reflected on the validity of the Rorschach index. Conversely, negative validity findings appear particularly likely to accumulate when discriminations or predictions are expected of the Rorschach in the absence of clearly specified theoretical formulations that justify these expectations.

The investigator who wishes to assess the construct validity of Rorschach indices needs first to identify the personality variables presumably measured by that index and then to select for his dependent variables specific behaviors or conditions presumably determined in significant part by those same personality variables. If he cannot decide with any confidence what personality variables are assessed by a Rorschach index, then that index cannot lend itself to adequate construct-validity studies and probably has little potential for widespread or sustained cross validation. If he is not satisfied that the behaviors he would like to use as his dependent variables are in fact significantly related to the personality variable measured by the

Rorschach index he wishes to study, then he needs to look further to find more adequate dependent variables. If none seems available, then he may have to decide that the Rorschach index, no matter how accurately it measures, is not measuring anything worthwhile, just like the often joked about treatment for which no disease has as yet been found.

THE UTILITY OF RORSCHACH APPLICATIONS

It is finally relevant to consider the differential utility of the Rorschach for clinical and research applications. Differential utility refers simply to what the Rorschach can and cannot be expected to do, and the assessment of utility involves certain extensions and refinements of usual validity considerations. The potential utility of a Rorschach index that has some demonstrable validity depends on three aspects of the specific situation in which it is to be applied: (1) whether it is primarily a clinical situation requiring discriminations among individuals or rather a research situation requiring distinctions between groups; (2) the degree to which distinctions achieved by the index improve on base-rate incidence and satisfy the tolerance for false-negative and false-positive indications in the specific situation; and (c) the extent to which the behavior under study is directly represented or merely symbolized by the Rorschach behavior used to measure it.

Clinical and Research Applications

Clinical and research applications of the Rorschach differ considerably in the precision of the discriminations they require. An investigator wishing to study the relationship between psychological maturity and impulse control in children may do well to compare Friedman's Rorschach developmental-level scores with scores on some valid measure of impulse control. Since *DL* scores validly reflect psychological maturation in children, a simple comparison of the median percent of genetically high Ws received by children equated for age but relatively high or low in impulse control would provide an appropriate test of the hypothesized relationship between maturity and impulse control.

Such group distinctions are seldom adequate for the clinical application of Rorschach indices. In estimates of suicidal potential or likelihood of schizophrenic or organic pathology, for example, utility for a Rorschach index is not indicated by a demonstrably valid association with one of these conditions (i.e., capacity to make significant discriminations between groups who do or do not have the condition), but rather by the percentage of subjects it can accurately classify as positive or negative for it. For research purposes a significant degree of association between two variables may be sufficient to demonstrate a conceptually meaningful hypothesized relationship between them; however, if this degree of association is not sufficiently powerful to allow accurate qualitative classification of a substantial percentage of subjects, its clinical utility is limited.

Thus the distinction between clinical and research applications pertains primarily to the problem of overlap mentioned in Chapter 1 and elsewhere, namely, that the precision necessary for idiographic applications of the Rorschach is greater than that required for nomothetic uses. A Rorschach index that discriminates between groups is satisfactory for application to individuals only if overlap between groups is sufficiently small to allow reasonable confidence in individual judgments based on the index. This consideration has often been overlooked in decisions to use the Rorschach for clinical purposes. Indices validated for group distinctions have frequently been put to the test of correctly identifying individual subjects, a task for which they are understandably likely to be found wanting.

It cannot be too strongly emphasized that significant mean differences between groups on a Rorschach diagnostic index, no matter how carefully the groups are defined, do not justify using that index for individual clinical diagnosis. The decision to use a Rorschach index for any idiographic purpose should be based on knowledge that the index has a reasonable likelihood of making the correct differentiation in a sufficient proportion of individual cases to satisfy the needs of the situation. This likelihood can be estimated only from appropriately designed research that indicates the percentage of correct judgments achieved by the index. *If such research is unavailable, as it is for many Rorschach indices, it is best to restrict the index to continued research applications and not to rely on it for clinical purposes.*

The clinical user of Rorschach indices must similarly be cautious in applying them to subjects who differ markedly from those on whom it was validated and for whom satisfactory percentages of correct judgments have been reported. For example, a Rorschach index for schizophrenia derived from and carefully cross validated with comparisons between blatantly schizophrenic patients and normal controls may elucidate general differences between the schizophrenic and the normal condition without necessarily having any utility for clinical judgments. The psychodiagnostic consultant is seldom asked to discriminate between normal and blatantly schizophrenic people; more frequently, his task is to differentiate patients with minimal or borderline schizophrenic deficits from nonschizophrenic patients who are nevertheless manifesting symptoms suggestive of schizophrenia. A Rorschach index that is highly successful in separating blatantly schizophrenic from normal subjects may be too gross to assist with the difficult and subtle diagnostic distinctions required in the clinical arena. The clinician needs accordingly to select diagnostic indices that have not only proved accurate in classifying easily separable groups, but also have achieved a satisfactory hit rate among clinically challenging subjects comparable to those with whom he intends to use it.

Base-Rate Considerations and Tolerance for Error

The concept of population base rates, as first elaborated by Meehl and Rosen (1955; see Chapter 1), implies that a valid test score or interpretation is useful only to the extent that it improves on the number of correct judgments that could be made without any differential assessment of the subjects. For a randomly distributed variable, any test index that can accurately classify a statistically significant proportion of subjects will, by definition, provide a useful improvement over chance judgments. However, the more the population incidence or base rate for a variable deviates from 50–50, the greater is the possibility that a test index which can identify its presence or absence in a significant percentage of a sample drawn from the population may still have no utility for making judgments about samples from that population.

Discussions in previous chapters have illustrated the manner in which valid Rorschach indices may fail to contribute meaningfully to clinical decisions. For example, a valid index of organicity that correctly classifies 65% of subjects as organically or nonorganically impaired will have no utility for evaluating patients referred from a neurological service on which the normative incidence of neuropathology is 70%. Simply regarding all patients on the service as having neurological disease will yield a higher percentage of correct identifications (70%) than will be realized from using the 65% accurate Rorschach index.

Decisions to use the Rorschach in a particular clinical or research situation should therefore include careful weighing of its demonstrated hit rate for the variables under study against the base-rate incidence of these variables in the population from which the subjects are selected. The clinician or researcher who applies the Rorschach in situations where its capacity for accurate discriminations falls short of population base rates may be in for disappointments that could have been avoided. The error will have lain not in the Rorschach, but in his asking it to do things he should not have expected it to do.

In view of these considerations, psychometric investigators should plan to collect and analyze their data in a manner that yields information related to base-rate expectancies. Where population base rates are known or can be determined, these values rather than chance should be used as the expected occurrence against which the obtained occurrence in individual samples is compared. When base-rate data are not available, it is important that the investigator attempt to make his sample as representative as possible of the population from which it is drawn. In the absence of detailed information about population parameters, this is often best done by total block sampling. Thus if an investigator were to study all patients seen for testing on a neurological service over some adequately long period of time, his subjects should constitute a representative sample of the population. Then any discriminatory power demonstrated by a test index within his sample could be presumed capable of similarly good discriminations in the population as a whole and among subsequent samples drawn from it—at least until such time as the nature of the population has changed in some significant way.

Concerning tolerance for error due to false-positive and false-negative indications, a valid test index will be useful only to the extent that its discriminatory power is congruent with the value judgments attached to the variable being measured. In the measurement of a positively valued trait, a relatively high percentage of false-negative indications can usually be tolerated, but false positives are costly; for a negatively valued trait, false positives are generally inconvenient at worst, whereas false negatives can be disastrous.

To illustrate, good prognosis for therapy can be considered a positively valued trait. Given the shortage of mental health manpower, there are usually more people applying for or in need of treatment than there are therapists to provide it. If a selection instrument identifies a large number of false negatives, that is, if it labels as poor treatment risks patients who in fact could have benefited from therapy, some patients will have been disadvantaged but the therapists' time may still be fully utilized. On the other hand, if the instrument errs heavily on the side of false positives, that is, if it selects for treatment many patients who drop out or otherwise do not benefit, then therapeutic effort will have been wasted and the patient population as a whole will not have received as much benefit as it would if the selection measure, whatever its incidence of false negatives, had not yielded any false positives.

The obverse situation obtains for negatively valued traits, of which suicidal potential is a good example. If an instrument for detecting suicidal risk overestimates the risk (false positives), unnecessary precautions may be taken for large numbers of people who would not have taken their lives. In terms of utility, however, this may be a price worth paying if the instrument is virtually free from false negatives, that is, if it almost always identifies people who, if not appropriately supervised, will kill themselves.

As this last example indicates, value judgments often combine with base-rate considerations to determine the utility of a psychometric instrument for a particular purpose. Because suicide is such a rare event, even a 90% correct test index is unlikely to improve on the statistical accuracy achieved by simply considering everyone nonsuicidal (see Chapter 8), and it is accordingly difficult to reconcile any clinical assessment of suicidal tendencies purely with base-rate considerations. From a value-judgment point of view, however, if a test index rarely yields a false negative, and if it is applied in a setting (e.g., psychiatric hospital) and to a population (e.g., depressed patients) where the base rate for suicide is considerably higher than among the population in general, the few instances in which it contributes to averting otherwise inevitable suicides may well be worth the extra effort caused by unnecessary suicide precautions.

In relation to error tolerance as well as base rates, then, the task is to select a test index that can be expected to do the required assessment job in the particular clinical or research situation where it is to be applied. If the clinician or investigator cannot specify base-rate or false-positive/false-negative expectations for his instruments in the situation he is studying, he needs either to search out such data or, in its absence, to refrain from criticising his measures should they fail to accomplish discriminations he had no right to expect of them.

Finally, the fact that clinical applications of the Rorschach usually involve situations in which either true-negative or true-positive indications are of prime importance has implications for validity research that are frequently overlooked. That is, in practice a test index is used to decide the likelihood either that a given condition is present or that it is not, and the alternative to either option is usually no decision at all. Thus a critical incidence of Piotrowski's signs is in some situations strongly suggestive of cerebral brain dysfunction, but absence of the signs does not rule out organicity, since the measure is known to yield a relatively high (but tolerable) number of false negatives (see Chapter 11). The most appropriate use of the Piotrowski index is to suggest organicity when it is present and to make no decision when it is not.

Accordingly, validating research with Piotrowski signs should allow a no-decision option, in order that the known propensity of the measure to elicit false negatives is not equally weighted with and allowed to obscure the potential utility of its true-positive indications. The notion of a no-decision category has rarely been appreciated and included in studies of Rorschach validity. Just as the sophisticated clinician recognizes that at times his Rorschach data are too ambiguous to allow him to answer a clinical question, validity studies need to provide a no-decision option rather than force all the obtained protocols into yes-no categories.

Symbolic and Representative Behavior

Finally, the user of the Rorschach needs to be guided by the extent to which the personality variables he is studying are directly represented or merely symbolized by the Rorschach behavior that measures them. In general, the more closely a Rorschach index parallels the actual behavior it will be used to understand, discriminate, or predict, the greater the likelihood that it will be capable of the task. On the other hand, the more the Rorschach index is symbolic of the behavior being studied, the wider is the latitude for the kinds of unknown or uncontrolled sources of error variance that generally complicate symbolic interpretations of behavior.

The differences between representative and symbolic indices can be elaborated in relation to whether the Rorschach is conceived of primarily as a perceptual-cognitive task, as a structured interview, or as a stimulus to fantasy productions. These conceptions of the Rorschach are not mutually exclusive, and most clinicians and researchers would agree that all three contribute to an understanding of the Rorschach situation. However, Rorschach examiners differ in which of the three they emphasize in approaching their test data, and most Rorschach indices relate primarily to one and not the other two. The following brief discussion of these conceptions clarifies the relationship of various Rorschach indices to each and elaborates the extent to which an index is accordingly representative or symbolic of behavior.

THE RORSCHACH AS A PERCEPTUAL-COGNITIVE TASK. From this perspective the Rorschach is a variegated stimulus field on which the subject is asked to impose some structure and organization. Since the task of responding to the Rorschach requires the subject to exercise his perceptual-cognitive abilities and preferences, Rorschach responses are by definition a reflection of these abilities and preferences, and the Rorschach situation bears an isomorphic relationship to other situations or conditions in which elicited behavior is significantly influenced by aspects of cognitive style and perceptual organization. Thus, Friedman's developmental-level scoring, because it is based on Rorschach behavior that directly represents perceptual organization, has a good likelihood of adequately measuring cognitive maturation, in which level of perceptual organization plays a major role.

Similar perceptual-cognitive parallels between Rorschach behavior and actual behavior are apparent for many clinical diagnostic indices. Since schizophrenic disturbance is defined in part by impaired reality testing, and form-level scores for the Rorschach represent the accuracy of an individual's perceptions, poor form level has a reasonably good chance of measuring extent of schizophrenic impairment. Likewise, because perseverative percepts on the Rorschach are directly representative of the kinds of perseverative behavior generally associated with organic brain dysfunction, Rorschach perseveration can be expected to contribute significantly to the identification of organicity.

In general, then, a Rorschach index based on perceptual-cognitive aspects of responding to the test has good potential for measuring personality characteristics reflected in perceptual-cognitive behavior patterns.

THE RORSCHACH AS A STRUCTURED INTERVIEW. Within this frame of reference the Rorschach administration constitutes a relatively structured interview, and verbal responses elicited by the standard inquiries—"What do you see?"; "Where do you see it?"; "What helps you see it that way?"—are to be interpreted in the same way as any other verbal productions. To the extent that an individual's speech style and language usage reflect features of his personality, then formal aspects of his Rorschach verbalizations, as a representative sample of his speech and language, will be likely to measure those personality features.

Direct Rorschach representation of diagnostically significant speech and language behavior is illustrated by a variety of verbalization patterns that are presumed to reflect psychological disturbance. Blocking, for example, which is one of the cardinal elements of schizophrenic thinking, is typically inferred from characteristically blocked speech patterns that may appear whenever verbal responses are demanded, whether to the Rorschach or any other form of inquiry. Dissociation is similarly a defining characteristic of schizophrenic thinking that is apparent primarily in the discontinuity of verbal productions, and the Rorschach provides a directly representative verbal sample of the logical sequence of a subject's ideas.

Organic brain dysfunction, obsessive-compulsive defensive style, level of language skill, and a host of other cognitive and personality variables can be assessed at least partly from verbal productions, whatever the situation used to elicit them. Automatic phrasing as an index of brain dysfunction, pedantry as a clue to an obsessive-compulsive style, and ungrammatical speech as an indication of limited language skill can be observed in Rorschach responses just as they are in any verbal production. Any Rorschach index based on those aspects of the Rorschach examination which liken it to an interview situation will similarly provide a direct representation of diagnostically meaningful aspects of speech and language.

THE RORSCHACH AS A STIMULUS TO FANTASY PRODUCTIONS. It is finally possible to focus on the Rorschach primarily as a stimulus to fantasy productions. From this point of view the most salient Rorschach data lie in the content of the responses, that is, *what* the subject sees rather than *how* he sees it or how he *verbalizes* his impressions. Whereas the Rorschach as a perceptual-cognitive task relates generally to theories and measures of cognitive functioning, and the Rorschach as a structured interview shares common principles with the formal analysis of verbal productions, the view of the Rorschach as a stimulus to fantasy productions has most in common with the general class of symbolic interpretations of behavior. As such, its parallels are in other efforts to understand behavior as symbolic or derivative of underlying or unconscious needs, attitudes, feelings, and motives, the best examples of which are id-psychoanalytic approaches to the interpretation of dreams, mannerisms of speech and gesture, and artistic and literary forms of self-expression.

It is important to differentiate Rorschach indices that symbolize behavior from those that directly represent it. The major difference is that whereas a representative index like developmental level is based on the operations it is intended to measure (i.e., perceptual organization), a symbolic index has no such direct relationship to the behavior it is presumed to measure and is based on indirect levels of inference.

For example, the perception of "a man with his back turned" or "buttocks" as an index of homosexual tendencies is a symbolic interpretation of content and not a direct representation of behavior associated with homosexuality. Unless he is actively hallucinating, the homosexual is not constantly in the process of perceiving buttocks, at least not in the same sense as he is constantly in the process of organizing his perceptual experience. Rather, his perception of buttocks is a behavior unique to the Rorschach situation, and the inference of homosexual tendencies from this Rorschach response involves a chain of inferences based on what are expected to be the persistent, defining characteristics of homosexuality: For example, homosexual men are preoccupied with the prospect of sexual relationships with other men; anal intercourse is a common modality of male homosexuality; therefore, homosexual men are more likely than other people to perceive ambiguous stimuli as "men seen from behind" or "buttocks," and such percepts in the Rorschach are a clue to homosexual tendencies.

Whatever their content, such chains of inference are operative whenever Rorschach indices are symbolic rather than directly representative of the behavior they are presumed to measure, and symbolic interpretations of the Rorschach are involved whenever the content of a response, rather than any of its formal qualities, provides the basis for scoring an index. However, it is important to note that content interpretations differ in the extent to which they are symbolic and accordingly in the length and complexity of the chain of inferences necessary to provide a rationale for them.

Thus the relationship between the perception of "buttocks" and homosexuality has no face validity and can be explained only by a long leap across several levels of inference.[1] In scoring for body boundaries (see Chapter 6), the presumed relationship between the perception of a turtle or other hard-shelled animal and the view of one's body boundary as definite and relatively impenetrable involves a symbolic interpretation of Rorschach behavior but requires a less tortuous chain of logic than is necessary to connect "buttocks" with homosexual tendencies. To go one step further, the presumed relationship between a percept of "two people arguing" and hostility level (see Chapter 5) is symbolic but involves an almost direct parallel between the measure and the characteristic measured. The hostility-level score for "two people arguing" is not directly representative of behavior, since the characteristic being measured is underlying hostility level and not the propensity for seeing people as arguing. Yet the compelling face validity of the score reflects the fact that only a very modest chain of inference suffices to account for how the perception of people arguing can measure hostility level.

The point of making such distinctions is that the more extensively a Rorschach index symbolizes the behavior it is intended to measure, that is, the less its face validity and the more numerous and complex the levels of inference necessary to provide a rationale for it, the greater are the possibilities for errors of measurement. In the first place, any symbolic interpretation of Rorschach content shares with all symbolic interpretations of behavior the problem of idiosyncratic symbol formation and selection. Despite some arguments for the universality of symbolic meanings, it seems clear that people who differ in age, sex, ethnic origin, and other demographic variables differ in at least some of the symbolic meanings they attach to their experience, and furthermore that most individuals are capable of highly unique symbolic interpretations of what they see. Hence extensive research is necessary to determine the applicability of symbolic interpretations of behavior. Just as a dream of falling may symbolize fear of becoming a prostitute ("fallen women") for a particular woman and fear of losing his job ("fallen from grace") for a particular man, and neither of these for some other man or woman, Rorschach indices symbolic of behavior may or may not be broadly applicable.

Second, since each level of inference in constructing a hypothesis involves some possibility of error, each additional level of inference adds to the total degree of error that may inhere in presuming a relationship between two events. Thus, the lengthier the rationale necessary to account for the presumed relationship between a Rorschach index and a behavioral characteristic, the greater are the odds against demonstrating validity and utility for that index (Goldfried and Kent, 1971).

[1] As noted in Table 7.1 (see p. 196), references to anality are probably good indicators of homosexuality, according to available data. However, Chapman and Chapman (1969) have recently presented evidence that clinicians are likely to place considerable weight on some Wheeler signs for homosexuality that have failed to receive empirical confirmation, and they comment on the unfortunate "persistence of illusory correlation in the face of contradictory reality."

These important considerations in assessing the potential utility of Rorschach indices that are symbolic of behavior do not necessarily imply that such indices should be discarded or presumed useless. A Rorschach index that is broadly symbolic of the characteristic being measured, or at least is demonstrably so for the particular group to which the index is applied, and that can be related to that characteristic through highly precise and accurate levels of inference may be as likely to be valid and useful as any index that is directly representative of the characteristic being measured. However, the user of symbolic indices must recognize that this is not always the case. Symbolic Rorschach indices involve the same kinds of risks for measurement error that attend other symbolic interpretations of behavior. Although they may do the assessment job asked of them, they cannot as readily be presumed adequate to the task as are more directly representative indices.

In summary, then, the Rorschach may be approached either as a perceptual-cognitive task, as a structured interview, or as a stimulus to fantasy productions, and Rorschach indices all relate primarily to one or another of these approaches. Indices based on the first two approaches emphasize the subject's manner of structuring his percepts and verbalizing his responses, and these indices are fairly directly representative of behavior; indices based on the third approach concern response content and constitute symbolic representation of behavior. It is the directly representative indices that offer the most promise for cross validation and broad applicability, whereas symbolic indices appear particularly prone to errors of measurement and the persistence of illusory correlation despite empirical contradiction.

REFERENCES

Abrams, S. 1964. A validation of Piotrowski's Alpha Formula with schizophrenics varying in duration of illness. *American Journal of Psychiatry,* **121,** 45–47.

Adams, H. B. 1964. Therapeutic potentialities of sensory deprivation procedures. *International Mental Health Research Newsletter,* **6,** 7–9.

Adams, H. B., and Cooper, G. D. 1962. Three measures of ego strength and prognosis for psychotherapy. *Journal of Clinical Psychology,* **18,** 490–494.

Adams, H. B., Cooper, G. D., and Carrera, R. N. 1963. The Rorschach and the MMPI: A concurrent validity study. *Journal of Projective Techniques,* **27,** 23–34.

Affleck, D. C., and Mednick, S. A. 1959. The use of the Rorschach test in the prediction of the abrupt terminator in individual psychotherapy. *Journal of Consulting Psychology,* **23,** 125–128.

Ainsworth, M. D., and Klopfer, B. 1954. Evalution of intellectual level, control, creative potential, and the introversive-extratensive relationship. In B. Klopfer et al., *Developments in the Rorschach technique, Vol. I: Technique and Theory.* Yonkers, N. Y.: World Book, pp. 352–375.

Aita, J. A., Reitan, R. M. and Ruth, J. M. 1947. Rorschach's test as a diagnostic aid in brain injury. *American Journal of Psychiatry,* **103,** 770–779.

Allison, H. W., and Allison, S. G. 1954. Personality changes following transorbital lobotomy. *Journal of Abnormal and Social Psychology,* **49,** 219–223.

Allison, J., and Blatt, S. J. 1964. The relationship of Rorschach whole responses to intelligence. *Journal of Projective Techniques and Personality Assessment,* **28,** 255–260.

American Psychological Association. 1954. *Technical recommendations for psychological tests and diagnostic techniques.* Washington, D. C.: APA.

American Psychological Association. 1966. *Standards for educational and psychological tests and manuals.* Washington, D. C.: APA.

AMES, L. B., LEARNED, J., METRAUX, R. W., and WALKER, R. N. 1954. *Rorschach responses in old age.* New York: Hoeber-Harper.

ANDERSEN, I., and MUNROE, R. 1948. Personality factors involved in student concentration on creative painting and commercial art. *Rorschach Research Exchange and Journal of Projective Techniques,* **12,** 141–154.

APPELBAUM, S. A. 1963. The problem-solving aspect of suicide. *Journal of Projective Techniques and Personality Assessment,* **27,** 259–268.

APPELBAUM, S. A., and COLSON, D. B. 1968. A reexamination of the color-shading Rorschach test response. *Journal of Projective Techniques and Personality Assessment,* **32,** 160–164.

APPELBAUM, S. A., and HOLZMAN, P. S. 1962. The color-shading response and suicide. *Journal of Projective Techniques,* **26,** 155–161.

APPLEBY, L. 1956. The relationship of Rorschach Barrier typology to other behavioral measures. Unpublished doctoral dissertation, University of Houston, Houston, Texas.

ARMON, V. 1960. Some personality variables in overt female homosexuality. *Journal of Projective Techniques,* **24,** 292–309.

ARMSTRONG, H. 1964. The relationship between a dimension of body-image and two dimensions of conditioning. Unpublished doctoral dissertation, Syracuse University, Syracuse, N.Y.

ARNAUD, S. H. 1959. A system for deriving quantitative Rorschach measures of certain psychological variables for group comparisons. *Journal of Projective Techniques,* **23,** 403–411.

ARNHOLTER, E. G. 1962. The validity of Fisher's maladjustment and rigidity scales as an indicator of rehabilitation. *Personnel and Guidance Journal,* **40,** 634–637.

ARONSON, M. L. 1952. A study of the Freudian theory of paranoia by means of the Rorschach test. *Journal of Projective Techniques,* **16,** 397–411.

AULD, F., JR., and ERON, L. D. 1953. The use of Rorschach scores to predict whether patients will continue psychotherapy. *Journal of Consulting Psychology,* **17,** 104–109.

BAKER, G. 1956. Diagnosis of organic brain damage in the adult. In B. Klopfer et al., *Developments in the Rorschach technique, Vol. II: Fields of application.* Yonkers, N. Y.: World Book, pp. 318–375.

BANDURA, A., and WALTERS, R. H. 1959. *Adolescent aggression.* New York: Ronald Press.

BARRON, F. 1953a. Some test correlates of response to psychotherapy. *Journal of Consulting Psychology,* **17,** 235–241.

BARRON, F. 1953b. An ego-strength scale which predicts response to psychotherapy. *Journal of Consulting Psychology,* **17,** 327–333.

BARRY, J. R., BLYTH, D. D., and ALBRECHT, R. 1952. Relationships between Rorschach scores and adjustment level. *Journal of Consulting Psychology,* **16,** 30–36.

BECHTOLDT, H. P. 1959. Construct validity: A critique. *American Psychologist,* **14,** 619–630.

BECK, S. J. 1945. *Rorschach's test, Vol. II: A variety of personality pictures.* New York: Grune and Stratton.

BECK, S. J. 1949. *Rorschach's test, Vol. I: Basic processes* (2nd ed.). New York: Grune and Stratton.

Beck, S. J., Beck, A. G., Levitt, E. E., and Molish, H. B. 1961. *Rorschach's test, Vol. I: Basic processes* (3rd ed.). New York: Grune and Stratton.

Beck, S. J., Rabin, A. I., Thiesen, W. G., Molish, H. B., and Thetford, W. N. 1950. The normal personality as projected in the Rorschach test. *Journal of Psychology,* **30,** 241–298.

Becker, W. C. 1956. A genetic approach to the interpretation and evaluation of the process-reactive distinction in schizophrenia. *Journal of Abnormal and Social Psychology,* **53,** 229–236.

Becker, W. C. 1959. The process-reactive distinction: A key to the problem of schizophrenia? *Journal of Nervous and Mental Disease,* **129,** 442–449.

Bergmann, M. S. 1945. Homosexuality on the Rorschach test. *Bulletin of the Menninger Clinic,* **9,** 78–83.

Berk, N. 1949. A personality study of suicidal schizophrenics. Unpublished doctoral dissertation, New York University, New York.

Berkowitz, M., and Levine, J. 1953. Rorschach scoring categories as diagnostic "signs." *Journal of Consulting Psychology,* **17,** 110–112.

Birch, H. G., and Diller, L. 1959. Rorschach signs of "organicity": A physiological basis for perceptual disturbances. *Journal of Projective Techniques,* **23,** 184–197.

Blatt, E. F. 1963. Body image and psychosomatic illness. Paper read at American Psychological Association, Philadelphia.

Bloom, B. L. 1956. Prognostic significance of the underproductive Rorschach. *Journal of Projective Techniques,* **20,** 366–371.

Bordin, E. S. 1966. Personality and free association. *Journal of Consulting Psychology,* **30,** 30–38.

Borgatta, E. F. 1959. The new principle of psychotherapy. *Journal of Clinical Psychology,* **15,** 330–334.

Brackbill, G. A., and Fine, H. J. 1956. Schizophrenia and central nervous system pathology. *Journal of Abnormal and Social Psychology,* **52,** 310–313.

Bradway, K. P., Lion, E. G., and Corrigan, H. G. 1946. The use of the Rorschach in a psychiatric study of promiscuous girls. *Rorschach Research Exchange,* **10,** 105–110.

Brawer, F. B., and Cohen, A. M. 1966. Global and sign approaches to Rorschach assessment of beginning teachers. *Journal of Projective Techniques and Personality Assessment,* **30,** 536–542.

Brockway, A. L., Gleser, G. C., and Ulett, G. A. 1954. Rorschach concepts of normality. *Journal of Consulting Psychology,* **18,** 259–265.

Broida, D. C. 1954. An investigation of certain psychodiagnostic indications of suicidal tendencies and depression in mental hospital patients. *Psychiatric Quarterly,* **28,** 453–464.

Brooks, M. O., and Phillips, L. 1958. The cognitive significance of Rorschach developmental scores. *Journal of Personality,* **26,** 268–290.

Brown, D. G. 1959. Psychosomatic correlates in contact dermatitis: A pilot study. *Journal of Psychosomatic Research,* **4,** 132–139.

Brussel, J. A., Grassi, J. R., and Melnicker, A. A. 1942. The Rorschach method and postconcussion syndrome. *Psychiatric Quarterly,* **16,** 707–743.

Buss, A. H. 1961. *The psychology of aggression.* New York: John Wiley.

Buss, A. H., and Durkee, A. 1957. An inventory for assessing different kinds of hostility. *Journal of Consulting Psychology,* **21,** 343–349.

Buss, A. H., Fischer, H., and Simmons, A. S. 1962. Aggression and hostility in psychiatric patients. *Journal of Consulting Psychology,* **26,** 84–89.

Butler, J. M., and Fiske, D. W. 1955. Theory and techniques of assessment. *Annual Review of Psychology*, **6,** 327–356.

Campbell, D. T. 1960. Recommendations for APA test standards regarding construct, trait, or discriminant validity. *American Psychologist,* **15,** 546–553.

Campbell, D. T., and Fiske, D. W. 1959. Convergent and discriminant validation by the multitrait-multimethod matrix. *Psychological Bulletin,* **56,** 81–105.

Carr, A. C. 1949. An evalution of nine nondirective psychotherapy cases by means of the Rorschach. *Journal of Consulting Psychology*, **13,** 196–205.

Cartwright, R. D. 1958. Predicting response to client-centered therapy with the Rorschach PR Scale. *Journal of Counseling Psychology,* **5,** 11–17.

Cassell, W. A. 1964. A projective index of body-interior awareness. *Psychosomatic Medicine,* **26,** 172–177.

Cassell, W. A., and Fisher, S. 1963. Body-image boundaries and histamine flare reaction. *Psychosomatic Medicine*, **25,** 344–350.

Chapman, A. H., and Reese, D. G. 1953. Homosexual signs in Rorschachs of early schizophrenics. *Journal of Clinical Psychology*, **9,** 30–32.

Chapman, L. F., and Wolff, H. G. 1959. The cerebral hemispheres and the highest integrative functions of man. *Archives of Neurology*, **1,** 357–424.

Chapman, L. J., and Chapman, J. P. 1969. Illusory correlation as an obstacle to the use of valid psychodiagnostic signs. *Journal of Abnormal Psychology,* **74,** 271–280.

Chesrow, E. J., Wosika, R. H., and Reinitz, A. H. 1949. A psychometric evaluation of aged white males. *Geriatrics*, **4,** 169–177.

Chodorkoff, B. 1954. Self-perception, perceptual defense, and adjustment. *Journal of Abnormal and Social Psychology*, **49,** 508–512.

Cleveland, S. E. 1960. Body image changes associated with personality reorganization. *Journal of Consulting Psychology*, **24,** 256–261.

Cleveland, S. E., and Fisher, S. 1956. Psychological factors in the neurodermatoses. *Psychosomatic Medicine*, **18,** 209–220.

Cleveland, S. E., and Fisher, S. 1957. Predicting of small group behavior from a body image schema. *Human Relations*, **10,** 223–233.

Cleveland, S. E., and Johnson, D. C. 1962. Personality patterns in young males with coronary diseases. *Psychosomatic Medicine*, **24,** 600–610.

Cleveland, S. E., Reitman, E. E., and Brewer, E. J. 1964. Psychological problems in juvenile rheumatoid arthritis. Paper read at American Psychological Association, Los Angeles.

Cohen, D. 1954. Rorschach scores, prognosis, and course of illness in pulmonary tuberculosis. *Journal of Consulting Psychology*, **18,** 405–408.

Coleman, J. C. 1967. Stimulus factors in the relation between fantasy and behavior. *Journal of Projective Techniques and Personality Assessment*, **31,** 68–73.

Compton, H. 1964. Body image boundaries in relation to clothing fabric and design preferences of a group of hospitalized psychotic women. *Journal of Home Economics*, **56,** 40–45.

Conquest, R. A. 1963. An investigation of body image variables in patients with the diagnosis of schizophrenic reaction. Unpublished doctoral dissertation, Case Western Reserve University, Cleveland, Ohio.

Cooper, A. 1961. Correlates of musical creativity obtained under standard and additional administration of the Rorschach. Unpublished doctoral dissertation, University of Rochester, Rochester, N. Y.

Cooper, G. D., Adams, H. B., and Gibby, R. G. 1962. Ego strength changes following perceptual deprivation. *Archives of General Psychiatry*, **7**, 213–217.

Cooper, G. W., Jr., Bernstein, L., and Hart, C. 1965. Predicting suicidal ideation from the Rorschach: An attempt to cross-validate. *Journal of Projective Techniques and Personality Assessment*, **29**, 168–170.

Cooper, J. G. 1955. The inspection Rorschach in the prediction of college success. *Journal of Educational Research*, **49**, 275–282.

Corsini, R. J., Severson, W. E., Tunney, T. E., and Uehling, H. F. 1955. The separation capacity of the Rorschach. *Journal of Consulting Psychology*, **19**, 194–196.

Corsini, R. J., and Uehling, H. F. 1954. A cross validation of Davidson's Rorschach adjustment scale. *Journal of Consulting Psychology*, **18**, 277–279.

Costello, C. G. 1958. The Rorschach records of suicidal patients: An application of a comparative matching technique. *Journal of Projective Techniques*, **22**, 272–275.

Crasilneck, H. B. 1954. An analysis of differences between suicidal and pseudo-suicidal patients through the use of projective techniques. Unpublished doctoral dissertation, University of Houston, Houston, Texas.

Cronbach, L. J. 1949. Statistical methods applied to Rorschach scores: A review. *Psychological Bulletin*, **46**, 392–429.

Cronbach, L. J., and Meehl, P. E. 1955. Construct validity in psychological tests. *Psychological Bulletin*, **52**, 281–302.

Cummings, C. P. 1954. The role of various psychological variables in children's nailbiting behavior. Unpublished doctoral dissertation, Pennsylvania State University, University Park, Pa.

Cutter, F., Jorgensen, M., and Farberow, N. L. 1968. Replicability of Rorschach signs with known degrees of suicidal intent. *Journal of Projective Techniques and Personality Assessment*, **32**, 428–434.

Dahlstrom, W. G., and Welsh, G. S. 1960. *An MMPI handbook*. Minneapolis: University of Minnesota Press.

Daston, P. G., and McConnell, O. L. 1962. Stability of Rorschach penetration and barrier scores over time. *Journal of Consulting Psychology*, **26**, 104.

Daston, P. G., and Sakheim, G. A. 1960. Prediction of successful suicide from the Rorschach test, using a sign approach. *Journal of Projective Techniques*, **24**, 355–361.

Davids, A., Joelson, M., and McArthur, C. 1956. Rorschach and TAT indices of homosexuality in overt homosexuals, neurotics, and normal males. *Journal of Abnormal and Social Psychology*, **53**, 161–173.

Davids, A., and Talmadge, M. 1963. A study of Rorschach signs of adjustment in mothers of institutionalized emotionally disturbed children. *Journal of Projective Techniques*, **27**, 292–296.

Davids, A., and Talmadge, M. 1964. Utility of the Rorschach in predicting movement in psychiatric casework. *Journal of Consulting Psychology*, **28**, 311–316.

Davidson, H. 1943. *Personality and economic background*. New York: King's Crown Press.

Davidson, H. 1950. A measure of adjustment obtained from the Rorschach protocol. *Journal of Projective Techniques*, **14,** 31–38.

Davis, A. D. 1960. Some physiological correlates of Rorschach body image productions. *Journal of Abnormal and Social Psychology*, **60,** 432–436.

DeLuca, J. N. 1966. The structure of homosexuality. *Journal of Projective Techniques and Personality Assessment*, **30,** 187–191.

DeVos, G. 1952. A quantitative approach to affective symbolism in Rorschach responses. *Journal of Projective Techniques*, **16,** 133–150.

DeVos, G. 1954. A comparison of the personality differences in two generations of Japanese-Americans by means of the Rorschach test. *Nagoya Journal of Medical Science*, **17,** 153–265.

DeVos, G. 1955. A quantitative Rorschach assessment of maladjustment and rigidity in acculturating Japanese Americans. *Genetic Psychology Monographs*, **52,** 51–87.

Diers, W. C., and Brown, C. C. 1951. Rorschach "organic signs" and intelligence level. *Journal of Consulting Psychology*, **15,** 343–345.

Dollard, J., Doob, L. W., Miller, N. E., Mowrer, O. H., and Sears, R. R. 1939. *Frustration and aggression.* New Haven: Yale University Press.

Dollard, J., and Miller, N. E. 1950. *Personality and psychotherapy.* New York: McGraw-Hill.

Dörken, H., and Kral, V. A. 1952. The psychological differentiation of organic brain lesions and their localization by means of the Rorschach test. *American Journal of Psychiatry*, **108,** 764–771.

Drake, A. K., and Rusnak, A. W. 1966. An indicator of suicidal ideation on the Rorschach: A replication. *Journal of Projective Techniques and Personality Assessment*, **30,** 543–544.

Dublin, L. I. 1963. *Suicide: A sociological and statistical study.* New York: Ronald Press.

Due, F. O., and Wright, M. E. 1945. The use of content analysis in Rorschach interpretation: I. Differential characteristics of male homosexuals. *Rorschach Research Exchange*, **9,** 169–177.

Eckhardt, W. 1961. Piotrowski's signs: Organic or functional? *Journal of Clinical Psychology*, **17,** 36–38.

Eigenbrode, C. R., and Shipman, W. G. 1960. The body image barrier concept. *Journal of Abnormal and Social Psychology*, **60,** 450–452.

Eisdorfer, C. 1960. Developmental level and sensory impairment in the aged. *Journal of Projective Techniques*, **24,** 129–132.

Elizur, A. 1949. Content analysis of the Rorschach with regard to anxiety and hostility. *Rorschach Research Exchange and Journal of Projective Techniques*, **13,** 247–284.

Elkins, E. 1958. The diagnostic validity of the Ames "Danger Signals." *Journal of Consulting Psychology*, **22,** 281–287.

Endicott, N. A., and Endicott, J. 1963. "Improvement" in untreated psychiatric patients. *Archives of General Psychiatry,* **9,** 575–585.

Endicott, N. A., and Endicott, J. 1964. Prediction of improvement in treated and untreated patients using the Rorschach Prognostic Rating Scale. *Journal of Consulting Psychology*, **28,** 342–348.

Epstein, S., Nelson, J. V., and Tanofsky, R. 1957. Responses to inkblots as measures of individual differences. *Journal of Consulting Psychology*, **21,** 211–215.

EVANS, R. B., and MARMORSTON, J. 1963a. Psychological test signs of brain damage in cerebral thrombosis. *Psychological Reports*, **12,** 915–930.

EVANS, R. B., and MARMORSTON, J. 1963b. Improved mental functioning with Premarin therapy in atherosclerosis. *Proceedings for the Society of Experimental Biology and Medicine*, **113,** 698–703.

EVANS, R. B., and MARMORSTON, J. 1964. Rorschach signs of brain damage in cerebral thrombosis. *Perceptual Motor Skills*, **18,** 977–988.

EVANS, R. B., and MARMORSTON, J. 1965. Mental functioning and Premarin therapy in cardiovascular and cerebrovascular disease. *Proceedings of the Society for Experimental Biology and Medicine*, **118,** 529–533.

EXNER, J. E. 1969. *The Rorschach systems.* New York: Grune and Stratton.

EYSENCK, H. J. 1960. The concept of statistical significance and the controversy about one-tailed tests. *Psychological Review,* **67,** 269–271.

FARBEROW, N. L. 1950. Personality patterns of suicidal mental patients. *Genetic Psychology Monographs*, **42,** 3–79.

FARBEROW, N. L., and SHNEIDMAN, E. S. (eds.). 1961. *The cry for help.* New York: McGraw-Hill.

FEFFER, M. H. 1959. The cognitive implications of role taking behavior. *Journal of Personality*, **27,** 152–168.

FEIN, L. G. 1950. Rorschach signs of homosexuality in male college students. *Journal of Clinical Psychology*, **6,** 248–253.

FERRACUTI, F., and RIZZO, G. B. 1956. Analisi del volore discriminativo di alcuni segni di omosessualita rilevabili attraverso techniche proittive. *Bollettino di Psicologia e Sociologia Applicata*, **13–16,** 128–134.

FERRACUTI, F., and RIZZO, G. B. 1958. Signos sobresalientes de homosexualidad en una poblacion penitenciaria feminina, obtenidos mediante la aplicacion de tecnicas de proyeccion. *Revista de Ciencias Sociales*, **2,** 469–479.

FILMER-BENNETT, G. 1952. Prognostic indices in the Rorschach records of hospitalized patients. *Journal of Abnormal and Social Psychology*, **47,** 502–506.

FILMER-BENNETT, G. 1955. The Rorschach as a means of predicting treatment outcome. *Journal of Consulting Psychology*, **19,** 331–334.

FINE, H. J., FULKERSON, S. C., and PHILLIPS, L. 1955. Maladjustment and social attainment. *Journal of Abnormal and Social Psychology*, **50,** 33–35.

FINE, H. J., and ZIMET, C. N. 1959. Process-reactive schizophrenia and genetic levels of perception. *Journal of Abnormal and Social Psychology*, **59,** 83–86.

FINE, R. 1948. Manual for a scoring scheme for verbal projective techniques (TAT, MAPS, stories and the like). Unpublished manuscript, University of Southern California, Los Angeles [subsequently published in *Journal of Projective Techniques*, **19,** 306–316 (1955)].

FINNEY, B. C. 1955. Rorschach test correlates of assaultive behavior. *Journal of Projective Techniques*, **19,** 6–16.

FISH, J. E. 1960. An exploration of developmental aspects of body scheme and of ideas about adulthood in grade school children. Unpublished doctoral dissertation, University of Kansas, Lawrence, Kansas.

FISHER, J. 1959. The twisted pear and the prediction of behavior. *Journal of Consulting Psychology*, **23,** 400–405.

FISHER, J., and GONDA, T. 1955. Neurologic techniques and Rorschach test in detecting brain pathology. *Archives of Neurology and Psychiatry*, **74,** 117–124.

FISHER, J., GONDA, T., and LITTLE, K. B. 1955. The Rorschach and central nervous system pathology. *American Journal of Psychiatry*, **111,** 486–492.

FISHER, R. L. 1958. The effect of a disturbing situation upon the stability of various projective tests. *Psychological Monographs*, **72** (all of No. 467).

FISHER, S. 1950. Patterns of personality rigidity and some of their determinants. *Psychological Monographs*, **64** (all of No. 307).

FISHER, S. 1951. The value of the Rorschach for detecting suicidal trends. *Journal of Projective Techniques*, **15**, 250–254.

FISHER, S. 1959a. Prediction of body exterior vs. body interior reactivity from a body image schema. *Journal of Personality*, **27**, 56–62.

FISHER, S. 1959b. Body image boundaries in the aged. *Journal of Psychology*, **48**, 315–318.

FISHER, S. 1960. Right-left gradients in body image, body reactivity, and perception. *Genetic Psychology Monographs*, **61**, 197–228.

FISHER, S. 1964a. The body boundary and judged behavioral patterns in an interview situation. *Journal of Projective Techniques and Personality Assessment*, **28**, 181–184.

FISHER, S. 1964b. Sex differences in body perception. *Psychological Monographs*, **78** (all of No. 591).

FISHER, S., BOYD, I., WALKER, O., and SHEER, D. 1959. Parents of schizophrenics, neurotics, and normals. *Archives of General Psychiatry*, **1**, 149–166.

FISHER, S., and CLEVELAND, S. E. 1955. The role of body image in psychosomatic symptom choice. *Psychological Monographs*, **69** (all of No. 402).

FISHER, S., and CLEVELAND, S. E. 1956a. Relationship of body image boundaries to memory for completed and incompleted tasks. *Journal of Psychology*, **42**, 35–41.

FISHER, S., and CLEVELAND, S. E. 1956b. Body-image boundaries and style of life. *Journal of Abnormal and Social Psychology*, **52**, 373–379.

FISHER, S., and CLEVELAND, S. E. 1956c. Relationship of body image to site of cancer. *Psychosomatic Medicine*, **18**, 304–309.

FISHER, S., and CLEVELAND, S. E. 1957. An approach to physiological reactivity in terms of a body-image schema. *Psychological Review*, **64**, 26–37.

FISHER, S., and CLEVELAND, S. E. 1958a. Body image boundaries and sexual behavior. *Journal of Psychology*, **45**, 207–211.

FISHER, S., and CLEVELAND, S. E. 1958b. *Body image and personality*. New York: Van Nostrand Reinhold.

FISHER, S., and FISHER, R. L. 1959. A developmental analysis of some body image and body reactivity dimensions. *Child Development*, **30**, 389–402.

FISHER, S., and FISHER, R. L. 1964. Body image boundaries and patterns of body perception. *Journal of Abnormal and Social Psychology*, **68**, 255–262.

FISHER, S., and HINDS, E. 1951. The organization of hostility controls in various personality structures. *Genetic Psychology Monographs*, **44**, 3–68.

FISKE, D. W., CARTWRIGHT, D. S., and KIRTNER, W. L. 1964. Are psychotherapeutic changes predictable? *Journal of Abnormal and Social Psychology*, **69**, 418–426.

FLAVELL, J. H. 1963. *The developmental psychology of Jean Piaget*. New York: Van Nostrand Reinhold.

FLAVELL, J. H., DRAGUNS, J., FEINBERG, L. D., and BUDIN, W. 1958. A microgenetic approach to word association. *Journal of Abnormal and Social Psychology*, **57**, 1–7.

FLEISCHER, M. S. 1957. Differential Rorschach configurations of suicidal psychiatric patients: A psychological study of threatened, attempted, and successful suicides. Unpublished doctoral dissertation, Yeshiva University, New York.

FORER, B. R., FARBEROW, N. L., MEYER, M. M., and TOLMAN, R. S. 1952. Consistency and agreement in the judgment of Rorschach signs. *Journal of Projective Techniques*, **16,** 346–351.

FORSYTH, R. P. 1959. The influences of color, shading and Welsh anxiety level on Elizur Rorschach content test analyses of anxiety and hostility. *Journal of Projective Techniques*, **23,** 207–213.

FOWLER, R. D., JR. 1957. Psychopathology and social adequacy: A Rorschach developmental study. Unpublished doctoral dissertation, Pennsylvania State University, University Park, Pa.

FRAMO, J. L. 1952. Structural aspects of perceptual development in normal adults: A tachistoscopic study with the Rorschach technique. Unpublished doctoral dissertation, University of Texas, Austin, Texas.

FRANK, I. H. 1952. A genetic evaluation of perceptual structurization in certain psychoneurotic disorders by means of the Rorschach technique. Unpublished doctoral dissertation, Boston University, Boston.

FRANK, J. D. 1961. *Persuasion and healing: A comparative study of psychotherapy.* Baltimore: Johns Hopkins Press.

FREED, E. 1952. Perceptual differentiation in schizophrenia: A tachistoscopic study of structural Rorschach elements. Unpublished doctoral dissertation, Syracuse University, Syracuse, N. Y.

FREUD, S. 1955. *Beyond the pleasure principle. Standard Edition, Vol. XVIII.* London: Hogarth, pp. 7–64.

FREUD, S. 1959. *Inhibitions, symptoms and anxiety. Standard Edition, Vol. XX.* London: Hogarth, pp. 87–172.

FRIEDMAN, H. 1952. Perceptual regression in schizophrenia: An hypothesis suggested by the use of the Rorschach test. *Journal of Genetic Psychology,* **81,** 63–98.

FRIEDMAN, H. 1953. Perceptual regression in schizophrenia: An hypothesis suggested by the use of the Rorschach test. *Journal of Projective Techniques,* **17,** 171–185.

FRIEDMAN, H. 1956. The structural aspects of schizophrenic responses to auditory stimuli. *Journal of Genetic Psychology*, **89,** 221–230.

FRIEDMAN, H. 1958. A comparison of action patterns of schizophrenic and normal adults. *Journal of Clinical Psychology*, **14,** 142–146.

FRIEDMAN, H. 1960. A note on the revised Rorschach developmental scoring system. *Journal of Clinical Psychology*, **16,** 52–54.

FRIEDMAN, H., and ORGEL, S. A. 1964. Rorschach developmental scores and intelligence level. *Journal of Projective Techniques and Personality Assessment,* **28,** 425–428.

FROMM, E. O., and ELONEN, A. S. 1951. The use of projective techniques in the study of a case of female homosexuality. *Journal of Projective Techniques,* **15,** 185–230.

FULKERSON, S. C., and BARRY, J. R. 1961. Methodology and research on the prognostic use of psychological tests. *Psychological Bulletin*, **58,** 177–204.

FUNKENSTEIN, D. H., KING, S. H., and DROLETTE, M. A. 1959. The direction of anger during a laboratory stress-inducing situation. *Psychosomatic Medicine,* **16,** 404–413.

FUTTERMAN, S., KIRKNER, F. J., and MEYER, M. M. 1947. First year analysis of veterans treated in a Mental Hygiene Clinic of the Veterans Administration. *American Journal of Psychiatry*, **104,** 298–305.

GAIR, M. 1944. Rorschach characteristics of a group of very superior seven year old children. *Rorschach Research Exchange*, **8,** 31–37

GALLAGHER, J. J. 1954. Test indicators for therapy prognosis. *Journal of Consulting Psychology*, **18,** 409–413.

GARFIELD, S. L. 1947. The Rorschach test in clinical diagnosis. *Journal of Clinical Psychology*, **3,** 375–381.

GIBBY, R. G., STOTSKY, B. A., HILER, E. W., and MILLER, D. R. 1954. Validation of Rorschach criteria for predicting duration of therapy. *Journal of Consulting Psychology*, **18,** 185–191.

GIBBY, R. G., STOTSKY, B. A., MILLER, D. R., and HILER, E. W. 1953. Prediction of duration of therapy from the Rorschach test. *Journal of Consulting Psychology*, **17,** 348–354.

GLUCK, M. R. 1955. Rorschach content and hostile behavior. *Journal of Consulting Psychology*, **19,** 475–478.

GOLDBERG, P. A. 1959. Differential diagnosis and the Rorschach: Fact, fiction, and foolishness. Unpublished manuscript, State University of New York at Buffalo, Buffalo, N .Y.

GOLDFRIED, M R. 1959. One-tailed tests and "unexpected results." *Psychological Review*, **66,** 79–80.

GOLDFRIED, M. R. 1961. The effect of sensory deprivation on developmental level of perceptual organization. Unpublished doctoral dissertation, State University of New York at Buffalo, Buffalo, N. Y.

GOLDFRIED, M. R. 1962a. Rorschach developmental level and the MMPI as measures of severity of psychological disturbance. *Journal of Projective Techniques*, **26,** 187–192.

GOLDFRIED, M. R. 1962b. Some normative data on Rorschach developmental level "card pull" in a psychiatric population. *Journal of Projective Techniques*, **26,** 283–287.

GOLDFRIED, M. R. and KENT, R. N. 1971. Traditional vs. behavioral assessment: A comparison of methodological and theoretical assumptions. *Psychological Bulletin,* in press.

GOLDFRIED, M. R., and POMERANZ, D. M. 1968. Role of assessment in behavior modification. *Psychological Reports*, **23,** 75–87.

GOLDFRIED, M. R., and ZAX, M. 1965. The stimulus value of the TAT. *Journal of Projective Techniques and Personality Assessment*, **29,** 46–57.

GOLDMAN, R. 1960. Changes in Rorschach performance and clinical improvement in schizophrenia. *Journal of Consulting Psychology*, **24,** 403–407.

GOODENOUGH, F. L. 1949. *Mental testing.* New York: Rinehart.

GOODSTEIN, L. D. 1954. Interrelationships among several measures of anxiety and hostility. *Journal of Consulting Psychology*, **18,** 35–39.

GOODSTEIN, L. D., and GOLDBERGER, L. 1955. Manifest anxiety and Rorschach performance in a chronic patient population. *Journal of Consulting Psychology*, **19,** 339–344.

GORLOW, L., ZIMET, C. N., and FINE, H. J. 1952. The validity of anxiety and hostility Rorschach content scores among adolescents. *Journal of Consulting Psychology*, **16,** 73–75.

Gottlieb, A. L., and Parsons, O. A. 1960. A coaction compass evaluation of Rorschach determinants in brain damaged individuals. *Journal of Consulting Psychology*, **24**, 54–60.

Grace, N. B. 1956. A developmental comparison of word usage with structural aspects of perception and social adjustment. Unpublished doctoral dissertation, Duke University, Durham, N. C.

Grant, M. Q., Ives, V., and Ranzoni, J. H. 1952. Reliability and validity of judges' ratings of adjustment on the Rorschach. *Psychological Monographs*, **66** (all of No. 334).

Grauer, D. 1953. Prognosis in paranoid schizophrenia on the basis of the Rorschach. *Journal of Consulting Psychology*, **17**, 199–205.

Grauer, D. 1954. Homosexuality in paranoid schizophrenia as revealed by the Rorschach test. *Journal of Consulting Psychology*, **18**, 459–462.

Greenberg, N. 1969. The use of the Rorschach Prognostic Rating Scale with foster-home children. *Journal of Projective Techniques and Personality Assessment*, **33**, 451–453.

Haber, W. B. 1954. Effects of loss of limb on sensory organization and phantom limb phenomena. Unpublished Ph.D. dissertation, New York University, New York.

Hafner, A. J., and Kaplan, A. M. 1960. Hostility content analysis of the Rorschach and TAT. *Journal of Projective Technique*, **24**, 137–143.

Haimowitz, N. R., and Haimowitz, M. L. 1952. Personality changes in client-centered therapy. In W. Wolff and J. A. Precker (eds.), *Success in psychotherapy*. New York: Grune and Stratton, pp. 63–93.

Hallowell, A. I. 1951. The use of projective techniques in the study of the socio-psychological aspects of acculturation. *Journal of Projective Techniques*, **15**, 27–44.

Hamlin, R. M., and Albee, G. W. 1948. Muench's test before and after non-directive theory: A control group for his subjects. *Journal of Consulting Psychology*, **12**, 412–416.

Hamlin, R. M., Albee, G. W., and Leland, E. M. 1950. Objective Rorschach "signs" for groups of normal, maladjusted and neuropsychiatric subjects. *Journal of Consulting Psychology*, **14**, 276–282.

Hamlin, R. M., Berger, B., and Cummings, S. T. 1952. Changes in adjustment following psychotherapy as reflected in Rorschach signs. In W. Wolff and J. A. Precker (eds.), *Success in psychotherapy*. New York: Grune and Stratton, 1954. pp. 94–111.

Hammond, K. R. 1954. Representative vs. systematic design in clinical psychology. *Psychological Bulletin*, **51**, 150–159.

Harris, J. G., Jr. 1960. Validity: The search for a constant in a universe of variables. In M. A. Rickers-Ovsiankina (ed.), *Rorschach psychology*. New York: Wiley, pp. 380–439.

Harris, R. E., and Christiansen, C. 1946. Prediction of response to brief psychotherapy. *Journal of Psychology*, **21**, 269–284.

Harrower-Erickson, M. R. 1942. The value and limitations of the so-called "neurotic signs." *Rorschach Research Exchange*, **6**, 109–114.

Harrower-Erickson, M. R. 1943. Diagnosis of psychogenic factors in disease by means of the Rorschach method. *Psychiatric Quarterly*, **17**, 57–66.

Haskell, R. J., Jr. 1961. Relationship between aggressive behavior and psychological tests. *Journal of Projective Techniques*, **25**, 431–440.

HAWARD, L. R. C., and MARSZALEK, K. 1958. The Munroe check list: A note on its validity in clinical research. *Journal of Mental Science*, **104,** 483–484.

HEMMENDINGER, L. 1953. Perceptual organization and development as reflected in the structure of Rorschach test responses. *Journal of Projective Techniques,* **17,** 162–170.

HERRING, F. H. 1956. Response during anesthesia and surgery. *Psychosomatic Medicine*, **18,** 243–251.

HERSCH, C. 1962. The cognitive functioning of the creative person: A developmental analysis. *Journal of Projective Techniques*, **26,** 193–200.

HERTZ, M. R. 1938. Scoring the Rorschach ink-blot test. *Journal of Genetic Psychology*, **52,** 15–64.

HERTZ, M. R. 1948. Suicidal configurations in Rorschach records. *Rorschach Research Exchange and Journal of Projective Techniques*, **12,** 3–58.

HERTZ, M. R. 1949. Further study of "suicidal" configurations in Rorschach records. *Rorschach Research Exchange and Journal of Projective Techniques,* **13,** 44–73.

HERTZ, M. R. 1951. *Frequency tables for scoring responses to the Rorschach inkblot test* (3rd ed.). Cleveland: Case Western Reserve University Press.

HERTZ, M. R., and LOEHRKE, L. M. 1954. The application of the Piotrowski and Hughes signs of organic defect to a group of patients suffering from post-traumatic encephalopathy. *Journal of Projective Techniques*, **18,** 183–196.

HERTZMAN, M., and MARGULIES, H. 1943. Developmental changes as reflected in Rorschach test responses. *Journal of Genetic Psychology*, **62,** 189–215.

HERTZMAN, M., and SEITZ, C. P. 1942. Rorschach reactions at high altitudes. *Journal of Psychology*, **14,** 245–257.

HOLT, R. R. 1966. Measuring libidinal and aggressive motives and their controls by means of the Rorschach test. In D. Levine (ed.), *Nebraska symposium on motivation*. Lincoln, Neb.: University of Nebraska Press.

HOLT, R. R. (ed.). 1968. *Diagnostic psychological testing* (rev. ed.). New York: International Universities Press.

HOLT, R. R. 1970. Yet another look at clinical and statistical prediction: Or, is clinical psychology worthwhile? *American Psychologist*, **25,** 337–349.

HOLT, R. R., and HAVEL, J. 1960. A method for assessing primary and secondary processes in the Rorschach. In M. A. Rickers-Ovsiankina (ed.), *Rorschach psychology*. New York: John Wiley, pp. 263–318.

HOLTZMAN, W. H. 1952. Adjustment and leadership: A study of the Rorschach test. *Journal of Social Psychology*, **36,** 179–189.

HOLZBERG, J. D. 1960. Reliability re-examined. In M. A. Rickers-Ovsiankina (ed.), *Rorschach psychology*. New York: John Wiley, pp. 361–379.

HOOKER, E. 1957. The adjustment of the male overt homosexual. *Journal of Projective Techniques*, **21,** 18–31.

HOOKER, E. 1958. Male homosexuality in the Rorschach. *Journal of Projective Techniques*, **22,** 33–54.

HOOKER, E. 1959. What is a criterion? *Journal of Projective Techniques,* **23,** 278–281.

HOOKER, E. 1963. Male homosexuality. In N. L. Farberow (ed.), *Taboo topics*. New York: Atherton Press, pp. 44–55.

HORRALL, B. M. 1957. Academic performance and personality adjustments of highly intelligent college students. *Genetic Psychology Monographs,* **55,** 3–83.

HOYT, T. F., and BARON, M. R. 1959. Anxiety indices in same-sex drawings of psychiatric patients with high and low MAS scores. *Journal of Consulting Psychology,* **23,** 448–452.

HUGHES, R. M. 1948. Rorschach signs for the diagnosis of organic pathology. *Rorschach Research Exchange and Journal of Projective Techniques,* **12,** 165–167.

HUGHES, R. M. 1950. A factor analysis of Rorschach diagnostic signs. *Journal of General Psychology,* **43,** 85–103.

HUNT, J. McV., and KOGAN, L. S. 1950. *Assessing the results of social case work: A manual on judging movement.* New York: Family Service Association of America.

HUNT, W. A. 1959. An actuarial approach to clinical judgment. In B. M. Bass and I. A. Berg (eds.), *Objective approaches to personality assessment.* New York: Van Nostrand Reinhold, pp. 169–191.

HUNT, W. A., and JONES, N. F. 1962. The experimental investigation of clinical judgment. In A. Bachrach (ed.), *Experimental foundations of clinical psychology.* New York: Basic Books, pp. 26–51.

HUNTER, M., SCHOOLER, C., and SPOHN, H. E. 1962. The measurement of characteristic patterns of ward behavior in chronic schizophrenics. *Journal of Consulting Psychology,* **26,** 69–73.

HURWITZ, I. 1954. A developmental study of the relationship between motor activity and perceptual processes as measured by the Rorschach test. Unpublished doctoral dissertation, Clark University, Worcester, Mass.

IVES, V., GRANT, M. Q., and RANZONI, J. H. 1953. The "neurotic" Rorschachs of normal adolescents. *Journal of Genetic Psychology,* **83,** 31–61.

JASKAR, R. O., and REED, M. R. 1963. Assessment of body image organization of hospitalized and non-hospitalized subjects. *Journal of Projective Techniques and Personality Assessment,* **27,** 185–190.

JESSOR, R., and HAMMOND, K. R. 1957. Construct validity and the Taylor Anxiety Scale. *Psychological Bulletin,* **54,** 161–170.

JOHNSON, E. Z. 1953. Klopfer's Prognostic Scale used with Raven's Progressive Matrices in play therapy prognosis. *Journal of Projective Techniques,* **17,** 320–326.

JOHNSON, H. M. 1954. On verifying hypotheses by verifying their implicates. *American Journal of Psychology,* **67,** 723–727.

JORDON, E. J., JR., and PHILLIPS, L. 1959. Dimensions of social maturity. Unpublished manuscript.

JOURARD, S. M. 1954. Ego strength and the recall of tasks. *Journal of Abnormal and Social Psychology,* **49,** 51–58.

JOURARD, S. M., and SECORD, P. F. 1955. Body-cathexis and the ideal female figure. *Journal of Abnormal and Social Psychology,* **50,** 243–246.

JUDSON, A. J., and KATAHN, M. 1964. Levels of personality organization and production of associative sequences in process-reactive schizophrenia. *Journal of Consulting Psychology,* **28,** 208–213.

KADEN, S. 1968. The relationship between interpersonal interaction in marriage and developmental level of perceptual functioning. Paper read at American Psychological Association, Washington, D. C.

KADEN, S., and LIPTON, H. 1960. Rorschach developmental scores and post-hospital adjustment of married male schizophrenics. *Journal of Projective Techniques,* **24,** 144–147.

KADEN, S., and LIPTON, H. 1962. A comparison of married male schizophrenics and their wives on biographical and psychological test variables. Paper read at Eastern Psychological Association, Atlantic City, N.J.

KAPLAN, B. 1956. *Primary records in culture and personality,* Vol. I. Madison, Wisconsin: Microcard Foundation.

KATAGUCHI, Y. 1959. Rorschach schizophrenic score (RSS). *Journal of Projective Techniques,* **23,** 214–222.

KATES, S. L. 1950a. Rorschach responses related to vocational interests and job satisfaction. *Psychological Monographs,* **64,** (all of No. 308).

KATES, S. L. 1950b. Objective Rorschach patterns differentiating anxiety reactions from obsessive-compulsive reactions. *Journal of Consulting Psychology,* **14,** 226–229.

KATES, S. L. 1950c. Rorschach responses, Strong blank scales, and job satisfaction among policemen. *Journal of Applied Psychology,* **34,** 249–254.

KATES, S. L., and SCHWARTZ, F. 1958. Stress, anxiety and response complexity on the Rorschach test. *Journal of Projective Techniques* **22,** 64–69.

KELLEY, D. M., and KLOPFER, B. 1938. Application of the Rorschach method to research in schizophrenia. *Rorschach Research Exchange,* **3,** 55–66.

KELLY, E. L., and FISKE, D. W. 1951. *The prediction of performance in clinical psychology.* Ann Arbor, Michigan: University of Michigan Press.

KELLY, G. A. 1958. The theory and technique of assessment. In P. R. Farnsworth and Q. McNemar (eds.), *Annual review of psychology.* Palo Alto, Cal.: Annual Reviews, pp. 323–352.

KIMBLE, G. A., and POSNICK, G. M. 1967. Anxiety? *Journal of Personality and Social Psychology,* **7,** 108–110.

KINSEY, A. C., POMEROY, W. B., and MARTIN, C. E. 1948. *Sexual behavior in the human male.* Philadelphia: Saunders.

KIRKNER, F. J., WISHAM, W. W., and GIEDT, F. H. 1953. A report on the validity of the Rorschach Prognostic Rating Scale. *Journal of Projective Techniques,* **17,** 465–470.

KISSEL, S. 1965. A brief note on the relationship between Rorschach developmental level and intelligence. *Journal of Projective Techniques and Personality Assessment,* **29,** 454–455.

KISSEL, S., and REISMAN, J. M. 1963. A genetic comparison between social and solitary delinquents. Unpublished manuscript.

KLINGER, E., and ROTH, I. 1964. Diagnosing schizophrenia with Rorschach color responses. *Journal of Clinical Psychology,* **20,** 386–388.

KLOPFER, B. 1954. Rorschach hypotheses and ego psychology. In B. Klopfer, M. D. Ainsworth, W. G. Klopfer, and R. R. Holt, *Developments in the Rorschach technique, Vol. I: Technique and theory.* Yonkers, N.Y.: World Book, pp. 561–598.

KLOPFER, B., AINSWORTH, M. D., KLOPFER, W. G., and HOLT, R. R. 1954. *Developments in the Rorschach technique, Vol. I: Technique and theory.* Yonkers, N.Y.: World Book.

KLOPFER, B., KIRKNER, F. J., WISHAM, W., and BAKER, G. 1951. Rorschach prognostic rating scale. *Journal of Projective Techniques,* **15,** 425–428.

KOFF, S. A. 1946. The Rorschach test in differential diagnosis of cerebral concussion and psychoneurosis. *Bulletin of United States Army Medical Department,* **5,** 170–173.

KOTKOV, B., and MEADOW, A. 1952. Rorschach criteria for continuing group psychotherapy. *International Journal of Group Psychotherapy,* **2,** 324–333.

KOTKOV, B., and MEADOW, A. 1953. Rorschach criteria for predicting continuation in individual psychotherapy. *Journal of Consulting Psychology,* **17,** 16–20.

KREINHEDER, A. 1952. Objective measurement of reality-contact weakness. *Psychological Monographs,* **66** (all of No. 343).

KRUGER, A. K. 1954. Direct and substitutive modes of tension-reduction in terms of developmental level: An experimental analysis by means of the Rorschach test. Unpublished doctoral dissertation, Clark University, Worcester, Mass.

LANDAU, M. F. 1960. Body image in paraplegia as a variable in adjustment to physical handicap. Unpublished doctoral dissertation, Columbia University, New York.

LANE, J. E. 1955. Social effectiveness and developmental level. *Journal of Personality,* **23,** 274–284.

LAZARUS, R. S. 1966. *Psychological stress and the coping process.* New York: McGraw-Hill.

LEBO, D., TOAL, R., and BRICK, H. 1960. Rorschach performance in the amelioration and continuation of observable anxiety. *Journal of General Psychology,* **63,** 75–80.

LEBOWITZ, A. 1963. Patterns of perceptual and motor organization. *Journal of Projective Techniques,* **27,** 302–308.

LERNER, P. M. 1965. Resolution of intrafamilial role conflict in families of schizophrenic patients. Paper presented at the meeting of the American Psychological Association, Chicago.

LESSING, E. E. 1960. Prognostic value of the Rorschach in a child guidance clinic. *Journal of Projective Techniques,* **24,** 310–321.

LEVINE, D. 1959. Rorschach genetic level and mental disorder. *Journal of Projective Techniques,* **23,** 436-439.

LEVINE, D. 1960. Rorschach genetic level and psychotic symptomatology. *Journal of Clinical Psychology,* **16,** 164–167.

LEVINE, D., and COHEN, J. 1962. Symptoms and ego strength measures as predictors of the outcome of hospitalization in functional psychoses. *Journal of Consulting Psychology,* **26,** 246–250.

LEVINE, M., and SPIVACK, A. 1964. *The Rorschach index of repressive style.* Springfield, Ill.: Charles C. Thomas.

LEVY, L. H., and ORR, T. B. 1959. The social psychology of Rorschach validity research. *Journal of Abnormal and Social Psychology,* **58,** 79–83.

LINDNER, R. M. 1946. Content analysis in Rorschach work. *Rorschach Research Exchange,* **10,** 121–129.

LINDZEY, G., TEJESSY, C., DAVIDS, A., and HEINEMANN, S. 1952. Thematic Apperception Test: A summary of empirical generalizations. Unpublished manuscript, Harvard University, Cambridge, Mass.

LIPTON, H., KADEN, S., and PHILLIPS, L. 1958. Rorschach scores and decontextualization: A developmental view. *Journal of Personality,* **26,** 291–302.

LISANSKY, E. S. 1948. Convulsive disorders and personality. *Journal of Abnormal and Social Psychology*, **43,** 29–37.

LIT, J. 1956. Formal and content factors of projective tests in relation to academic achievement. Unpublished doctoral dissertation, Temple University, Philadelphia, Pa.

LITMAN, R. C., and FARBEROW, N. L. 1961. Emergency evaluation of self-destructive potentiality. In N. L. Farberow and E. S. Shneidman (eds.), *The cry for help*. New York: McGraw-Hill, pp. 48–59.

LIVERANT, S. 1958. The use of Rotter's social learning theory in developing a personality inventory. *Psychological Monographs*, **72** (all of No. 455).

LOEVINGER, J. 1957. Objective tests as instruments of psychological theory. *Psychological Reports*, **3,** 635–694.

LOFCHIE, S. H. 1955. The performance of adults under distraction stress: A developmental approach. *Journal of Psychology*, **39,** 109–116.

LONDON, I. D. 1946. Some consequences for history and psychology of Langmuir's concept of divergence and convergence of phenomena. *Psychological Review*, **53,** 170–188.

LOVELAND, N. T. 1961. Epileptic personality and cognitive functioning. *Journal of Projective Techniques*, **25,** 54–68.

LUCAS, W. B. 1961. The effects of frustration on the Rorschach responses of nine year old children. *Journal of Projective Techniques*, **25,** 199–204.

McCONNELL, O. L., and DASTON, P. G. 1961. Body image changes in pregnancy. *Journal of Projective Techniques*, **25,** 451–456.

McFARLANE, J. W., and TUDDENHAM, R. D. 1951. Problems in the validation of projective techniques. In H. H. Anderson and G. L. Anderson (eds.), *An introduction to projective techniques*. Englewood Cliffs, N.J.: Prentice-Hall, Inc., pp. 26–54.

MACHOVER, S., PUZZO, F. S., MACHOVER, K., and PLUMEAU, F. 1959. Clinical and objective studies of personality variables in alcoholism. III. An objective study of homosexuality in alcoholism. *Quarterly Journal of Studies in Alcohol*, **20,** 528–542.

McREYNOLDS, P. (ed.). 1968. *Advances in psychological assessment, Vol. I.* Palo Alto, Calif.: Science and Behavior Books.

MARGOLIS, R., ENGELHARDT, D. M., FREEDMAN, N., HANKOFF, L. D., and MANN, D. 1960. Rorschach cognitive development scores as an approach to classifying schizophrenic outpatients. Paper read at American Psychological Association, Chicago.

MARGULIES, H. 1942. Rorschach responses of successful and unsuccessful students. *Archives of Psychology*, **36,** 1–61.

MARQUIS, D. P., SINNETT, E. R., and WINTER, W. D. 1952. A psychological study of peptic ulcer patients. *Journal of Clinical Psychology*, **8,** 266–272.

MARTIN, H. 1951. A Rorschach study of suicide. Unpublished doctoral dissertation, University of Kentucky, Lexington, Ky.

MASSON, R. L. 1963. An investigation of the relationship between body-image and attitudes expressed toward visibly disabled persons. Unpublished doctoral dissertation, State University of New York at Buffalo, Buffalo, N.Y.

MEDNICK, S. 1959. The body's barriers go Rorschach. *Contemporary Psychology*, **4,** 276–277.

MEEHL, P. E., and DAHLSTROM, W. G. 1960. Objective configural rules for discriminating psychotic from neurotic MMPI profiles. *Journal of Consulting Psychology*, **24,** 375–387.

MEEHL, P. E., and ROSEN, A. 1955. Antecedent probability and the efficiency of psychometric signs, patterns, or cutting scores. *Psychological Bulletin*, **52,** 194–216.

MEKETON, B. W., GRIFFITH, R. M., TAYLOR, V. H., and WIEDEMAN, J. S. 1962. Rorschach homosexual signs in paranoid schizophrenics. *Journal of Abnormal and Social Psychology*, **65,** 280–284.

MIALE, F. R., and HARROWER-ERICKSON, M. R. 1940. Personality structure in the psychoneuroses. *Rorschach Research Exchange*, **4,** 71–74.

MILES, H. H. W., BARRABEE, E., and FINESINGER, J. E. 1951. Evaluation of psychotherapy. *Psychosomatic Medicine*, **13,** 82–105.

MILLS, E. S. 1955a. Personality adjustment and the study of abnormal psychology. *Journal of Applied Psychology*, **39,** 358–361.

MILLS, E. S. 1955b. Abnormal psychology as a selective factor in the college curriculum. *Journal of Educational Psychology*, **46,** 101–111.

MINDESS, H. 1953. Predicting patients' responses to psychotherapy: A preliminary study designed to investigate the validity of the "Rorschach Prognostic Rating Scale." *Journal of Projective Techniques*, **17,** 327–334.

MINDESS, H. 1957. Psychological indices in the selection of student nurses. *Journal of Projective Techniques*, **21,** 37–39.

MINER, H. M., and DEVOS, G. 1960. *Oasis and Casbah: Algerian culture and personality in change*. Ann Arbor, Mich.: University of Michigan Press.

MISCH, R. C. 1954. The relationship of motoric inhibition to developmental level and ideational functioning: An analysis by means of the Rorschach test. Unpublished doctoral dissertation, Clark University, Worcester, Mass.

MISCHEL, W. 1968. *Personality and assessment*. New York: John Wiley.

MOGAR, R. E. 1962. Anxiety indices in human figure drawings: A replication and extension. *Journal of Consulting Psychology*, **26,** 108.

MONTALTO, F. D. 1946. An application of the Group Rorschach Technique to the problem of achievement in college. *Journal of Clinical Psychology*, **3,** 254–260.

MONTALTO, F. D. 1952. Maternal behavior and child personality: A Rorschach study. *Journal of Projective Techniques*, **16,** 151–178.

MUELLER, A. D., and LEFKOVITS, A. M. 1956. Personality structure and dynamics of patients with rheumatoid arthritis. *Journal of Clinical Psychology*, **12,** 143–147.

MUENCH, G. A. 1947. An evaluation of non-directive psychotherapy by means of the Rorschach and other tests. *Applied Psychological Monographs*, **13,** 1–163.

MUNROE, R. L. 1941. Inspection techniques. *Rorschach Research Exchange*, **5,** 166–191.

MUNROE, R. L. 1944. The inspection technique: A method of rapid evaluation of the Rorschach protocol. *Rorschach Research Exchange*, **8,** 46–70.

MUNROE, R. L. 1945a. Objective methods and the Rorschach blots. *Rorschach Research Exchange*, **9,** 59–73.

MUNROE, R. L. 1945b. Prediction of the adjustment and academic performance of college students. *Applied Psychology Monographs*, **7,** 1–104.

MUNROE, R. L. 1946. Rorschach findings on college students showing different constellations of subscores on the ACE. *Journal of Consulting Psychology*, **10,** 301–316.

MUNROE, R. L., LEWINSON, T. S., and WAEHNER, T. S. 1944. A comparison of three projective methods. *Character and Personality*, **13,** 1–21.

MURSTEIN, B. I. 1956. The projection of hostility on the Rorschach and as a result of ego-threat. *Journal of Projective Techniques*, **20,** 418–428.

MURSTEIN, B. I. 1958. Some determinants of the perception of hostility. *Journal of Consulting Psychology*, **22,** 65–69.

NADEL, A. B. 1938. A qualitative analysis of behavior following cerebral lesions. *Archives of Psychology*, **32,** 60.

NEFF, W. S. 1955. The use of the Rorschach in distinguishing vocationally rehabilitable groups. *Journal of Counseling Psychology*, **2,** 207–211.

NEFF, W. S., and GLASER, N. M. 1954. Normative data on the Rorschach. *Journal of Psychology*, **37,** 95–104.

NEFF, W. S., and LIDZ, T. 1951. Rorschach pattern of normal subjects of graded intelligence. *Journal of Projective Techniques*, **15,** 45–57.

NEIGER, S., SLEMON, A. G., and QUIRK, D. A. 1962. The performance of chronic schizophrenic patients on Piotrowski's Rorschach sign list for organic CNS pathology. *Journal of Projective Techniques*, **26,** 419–428.

NEURINGER, C. 1962. Methodological problems in suicide research. *Journal of Consulting Psychology*, **26,** 273–278.

NEURINGER, C. 1964. The Rorschach test as a research device for the identification, prediction and understanding of suicidal ideation and behavior. *Journal of Projective Techniques and Personality Assessment*, **28,** 71–82.

NEURINGER, C., MCEVOY, T. L., and SCHLESINGER, R. J. 1965. The identification of suicidal behavior in females by the use of the Rorschach. *Journal of General Psychology*, **72,** 127–133.

NICKEL, H. 1957. Developmental analysis of the effects of a stressor condition on perceptual functioning. Unpublished master's thesis, Clark University, Worcester, Mass.

NITSCHE, C. J., ROBINSON, J. F., and PARSONS, E. T. 1956. Homosexuality and the Rorschach. *Journal of Consulting Psychology*, **20,** 196.

NOVICK, J. I. 1962. Effectiveness of the Rorschach Prognostic Rating Scale for predicting behavior change in children following brief psychotherapy. Paper read at American Psychological Association, St. Louis.

OLTEAN, M. 1952. Organic pathology accompanying diabetes mellitus as indicated by Rorschach. *Journal of Projective Techniques*, **16,** 485–488.

ORBACH, C. E., and TALLENT, N. 1965. Modification of perceived body and of body concepts. *Archives of General Psychiatry,* **12,** 126–135.

ORME, J. E. 1964. A study of Weiner's Rorschach schizophrenic indicators. *Journal of Clinical Psychology,* **20,** 531–532.

ORME, J. E. 1966. A further comment on Weiner's Rorschach color indicators. *Journal of Clinical Psychology*, **22,** 223.

OSBORNE, R. T., and SANDERS, W. B. 1950. Rorschach characteristics of duodenal ulcer patients. *Journal of Clinical Psychology*, **6,** 258–262.

PAGE, H. A. 1957. Studies in fantasy—daydreaming frequency and Rorschach scoring categories. *Journal of Consulting Psychology*, **21,** 111–114.

PATTIE, F. A. 1954. The effect of hypnotically induced hostility on Rorschach responses. *Journal of Clinical Psychology*, **10,** 161–164.

PAUKER, J. D. 1962. Base rates in the prediction of suicide: A note on Appelbaum's and Holzman's "The color-shading response and suicide." *Journal of Projective Techniques*, **26,** 429.

PEÑA, C. D. 1953. A genetic evaluation of perceptual structuralization in cerebral pathology: An investigation by means of the Rorschach test. *Journal of Projective Techniques*, **17,** 186–199.

PETERSON, A. O. D. 1954. A comparative study of Rorschach scoring methods in evaluating personality changes resulting from psychotherapy. *Journal of Clinical Psychology*, **10,** 190–192.

PHILLIPS, L. 1953. Case history data and prognosis in schizophrenia. *Journal of Nervous and Mental Disease*, **117,** 515–525.

PHILLIPS, L. 1959. The Worcester Rorschach developmental scores. Paper read at Eastern Psychological Association, Atlantic City.

PHILLIPS, L., and COWITZ, B. 1953. Social attainment and reaction to stress. *Journal of Personality*, **22,** 270–283.

PHILLIPS, L., and FRAMO, J. L. 1954. Developmental theory applied to normal and psychopathological perception. *Journal of Personality*, **22,** 464–474.

PHILLIPS, L., KADEN, S., and WALDMAN, M. 1959. Rorschach indices of developmental level. *Journal of Genetic Psychology*, **94,** 267–285.

PHILLIPS, L., and SMITH, J. G. 1953. *Rorschach interpretation: Advanced technique.* New York: Grune and Stratton.

PIOTROWSKI, Z. A. 1937. The Rorschach inkblot method in organic disturbances of the central nervous system. *Journal of Nervous and Mental Disease*, **86,** 525–537.

PIOTROWSKI, Z. A. 1940. Positive and negative Rorschach organic reactions. *Rorschach Research Exchange*, **4,** 147–151.

PIOTROWSKI, Z. A. 1950. A Rorschach compendium, revised and enlarged. *Psychiatric Quarterly*, **24,** 543–596.

PIOTROWSKI, Z. A. 1957. *Perceptanalysis.* New York: Macmillan.

PIOTROWSKI, Z. A., and BERG, D. A. 1955. Verification of the Rorschach Alpha diagnostic formula for underactive schizophrenics. *American Journal of Psychiatry*, **112,** 443–450.

PIOTROWSKI, Z. A., and LEWIS, N. D. C. 1950. An experimental Rorschach diagnostic aid for some forms of schizophrenia. *American Journal of Psychiatry*, **107,** 360–366.

PODELL, J. E., and PHILLIPS, L. 1959. A developmental analysis of cognition as observed in dimensions of Rorschach and objective test performance. *Journal of Personality*, **27,** 439–463.

POKORNY, A. D. 1964. Suicide rates in various psychiatric disorders. *Journal of Nervous and Mental Disease*, **139,** 499–506.

POPE, B., and JENSEN, A. R. 1957. The Rorschach as an index of pathological thinking. *Journal of Projective Techniques*, **21,** 54–62.

POWERS, W. T., and HAMLIN, R. M. 1955. Relationship between diagnostic category and deviant verbalizations on the Rorschach. *Journal of Consulting Psychology*, **19,** 120–124.

PRATT, C. 1951. A validation study of intropunitive and extrapunitive signs on the Rorschach test, based upon records given by suicidal and homicidal patients. Unpublished doctoral dissertation, Purdue University, Lafayette, Ind.

PURCELL, K. 1958. Some shortcomings in projective test validation. *Journal of Abnormal and Social Psychology*, **57**, 115–118.

QUIRK, D. A., QUARRINGTON, M., NEIGER, S., and SLEMON, A. G. 1962. The performance of acute psychotic patients on the index of pathological thinking and on selected signs of idiosyncracy on the Rorschach. *Journal of Projective Techniques*, **26**, 431–441.

RABIN, A. I. 1946. Homicide and attempted suicide: A Rorschach study. *American Journal of Orthopsychiatry*, **16**, 516–524.

RABIN, A. I. 1968. *Projective techniques in personality assessment.* New York: Springer-Verlag.

RABINOVITCH, M. S., KENNARD, M. A., and FISTER, W. P. 1955. Personality correlates of electroencephalographic patterns: Rorschach findings. *Canadian Journal of Psychology*, **9**, 29–41.

RADER, G. E. 1957. The prediction of overt aggressive verbal behavior from Rorschach content. *Journal of Projective Techniques*, **21**, 294–306.

RAMER, J. 1963. The Rorschach barrier score and social behavior. *Journal of Consulting Psychology*, **27**, 525–531.

RAMZY, I., and PICKARD, P. M. 1949. A study in the reliability of scoring the Rorschach inkblot test. *Journal of General Psychology*, **40**, 3–10.

RAPAPORT, D., GILL, M., and SCHAFER, R. 1946. *Diagnostic psychological testing, Vol. II.* Chicago: Year Book Publishers.

REITAN, R. M. 1954. The performance of aphasic, non-aphasic, and control subjects on the Rorschach test. *Journal of General Psychology*, **51**, 199–212.

REITAN, R. M. 1955a. Evaluation of the postconcussion syndrome with the Rorschach test. *Journal of Nervous and Mental Disease*, **121**, 463–467.

REITAN, R. M. 1955b. Validity of the Rorschach test as a measure of psychological effects of brain damage. *Archives of Neurology and Psychiatry*, **73**, 445–451.

REITAN, R. M. 1962. Psychological deficit. *Annual Review of Psychology*, **13**, 415–444.

REITZELL, J. M. 1949. A comparative study of hysterics, homosexuals, and alcoholics using content analysis of Rorschach responses. *Rorschach Research Exchange and Journal of Projective Techniques*, **13**, 127–141.

RIEMAN, G. W. 1953. The effectiveness of Rorschach elements in the discrimination between neurotic and ambulatory schizophrenic subjects. *Journal of Consulting Psychology*, **17**, 25–31.

ROBERTS, L. K. 1954. The failure of some Rorschach indices to predict the outcome of psychotherapy. *Journal of Consulting Psychology*, **18**, 96–98.

ROCHWARG, H. 1954. Changes in the structural aspects of perception in the aged: An analysis by means of the Rorschach test. Unpublished doctoral dissertation, Michigan State University, East Lansing, Mich.

ROCKBERGER, H. 1953. The effectiveness of a Rorschach prognostic scale for predicting results in psychotherapy. Unpublished doctoral dissertation, New York University, New York.

ROE, A. 1946a. Alcohol and creative work. *Quarterly Journal of Studies on Alcohol*, **6**, 415–467.

ROE, A. 1946b. Painting and personality. *Rorschach Research Exchange*, **10**, 86–100.

ROE, A. 1946c. A Rorschach study of a group of scientists and technicians. *Journal of Consulting Psychology*, **10,** 317–327.

ROE, A. 1949. Psychological examinations of eminent biologists. *Journal of Consulting Psychology*, **13,** 225–246.

ROE, A. 1951. A psychological study of eminent physical scientists. *Genetic Psychological Monographs*, **43,** 121–239.

ROE, A. 1952a. Two Rorschach scoring techniques: The inspection technique and the basic Rorschach. *Journal of Abnormal and Social Psychology*, **47,** 263–264.

ROE, A. 1952b. Group Rorschachs of university faculties. *Journal of Consulting Psychology*, **16,** 18–22.

ROE, A. 1953. A psychological study of eminent psychologists and anthropologists, and a comparison with biological and physical scientists. *Psychological Monographs*, **67** (all of No. 352).

ROGERS, L. S., and HAMMOND, K. R. 1953. Prediction of the results of therapy by means of the Rorschach test. *Journal of Consulting Psychology*, **17,** 8–15.

ROGERS, L. S., KNAUSS, J., and HAMMOND, K. R. 1951. Predicting continuation in therapy by means of the Rorschach test. *Journal of Consulting Psychology*, **15,** 368–371.

ROSEN, A. 1954. Detection of suicidal patients: An example of some limitations in the prediction of infrequent events. *Journal of Consulting Psychology*, **18,** 397–403.

ROSEN, A., HALLES, W. M., and SIMON, W. 1954. Classification of "suicidal" patients. *Journal of Consulting Psychology*, **18,** 359–362.

ROSENBLATT, B., and SOLOMON, P. 1954. Structural and genetic aspects of Rorschach responses in mental deficiency. *Journal of Projective Techniques*, **18,** 496–506.

ROSENTHAL, D., and FRANK, J. D. 1956. Psychotherapy and the placebo effect. *Psychological Bulletin*, **53,** 294–302.

ROSENTHAL, R. 1966. *Experimenter effects in behavioral research.* New York: Appleton-Century-Crofts.

ROSENWALD, G. C. 1961. The assessment of anxiety in psychological experimentation. *Journal of Abnormal and Social Psychology*, **62,** 666–673.

ROSS, W. D. 1940. Anatomical perseveration in Rorschach records. *Rorschach Research Exchange*, **4,** 138–145.

ROSS, W. D. 1941a. The contribution of the Rorschach method to clinical diagnosis. *Journal of Mental Science*, **87,** 331–348.

ROSS, W. D. 1941b. The incidence of some signs elicited by the Rorschach method. *Bulletin of the Canadian Psychological Association*, **2,** 21–22.

ROSS, W. D. 1942. Notes on Rorschach "signs" in diagnosis and research. *Rorschach Research Exchange*, **6,** 115–116.

ROSS, W. D., and ROSS, S. 1944. Some Rorschach ratings of clinical value. *Rorschach Research Exchange*, **8,** 1–9.

RUBIN, H., and LONSTEIN, M. 1953. A cross-validation of suggested Rorschach patterns with schizophrenia. *Journal of Consulting Psychology*, **17,** 371–372.

RUST, R. M., and RYAN, F. J. 1953. The relationship of some Rorschach variables to academic behavior. *Journal of Personality*, **21,** 441–456.

SAKHEIM, G. A. 1955. Suicidal responses on the Rorschach test: A validation study. *Journal of Nervous and Mental Disease*, **122,** 332–344.

Salfield, O. S. 1950. An attempt at a numerical evaluation of Rorschach test results. *Journal of General Psychology*, **43,** 305–311.

Sanders, R., and Cleveland, S. E. 1953. The relationship between certain examiner personality variables and subjects' Rorschach scores. *Journal of Projective Techniques*, **17,** 34–50.

Sandifer, M. G., Pettus, C., and Quade, D. 1964. A study of psychiatric diagnosis. *Journal of Nervous and Mental Disease*, **139,** 350–356.

Sapolsky, A. 1963. An indicator of suicidal ideation on the Rorschach test. *Journal of Projective Techniques and Personality Assessment*, **27,** 332–335.

Sarason, I. G. 1960. Empirical findings and theoretical problems in the use of anxiety scales. *Psychological Bulletin*, **57,** 403–415.

Saslow, G. 1965. Personal communication.

Saslow, H. L., and Shipman, W. C. 1957. The tendency of the Dörken and Kral brain damage measure to score false positives. *Journal of Consulting Psychology*, **21,** 434.

Schafer, R. 1954. *Psychoanalytic interpretation in Rorschach testing.* New York: Grune and Stratton.

Schatia, V. 1941. The incidence of neurosis in cases of bronchial asthma as determined by the Rorschach test with psychiatric examination. *Psychosomatic Medicine*, **3,** 157–169.

Schmeidler, G. R., Melson, M. J., and Bristol, M. 1959. Freshmen Rorschachs and college performance. *Genetic Psychological Monographs*, **59,** 3–43.

Schmidt, H. O., and Fonda, C. P. 1956. The reliability of psychiatric diagnosis: A new look. *Journal of Abnormal and Social Psychology*, **52,** 262–267.

Schulman, R. E. 1963. Use of the Rorschach Prognostic Rating Scale in predicting movement in counseling. *Journal of Counseling Psychology*, **10,** 198–199.

Secord, P. F. 1953. Objectification of word-association procedures by the use of homonyms: A measure of body cathexis. *Journal of Personality*, **21,** 479–495.

Seeman, J. 1954. Counselor judgments of therapeutic process and outcome. In C. R. Rogers and R. Dymond (eds.), *Psychotherapy and personality change.* Chicago: University of Chicago Press, pp. 99–108.

Seidel, C. 1960. The relationship between Klopfer's Rorschach Prognostic Scale and Phillips' case history prognosis rating scale. *Journal of Counseling Psychology,* **24,** 46–49.

Shah, S. A. 1957. Use of the inspection Rorschach technique in analyzing missionary success and failure. *Journal of Projective Techniques*, **21,** 69–72.

Sheehan, J. G., Frederick, C. J., Rosevear, W. H., and Spiegelman, M. 1954. A validity study of the Rorschach Prognostic Rating Scale. *Journal of Projective Techniques*, **18,** 233–239.

Shipman, W. G., Oken, D., Goldstein, I. B., Grinker, R. S., and Heath, H. A. 1964. Study in psychophysiology of muscle tension: II. Personality factors. *Archives of General Psychiatry*, **11,** 330–345.

Shneidman, E. S. 1959. Suggestions for the delineation of validation studies. *Journal of Projective Techniques*, **23,** 259–263.

Shneidman, E. S. 1963. Suicide. In N. L. Farberow (ed.), *Taboo topics.* New York: Atherton Press, pp. 33–43.

Shneidman, E. S., and Farberow, N. L. (eds.), 1957. *Clues to suicide.* New York: McGraw-Hill.

SIEGEL, E. L. 1953. Genetic parallels of perceptual structuralization in paranoid schizophrenia: An analysis by means of the Rorschach technique. *Journal of Projective Techniques*, **17**, 151–161.

SIEGEL, S. M. 1956. The relationship of hostility to authoritarianism. *Journal of Abnormal and Social Psychology*, **52**, 368–372.

SIERACKI, E. R. 1963. Body-image as a variable in the acceptance of disability and vocational interests of the physically disabled. Unpublished doctoral dissertation, State University of New York at Buffalo, Buffalo, N.Y.

SINGER, M. T., and WYNNE, L. C. 1963. Differentiating characteristics of parents of childhood schizophrenics, childhood neurotics, and young adult schizophrenics. *American Journal of Psychiatry*, **120**, 233–243.

SIPPRELLE, C. 1955. An empirical test of Pascal's formula. *Journal of Personality*, **23**, 195–206.

SJOSTEDT, E. M., and HURWITZ, I. 1959. A developmental study of sexual functioning by means of a cognitive analysis. *Journal of Projective Techniques*, **23**, 237–246.

SMITH, A. 1962. Ambiguities in concepts and studies of "brain damage" and "organicity." *Journal of Nervous and Mental Disease*, **135**, 311–326.

SMITH, J. R., and COLEMAN, J. C. 1956. The relationship between manifestations of hostility in projective tests and overt behavior. *Journal of Projective Techniques*, **20**, 326–334.

SMITH, L. C., JR., and PHILLIPS, L. 1959. Social effectiveness and developmental level in adolescence. *Journal of Personality*, **27**, 239–249.

SOLOMON, P. 1955. Differential Rorschach scores of successfully and unsuccessfully placed mental defectives. *Journal of Clinical Psychology*, **11**, 294–297.

SPIELBERGER, C. D. 1966. Theory and research on anxiety. In C. D. Spielberger (ed.), *Anxiety and behavior*. New York: Academic Press, pp. 3–20.

STEISEL, I. 1952. The Rorschach test and suggestibility. *Journal of Abnormal and Social Psychology*, **47**, 607–614.

STEWART, B. M. 1950. A study of the relationship between clinical manifestations of neurotic anxiety and Rorschach test performance. Unpublished doctoral dissertation, University of Southern California, Los Angeles.

STOTSKY, B. A. 1952. A comparison of remitting and nonremitting schizophrenics on psychological tests. *Journal of Abnormal and Social Psychology*, **47**, 489–496.

STRUPP, H. H. 1962. Psychotherapy. *Annual Review of Psychology*, **13**, 445–478.

SULLIVAN, H. S. 1953. *The interpersonal theory of psychiatry*. New York: Norton.

TAULBEE, E. S. 1958. Relationship between certain personality variables and continuation in therapy. *Journal of Consulting Psychology*, **22**, 83–89.

TAULBEE, E. S. 1961. The relationship between Rorschach flexor and extensor M responses and the MMPI and psychotherapy. *Journal of Projective Techniques*, **25**, 477–479.

TAULBEE, E. S., and SISSON, B. D. 1954. Rorschach pattern analysis in schizophrenia: A cross-validation study. *Journal of Clinical Psychology*, **10**, 80–82.

TEMOCHE, A., PUGH, T., and MACMAHON, B. 1964. Suicide rates among current and former mental institution patients. *Journal of Nervous and Mental Disease*, **138**, 124–130.

THETFORD, W., and DEVOS, G. 1951. A Rorschach study of clinical groups by means of Fisher's maladjustment scale. Paper read at Midwestern Psychological Association, Chicago, Illinois.

THIESEN, J. W. 1952. A pattern analysis of structural characteristics of the Rorschach test in schizophrenia. *Journal of Consulting Psychology*, **16**, 365–370.

TOWBIN, A. P. 1959. Hostility in Rorschach content and overt aggressive behavior. *Journal of Abnormal and Social Psychology*, **58**, 312–316.

TRAVIS, L. E., and BENNETT, C. L. 1953. The relationship between the electroencephalogram and scores in certain Rorschach categories. (Abstr.) *Electroencephalogram and Clinical Neurophysiology*, **5**, 474.

ULETT, G. A. 1950. *Rorschach introductory manual.* St. Louis: Educational Publishers.

ULETT, G. A., MARTIN, D. W., and MCBRIDE, J. R. 1950. The Rorschach findings in a case of suicide. *American Journal of Orthopsychiatry*, **20**, 817–827.

ULLMANN, L. P., and HUNRICHS, W. A. 1958. The role of anxiety in psychodiagnosis: Replication and extension. *Journal of Clinical Psychology*, **14**, 276–279.

VERNALLIS, F. F. 1955. Teeth-grinding: Some relationships to anxiety, hostility, and hyperactivity. *Journal of Clinical Psychology,* **11**, 389–391.

VETTER, H. J. 1955. The prediction of Rorschach content from the psychoanalytic theory of obsessive-compulsive neurosis. Unpublished doctoral dissertation, State University of New York at Buffalo, Buffalo, N.Y.

WALKER, R. G. 1951. A comparison of clinical manifestations of hostility with Rorschach and MAPS test performance. *Journal of Projective Techniques*, **15**, 444–460.

WALLACE, J. 1966. An abilities conception of personality: Some implications for personality measurement. *American Psychologist*, **21**, 132–138.

WARE, K., FISHER, S., and CLEVELAND, S. 1957. Body-image boundaries and adjustment to poliomyelitis. *Journal of Abnormal and Social Psychology,* **55**, 88–93.

WATKINS, J. G., and STAUFFACHER, J. C. 1952. An index of pathological thinking in the Rorschach. *Journal of Projective Techniques*, **16**, 276–286.

WEINER, I. B. 1961a. Cross-validation of a Rorschach checklist associated with suicidal tendencies. *Journal of Consulting Psychology*, **25**, 312–315.

WEINER, I. B. 1961b. Three Rorschach scores indicative of schizophrenia. *Journal of Consulting Psychology*, **25**, 436–439.

WEINER, I. B. 1962. Rorschach tempo as a schizophrenic indicator. *Perceptual and Motor Skills*, **15**, 139–141.

WEINER, I. B. 1964. Pure C and color stress as Rorschach indicators of schizophrenia. *Perceptual and Motor Skills,* **18**, 484.

WEINER, I. B. 1965a. Follow-up validation of Rorschach tempo and color use indicators of schizophrenia. *Journal of Projective Techniques and Personality Assessment*, **29**, 387–391.

WEINER, I. B. 1965b. Rorschach color stress as a schizophrenic indicator—A reply. *Journal of Clinical Psychology*, **21**, 313–314.

WEINER, I. B. 1966. *Psychodiagnosis in schizophrenia.* New York: John Wiley.

WEINER, I. B. 1968. Rorschach diagnosis of schizophrenia: Empirical validation. Presented at Seventh International Congress of Rorschach and other Projective Techniques, London.

WERNER, H. 1945. Motion and motion perception: A study in vicarious functioning. *Journal of Psychology,* **19,** 317–327.

WERNER, H. 1948. *Comparative psychology of mental development* (rev. ed.). Chicago: Follett.

WERNER, H. 1957. The concept of development from a comparative and organismic point of view. In D. B. Harris (ed.), *The concept of development.* Minneapolis, Minn.: University of Minnesota Press, pp. 125–148.

WERTHEIMER, R., and BACHELIS, L. A. 1966. Individual discrimination as a cognitive variable. Paper read at Eastern Psychological Association, New York.

WESTROPE, M. R. 1953. Relations among Rorschach indices, manifest anxiety, and performance under stress. *Journal of Abnormal and Social Psychology,* **48,** 515–524.

WHEELER, W. M. 1949. An analysis of Rorschach indices of male homosexuality. *Rorschach Research Exchange and Journal of Projective Techniques,* **13,** 97–126.

WHITE, M. A., and SCHREIBER, H. 1952. Diagnosing "suicide risks" on the Rorschach. *Psychiatric Quarterly Supplement,* **26,** 161–189.

WILENSKY, H. 1959a. Rorschach developmental level and social participation of chronic schizophrenics. *Journal of Projective Techniques,* **23,** 87–92.

WILENSKY, H. 1959b. Developmental scoring of Rorschachs of schizophrenics. Paper read at Eastern Psychological Association, Atlantic City.

WILLIAMS, G. J., MONDER, R., and RYCHLAK, J. F. 1967. A one-year concurrent validity study of the Rorschach Prognostic Rating Scale. *Journal of Projective Techniques and Personality Assessment,* **31,** 30–33.

WILLIAMS, R. L. 1962. The relationship of body image to some physiological reactivity patterns in peptic ulcer and rheumatoid arthritic patients. Paper read at American Psychological Association, St. Louis.

WILSON, M. T. 1954. Regression in perceptual organization: A study of adolescent performance on the Rorschach test. Unpublished doctoral dissertation, Clark University, Worcester, Mass.

WINDLE, C. 1952. Psychological tests in psychopathological prognosis. *Psychological Bulletin,* **49,** 451–482.

WITKIN, H. A., DYK, R. B., FATERSON, H. F., GOODENOUGH, D. R., and KARP, S. A. 1962. *Psychological differentiation.* New York: John Wiley.

WITKIN, H. A., LEWIS, H. B., HERTZMAN, M., MACHOVER, K., MEISSNER, P. B., and WAGNER, S. 1954. *Personality through perception.* New York: Harper & Row.

WITTMAN, P. 1941. Scale for measuring prognosis in schizophrenic patients. *Elgin State Hospital Papers,* **4,** 20–33.

WOLF, I. 1957. Hostile acting out and Rorschach test content. *Journal of Projective Techniques,* **21,** 414–419.

YAMAHIRO, R. S., and GRIFFITH, R. M. 1960. Validity of two indices of sexual deviancy. *Journal of Clinical Psychology,* **16,** 21–24.

YATES, A. J. 1954. The validity of some psychological tests of brain damage. *Psychological Bulletin,* **51,** 359–379.

YULE, G. U. 1924. *An introduction to the theory of statistics.* London: Griffin.

ZAX, M., and KLEIN, A. 1960. Measurement of personality and behavior changes following psychotherapy. *Psychological Bulletin,* **57,** 435–448.

Zigler, E., and Phillips, L. 1960. Social effectiveness and symptomatic behaviors. *Journal of Abnormal and Social Psychology*, **61,** 231–238.

Zilboorg, G. 1936. Suicide among civilized and primitive races. *American Journal of Psychiatry*, **92,** 1350–1368.

Zimet, C. N., and Brackbill, G. A. 1956. The role of anxiety in psychodiagnosis. *Journal of Clinical Psychology*, **12,** 173–177.

Zimet, C. N., and Fine, H. J. 1959. Perceptual differentiation and two dimensions of schizophrenia. *Journal of Nervous and Mental Disease*, **129,** 435–441.

Zubin, J., Eron, L. D., and Schumer, F. 1965. *An experimental approach to projective techniques.* New York: John Wiley.

AUTHOR INDEX

SUBJECT INDEX